Cambodge

Southeast Asia

POLITICS, MEANING, AND MEMORY

David Chandler and Rita Smith Kipp

SERIES EDITORS

OTHER VOLUMES IN THE SERIES

Cambodge

The Cultivation of a Nation, 1860–1945

PENNY EDWARDS

UNIVERSITY OF HAWAI'I PRESS   *Honolulu*

For my parents

Library of Congress Cataloging-in-Publication Data

Edwards, Penny.

Cambodge : the cultivation of a nation, 1860–1945 /
Penny Edwards.

    p.   cm.—(Southeast Asia—politics, meaning, memory)

Includes bibliographical references and index.

ISBN-13: 978-0-8248-2923-0 (hardcover : alk. paper)

ISBN-10: 0-8248-2923-9 (hardcover : alk. paper)

1. Cambodia—Intellectual life—19th century.   2. Cambodia—
Intellectual life—20th century.   3. Nationalism—Cambodia—
History.   4. Cambodia—History—1863–1953.   I. Title.
II. Series.

  DS554.7.E39 2006

  959.6'03—dc22

                        2006000837

Series designed by Richard Hendel

Printed by The Maple-Vail Book Manufacturing Group

CONTENTS

ACKNOWLEDGMENTS

Historians are ventriloquists, giving voice to plural pasts. We're also soliloquists. Throughout this project, my inspirational and irresistible husband, Peter Bartu, and our radiant children, Benjamin, Maxine, and Lorenza, have all pulled me incessantly out of the past with their zest for the present, bringing light and fresh insights to what might otherwise have remained a quiet conversation between me and the men and women who walk the pages of this book.

How, why, and with what effect people and ideas travel across time and space is a central focus of this book. In its various incarnations, the book's manuscript travelled to and through France, Australia, Cambodia, Burma, and America. Our journey began with a wrong turn in a library. Fresh from a year as a media analyst with the United Nations Transitional Authority in Cambodia, I was browsing the Southeast Asia stacks in Cornell University's Kroch collection in 1993, gathering materials for a planned PhD on Sino-Cambodian relations, when the gilded spines of some old French tomes caught my eye. Behind their quaint jackets, I found statements about the Khmer character and the temples of Angkor similar to the nationalist diatribes broadcast by the Khmer Rouge, the Cambodian People's Party, the royalist party Funcinpec, and the Buddhist Liberal Democrat Party whose propaganda it had been my job, as a United Nations officer, to analyze and summarize. That frisson of déjà-vu stretched into more than a decade of research, whose final outcome is this book.

I could have found no better tutor at this juncture than Benedict Anderson, whose legendary course on Plural Societies framed my first analytical encounters with European colonialism, and who provided thought-provoking feedback on my initial scribblings. No less important were Vaddey and Blake Ratner, whose creative talents, powers of perception, and great humor warmed and have long outlasted my Ithaca winter. In 1994 I travelled to Australia to join my fiancé, Peter Bartu, who had become an inseparable part of my life and adventures since we first met over frogs legs and beer in Phnom Penh. We were married two years later. Peter's intuitive grasp of the human condition, his sense of the Cambodian landscape, his gift for deciphering political machinations, his eclectic music and literature collection, his penchant for new adventures, and his unwavering enthusiasm for my work have all been vital ingredients of this book.

My most significant other willing accomplice has been David Chandler, who supervised my doctoral dissertation at Monash University. David's energy, his passion for history, and his generosity with ideas and materials added greatly to my thesis. Ian Mabbett's erudite feedback on my dissertation, and insightful critiques by my examiners Thongchai Winichakul and Tony Reid all helped sculpt this book.

In France in 1996, Michael Vann and David Deltesta guided me through colonial archives, and Christopher Goscha, Nasir Abdoul-Carime, and Serge Thion all gave generously of their time.

Much of this book is in dialogue with the work of the brilliant art historian Ingrid Muan. This conversation was cut brutally short when Ingrid died, far too young, in Phnom Penh, in January 2005. Ingrid and I met in Phnom Penh in late 1999, and while I was juggling research and babies in later years, she generously shared her notes from the National Archives of Cambodia. Her scholarship informs much of what follows.

My parents, John and Felicity, whose love of travel and books first stoked my curiosity for new places and strange tales, encouraged and indulged my interest in Cambodge with mailings of rare books, news clippings, long hours at photocopy shops, and visits to my research sites.

Demelza Stubbing's enterprise first got me to Cambodia in 1991, and her incisive intellect and political savvy have helped me to make sense of much of what I have found since. Demetra Tzanaki opened up new ways of thinking about culture and nationalism.

Several sponsors backed my global roamings. A postdoctoral fellowship at the Centre for Cross-Cultural Research 2000–2002, a Discovery Project Fellowship from the Australia Research Council 2003–2005, and a Harold White Fellowship at the National Library of Australia sustained the bulk of this book's long gestation. A Fulbright Travel and Maintenance Award financed my year at Cornell. My PhD was funded by a Commonwealth Scholarship, a Robert Menzies Travel Award, a Monash Graduate Scholarship, and, when all that ran out in the months before completion, the Felicity Edwards Drifting Daughter's Tuition Award and a John T. and Catherine D. Macarthur Research and Writing Grant.

In Cambodia, the Khmer Institute of Democracy, the Buddhist Institute, and the Centre for Khmer Studies all provided essential writing and thinking space. The staff of the National Archives of Cambodia and of numerous libraries and archives worldwide gave invaluable assistance.

I also owe thanks to Michel Antelme, Olivier de Bernon, Dipesh Chakrabarty, Murray Cox, Ly Dary, Erik Davis, Noël Deschamps, May Ebihara, Jaqueline Filliozat, Kate Frieson, Christopher Goscha, Peter Gyallay-Pap, Anne Hansen, Ian Harris, Marie-Paul Ha, Stephen Heder, Peter Heehs, Julio Jeldres, Henri Locard, John Marston, Gregor Muller, Jacques Népote, Khing Hoc Dy, Panivong Norindr, Leakthina Chaupech Ollier, Ashley Thompson, and to my many fabulous colleagues at the Centre for Cross-Cultural Research.

Finally, I have the talented team at the University of Hawai'i Press to thank for its professionalism and painstaking production of this book. Needless to say, I have only myself to blame for any surviving errors.

Introduction

Originations

In 1952, two years before Cambodia gained independence from French rule, a letter comparing democracy and diamonds appeared in the Khmer-language press, under the nom de plume "The Original Khmer" (Kmae daem).[1] The writer would assume other names, but his self-identification as a Kmae daem was not so easily shrugged off. At the height of his political career, from 1975 to 1977, he practiced John Doe politics, ruling under the mantle of anonymity, in the shadows of the invisible but brutally omnipresent Angkaa (the "organization"). This bizarre preemption of Maurice Blanchot's description of the holocaust as the "unknown name, alien to naming" ensured that no names or faces could be put to his regime, making it harder to translate the terror into political opposition.[2] In a famous public speech delivered in late September 1977, he unmasked Angkaa as the Cambodian Communist Party and identified himself as Pol Pot, another pseudonym. The man behind this masquerade was born as Saloth Sar.

In its attempt to transform Cambodia's culturally diverse terrain into an ethnically homogeneous, revolutionary utopia, Saloth Sar's murderous regime of Democratic Kampuchea (DK, 1975–1978) criminalized superstition, tradition, religion, and the linguistic, sartorial, and culinary expressions of ethnic difference. As he indicated with pride in a 1978 interview, Saloth Sar equated the assimilation of Cambodia's upland tribal groups with their modernization, declaring that while these "national minorities" were very miserable before, "now one cannot distinguish them from the other people. They wear the same dress and live like every one." In many respects, the DK regime was one where the right to life was determined by one's powers of mimicry. It was not enough to *be* a Cambodian, born on the land: one had to speak, act, dress, and perform according to an ideal—that of the Original Khmer.

The curious ideological mix of the DK combined the rejection of modernity with the quest for a return to a prefeudal past and the simultaneous search for a progressive future. In internal policy documents and public pronouncements, boasts that the DK could outleap Mao Zedong's Great Leap Forward sat alongside explicit appeals to the "masses" to prove their mettle as worthy descendants of the builders of the twelfth-century temple complex of Angkor Vat, and implicit exhortations to return modern Cambodia to its past glory. Whereas Marx had set out to turn all peasants into citizens, Saloth Sar was determined to turn all citizens into peasants, viewing their potential to build anew as an atavistic trait exemplified in the prototypes for his earlier masquerade as the Original Khmer: the builders of Angkor.

Like many others in his cohort, Saloth Sar was pale in complexion. His parents were well-to-do farmers in the province of Kompong Thom, but he had spent his formative years in the elite enclaves of Phnom Penh and Paris, moving between the Palace, cafés, and colonial schools. The farther he travelled from the site and status of his birth, the more seductively the role of "the Original Khmer" must have beckoned, offering fixity in a time of political and personal transition, and enabling Saloth Sar and his coterie to stamp Cambodia's budding communist movement as "national." It was precisely his departure from his rural origins and his coaching in foreign institutions that inspired him first to hanker after this *dramatis persona* and then, after decades in the Cambodian wilderness *(priy)*, to emerge with his hands dirtied, and bloodied, and closer in image to this fictive persona.[3]

The Kmae Daem has dark skin, a pure soul. He is a son of the soil, but the blood of Angkor's builders courses through his veins. An apparition that vanishes on attempt to translate it into the flesh and blood of the everyday, "the Original Khmer" is the conjunction of two notions—Khmerness and a state of origin, or before-ness. This book is an attempt to map the fractured genealogy of this split personality— the modern Kmae daem—and to detail how this figure of fiction emerged in the twilight of colonialism, and whence it drew its authority.

MAKING HISTORY

Saloth Sar was apparently untroubled by the contradictions inherent in his blend of Angkorean antiquity and revolutionary modernity, or by its intellectual genealogy, which sat oddly alongside the DK's robust anticolonial vitriol. As would have been well known to Saloth Sar and such members of his inner circle as Khieu Samphan, Ieng Sary, and Khieu Thirith, the French Protectorate (1863–1954) had used the trope of fallen race and the lodestone of Angkor to indicate what heights the Khmers could achieve with the correct (French) tuition. Saloth Sar used the same tropes, but "independence mastery" was his motto. This skewed translation of colonial historiography was conducted with a peculiar eye to posterity.

In DK, the past was banned in many ways. Nostalgia was renamed memory sickness *(cheu satearum),* a counterrevolutionary condition treatable by execution, as if history had become literally embodied in particular people, whose annihilation could eradicate the country's polluted past.[4] Pre-DK songs were forbidden, as was money.[5] But when questioned about such moves, Saloth Sar furnished historical examples, aligning his regime with the precolonial era, when barter and work in kind were still common. "At certain times in Cambodian history," he responded in a 1978 interview, "we have not needed money." The "we" placed him on a continuum with his ancestors and bracketed him with the mythical persona onto which he projected his political desires: the Original Khmer.

We see a glimpse of Pol Pot's yearning for a place for himself and his regime in *la longue durée* at his coming-out speech in 1977, in which he celebrated the "powerful historical tide" of world revolution and urged the people of Kampuchea to take their place in this forward push of history. Anthropologist Michael Herzfeld has argued that, when history becomes the discourse of any totalizing regime, it acquires "precisely that capacity for suppressing time that Lévi-Strauss identified as the specific property of myth," encouraging a "creative rethinking of pasts mythologized in very different fashions by previous sources of authority."[6] DK historiography shared with that of other postcolonial regimes a common capacity for suppressing what Herzfeld calls time's specificity, most notably through the erasure of the colonial encounter from the idea of Cambodian history. Paradoxically, this negation of time in itself reveals the enduring hegemony and mythic hold of the rethinking of time that occurred among Cambodians in the French Protectorate.

The DK leadership's notions of history survived the regime's collapse. In late 1978, tank columns accompanied by a Vietnamese-backed Cambodian resistance group rolled across the eastern border, pushing the DK leaders and captive populations west into Thailand, where they set up camp on the Thai–Cambodian border. In 1988, a document emerged from one such DK camp, allegedly written by the DK leadership to provide ideological guidance to cadre. The style of Khmer language used suggested it had been written first in French, which in itself is unsurprising, given that the inner circle of the DK leadership were mostly educated in Paris and in the colonial school system in the French Protectorate.[7] The document rationalizes attacks on the DK as a case of historical envy, asserting that enemies desired to "crush" them "because they do not want us to let the world know our history," and aim to deny us (the DK) "our place in history" and to "crush us until we, our name, our forces, and this history no longer exist." It contextualizes the DK's successes in light of historic heroes. First on the list is Napoleon, closely followed by three famous monks and the Cambodian prince Sivutha, who led uprisings against the French in the late nineteenth century. But the DK dismisses these examples as unimportant. Napoleon made mistakes. The Khmer resistance leaders were not communists. "The History" also repeatedly emphasizes that the DK failings were a matter of *time*. The DK only had three and a half years before it fell, yet it was being compared with regimes and dynasties hundreds of years old. In truth, therefore, the "DK is far better than all of those historical heroes" and its "virtue, quality, true character and value" are the best in Cambodian and world history—a world history shrunk to the span of the French history that would have been taught in those schools and *lycées* where the DK leaders gained their education.

Another, macabre collection of DK historiography dates from the regime itself, in the files of its notorious secret prison at Tuol Sleng/S-21, which sent some sixteen thousand Cambodians to their deaths after excruciating torture and the extraction of so-called confessions. Writing on modernity, Dipesh Chakrabarty has illuminated the nexus between violence and idealism underpinning the process by which the narratives of citizenship and modernity come to find a natural home in "history."[8] Like the colonial prisons noted by Chakrabarty, S-21 also functioned in part as a labora-tory of knowledge whose deeply disturbing archive, analyzed in depth elsewhere by David Chandler, Judy Ledgerwood, and Stephen Heder, raises troubling questions about the role of texts in constructing modern regime narratives of "truth" and na-tional identity.

Extracted under hideous torture, the confessions were transcribed by a clerk and subseqently scrutinized by the prison head, Khang Khek Ieu, who added his own marginalia to many of the thousands of pages so generated. In this bizarre chain of audiences, the role of the victim's interrogator is complicated by the quest to salvage memories in a regime that has banned nostalgia and who is framing his questions in the knowledge they will be subsequently examined by his superiors, and ulti-mately by the all-seeing and all-knowing Angkaa. Once the required knowledge is extracted, the prisoner is executed, the report filed. The files accumulate and become an extensive archive whose meticulous documentation is all the more extraordinary in a regime that placed a virtual ban on reading.

Why was this archive built? Why were the confessions sought? Stephen Heder has offered the most persuasive explanation, arguing that it was compiled "to provide the Party Centre with raw material for a massive, unwritten history of the Party. . . . because everyone held at S21 was eventually 'smashed' their confessions would testify not only to their crimes but also to the Party's power and omniscience."[9] David Chan-dler has called these confessions "induced historical texts," which provided the party's leaders with intriguingly dark areas that threw "the triumphal history of the party into sharp relief." The confessions were testaments to the omniscience of the Com-munist Party of Kampuchea (CPK), designed to demonstrate its leaders' "consum-mate ability to grasp the wheel of history and thereby create and control the Party's triumphant narrative."[10]

Literary critic Homi Bhaba has noted a similar demand for narrative in colonial regimes, where much of the drive for collecting indigenous versions of the "truth" was driven by the search for validation and the need to hear, from the colonized, why "we," the colonials, are "here."[11] Although it seems a far cry from the brutality of DK to colonial Cambodia, in some respects the clerks in Tuol Sleng bore more relation to colonial bureaucrats than to traditional scribes. In precolonial Cambodia, writing was invested with sacred meaning, and transcription was a deeply spiritual transaction. Manuscripts were created to be read aloud, and the act of listening to a monk's reci-tation of scriptures was a means of gaining merit. The scribes of Tuol Sleng worked to a reverse formula. The subject was made to speak so that her or his loudness could be made silent, absorbed on paper, sandwiched between cardboard, stacked on a shelf. The subsequent execution of the subject of the history thus produced gave the institution—Tuol Sleng—and by extension DK, the nation-state on whose territory and in whose conceptual framework that institution resided—an immortality.

Drawing on the work of Holocaust scholars Erving Goffman and Irving Horo-witz, Chandler likens the DK regime itself to a total institution, which became a "sealed environment" cut off from the outside world.[12] This insulation of DK has gained a curious immortality of its own, in part through museology. In 1979, one of the first priorities of the newly installed regime of the People's Republic of Kampuchea was to turn Tuol Sleng into a museum of genocide, so localizing the DK experience, excising it from the present and consigning it to a place marked "past." In the same curatorial spirit, a number of commentators have emphasized DK's isolation from our world, denying Saloth Sar the glory of posterity by relegating him and his regime to a place outside of history: it is comforting to consider the DK as an anomalous and totally alien elsewhere. But, as others have noted, several key nationalist notions that drove Saloth Sar's murderous revolution have found a place in the ideological armature of all Cambodia's postcolonial regimes. Sihanouk's royalist Sangkum Reastr Niyum (1955–1970), Lon Nol's Khmer Republic (1970–1975), Saloth Sar's communist Democratic Kampuchea (1975–1978), Heng Samrin's socialist People's Republic of Kampuchea (1979–1989), Hun Sen's State of Cambodia (1989–1993), and the Kingdom of Cambodia (1993–) have all sought legitimacy in imagery of Angkor Vat. Idealized in national anthems, flags, and ceremony, this emblem of antiquity has come to signify Cambodian sovereignty. Today, its tricorn towers stand as political shorthand for two enduring nationalist tropes, symbolizing faith in Cambodia's past glory and fears of that country's future disappearance.

These abstractions share a common point of origin. Forged in the French Protectorate, they have spilled across that false and seductively simple line staving off colonial from postcolonial time, carried in images and intellects, embodied in a panoply of forms, from the "national-style" architecture that survived the iconoclasm of the DK to the logoization of Angkor as national monument. Some, notably the notion of Buddhism as the Khmer national religion, were not admitted into Saloth Sar's vision of the Original Khmer. However, the fact that they survived the destructive policies of the DK and remain central constructs of Khmer nationhood today attests to their longevity. This book is a history of these ideas, and of the individuals and historical circumstances that brought them into being.

COLONIALISM, NATIONALISM, AND SYMBOLISM

The hypnotic appeal of Angkor Vat as a sacred symbol uniting Khmers in time and space has seduced some observers of modern Cambodian history into accepting nationalist myth as historical fact. Until recently, Cambodian nationalism was commonly conceived of as a primordial web of memory linking "pre- and postcolonial Cambodia" via an unbroken chain of pride in the golden age of Angkor.[13] Implying that this atavistic pride had simmered beyond the reach of history for centuries, several scholars have pinpointed its sudden mutation into modern nationalism to the 1930s and 1940s.[14] Such analyses are anchored in two specific developments. First is the launch, in 1936, of the Khmer-language newspaper *Nagaravatta* (Angkor Vat). Often wrongly described as the first Khmer newspaper, *Nagaravatta* is now widely regarded as the birth certificate of modern Cambodian nationalism. Second is the

"Umbrella War" of 1942, an anti-French demonstration by several thousand monks and laypeople in the Cambodian capital of Phnom Penh.[15]

This preoccupation with the political manifestations of nationalism as opposed to cultural content has fostered a popular view of Cambodian nationalism as a creature of discontent—a knee-jerk reaction to the political repression, economic injustice, and educational denial commonly equated with the French Protectorate (1863–1954). Such analyses hinge on a common interpretation of "nation" as an essentially political construct. However the nation is very much "a system of cultural signification" whose "national traditions," as Bhabha has argued, stem from a complex nexus of "acts of affiliation . . . establishment . . . disavowal, displacement, exclusion and cultural contestation."[16] Despite such linkages, much current scholarship on nationalism continues to depict culture and politics as mutually exclusive spheres of activity.

One of the first champions of two distinct brands of cultural and political nationalism was the French intellectual Antonin Artaud. In 1936, when a small group of Cambodian civil servants were furtively penning articles for *Nagaravatta* on issues ranging from Khmer national culture to the economic virtues of Chinese immigrants, Artaud contrasted "cultural nationalism," which asserts the unique features of a nation, with a rival brand of "civic nationalism" characterized by customs restrictions, economic conflict, and military engagement.[17] The following decade, as the Governor General of Indochina recruited politically dependable cultural experts to concoct Vichy propaganda, the European historian Hans Kohn conflated these conceptual boundaries with geographic borders, arguing that only "outside the western world" was nationalism first expressed "in the cultural field," originating as "a venture in education and propaganda" orchestrated by scholars and poets. Western nationalism, by contrast, was a political construct, concerned with "policy-shaping and government."[18] In the 1980s, when fighting Cambodian factions staked out their claims with different flags, each bearing the image of Angkor, Kohn's bipolar view resonated in the work of John Hutchinson, who argued for two "quite different types of nationalism—cultural and political." Hutchinson defines cultural nationalism as the brainchild of historical scholars and artists who form cultural and academic societies, and argues that it is concerned exclusively with the articulation of a nation's unique civilization, history, culture, and geography. Political nationalism, in contrast, is the creature of legislators and politicians, who aspire to uproot the status quo and to realize a civic polity.[19] This compartmentalization of culture and politics has also featured in recent scholarship on national identity formation in colonial states. In his pathbreaking study of nationalism in British India, for example, Partha Chatterjee posits an inviolable "spiritual" space enshrining language, religion, and family life, which Indian nationalists sought to insulate from European influence and to preserve as a sovereign domain of cultural difference. This he contrasts with the outer "material" domain of law, administration, economics, and statecraft, in which nationalists fought to erase substantive difference. Indian nationalism, asserts Chatterjee, allowed "no encroachment by the colonizer" on the "inner core of the national culture."[20] In Cambodge, such notions become unstuck: the very notion of a national culture, let alone its inner core, were products of the colonial encounter. In the protectorate, precisely those domains marked as separate by Chatterjee in India became entangled, both in mutually constitutive processes (there could be no "public," itself a product of modernity, without a clear demarcation of what was "private" and "native") and through the personal journeys of key interlocutors and vectors of cultural transition that crisscrossed these spiritual and material, colonial and colonized, public and private realms. Despite, or because of, such efforts to categorize and compartmentalize, these spheres became intertwined in inseparable ways as nationalism developed. The dynamic intersection of European and indigenous worldviews fostered a self-conscious demarcation of a national religion, a national space, a national past, and a national culture. The last, open to manipulation and veneration, became not so much an inner core as an outer shell.

In the protectorate, the multistranded construction of a national, geocultural body of Cambodge would gradually and imperceptibly extend the rural majority's boundary markers beyond the local landmarks of temple, forest, and folklore and expand the horizons of individual belonging from a local to a national community, bounded by the monumental regalia of Angkor Vat, framed in a national space defined by modern mapping, and unified by a "national" heritage, history, religion, and literature. Cultural parameters became contiguous with territorial borders, binding socially and regionally disparate groups into an "imagined community," in Benedict Anderson's famous phrase. While Anderson defines a nation as an "imagined political community," the anthropologist Bruce Kapferer has highlighted its cultural dimensions, arguing that Sri Lanka's nationalists made a "fetish of culture."[21]

In Cambodge, nationalists did not *produce* a national culture. Rather, the elaboration of a national culture by French and Cambodian literati eventually produced nationalists. As the philosopher Tzvetan Todorov has argued, the development of a national cultural consciousness is a critical prelude to the evolution of the idea of political autonomy.[22] In Cambodge, as in the Europe studied by Miroslav Hroch and Eric Hobsbawm, the initial developmental phase of nationalism in the nineteenth century was "purely cultural, literary and folkloric," with "no particular political . . . implications"; as in Europe, the elaboration of this self-conscious cultural identity subsequently became politicized and promoted by "militant pioneers" of the "national idea."[23] Elaborated, contested, and revised by indigenous intellectuals, this early colonial synthesis of cultural and social practice, ancient monuments, and present customs into a narrative of Khmer national history provided the blueprint upon which future nationalists would build.[24] Like their counterparts in the India studied by Marinalini Sinha and Chatterjee, Cambodge's budding nationalists structured their arguments for social reform around notions of Cambodia's decline from a glorious past.[25] These notions of decay would fuel an enduring theme in modern Cambodian nationalism: the fear that Cambodia could disappear.[26]

As the notion of "Cambodge" took root, the theater of "the Protectorate" became dislodged from a specifically Southeast Asian location to a broader arena of trends and ideas reaching back and forth into the Métropole, or Paris. Recent scholarship by Edward Said, Antoinette Burton, and Ann Stoler, has highlighted the elasticity of the notion of national cultural consciousness by stimulating recognition of the interdependency of "Imperial and national identities" and exploring the connectivity between Metropolitan and colonial ideologies and anxieties.[27] The emergence of Cambodian nationalism was fraught with just such a traffic in ideas and images, and this study is framed with as much attention to the "cultural topography" of colonies and the "imaginary scaffoldings" of empire explored by literary critic Panivong Norindr as to the charting of a linear chronology.[28] In broadening our understanding of the workings of colonialism, this focus on the crosscurrents between Europe and Cambodge simultaneously threatens to discount or elide the influence and rich exchange of ideas between China, Siam, Japan, and other countries, colonies, and individuals in the region. Regrettably, the scope of this project has not allowed for more than passing reference to such exchanges, which merit far more extensive scholarly attention.[29]

The dominant paradigm of Khmer national sentiment as a primordial continuum linking pre- and postcolonial Cambodia is a shibboleth. Cambodian culture was, and remains, a dynamic field of change that evolved in the colonial era via a process of "creative adaptation," to use John Smail's diagnosis of parallel developments in the Dutch East Indies.[30] Chandler has long hinted at the crucial place of colonial culture in forging modern Cambodian nationalism, arguing that the contradictions between French conceptions of past glory and present decay led to a crisis of identity among educated Khmers in the 1930s and 1940s and so catalyzed Cambodian nationalism.[31] Locating the origins of Chandler's crisis of identity in the late nineteenth and early twentieth century, when the clinical gaze of colonial rule and the telescopic eye of Western historiography forced indigenous literati to reassess their culture and history, this book shows how Cambodian nationalism was shaped, not in the pages of *Nagaravatta,* but in colonial offices, schoolrooms, research institutes, and museums. In stark contrast to the "cultural asphyxia" that French rule inflicted upon Algeria, the protectorate of Cambodge saw a redefinition of Khmer culture and its emergence into the public sphere of the modern nation.[32] This controversial claim flies in the face of much existing scholarship and most nationalist historiography. A case in point is the assertion by former minister of cults and religion Bunchan Mul that Khmer "literature and culture ran and hid in the pagoda" during colonial rule, and that Khmer monks alone "preserved, supported, and kept it intact."[33]

In fact, European scholarship and colonial cultural institutions in France and Cambodge opened up new space for the reform of Buddhism, while sponsoring new forms for its conservation in palm-leaf manuscript or printed book. For the most part, these activities and the conversations they generated with indigenous monks bore the heavy imprint of individual initiatives. Despite such dialogues, the colonial period was long treated by Khmer scholars and politicians as nonhistory, an act of exile earlier seen in DK historiography. Chandler has noted how the Cambodian Palace Chronicles of 1927–1949 did not consider the colonial era "as a phase of Cambodian history worth examining by itself." The first entry to break this trend, made in July 1945, a month before the fall of Vichy Indochina when Cambodge was under temporary Japanese military control, implicitly disowned the period as an era of *Cambodian* history, alleging that Cambodians had been rendered "unconscious" under colonial rule by policies privileging French values, culture, and language. A later entry from the same year reinserted Cambodians into the period, mapping a time line of heroes from the antimonarchic revolts of 1860 and 1866, the anti-French revolt of 1884–1885, the demonstrations of 1916, the assassination of Résident Bardez in 1925, and the demonstration of 1942. But these Cambodians were still on the margins of history, looking in at institutions of monarchical or colonial power from the invisible and otherwise undocumented realm of non-kings and non-Résidents. This version of the past, set aside once the French returned to Cambodia in 1945, still did not resolve the questions raised by Chandler: what were Cambodian values, and what was Cambodian history?[34] Postcolonial Khmer historiography has commonly depicted Cambodian history as a thread running from Funan to Angkor to the reign of Ang Duong, suddenly ruptured by the establishment of the French Protectorate in 1863 and mysteriously mended and tied to a new, true chapter of Cambodian history upon independence in 1954.[35] Although variations on this theme have emerged, most notably in DK historiography, which blanketed two thousand years of history prior to the revolution as a period of feudal rule, all regimes have promoted the view of the colonial era as a chapter outside the passage of Cambodian time.

Riding on the wings of postcolonial guilt, this version of history gained a mysterious credibility among Western audiences. Until recently, most scholars cold-shouldered the period, as if Cambodia's entanglement with Europeans from 1863 to 1954 rendered it somehow impure. Brief flirtations with the period en route from or to other eras yielded superficial conclusions, many of which have gained common currency, notably the portrayal of Cambodge as a "backwater" of French Indochina.[36] The colonial impact is generally described in negative terms, such as a "severe decline in traditional intellectual institutions" or a "barren legacy" in education, depicting Cambodge as culturally and socially stagnant when contrasted with the supposedly born-again Cambodia that emerged after 1954.[37] This academic neglect and the resultant knowledge deficit allowed even the most learned scholars of Cambodian society and culture to pole-vault this near-century of events and ideas with such sweeping statements as "[Khmer] girls did not go to school" before Independence.[38] Such leapfrogging of the colonial era fostered the perception of postcolonial currents of thought, and most notably Sihanouk's backward-looking, Angkor-centric nationalism, as a continuation of traditional monarchical political and religious institutions bridging pre- and post-colonial Cambodia. The theme of continuity is privileged, suggesting that the colonial era is some inauthentic abyss, an aberration for which the French can be blamed but that is not to be claimed as an integral or "authentic" passage in Cambodian history. Ironically, this interpretation buys into French colonial propaganda, which held that Cambodians were changeless, suspended in cultural time and political space.[39]

This academic lacuna finds its antithesis in popular culture. Since the early 1990s, bookshops and cinemas in France and Indochina have yielded increasing shelf space and screen time to the literature and cinema of colonial nostalgia. A boom in re-releases of such exotica as Pierre Loti's *Un pèlerin d'Angkor* (1911) and Roland Meyer's *Saramani: Danseuse cambodgienne* (1919), exhibitions of colonial photographs, and such films as *Indochine* and *L'amant* all demonstrate a belated backwash of the dissolution of empire. This literary and cinematic afterglow has submerged a period of oppressive rule in an overpowering "aura of nostalgia."[40] This new wave of colonial *chic*—or *Indochic,* to quote Norindr—calls for a reevocation of the context that produced such images. Glamorized and excised from their historical context, such memorabilia foster the view of colonial society as a romantic interlude, an exotic escape from the frenetic pace of life in the West, where races and cultures coalesced in a generally free and happy fashion. Such quaint imagery not only diverts attention from the less picturesque agendas of colonial rule; it also projects the deluded notion that Europeans were the exclusive architects of cultural life in the colonies. The net effect of these competing views of colonial history is to deny Cambodians agency in a highly significant era of social, cultural, and political change, which saw the crystallization of the very notion of the Cambodian nation and the self-conscious articulation of a national culture.[41]

In the past decade, new scholarship on the colonial period has brought this long-neglected era into new focus. An outstanding doctoral dissertation by the late art historian Ingrid Muan has put colonial arts education and its legacies of Angkorean reproduction in a fresh and critical perspective. In his forthcoming biography of a small-time entrepreneur whose late-nineteenth-century antics reveal a robust energy, obstinacy, and commercial savvy, alternating with bouts of delusion, historian Greg Müller has lent rare life and complexity to the colonial period. Scholar of religion Anne Hansen has also shed important light on shifts in the conceptual, intellectual, and literary register of a leading Khmer poet, Suttantaprija In. This small but growing body of nuanced scholarship is changing perceptions of the protectorate as either monolithic or culturally static.

As Jan Nederveen Pieterse and Bhikhu Parekh have argued, colonialism generated a heightened self-consciousness among colonized intellectuals, forcing them to confront questions about their history, society, and themselves. Cultural practices that had long been "lived" and thus taken for granted were now refracted through the lens of Orientalist preoccupations with authenticity and reframed in European paradigms of race and nation.[42] This new scrutiny resulted in the identification of a panoply of cultural forms and practices, from ritual objects to court dance, as signifiers of national belonging. Indigenous intellectuals in Cambodge, like their counterparts in British India, played a vital role in structuring and shaping this cultural production through a complex web of exchange best described by Aijaz Ahmad as a "wilderness of mirrors."[43]

In Cambodge, the mirror becomes a particularly compelling metaphor. Khmers in the French Protectorate, repeatedly told they were a vanished race, were tasked not with imitating European colonialists, in the spirit of Lord Macaulay's "class of persons Indian in blood and colour, but English in taste . . . and in intellect," Rudyard Kipling's "Hurreë Babu," or V. S. Naipaul's "mimic men," but with mimicking their ancestors. Before Khmers could perform this task to the satisfaction of their colonial tutors, the latter had to ascertain the ethnocultural dimensions of the "authentic" Khmer, whom both painstaking scholarship and amateur antiquarianism located in the temples of Angkor, after an initial misdiagnosis that the Khmers had vanished, and that the Cambodians who now walked the land were some distant and degenerate offshoots. Bas-reliefs, sculptures, inscriptions, and decorations were the materials from which the French would mold the template of the Original Khmer and chart the specific coordinates of the Khmer race, temperament, and nationality. In this hall of ancestral mirrors, mimicry became inextricably tied up with questions of nation, authentication, and anticipation.

Had Khmerness been identified as something inhering in the contemporary, this dilemma might never have emerged. But most early European visitors were, quite naturally, drawn to Cambodge's ancient temples and monuments, and subscribed to the view that "the Khmers" had vanished, and that Cambodge's current inhabitants were the detritus of Angkor's builders. From 1860 to the 1910s, at precisely the time when preoccupations with France's falling birthrate dogged politicians and technocrats in the Métropole, this trope of the vanishing Khmer dominated colonial discourse. As if to compensate for this presumed absence, a model of what was authentically Khmer began to be sculpted onto the colonial aesthetic. Stamps, banknotes, exhibition and museum displays, art, photography, poetry and literature, architecture and urban sculpture, provided multiple arenas for the projection and expression of imaginings about Cambodge. The more "scientific" material and "documentary" evidence those working for and with the protectorate dredged up from the past, the more entrenched and irreversible the notion of the Khmer became. By the 1900s, these notions had become, quite literally, set in stone, informing monuments to Khmerness that still exist, at the time of writing, in Phnom Penh and Marseille. This colonial aesthetic enjoyed currency largely among Metropolitan museum goers and exhibition visitors, subscribers to such journals as the Parisian daily *l'Illustration,* and tourists or civil servants in Cambodge. It was also woven into the lives of elite Cambodians.

French scholar-officials and native literati did not simply dislocate such elements as dress, coiffure, architecture, and art from the social, historical, and cultural network in which they were embedded. Some labored to produce icons of Khmerness, which simultaneously hailed back to the imagery of, or assumptions about, Angkor and also catered to the expectations and tastes of contemporary Europeans. In colonial exhibitions, court dance was truncated into manageable performances. In the new art school, decorative emblems from Angkor were conflated with ritual objects. In the capital's new "national" monument, a spiritually imbued toponym and Buddhist pagoda were teamed with Angkorean motifs and a statue of King Sisowath flanked by a bas-relief of a Cambodian militiaman sporting a beret. Clothes for women were translated into a so-called national costume in part modelled on the European skirt, while monks who wore robes of European cloth were reprimanded as "un-Cambodian." Like the stereotypes enumerated by Nicholas Thomas in his study of colonial culture in the South Pacific, such cultural constructions performed a legislative function "by privileging certain identities and stigmatizing others as inauthentic."[44]

The notion of authenticity had a particular currency by the 1910s to 1930s. As James Clifford writes, what "matters politically is who deploys nationality or trans-nationality, authenticity or hybridity, against whom, with what relative power and ability to sustain a hegemony."[45] Under the French Protectorate, a narrative of authenticity emerged as a hegemonic discourse. This was not simply a word-based narrative, in Bhaba's earlier sense. It was created through a traffic in ideas, images, and artifacts. This rich visual, material, and textual discourse, generated by both colonizers and colonized, gained a momentum of its own, securing converts among those Cambodians and Europeans who felt dislocated by the social upheavals of colonialism and the global turmoil wrought by industrialism, modernity, and the devastation of the First and Second World Wars. Many Cambodians, both in the civil administration and in the *sangha* (monkhood), enthusiastically participated in the identification and delineation of an authentic Khmerness and transcribed this notion into diverse spheres of activity and contesting schools of nationalism. After Independence, this authenticity discourse was deployed by successive regimes, which asserted their claims to political legitimacy and national moral authority by deploying the notion of their "Original Khmerness" both to vilify "other" ethnic groups, countries, or ideologies and to assert their regime's "sameness" with the tropes of Angkor and the Original Khmer.

The authentication of a particular body of culture as "the Khmer nation" represented a radical deviation from previous notions of identity within the territory now under the Tricolour. The cultural foundations of this modern construct were by no means new; much of the literature, art, sculpture, language, and religious scriptures mobilized to form the modern nation predated the colonial encounter by hundreds, and in some cases over a thousand, years. What was new were the terms of reference framing these linguistic, religious, and artistic expressions. Like Malays under colonial rule, Cambodians played a pivotal role in the articulation of concepts of a national community that would last well after the withdrawal of the French administration, including concepts of nationalism, of a territorially defined nation-state, and of Khmerness itself.[46] Central to this process was a changing vocabulary of "nation."

NATION AND TRANSLATION

The concept of nation was pushed to the forefront of intellectual inquiry in France in the early 1880s, with the appearance of Ernest Renan's essay *Qu'est-ce qu'une nation?* (What is a nation?). Renan, whose emphasis on the monumental manifestations of a national essence were partly shaped by a tour of the Pyramids in colonized Egypt, defined the nation as "a soul, a spiritual principle," whose two essential constituents were "a rich legacy of remembrances" and "the will to continue to value [a common] heritage."[47] Although not published until 1882, Renan's exegesis gave verbal form to a concept of cultural nationhood that had been brewing in France as elsewhere in western Europe for the best part of a century. In two earlier publications, Renan had identified temples and traditions as vital constituents of each nation's "great soul" and invoked the "ancestors" and a "common past" as a thread linking "plebeians" and "patricians" into a national culture.[48] While Renan focused on a nation's cultural complexion, his influential contemporary Jules Michelet emphasized its geographic dimension, cultivating a new awareness of landscape and place as repositories of a nation's essence and its past.[49]

In reporting signs of "national" identity in late-nineteenth-century Cambodge, French explorers and observers were unwittingly transporting this vocabulary to a country where patterns of identification were still governed by a very different cosmology.[50] A prime example of this tendency to box indigenous thought worlds into European frames of reference is the observation by the scholar-offical Étienne Aymonier, published in 1896, that "The *nation* has long been accustomed to the idea of not separating its own existence to that of the royal house. The monarch is the living incarnation, the august and supreme personification of *nationality*."[51] Reading such colonial commentaries as testimony to the existence of a "*national* religion" and "*nationalist* pride" in nineteenth-century Cambodia risks obscuring indigenous patterns of identification.[52] Khmer sources indicate that concepts of "nation" and "nationality" as understood by Aymonier and his contemporaries did not percolate down into Cambodian consciousness until the first decades of this century, and then only into elite circles. Although the current Khmer term for nation, *jiet,* was used during the nineteenth century, its meaning differed markedly from contemporary usage. *Jiet* (Pali: *jati,* root meaning "birth") was a moral and cosmological term that literally had to do with one's birth, and whose late-nineteenth- and early-twentieth-century usage encompassed a multiplicity of concepts, including ethnic identity and social status.[53] In nineteenth-century France, "birth" was one of the many meanings of the term *race,* which was used in multiple contexts to denote social and professional groups, sex, nation, and ethnicity.[54] In the first decades of the twentieth century, secular literati and the *sangha* in Cambodge increasingly used *jiet* to signify both race and nation, echoing the interchangeability of *nation* and *race* in contemporary French discourse and paralleling the development and deployment of similarly fluid formulations for race/nation elsewhere in Asia.[55]

Colonial education was one means of inculcating such notions. Schooled in Phnom Penh and Hanoi in the 1910s, the teenage Prince Areno Iukanthor defined the term *ma pauvre Race* as *mon peuple* (my people) and their *héritage* (heritage).[56] The establishment of the first Khmer-language newspapers and journals in the 1920s would provide new forums for the translation and formulation of such ideas, while the continued role of monks as interpreters of this Khmer media to their rural constituencies, ensured the percolation of such concepts beyond the small nucleus of the educated elite.

But the shifting meaning of *jiet* cannot entirely be ascribed to pedagogy or print media. Native participation in the adaptation and elaboration of colonial forms of knowledge engineered new ways of relating to both space and time. Of key significance here was the introduction of European notions of history as a sliding scale of time, which encouraged the elite to relate to the past as both a separate realm and a national, rather than purely dynastic, terrain. Prior to the eighteenth century, Western chronicles of history, like their counterparts in the preindustrial societies of nineteenth-century Southeast Asia, depicted the past with an "immediacy and intimacy" that reflected its presumed likeness to the present.[57] In Cambodge, as in Malaya, India, and countless other territories under European rule, history writing evolved from the "flat canvas" of traditional texts, which had plotted important incidents around particular reigns, to a linear narrative of nation that fused concepts of country, people, sovereignty, and statehood.[58] The resultant shift in literary focus from the "history of kings" to the "history of this country" was coupled with a distinction between the "legends and fabulous tales" of indigenous sources and the new, "true historical account" reflecting the criteria of Western scholarship.[59]

Late-nineteenth-century European preoccupations with themes of decadence and decline exaggerated this process, leading colonial and metropolitan scholars, administrators and writers to extol the antique civilizations of colonized countries, juxtaposing past golden eras with present degeneracy, as in Renan's earlier mentioned reflections on Egypt. In Cambodge, the ancient temples of Angkor were seized upon as the apotheosis of past glory and presented as the pinnacle of national endeavor in scholarly works, official pronouncements, visual arts, and plastic representations that collectively plotted monuments and moments in Cambodian history as part of "a national (in the sense of a nation-state) continuity" and cast "the Khmer as a people sliding down a millennial incline."[60]

These preoccupations with vanishing and decline stemmed in part from a growing tendency on the part of Europeans, bound up with the rise of national heritage movements in nineteenth-century France, England, and elsewhere, to equate the existence of the Cambodian nation with the maintenance of its "traditional" culture, a mentality seen in scholar-offical Roland Meyer's novel *Saramani: Une danseuse cambodgienne* (1919). When Meyer began his novel in 1910, the Khmer population of Cambodge had nearly tripled since the establishment of the French Protectorate. Yet *Saramani* portrays the Khmers as a people on the brink of extinction, destined to die out under the barrage of European, Chinese, and Annamite influence—despite the fact that these non-Khmer groups then formed a mere fraction of the population. Meyer's concern was not that actual persons would die or disappear, but that their customs and culture might vanish. Similar preoccupations dictated a policy of cultural containment in education, religion, publications, the pictorial, plastic, and performing arts, museology, and archaeology. In these areas, French conceptions of Cambodge gained tangible form and were made accessible to Cambodge's slowly expanding, educated urban elite.

Nagaravatta, whose title reflected both the validation of the temples of Angkor as an emblem of that "newly imagined collectivity"—the nation—and the identification of the newspaper's founders as the rightful heirs and guardians of that nation, provided a forum for the coinage and circulation of a new, nationalist vocabulary.[61] By the time of *Nagaravatta's* establishment in the 1930s, *jiet* had become the principal term for race/nation in the rhetoric of both secular intellegentsia and reformist *sangha.* The popularity of such pen names as Kmae botra (Son of the Khmers) and Kmae daem (Original Khmer) reflected the new primacy of ethnicity as a locus of identity. As defined by one self-styled "Son of the Khmers," *jiet* denoted race *(la race).*[62] However, it also signified nation, as in such compounds as *sasana-jiet* (national-religion) and *jun-jiet* (nationality). Editorials regularly urged readers to *sralan jiet* (love the race-nation). Coverage of such abstract notions as race and nation vastly eclipsed the attention given to the monarchy in *Nagaravatta* and its predecessors. The linkage of the term *bangsaa* (race/family/lineage) to such terms as *yeung* (our) and *kmae* (Khmer) reflected a shift in focus from royal ancestry to national genealogy, indicating that in Cambodge, as in Malaya and other colonial dominions, race and nation were competing with and in some cases superseding royalty as a primary object of loyalty.[63] As we shall see, these developments were tied up with the shifting meaning of the Khmer term *sasana.* Used to denote religion at the turn of the century, *sasana* had broadened by the late 1930s to encompass notions of race and ethnicity, reflecting the elevation of nation to a quasi-religious site.[64] By 1937, *sasana-kee* (lit.: the religion of others) was used to mean other races, and *sasana-kmae* (Khmer religion) to denote both Buddhism and the Khmer race.[65]

From the earliest Khmer newspapers to the 1952 essay on democracy and diamonds by the "Original Khmer" Saloth Sar, pseudonyms emerged as a popular strategy among Cambodian intellectuals, allowing these graduates of colonial modernity simultaneously to shield their identity from the scrutiny of the Sûreté, and to bask in the fantasy of antiquity through such alter egos as Son of the Khmers and the Original Khmer. These names not only concealed their author's identity and revealed their aspirations, they also reflected back at the protectorate its description of Khmers as talented copyists.

From the 1930s to mid-1940s, these abstract notions of Cambodge and attempts to personify Angkorean glory through such individual and national acts of naming, were circulated through a growing number of school clubs, newspaper groups, and literary associations. Barely visible in these early nationalist organizations were the future foreign minister of Democratic Kampuchea Ieng Sary, a young Saloth Sar, and his future wife and mentor, Khieu Ponnary. These and other secular intellectuals would carry the conceptual legacy of Cambodge into the postcolonial era.

CHAPTER AND VERSE

As a history of ideas, this book is organized with more attention to the circulation and translation of abstractions than to the strict sequence of events. Three chapters focus on interventions at Angkor and three on the monkhood, while three deal with more urbane themes. But rather than group these chapters into a thematic tryptich, I have interleaved them to create a sense of the interconnectedness of these spheres of activity, and to emphasize the plurality of actors and ideas engaged in the "cultivation of a nation" in Cambodge.

Following on from this introduction, Chapter 1 explores Angkor as a site for the generation of European imaginings about Cambodge, from the arrival of the explorer Henri Mouhot in 1860 to the construction of an Angkor pavilion at Marseille in 1906. Interleaving Cambodge and the Métropole, museums and monuments, exhibitions and excavations, it explores the influence of European heritage movements and historicist paradigms in shaping Angkor Vat's transition from a primarily sacred site to an emblem of the modern nation-state. Moving to the colonial capital of Phnom Penh, Chapter 2 explores the translation of these visions into the built environment, the authentication of a Khmer "national style," and the cult of "verisimilitude" that saw the integration of Angkorean symbols into the new Cambodian capital as well as Paris. Turning from European designs to Cambodian interlocutors, the third chapter of this book explores the emergence of two key transitional figures who marked the emergence of an indigenous secular literati, and who participated in the initial scripting of a Khmer nation for European and Cambodian audiences. Turning to the domain of religious practice and Buddhist texts, Chapter 4 explores the impact of colonial intervention on the Cambodian *sangha,* or monkhood, and charts the cultivation of Buddhism as a national religion by French scholars and reformist *sangha* from the establishment of the protectorate to the 1920s. Chapter 5 examines the "Hinduization" and desecralization of Angkor in situ and the reverberations between metropolitan and indigenous fund-raising schemes to conserve the temples, following the establishment of a formal conservation program in 1907. Examining the impact of colonial excavations of Angkor on indigenous belief systems through the work of a noted Khmer poet, the chapter also explores the involvement of Cambodian donors, committee members, and laborers, in the temple complex's rehabilitation. Focusing on the School of Fine Arts established by the protectorate, Chapter 6 examines colonial prescriptions both for visions of Khmerness and for the field of Khmer vision, and explores the emergence of particular artistic products as embodiments of the Khmer "national style."

Chapter 7 moves to the secularisation of the *sangha,* and explores how administrative suspicions of the *sangha* fostered strategies to tax, school, and card that mirrored metropolitan concerns to segregate church and state, and also cohered with the visions of Cambodian reformist monks, to create an ethnolinguistic Khmer nation. Chapter 8 examines the role of other key cultural and educational institutes established by the protectorate, notably the Royal Library and the Buddhist Institute, which were established with the dual aims of insulating the Cambodian *sangha* from Siamese influence and articulating and conserving a specifically Khmer branch of Buddhism.[66] Chapter 9 explores the convergence of these trends and arenas in a vital, dynamic decade, when the *sangha,* secular intellectuals, print media, and clubhouse became conjoined in the translation of the conceptual rubric of Cambodge into a modern nationalist movement, from 1935 to 1945. Chapter 10 briefly reflects upon the ramifications of colonialism's "temple complex" for postcolonial politics and sketches the longevity of "Cambodge," and its attendant fantasies, in regime discourses after Independence.

SOURCES AND TERMINOLOGY

In attempting to recreate a feel for the social, cultural, and intellectual climate in Cambodge, this book draws on a range of French and Khmer literary, archival, and news materials, as well as illustrations and photographs. Rather than looking in at the period from the "master narrative of nationalism," I have tried to shed light on the mindsets of French and Cambodian actors by peering out from their piecemeal trail of articles, literature, memoirs, and letters, and mapping the outbound trajectory of their notions through their translation into colonial policy, intellectual practice, and nationalist politics.[67] This approach has its obvious shortcomings. Like the letters exchanged by an estranged couple in Siri Hustvedt's recent novel, all texts are "skewed by invisible perforations, the small holes of the unwritten but not the unthought."[68] My main Khmer sources are journals, newspapers, and administrative reports, which passed the scrutiny of the Sûreté but were still perforated by the individual acts of self-censorship common to all authoritarian states. My main research sites—national and colonial archives—are no less flawed. This is not only because their contents are imprinted with the ideologies of their writers and the imprint of their supposed spectator, nor is it purely because they have been scrutinized, culled, and ordered in a particular way. The holdings of colonial and national archives, long held in awe as bastions of historical evidence, are complicated by their simultaneous function as "the outcome of historical process and the very conditions for the production of historical knowledge."[69] Moreover, as Stoler convincingly demonstrates, many of the documents stored in these monumental spaces are not records of past events but plans and prescriptions expressing often unrealized colonial desires. These "colonial utopias" and "historical negatives," Stoler argues, are not so much paradigms of conquest as distress signals, pointing to "the disjuncture between what was possible to think and impossible to implement."[70] Despite these restrictions, however, in between Stoler's "blueprints of distress" and Hustvedt's "perforations" the marvellous vagaries of human error and individual eccentricities have infused my own experience of archival and library research in Paris, Marseille, London, Rangoon, Canberra, and Phnom Penh with a taste of the subversive potential of archived materials to transcend and elude the categories under which they are filed. Random photos, misplaced letters, eclectic collections of news cuttings, scrawled notes on visiting cards, personal dedications in the flyleafs of crumbling books, are just some of the sources undermining the presumed rigor and monumentality of the archive. The rigorous scrutiny of the Sûreté, particularly in the late 1930s and during the Vichy regime, acted as a lens on both the paranoid machinations of the regime and the everyday, ensuring the obsessive conservation of many personal letters of both Europeans and Cambodians. Nineteenth- and early-twentieth-century French and Khmer media produced in Indochina, Paris, and Marseille, as well as colonial novels, travelogues, poetry, and photographs, also figure throughout this book.

However, like many other works on colonized domains, this book remains captive to the conundrum of its reliance on the very European colonial sources whose fundamental assumptions it sets out to question. Since I am writing about exchanges in ideas and images between Cambodians and Europeans, such materials are essential to my project. Too easily lumped together as a hegemonic and homogeneous narrative, works by Europeans were themselves caught up in a complex circuit of knowledge production, involving indigenous actors, the transmission of new modalities and technologies of knowledge and print production, and a multiplicity of sponsors, audiences, and motivations for publication. To emphasize colonialism's often fractured chorus of voices and to alert readers as to their origin, I have tried, as far as possible without disrupting narrative flow, to signal the authorship and genre of documents cited in the main body of the text.

I use the term "Cambodge" throughout the book, as in its title, to denote the political life span and geographic domain of the protectorate, and the conceptual rubric of nation structured within this temporal and territorial frame.[71] Like the Indochina described by Norindr, I see Cambodge as a product of the "identification," "conflation, and confusion" of French imaginings with the political and geographic structure of the protectorate.[72] I use the term "colonial" broadly to describe the regime, policy, personnel, and European residents of the Protectorate of Cambodge. I do so, not to denote "the colonial" as a monolithic category, but in an adjectival sense, to connect such figures in time and place with the colonial enterprise. When writing about Cambodge, the majority of French administrators and scholars used the term *le Cambodgien* to refer, not to an inhabitant of Cambodge, but to the majority Khmer ethnic group as distinct from *le Chinois* or *l'Annamite*. To avoid confusion with the current English usage of "Cambodian," which denotes a resident of Cambodia regardless of ethnicity, I have rendered the French term *Cambodgien* as "Khmer" where context so requires. I have kept Annamite as used in the French period—the preferred blanket term referring to those people later identified as "Vietnamese" living in Cochinchina, Tonkin, and Annam.[73] When discussing relations and correspondence between administrations and individuals on the mainland and the Protectorate of Cambodge, I often use the term "Métropole" to refer to France. I use the term *savant* interchangeably with the nearest English equivalent, scholar, to describe those colonial personalities of various professional backgrounds who held a lasting scholarly and cultural interest in Cambodge. A full glossary of French and Khmer terms appears at the back of this book. Unless otherwise stated, all translations of Khmer and French sources are my own.

I | The Temple Complex

Angkor and the Archaeology of Colonial Fantasy, 1860–1906

In 1860, a team of Chinese coolies and Siamese guides escorted a young French naturalist named Henri Mouhot through the dense jungle undergrowth surrounding the former seat of the Khmer Empire at Siem Reap, named after the decisive battle that had seen its annexation by Siam in the fifteenth century. Before the year was out, he was dead, but what he saw on this Siamese side trip as a naturalist turned accidental tourist filled him with wonder and catapulted him to posthumous fame.

Mouhot's guides may well have marvelled at his wonder, for there was no novelty for them and many others in the vicinity in the site to which they led him. But to Mouhot this was the paradigmatic moment of discovery, a moment whose mixture of joy, shock, and gravitas must have turned him giddy with prospects of academic fame. Before him were ancient trees and vines and dense brush, whispering with wildlife and teeming with a wealth of natural specimens. Ordinarily, he might have stopped to sketch this or that life-form in his sketchbook, trapping a bug, or snaring an exotic butterfly. But what he saw blinded him to such minutiae. Here were the sandstone corpses of a civilization, the huge and sprawling ruins of an abandoned city.

Mouhot was barely known at the time and had failed in his first grant application to the French government. Aided by his marriage to an Englishwoman, he had secured funding from the Royal Geographical Society of Britain, which had every interest in seeing such "blank patches" on Britain's map of Southeast Asia filled. Eight years after the Second Anglo-Burmese War (1852), the vast tract of land stretching southeast of Rangoon through Siam and across to Saigon was as yet unspoken for, at least by European powers. The year of Mouhot's discovery coincided with the launch of France's first travel journal, *Tour du Monde* (World tour), designed to inform the public and politicians of the value and potential of overseas countries and peoples, so that France might better decide "what we should take, and what we should leave."[1]

As he regained focus and continued his tour of this place known in Khmer as Nokor Vat (temple city), Mouhot would have seen Buddhist monks traversing part of the complex, tending to shrines, and their dwellings. His hurried, fluid sketches of the ruins contrast with the exactitude of his depictions of natural specimens, betraying both the excitement of his discovery and his awe at the impossibility of ever adequately representing its enormity. Perhaps to indicate scale, Mouhot included people in his sketches: solitary figures leaning against a lintel or groups of two clad in monkish robes. Sketched at a distance, their ethnicity is indiscernible, but their contemporaneity is immediately apparent. To Mouhot, these people, however few and far between, were part of the picture. As a naturalist, he recorded what he saw. But Angkor would no doubt remain in his imagination as it became in European conceptions and as it first appeared to him in that moment of awed discovery: as the fantastic, picturesque burial ground of a "dead" civilization.

Several months later, a severe bout of malaria dispatched the exhausted Mouhot to an early jungle grave in Laos, but his memoir was compressed into a travelogue and published posthumously by a family friend.[2] In January 1863, the *Revue Maritime et Coloniale* (Naval and colonial review) published an account by Vice Admiral Bonard, governor of Cochinchina, describing his voyage from Saigon to Angkor aboard "the first European steamboat to have flown a [French] flag" on the Tonle Sap lake.[3] Bonard stressed the potential of Cambodge's people and the untapped archive of its Angkorean past.[4] Rehashed by a ghostwriter and embellished with elaborate engravings, Mouhot's diary was serialized later that year in the *Tour du Monde,* firing the imaginations of France's growing colonial lobby and inviting comparison with the monuments of British India.[5] Extolling Cambodge's rich natural resources, Mouhot urged France to add this "jewel" to its "colonial crown" before Britain snatched it.[6]

Many of Mouhot's sketches were excluded from the text, thus banishing those human figures—the presence of the present—which had been recorded in the young naturalist's first impressions, from public view. In their place were lavish interpretations of his original line drawings by the noted European engravers Sabatier, Boucourt, Rousseau, Thérond, Beaumont, Hanet, Lange, and Catenaccis, most of which bore little relation to the text itself.[7] The 1863 *Tour du Monde* enhanced Mouhot's drawings with stormy skies or excised native figures, reinforcing the message that the Khmers were a vanished race. Contrasting Cambodge's "degenerate" present with the majesty of Angkor, scholars, explorers, administrators, and novelists mistakenly concluded that the Khmers who had built Angkor were now extinct.[8] Some, like the young explorer Francis Garnier, would apply this rubric to an entire civilization, declaring that all Khmer social and political organization, as well as literature, had vanished.[9] This spectre of erasure of the past as a warning of imminent vanishing remained a key trope in colonial art, literature, and propaganda, and would be worked into national imaginings as a keystone of postcolonial nationalism.[10] Ravaged by tropical decay and neglect, Mouhot's Angkor entered *l'imaginaire français* as an emblem of the fate awaiting empires—and civilizations—in decline.[11] The temples epitomized the dangers of decadence and symbolized France's moral destiny in Indochina. Angkor's location in Siem Reap, annexed by Siam in 1794 and regularly referred to along with neighboring Battambang and Sisophon as Cambodge's "Alsace-Lorraine," reinforced its role as a repository of yearning for a lost golden age. While talk of Mouhot's and Bonard's discoveries made the rounds of Parisian salons and colonial barracks, a trio of young Frenchmen posted in Cochinchine were constructing a different case for expansion in Indochina. Headed by the twenty-three-year-old naval officer Francis Garnier, the group lobbied Minister of Marine Chasseloup Laubat to open up the still uncharted Mekong River as France's trade route into China.[12]

Mindful of Cambodge's cultural potential and its strategic location as a counterweight to what was considered a British zone of influence in Siam, France's representative in Cambodge, the naval commander Ernest-Marc-Louis de Gonzague Doudart de Lagrée, secured King Norodom I's signature on an 1863 Treaty of Protectorate—so named because it embodied France's pledge to protect Norodom's throne from rival claims and from the threat of control by his historically avaricious neighbors, Vietnam and Siam. In an early indication of just whose interests France was protecting, Norodom's subsequent attempt to outmaneuver France through secret negotiations with Siam met with the swift dispatch of a gunboat. This initial swagger presaged a policy that became more entrenched and complex as colonial rule progressed, namely, that of severing Siamese scholarly and religious connections with Cambodge.

Until the retrocession of Siem Reap to Cambodge in 1907, the twelfth-century temple complex of Angkor had remained on Siamese territory. However, France used its new foothold in the region and its ally, the Cambodian monarchy, to win privileged access to the temples. Through persuasion, diplomacy, coercion, and deception, French explorers, administrators, and scholars acquired numerous relics from Angkor. By the turn of the century, before a blueprint had been drawn up for a museum in Phnom Penh, Paris boasted the world's most elaborate museum exhibits of ancient Khmer sculpture and architecture. These collections, and the establishment of the École Française d'Extrême Orient (EFEO) in Saigon in 1901, gave France a monopoly on the production of knowledge about Angkor.

As French scholarship expanded, Western depictions of the temples changed. Plastic and textual representations rebuilt Angkor as a totem of the Western imagination, erasing contemporary residents from temple views or dramatizing them by the addition of helmets, spears, and a bizarre Roman-Angkorean regalia designed, apparently, to signal grandeur, themes of glory and decline, and a knowledge intimated by the artist or writer to the viewer/reader, of an-other time. By the 1880s, elaborate engravings as well as material reconstructions of Angkor at colonial and national exhibitions had antiquarianized the rambling, wondrous ruins witnessed by Mouhot, transforming them into a perfect citadel, peopled by figures from the temple's bas-reliefs.[13] Maps, journals, travelogues, and exotic novels embroidered Angkor onto the French consciousness as a peripheral emblem of empire, demarcating France's geographic and scholastic reach in the Orient. These conceptions were reinforced by concrete configurations of Angkor. Plaster casts, miniature models, massive pavilions, and purloined relics in Paris and Marseille all wove the art and architecture of Angkor into France's national fabric. While the ephemeral displays at these mostly temporary exhibitions reenacted the mythical vanishing acts of Angkorean civilization, the permanent halls and exhibits at museums in Paris and Phnom Penh provided a sort of cultural formaldehyde in which conceptions of Cambodge hung suspended and unchallenged.

The incorporation of Angkor into France's national heritage, or *patrimoine,* was paralleled by a far more subtle process in Cambodge. The temple had remained a central point of reference in Khmer cultural and spiritual life since its construction. However, the processes through which colonial policy and scholarly practice carved out a niche for Angkor in the French national imagination also fostered a fundamental shift in Cambodian perceptions of, and relationships to, the temples. In part the result of European scholarship and colonial propaganda, but also informed by similar developments in Siam, this "changed consciousness" transcribed Suryavarman II's celestial city with national meaning.[14]

From 1863 until the absorption of Siem Reap into Cambodge in 1907, French scholars and administrators, unable to claim sovereignty over the actual site of Angkor, began to stake out an intellectual and cultural sovereignty in the Metropolitan domains of exhibitions, museums, and monuments. Here, representations, fragments, replications, restorations, and images of Angkor acted as surrogate sites, which can in and of themselves be mined as archaeologies of colonial fantasy. These were physical transactions, and the manner in which they were carried out, by whom, and with what purpose—in short, their normative framework and the new field of meanings such transactions created in their rejection of or intersection with indigenous patterns of behavior and belief—had lasting ramifications for the shaping of Khmer nationalism, and infused that nationalism with both an inexorable longing for a return to the past and a keen desire to prove the potency of that past through a merging of antiquity and modernity.

ANGKOR AS A SPIRITUAL SITE

The reign of Jayavarman II, who founded the Khmer Empire in 802 AD, saw the revitalization of sculpture, art, and architecture and the inauguration of a monumental tradition at his new capital of Mahendraparvata, centering at first on the lingam.[15] A symbol of the god Siva and his own royal divinity, the lingam and other dedicated statuary would prove essential to the maintenance of the Devaraja cult. Although in time Devaraja came to denote "God-King" in popular usage, inscriptions from the Angkor period clearly describe the *devaraja* as a sacred object—perhaps a lingam or a statue—that travelled to each successive capital with each successive king. The resultant conflation of sovereignty and statuary is reflected in an eleventh-century inscription describing the king as possessing a "subtle inner self" that actually resided in a lingam found in his temple.[16]

In Khmer culture as in the Javanese belief systems described by Anderson, power was traditionally perceived as a "concrete, homogeneous" feature of the spiritual cosmos to be "accumulated" and "concentrated" through such acts as the erection of temples and other holy monuments.[17] The temples of Angkor, built as funeral complexes to house the ashes and spirits of kings, both perpetuated the divine powers of their builders after death and augmented their power during their lives. Modelled on a celestial city, Angkor Vat was itself revered as a pivot between heaven and earth. At its center was a monument to Vishnu, the avatar of the god-king Surya-varman II who built and controlled it.[18] In traditional Khmer cosmology, as in the belief systems of neighboring kingdoms, the temples thus acted as both signs and stores of power.[19] Khmers did not conceive of these early temples as a meeting place for the faithful, but as the home of the god to which each temple was dedicated, and who was thought to inhabit the temple in the form of his sacred image. Temple architecture was strongly symbolic, and mirrored the Hindic firmament. Replicating Mount Mehru as the cosmic *axis mundi,* the central feature of each temple was a tower *(prasat)* enshrining the principal deity. Radiating out from this central point was a highly symmetrical pattern of subordinate towers, one or more of which were dedicated to the god's spouse and his "vehicle." Secondary constructions, designed to preserve cult objects and everything connected with the liturgy and exegesis formed the periphery to this core.[20]

The spiritual power of the city of Angkor as the seat of the Khmer Empire was progressively developed through ritual, art, and literature from the ninth to thirteenth centuries. In a bid to retain this power, and to perpetuate their divinity and sovereignty, Khmer royalty took sacred statuary with them as they moved southward to escape Siam's reach, transplanting fragments of Angkor to their new capitals at Longvek and, subsequently, Oudong. Its power sustained by statuary and story, Angkor would reverberate at the heart of Khmer culture even as the Khmer Empire splintered and fragmented in the shadow of Siam, Vietnam, and the power plays of rival royal factions. Indeed, as cultural historian Ashley Thompson has suggested, the physical abandonment of the temple city might even be said to have magnified the mystical power and regional orbit of Angkor as a cultural and political concept.[21] From the Siamese victory until the sixteenth century, when Theravadan Buddhists led a movement to "reappropriate ancient space" through the conceptual and physical revitalization of the Angkor heritage, artists and laity had perpetuated remembrance of Angkor in works of architecture, art, and literature.[22] In the late sixteenth century that reappropriation also took the form of renovation. "The King restored the walls of the building, stone by stone, [and] rebuilt its roof" reads a 1579 inscription at Angkor Vat.[23] The harmonization of that Brahmanic heritage and Theravadan ideology is reflected in *Lpoek Nokor* (The construction of Angkor). Variously dated 1598 and 1620 and attributed to Neak Pang, the poem unfolds the Khmer version of the Ramayana (Reamker) through vivid poetic images describing the bas-reliefs at Angkor Vat.[24] The early seventeenth century also saw the sculpting of fresh bas-reliefs on the north-facing wall in the eastern wing of Angkor Vat.[25] Sixteenth-, seventeenth-, and eighteenth-century inscriptions by Khmer royalty on the temple testify to the lasting identification of Khmer queens and kings with Angkor, and to its emerging significance as a site of Buddhist ritual.[26] In 1835, Angkor's continued relevance as an emblem of royalty was reflected in the issue of coins bearing the facade of Angkor Vat.[27] During the 1850s, the French missionary Bouillevaux found a number of monks practicing in Angkor Vat.[28] As earlier noted, Mouhot also witnessed active worship in and around the temples.[29] After the coronation of King Norodom I in 1860, chief monks continued to make annual pilgrimages to Angkor.[30]

Through the prism of twentieth-century notions of nationhood, these royal and religious pilgrimages have been interpreted as evidence of Khmer identification with Angkor as national heritage. Writing in 1900, one French analyst linked religious pilgrimages to Angkor to the maintenance of "a certain nationalist spirit" among the Khmer population in Siem Reap.[31] Mme de Coral Rémusat later concluded that the temple functioned continuously as a "national shrine," while Australian museum curator Michael Brand has stressed its lasting significance as a national treasure.[32] But the fact that non-Khmers also made such pilgrimages, and that non-Khmer monarchs also sought to identify with Angkor, undermine such unequivocal interpretations of Angkor's significance as a locus of nation.

Such naturalizations of Angkor as a symbol of Khmer identity are further complicated by the temple's genealogy. Thai and Cham prisoners of war were allegedly involved in Angkor's construction.[33] Chinese symbols were incorporated into Khmer art and sculpture during the Angkorean period, and an entire Chinese edifice into the temple site of Vat Nokor in Kompong Cham during the thirteenth century.[34] After the sacking of Angkor, the king of Siam ordered the removal of statuary from the temple complex to his capital at Ayuthaya.[35] This symbolic act of transfer prefigured the emergence of Angkor as a model of Siamese statecraft during the fifteenth century, the identification of Siamese kings with Rama, and the adoption and adaptation of Angkorean dance and language by the Siamese court.[36] Stylistic evidence suggests that the bas-reliefs added to the eastern wall of Angkor in the seventeenth century were fashioned by Chinese artisans.[37] The Ayuthaya kingdom drew heavily on the Angkor heritage. When Burma sacked Ayuthaya in the early eighteenth century, Siam's collection of Angkorean statuary was moved to Mandalay.[38] Khmer folklore describes a nineteenth-century attempt by a Khmer mandarin to dismantle part of the Ta Prohm temple so as to transfer it to Bangkok by request of the Siamese king, who wished to resurrect a segment of Angkor in his capital.[39] This version of events resonates with other legends encompassing Ta Prohm and Ta Nei.[40] While all may be apocryphal, we do know that after his accession to the throne, King Mongkut (r. 1851–1868) had a replica of Angkor constructed near the shrine of the Emerald Buddha at the grand palace in Bangkok. Led by Mongkut, Siamese literati began to investigate the historical origins of Siam and to "discover" the significance of Angkor in Siam's national heritage, perhaps in part to bolster the legitimacy of Siamese claims to the western provinces in response to France's expansionist aims in the region.[41] In 1865, a Lao dignitary visited Angkor with a sizeable retinue on a pilgrimage.[42]

This backdrop of cross-fertilization, cultural transfer, and ritual restoration lends a dissembling air of continuity to the French appropriation and relocation of Angkorean artifacts. Examined in strict chronological sequence, the colonial intervention in Khmer monumental space might appear to have been part of a long-standing pattern. Continuing along this monofocal chronology to the postcolonial era, we might also conclude that the modern Cambodian celebration of Angkor as a national monument is but another act of continuity with the past. Such assumptions skirt vital differences in belief systems.

The sixteenth- and seventeenth-century embellishments of Angkor by Khmer monarchs were projects to honor sacred beings and accumulate spiritual power. In this they differed markedly from later projects by the French state and its institutions to restore Angkor as a historical monument. In contrast to nineteenth- and twentieth-century individual and institutional collectors of Khmer art, Siamese and Burmese monarchs coveted Angkorean statuary, not for its documentary value as a repository of history or for its market value, but for the divine power of Khmer god-kings concentrated therein.[43] While Angkor remained an active site of worship and of pilgrimage for both Khmers and non-Khmers, there is no evidence to suggest that the monument functioned as a symbol of one nation. Rather, like the generic monument described by the political geographer Jean Lefebvre, the temples of Angkor are likely to have possessed a "shifting hierarchy" of meanings.[44]

The apparent absence of a linear historical perspective in indigenous accounts of Angkor fostered an enduring assumption, on the part of European observers, that Angkor was a place *sans memoire*. "Here, in this point of the Far-East," wrote Louis de Carné of the ruins of Angkor, "all is dead, even the memory of this brilliant theocracy."[45] Describing his visit to Angkor in the late 1860s, Ch. Lemire writes that "The Cambodians have no memory of their past grandeur."[46] Recycled in later tomes, such assertions gained documentary status. "Cambodians haven't even kept the memory of their grand past," proclaimed one scholar-official in 1905.[47] Theories abounded that the Khmers who had built Angkor were a vanished race, their tracks covered by the degenerate crop of "Cambodgiens" who had risen in their wake.[48]

While unable or unwilling to furnish colonial savants with the hard historical data after which they hankered, Khmer monks and laypeople interviewed by nineteenth-century French explorers all shared a rich repertoire of local lore. All appeared deeply aware of Angkor as a place of great magical significance; none replied that "the Khmers" had built it. The French missionary Bouillevaux related that the Cambodians he met in the 1840s and 1850s knew Angkor as an old city "long ago populated by people of their race, and built by a Leper King."[49] Mouhot's search for the builders of Angkor elicited four standard responses: Pra-eun, the King of the Angels; giants; leprous kings; and "It made itself."[50] Twenty years later, members of the Mekong Exploration Commission elicited similar responses.[51] Another legend held that the temple of Angkor was built under the reign of Prah Ket Mealea (Blossoming Light), the son of Queen Vong and the god Indra, whose father Indra placed a heavenly architect at his disposal, Popusnakar, the Viçakarman of Hindu tales.[52] Allusions to Angkor also persisted in Khmer folk songs that may have long predated French rule.[53] Chandler has interpreted these responses to mean that, while Cambodians had been aware of Angkor at the time of the French discovery, they did not see the ruins as "evidence of a *Cambodian* kingdom."[54]

Khmers questioned by these European travellers may have been reticent to reveal their real beliefs and feelings about the temples. Moreover, poetic license and romantic embellishment doubtless interfered with accurate reporting, and colonial writers were not averse to poaching the prose of earlier explorers to authenticate their own accounts. However, the commonality of outlook reflected in the diverse range of testimonies recorded by Mouhot and others provides some indication of how Khmers in the late-nineteenth century related to Angkor, and supports Chandler's conclusion that Khmers living in the vicinity of the temple did not identify with Angkor as a monument of Khmer nationhood or a lodestone of *national* pride, but rather as a religious site connected in popular belief-systems with celebrated monarchs and mythical figures.

While colonial savants eschewed such accounts as fantasy and fairytale, many such oral histories were remarkably well informed, testifying to the continued interest that Angkor had evoked throughout the centuries.[55] As Chandler has noted, many of the monuments and statuary "discovered" by the Europeans, and supposedly rescued by them from a widely diagnosed Khmer amnesia, bore Cambodian names, pointing to a continuity in folk memories that served as popular transmitters of undocumented fact.[56] Thompson has corroborated this view through research tracing the inheritance and perpetuation of the cults of Angkor Vat by temple caretakers and local worshippers whose rituals have traversed centuries, guided by memory, not text.[57]

Colonial intervention would subsume this multiplicity of meanings into a homogenizing, national narrative. As described in 1951 by Director Louis Malleret, the EFEO "restored a chronology, disengaged the past from its legend, and recovered dynastic lines, giving a new éclat to great reigns like those of Jayavarman II and Jayavarman VII."[58] By inserting Angkor into a sliding scale of time, grooming, landscaping, restoring, and depicting the ruins in ways that privileged European aesthetic standards, and authenticating it as a ledger of national history, the protectorate would first assert, and then sublimate, Angkor's status as a national monument. This totalizing, secular frame of reference would radically alter Cambodian relations to, and perceptions of, the temple complex. Paradoxically, this rupture with past practice was brought about by French attempts to establish a continuity between Cambodge and its Angkorean past through historiography, archaeology, and museology.

HOLY PATRIMONY: MUSEUMS, EXPOSITIONS, AND NATIONAL HERITAGE IN EUROPE AND EMPIRE

Museums and exhibitions provided the principal stages onto which colonial fantasies of Angkor were projected into Metropolitan cultural life.[59] In the earliest days of imperial exploration, the destination of biological specimens and cultural artifacts collected by missionaries, merchants, and naturalists had been "curiosity chests," a fashionable feature of wealthy eighteenth-century households. During the nineteenth century, the movement of museum from domestic and religious spheres to the public domain brought these exotica into the public gaze, while the acquisition of foreign cultural "patrimony" (patrimoine) was deeply enmeshed with Europe's growing preoccupations with national identity.[60] Unlike its private, royal, and religious antecedents, the modern museum identified with the state and nation. By promoting the "genius" of national schools, and embodying "national" character in art and artifact, public museums promoted both state power and national identity. The neat chronologies and national categories of these new institutions effectively converted the contents of curiosity boxes to "repositories of spiritual treasure—the heritage and pride of the whole nation."[61] But the transformative power of France's new museums was not restricted to objects. By engaging visitors in a designated national arena of culture, these new "civic temples" also constructed national subjects, thus helping to create a "national public."[62] The Revolution of 1789 laid the ground for future attempts to institutionalize and nationalize history and heritage and for the emergence of a new historiography that chronicled a "community of shared memory."[63] In the absence of a French nation—whose characteristics and parameters had yet to be properly defined and constituted—early-nineteenth-century French historians deplored the absence of a national history. This new passion for history and nation, and the desire to embed the one in the other, informed a drive to conserve, identify, and catalogue the past. Old relics were infused with new meaning as icons of communal identity, continuity, and aspiration.[64]

The term "historic monument" (monument historique) first appeared in France in a 1790 compendium of "national antiquities," to refer to buildings, statues, tombs, and anything able to "determine, illustrate and clarify national history."[65] Forty years later, France's first state office for the protection and management of French heritage (patrimoine français) was born.[66] Created by the eminent historian Guizot, the Inspectorate of Historic Monuments had a dual mandate of recovering antiquity and discovering the modern French nation.[67] Led by Prosper Merimée and Eugène Viollet-le-Duc, the French government began to catalogue and classify monuments according to their historic and aesthetic importance, and to develop a methodology of conservation and restoration that placed classified monuments under government protection.[68] A Commission of Historic Monuments, established in 1836, became the nodal point for France's growing network of scholarly societies (sociétés savants) and local archaeological commissions.[69] Although earnestly committed to conserving past heritage, these groups often elaborated new pasts for their locality, region, and nation.[70] Across France, heritage societies mushroomed. The valorization of objects as historical records was reflected in the French term document, commonly used in the late nineteenth century by explorers and museographers to refer to sculpture, architecture, and artifacts.

Fin de siècle fears of degeneration and decadence intensified the drive to define and conserve a national heritage through monument and museum not just in France but throughout Europe. The British composers and songwriters Gilbert and Sullivan captured this mood in their lines "There's a fascination frantic/In a ruin that's romantic;/Do you think you are sufficiently decayed?"[71] These fears were particularly pervasive in France, where a burgeoning working class, Prussia's amputation of Alsace-Lorraine in 1870, and falling birth rates exacerbated bourgeois fears of national disappearance and racial decline.[72]

But what was the nexus between museums and empire? First, these preoccupations with social and national entropy at home could only have exacerbated the trend towards conservation in France and the colonies, and encouraged the transplantation of discourses of vanishing and decline to newly conquered cultures. Second, as Said has argued, "the French empire was uniquely connected to the French national identity, its brilliance [and] civilizational energy" in the minds of novelists, lobbyists, and savants.[73] Domiciled in France, the plant, animal, mineral, and cultural products of distant regions were absorbed into France's *patrimoine* as signifiers of scientific strength and territorial reach. In this context, museums emerged as indices of their host country's commitment to cultural conservation and national education. They also created a strong centripetal current by focusing the minds of explorers and archaeologists on obtaining Oriental antiquities to enrich their "national" heritage.[74]

The new phenomenon of world fairs *(expositions universelles)* encouraged the conflation of history, territory, monument, and nation through displays of French *patrimoine* both within and outside France's borders.[75] Launched in 1851 by the London Crystal Palace Exhibition, these events far surpassed museums in their scope, scale, and visibility, performing a similar function as crucibles of British, Dutch, and French national identity, but within an international context.[76] Diverse national exhibits fuelled competition, comparison, and speculation as to the defining characteristics of participating nations, enabling one French commentator on the International Exhibition in London 1862 to declare the British an "industrial" race and the French "an artistic race" on the basis of goods displayed.[77] On a larger scale, the exhibitions themselves served as grandiose displays of their host country's power and influence. The Universal Exposition of Paris in 1867, France's answer to Crystal Palace, attracted seven million visitors—approximately seven times the entire population of Paris, and close to six times more than the population of Cambodge. The exhibition symbolized the ambitions of the Second Empire in its attempt to "classify and organise every branch of human activity and to invest that activity with moral purpose."[78] This was the first exhibition to integrate nations and products into one comprehensive system, the first to feature anthropology as a separate discipline, and the first to feature foreign pavilions built in various "national" architectural styles.[79]

As empire expanded, so too did the floor space dedicated to colonial exhibits. Through exotic pavilions and eclectic displays combining cultural artifacts, scholarly achievements, and raw materials, empires sought to eclipse the *patrimoine* and productivity of their rivals. Although the exhibitions lasted for no longer than a year, each was preceded by a concentrated flurry of activity linking colony and Métropole through the creation of committees and the appointment of commissioners, and many left permanent traces in the collections of Metropolitan museums. These exhibitions offered a collective, participatory experience of empire, which threw together not only

French and British but Cambodians, Madagascans, Laotians, and Indians. Modern print media may have cemented and spread elite conceptions of different nations, but it was the exhibitions that provided the "intellectual, economic and cultural sinews of empire" and fostered the training and travels of a cultural elite. Cambodian nationalists were slower to expropriate the exhibitionary mode than officials of the Indian Congress, who, from the early 1900s, sponsored shows to demonstrate the "national style" and cultural prowess of India.[80]

ANTIQUARIANIZING ANGKOR

Excavations of colonial cultures extended the boundaries of France's *patrimoine*.[81] Imperial conquest of the "Orient" and improved modes of transportation opened up new fields for the development of archaeological expertise, which in turn incorporated the ancient monuments of colonial possessions into the cultural and architectural map of greater France. Colonization of North Africa further expanded the frontiers of French archaeology, and by the end of the century champions of *la mission civilisatrice* had declared Algeria's heritage as the "Patrimoine de la Civilisation."[82] France would declare itself heir to Angkor in the same vein, staking its reputation as a guardian of global civilization on its claims to be salvaging and reclaiming the temple ruins "from the uncivilized for the greater benefit of humanity."[83]

These gains assuaged an archaeological angst dating to France's loss of India and Egypt to the British in the eighteenth and early nineteenth centuries. Lost scholarly opportunity and the British plunder of Napoleon II's cultural conquests were symbolized by the presence of the Rosetta Stone in the British Museum and by its glaring absence from the Louvre.[84] Said has traced the French "Orient of memories, suggestive ruins, [and] forgotten secrets" to this history of loss.[85] Angkor's location gave the temple a special place in Anglo–Gallic rivalry, while its archaeological import offered French scholars compensation for the "lamentable loss of India."[86]

From 1878 onward, increasingly elaborate props and replicas at museums and exhibitions in Paris and Marseille proclaimed Angkor as a sign of empire, encouraging its incorporation into the French psyche long before the temple complex's actual recovery from Siam. As the century wore on, the Cambodge pavilions grew in size and scope, and bent to the organizing imperatives of an increasingly unified colonial and metropolitan bureaucracy. Colonial exhibitions at Marseille in 1906 and 1922, and at Paris in 1931, provided a central stage for the enactment of French fantasies of Cambodge through pavilions and performances that invariably revolved around the architecture and archaeology of Angkor. Reproduced from casts taken at the temples, these structures reconfigured Angkor in pristine displays that celebrated the golden age of Khmer empire and the restorative powers of colonial rule. Emblazoned on many young imaginations, such images helped to establish Angkor as one of the "privileged reference points" in the "French literary imaginary on the Far East."[87] The circularity of this process is neatly illustrated by Pierre Loti. Leafing through a faded colonial revue in Provence in the 1860s, a young Loti was transfixed by an illustration of Angkor, which, he later claimed, gave him his first presentiment of a travelling life.[88] Loti subsequently became France's leading exotic novelist and travel writer. Among his more than thirty books was an account of his "pilgrimage" to Angkor. Such literary treatments of the temples, like the visual extravaganzas at the international exhibitions, facilitated further armchair travel to Angkor from Europe, so shaping the Indochina-bound trajectory of future colonial employees.[89] As the ultimate "lost" city, whose vanishing into myth and subsequent recovery fired the imagination like Petra and Pompeii, Angkor lent itself well to romanticization and embellishment. Collectively, the works of Loti and others formed a shimmering mosaic of mirrors through which, increasingly, Europeans came to anticipate Angkor as a perfect simulacrum of a vanished past.

Taking up Mouhot's trail, the Englishmen Kennedy and King travelled to Angkor from Bangkok in 1864. Their trip, documented by photographs, prompted the British government to ask King Mongkut (r. 1851–1868) of Siam for permission to carry away statues and sculptures. Mongkut, who was developing his own interest in deciphering the national historical significance of inscriptions and monuments, refused. From 1864 to 1865, Captain Doudart de Lagrée, France's representative in Cambodge, made numerous trips to the temples during which he discovered new relics, mapped the monuments, collected local legends, and deciphered inscriptions, in a bid to trace the origins of Khmer art and civilization.[90]

In June 1865, de Lagrée led another mission to Angkor as head of the newly established Mekong Exploration Commission. At Battambang and Angkor, he and his colleagues discovered new monuments and tried to amass native documentation of their history. "I could wish for nothing more than to be named the curator of these ruins," wrote Garnier on his arrival at the temples.[91] His dream was subsequently realized by a young naval officer on the mission, Louis Delaporte. A newcomer to the East, the gaunt Delaporte emerged as the mission's artist and musician and later claimed that this first visit to Angkor gave him the idea of "enriching our national museum with some of these artistic treasures."[92] In December 1871, Vice Admiral Duprés, governor of Cochinchina, visited Angkor. Struck by the overgrowth invading the ruins, Duprés remarked on Siam's failure to conserve the temples and declared that France alone could and should preserve Angkor for posterity.[93]

The following year, Delaporte wrote to the Ministry of Education seeking support for a return expedition to Angkor, to acquire for the Louvre

> a collection of statues, bas-reliefs, real and fantastic animals, pillars, ornamental sculptures, all entirely new [to Europe], and of the greatest artistic and archeological value. . . . Where England failed, France can succeed with ease and at little cost. . . . Our protégé and friend the king of Cambodge will undoubtedly put the statues we covet . . . at our disposal, and will even help us transport them through the forest.

His proposed mission would stay at Angkor, collecting inscriptions and maps, so as to "enrich [France's] national museum with a completely new collection that would attract strong scholarly and artistic interest in a . . . great and vanished people."[94] In

1872, France's Ministry of Public Education, Religion, and Fine Arts awarded Delaporte a grant of ten thousand francs to collect statues, bas-reliefs, columns, and other architectural monuments or statuary from Cambodge for France's national museums.[95] Before leaving for Cambodge, Delaporte convinced the ministry to provide him with reproductions of such works as Raphael's *Adam and Eve* and Poussin's *Bacchanale* for presentation to King Norodom and key dignitaries, so as to "vanquish the few religious scruples"[96] of the people of Cambodia and gain access to Cambodian monuments.[97] Pleading sickness, King Norodom declined to give the mission an official reception, thus publicly distancing himself from the venture. However, he met privately with Delaporte, accepted his gifts, and wrote letters of support asking provincial governors to assist him in his mission.[98]

Backed up by a gunboat and some fifty coolies, and aided by a Khmer-speaking French entrepreneur named Félix Gaspard Faraut, Delaporte explored the waterways of Kompong Thom en route to the temple ruins of Preah Khan and Beng Mealea. At each site he decided "which sculptures to remove," hacking and chiselling away at various monuments until, in his own words, the "resources of the province were exhausted."[99] At Angkor, Delaporte abused the hospitality of the provincial governor, who expressly forbade the mission to remove sculptures or statuary on the permanent order of Mongkut's son and successor as king of Siam, Chulalongkorn (r. 1868–1910). Despite assuring the governor that his intention was merely to take rubbings and make casts, Delaporte used the labor teams supplied by his host to dislodge some seventy pieces of antique statuary. He then shipped them to France, together with casts and rubbings made on site.[100]

Due to a lack of space in its "proper" home, the Louvre, Delaporte's collection was grouped at the Palais de Compiègne.[101] Delaporte was appointed chief curator of the newly formed Musée Compiègne, which was opened to the public in 1874. The same year, in Bangkok, Chulalongkorn turned his father's private collection of European and Chinese curiosities into a small public museum.[102] From 1875 to 1876, the Ministry of Marine and Colonies seconded Delaporte to the Ministry of Public Education to write up his research on Cambodian monuments.[103] In 1876, the Ministry of Public Education funded him on a mission to India to study the relationship between Hindu and Cambodian art.[104] The following year, Delaporte was suspended from the Ministry of Marine and Colonies on the ground of "temporary illness."[105] He devoted the rest of his life to the study, procurement, conservation, and popularization of Khmer antiquities. Passion, not profit, shaped his new career. Like his colleagues in the museums of late-nineteenth-century France, he received scant compensation.[106]

In 1878, Delaporte moved his collection to Paris for display at that year's Exposition Universelle. "Here are the casts taken from Angkor-Vat, that dead city of Cambodge" wrote one reporter, while another marvelled at two "huge statues . . . curious specimens of Khmer or Cambodian art," and a third compared the arcane inscriptions on the "mysterious monuments" of Cambodge with the Rosetta Stone, declaring that Cambodge would soon find its Champollion to help lift the "mists covering this disappeared civilization."[107] Although Delaporte had sought to impress France's desire for the "beautiful works of far-off lands" on King Norodom through his earlier gifts of French art, the arts of colonial territories were still not treated on a par with European art, but catalogued as anthropological and scientific evidence.[108] Excluded from the Europe-only Sculpture Salon, Cambodian statues were displayed in the "Ethnographic Exhibit of Scientific Missions" near to the Cambodian skulls and skeletons labelled "Exotic Types" in the Anthropology Pavilion.[109] This cataloguing contrasted oddly with Britain's "Indian Section of Arts and Manufactures," organized by Rudyard Kipling's father. As he wandered through the various stalls, the future author, like many others at the exhibit, was more conscious of color and sensation than exhibition labels. While curators might spend hours designing labels and schemes, the exhibition experience was probably less easily distilled to such fragments by its millions of visitors. By 1878, the exhibition had emerged as a world of "ritualised and participatory fantasy," one that converted the rude truths of colonial conquest into an Oriental bazaar of "mosques and minarets."[110] Compared to the genteel confines of France's private and fledgling public museums, this marriage of theatre, circus, sculpture, taste, smells, textures, and art would have been experienced as a massive assault on the senses.

Among this vast conglomeration, next to the Delaporte display, stood Delaporte's most ambitious project: a life-size model of part of the Giant's Causeway, the main gateway to Angkor Thom, fashioned from one of Delaporte's plaster casts. Three perfect, unchipped, and untarnished gods rode the divine serpent *(Naga)*, their contemporary imperfections perhaps erased with putty.[111] After the exhibition, the Khmer statuary was stored in the basement of the Trocadero, out of sight of visitors but open prey to mold and damp. In 1879, an ethnographic museum was founded at the Trocadero, with provisions for a special gallery for the Khmer collection—dubbed the Musée khmer—and a curatorship for Delaporte.[112] In 1881, France's minister of public education Jules Ferry mandated Delaporte's return to Indochina to complete an artistic and archaeological study of ancient Khmer monuments and to collect works of sculpture and architecture for his existing Musée khmer, for the museum of archaeology then under construction in Saigon, and for the next Exposition universelle, scheduled for 1889. Delaporte visited another fifteen Khmer temples and amassed a considerable collection of antiques and casts, which, he argued, would enable France to "maintain the superiority of French art."[113]

A more immediate objective for the colonial government of Indochina was to project superior imagery of Cochinchina and Cambodge to rival European powers. "Now that we are asserting our action in the Far East, it is imperative that Cochinchine and Cambodge . . . be brilliantly represented in the Universal Exposition at Anvers," wrote the governor of Cochinchina Charles Thomson in 1884.[114] F. Faure, Under-Secretary of State for Marine and Colonies, stressed the political benefits of a Cambodge display involving photographs of Cambodian monuments and archaeological relics.[115] Here, colonial archaeology was unashamedly flaunted as a trophy of French colonial success, and Cambodge's newly acquired *patrimoine* became conflated with French national cultural eloquence. In an indication of the importance also attached to home audiences, in 1885 the Ministry of Marine and Colonies issued a ministerial despatch to all colonial administrations asking them to purchase local objects for display in the Métropole. Governor of Cochinchina Begin subsequently allocated a thousand piastres to the Resident General of France in Cambodge, Badens, to buy objects from Cambodge for display in the principal towns of France, and authorized him to assemble a collection for both the protectorate of Cambodge and the Musée de Saigon.[116]

These acts of conservation were paralleled by publications justifying France's violent repression of the Sivutha rebellion in the name of "regenerating a people and renovating a once glorious past."[117] Returning to Cambodge in 1887, Delaporte was warmly welcomed by Myre de Vilers, who applauded the importance of his mission, both for the *monde savant* and for France's "legitimate influence in Indochina."[118] In June 1889, a month before the colonial architect Daniel Fabre left Phnom Penh for Paris to construct a "Cambodge" pavilion at that year's Exposition Universelle, the Cambodian gallery of the newly launched Musée indochinois at the Palais de Trocadero opened to the public, with Delaporte as curator.[119]

Delaporte's collection provided the ornamental and architectural motif for Fabre's pavilion in the form of casts, photographs, and rubbings.[120] Reflecting the prevailing European obsession with golden ages, the Cambodge pavilion was "painted and gilded, so as to reproduce, with the most scrupulous realism, the decor of these sumptuous Khmer buildings whose beauty, pomp and brightness still shine upon us."[121] But "Angkor" was not only catapulted forward in time with a new golden sheen; spatial restrictions and aesthetic standards also led to the divine city's dissection. Fabre's pavilion was a replica of the heart of the temple complex, the innermost, uppermost sanctuary to which only the king and the high priest had been allowed access in the Angkorean era. This central sanctum was recreated as a freestanding structure on the Esplanade des Invalides, closer in appearance to a Catholic cathedral than to the Angkor temples. The steep staircase that in fact led up to the original was shrunk to twenty or so steps, easily negotiated by the weary tourist.[122] Despite Fabre's stated commitment to honor the "traditions, organization, and devices of the grand Khmer art," the pavilion was a potpourri of Angkorean ornament, which privileged the temple's dancing girls, ornamental pediments, steles, and bas-reliefs.[123] But in the eyes of the French government and the twenty-six million visitors to the fair, the pavilion *was* Cambodge. Its authenticity was bolstered by the deployment of Cambodians—possibly the artists who had built it—in the villages, temples, and markets of the colonial section.[124] Here, contemplating Lucien Fournerau's evocative watercolors of Khmer ruins, a thirteen-year-old Henri Marchal (1876–1970) first dreamed of his future vocation. Greatly taken by these and other representations of Angkor at the exhibition, the teenager's visions were reinforced by his readings of Mouhot, Captain Doudard de Lagrée, and others. On this basis, he later wrote, "My decision was made, I knew that one day I, too, would go [to Angkor]."[125] Marchal was to achieve lasting fame as the longest-serving curator of Angkor.[126] "The public,

FIGURE 1. Angkor in Paris, 1889. *L'Illustration.*

which had so much difficulty in understanding the necessity of Greater France, is finally fascinated by it," proclaimed one newspaper.[127]

Various objects from the Tonkin and Cambodge pavilions were transferred to Delaporte's museum the following year, where they joined other recent donations of originals and replicas of Khmer art by colonial administrators. The scholar-administrator Adhémard Leclère gave Delaporte a Buddha's head taken from the Vat Pnum in Phnom Penh, and the artist and sculptor Fournereau donated various acquisitions from his missions to Cambodge.[128] In 1886, France's representative in Cambodge, Moura, and the governor of Cochinchina, Myre de Vilers, both entrusted pieces of Khmer antiquity to Delaporte's care.[129]

In April 1890, the minister of public education and fine arts commissioned a sculptor named Raffegeaud to make a second batch of casts in Cambodge to complete the collections of the Musée khmer.[130] Later that year, the Résident supérieur du Cambodge asked King Norodom to instruct the provincial authorities to supply Raffegeaud with guides and porters, and to give him his royal authorization to make moldings and take certain original pieces from the northern provinces. In the first recorded instance of overt Cambodian obstruction of such missions, Norodom asserted the impossibility of mobilizing the corvée labor commonly used by archaeologists and explorers as guides and porters, due to a drought, poor harvest, and famine.[131] As we shall see later in this book, Norodom also raised distinct objections on religious grounds. Despite such obstructions, and the king's blockade of the transport of a particular collection of original pieces of statuary, Raffegaud nonetheless succeeded in shipping thirty-two cases of monuments from Siem Reap to Saigon. First destined for the Trocadero Museum of Ethnography, the items ended up at the Musée Guimet, a museum of religion opened in Paris in 1889, where six prominent Asia collections were centralized in 1891, including some fine specimens of Cambodian sculpture.[132]

Six years later, while King Chulalongkorn was touring the Musée Guimet, an eminent politician and former finance minister Paul Doumer visited Angkor on his way to assume the reins of power as governor-general of Indochina (1987–1902).[133] Contemplating Angkor Thom, the former French finance minister declared its builders a "strong, courageous, artistic race" who had "achieved a high degree of civilization" and bore no relation to contemporary Cambodians, who had "erased" them. Overcome with emotion for a "beautiful civilization destroyed, and melancholy at its demise," Doumer was struck by Angkor's potential as a tool for educating French youth about the dangers of degeneration and stressed the urgency of doing "everything in our power to prevent [France] . . . from slithering down the slope of decadence, which ends only in ruin."[134] Although Doumer never succeeded in organizing school trips from France to Siem Reap, his active support of representations of Indochina at museums and expositions in the Métropole did accomplish partial realization of his aspirations to educate French youth in Angkor's image.

Doumer's preoccupations with decadence were probably reinforced by his association with the Musée Social, a republican think tank whose goals included raising public awareness of such social problems as "degeneration"[135] and increasing governmental knowledge about indigenous cultures so as to ease French subjugation of native societies.[136] In 1898, Doumer established a "Permanent Archaeological Mission" (Mission Archéologique Permanente) in Saigon "to make the stones [of Angkor] speak."[137] Serving the goals of the Musée Social, and inspired by his personal reflections on the temples, Doumer's initiative inaugurated a new phase of colonial conquest in Indochina.

EXCAVATING ANGKOR

On 9 March 1900, Doumer established the first official conservation order on historic monuments in Indochina. Within months, the newly formed Permanent Archaeological Mission had dispatched Captain Étienne Lunet de la Jonquière, a Thai speaker serving with the French infantry in Indochina, to map Cambodge's ancient temples.[138] In 1901, a presidential decree transformed the mission into the École française d'Extrême-Orient (EFEO).[139] Modelled on the prestigious French schools at Rome, Athens, and Cairo, the EFEO was also designed to mirror, and ultimately to eclipse, the knowledge projects of the British and Dutch empires in Southeast Asia, as embodied in the Archaeological Department of Burma, established in 1899, and the Dutch Colonial Antiquities Commission, founded in 1901.[140]

The EFEO's first president, Louis Finot was France's premier Indologist.[141] In his inaugural address, Finot warned that neglect of scholarship in French Indochina had made this territory easy prey for Orientalists from rival empires; a Dutchman had translated the first Khmer inscription, while a German had produced the first study of Cham grammar. To preempt further such trespassing on Greater France's intellectual terrain, the school would study that part of Indochina which owed "its monuments, its customs and its culture to India"—that is, Cambodge. Finot gave the EFEO a mandate at once pragmatic, romantic, and academic. The school would provide the colony with precise information about the colonized, their languages, morals, and traditions; enable France to realize its "duty" to the "civilized world" by conserving and studying the ancient monuments in its possession; and rescue French orientalism from the death grip of theory through studies grounded in the realities of contemporary life. "To know . . . the past," reasoned Finot, "we must have seen the present, which reflects and echoes the colors and voices of the past."[142]

Despite Finot's insistence on the value of the present, the focus of the EFEO was overwhelmingly on antiquity. Charles Carpaux (1870–1904) was appointed head of EFEO fieldwork and assigned to complete a study of the Bayon.[143] In 1901, the Ministry of Public Education funded a research trip by the young scholar Jean Ajalbert to study Cambodian antiquities,[144] the Société pour la conservation des monuments anciens de l'Indo-Chine was founded in Paris to further the conservation and study of monuments in Indochina, and Lajonquière's *Atlas archéologique de l'Indo-Chine* was published in Paris.[145] First installed in Saigon, the EFEO moved to Hanoi when the Gouvernement Général relocated there in 1902.[146] That year, the Indologist Alfred Foucher, recently appointed deputy director of the EFEO, supervised the publication of Lajonquière's sequel, the *Inventaire archéologique des monuments du Cambodge*.[147] In August 1902 the EFEO requested Lajonquière's transfer from the army to the academy, so that he might catalogue the Angkor monuments, pending the peaceful resolution of the "Siamese situation."[148] The following month, Foucher wrote to the GGI stressing the EFEO's determination to take over the conservation of Angkor.[149] Angkor was not the sole field of EFEO archaeological enquiry. The school also undertook massive excavations of fifteenth-century Cham brick-and stone-sculptures in

Annam. However, Angkor remained the centerpiece of EFEO endeavors, a position reiterated in its function as the central attraction of colonial exhibitions. Nguyén-Ba Long, a former employee of the EFEO, has located this preference in Angkor's magnificence and elaborate stonework, which better suited the French taste for majesty and nobility.[150]

With its microcosm of empire juxtaposing formidable Dutch Indies and British imperial pavilions with Indochinese exhibits, the Exposition universelle in Paris 1900 had particular resonance with Doumer's and Finot's strategic and scholarly quests. Following accusations of unfairness from other imperial centers at the 1889 Exposition Universelle, which had restricted its colonial section to French territories, the 1900 event opened itself to rival nations with the creation of a separate display category, "Colonization."[151] Unprecedented in scale and scope, the exposition celebrated European industrial and imperial achievements in a vast medley of architectural fantasia, entertainment, and consumer products, within which the Indo-Chinese exposition earned a ranking by one journalist as the pièce de resistance of the French colonial displays.[152]

Reflecting the creation of the Indochina Union in 1898, Cambodge, Tonkin, Annam, Cochinchina, and Laos were grouped together to convey the "administrative, economic and moral unity of our great Asian colony"[153] However, an exception was made to this organizing principle in the exaggerated place given to Cambodge, which was represented by a replica of Phnom Penh's chief landmark and namesake, the Vat Pnum, whose construction and meaning I shall consider in the next chapter. The prestigious daily *L'Illustration* billed the Pnum as "the most important, and most interesting, of the French colonial constructions."[154] However, these representations of Cambodge appear to have made little mark on King Norodom's delegate to the 1900 exposition. To the reported chagrin of his French hosts, Prince Yukanthor allegedly ranked a group of Swiss chalets as the exposition's star attraction.[155] However, as we shall see in Chapter 3, they moved another Khmer visitor to poetry.

In 1901, Loti realized his boyhood fantasy of visiting Angkor and dedicated his account of that voyage, *Un pèlerin d'Angkor* (A pilgrim of Angkor) to Doumer.[156] Cambodge continued to exist as a site of exploration and a place *sans histoire* in Orientalist imaginings.[157] The first synoptic history of Angkor, *L'Empire khmèr: Histoire et documents* (The Khmer Empire: History and documents) was produced in 1904 by George Maspèro, son of the eminent Egyptologist Gaston.[158] In his preface, Maspèro claimed that "the painstaking research of savants, historians, epigraphists, and travellers has almost completely dispelled the darkness which desecrated the Khmer past, and promised to make their secrets accessible to the French public."[159]

This curious claim belittled the expansion of Metropolitan and colonial museums and exhibitions, which several of Maspèro's peers and superiors had identified as key means of filtering the Khmer past to the French populace. Both Finot and the scholar-administrator Adhémard Leclère had been actively involved in promoting knowledge of Cambodge, and the achievements of the EFEO, at the Hanoi Exposition of 1902.[160] By 1904, Étienne Aymonier, now director of the École Coloniale,

Finot, director of the EFEO, the sculptor and artist Fournereau, a seasoned hand on Delaporte's archaeological missions, and Leclère all had become recognized patrons of the Musée Guimet.[161] Along with the Trocadero, the Guimet provided a key window onto French conceptions of Cambodge to those few elite Cambodian students studying at the École coloniale in Paris, on their weekly tours of Paris and its museums.[162] The establishment of a Musée khmer in Phnom Penh in 1905 would provide Cambodians in the capital with their first window onto modern European museology.

In 1905, RSC Jules Morel established a Commission of Antiquities in Cambodge "to make an inventory of monuments or objects of historic or artistic value, proposing measures to assure their conservation . . . signalling discoveries, contributing by all means in its power to the knowledge of the history, archaeology and ethnography of Cambodge."[163] The commission was subsequently charged with the surveillance of buildings and other antiques classified as historic monuments in Cambodge.[164] Like their counterparts in Europe and Siam, the museum and heritage commission would gradually but steadily imbue religious monuments with national significance, so that, in the eyes of Cambodge's nascent, Western-educated elite, ruins would no longer constitute "evidence of the Buddhist law of impermanence (anit-cang), but material proof of the imported idea of linear historical development centered on the nation state."[165] This listing of monuments for conservation coincided with the dispatch of some thirty indigenous masons, decorators, and painters from Saigon to Marseille to construct and decorate the Indochina pavilion for the 1906 Exposition coloniale.[166]

Conceived by colonial lobbyist Joseph Chailley-Bert, founder of the Union Coloniale, the Marseille exposition was landscaped to reflect both the administrative organization of empire and the rank order of France's colonial possessions.[167] Pavilions were grouped in the five major units of empire—Indochina, West Africa, Madagascar, Algeria, and Tunisia—and participating colonies were asked to emphasize natural resources and economic potential, in line with the ascendance of *mise en valeur* policies. Although mines, public works, and cartography all featured in the Indochina exhibit, its focus was predominantly cultural, reflecting the interests and identities of its organizers.

Indochina afficionados Aymonier, Doumer, Paul Beau, and Myre de Vilers all shaped representations of Indochina at the exposition.[168] The Cambodge pavilion, a replica of part of the Bayon temple, was modelled on a new series of casts and the now expanded Delaporte collection at the Musée du Trocadero. An EFEO exhibition hall displayed an elaborate model of Angkor made by EFEO Deputy Director Dufour and Charles Carpaux.[169] Angkor appeared again in the Cambodian section of an "Indochinese diorama."[170] Finally, Angkor was brought to life in the imaginations of many exhibition goers by the performances of the Cambodian royal ballet.

Dances had long been performed at Angkor as part of local festivities and ceremonies. In April 1902, a young scholar named Charles Carpaux had witnessed "hundreds of Cambodian men and women dressed in bright scarves walking in the usually deserted ruins. They [were] singing and dancing. . . . in the cruciform gallery

. . . in a long line, chanting very slowly and taking one step forward, one step back," in front of two men in monkey masks who held up the focal performer, a man in a horned deer mask.[171] But a different, highly stylized form of performing "Angkor" was proposed for representing Cambodge to the outside world. The same month, the RSC had called for the dispatch of a "dancing troupe that recalls the bas-reliefs of Khmer monuments" to the 1902 exposition in Hanoi.[172] Four years later, in Marseille and Paris, Sisowath's royal dance corps, traditional mediators between the king and heaven, performed in public for the first time.[173] This representation of Cambodge was decided upon by Khmer and French administrators, among them a rising star named Thiounn, whose career commands closer attention in Chapter 3. Although Apsaras figured prominently among the rich figurative art on Angkor's bas-reliefs, this reenactment of Angkorean bas-reliefs *as* dance was clearly new.

Directed by Sisowath's daughter Princess Samphoudry, the royal dance corps performed at Marseille, at the Château d'If, and at Notre Dame de la Garde before moving to Paris, where they perfomed at the president's garden party in the Elysée and for the Minister of the Colonies in the Bois de Boulogne, where an "artistic gala" sandwiched the royal ballet between classical Greek dance and eighteenth-century dances.[174] A review in *l'Illustration* described Cambodge as "a fallen country, which has preserved only two parts of its glorious past: its improbably grandiose ruins and its dancers, strange relics of a dead past."[175] The sculptor Auguste Rodin was so mesmerized by the performance that he followed the dancers back to Marseille, where he completed a pen and watercolor series, *Les danseuses cambodgiennes.*[176] The Cambodian dancers also left an indelible imprint on another member of their audience. Impressed by their delicate grace and mysterious demeanor, and apparently equally enthralled by the various representations of Angkor at the exposition, the seventeen-year-old Roland Meyer resolved to shape his future in Indochina as the first "Frenchman of Asia" to write the "book of Angkor."[177] Two years later, he set sail for Saigon and, in 1908, arrived in Phnom Penh. Here he joined a new wave of scholar-administrators, among them George Groslier (1887–1945), born in Phnom Penh but schooled in Paris, where he may well have joined the throngs at the 1900 Exposition universelle. These architects of "phantasmatic Indochina"—to use Norindr's evocative term— were part and parcel of the fantasies they documented in their work and art. Angkor was a key compass point in their own quests to define their identity vis-à-vis the French Métropole and the colonized population. By the time they arrived in Phnom Penh, Angkor and echoes of the majesty of Suryavarman II and Jayavarman VII were already firmly ensconced in the colonial capital.

2 | Urban Legend

Capitalizing on Angkor

On moving from Phnom Penh to the Métropole in the 1910s, a teenager of royal descent named Atman (Khmer for "soul") wrestles a fit of depression encapsulating many of the contradictions inherent in colonial and postcolonial visions of the Cambodian nation. As she travels through the streets, eyeing major monuments, the immensity of her surroundings overwhelms her, stoking deep emotions and sparking a vision in which "all the capitals of my Khmer ancestors" issue forth from Paris. On passing the Seine, the Mekong floods her soul. "Ordinarily," she ponders, "though it is their only valid measure, Asiatics in Europe do not immediately perceive this time of their ancestors, of which they were ignorant in Cambodia. They must first be transfused with the earth of Europe. . . . It is in absorbing Europe's grandeur that they bring forth the grandeur of Asia." Her lungs have barely filled with Parisian air when, gazing at the towers of Notre Dame, she issues a "long, low, heartrending cry." This, she tells us with the clinical detachment of an obstetrician, was "my soul, giving birth to Angkor Wat." The "grandeur of Angkor" chokes her, "demanding of me things beyond my age," and, with poignant prescience, she wonders whether the weight of this Angkorean epoch will one day "destroy my future society."

Atman is a fiction. The chief protagonist of a novel *The Last Concubine* (1942) by the Franco-Cambodian writer Pierrette Guesde (also known as Makhâli Phal), she is the time-travelling daughter of the Khmer emperor Jayavarman VII. Her attempts to adapt to modernity are strained by the ever-present shadow of her ancestry and are informed by her encounters with another character: the recently renovated capital of Phnom Penh. In her split trajectory, Phnom Penh functions as a spatial and temporal axis between Asia and Europe, Cambodia and Paris, past and present, slowness and speed, allowing her "Khmer soul" to straddle these different worlds. Towards the end of her tumultuous journey through time, Atman thanks "France for my discovery of Angkor, for my discovery of the Khmer grandeur, and for my opportunity to preserve the nobility of the Khmer race."[1] Years later, after Independence, Atman's creator wrote to the doyen of Cambodian history and ethnology, George Coedès, expressing her gratitude and admiration for his "immense work which has allowed me to know my Khmer ancestors."[2] Like Malcolm McLaren's twenty-first-century Paris, Makhâli Phal's metroscape is a city where you can live yesterday tomorrow.[3] Getting to know the ancestors, colonial style, involved the translation of signs of Angkor and sighs of Paris into the urban environment through museology, town planning, and architecture.

Elsewhere in French empire, the spatial and architectural foundations of colonial cities encouraged the possibility of combining modernism and tradition.[4] In Cambodge, colonial architecture and town planning had a reverse effect. By promoting notions of the incompatibility of Khmer and non-Khmer symbols of nation, grouped as these were in distinct milieux, they also implicitly segregated notions of antiquity (associated with Angkor and "Khmerness") from modernity (associated with the French Quarter and the protectorate's government offices). In 1889, a French visitor to Phnom Penh dismissed the colonial capital as "a place of transit," preempting ethnologist Claude Lévi-Strauss' condemnation of the new Brazilian city of Goiânia, some forty years later, as a "place of transit—not of residence."[5] This trope of transience tallied with common colonial castings of indigenous lives and spaces as ephemeral, fleeting, shadowy, and transgressive. Clear distinctions were made between the indigenously built environment of the "golden age" of Angkor—which was deemed, like one of many twelfth- and thirteenth-century stone structures that had survived, as marking a stage of "civilization" from which Cambodians had ever since been in a state of flight, like nomads of history who had not yet found a firm footing in firm structures and the present, seen as unanchored, both in its predominant form— flammable wood—and design. Considering Khmer palaces too makeshift to represent real power, European planners were brought in to supervise the construction of lasting monuments to "majesty" in stone, brick, cement, and concrete.[6] A primary facet of this transformation was the development of a "national style," first articulated as such in the national pavilions designed in a presumed "purely Cambodian style" for Europe's grand nineteenth-century exhibitions.

Like other French colonial cities, Phnom Penh's emerging geometric cityscape paid tribute to René Descarte's vision of a "well-ordered" town laid out "on a vacant plane as suits [the engineer's] fancy."[7] Colonial approaches to the city also reiterated notions of an unspoiled rural essence versus a corrupting urbane environment. Constructing a Cambodian quarter was one way of quarantining that quintessential, rural Khmerness within the modern urban environment. But in reducing Khmerness to ornamentation, and in taking the ancestral and Angkorean as the model for that Khmerness, colonial planners inscribed the notion of the vanished Khmer on the very Quartier cambodgien (Cambodian quarter) that they built. The grafting of Angkorean symbols onto the new capital's streetscape correlated with the crafting of a new profile for the Khmer monarchy, with Angkorean undertones and opulent dimensions, through palace construction and ceremonial function that allowed King Norodom I and his successors to embody the splendor—but not the substance—of kingship on a scale unseen since the fall of Angkor.[8]

THE REGALITY EFFECT: MAKING A MAJESTIC PHNOM PENH

On the establishment of the French Protectorate in 1863, King Norodom I and his court were resident in Oudong, a small range of stupa-crested hills, saturated with memories and associations emanating from the stupas containing the remains of royalty, and from the hills themselves, held to be the home of powerful *naga*. Three years later, the capital would be relocated to Phnom Penh, and the house of Norodom would at once be demoted to flatland and increased in ostentation. This was no empty site: Phnom Penh had been founded as a royal capital by King Ponhea Yat in 1431, and shortly thereafter reconstruction began of the city's first temple, a *vat* erected in 1372 on a hill (Phnom) to house four statues of Buddha discovered in a tree on the site by a woman named Dame Penh. Although the city was subsequently abandoned as a royal capital, its position at the confluence of the Mekong and Bassac rivers made it, besides the coastal town of Kampot, Cambodia's most vibrant commercial conduit, and its long-standing community of Chinese, Malay, Indian and other traders secured its status as Cambodia's economic capital.[9] The Vat Pnum retained an active temple, and this, in conjunction with animist beliefs in the spirited powers of toponyms and its place as the small trading town's only hill, probably sealed its status as the city's spiritual nucleus.

From its earliest official establishment in Phnom Penh, the protectorate displayed a canny sensitivity to the spirituality associated with such sites, locating the French *Résidence* immediately opposite the Vat Pnum in two buildings whose transfer Doudart de Lagrée negotiated from Norodom under the 1863 treaty.[10] It has been argued of South Asia that the colonial city not only moved the locus of power but shifted it "from a religious to a secular basis."[11] In Phnom Penh, the protectorate did not so much displace religious power as fuse it with new layers of secular authority. In addition to its symbolic value, Vat Pnum provided an excellent vantage point for French naval personnel, who transformed the stupa into a surveillance tower.[12] By moving his court some thirty kilometers to Phnom Penh, Norodom stamped the royal seal of approval on the protectorate's chosen capital, conjoining his charismatic authority with French military might.

At the time, Paris was in the final stages of Baron von Haussmann's "draconian . . . retrofit," a grandiose public works program that paved the way, both politically and spatially, for the incubation of the Paris Commune in 1871. Security concerns fused with aesthetic prescriptions, and Haussmann's plan turned Paris into "spectacle."[13] Next to the urban theatre of Paris, Phnom Penh was far from spectacular, and wheels were soon set in motion to create what one governor of Cochinchina called a "real" capital. The creation of this urban legend involved both the translation of Parisian grandeur and the lifting of ancestral genius from the temples of Angkor. The resultant bricolage formed part of that curious process of anticipation and replication from which the Kmae daem would emerge. Phnom Penh's renovation ushered in a new era, central to which was the material display of royal and colonial power through architecture and public festival, and the parallel dilution of official, political, and financial indigenous power and substance.

In the first two decades of the protectorate, the king retained complete power over the treasury, as well as the farming of opium, fisheries, pig farms, gambling, and other concessions, and he was the undisputed owner of all land in the kingdom. At Oudong, as in previous royal capitals, wood and thatch housed royalty, mandarins, and peasants, while masonry was generally reserved for temples, reliquary stupas, and funereal monuments.[14] Wood had been used by royalty and peasants alike since at least the third century, and early Chinese accounts note that rulers in the region lived in tiered, wooden buildings, while commoners resided in thatched wooden houses raised on stilts, known in French as *paillotes*.[15] This trend continued after the fall of the Khmer capital at Lovek in 1594, with the construction of the new royal palace at Oudong as a walled compound of wooden buildings. Most elaborate was the house of the queen mother, who remained at Oudong after the transfer of the royal capital to Phnom Penh in 1864.[16]

The quality of building materials—which ranged from bamboo matting and thatch to fine timbers—and craftsmanship varied from one dwelling to another according to the rank and status of their owners. But the location of a residence and its proximity to sacred sites acted as more significant indicators of power and status. Centuries of upheaval, the perennial threat of war and relocation, and indigenous notions of power all ensured that political potency was vested in enduring ceremonial items and human constellations of kin and clientele, both of which could be quickly mobilized, rather than elaborate palace complexes or lavish personal abodes. Displays of power and ways to earn and express merit in the built environment took the form of the construction or renovation of a Buddhist monastery or ancestral temple, hospice, or library.

This lack of spectacle disappointed Europeans. In 1884, a visiting administrator reporting to the governor of Cochinchina dismissed the queen mother's residence as a few "tiled, undecorated wooden buildings . . . nearly as badly maintained as any other Cambodian huts, [and] just as poor inside," which "give the visitor a very sorry picture of the majesty of Khmer monarchs."[17] Underlying the colonial imperatives to improve the picture of such majesty was a fascination with Khmer royalty. France's dependence on the monarchy as a legitimating conduit in Cambodge, and Orientalist stereotypes of despotic, opulent sovereigns intensified this attraction. So, too, did the thinly veiled nostalgia among the many conservative, antirepublican naval and military officials who formed the bulk of the protectorate's early policy makers and enforcers for kings, queens, and emperors, and for royalty in general as an institution. Prior to the fall of Emperor Napoleon II in 1870, administrators had held him up as a model for King Norodom. After Napoleon's demise, and against the background of an ostentatiously royalist Britannia, the most pertinent legitimate symbol of imperial majesty that cohered with France's agenda in Cambodge was found not in the Métropole but at Angkor, in the figures of Suryavarman II and Jayavarman VII.

The protectorate's first involvement in royal spectacle was at Norodom I's coronation at Oudong in 1864, where one side of the crown was held by an officer of the French navy, and the other by an ambassador from Siam. Naval captain Desmoulins gave an energetic speech, so establishing France's "supremacy vis-à-vis the king whom we were delivering, so to speak, from Siamese tutelage."[18] Eight years later, the French government awarded King Norodom a Grand Cross of the Légion d'honneur to "elevate the prestige of our protégé, over whom the king of Siam has long pretended to exercise a right of suzerainty" and to "recognize the king's attachment to France."[19] The award was clearly no good-conduct medal. Norodom's nominators had more than once condemned him for barbarism, inhumanity, mass unpopularity, and butchery.[20] The following year, the French administration nominated Obbereach Sisowath for the Legion of Honor as a mark of gratitude for his cooperation in securing the king's signature on the 15 July 1873 agreement on the Cambodian–Cochinchinese boundaries.[21] By the turn of the century, with the ascendance of an indigenous, secular elite, French decorations had emerged as highly prized status symbols. Addressing a colonial congress in Marseille in 1906, the colonial administrator Pasquier freely admitted that in Cambodge "the king reigns, but the Résident Supérieur rules [lit.: holds the real power]" and stressed the importance of giving Cambodian mandarins the impression, or appearance, of power.[22]

The desire to increase the "appearance" of power would prove a central preoccupation of the protectorate, which, like the French protectorates of Tunisia and Morocco, sought to bolster its own superimposed order in Cambodge by buttressing what it considered to be "traditional rituals, spatial patterns, and architectural ornament."[23] The erection of an opulent palace in the center of Phnom Penh in the 1860s, and its elaboration and expansion during following decades, provided both a major tourist attraction and convenient window dressing for policies that vastly decreased the financial clout and political power of both the monarchy and the mandarins. Perhaps partly to compensate for that decline, and also to participate in the prestige systems established by Europeans, Khmer royalty and dignitaries mortgaged their threadbare political power in exchange for its trappings.[24]

Opened in 1870 and designed by French architects, the palace spoke as much of innovation as preservation.[25] Brick, cement, and tile contracted from a Chinese firm in Saigon supplemented wood.[26] Under the cosmetic enhancement of a "Khmer" roof, the palace featured a barracks for the king's Tagal armed guard, offices, workshops, private apartments for the king and his family, a throne room, and a performance hall for the royal dancers. One scholar has estimated the cost as one million piastres.[27] It was less a palace, in the European sense of the word, than a miniature city within whose walls Norodom reigned supreme over thousands of courtiers, courtesans, and other servants of the crown.[28] Opening the palace on 14 February 1870, Representative Moura congratulated Norodom on his modernist aspirations, encouraged him to continue on the "road to progress," and exhorted Cambodian dignitaries and commoners to build brick dwellings instead of the traditional wooden houses, which he condemned as "unhygienic, highly flammable, and lacking in basic comfort."[29] It had taken three years of persuasion, wrote one French entrepreneur, before the king "finally decided to build the town in brick," landing le Faucheur a contract for three hundred brick buildings, including a police station, a covered market, and villas for ambassadors, all to be finished by the end of 1872.[30]

In 1884, the French Protectorate, anxious to end its dependence on the king's gift or loan of land and buildings, dealt a fiscal deathblow to the Cambodian monarchy in the form of a convention that established four categories of property ownership: royal property, public property, inalienable public reserves that could be leased, and inalienable private property.[31] In October 1889, to achieve his goal of "sanitizing, developing, and embellishing" Phnom Penh, RSC de Verneville issued a new convention securing the protectorate long-coveted development rights over Phnom Penh, whereby Norodom ceded all land and property rights in Phnom Penh to the protectorate, in exchange for an annual rent of thirty thousand piastres.[32]

Norodom had the palace remodelled in the 1880s, adding a state room and a funeral building, and renovating his private apartments. "There are three things of interest to see in Phnom Penh," wrote a 1900 traveller, "The Phnom, the Royal Palace . . . and the king. . . ." A bronze statue of Norodom on horseback, in the trappings of a French general, graced the palace grounds: a gift from the French government, this former statue of Napoleon II had been decapitated and recapped with a bust of Norodom chiselled up from a portrait.[33] This cosmetic surgery symbolized French visions of Norodom as a figurehead of the protectorate's body politic. Despite its hybrid origins, the palace soon came to symbolize the pristine essence of Cambodge in the eyes of certain scholar-administrators. In 1912, Norodom's successor, King Sisowath, petitioned the French administration for the reconstruction of many of its now dilapidated buildings. Gouverneur Général d'Indochine (GGI) Albert Sarraut allocated funds for the desired renovations, so rewarding the king's cooperation with the protectorate's modernizing agendas and signaling Sarraut's own commitment to the conservation of indigenous cultures under his new politics of association.[34] Where the late-nineteenth-century imperative to entrench French power had seen the architectural assertion of "la nationalité française," the early twentieth century saw the emergence of new proclamations by French colonial officials of their tolerance and appreciation of other cultures, and their respect for tradition.[35] These principles shaped the wording of the palace's invitation to tender for the new "Salle des fêtes," which invited submissions "inspired by the Cambodian style," particularly in their roof and décor. Palace Minister Thiounn pledged to provide the successful bidder with Cambodian workers so as to ensure a "work of Khmer art."[36] At the inauguration of the new hall, RSC Lamothe celebrated it as an example of "the most pure Cambodian style."[37] But even before Sarraut set this new agenda, architecture had emerged as something in which "the Cambodian nationality" could be vested and displayed in much the same way as Le Myre de Vilers had visualized encapsulating *la nationalité française* in public buildings.

DEFINING A NATIONAL STYLE

The first mention of a "national style" for Cambodian architecture appears to date to the mid-1880s and arose in the context of plans for the representation of Cambodge at the Exposition universelle in Paris in 1889. Closely following the Sivutha rebellion, which had massively damaged France's moral authority in Cambodge, the exposition offered the protectorate and the Ministry of Colonies a means of flattering the monarchy and shoring up its prestige. As in India following the Sepoy Mutiny, a policy promoting exhibitions and celebrations of antiquity formed part of broader designs to reinvent traditional society while promoting the image of imperial patronage.[38] Stripped of financial power by the 1884 convention, Norodom would increasingly cling to such symbolic assertions of sovereignty. This was the first international exhibition to include a separate section for the colonies, and the first at which Cambodge was represented as a single category.[39]

To mobilize participation in this Parisian spectacle, the colonial lobbyist de Lanassan toured Indochina in 1887 emphasizing the need for each territory to appear as an individual entity.[40] A Cambodge exhibition committee was duly formed in 1887, under Norodom's auspices, and it recommended a "completely distinct and separate exhibit" for Cambodge.[41] This emphasis on individual representation was complicated by the realities of administrative power in Indochina, where Cambodge had long been regarded and ruled as a prefecture of neighboring Cochinchina. "From the political point of view I think that there is a great interest in having just one single exposition for Cochinchine and Cambodge," wrote Governor of Cochinchina Filippine in 1887, forwarding a plan for a hybrid Khmer–Annamite pavilion to his subordinate in Cambodge. "I would prefer two separate pavilions," responded Resident General Piquet. "Each one representing the national style."

Piquet subsequently stressed the political advantages of granting Norodom's wish.[42] The Ministry of Colonies concurred. "It would be good politics to allow the king to have a special, purely Cambodian pavilion," wrote Under-Secretary of State Eugene Étienne to Filippine, stressing the need to tighten Cambodge's links to France.[43] Bowing to the ministry, and in a bid to secure Norodom's goodwill, Fillippine gave the protectorate permission to erect its own pavilion.[44] In 1888, Piquet commissioned Fabre, head of the Department of Public Works and principal planner and landscaper of Phnom Penh, to design an exclusively "Khmer" pavilion that would attract both public interest and academic attention, and would conform to Metropolitan desires to see an "absolutely Cambodian style."[45] But how was that style to be defined? "A page of history," Fabre's blueprint replicated the dimensions and artistic motifs of Angkor Vat, so as to recall "the master builders of generations past."[46] Fabre left for Paris in July 1889 to construct the Cambodge pavilion, and was later joined by a group of Cambodian artisans including ten painters, eight sculptors, and four builders.[47]

Developed in concert with French architects, artists, and engineers, and for a Parisian and international audience, this "national style" would increasingly make itself felt in the capital through monument, architecture, and landscaping over the next two decades. The protectorate drew its inspiration for such projects from Europe, where town planners were focusing on the use of public space and national monument to strengthen national pride, leading to a veritable "statuomania." Elite and middle-class fears about the formlessness of society in fin de siècle France led to a search for unifying symbols and rituals.[48] Though the Cambodge pavilion made an impact in the French capital, an 1889 publication bemoaned the absence of any artistic monument in the new capital of Phnom Penh.[49]

Perhaps inspired by the 1889 exhibition, GGI de Lanessan made it his mission on his appointment in 1891 "to enhance our prestige, and that of Norodom, in the eyes of his subjects and of foreigners, by making Phnom Penh a real capital."[50] Fabre was the principal architect of this transformation, providing artistic direction for the entrepreneurial engineer Félix Gaspard Faraut (d. 1911). Together they oversaw the expansion and embellishment of Phnom Penh, marking out roads, building houses and offices. "Taciturn, a little detached," tall and thickset, an avid cardsharp, Faraut had settled in Cambodge in the 1870s, then married a Lao princess, had two sons, learned Khmer in a temple, and returned to France once every seven or eight years.[51]

With de Lanessan's backing, RSC de Verneville began work on a canal that flowed into the Tonle Bassac River to form a triangular moat around the French quarter, thus protecting and isolating Phnom Penh's European population. The resultant landfill transformed large tracts of swampland into the foundations of future roads and streets. The Bank of Indochina built a new Phnom Penh branch, and the Compagnie des messageries fluviales de Cochinchine (CMF) established a handsome new office. A new printing house, treasury, pharmacy, customs house, and new streets completed the capital's transformation from a rambling morass into a highly segregated and hierarchical city.[52] A recognizable French quarter had emerged, arraying European offices and houses around its central landmark, the Vat Pnum. Also known as the Administrative District, this was the stamping ground of French administrators, Khmer royalty, and native dignitaries, and was connected to the Cambodian and Chinese quarters in the south by a "Naga" bridge spanning the newly built canal.[53] Designed by Fabre and finished in 1892 at a cost of thirty thousand piastres, this "Naga bridge" was modelled on the serpent's arching body, with two hooded *naga* heads flanking each end. The visual effect, especially when viewed from the south with the Pnum rearing up like a parapet in the middle of the line of vision, was a modernized version of the Giants causeway crossing the moat to Angkor Thom.[54]

Fabre also oversaw the renovation and landscaping of the Vat Pnum, and its effective transformation into a national monumental place that was officially opened on 1 January 1894 as the *pagode nationale* (national pagoda). Replicas of Angkorean statuary were sculpted along a newly constructed stairway leading to the stupas, steles, and renovated temple on the hilltop.[55] Fabre, that author of the national style in Paris in 1889—a feat involving the extraction of a Buddha's head from the Vat Pnum in Cambodge for display in his Parisian pavilion—was subsequently credited with creating "a real Cambodian jewel" in Phnom Penh, whose monumental stairway, complete with castings taken from Angkor's bas-relief, were in a "pure Khmer style."[56] A small zoo showcased "national fauna," including Cambodian tigers, panthers, monkeys, serpents, boas, and cobras.[57] Norodom and other Cambodians reputedly attached the greatest importance to this work, heralding the renovated site as a portent of future glory.[58] Until at least 1900, monks attached to the hilltop temple lived at the foot of Vat Pnum in tiny huts beneath shady trees.

When the authentic meets the nonauthentic, mathematical logic would indicate a multiplication. But colonial narratives saw in terms of subtractions and vanishings, of dying races and disappearing cultures. The quest for the authentic Khmer was at once troubled and exacerbated by the perceived corruption of the remnants of the ancestral Angkorean Khmer ideal, such as they existed in the "detritus" of the present, by the influx of foreign, non-Khmer elements, from the West and elsewhere. Stripped of this mystery, his oral histories, his cosmology, all that was observed as foreign, decadent, and impure, the Cambodian was indeed "vanished" and void. Where artists absented contemporary Khmers from their illustrations to the works of Mouhot, Delaporte, and others, town planners transcribed this vanishing act to the built environment through the erection of European and other quarters, and the deployment of Angkorean motifs.

The recurring mimicry in which these Angkorean templates of Cambodge were entangled is demonstrated with brilliant clarity by the exhibition of a simulacrum of the Vat Pnum at the 1900 Cambodge pavilion in Paris. Here, visitors were invited to experience Cambodge through a reconstruction of a colonial construction incorporating moldings and imagery of an Angkor that was as yet in reality far from being reconstructed to cohere with such imaginings. Covering two thousand square meters, the reconstructed hill and pagoda at the 1900 exposition were merged in a fairytale pavilion whose vast, hollowed-out frame was filled with Angkorean imagery and Khmer cultural memorabilia.[59] In keeping with France's reading of Angkor as compensation for the loss of India, this subterranean extravaganza was compared to the "underground Ellora temples" in India. In a celebration of the guiding hand of French explorers, the corridor leading into this oriental grotto sported an exhibition about Auguste Pavie and his cartographic missions in Cambodge and Laos.[60]

The prestigious daily *l'Illustration* billed the Pnum as "the most important, and most interesting, of the French colonial constructions."[61] Alexandre Marcel, government architect, and Louis Dumoulin, painter at the Ministry of the Marine, had decided upon the Pnum as the best means of "attracting the greatest possible public attention." "By dint of its sheer size and its silhouette," an exact replica of the Pnum, they felt, would "capture the imagination from afar" and was thus the natural choice for the centerpiece of the Indochina exhibit. Designed as the principal crowd puller of the Indochina section, this "Khmer" exhibit would have left most spectators with the impression that Cambodge was the cultural apotheosis of Indochina.[62] In 1900, the sculptor Auguste Rodin visited the Exposition Universelle and was impressed above all by the stairway to the Cambodian pavilion, which he credited with revealing a "hitherto unknown art."[63] As we have just seen, this so-called Cambodian landmark was revamped to French specifications during the 1890s face-lift of the capital. Marcel's Cambodge pavilion at the 1900 exhibition was thus a Parisian reproduction of a protectorate production. One journalist described it as Indochina's "Indian" face, but in Cambodge, the Vat Pnum was evidently achieving its own prescribed

(194) CAMBODGE : Pnom-Penh – Arbre du voyageur
et escalier du Pnom.

FIGURE 2. Vat Pnum, early 1900s. Courtesy of Joel Montague.

vocation, at least in European eyes, as a central artistic and national monument. In 1906, the protectorate lauded Daniel Fabre as the "incontestable creator of the city of Phnom Penh" and praised his marvellous assimilation and adaptation of Khmer art to French architecture.[64] The same year, the Vat Pnum moved one young French-woman to poetry. Mary Gerny-Marchal, recently arrived in Cambodge, where she would spend the next thirty years with her husband, curator Henri Marchal, wrote ten verses on the Pnum, extolling its atmosphere of serenity and architectural elegance while lamenting that the "skeptical West" was pushing the "sons" of Buddha towards new routes.[65] Hers was not a lone voice.

PURIFYING PHNOM PENH

Concerns to segregate European from Khmer art and architecture became increasingly apparent around the turn of the century. In 1900, a report commissioned by the Colonial Ministry complained that the balustrade around the Vat Pnum evoked the gardens of suburban Paris and complained that European art had begun to "invade" the royal palace.[66] Another visitor to Phnom Penh in 1912 dismissed the Royal Palace as a mass of "semi-Cambodian, semi-French" buildings.[67] Writing in the 1910s, the colonial administrator Roland Meyer decried the westernization of Phnom Penh, warning that "Soon the palace itself would be invaded by a wave of modernization. But that was a minor concern; for the poison of new ideas would get there before the builders, eating away at hearts much as termites devour the inner-most core of a tree, causing it to fall. Then what would become of the old, forgot-ten Cambodge? A few ruined pagodas, a few old men . . . "[68] Meyer's notion of the dangers of architectural mixing between West and East tallied with his views of the damaging effect of such cross-cultural enterprises as the learning of French by Khmer girls. Similar tirades against experiments by Khmer women with Western dress or accoutrements figured in the works of that other arch critic of architectural and artistic hybridity, George Groslier. In Meyer's and Groslier's reading, women are consistently the agents of cultural transmission, Cambodge's copyists par excel-lence. These readings implicitly take the countryside as pure (and female), the urbane as corrupting (and male). The conflation of cities with modernity and of rural out-reaches, particularly those housing the ancient temple complexes, as loci of ancient time and Edenic innocence was a core theme in much colonial writing.

Meyer's portrayal of the Khmers as a "swamped" race resonated with similar descriptions in official and romantic literature on Cambodge during the first half of this century. Such perceptions were formed and strengthened by the urban horizons of most colonial officials and by turn-of-the-century preoccupations in the Métro-pole with France's own falling birth rate. French civil servants were largely concen-trated in the towns where European, Vietnamese, Chinese, Indian, and Cham popu-lations were in the majority. From this we can see how an ornate Khmer quarter announced the presence of Khmers, but architectural features of the quarter were cited as proof of the vanishing of Khmers. In the calculations of France's pioneer of heritage, Eugène Viollet-le-Duc, monuments could never succeed in recapturing pristine moments of past grandeur through present renovations. Similarly, Cambodians could only always fail to realize the facsimile of their authentic but vanished progenitors and remain taunted by a national identity whose realization they were denied, baited by what Dipesh Chakrabarty has termed the ever-receding horizon of Khmerness.[69] As Anderson has argued, it was precisely this notion of hybridity that would produce "nationalism's purities" and its cleansings.[70]

Despite this horror of hybridity, European art forms, particularly sculpture, were routinely used to capture the national character of Cambodge and its inhabitants in public monuments. In 1907, to commemorate the retrocession of Battambang, Sisophon, and Siem Reap from Siam, GGI Beau commissioned the sculptor Théodore Rivière to design a monument for installation on the Vat Pnum.[71] Conceived in Phnom Penh, executed in Paris, and transported to Phnom Penh in 1908, where finishing touches were added by Cambodian craftsmen, the monument was inaugurated on 21 February 1909.[72] At the opening ceremony, RSC Luce heralded Rivière's image of a "generous and debonnaire prince" flanked by three women, personifying the provinces, and a Cambodian militia saluting the Tricolour, symbolizing Cambodge's loyalty to France.[73]

Such material landmarks signed the protectorate with a new vocabulary of monument and architecture that was neither Khmer nor French, but strictly Cambodge. Passing through the Angkor replicas in Phnom Penh, having earlier seen other replicas or illustrations in the journals, museums, and exhibitions of Europe, tourists were whetting their appetites for the "real" experience of the renovated sites of Angkor itself. The anticipatory effect engendered by these cross-references to Angkor between Paris and Phnom Penh is captured in one 1905 publication; it described the restored Phnom, the Royal Palace, and the Naga Bridge as monuments that would give the traveller "a foretaste of the wonders of Angkor."[74] Whatever their point of origin, European and American tourists to Angkor and Cambodia are likely to have demanded that their experiences live up to the mirage of the "real" aroused by the replicas of Angkor they had encountered either in the capital and/or in journals, books, museums, and exhibitions. Erected in Phnom Penh, on bridges, stairways, and other principal places of passage and transit, replicas of Angkor would give those who traversed them a sense of crossing both time and place, whether it be the bridge linking the Cambodian quarter to the French quarter, or the stairway to the Vat Pnum.

In the late 1910s, the protectorate's political and aesthetic prescriptions for the architectural dimensions of the Cambodian nation, and specifically its indigenous elite, were circulated by RSC François Baudoin in his Circular no. 82, "Various buildings." Stressing the importance of restoring to Cambodian buildings some of the unique architectural appeal that distinguishes Cambodge from the rest of Indochina, and voicing his concern over the veritable genius of "native officials" for neglecting "customs," Baudoin instructed *Résidents* and engineers to be inspired by "tradition" in the design and management of diverse structures. Apart from bridges, all of the structures listed were those used predominantly by the Cambodian population and the indigenous administration: *salaas* (travellers' way stations), the houses and offices of governors, and courts.[75] Recognizing that there were generally no Cambodian architects in the residential districts, and that the natives themselves had "submitted to Siamese, Chinese, and Vietnamese influences," often adapting imitations of "European conceptions," Baudoin announced the forthcoming creation in Phnom Penh of a "central organization whose aim will be precisely to recall and to fix with certainty the fundamental principles and traditions of the Cambodian arts, in the light of ancient monuments and textual documents." In the meantime, the circular's addressees should refer to three sketches. Bridges were the order of priority, as these were the literal and conceptual passageways to tourist perceptions of Cambodge. Molds of such "easy and inexpensive" options as the "Nagas and lions" would be available on demand according to the preferred type (model 1, 2, or 3,) to embellish the protectorate's increasing arteries of tourist traffic with such "purely Cambodian" models as the "Spean Sreng" or "Spean Toeup." Next on the list were buildings: first, the governor's home and office; second, the native court; and third, *salaas,* and sketches of these would arrive in due course. Such measures, Baudoin concluded, would exert an indisputable moral effect on the natives, who "will see tradition continue in this remarkable architectural art whose vestiges, as you know, provoke general admiration," while "the local administration will obtain a homogeneous and truly Cambodian aspect."[76]

Baudoin's circular had been drafted by Georges Groslier, founder of the Cambodian school of arts. Groslier's accompanying designs, of "decorative bridges in the Cambodian style" were borrowed from the balustrades of footbridges and the perrons of "ancient monuments." Groslier's plan and sketches formed the basis for Circulaire no. 64, "Des constructions du style Cambodgien," issued in August 1918, which provided Residents, heads of districts, and the Public Works Department with a model-type for the house of a governor, designed by the Cambodian School of Arts, and inspired by "adapted Cambodian traditions."[77] The following June, Baudoin released a new circular and plans, drawn up by Groslier, for the houses of Cambodian governors. Designed with reference to the "laws of Cambodian architecture" as gleaned by Groslier from the dwellings of Cambodian notables, and modified by him to provide more air and light, these blueprints for real Khmer architecture were drawn as simply as possible, with Khmer notations, so that Cambodian carpenters, not used to consulting such visuals, might better understand them. Groslier also pledged free on-site assistance from "architect, monitors or foremen" from the school as demand arose.[78]

The adaptation of tradition and the colonial capacity for spectacle was acknowledged and mastered by Palace Minister Thiounn. Inside the palace grounds in 1920, Thiounn thanked France, on behalf of the king and the "ancient and noble" country of the Khmers, for the "moving spectacle unfolding before our eyes." He was referring specifically to the laying of the first foundation stone of the new Throne Room and associated buildings at the Royal Palace, for which he had prescribed Cambodian craftsmen and a "pure Cambodian style" in his call for tenders, but also to two broader forms of spectacle—that embodied in the "magnificent works" undertaken in the palace complex, and an item on the ceremonial program: the expressions of royalty, loyalty, patronage, and protection about to be performed "by artists of the royal ballet."[79]

PERFORMING THE COLONIAL NATION

In addition to material trappings of power, the protectorate had relied on the choreography of elaborate "traditional" ceremonies to buttress royal authority and cement Phnom Penh's status as a "real" capital. As one French writer lamented, Asian gambling games could not replace the "parties, theaters and other pleasures to which we [French] are accustomed."[80] Despite the expense lavished on Phnom Penh's facelift, the city continued to "exude melancholy," and only escaped its stupor on such rare occasions as New Year's and Bastille Day.[81] The pomp and circumstance of such events increased in inverse proportion to the king's actual power. Such festivities also projected *la nationalité française* while cementing ties with Cambodge's indigenous elite and showcasing the protectorate's alliance with royalty. The most important was Bastille Day. Established by the Third Republic in 1880, this new tradition was soon transported to the colonies, where, as in the Métropole, officially choreographed demonstrations, fireworks, and street dancing merged in an annual assertion of the French nation.[82]

On 14 July 1885, while much of the Cambodian countryside was reeling from the ravages of Sivutha's rebellion and the colonial army's brutal response to it, the Second King (Obbareach) Sisowath, princes, and mandarins brought out mats and ornaments reserved for *royal* ceremonies and helped decorate the capital's state buildings for this *national* festival. All Europeans were invited, Sisowath toasted the president of the Republic, and the festivities went "brilliantly."[83] The "Marseillaise" was a feature of such celebrations from the 1870s onward.[84] The importance of such public festivals was reflected in Phnom Penh's annual budget, which in 1902 earmarked a thousand piastres for public festivals, the same amount slated for education.[85] From the 1880s onward, the protectorate orchestrated increasingly lavish public celebrations of the Tang Toc (king's birthday).[86] A paradoxical effect of this new public ceremony, which occurred outside palace walls, was that Norodom, who had once regularly invited French administrators and entrepreneurs to dine and attend "intimate festivals" in the palace, became increasingly cloistered, leaving the palace only to make "obligatory visits to the Resident and key officials" and to attend such public functions as the water festival.

By the early 1900s, the water festival offered a particularly lavish diversion from office routine.[87] The king and high-ranking Cambodian dignitaries mingled with the Résident supérieur and other senior French administrators. Royal "festival halls" were constructed on the riverfront, from which Europeans gazed on glittering floats

and lantern-festooned boats as they lolled back in their armchairs, puffing on fine ci-
gars and sipping champagne from Norodom's best crystal.[88] In death as in life, the
monarchy was celebrated with great pomp. King Ang Duong's cremation had been
a modest affair that drew scant attention. In 1906, Norodom's cremation attracted
masses of people to Phnom Penh and was conducted with unprecedented éclat.[89] But
whereas Ang Duong had died with the monarchy intact as a political institution,
Norodom had witnessed its diminishment to little more than a figurehead.

By 1920, when Palace Minister Thiounn waxed lyrical about the benefits of protection, the French Protectorate had been worked into Cambodian performances of
nation, through choreography involving the "presentation of offerings, on a gold or
silver platter, . . . to protective Divinities *(Divinités protectrices)*" by artists from the
royal ballet, "representing Princes, Princesses, and Yaks *{yeaks}*" to an altar embellished with flowers and lit with incense and candles. In the context of Thiounn's
speech, there was no mistaking the transfer of divine protective power, in his design
of this ceremony, to the French Protectorate and France, extolled by Thiounn as "our
powerful and generous protector" *(notre puissante et généreuse protectrice),* although some
Cambodians in the performance and the audience may have more readily identified
France's representatives with the dramatis personae of the *yeak,* a term applied by
Cambodians to the bulky, whey-faced Europeans.

Multiple festivals and traditions were crafted around officially sponsored king's
birthday celebrations, which had become a major popular attraction in Phnom Penh
by the mid-1920s, drawing provincial and local crowds.[90] In return for the protectorate's sponsorship of these increasingly lavish Tang Toc celebrations, the king and
his ministers made a strong show of support for France on Bastille Day and, after the
First World War, at annual ceremonies to honor the war dead.[91] This ceremony was
concentrated in Phnom Penh, augmenting its status as a real capital, while limits
were also placed on the performance of alternative ethnicities, as reflected in the imposition by the municipality of Phnom Penh, in the early 1900s, of a levy on Chinese
and Vietnamese New Year festivities. Khmer holidays, Christmas celebrations, and
"national" festivities such as Bastille Day, were apparently exempt.[92]

PLACING RACE AND CLASS

Beneath the veneer of European unity and cultural cohesion, petty rivalries
flourished in the colonial capital, magnified by the bell jar of expatriate existence.[93]
Protocol demanded that newcomers present themselves to the RSC, the priest, the
president of the Appeals Court, the president of the French Court, the public prosecutor, the chief doctor, the head of public works, the head of posts, telegraphs and
telecommunications, and finally to the treasurer-paymaster, who would advise on
which compatriots should be avoided.[94] By 1888, the administrative elite had formed
notions of an underclass of European undesirables who frequented the cafés of Phnom
Penh and who cohabited, or conversed with, Cambodians outside the course of official

duty, encouraging the growth of a third "class" that blurred colonialism's neat divisions: the *déclassés*. This badge of dishonor embraced "social misfits," young Cambodian women led astray, Cambodian students who had journeyed to France in search of education and returned with new vices and misplaced airs and graces, and what one French administrator referred to as our "most despicable European colonials."[95] In a bid to deplete the ranks of such *déclassés,* the GGI and the Résidents supérieurs issued a number of circulars from the late 1890s onward banning cohabitation between European employees of the colonial state and indigenous women.[96] These attempts to direct the traffic between Europeans and Cambodians were mirrored on the ground by the construction of new material divisions in the urban landscape, lessening the room for social and cross-cultural maneuver enjoyed by figures like the engineer Félix Faraut, who had enjoyed dual status within the Cambodian court and the French administration in the first decades of the protectorate.

Social hierarchies also surfaced in the tension between the protectorate's administrators and investors. Until the turn of the century, when GGI Paul Doumer (1897–1902) oriented the administration in a new, business-friendly direction, European entrepreneurs—men such as Faraut and the flamboyant Vandelet—preferred to frequent the "Cambodian town" across the bridge, with its palace, dancers, princes, mandarins, and dignitaries.[97] These crossings between milieux correlated with the fluid movements across Cambodge's boundaries long demonstrated by the mobility of the Cambodian monkhood in their search for erudition in Siam and, farther afield, in Sri Lanka—movement that the government of Indochina was determined to stop.

Cartography's dual abstraction and contraction of Cambodge and neighboring places and peoples were materialized in microcosm through the construction of culturally and ethnically distinct milieux in Phnom Penh. The concept of "milieu" encompassed climate, disease, hygiene, pestilence, criminality, class, and sexuality. In the Métropole, policies to contain and police the milieu focused French architects and intellects on social integration in the urban environment. The demography of the colonies, with their minority white populations, focused architectural, intellectual, social, and medical attention overwhelmingly on issues of racial segregation. In 1906, the future governor-general of Indochina, Pierre Pasquier, noted with alarm that the French official in Indochina sometimes lost his Western outlook and developed "a new mentality close to that of the colonized people, which threatens to destroy his personality and even his morality." Pasquier exhorted his peers "to conserve all the qualities of [their] race" so as to prevent their absorption by the native milieu.[98] As a preventative measure against such absorption, late-nineteenth- and early-twentieth-century designs for the new colonial capital in Cambodge included the construction of a French quarter, designed to reinforce the "Frenchness" of its residents.[99] In turn, legislation and urban planning encouraged the segregation of the diverse "races" of the colonies—Khmers, Chinese, Vietnamese, Indians, and Chams—into culturally specific, economically stratified, and racially segregated milieux within which each of these groups could thrive uncontaminated by the degenerative cultural influences of other groups.[100] These milieux, or "quarters," were the built equivalents of cartography's blind patchwork.

The beginnings of a separate quarter for Europeans in Phnom Penh can be traced to 1866, when, soon after the decision to move the capital there, France's representative in Cambodge, Doudart de Lagrée, advised Europeans to set up their homes near his offices, so as to create a special district. This directive was based more on concern about creating safety in numbers against the new capital's high crime rate and frequent fires than in elaborate theories of race.[101] However, with the installation of fire hydrants, an improved security environment, and the growth in Phnom Penh's population, fire hazards were increasingly displaced by racial anxieties and ideas of national difference as the leading preoccupation of urban administrators.

In 1879, the minister of Marine and Colonies wrote to Myre de Vilers, governor of Cochinchina, stressing the importance of "affirming the idea of *la nationalité française* so as to leave [the natives] in no doubt" of the depth and durability of France's presence and power. To this end, Myre de Vilers allocated considerable funds for the construction of grandiose government buildings in Cambodge and Cochinchine.[102] In 1889, the French still comprised a tiny minority in the capital. Budgetary constraints meant that the protectorate could barely afford the maintenance or lighting of Phnom Penh's only road. This 1,800-meter thoroughfare stretched from the mission to the royal palace, linking the Chinese quarter, the French barracks, and the seat of French power in Cambodge, the Hôtel du Protectorat. All but the wealthiest and most powerful Europeans rented the narrow, two-story shop-houses (*pteah lveeng*) favored by Chinese merchants. Built to Norodom's specifications in the late 1860s, these had degenerated into "deplorable slums" by 1891.[103] The city was best known for its vast tracts of mosquito-infested swampland, the stench of stagnant water and human waste, and frequent outbreaks of cholera. In the wet season, boat travel was necessary between different sections of Phnom Penh.[104]

Distinct ethnic settlements had been a feature of Cambodian social organization for several centuries preceding the establishment of the protectorate.[105] Prized by Khmer kings for their energy, bravery, and discipline, many Chams served at Ang Duong's and Norodom's courts in Oudong as high-ranking functionaries and soldiers. When Norodom moved his capital to Phnom Penh, a large number of Chams abandoned their settlement and followed him.[106] On establishing the new capital in 1867, Norodom assigned a portion of land to the Catholic Annamite community.[107] The area, Russey Keo district, soon became a gathering point for Annamites of all religious persuasions, the home of Phnom Penh cathedral and many pagodas.[108] Shortly after relocating to Phnom Penh, Norodom built a street of shop-houses in Phnom Penh and rented them out to Chinese traders.[109] By the turn of the century, the capital's segmentation into distinct French, Cambodian, Chinese, and Vietnamese districts had disentangled and ossified the ad hoc arrangements of space and race that had characterized Phnom Penh as well as native–European relations during the first decades of colonial rule. This urban zoning was compounded by the allocation of resources and the selective use of legislation. An electricity generator provided lighting for the European and central Cambodian quarter, although "shadowy streets" characterized the Cambodian villages on the city's outskirts, colloquially known as "little Takeo."[110] Here, under legislation enacted in 1884, Cambodians and Asiatics, but not Europeans, lived under a curfew of light and were not allowed to venture outdoors after 9 p.m. without a lantern.[111]

Phnom Penh's European population expanded from 150 in 1900, to approximately 350 in 1903, to 530 in 1904, a trend in part reflecting the growth in female emigration from France to the colonies.[112] The growing community was served by four insurance companies, two banks, one hairdresser, two entrepreneurs, an ice maker, a hotel owner, a lemonade maker, a bookshop, a pharmacist, an ironmonger, a mechanic, and four import/export businesses.[113] This demographic shift, coupled with the rise of methodologies of housing, town planning, and hygiene in the Métropole, led to increasing demands by the administration for a European quarter. In 1905, the protectorate's new emphasis on providing "comfortable, but simple residences" for Europeans, had led to the design and installation of the first freestanding villas for whites.[114] On the ground, however, prescriptions for a specifically European milieu were hampered by economic realities. Few but the highest-ranking Europeans could afford to live in the European quarter, prompting RSC Jules Morel to write to the GGI in 1905. The rapid growth in the European population had seen no corresponding provision of appropriate housing, argued Morel, and expansion of such properties was urgently needed.

Anomalies persisted, however, notably around the Vat Pnum. Despite its branding as a "national monument," certain attractions at the Vat Pnum were developed specifically for Phnom Penh's European population, and the Vat Pnum was increasingly incorporated into conceptions of the "Quartier Européen." This positioning is evident in a string of correspondence about the small zoological gardens. In May 1907, Paul Collard, mayor of Phnom Penh, chased up an offer of wild animals from Stung Treng and elsewhere. Noting a small "grotto" he had prepared for sun bears, and a larger enclosure for panthers, he stressed the benefits of acquiring "miniature monkeys" for the amusement of the European children who were regular visitors to the gardens. The more live specimens the merrier; such animals would provide a welcome distraction to "the French children of the town."[115] By 1905, the proper maintenance of Vat Pnum relied on the seventy-two workmen, gardeners, coolies, and sweepers on the protectorate's payroll. But as the notion of Vat Pnum as a European domain crystallized, larger movements of native workers to and through this area elicited increasingly less favor.[116]

The Vat Pnum's role as a strolling grounds for bored Europeans had by this time surpassed its earlier strategic function as a surveillance post. The presence of the RSC offices had made it the obvious site, at the peak of the Sivutha rebellion, for the stationing of the fledgling Cambodian infantry. From 1885 to 1891, the *garde indigène* (native guard) had moved from pillar to post around this area, making way for the Treasury and the tennis courts at the Société Sportive, until wooden barracks were built in 1891 alongside the Vat Pnum. "At this time," wrote the mayor of Phnom

Penh, "the town was not yet traced out, the edges of the Pnum were poorly delineated, being rimmed by thick bush and tracts of swamp," and the gardens at the Pnum and the European quarter were not yet fully developed. But by 1914, at the July session of the Municipal Committee, it was decided to be a matter of aesthetic preference and public order to move the native guard from the vicinity of the Vat Pnum. "With their noisy life, . . . their calls to exercises, the inevitable burgeoning of people and things, . . . the kitchens and street sellers who find here ready customers, . . . the indigenous barracks have no place in the prettiest and most pleasant district of the town, next to public gardens, European dwellings, and government offices." Now that Phnom Penh had been made a real capital, this unruly hive of indigenous activity must be moved from the center to the periphery.[117] In the April 1915 meeting of the Municipal Committee, there was unanimous agreement that shops and workshops, with their attendant dust, noise, and comings and goings of numerous natives had no place in the European quarter, and would have to be moved to the outskirts of the city.[118]

By this stage, it had become clear that investors favored the construction of Chinese-style apartment buildings over European construction. The scarcity of the latter and rapid rental increases had led to a veritable crisis of rental buildings for both Cambodians and Europeans. Of immediate concern to the municipality were the strategic and aesthetic dimensions of this crisis. In October 1914, dismayed at the hurried and horrid "houses of Beng Dechor," built any which way by get-rich-quick developers, with scant regard for the lie of land and of "the most bizarre materials," the mayor of Phnom Penh proposed restricting new construction to "model types of indigenous buildings." Beng Dechor was not only an eyesore—a "spectacle" of poor taste that had no place in the more grandiose plans for the spectacle of a national capital—but a public-health risk, offering an ideal breeding ground for epidemics. Since it was about to undergo a revamping through landfill, now was the time to establish new standards of indigenous construction. Land purchase would from now on be tied to a commitment to build model types of indigenous houses. Later, similar restrictions for the construction of two-story brick apartment buildings (*pteah lveeng*) could be applied. Here, presumably, was the background to Baudoin's and Groslier's circulars of 1917 and 1918. The bête noire of these architectural freeze-frames for European or Khmer houses was the Chinese shop-house, namely, housing compounds of narrow, storied, vertical units. It was not just that these affordable solutions to the housing crisis were unsightly and unhealthy. Worse still, they cropped up outside of the Quartier Chinois.

In December 1914, a report apparently authored by the public works department of Phnom Penh expressed frustration at the inability to realize these neat visions of segregated milieus. Stating that the administration's efforts should focus on the "creation of indigenous villages" in Phnom Penh, the report named the roads bounding distinct districts for the Cambodian, the Vietnamese, and the Chinese, and welcomed a proposal for the landfill of Beng Dechor, an area adjacent to the Chinese quarter, as a means of enlarging this ethnic district, which was currently squeezed to the limit and threatened to spread its population and style farther from its designated zone into the palace district through the further construction of apartment buildings. So as to regulate the aesthetic and spatial makeup of any such expansion, acquisitions of land in the proposed area would be carefully monitored to allow for the construction of freestanding villas.[119]

By 1916, Phnom Penh's European population had risen to sixteen hundred. A passable hotel catered to the expanding tourist market, and the capital also boasted a small cinema and extensive electric lighting, although this ended somewhat abruptly at the capital's perimeter.[120] Rather than dispersing throughout the town, European residents remained concentrated in white enclaves, and most were apparently convinced of the hygienic and social necessity of maintaining such distinct milieux. The dangers of transgressing one's "proper" sphere comprised a popular theme in colonial literature.[121] In circa 1916, the French administrator Roland Meyer's decision to live in the Cambodian Quarter earned him "pariah" status among French colleagues, who allegedly despised his "wild retreat" into this native space. In turn, Meyer's literary alter ego, Komlah, mocked the "rootless whites" who "curse[d] and ignore[d]" Cambodge from the confines of the European quarter, where they "preserve[d] the puerile manias of their civilized life."[122] But these attempts to bolster "Frenchness" often exerted little more than a superficial pressure on those many Europeans who, having been long settled in the protectorate, remained in many respects the internal exiles of the French imperial experience. In the 1920s, locally produced French newspapers carried cartoons of pointy-nosed, round-eyed Phnompenhois, comical incarnations of the complex identifications best captured by the poet and administrator Albert de Pouvourville. I am "a different man" with "a different look in my eyes," wrote de Pouvourville, and different blood courses through my veins since I traded "the damp, gray land" of my birth for the diamantine dykes, opalescent mornings, and golden dust of Indochine.[123]

The consolidation of the French Quarter, and its inland equivalent—the hill station of Bokor, constructed in the southern coastal province of Kampot in the early 1920s and designed to reconcile the European taste for travel and a cool climate with fears of natives and pestilence—accentuated the material difference and social distance between European and native, allowing Europeans to perpetuate the myth of the somnolent, changeless Khmer. New communications channels facilitated the circulation of these myths. As the bureaucratization of colonial life dissipated the adventure and romance of serving in Cambodia, the clichés French scholar-officials used to describe the colonized became increasingly "fuzzy and romantic."[124] The cumulative weight of legal statutes, bureaucratic practice, social convention, and attempts to police native–European sexual relations, all circumscribed the world of colonial administrators, shrinking their span of vision to a fairytale Cambodge. The ornate and elaborate world of the Cambodian Quarter gave a tangible dimension to that fantasy. Its central cultural axis was the Royal Palace.

During the late 1910s and 1920s the Pali School, the Musée khmer, the School of Fine Arts, the Royal Library, and several elite schools were added to the Cambodian Quarter. These institutes, and the buildings in which they were housed, were founded and designed wholly or in part by French architects and savants. Yet these manifestations of colonial imaginings became the cultural coordinates around which Cambodge's educated elite would map their visions of nation. Ly Canne, a Khmer Kraom (an ethnic Khmer from Cochinchina) who witnessed King Monivong's spectacular coronation festivities and his "famous promenade" through the Khmer cultural heartland in 1928, was suitably irked when, waiting for the king's cortege outside the Royal Library, his camera at the ready, he was told, "You have no right to take a photograph." On seeing the library's French curator, Mlle Karpelès, "snapping away on her Kodak several meters" away, this "Cambodian from Cochinchina" decided against becoming a royalist, as "the king continues to live off his Royalty in his palace . . . while this Cochinchinese stays at home to plant his rice and make poems."[125] Despite this power of the colonial template of Khmerness—as performed by Monivong parading past the Royal Library in sight of its curator Karpelès—to kindle anomie in an ethnic Khmer from Cochinchina, by the end of the following decade, in part due to Karpelès' projects, Phnom Penh had emerged as not only the capital of Cambodge but as a cultural magnet for much of Cochinchina's educated, ethnic Khmers. The standard-bearers of Cambodian nationalism spent formative phases of their youth and intellectual development here, among them Son Ngoc Thanh and Pach Choeun. So, too, did Saloth Sar, whose exposure to Phnom Penh's Cambodian Quarter in the late 1930s and early 1940s may well have sharpened his feeling of being "a Khmer, unattached to the Chinese and Vietnamese."[126]

The Cambodian Quarter's place as part of a larger, ethnic gridiron juxtaposing distinct Chinese, Vietnamese, and Cham living areas would have reinforced such sentiments, further tilting the slant towards an exclusively Khmer model of nation among the privileged residents of the Cambodian Quarter. Colonial statutes on the legal identity of "alien" Asians, and the bureaucratic calculus of census and congregation, undergirded and buttressed these psychological and physical boundaries. To some extent, the ethnic segregation of town plans and colonial policy was a fiction. "Wander into the Chinese Quarter," wrote one visitor to 1920s Phnom Penh, "in your first four steps you'll see characters give way to quoc-ngu . . . these are the streets colonized by Annamites. . . . Everywhere vast, thick crowds of Yellows, among whom [you'll see] the close-cropped hair of Cambodians floating by, and the velvet caps of Malays, and Hindu chignons. This hotchpotch of races is at its most dense in the market."[127] A Cambodian song from the early 1900s celebrated the "pretty stone house" in which Chinese in the market could sell their products to "everyone, Annamites, Chams, Malays, Burmans, without exception."[128] Thousands of Indians from French Pondichéry as well as British India had made their way to Cambodge, engaging in a variety of professions from moneylenders to school teachers; those from French territories became known by Khmer nationalists as "black Frenchmen."[129] Attempts to separate European and native spaces were further complicated by the increasing presence of colonial troops from Africa and elsewhere stationed in the French

Quarter. An American visitor to Phnom Penh in 1926 noted that "whites were few, but there were plenty of other foreigners—black and brown French soldiers from other colonies, representations of nearly all the lands of the Far East."[130] Excluding troops, Phnom Penh's European population numbered 1,450 in 1928.[131]

The Chinese Quarter was chosen by the architect Ernest Hébrard as the site for Phnom Penh's colossal indoor Grand Market, built between 1935 and 1937.[132] Its dome-shaped design presented a modern variation on the mandala principle, marrying the geometry of Mount Mehru with Hébrard's new colonial style. Despite its negative reception by a grouchy RSC Thibaudeau, who condemned the market as an exercise in bad planning, the Grand Market would become a major landmark of Phnom Penh, symbolizing its status as a commercial capital.[133] By 1936, the capital's population exceeded 100,000, including 1,510 French citizens, 47,911 Cambodians, some 28,000 Vietnamese, 21,309 Chinese, and 3,363 Malay or Cham.[134] Despite Phnom Penh's divisions into ethnically distinct districts, reported Groslier in 1931, "a Chinese temple and Chinese grocers can be found in the European quarter between the two banks" and "the large garages and part of the French Administration's departments are installed in the Chinese quarter."[135] For the most part, however, such transgressions appear to have been minor infringements upon the pristine geometry of race enshrined in colonial institutions and town plans.

CONCLUSION

Next to continuing notions of a dead Angkorean civilization, the modern capital emerged as a totem of French powers of resuscitation. By the late 1920s, the "seven-headed cobras" guarding its bridges had secured Phnom Penh's status as a "reliquary of the culture that was Angkor."[136] A 1930s study of Indochina's economic history ranked "the metamorphosis of old Phnom-Penh into a modern metropolis" as the French Protectorate's most significant achievement.[137] Ultimately, colonial town planning and the corresponding stratification of Cambodge into "urban," "suburban," and "rural" spaces would lead to massive social cleavage, laying the groundwork for the iconoclastic antiurbanism of the Khmer Rouge.[138] But Phnom Penh's metamorphosis would have equally important ramifications for national imaginings. Embedded in the communal space of a park, garden, or square, statues and symbols can act as a "collective mirror," welding bonds of identity between individuals and society in the image of a nation.[139] In the colonial context, however, this was a frozen mirror, fashioned largely by Europeans, in which Khmers saw not themselves but the perfected projections of French imaginings. Looking at colonialism's mirror, in its monumental, museological, textual, and cartographic forms, Khmers were constantly reminded of what was to become a core preoccupation of postcolonial nationalism. What they saw was their own absence, the daily reiteration of their status—the status of contemporary Cambodians—as vanished.

How was this so? The juxtaposition of "national style" replicas of Angkor and "the modern" reproduced in the urban landscape the fraught tension between old and new played out in the conservation and museumization of Angkor. Saloth Sar, growing up in the Cambodian Quarter, would not simply have felt "more" Cambodian and "less" Chinese and Vietnamese. Rather, like the Khmer Kraom whose encounter with the late 1920s capital left him thinking that Cochinchina, and not here, was home, he would have increasingly felt less Cambodian and more compelled to stake out and prove his authenticity as a Khmer precisely because the daily paragons of Khmerness that he experienced were impossible ideals.

Urban planning did not influence just national imaginings. Together with the protectorate's reshaping of the political terrain, it had a marked impact on the local semiotics of status. The royal palace's construction and the lavish examples of colonial architecture encouraged Cambodian officials to view both private and public residences as markers of prestige. By the 1930s, many wealthy Cambodians and retired Chinese business tycoons preferred to build ornate European villas in what the arts administrator George Groslier termed the "comprador style."[140] That decade, an article in *Nagaravatta* promoted the rights of Cambodian civil servants to homes and offices in keeping with their social status and asked the administration to ensure that the offices of Khmer officials be "of a grandeur befitting [their] rank."[141] In their hybrid forms, these architectural embodiments of Indochinoiserie represented a transitional space between *la nationalité française* and the "purely Cambodian style."

Central to this tension between the real and the ideal was the notion of Khmerness as an impossibly fractured space between past and present, a notion given prominent treatment by Makhâli Phal, whose examination of Paris and Angkor led us into this chapter. In Paris, "the time of Angkor" had seized Atman by the throat, ruining the "delicate atmosphere" of her beautiful house, and arousing "the insensate desire to live in a tower erected on twelve tiers of stone—to live with a black idol, on the shores of a lake." This time of Angkor that would not relax its spectral grip or cease its whisperings, also allowed her to appreciate the order and cleanliness of her European house, leading her to contrast "Asia's squalor" with the refinement and simplicity of old Cambodian, Indian, and Chinese houses and contemporary French homes. In other words, the modern in Asia was a mess: beauty was only possible in the European present or in the Asian past. But that past forbade her from appreciating the modern. "Without this recaptured time of my ancestors, this grandeur of Angkor, I should have loved deeply my sober, clean, harmoniously arranged Parisian dwelling."[142]

Saloth Sar did not share Phal's mixed parentage—she was the child of a French father and a Cambodian mother. However, like many Cambodians born into the era of high colonialism, he grew up similarly challenged by Cambodge's architectural and archaeological motifs, their vacillation between two eras, and between Angkorean and European forms. As we have seen, colonial archaeology was central to this "extemporization" of Cambodge and intimately allied to the creation of a "national style." But the construction of a national *patrimoine* for Cambodge was as much a product of text, translation, and reiteration as it was a matter of bricks and mortar. Overseeing the narration of these physical and cultural manifestations of the emergent Khmer nation were figures like Thiounn, whom we encountered fleetingly in this chapter as the scriptwriter for both the palace tender for buildings in a "pure Cambodian style" and the ceremony for laying the first stone.

3 | Les fidèles Cambodgiens and les Khmèrophiles

Scripting a Khmer Nation, 1870–1935

Crossing the rural landscape for the first time, Son Diep is filled with a certain melancholy. Later, his heart lifts. The dancing girls, exotic angels descended from paradise, fill his dreams. Heavenly creatures on the stage, they are no less "superb" on the streets. He finds their faces magnificent, their bodies like the *kinnari,* the feather-bodied, winged women who haunt Khmer mythology and folklore. The metaphor captures his own sense of giddy flight. He sees them in the Opéra, in the Moulin Rouge. He might also see them, disguised in Oriental garb, at the 1900 Exposition universelle in the Indochinese Theater, whose manager has failed to procure the Cambodian ballet and has contracted Mlle Cleo de Mérode, the future mistress of King Leopold of Belgium, to perform as a Cambodian dancer.

And the monuments—what beauty! One in particular, that much maligned metallic lodestone of French national character, stirs his fantasy. To Son Diep, the Tour d'Eiffel looms like a celestial palace of gold. For three days he wanders through the exhibition, mesmerized by the magnificent pavilions, each built "like a palace . . . in the style of each country." He confuses Malays and Madagascans, but is careful to distinguish between the polite, soft-spoken, and upright French and those "bad, dishonest, thieving immigrants, people from elsewhere." The exhibition commissioner, Pierre Nicolas, was warm enough when they met; we can assume that he is armed with a leatherbound copy of Nicolas' guide, complete with its detailed maps of the Indochina section and a glorious aquatint of the Vat Pnum. The casts of Angkorean statuary don't stir quite the passion they kindled in Rodin, but more the instincts of a curator. He lists them by name, "the sculptures, the *naga,* the *garuda,* the demons," figures from the churning of the sea of milk, and Rama's father, Dasarath.[1] To reach this subterranean display, he must have walked the length of an exhibit celebrating some fifteen years of mapping missions in Cambodge and Laos by the arch cartographer Auguste Pavie (1847–1925). It was no accident that you had to pass the Pavie exhibit en route to the replicas of Angkor. To Nicolas, the commissioner of the Indochina section, Pavie had "lifted the veils of the past on this ancient Indo-Chine, still mysterious, a cradle of all the people who were prosperous, right up to the apotheosis of Ang-Kor; the tomb of so many kings forgotten in the sleep of decadence."[2] Did he stop to look for his own image among the Pavie displays? Or sigh or smile in recognition of a particular line or location on the map, thinking, I was there. And how

FIGURE 3. Auguste Pavie *(center right)* and "les fidèles Cambodgiens," circa 1884. Courtesy of the National Archives of Cambodia.

did he react to that photo, taken in 1884?—a booted, suited Pavie, two unnamed Europeans in military dress, and four people described in Pavie's sloping hand as *"les fidèles Cambodgiens"* (the faithful Cambodians) gathered on a neatly cropped lawn.[3] A monacle adorns Pavie's neck, and his eyes stare off into the middle distance, piercing the gloom cast by his trademark broad-brimmed felt hat.

Son Diep (ca. 1855–1934) may have been absent from the frame, but he would have recognized himself in the caption. He would also have recognized Thiounn Sambath, perhaps with a mixture of camaraderie, admiration, and a tinge of professional envy. Stalwart, moustached, his neat colonial uniform accentuating his upright posture, an unnamed but readily identifiable Thiounn Sambath (ca. 1864–1950) meets the eye of the camera with cheerful confidence. Educated at the École franco-cambodgienne in Phnom Penh and the Chasseloup-Laubat Collège in Saigon, Thiounn entered the French administration on 15 February 1883 and was assigned as a guide on Pavie's survey of Kompong Chhnang the following year.[4] Here, Pavie cuts a military figure. Off duty, he would don a *sampot* and a white vest and supplement his surveyor's notebooks with folktales gathered from the crowd, through his interpreters. The tour to Kompong Chhnang was part of a plan to revise the internal political map of Cambodge and extend French powers into the *intérieur* under a controversial *convention* foisted on King Norodom.[5] Designed to radically prune royal powers, remove the monarchy's capacity for independent revenue raising, and escalate French control over state affairs, the 1884 *convention,* and the governor of Cochin-china's heavy-handed attempts at its enforcement, provoked a wave of confrontation and coalition building.

On one side stood the monarchy symbolized by Norodom and his nephew Prince Sivutha, who led a military uprising against the French; on the other, the French administration. Between them stood a new, reformist wave of Francophile officials and royalty, headed by Norodom's brother Obbareach (Second King) Sisowath, who was appointed to lead the battle against Sivutha, and individuals like Thiounn, who identified with aspects of the old order but aligned themselves with French power. This was a protracted, bloody conflict, embroiling some four thousand colonial troops from France and Annam in campaigns throughout much of central Cambodia. Son Diep, whose wanderings through fin-de-siècle Paris led us into this chapter, served at the spearhead of Sisowath's "pacification" campaign and later became a correspondent of Pavie.[6]

Like Son Diep, Thiounn proved his fidelity to the French as an interpreter and guide on a number of military expeditions against Sivutha and later claimed to have "always march[ed] at the front with commanding officers."[7] This was the start of an extraordinary move through colonial ranks that culminated in Thiounn's appointment as Cambodge's most powerful civil servant, palace minister, a post he retained until 1941. But the object of Thiounn's faith was more complex than Pavie's caption—*les fidèles Cambodgiens*—suggests. Popularly dubbed "collaborators" or "compradors," figures such as Thiounn were cooperating with more than an occupying European power. They were also accommodating and adopting new ways of thinking about power itself, about government and its constituency, and about the exercise of knowledge.

Son Diep was born in 1855 in Nham Lang village, Soc Trang. His first taste of education was in Bassac Province, first as a novice at a temple in Chrien Village, and later learning "French letters" from Catholic missionaries, before entering the École Normale in Saigon. We know little about his family, other than that his father, Son-Tâp, had acted as an adviser to the court of Ang Duong. In 1873, when Son Diep was still a teenager, the area that later became dubbed Kampuchea Kraom (lower Cambodia) and its sizeable ethnic Khmer communities was detached from Cambodge by a new political boundary, drawn up by the French, and incorporated into Cochinchina. For the young Son Diep, boundary created opportunity. That year, he became a teacher of "writing and Khmer language" at the College for Administrators at Saigon, where he met a talented French administrator named Étienne Aymonier (1844–1929). In 1877, the school closed, and Son Diep was twice assigned to serve as an interpreter on a river mission to Angkor Vat, returning to Saigon at the end of each mission. In Saigon, from 1877 to 1880, he helped Aymonier with the publication of his French-Khmer dictionary, and with the translation of Khmer stories, for use as Khmer-language texts for French students of Khmer. In 1881, Son Diep was appointed as an interpreter to the French Protectorate in Phnom Penh, and in 1884 he acted as interpreter for Governor of Cochinchina Charles Thompson when he presented to King Norodom the convention that would spark the largest and longest armed struggle in the protectorate's history. After this meeting, Thompson proclaimed, in front of Pavie, "Diep, the French Administration will not forget what you have done today, and will certainly reward you."[8]

In 1884, the year in which Son Diep married Lam-thi-ly (Soumali), the French assigned him to conduct a "ghost-hunt" in Cambodge to find the corpse of a French engineer, Bruel, and arrest the culprits for his murder. From 1885 to 1886 he traveled with Obbareach Sisowath on a mission of "pacification" to Prey Veng, Takeo, and Babaur, securing the surrender and disarmament of a "fearful" leader of the rebellion in Prey Veng in 1885 and restoring peace in east and southeastern Cambodge. In 1887, he joined Sisowath on a mission to the north and, as royal messenger, requested Sivutha's return to Phnom Penh. Sivutha refused. In recognition of his service, Son Diep won a gold medal and the status of a high-ranking *Oknya* from Sisowath, and a second gold medal from the French. On his return to Phnom Penh where, as he writes, "the French administration of Cambodge had been returned to the king by the French government," he asked to return to Soctrang. Here, he served as first Huyên and Phu, and in 1900 was chosen by the administration "to see the Exposition universelle de Paris." In Paris, Pierre Nicolas, commisioner general of the exposition, recommended him for a Chevalier de la Légion d'honneur, but to no avail. Son Diep returned to Soc Trang to continue with his duties.[9]

Thiounn Sambath was a child of providence, with no apparent familial ties to the court. He described himself as the son of a Cambodian businessman born in Kompong Cham.[10] Perhaps because such mundane origins shortchanged his prodigal political career, rumors circulated in the 1930s, as in the 1960s, that he had been abandoned as a baby on the doorstep of a city mansion, and that he was a *métis,* a term used to describe Cambodians of Sino-Khmer or Franco-Khmer descent. Whatever his real ancestry, his journey to government, without the apparent benefits of political lineage or royal patronage, was acutely symbolic of a new regime of power whose principal currency was secular, certified knowledge of the type acquired in colonial schools and vouchsafed by diplomas. But Thiounn and Son Diep were also privy to another, less formal, and less readily defined currency of power—that resulting from their position as gateways between colonial and Khmer vocabularies and political authorities.

Both Thiounn and Son Diep's careers were shaped by a blend of personal ambition, adaptability, pragmatism, and their openness to new ideas. Both had a keen appetite for power, and each, at some stage, became involved in projects to commemorate, conserve, and celebrate aspects of a "national" culture. Like their Sino-Burmese contemporary, Taw Sein Ko (1864–1930), an archaeologist who reached high rank within the British administration in Burma, or the equally prolific Indian art historian and curator Trikolya Nath Mukharji, they represented a new clerisy of cultural specialists who, in their role as intermediaries between Asia and Europe, became active agents of cultural change.[11] Son Diep's writings indicate several identifications: as a Khmer Kraom, who distinguishes between the motivations and agricultural practices common in Cochinchina and those he found among the Khmers in Cambodge; as a loyal servant of the Khmer crown, as an ally of the French Protectorate, and a friend of "progress." We can only guess at the truly defining moments in these two men's life journeys, or how their trajectories, which encompassed Phnom Penh, Saigon, and Paris, shaped their personalities. As bureaucrats and embryonic nationalists, their stories are those of Cambodge's colonial transition to modern statecraft. They also give us a tantalizing glimpse of the ways in which power itself was reconfigured in the colonial encounter.

Indigenous belief and the traumas of constant war saw the ready accumulation and exercise of power through the custodianship and control of ritual or sacred objects and loyal populations, while sites such as Angkor became saturated with specific spiritual meaning which radiated outwards and through time as people, arts, and stories traveled. Two other fundamental arenas or repositories of power were land and literacy. The careers of both Son Diep and Thiounn, started in pagoda and early colonial schools, cultivated in the capitals of Cambodge, Cochinchine, and France, and colored by their participation in military expeditions, represented a regrounding of political power away from one's birthplace and ancestral region, and towards the abstraction of a modern national state. In Cambodge, the spatial altars of that abstraction were Angkor and Phnom Penh. For centuries, however, an intricate overlay of animist beliefs, feudal governance, agricultural rhythms, and kinship rings had fostered a deep attachment to place. The numerous *salaas,* or wayside shelters, dotted across Cambodia, provided ample testament to indigenous mobility. The colonial encounter, however, introduced the technical and conceptual frameworks for a new form of political mobility, vested in such figures as Thiounn and Son Diep, which simultaneously attenuated attachment to the land while centering devotion, and the allocation of rewards, on the abstract figure of the nation.

Increasingly, Cambodge's small nuclei of educated elite and colonial officials such as Thiounn and Son Diep would come to visualize power less in terms of individual influence based in charismatic aura and exerted over a personal following (*one's* people) in a particular place, and more in terms of an ungrounded, institutionalized power manifest in formal diplomas and rigidly delineated offices, and exercised over a national population (*the* people). These two systems were not mutually exclusive. As Milton Osborne has cautioned, the mere existence of Western-named institutions of government in Southeast Asia does not necessarily indicate the erasure of traditional concepts of rule.[12]

POWER AND LAND IN THE KHMER CONTEXT

In nineteenth-century Cambodia, money and merit were entangled in a Theravadan universe where high rank in the present was perceived as a reward for good behavior in a past life, and meritorious people were by definition those with money and power.[13] Official posts were open to purchase by the rich, whose wealthy status signified a meritorious inheritance and thus counted as a qualification to rule.[14] This complex interplay between merit, wealth, and power was enshrined in the language. The Khmer term for merit or good *(bon;* Sanskrit *punya)* also means "dignity, rank, grade, promotion," and appears in such compounds as *bon-amnaac* (power, authority) and *bon-sak* (rank).[15] Although most commonly associated with Buddhism, the notion of *bon,* its accumulation and circulation, was deeply entangled with other beliefs, and can be found on inscriptions long predating the official introduction of Buddhism into Cambodia.[16] Cambodian normative poems, or *chbap,* depict a world where power and merit are "coterminous" and nineteenth-century chronicles noted that "people of merit" *(neak sel)* were powerful.[17] Parents of bright boys and beautiful daughters would offer their progeny to high-ranking dignitaries, the king, or royalty so that their daughters might become concubines and their sons ministers "high or low, and enjoy fame."[18] Such fame, suffused with merit, would have radiated out to the parents in much the same way as merit acquired through religious service.[19]

But the popular equation of wealth and power with merit was problematic. As the late May Ebihara has noted, the Theravadan notions of merit and power that legitimated the Cambodian social hierarchy also sanctioned paternalistic rather than despotic rule.[20] The Khmer terms *samsak* (power/rank that is deserved) and *saksam* (deserving of power) have moral overtones.[21] Chandler reads the *chbap* as windows onto a moral universe vacillating between the ideal of "human, meritorious behaviour" and "wild, unacceptable behaviour"; to deviate from the path of proper conduct was to forfeit one's merit-based power.[22] But while this normative framework infused power with the burden of responsibility for people's welfare, the social framework of patron–client structures rendered one's moral obligations coterminous with the boundaries of one's clientele.[23] A powerful man was expected to take care of his followers; a powerful woman to look after the interests of her clan.[24] This seemingly top-down relationship was tempered by reciprocity, for power, like that accrued in objects, was transferred and accumulated through the dynamic of meritorious clan interaction. The care of numerous wives and children, the maintenance of dancing corps, artists, and orchestras, and the ability to mobilize large numbers of people for corvée labor and military service were all indices of moral and political power.

In Europe, by contrast, the locus of power had shifted during the eighteenth and nineteenth centuries from earlier, highly personalized displays of pomp and pageantry to an array of official procedures and institutions that were gradually consolidated into a "machinery that no-one owns"—bureaucracy.[25] Where the mandarinate of feudal or patrimonial rulers drew their status and legitimation from the "charismatic authority" of their patrons, Europe's new bureaucrats sought glory in the "ideological halo" of the state.[26] Although Cambodge was spared the "pulverization" of local institutions that occurred in settler colonies such as Algeria,[27] the French Protectorate engineered fundamental and lasting changes in the way the state and its servants exercised, gained, and displayed power.[28]

The notion of a "protectorate," although translated into Khmer as an empty phonetic (Prou-tek-to-rat), was not new, and was easily adapted to this framework in a broad conceptual sense: the Khmers were the protected clients of a powerful patron. The adoption of this colonial vocabulary, in Thiounn and Son Diep's letters and speeches, was no empty maneuver, but resonated with preexisting means of thinking about political and personal responsibility to which both would have been exposed in their early socialization and parental and temple education. What was new was the *impersonality* of political power, and the transference of the "charismatic authority" associated by Weber with feudal kings and overlords to the "personality" of the nation. Since the protectorate was itself ephemeral, its mandate vested in a rotating crew of people from a distant land about which Cambodians knew little; its insertion into these preexisting moral structures and its gradual erosion and displacement of monarchic power created a psychological vacuum. Lip service could be paid, through sycophantic speeches, to the glories of French power, and its monuments were increasingly visible. But here was power without enduring, personalized charisma. The legendary Pavie and his cohorts were all vibrant personalities and acted as patrons to Son Diep, Thiounn, and others. But in the absence of a greater, more enduring figure of charismatic authority through which such colonized intellectuals could make sense of their world, another naturally developed, its new role apparent in such nineteenth-century neologisms as "national character" and "national personality." France was a "protectorate" in more than name for those on the receiving end of scholarships, decorations, gun licenses, pensions, and the privileges of modernity. But the protectorate's crude truncating of royal power and the rearrangement of regional administrations in ways that disrupted or diverted preexisting circuits of power, problematized the notion of France and the protectorate as either a god-king *(deva-raja)* or a person of virtue *(neak-sel)*. Increasingly, the moral barometers of meritorious behavior would be transferred to the "national character," and it was by walking these parallel roads—serving France, serving a disempowered king, and honoring the national character of the ancient Khmer kingdom—that Thiounn, Son Diep, and others could make sense, and derive a merit-tinged glory, from their roles.

France was not injecting bureaucratic procedures into a void. A centralized bureaucratic tradition can be dated to the Angkorean era, when the Chinese emissary Zhou Daguan recorded a hierarchy of ministers, generals, astronomers, and other officials at the court of Angkor.[29] Some five centuries later, the scribe Nong's royal chronicle delineated the key holders of prestige and power in the kingdom as royalty, religious leaders including the chief monk *(sanghareach)*, Brahmins, literati, "sages, scholars, poets," and "high-ranking mandarins, the four ministers (of justice, finances and palace, land transport and war, and sea and water transport); and the functionaries and servants in their service."[30] King Ang Duong in particular is credited with having placed a high premium on court scholarship and with training a diplomatic corps.[31] However, the nature and structure of Cambodian power relations prejudiced the formation of an institutionalized bureaucracy.[32] Social order was predicated, not on individual obeisance to an artificially imposed machinery of government, but on the exercise of roles and duties determined by one's place in the social hierarchy, and particularly vis-à-vis one's patron.[33]

Formal social organizations and institutions were conspicuous by their absence, as was the very notion of society as a distinct sphere of activity. Rule was highly personalized, and a king's power maintained through "a regime based on interlocking pyramids of patron–client networks that kept [his] subjects in place and provided rewards to loyal followers."[34] Individuals, not offices, were the source and focus of authority and loyalty, and there was no notion of a state operating outside of personal relationships.[35] In 1872, de Carné described Cambodia's mandarins as "powerful and rich" kinsmen of King Norodom who supplemented their meagre "salaries" through "pitiless and arbitrary exactions" from the people.[36] Such exactions were probably seen as a legitimate source of revenue, and a dignitary's salary as a nominal figure of accessory value, tantamount to a badge of rank.[37] Officials stayed in power, not by managing governmental departments or delivering on social pledges, but by managing relationships and ensuring the continued loyalty of their clientele through the distribution of sufficient rewards. "The Kite flies because of the wind," reads a seventeenth-century *chbap:* "An official reaches the heights because his men support him."[38] Cambodian *chbap* enjoined youngers to obey clan elders, and clients to obey their patrons. This patron–client framework thwarted early French efforts to establish state-based loyalties.[39]

In nineteenth-century Cambodia, state office was no longer the exclusively princely prerogative it appeared to have been in the Angkor era.[40] Titles could be bought as well as inherited, the *sangha* straddled classes and provided an avenue of mobility for bright and dedicated pupils, and gifted children might be ingratiated into noble households. But such paths to power were rare. Most Cambodians were locked into social position as members of the royalty, the mandarinate, or the peasantry.[41] A fourth social class grouped hereditary slaves and criminals. The absence of a middle class in Cambodia struck Doudart de Lagrée, who noted in 1863 that the king divided his authority among "the class of mandarins" who, "two or three times as numerous as need be," exacted large sums from the populace under their jurisdiction.[42] In his novel *Samapheavi* (Phnom Penh, 1943) set in 1867, Cambodge's first modern novelist Rim Kin (1911–1959) portrays a Khmer administrator who uses his contacts and a bribe to secure a governorship.[43] Cast as a philanderer of dubious morals, this personification of Cambodia's traditional administration contrasted with another colonial figure of fiction, that of the nineteenth-century Western European model of meritocracy. The latter rested on a functional specialization of work, a sharp distinction between the private and public spheres of life, paid professional labor, and a system of promotion and reward based on individual merit rather than personal relations or financial transactions.[44]

During the first decades of colonial rule, the protectorate was characterized by personal favoritism and petty rivalries, and both Son Diep and Thiounn owed the beginnings of their ascent to the personal patronage of Pavie and Aymonier. The administration was dominated by the navy and military, many of whose officers deplored the demise of France's ancien régime on the fall of Napoleon III in 1870. In 1874, the economist Paul Leroy-Beaulieu recommended the creation of a corps of "specially selected and trained administrators" after British and Dutch models.[45] But over twenty years passed before the establishment of a formal colonial civil service. By this point the colonial administrations in Indochina were riddled with personal networks cultivated between colonial bureaucrats during what were sometimes astonishingly long periods of service in Cambodge. From 1870 to 1940, the average life span of a ministry in France was eight months.[46] In Indochine, by contrast, a number of high-ranking officials enjoyed far longer terms in power, ranging from years to decades. Although, strictly speaking, these officials were conduits of Metropolitan policy, the sheer length of their terms in office meant that, over time, the individual interpretations and intitiatives of a handful of key figures—Delaporte, Aymonier, Groslier, Finot, and Karpelès, to name a few—were critical in shaping the culture and structure of Cambodge.

Under colonialism, a process of cultural translation saw the partial displacement of specific artifacts and the adoption of European accoutrements, ranging from guns to handbags, as new markers of prestige, as well as the incorporation of such effects as school diplomas into recognized indigenous domains of power, and the layering of these domains through the introduction of a new standard of specifically European, bureaucratic civilization. By the second decade of this century, guns had become a primary status symbol among Cambodian administrators, who were eligible to apply for them if they were of clerical grade three or higher.[47] Personal defense against disgruntled tax victims and voracious bandits while on duty in the *intérieur* and in Phnom Penh was a major factor in requests for gun licenses, which formed one of the fattest files in the portfolio of Minister of War and Education Ponn; but common to all applicants, from palace officials, provincial administrators, members of the judiciary, and clerical staff, was the understanding that guns were a proper reward for long service.[48] Since the quest for a gun in colonial Cambodge entailed the quest for a gun license, a gun spelled not only physical might and financial wherewithal but also knowledge of colonial bureaucracies and, when wielded by those with such access, signaled the exercise of a civilized mode of violence, as opposed to that of the wild thieves, *chau-priy*, or bandits. In 1905, when listing his rewards for service, Son Diep proudly declared a rifle (*fusil gras*) alongside his 1885 gold medal.[49] This did not necessarily indicate an underlying rejection of indigenous notions of potency as vested in objects, but merely a shift in the range of material vessels or icons of such potency and the recognition of a new field of power—that of secular governance, with its paper-based iconography. Guns, of course, were not empty status symbols, and their popularity also reflected a sense of physical insecurity on the part of Cambodian servants of the protectorate.

KNOWLEDGE BROKERS

In precolonial Cambodia a high culture zealously guarded by a small literate elite coexisted with an oral culture transmitted from generation to generation with little assistance from full-time cultural specialists. During the 1900s and 1910s, the growth of a secular elite, the colonial patronage of reformist elements within the *sangha,* the gradual expansion of colonial schools, and the introduction of Khmer print production levelled this cultural terrain and facilitated the emergence of a "shared high culture"—a crucial element in the crystallization of national senti-ment.[50] At the turn of the century, only a few high-ranking ministers were involved in the colonial project to catalogue Khmer culture for libraries, exhibitions, and mu-seums. As more elite children attended French schools in Phnom Penh, the provinces, Saigon, and Paris, the theatre of involvement expanded to such indigenous forums as the Mutual Education Society, founded in 1905, and the Society for the Protection of Angkor, founded in 1907. Such forums opened up scope for a new type of pundit critical to the formation and transmission of nationalism: secular intellectuals and their professional disciples. This clerisy of cultural specialists would increasingly take over from priests, scribes, and other custodians of cultural traditions.[51]

Central to this process was the colonial provision of an official, and supposedly uniform, system of secular education. Although its catchment area was restricted to a small elite, Cambodge's secular school system had lasting ramifications for the na-ture of knowledge and its carriers. Where the elite cliques of precolonial Cambodia had shared common bonds of kinship, hereditary title, or royal favor, colonialism's nouveau elite enjoyed a different kind of favor, one purchased through proficiency in French and the demonstration of one's aptitude for modern government through the acquisition of a colonial education. What distinguished this new corps of *neak-cheh-doeng* from previous indigenous administrators was their lack of specialized religious or cultural knowledge and their grounding in a broad framework of "general knowl-edge," which, paradoxically, purchased them status as official translators and cultural advisers. Working to this reverse formula, Thiounn and Son Diep developed a way of seeing particular poems, folktales, and paintings not as a field of specialized art *tout court* but as a fragment of a larger whole, pieces of a loving portrait of their meritori-ous patron: the "national character" of Cambodge.

Couched in French language and taught by Europeans, a person seeking suc-cess in this system had to accept an understanding of himself and his own culture as the other, and thus the system cultivated a self-conscious appreciation of indigenous difference among intermediaries such as Thiounn, and later, to a far sharper extent, among the nationalists educated in colonial schools between the 1910s and 1930s. What was left behind in transactions between these canny beneficiaries of colonial-ism's new knowledge system and its institutions were those sediments of beliefs and cultural practice that resisted precise naming because they were still valued and lived by the vast majority of Cambodians beyond the reaches of colonial schoolrooms.

HOW TO BE A KHMER CIVIL SERVANT:
SCHOOLING AN AUXILIARY ELITE

In 1885, Governor of Cochinchina Charles Thomson stated his commitment to French-language education in Cambodge.[52] "Our foremost preoccupation," Thomson argued, "must be the formation of a native personnel whose services we can use quickly, and it is therefore advisable to give the Cambodians a basic education that will allow their soonest possible appointment to the posts of telegraphists and interpreters. It is by gradually excluding the Annamite element, and [placing] as many Cambodians as possible in our administrative life, that we can win the sympathies of a people who still distrust us."[53] Cambodge was poorly equipped to train such auxiliaries, its sole "school for natives" being a dismal affair started in 1873, bankrolled by Norodom, and prey to a succession of ill-qualified headmasters. Capitalizing on the readiness of Metropolitan and colonial government to reverse the massive damage to "native opinion" wrought by the brutal crushing of the Sivutha rebellion, Pavie garnered immediate financial and political backing for his new pet project: a Parisian school for Cambodian protégés.

In August 1885, Pavie set sail from Saigon to Paris with thirteen Cambodian males aged from thirteen to thirty-one.[54] Handpicked from the families of loyal governors, ministers, and mandarins, these were the founding class of Pavie's brainchild, and they signaled a new phase of policy.[55] Established in Paris in 1886 to "give the sons of leading mandarins a grounding in French language, to train auxiliaries devoted to [colonial] policies," and to cultivate Francophile sentiment among influential families, the École cambodgienne was the first school in France devoted to the education of the colonized.[56] The former governor of Cochinchina Myre de Vilers, a close friend of Pavie, and vice president of the school's founding committee, envisaged its eventual transformation into "a school of languages" for French youths aspiring to a colonial career.[57] But from 1885 to 1889, the École cambodgienne catered exclusively to Cambodians.

The protectorate's dependence on such students was exacerbated by the fact that most French officials, trained in naval academies in France, knew no Khmer. When the governor of Cochinchina visited Phnom Penh in 1886, colonial legend has it that he was unable to thank his host King Norodom because he lacked an interpreter.[58] Bright pupils were well placed to capitalize on this skills gap. The first students at the Parisian school included Ponn, future minister of war and Education, and Keth, future president of the Council of Administration.[59] Devised by Pavie and former Governor of Cochinchina Myre de Vilers, the school's curriculum included French language, a carefully edited history of France, and excursions to museums.[60] In 1886, King Norodom expressed his support for Pavie's project, and by 1887 many Cambodian mandarins had applied to send their sons to the school.[61] The very act of sending one's sons to study in Paris was soon seen as an avenue to parental promotion in court circles.[62]

Despite Pavie's scholarly intentions, the school rapidly gained a reputation as a finishing school for princes. Its graduates were social misfits, unable to blend back into Khmer society after their flirtation with Europe's high life, and inferior in practical skills to the graduates of the École franco-cambodgienne in Phnom Penh.[63] These sentiments were shared by at least one student.[64] In 1887 Penn, a former interpreter at the appeals court in Saigon, asked the GGI to transfer him from the École cambodgienne to a bona fide French school because his compatriots frittered away their days gabbling in Khmer.[65] In August 1889, three students at the school in Paris wrote to their fathers asking leave to return to their families.[66] Others fulfilled Pavie's aspirations, such as Ponn, the son of a dignitary, who joined the colonial administration on his return to Cambodge and went on to high office.[67] In November 1889, the École cambodgienne became the École coloniale. Opened to students from all of France's overseas territories as well as aspiring colonial civil servants from France, the new school aimed to nurture a steady stream of colonial personnel, but maintained a preferential quota for Cambodian students.[68]

Meanwhile, local facilities for the training of a "Cambodian administration" versed in French and such office skills as stenography, telegraphy, and dactylography, grew slowly. In 1888, the École franco-cambodgienne produced satisfactory candidates for clerical posts. But by 1901 the quality of teaching, and the French proficiency of the school's "subaltern" graduates, had deteriorated, leading the RSC to appoint a new headmaster to implement change.[69] Whereas Doumer had focused on administrative reform, his successor, GGI Paul Beau, made the systematization of colonial education his priority. By this time, business circles and chambers of commerce had also joined the thrall. Arguing that "more frequent contact with the European will allow Cambodians to adapt to our customs and the habits of our race much more quickly," the prominent entrepreneur Octave Vandelet lobbied for the establishment of more schools in the provinces, where a meagre three colonial schools were now functioning in Kampot, Takeo, and Kompong Cham, and proposed the creation of a technical college in Phnom Penh to train secretaries, telegraphists, teachers, and accountants.[70] In 1903, identifying the low calibre of teaching staff as part of the problem and hoping to combat the prevalent mentality in Indochina that "any old fool can teach the natives," GGI Beau issued an *arrêté* decreeing minimum qualifications for teachers.[71]

The accession of the reform-minded King Sisowath to the throne in 1904 hastened the spread of French education. In 1904, the École cambodgienne in Phnom Penh relocated to Sisowath's former residence and nearly doubled its student intake to 487 pupils. All students over twelve were transferred to a newly created École professionelle, founded to train native teachers and secretaries for various government departments and commercial offices.[72] New schools were established in Kompong Cham and Pursat. The first secular girls' schools in Cambodge were established later that decade.[73] The cultivation of elite ties through education continued. In 1907, Sisowath's son Prince Monivong was sent to the St. Maixent Military Academy in France.[74] In 1910, in a clear bid to win the loyalty of Khmer administrators in the newly acquired western provinces, the protectorate awarded three-year scholarships in France to the sons of the governor of Battambang and the chief judge of Battambang Court.[75] The following year, a Cambodian student at the École coloniale in Paris wrote to a former French teacher, complaining that the frivolous program was an impediment to serious study:

> Each day we're taught literature, geography, law . . . I find the literature very difficult. We only work two hours a day. . . . I tell you frankly, that after having spent two years in France I won't know a great deal. They make us go on outings instead of working. Each Thursday we're taken on an excursion, accompanied by a professor, either to the museum, or around Paris. . . .[76]

Sarin's letter subsequently came to the attention of RSC Ernest Outrey, who forwarded it to the GGI with a cover letter declaring the program a waste of government funds.[77] However, one student soon showed a return on the protectorate's investment. In 1914, Thiounn's son Thiounn Hol became the first Cambodian to successfully complete the first stage of his baccalaureate. The GGI's delegate at the Colonial Office in Paris held him up as a role model for the king's sons and grandsons.[78]

In 1916, called upon to explain mass peasant protests that had convulsed Cambodge, RSC Baudoin pointed the finger not at the protectorate's internal inadequacies but at an unreformed Khmer administration. As an antidote, the Cambodian School of Administration was established by Royal Ordinance in Phnom Penh in 1917. Construction began shortly thereafter, and the new school buildings neared completion in October 1918.[79] Proficiency in French and Khmer was a prerequisite for admission to the school, which offered a grounding in law, administration, and general culture, including Khmer art and public works.[80] The veteran civil administrator Sylvestre, who had served in Cochinchina since the 1870s, taught at the school for a number of years. Echoing Thomson's 1885 exhortation to create a "Khmer administration," Sylvestre wrote a training manual "Cours de connaissances administratives à l'usage des fonctionnaires Cambodgiens et des élèves de l'école d'administration Cambodgienne." Translated into Khmer and published in 1920, the book's long-winded French and Khmer titles were shrunk in popular usage to *Seavpov bangrien rattabal kmae* (Teaching manual for the Khmer administration). Dedicated by the author to RSC Baudoin, the book aimed to teach students "how to be a Khmer civil servant." Many of Sylvestre's students went on to work as junior and senior officials and ministers in various government departments, earning him a sympathetic obituary in *Nagaravatta*.[81] As a result of "progress in training natives for 'secondary-grade' jobs," natives in Indochina were now filling those stultifying posts once occupied by "European agents lacking in education," wrote one colonial civil servant in 1921.[82] That year, the director of public education in Indochina proposed a restructuring of the Cambodian School of Administration, but intake remained small.[83] In 1923, Humbert-Hesse, director of primary education in Cambodge, reported growing awareness among a "small minority" of Cambodians of the career benefits of proper schooling. Humbert-Hesse defined the goal of French education as "training élites and auxiliaries with a view to useful collaboration" and encouraging "the native spirit to open up to the glimmer of the West, while conserving its own traits."[84] In 1930, only fourteen newly trained civil servants graduated from the school.[85] But other candidates for posts lower down the career ladder emerged from the protectorate's secular schools, whose graduates shunned teaching in favor of positions in the judiciary and government administration.[86]

WHITE TAPE: COLONIAL BUREAUCRACY

The protectorate's crude assertion of military power in the battle against Sivutha was matched in civilian offices by a more insidious accretion of bureaucratic practice. One measure of this change was a stationery order by the mayor of the municipality of Phnom Penh in 1885 for fifty birth certificates, fifty marriage certificates, two hundred and fifty passports, and two hundred and fifty letterheads.[87] The volume of stationery ordered increased the following year.[88] By contrast, when in 1880 the forty-year-old entrepreneur and plantation owner Jean Thomas-Caraman finally decided to register the birth of his three-year-old son, Résident Étienne Aymonier had had to design and handwrite a birth certificate.[89] Although in motion, the trend towards full bureaucratization was still far from complete. The continued ad hoc nature of appointments and the lack of structured employment contracts encouraged a system run on arbitrary awards and favoritism, as attested by numerous personal appeals from widows and offspring of the protectorate's employees for pensions, grants, and other allowances.[90] Despite its own ad hoc approaches, the protectorate felt deep unease at the inscrutability and lack of bureaucratic process within the Khmer administration, as reflected in one French Résident's declaration that there was no way of proving rumor or hearsay since the king never wrote anything down, which in turn made the attempted surveillance and interception of letters a fruitless and frustrating task.[91]

In 1891, Thiounn, having recently served as an administrator of native affairs in Hatien and spent some time in the Cambodian School in Paris, was appointed second secretary to the Council of Ministers.[92] A purely secular engine of governance founded by the protectorate under the 1884 convention, this body grouped the five principal Cambodian ministers together to discuss matters of policy in the absence of their traditional arbiter, the king. In early 1897, RSC de Verneville announced himself chairman of the Council of Ministers. Months later, the newly installed GGI Paul Doumer, infuriated by de Verneville's arbitrary rule, removed him from office and overhauled what he described as Cambodge's "inert, purely decorative" French administration.[93] To all intents and purposes, Doumer declared, "the French administration [still] did not exist" in Cambodge.[94] Two years later, Doumer established the Indochinese Civil Service, bringing Cambodia, Cochinchine, Tonkin, and Annam under central control and unified bureaucratic procedures.[95] Indochina, once coveted as a free field of action by military and naval personnel wishing to escape the drudgery of public life in late-nineteenth-century France, was becoming increasingly bureaucratized.[96]

The transition was particularly marked in Cambodge, where de Verneville's departure signalled the end of an era of highly personalized rule. Within months of Doumer's appointment, the new RSC requested multiple copies of such manuals as *Formulaire des chancelleries diplomatiques de consulaires* (Formulary for diplomatic and consular chancelleries) and Lucien Roy's *Traité et formulaire des actes de l'état civil* (Treatise and formulary of registry office certificates) to meet the "pressing needs" of Résidents.[97] Doumer also sponsored an expanded volume of "Cambodian Laws" by Adhémard Leclère (1853–1917). A long-serving Résident in Kompong Cham, Leclère dedicated his work to "the Cambodian people" who had created these laws, and to Doumer, "who had wanted to make [these laws] known."[98] A new royal ordinance designed by Doumer gave the RSC full executive powers over the Cambodian Council of Ministers. Henceforth, royal ordinances and all of the king's decisions would require the RSC's signature before they could enter into force. A seasoned observer of Cambodge later described this two-track administration as "an optical illusion, a political fiction," which stamped a veneer of royal authority and indigenous authenticity on plans concocted in the offices of the Résident Supérieur, and subsequently issued in French and Khmer texts as royal ordinances.[99]

In bureaucratic terms, the effect of this new ruling would extend the paper trail from the protectorate's offices to the Khmer administration, ensuring the documentation and scripting of an "official" narrative, so filling the bureaucratic void that had earlier exasperated Résident Badens in his search for the "truth" about the Sivutha rebellion. Such documentation would create a parallel thread to the royal chronicles, which colonial officials disparaged as "untrue," and which were increasingly sidelined to perform a ceremonial function within colonial and national discourse, acquiring status as a "truly" Cambodian form of literature but not a "true" account of history.

Bhabha has branded the "irredeemable act of writing" a sign of colonial government, while novelist David Malouf sees transactions between European record keepers and native informants as a form of "colonial fairytale."[100] Transformed by the twin imps of invention and ignorance spiking many a nineteenth-century European pen, and transcribed into the modern if ephemeral equivalent of a temple stele, the voice of the questioned native becomes a silent tablet: ink marks in a pocketbook, notes for a file. Through such processes, Bhabha and Malouf suggest, indigenous narratives become simultaneously frozen in time and are given a new lease of life within bureaucratic, academic, literary, and or museological circuits—warped testimonials to both indigenous culture and colonial omniscience. In Malouf's account, the grand registers of imperial wisdom become chaotic and shambolic meters of European ignorance.

Typical of colonialism's record keepers in late-nineteenth-century Cambodge was the scholar-offiical Étienne Aymonier. In close concert with one, and perhaps more, Cambodians, Aymonier produced French treatises on Cambodian culture, history, and geography and several Khmer-language primers. His projects were catalyzed by individual initiatives outside of policy templates and institutional frameworks, the fruits of his own restless energy, and a desire to inscribe the literal tabula rasa, or blank slate, of Metropolitan knowledge about Cambodge. Typical here was Leclère, who hoped that the knowledge of indigenous customs and laws imparted by his work would impress itself upon the native so that "seeing that we know him, he will understand that we love him and that we are resolved to respect in him that which is respectable—his laws, his religion, the dignity of the people—and that we only intend to destroy that which no longer holds, that which is obsolete, which holds him back . . . which threatens to lose him completely."[101] Despite this explicit acknowledgement of the power of knowledge as an arbiter of colonial actions to both conserve and erase diverse aspects of indigenous social custom, Leclère shared with several of his contemporaries a passionate interest in translating Cambodge and making it known to Western audiences.

Motivating such figures was not only a scientific desire to catalogue and define Khmer culture and territory, but also the impulse to mediate between Cambodge and France, "East" and "West," through the explication of Khmer culture, geography, and religion. Inevitably, these transactions, alongside quests to discover Khmer manuscripts and relics so as to relocate them to Parisian museums and libraries, ensured the absorption of Cambodge into a French "national" knowledge bank, much as India was worked into the British imperial imagination. Like Thiounn, Son Diep, and other Cambodians who attempted to make sense of French mores and modes of governance for those within the Khmer administration, shaping the concept of "Cambodge" relayed to audiences in and outside the protectorate through their scripting, selection, and adaptation of a national lore, these Europeans were brokers of ideas and vectors of change. Their letters and publications are ample proof that the French Protectorate did not unilaterally "impose" an "already rigorously articulated" Orientalism on indigenous inhabitants, implant that knowledge into "Cambodian brains," or imprint French influence on "the Khmer soul."[102] Such language implies a form of cross-cultural surgery and a clear-cut anatomy of knowledge. Son Diep, Thiounn, and others in their circle were no empty receptacles. Their cultural introspection partly ensued from the climate of violent confrontation and rapid political flux, which may well have whet their appetites not only for power but for the power of change. In this atmosphere, they played with ideas, words, and language, creating something that, in their new roles, they might more meaningfully pay homage to than a defunct sovereign or a foreign power—namely, the very concept of "the Khmer soul" and its twin, the "national character."[103]

Instrumental in the negotiation and cultivation of such ideas were scholar-officials like Aymonier, whom the cartographer Lunet de Lajonquière aptly described as *Khmèrophiles,* noting wrily that "everyone has his 'philia' in Indochina."[104] As colonial rule became more entrenched, the status and identity of scholars and officials became increasingly embedded in their own administrative patch. By identifying and conserving a *patrimoine* for Cambodge through their research and collaboration with Cambodian scholars, Aymonier and others, many of whom were humanists fuelled by a sometimes obsessive quest for knowledge, could both make more sense of their own role and carve out an identity and a geography for the area they governed so as to distinguish it from other colonial plots. Working before the creation of the École française d'Extrême Orient, without academic training or scholarly recognition, such figures differed in style and, sometimes, substance from the later cadre of trained Orientalists. Their sometimes eccentric and generally energetic researches were driven by a blend of expediency, enterprise, and unrelenting curiosity. While some would later question the quality or veracity of these early colonial writings, the quantity of output, including articles, volumes, written reports, sketches, and fictional works, was often astonishing. Like their Cambodian interlocutors, they too were on the cusp of a new era.

Many saw themselves as the valiant saviours of a lost *patrimoine*.[105] The efforts by Delaporte, Aymonier, Meyer, Groslier, and other such *Khmèrophiles* to identify, salvage, and secure the boundaries of that *patrimoine* evinced both emotional attachment to and intellectual curiosity about Cambodge and were guided, not solely by thoughts of their own posterity or the long-term security of the Protectorate, but of "humanity." As such, they were among the many nineteenth-century pioneers of the concept of a global heritage subsequently enshrined in the statutes of UNESCO. For all their admirable intentions, their dogged passion, and their voluminous results, it is impossible to isolate their quest to unfold a narrative for Cambodge from the broader, insidious colonial impulse for complete possession through the transformation of the occupied territory into a tabula rasa upon which colonialism could write "anew."[106] In this context, the task of recording and recounting a colony's culture and history, and the interaction between European/indigenous scribes and indigenous/European storytellers, became a politically and psychologically vexed question of drawing boundaries and demarcating territory.[107] Colonialism's insistence on narrative—on the accumulation of a historical record through which the Métropole could at once proclaim its mastery of indigenous history while accumulating its own history for posterity—was compounded by the advent of print media. If the reading public, a relatively new concept in Europe, was growing, then so was a new panoply of public institutions that created an immediate and voracious demand for narrative. Public museums, public schools, public exhibitions, and a colonial civil service expanded public space and simultaneously demanded that narrative spaces be filled, through papers to read, bulletins to compile, forms to complete, lectures to give, journals to contribute to, exhibition pamphlets to write, and library shelves to fill.

Anderson has argued for the importance of "the proximity of real print encounters" in forging "nationalism's purities" by inculcating an awareness of "nativeness." Equally important were print encounters with "the real." Government sponsorship, through grants to scholars and publishing subsidies for works related to France's activities in the Orient, implicitly invested the production of an official narrative of nation in such amateur scholars, providing both the patina of institutional authority and a seal of authenticity to their versions of Cambodge. Just as the collector's net transforms a butterfly's airborne iridescence into a rigid specimen, so the printer's block transfixes such vibrant and ephemeral cultural forms as ceremonies, dances, oral histories, and folklore into an immutable testament, inscribing the national character onto paper.

TYPECASTING THE KHMER NATION

It was with the assistance of Son Diep, then an "Interpreter of the Second Grade," that Aymonier, an administrator of native affairs and director of the Student College in Cochinchina, compiled the first published collection of Khmer folktales as a lithograph in Saigon in 1878.[108] This bilingual French and Khmer lithograph juxtaposed popular tales, part of a rich oral repertoire of Khmer folklore recorded in the vernacular and perhaps here put to paper for the first time, with *satras* in literary Khmer dating to the sixteenth century, among them the Edification of Angkor Vat. Its eclectic contents were a mark of its youth: by the 1900s, folklore and history would become separated out in colonial scholarship, which cast folktales and animism as the nemeses of history and Buddhism. While recognizing the role of indigenous stories as a lens on "the language and mores of a people," Aymonier saw the primary value of his collection as residing in its illumination of the ancestral past, which could deepen European knowledge of "the remains of these former masters of Indochina," an account that implicitly equated the Khmers with their fallen monuments as a people in ruins.[109]

In his French–Khmer dictionary, compiled the same year with the assistance of Son Diep, Aymonier noted the problems of distorting the sonorous richness of the Khmer language by forcing it into the Latin straitjacket of twenty-six letters.[110] If transliteration is a risky business, then translation is more so, being rife with scope for anachronisms, misfits, and the stretching or squeezing of terms from one language to cohere with concepts from another.[111] However skewed, acts of translation generate new meanings and understandings across cultural axes. Son Diep's involvement in the first Khmer–French dictionary made him a partner in these early linguistic acrobatics. Was it he or Aymonier who decided to render the Khmer term *sasana* as "religion," "race," and *"nationalité"*? Who drew up the list of words for inclusion in the dictionary? We shall probably never know, but among them was *jiet,* the contemporary word for nation and race. This was translated, presumably with Son Diep's assistance, as *naissance, existence, generation, naturel; saveur, essence.*[112] Ten years later, when the priest Pierre Guesdon was posted to Soc Trang, he probably sought Son Diep's help with early drafts of his French–Khmer dictionary.[113]

A Catholic priest, Guesdon was also the father of Khmer print production. In train from the 1880s onward, the initial output was largely restricted to administrative circulars and missionary tracts. Indochina's first newspaper, the *Gia Dinh* (Cochinchina) journal, was founded by Governor of Cochinchina Roze in Saigon in 1865 to disseminate news among the native population and to inform them of "current cultural matters" as well as agricultural developments.[114] The *Courrier de Saïgon* appeared four years later. In 1880, Le Myre de Vilers (1833–1918), governor of Cochinchina, established the journal *Excursions et Reconnaissances,* which serialized Auguste Pavie's "Excursions dans le Cambodge et le royaume de Siam in 1881."[115] This was followed by *Bulletin du Comité d'études de Hanoi; Bulletin de la Société des Études Indo-Chinoises* (Saigon), and, in 1893, the *Revue Indochinoise* (Hanoi), the first illustrated Indochinese journal. Like its predecessors, the *Revue* aimed to popularize knowledge of Indochina in France, to trumpet the achievements of colonialism, and to illuminate "questions of linguistics, anthropology, morals, religious beliefs."[116] Circulated in Indochina and France, these publications mirrored and magnified imaginings of Cambodge, establishing new circuits of knowledge and exchange.

In 1895, the National Library commissioned Leclère (1853–1917), Résident of Kratie, to collect and have translated a representative selection of Cambodian literary and historical texts for deposition in Paris.[117] Five years later, Son Diep wrote a stylized Khmer travelogue recording his own journey to Paris, which was published in Soc Trang, Phnom Penh, and, owing to Guesdon's intervention, in an illustrated Khmer-language edition, in Paris. Entitled *Lpoek look daam pliw tiw srok parang she niw di dang tuu niw krong barih* (Voyage en France pendant l'Exposition universelle de 1900 à Paris), Son Diep's verse narrative reveals a passion for the modern.

Son Diep was as mesmerized by the Eiffel Tower as French travellers were by Angkor Vat. Was it his predisposition to Gallic grandeur that whetted this fascination, whereas Mohandas T. K. Gandhi, on a side trip from his legal training in England, felt nothing but disdain on visiting it ten years earlier?[118] Or was it an aesthetic sense that led to a ready association of the Tour d'Eiffel's skyward symmetry, like Makhâli Phâl's later celebration of Notre Dame, with Angkor's towers? What captivated Son Diep most, it appears, was its *novelty.* Written in a traditional verse form, his celebration of turn-of-the-century Paris dwells longer on the city's mechanical street art—slot machines in the form of horses, monkeys, and bears, which dispense cakes from their mouths when fed coins in the belly—and on its public baths with hot and cold water than on its ancient monuments. He is literally dazzled by the Eiffel Tower, which, garlanded with electric lights at night, combines the modern and the ethereal:

> The highest building of all
> Stands 3,600 feet tall, and has several floors,
> In the night, its pointed summit, with electric lighting,
> Appears as a heavenly palace of gold.
> A mechanical elevator runs constantly,
> Helping people to ascend and descend.
> I walk below, listening to the sounds of gongs and bells,
> On streets bordered with rose-filled gardens,
> A pool, with a clear scented fountain,
> Offers freshness and pleasure to passers-by.

This connection of modernity and divinity, which recurs throughout his poem, translates colonial privilege as good karma. To Son Diep, spectacle is real, and it becomes so because each piece of theater, each enticing woman, each electric tramcar, elevator, fragrant flower, and "gilded house" he encounters in Parisian streets and parks transports him to the verge of another world. His travel is proof of his own merit—*kusala* and *punnya*—qualities that he describes as prerequisites for access to this world and that are reflected in his accommodation in a coveted district, among "people of power and wealth" *(neak mien sak samboat)*. Here, the indigenous concepts of political power and moral standing discussed earlier in this chapter are applied to wealthy Parisians. Inserting Paris into this cosmology, and describing also "immigrants" of bad morals from other countries who should not be mistaken for the "honest" French, he opens this world to Cambodians who have acquired "merit." Such meritorious people, Khing Hoc Dy explains in his elegant analysis and translation of Son Diep's verse, are those who have learned French and assimilated to European culture.[119]

We do not know how Son Diep's verse narrative of his 1900 Paris visit was received in Soc Trang or Phnom Penh, although the subsequent commissioning of a similar form in 1923 by Minister Ouk, a court official attending the colonial exhibition in Marseille, indicates that it was favorably received in both French and Khmer quarters. Despite his use of a traditional verse form and elegant language including many Sanskrit terms, Son Diep's attention to the everyday and the way he threaded place and time into a chronology of his own wanderings broke with Khmer literary convention. Unwittingly or not, it is he, not France, who emerges as the central subject of the text. Descriptions of the sounds and smells he experienced at the foot of the Eiffel Tower, and such asides as "intelligent people will know what I mean," not only broke level ground with the French people he describes, but implicitly conferred upon him, more than the status of a scribe who had a duty to observe, that of a sovereign who has the power to make his opinion known. By inserting himself into the text as a first-person observer, Son Diep—author of the first modern Khmer literature published in book form and the first literary work using Khmer vocabulary and concepts to describe life in Paris—paved the way for the development of a vernacular, modern literature. Aspects of this participant-observer technique may well have been drawn from his travels through Cambodge, when he assisted Pavie and others to assemble information into reports of daily journeys and activities.

On the eve of Son Diep's Paris visit in December 1899, Thiounn, newly promoted to secretary-general of the recently reformed Council of Ministers, had written an effusive letter to Pavie. Apparently referring to a French anthology of Khmer, Siamese, and Lao folktales that Pavie had published in Paris in 1898, Thiounn thanked Pavie for his love of Cambodge and for "making [Cambodge] known" through his works.[120] As one of Pavie's interpreters on his 1880s mapping missions, Thiounn would have been sent off to explain to villagers in each new encampment, "Yes, it's a French man! And we are Khmers like you. . . . " Once a crowd had gathered, Pavie would tell a few stories about himself, then solicit them from Cambodians in return. He found Khmer literature remarkable for its "simplicity," its "clarity of style"—a product, he felt, of a scribal tradition that restricted expression to the bare minimum—and the way it drew its audience into the story through emotional expression.[121] In his letter of 1899, Thiounn reported on his own progress in translating more Khmer folktales for Pavie's next volume.[122] In 1903, the year after Son Diep's Khmer travelogue was published in Paris, Thiounn's translations were published there in a new anthology by Pavie.[123] Perhaps inspired by this project, Thiounn soon turned his hand to writing French-language pamphlets and articles documenting a body of "Cambodian" traditions and court rituals, among them a haircutting ritual extant in Siam and Laos and a ceremony for newly promoted ministers.[124] Such translations and reports fed into a larger process, whereby folklore, in which animist, Buddhist, and Hindu spirits and divinities joined forces and royal ceremony that was often attended by Brahmins and monks, increasingly became hived off from religious spheres and was secularized as an index of national culture.

Where Makhâli Phâl saw bipolarity in the monumental matrix of Notre Dame and Angkor, and Son Diep apparently located Angkor's and his own positioning in France as proofs of personal and national merit, Thiounn saw the twin hinges of progress as the distinctive genius of *les deux races,* the *protectrice* and *protégée.* These were no empty comparisons. Colonial travel and contact by such elite actors honed the notion of race as a distinct category through physical, material, and performed displays of difference. Linked to and buttressed by such supporting categories—protector and protected, France and Cambodge—race was more readily absorbed into indigenous cosmology. Speaking in 1920, Thiounn contrasted the "two races" and the dual genius respectively embodied in a "still young nation, whose glory and genius was in a process of constant renovation," and the "ancient and noble country of the Khmers." Here, the French race was represented by the RSC Maspéro, whose "brilliant personal qualities" were a sure guarantee of the "present and future of Cambodia," and the Khmer race by the "august monarch," a symbol of the kingly splendor of Cambodge's prestigious past.[125] As palace minister, whose professional raison d'être and political future constituted a bridge between these two races and their genius, Thiounn had good reason to play up their differences.

NEGOTIATING STATUS THROUGH KNOWLEDGE

By the turn of the century, Thiounn's common origins, his meteoric ascent, and his ambiguous loyalties had begun to rankle deeply with Cambodian royalty. In 1900, Prince Norodom Yukanthor accused the French Protectorate of substituting that *"métis,"* the "interpreter *boy* Thiounn" for the "legal and regular royal authorities" and called for his dismissal. Thiounn rebuffed the allegation. "I've never been a servant boy and have always carried out my service conscientiously and honestly," he wrote. "To me, the Protectorate represents the party of progress and social improvement. This party is very strong today because it stands for a future free of personal animosity."[126] Thiounn's promotion to minister of the palace in 1902 aroused strong personal animosity throughout and beyond his career, from the Norodoms in particular.[127] In November 1903 Thiounn interpreted for the king and Europeans at the boat festival in Phnom Penh, impressing one French observer as "an excellent mandarin . . . a greatly distinguished man of the world and charming company." In a telling indication of the hybrid cosmos inhabited by the Francophone mandarinate, Thiounn allegedly spent the three days at the festival "crouching down at the king's feet."[128] This was to be the last time Norodom I presided over the water festival. On 24 April 1904, he died of cancer.

Norodom's successor, Sisowath, who had sided openly with the French in the battles against Sivutha, proved more adept at navigating Cambodge's transition to modernity and embraced administrative and educational reform. On 3 February 1905, Keth, an alumni of the École cambodgienne, founded a Society for Mutual Education in Phnom Penh to promote "the practical study of French language, morals and customs" among Cambodian civil servants so as to "help the French administration . . . to raise the moral and intellectual level of the Cambodian people." The society, modeled on a similar venture in Tonkin, was supported by Son Diep.[129] In a nod towards European systems of administration and those long in place in China and Vietnam, Sisowath introduced entrance exams for the judiciary and other senior posts in the Cambodian administration. Cambodian ministers were given new, nationwide portfolios to replace the previous division of ministerial portfolios along regional lines.[130] Fresh attempts to cultivate state-based loyalties saw salary increases across the board for all civil servants and the introduction of regular salary reviews.[131] Ponn, one of Pavie's first protégés schooled at the École Cambodgienne in Paris, was given a taste of this new administration with his appointment to the post of Minister of War and Education.

Son Diep also benefited from these changes. Weeks after Norodom's death, he penned a letter to Pavie from Soc Trang. He was waiting for Sisowath to make good on a past pledge that, if he were ever made king, he would reward Son Diep's loyalty with a position in his court. On a recent visit to Phnom Penh, Son Diep had been nominated for the Cross of the Chevalier of the Légion d'honneur by Norodom and RSC de Lamothe, and had subseqently won promotion within the Cochinchinese administration. "Although stationed in Cochinchina, nearly three-quarters of my kith and kin are in the Kingdom of Cambodge," wrote Son Diep:

> I could be as useful to Cambodge as to the French government. I think that you
> have appreciated my conduct for a long time. Even if I were called to Cambodge,
> my body and soul [would] belong to France. I assure you that. . . . I would make
> every effort to get the Council of Ministers to propose projects beneficial to . . . the
> French Protectorate, such as building roads across the huge uninhabited regions
> which could be turned to farmland. . . . From the agricultural point of view I would
> do everything in my power to make Cambodge richer and more prosperous.[132]

By March 1905, Son Diep's ministerial ambitions were realized with his appointment to the position of general secretary of the palace. That year, the Machiavellian maneuverings behind such appointments surfaced in accusations by the RSC Jules

Morel that Son Diep had tried to engineer the disgrace of Minister of War Ponn, a former graduate of Pavie's Parisian school. In a thundering letter forbidding King Sisowath to promote Son Diep as acting minister of war, Morel told of objections by the French population to "Ponn's disgrace." Describing Ponn as a "good servant of Cambodge" who deserved the king's affection, Morel depicted Son Diep as a far from loyal subject. Citing the intrigues of individuals opposed to progress and enemies who envied his position, Morel blamed Ponn's downfall on a "party hostile to the Protectorate," headed by Son Diep. The latter's "debut" had been frowned upon by Cambodian and French functionaries alike, wrote Morel, and he himself had advised Son Diep not to try and take the place of Ponn. Morel would not support such an appointment as long as that ministry was funded by the protectorate. Furthermore, should Son Diep ever try to sabotage the "harmony" between the RSC and the king, Morel would send him back to Cochinchina. Allowing for the possibility that there was more to Son Diep than his dreadful reputation, Morel suggested that, should Son Diep ever convince him of his sincere devotion to the king and to "the cause of progress and the prosperity of Cambodge, to which I am passionately attached," we ("we" being the two-track administration) might find him a position. Having lambasted Son Diep as an enemy of progress, Morel concluded his letter by assenting to the king's wishes with respect to two other ministerial appointments of longer-serving figures, declaring that "the present *Résident supérieur* is not biased only towards French-speaking ministers, but also knows how to recognize services rendered to Cambodge by old Cambodians, even if some reproach them for not being sufficiently in favor of progress."[133]

As these shenanigans suggest, the "royal" administration was indeed a fiction; the protectorate exercised final political as well as financial control over the ministries. The reforms of 1904 did not erase indigenous, or French, patron–client networks and initiate a meritocracy overnight. French personnel files for native administrators still included sections for recording kinship links with top brass in the capital, the names of any children working for the administration or in the palace, and the names of any daughters married to royalty or high-ranking dignitaries.[134] Although a 1908 version of the form omitted these questions and focused instead on appraisals of conduct, morality, and health, the colonial bias towards recruiting elite progeny continued.[135] In 1905, Cambodian candidates for scholarships at the École coloniale were chosen not only on the basis of their "knowledge . . . merit, ability" but also for their "rank . . . and the favor in which they are held."[136] In the words of the colonial administrator and future GGI Pasquier, the protectorate's education policy aimed to "rally the Cambodian aristocracy firmly around us, and through them the Khmer people."[137] This subaltern elite was intended to serve "as an instrument of [French] government," Pasquier elaborated, acting within a token traditional administration while remaining "completely in [French] power."[138] Despite their 'elite' status, they were for many years required to furnish the administration with not only the names but also the fingerprints of their progeny, a requirement that infuriated Thiounn.

Coherence between elite Cambodian and French visions for Cambodge's uplift did not, however, amount to blind subservience to colonial government. Sometime between 1905 and 1907, Son Diep wrote a letter to Sisowath laying out, in impressive detail, his vision for Cambodge's agricultural development, and tying his ideas into his report of a royal tour on which the king had visited various temples to participate in celebrations of the Buddhist Kathen festival one October. Landfill, canals, dikes, the reward of arable land for work undertaken by "the Cambodian people"— six pages of recommendations, including ten days' corvée labor in lieu of taxes, the establishment of a Cambodian and European committee to decide on such projects, and plans for the expansion of Phnom Penh—were all elaborated by Son Diep. Travelling through France, he had shown particular sensitivity to the rural landscape; his correspondence to Pavie, the administration, and the king also reveals a keen feel for the land and for the seasonal rhythms and rainfalls affecting Cambodians, as well as for questions of urban planning that, presumably in part, were informed by his Parisian adventure.

We also see here a presentiment of a feeling that would be evinced more strongly by later figures in the nationalist movement who hailed from Cochinchina, such as Son Ngoc Tanh. Son Diep had a deep empathy for "les Cambodgiens," but felt somehow removed from them. Although he was clearly at ease in France, and with his French colleagues, and was a skilled writer in Khmer, his letters reveal a manifest intellectual and social orientation towards Cochinchina and Siam, which he sees as the most relevant models for Cambodge's future prosperity. Here, Son Diep writes, people see the value of "intellectual education and professional education," and those who can afford it due to agricultural surplus "will cultivate the minds of their children by sending them to school, either for special education, or professional education."[139] France, Son Diep argued, knew the benefits of "raising the moral and intellectual level of the Khmers" while he, personally, found "that the Cambodian people do not yet have enough of a taste for the expansion of industry and agriculture." Agricultural incentives were needed to "encourage the Cambodian element."[140]

In 1906, Son Diep and Thiounn returned to Paris, this time as escorts for King Sisowath on the first visit of a Cambodian monarch to France. They sailed with the royal dance corps and a delegation of ten Cambodian dignitaries from the provinces, and their first destination was the 1906 colonial exhibition in Marseille.[141] As guardian of the royal dance corps who performed on alternate days in the custom-built Indochinese theatre, Son Diep would have made regular visits to the exposition's Indochinese section, which was dominated by a replica of the Bayon and various Angkorean paraphernalia, as would Thiounn.[142] In contrast to their Vietnamese counterparts, who mingled freely with Marseille society, the Cambodian delegates reportedly kept to themselves.[143] As guardian of the royal dance corps, Son Diep would certainly have met, and possibly sat for, Auguste Rodin, who spent many hours sketching the dancers in Marseille, and whose numerous sketches and watercolors, which have since been catalogued as portraits of either King Norodom or the dancers, include several tantalizing sketches that may well have been of Son Diep, as well as one uncanny likeness to Thiounn. A cartoon in *La Vie Parisienne* con-

FIGURE 4. Palace Minister Thiounn. *L'Illustration,* 1906.

trasted Rodin, being pulled along in a cyclo by a Vietnamese in national dress, with Sisowath, sporting his diamond bowler, whizzing past him in the background in a chauffeur-driven automobile. Racial harmony is established through such exchanges, noted the caption, but asked: "Who's civilizing whom?"[144] In Paris, Thiounn was fêted by the fashionable journal *l'Illustration.* Next to a photo of a seated Thiounn, with numerous decorations and a trim moustache, a short article praised his erudition, his excellent French, and his deep devotion to France.[145]

To reward and retain such devotion, the protectorate sponsored Thiounn's son,

Thiounn Hol, and Son Diep's son, Son Diep Ketsari, to attend the École coloniale in Paris. As a further mark of favoritism, Thiounn's nephew Huot was appointed to teach Khmer at the school.[146] Hol and Ketsari were the only two nonroyals on a list of six students whom Pavie agreed to take into his personal care two years later.[147] However, as Son Diep learned later in that decade, the protectorate was less generous with scholarships for girls. Son Diep had sent his eldest daughter, Soumalay, to l'École primaire superièure des jeunes filles à Saigon, at his own expense. In 1919, his second youngest daughter turned twelve. She was enrolled at the École de la Princesse Sutharot, Phnom Penh's only school for Cambodian girls, where she had learned "Cambodian well enough, and passable French." When Son Diep sought assistance for her proposed move to Saigon to join her elder sister at the École primaire superièure des jeunes filles, so that she "could perfect her studies in the French language,"[148] RSC Baudoin declined assistance on the ground that scholarships were generally restricted to "needy" families.[149]

In 1908, Son Diep was appointed minister of marine, commerce, industry and agriculture. His new salary roughly equalled his entire earnings from the previous twenty years.[150] A French visitor to the palace in Phnom Penh in the early 1910s described Son Diep as an "eminent Cambodian" with fluent French and strong Khmer features; "quite at ease in his smoking-jacket, sporting a red ribbon (the Cross of the Knight of the Legion of Honor) in his buttonhole," he gave his guest a detailed description of a Buddhist ceremony taking place. In 1922, Son Diep became minister of justice, replacing the retired Chhun, and Sisowath Suphanouvong took over Son Diep's former post.[151] Son Diep retired in 1927, because of old age. The illness and death of King Sisowath in 1927 may well have precipitated his decision. In 1928, following the ascent of Sisowath's son, Monivong, to the throne, Thiounn was made president of the Permanent Committee of the Council of Ministers.[152]

From the 1910s to the mid-1920s, Thiounn spent considerable time, effort, and private investment in the completion of three illustrated bilingual volumes. Two recounted the Reamker "the Cambodian version of the Ramayana," showcasing turn-of-the-century artwork from the Silver Pagoda in the palace, and one the life of the Buddha. Thiounn, who had devoted ten years and a significant sum of money to the book, saw Cambodge as the primary destination for these works. "The story of the Ramayana is very interesting and much enjoyed by Cambodians," he wrote, and "no-one has been able to relate [it] as completely as myself."[153] The idea for the volume may well have been generated by Thiounn's choreography of a procession of one hundred Reamker figures for festivities surrounding the visit of GGI Albert Sarraut to Phnom Penh in 1911, complete with "parasols, banners, torches, fans, chariots, symbolic animals."[154]

Thiounn first presented his two-volume Ramayana and his *The Story of the Buddha,* to the acting governor-general, Baudoin, in June 1922, so that he could pass them on to Finot, director of the EFEO, for future publication in France. Thiounn was adamant that his works should not be printed purely as texts; the images, taken from the walls of the Silver Pagoda in Phnom Penh, were so vital that if "even one picture" could not be printed, in color or black-and-white, he would not consider publication.[155] Two leading Parisian publishers subsequently provided quotations for publication, while one declined, stating his preference for works on the "Monuments and arts of the past, such as the sculptures of Angkor-Vat" and categorizing Thiounn's compilation of relatively modern temple murals as lying outside of his area of specialization, namely, books related to "fine arts" and "archaeology."[156]

Subsequently, the Department of Press and Propaganda of the GGI suggested that Thiounn's text "would have to undergo revision" prior to publication. In September 1924, RSC Baudoin chased up the matter, arguing that Thiounn's work would be "interesting in as much as it popularizes the Cambodian version of the story of the Ramayana," whose comparisons with the Hindu classic would interest Indologists. On Baudoin's request, the GGI returned the file to him. In March 1925, Thiounn sent his manuscripts to Suzanne Karpelès, the curator at the Royal Library. As we shall see in greater detail in Chapter 8, they were never published. Thiounn's interest in exposing the Reamker reveals a relish for Khmer folk culture reminiscent of the early projects and interests of Aymonier and Pavie and, at this juncture, went beyond that espoused by Finot.

Thiounn's pictures subsequently generated interest in Paris, and in the late 1920s one of the organizers of the 1931 colonial exhibition wrote to Thiounn asking for his assistance in compiling a list of the "costumes and diverse accessories" mobilized for the 1911 Ramayana procession, and asking to borrow an "Album" mentioned by M. Pierre Guesde. The father of Makhâli Phal, Guesde was a member of the organizing committee of the 1931 colonial exhibition.[157] As the Ramayana file thickened, one American writer described Palace Minister Thiounn as "the real power in Cambodia," a "kind of political comprador" who was:

> An intelligent hard worker, supple, well informed, speaking French fluently now, he has made himself indispensable to the superficial and unstable French administrators . . . every day perfecting his double game between the king and the French *Résident,* peopling posts with his relatives and retainers, keeping his political fences in order. . . . Some *Résidents* have tried to outwit this now richest and most powerful man in the kingdom, but he always comes out the best. He is the real master; the other ministers, the crown prince, even [Sisowath] himself tremble before him, mute and resigned.[158]

Kiernan has since described Thiounn as a "comprador feudalist." Charles Meyer sees him as something of "the shogun" of the reigns of Norodom I and the two Sisowaths. Neither label captures the complexity of his role.[159] Closer to the mark is Michael Vickery, who bills Thiounn as "the epitome of the colonial subject who quickly saw how to turn the new regime" to new advantage.[160] It is certainly true that, as the king's political powers had diminished over the past four decades Thiounn's fortunes had risen, and his trajectory to office is ample testimony to his ambitions for wealth and power. Equally evident, but largely absent from the political arena in which most observed him, was his commitment to the conservation, translation, and reproduction of Khmer culture. An advocate of modern values and an amateur scholar of traditional ceremony, borne to power through French rather than royal patronage, Thiounn represented an early incarnation of that omnipresent feature of postcolonial Cambodian politics, the secular intellectual or *neak-cheh-doeng* (person with know-how and knowledge).[161]

In early-twentieth-century China, the term *zhi-shi-fenzi* (people with knowledge) was coined to describe a similar phalanx of "modern . . . professionalized intellectual[s]" whose self-conscious regard for "once robust conventions" allowed a similar reification of traditions.[162] Identified by Edward Shils as a "unique phenomenon in human history," such secular intellectuals, were defined by Shils as people possessing "an advanced modern education and the intellectual concerns and skills ordinarily associated with it." In Asia as in Africa, many such figures sought a solution to their own positions at the interstices of established and emerging orders by seeking the salvation "of their own souls and their own society" in the cultivation and elaboration of such concepts as the national "soul."[163] Like their counterparts in British Ceylon studied by Bruce Kapferer, and in concert with scholars such as Pavie, they helped to weld the fragmented cultural landscape of the precolonial era into a bounded body of culture that would become the focus of nationalist devotion.[164]

The earliest recorded usage of the term *neak-cheh-doeng* in modern Khmer print media appears in a *Kambuja Surya* transcript of a speech made by the Supreme Patriarch in 1927, which identifies *neak-cheh-doeng* as one of the social groups, alongside the *sangha,* royalty, and French administrators, responsible for the recent transformation of Pali education in Cambodge.[165] Immediately preceding this speech is a Khmer vernacular rendition of Jataka tales, prepared for publication by Thiounn and serialized over several issues of *Kambuja Surya.* These, perhaps, were taken from Thiounn's *L'histoire du Bouddha.*[166] Not long thereafter, Thiounn coauthored a French-language study of Cambodian customs and the royal ballet.[167] As palace minister, Thiounn made the collection and recording of "traditional tales and poems" an official duty of court scribes.[168] Together with the cultural institutes such as the Royal Library, which I shall explore in later chapters, these initiatives would gradually construct a body of national literature, so that folk tradition would become generalized into the history of a nation.[169] As Serge Thion has argued, such preoccupations with cataloguing traditions, and concerns that particular "national" traditions and cultures might become extinct, are generally the preserve of an intellectual elite for whom such traditions are already "dead" inasmuch as they have passed out of the domain of unselfconscious practice to that of scrutiny and labelling.[170]

CONCLUSION

In precolonial Cambodian society each successive reign inaugurated a new network of patronage through the promotion, demotion, appointment, or displacement of particular elite factions and regional fiefdoms.[171] As a supra-patron overarching traditional indigenous power structures and dynastic loyalties, the French Protector-ate created room for the emergence of a secular literati tied not to kings or individu-als but to the state administration. The continuity of Thiounn's ascent through three separate reigns (King Norodom I, King Sisowath, King Monivong) mirrored the gradual consolidation of a bureaucratic apparatus linked to the concept of a nation-state as opposed to individual dynasties. At the same time, Thiounn's writings on Khmer ceremonies for turn-of-the-century French journals, his work in translating Khmer folktales for publication, his work on the Reamker, and his later editions of Jataka tales, provided a literary framework for the notions of nation that would be elaborated by a rising, overtly nationalist wave of *neak-cheh-doeng* in the late 1930s and early 1940s.

Similarly, although most intimately allied with a single Cambodian patron, King Sisowath, Son Diep's path to power helped to carve out a space for future *neak-cheh-doeng.* The Chevalier du Légion d'honneur he so coveted had eluded him, but he had acquired over thirteen decorations, including French titles and honors, gold medals from Norodom, Sisowath, and the king of Laos, and the title Samdec Préa Potvisal Réach, conferred on high-ranking Buddhist scholars by the king. He carried these honors to the grave, but within two days of his death, the mayor of Phnom Penh wrote to the RSC demanding the return of his hunting rifle and his gun license.[172]

Thiounn's handiwork was evident in the bilingual biography that was prepared for circulation at his funeral and in arrangements for Son Diep's funeral procession, a magnificent affair that began at his home and ended at the *viel men,* the large lawn adjacent to the palace and in front of the recently built Musée Albert Sarraut, re-served for royal ceremony and ritual. This was no empty choreography as Thiounn had concocted for Sarraut and the colonial exhibitions. On this occasion, the *pavil-lons cambodgiens* leading the procession, and their thirty porters, were not designed as markers of a "national style" but expressions of a spirit of active mourning. The five orchestras included one Chinese band. Towards the front of the procession, four monks carried the Tripitaka on a sedan; not far behind, a family member threw rice and coins from a sedan. Behind them filed countless functionaries, friends, relatives, palace dignitaries, the Native Garde, and the Royale Garde; the bearers of the vari-ous pavilions, fans, and monks' robes numbered over one hundred and ninety. After eighty monks had recited prayers, King Sisowath lit the cremation pyre and a volley of cannon fire marked the end of the festival.[173]

This lavish ceremony belied Son Diep's own straitened circumstances. He had died "in misery" at home. The wealth he had accumulated during his career had been gambled away by his hard-living son-in-law, a European officer of the colonial infantry, and his last years were spent in the grip of an Indian loan shark.[174] In a mov-ing testimony in support of Son Diep's widow's application for a pension in August 1937, a Monsieur Hoareau argued that Son Diep had "shown tremendous activity and a sincere devotion to the French cause."[175] We can only assume that his widow received her pension, and that it was she who financed a memorial service for her husband later that year in the Royal Library in Phnom Penh, also home of the Buddhist Institute. Twenty-three members of the Buddhist Institute Commission on the Tripitaka payed homage to his memory and his "supreme knowledge" before a photograph of Diep, next to which were piled his various Khmer and French insignia of rank.[176] This confluence of French medals and Khmer savants in a center of Khmer studies established by the French Protectorate nicely captured Diep's identity. In his capacity as scholar and administrator, through his studied grasp of the French language and his self-conscious promotion of Khmer culture, Son Diep helped to bridge Cambodge's passage to modernity and played a key role in the early articulation of a Khmer national cosmos.

The year after Son Diep's demise, in 1935 Thiounn's son Thiounn Hol was promoted to secretary-general of the Council of Ministers.[177] Six years later, in 1941, under pressure from Admiral Decoux's Vichy government, Thiounn retired from office, terminating a fifty-eight-year career in the civil service. With Thiounn's removal, Decoux hoped to assume full French control over the Khmer administration and crown, shortly to be vested in the boy-king Norodom Sihanouk. The French and Khmer press heralded Thiounn as one of the new company of men who had steered Cambodge back to greatness and progress. An article in *Nagaravatta* praised his rare depth of wisdom and far-sighted knowledge *(pracnya cheh-doeng vieng-vae)*.[178] The notion that this modern, Western-educated figure had steered Cambodge "back to the future," to borrow the title of a 1980s Hollywood blockbuster, from an inadequate present to a past that also represented the full glory and potential of Cambodge, epitomized the contradictory space between the colony and the nation, the past and the present, inhabited by Thiounn. More than their successors and descendants, and to a greater extent than those whose careers overlapped with and outlasted their own, Thiounn and Son Diep found themselves growing up *with* the protectorate rather than being born into a fully formed idea. They participated in and witnessed the emergence of maps, secular schools, colonial exhibitions, new communication routes, and the distillation of Cambodge's cultural essence into texts written independently or in concert with colonial administrators, such as the folktales collected by Pavie.

The careers of these two men carved out a critical space for the *neak-cheh-doeng* in the colonial and national projects. But their celebration of Cambodian nationhood placed Cambodge, its cultural institutions and history, in the shadow of their own status—as a secondary subject-citizen to France and the Métropole. To Thiounn, Khmer was a secondary language of government, and proficiency in it an essential means of communicating colonial schemes, plans, and desires, first coined and articulated in French, to the Khmer masses. Khmer folktales were treasures for European collectors' curiosity chests and Parisian libraries. Both projects—that of publishing Khmer folktales as told in oral lore and that of devising mass Khmer circulars to relay central messages to rural audiences—represented merely first stages in what would become a key project of Khmer nationalism: namely, the print production of a national, vernacular literature.

Thiounn and Son Diep acted not only as brokers across cultures and political systems but between eras. As vectors of change, they helped to bridge the transition to a bureaucratic, state-centered notion of governance, and to a print culture. The twilight of their careers overlapped with the ascendance of a new cohort of men and women who would carry the concept of the "Khmer nation" into an intense phase of politicization. However, their story is only a fragment in a larger picture. From the 1860s to 1880s, French officials had focused their energies on reducing the king to little more than a figurehead. During the 1880s to 1900s, the fledgling administration had successfully met the challenge of grooming a new secular elite. With these challenges behind them, the protectorate was forced to direct its attention to a third arena of power: that of the monkhood, or *sangha*. The *sangha*'s spiritual appeal, like that of the nation to which Thiounn and Son Diep subscribed, could only have increased as a result of the displacement of kingly authority and the stoking of popular anxieties by the turbulence and uncertainties of modernity and the erection of a new, foreign "protector." These factors contributed to the political potency of the *sangha,* while the embracing of reformist ideas from Sri Lanka, Siam, and elsewhere by figures within the *sangha* also heightened their receptivity to various modernizing projects. From the 1900s to the 1930s, the most dynamic theatre of transition, and one that would expand print culture from the corridors of a fledgling bureaucracy to a broader public while mobilizing a notion of the Khmer nation, was the *sangha.*

4 | Colonialism and Its Demerits

Bringing Buddhism to Book, 1863–1922

The identification and authentication of a national religion, or *sasana-jiet,* for Cambodge was a complex process. Khmer monks, sponsors of reform within the Khmer court, French-educated notables, and French scholars and museologists collectively mapped the contours of a particular type of Buddhism as the national religion in textual and material realms. The most prominent architects of this transformation were Chuon Nath (1883–1969) and Huot Tath (1891–1975). Widely iconized in Khmer temples today, by the early 1940s Nath and Tath had emerged as leading figures of the Khmer nationalist movement. Intellectual curiosity led them in unorthodox directions. They were already in their twenties when they met the Indologist Louis Finot, one of several talented French scholars who would play a major role in leading this reformist group from the intellectual margins of Khmer Buddhism into an institutional mainstream.[1]

Ordained in the mass-based Mahanikay sect, Nath and Tath applied their own readings of Pali scriptures in sermons criticizing what they saw as the laxness of older members of the order and their departure from the "authentic" Buddhist discipline laid out in the Pali canon.[2] Nath and Tath sought to make the Buddhist dhamma intelligible and accessible to laypeople and novice monks through the translation and publication of religious texts. A critical facet of this process, and one that gave Cambodge's nascent nationalism a linguistic dimension cordoning it off from Laos, Thailand, and Vietnam, was the publication of such texts in modern print form and the linked promotion of a national language *(piesaa-jiet)*—that is, Khmer.[3] During the 1910s and 1920s, Tath's and Nath's keen intelligence and moral probity stimulated a reevaluation and reform of the principles and practices of the Mahanikay. In their embrace of modern scientific methods of scholarship, their emphasis on the Pali canon, and their rejection of superstition, Chuon Nath and Huot Tath drew partly on the Thommayuth traditions of Buddhist scholarship laid down by Prince Mongkut in early- to mid-nineteenth-century Siam.

In some ways, their reaction to modernity can be likened to Son Diep's and Thiounn's accommodations to a changing order. Emerging from within the Mahanikay, Nath and Tath's reform movement stressed the value of personal engagement with, and reflection on, the Buddha's teachings. Their adoption of imported media (the printed book) and accommodation of Orientalist conceptualizations of religion contrasted strongly with the shape and aims of late-nineteenth-century millenarian movements: whereas modernity's promise of other ways of seeing and being stirred Nath and Tath, others responded to it as presenting a threat. Led by charismatic religious leaders termed *neak-mien-bon* (those possessing merit), who linked their religious authority to prophecies and Buddhist texts predicting the birth of the epoch of the Buddha to come, Maitreya, and the ideal of the *cakkavattin,* or wheel-turning dhamma king associated with Maitreya's epoch, Cambodge's millenarian movements were born out of the cosmological dislocation associated with modernity. As Hansen writes, their millenarian nature resided in the belief that "in the midst of social turmoil, the arising of a righteous leader would usher in a new golden age of justice and dhamma, paving the way for the coming of Buddha." As in British Burma and northeast Thailand, these movements were dismissed as banditry and were criminalized and ridiculed for their espousal of magic and amulets, but they may also be read as early organized, political responses to colonial occupation. Bloody confrontations resulted when millenarian followers armed primarily with protective tattoos, amulets, and mantras were slaughtered by conventionally armed government troops.[4]

Nath and Tath were quartered in Vat Ounaloum and had moved to the capital at a dynamic period in its transformation to a modern colonial city, complete with printing presses, secular schools, and monuments and buildings in the "national style." Their movement emerged at a critical juncture in the growth of colonial education. In allowing for a synergy between the sciences taught in the colonial curriculum, in offering a more stimulating and engaged approach to Buddhist texts than that employed in traditional Mahanikay monasteries, and in making those texts available in Khmer, Nath and Tath's reform movement provided a vital stimulus to Buddhism, most importantly through its appeal to youth.

In their desire to define the "new" and fashion the future through a reversion to the purity of the past, Nath and Tath shared with Orientalists like Finot a quasi-curatorial commitment to revive and enlist the past in the service of the present. Although this vision of the past as the blueprint for a better future resonated with Buddhist conceptions of time, its strict emphasis on a scriptural tradition confined to the Pali canon disrupted the holistic field of Cambodian religion. The concept of "tradition" and of "religion" informing such critiques was partly a feature of Orientalist imaginings. However, to describe these notions of authenticity as purely European, and to relegate them to the realm of fantasy, would be to deny the aspirations and beliefs of such figures as Chuon Nath and Huot Tath, who began to apply their own rigorous scrutiny to Mahanikay practices in Cambodge in the 1910s.

Engineered by Nath and Tath with the financial or intellectual sponsorship of Cambodian officials, figures of royalty, and intellectuals, as well as European scholars and administrators, the Buddhist reform movement of the 1910s to 1920s aligned secular and spiritual arenas. Emerging concepts of nation, cultural distinction, and religious difference were conflated in a new category: "national religion" *(sasana-jiet).* In the precolonial lexicon, this compound would have made little sense, since each of its constituents *sasana,* and *jiet,* denoted similarly expansive concepts related to genera, origin, and genealogy. The colonial experience and Cambodge's multivalent encounters with modernity across regional as well as global frontiers, whittled away the common ground beneath such indigenous concepts. As new museological, literary, and other projects carved out a space for "national culture," the concept of *sasana-jiet* also became possible. Linking these exercises to the monumentalization of Angkor and the development of a visual and material rhetoric of "Khmerness" was a celebration of the "authentic" and the "pure." The monastic quest to restore the uncorrupted text and the original words, meanings, or practices of the Buddha in addition to the scholarly projects to retrieve past purity, conservation, and the explicit or implicit fear of "vanishing" would all emerge as critical themes in Khmer nationalism.

BUDDHISM BEFORE THE PROTECTORATE

By the start of the protectorate, the Mahanikay sect was far from homogeneous in structure or belief. Its monasteries could be roughly divided among those focusing on Gantathura, or the teachings of the Tripitaka, and those pursuing Vipassana-thura, or insight meditation. But numerous other branches also sprang up. As later described by the minister of religion, K. Chea: "Some monks . . . know magic spells, the art of containing demons, of warning against misfortunes. . . . Certain monks knew necromancy, the art of seeing demons with their own eyes, of seeing their long-dead parents, knowing the secret of the Thirty-six Beasts [a popular gambling game], the secrets of various other games, etc. Some have mastered the profession of shoring up the honor of others, so that they might succeed in all [their] enterprises."[5] K. Chea dismissed these as "erroneous sciences, far from being accepted by the [Buddhist] religion," but what concerned him was their hold over both the lay public and members of the *sangha,* who "hid these sciences under the shell of religion, considering them a branch of Buddhist teaching." K. Chea was writing in the 1930s, and his horror of magic's perceived trespass on Buddhism was partly a product of the reformist beliefs and movements considered in this and following chapters. But his report, which opens with a fairly detailed history of Cambodian religion until the early twentieth century, also reveals both the multiple forms and functions of religion *(sasana)* and the extent of Buddhist fusion, in practice and popular perception, with preexisting and later areas of belief.

Literally meaning "community," *sangha* was the term adopted by the body of disciples of Gautama, who committed their lives to practicing and transmitting the Buddha's teachings. Buddhist missionaries travelled to and through pre-Angkorean kingdoms from India, and Theravada Buddhism became increasingly firmly established from the twelfth century onward. The success with which Theravada Buddhism spread and took hold over the next few centuries in Cambodia was undoubtedly tied to a selective adaptation and integration, dictated by both monks and their lay constituencies, of existing animist and Brahminist practices. By the nineteenth century, religion as practiced by monks and members of Cambodia's Mahanikay (literally, "great sect") incorporated a broad spectrum of popular traditions and folk beliefs. Khmer cosmology fused a panoply of *yeak* (demons) and *neak-ta* (spirits) with the Buddhist pantheon.[6] The interface between mortals and this spirit world were Achars, lay preceptors who made the world intelligible to villagers by performing cyclical rituals in local temples *(vats)* and spirit mediums.[7] Shiva, Vishnu, and other Brahmanic and Hindu deities were added to this syncretic pantheon, and Brahmanic rituals were maintained at the court. Animist beliefs were a vital corollary of Buddhist faith, the two combining to form a cosmos where the untamed world of the "priy," home of ghouls and beasts, was in perpetual counterbalance with the realm of the srok (district), where king and the Buddha held sway through the mediation of mandarins and monks.[8] In its hierarchical ordering of living beings into a vertical grid according to their karma—the "physical, cognitive, and verbal actions of past lives"—Buddhist cosmography proved compatible, in Cambodia as in many other mainland Southeast Asian societies, with such animist beliefs.[9] Animist beliefs also shaped relations to space through the worship of mountains and other toponyms and tumuli, including termite hills, believed to be inhabited by territorial spirits or other supernatural powers. While Buddhism read one's destiny as partly preconditioned by one's karmic legacy, supernatural deities were seen as shapers of destiny who could prevent accident, danger, drought, and illness and ensure well-being and wealth. The king was seen as the "greatest territorial spirit of the land," embodied by a temple conceived as a replica of Mount Mehru, which in turn, as Hang Chan Sophea writes, sheltered statues representing the most powerful divinities.[10]

To describe this synergy as "syncretism" presupposes the indigenous compartmentalization of different beliefs as Buddhist or animist, but the gradual fusion and layering of diverse religious movements over time probably led many monastic and lay practitioners to see, not in terms of "a syncretism of two religions, but as a whole."[11] This holistic view is underscored in such phenomena as the presence of *neak-ta* shelters in the grounds of Buddhist temples, the incorporation of Buddhist symbols in places of worship established by spirit mediums, and the latters' invocation of the Buddhist trinity and the three jewels of the Dhamma in rituals.[12] Overlaid on centuries of ongoing animist practice, Brahminic beliefs, and worship of Hindu deities, Buddhism became integrated into the worldviews and daily lives of Cambodian farmers in much the same way that Buddhism was adopted in the Siamese kingdom of Sukhothai.[13] Despite the unifying cosmological structures of the Buddhist calendar and the doctrinal homogeneity of the Buddhist canon, through their later reliance on local craftsmen, architects, and artists, and their recruiting of lay preceptors, or *achar,* from among village communities, the *sangha* necessarily acquired, and were attributed with, extraneous roles, powers, and a cultural vocabulary. Indeed, to communicate the Buddha's teachings to their constituency, the adoption and adaptation of local oral and visual cultural forms was essential. Animist beliefs and reverence for Hindu deities and legends were worked into this new order in ways that suggest, not the casual streamlining of parallel threads, but a layered, thoughtful interweaving and absorption of diverse elements into a broad field of belief and practice. As Forest notes, the *neak-ta* tree became a fig tree; animal sacrifices and offerings of meat and wine were abandoned. Scenes from the Reamker, the Cambodian version of the Hindu epic Ramayana, became a popular didactic and decorative device in Buddhist temple murals.[14] As in Siam, these processes of grafting and fusion, and the strength of indigenous beliefs in the magical powers of good and evil spirits, ensured that the rites of Buddhism were often regarded animistically. It followed from this that monks came to be seen, not solely as those who personified the Buddha's teachings or as conduits of merit, but as sources of "protective, beneficial power."[15] Buddhist iconography also developed a significance beyond the purely representative. Particular statues and images of the Buddha, as well as reliquary sites and stupas believed to hold remnants of his physical presence on earth, became attributed with divine powers of their own, attracting pilgrims and material offerings. Buddhist monasteries were linked into the broader sacred topography of Khmer kingdoms through the erection of boundary stones *(sima),* the laying of which was the subject of great ceremony and is unlikely to have taken place without consultation with other local specialists, including astrologers.

Another dimension of this eclecticism was regional diversity. Nineteenth-century Cambodge possessed, in the words of Leclère, "no church, no national sangha," but a multitude of *sangha* whose primary geographic loci of identity were the villages, districts, or provincial centers where their *vat* was located, and not the nation.[16] In addition to their much vaunted role as centers of education, curators of Buddhist scriptures, and diffusers of a socially binding culture, monasteries also tied isolated districts *(sroks)* into a loosely knit conglomeration at whose apex stood the Buddhist monarch, in whom temporal power was vested. Equilibrium between these diverse spheres of spirituality, status, and duties was maintained without benefit of rigid institutional structures; but with monasteries came a unifying Buddhist calendar and the harmonization of gestures and rites.

As teachers and practitioners, the *sangha* could not mediate with divinities. Rather, their role vis-à-vis the laity was as exemplars of the Buddha through their strict observance of the *vinaya,* or Buddhist code of conduct. Devotion to a monastic life, together with meditation, could lead to nirvana, the moment of enlightenment that brought salvation or the cessation of suffering. Nirvana, however, was not the goal of lay Buddhists, who more commonly aspired to a better life in their next incarnation. Theravada Buddhism was integrated into Khmer mundane practice through the concept of *bon,* from the Sanskrit, *punnya,* denoting karmic merit. Karmic merit was not something that was directly "transferred" through binary transactions, but rather something that could be accumulated through good deeds, and its dividends passed on to "sentient beings," including humans, animals, ancestors, or spirits. It was this elasticity of merit, argues Saveros Pou, that ensured the adaptability of Buddhist beliefs and practices to modernity's constantly changing institutions.[17] It was as generators and mediators of merit that the *sangha* gained much of their value and status among laity and royalty, over and above their canonical roles as practitioners and teachers. In their quest for merit, Khmer laity commonly sought, not nirvana, but a more propitious rebirth in the next world. Lay search for merit guided myriad transactions.

One broad field of achieving merit encompassed monastic scholarship: offering one's son to a temple, sponsoring an ordination ceremony, and the act of learning in temple schools were all means of accumulating merit for kith and kin. A tangible act of acquiring merit, and that through which the wealthy and elite also gained considerable current status, was temple construction or restoration. Other material merit-based transactions were the donation of alms to monks and the honoring, through incense and gifts of fruit and food, of Buddhist icons. A more abstract means of acquiring merit involved listening to sermons. The concept of karmic merit conveys part, but not the entirety, of the Khmer Buddhist universe as experienced by lay practitioners. The search for it was both plural and sensual, involving both alert attention to the lively performance of sermons and Buddha birth tales (jataka) and observance of holy days, which, as in many religions, were marked in the lives of laity not by abstention but by indulgence—by bodily adornment, feasting, and merriment.

In Cambodia, Laos, and Siam, notes Keyes, the nativity tale concerning the life of Prince Vessantara, the last incarnation of the Buddha before his rebirth as Siddhatha Gautama, provided an important vehicle of merit to attentive listeners.[18] Known as *Mahavesantarajatak* in Pali and *Mahavesantajietok* in Khmer, and by its abbreviated Thai form *Maha Ch'at,* and hereafter simply as the Maha Jataka, this story tells of how Vessantara donated his own wife and children as alms. The best loved of all Jataka tales in Cambodia, it was celebrated in a festival held at the end of the *uesaa* retreat in most Mahanikay vats.[19] In late-nineteenth- and early-twentieth-century Cambodge, as in northeastern Siam, the very act of listening to the Maha Jataka was considered particularly meritorious.[20] The centrality of this Maha Jataka in Buddhist life and the elasticity of merit as described by Pou are reflected in one seventeenth-century inscription at Angkor studied by Chandler. "Then the congregation was asked to recite the great Jataka (Maha Jataka). . . . All of these people were eager to gain merit, and made these offerings to their parents and ancestors, to seven degrees of kinship." For their services in reciting prayers and the great Jataka, monks at the temple were given silver, cloth, and other objects. The sponsors of this ceremony also offered an eight-year-old boy up to the monkhood, and a sum of money.[21] As Chandler reminds us, this extensive inscription, dated 1747, indicates not only the significance of the Maha Jataka but the importance of Angkor in Cambodian religious life long before its "discovery" by the French.

Within the monkhood, merit could be accumulated through the exercise of such specialist skills as the crafting of Buddhist manuscripts. Underpinning the power of the *sangha* in Cambodia, as in other Buddhist societies in Southeast Asia, was the "symbolic, magico-religious value" of writing.[22] Scribes and monks recorded, copied, and preserved religious and royal announcements and literature for posterity through stone inscriptions, palm-leaf manuscripts, and concertina-like manuscripts of stiff card.[23] Due to their long-standing use as the tangible vehicles of Buddhist teachings or *dhamma*, palm-leaf manuscripts became objects of sacred power in their own right in the Buddhist societies of Southeast Asia.[24]

The preparation, transfer, and maintenance of Buddhist manuscripts involved acts of consecration, dedication, and presentation centering on the notion of the manuscript's intrinsic and accumulated merit. As Hansen asserts:

> [w]riting, in and of itself, was highly valued and spiritually potent . . . surrounded by rituals for preparing the palm-leaves, and ceremonies and regulations that had to be observed by the monks who inscribed them.
>
> Finished manuscripts were consecrated and the presentation of the manuscript to a monastery required a ritual presentation of robes to the monk-scribe in order to effect the passing of merit to the donor of the manuscript. The quality and efficacy of the manuscript depended in part on the beauty of its written words, which in turn reflected the mindfulness of the monk who inscribed it, since in many cases, written syllables of the teachings were considered as microcosmic representations of the Buddha.[25]

Deposited in European libraries and isolated from the popular practices in which they had long been embedded, such texts allowed the European construction of Buddhism as a "transhistorical and self-identical essence that had benevolently descended on various cultures over the course of history, its instantiations, however, always imperfect."[26]

BUDDHOLOGY

The Western search for a pure, canonical Buddhism was not solely a scientific endeavor. It was also in part a quest for European spiritual redemption, which dated to the Enlightenment. By the late nineteenth century, the crisis of faith sparked by Charles Darwin's *On the Origin of Species* (1857), and exacerbated by rapid industrialization and social change in Europe, coupled with the expanding ken of "Oriental" cultures through the distorting prisms of metropolitan museums and exhibitions, had fostered a number of societies committed to discovering, or inculcating, alternative religions. Most prominent was the Theosophical Society, established in New York City in 1871. Where the spectres of European fears of social "decadence" haunted colonial conservation campaigns, and the armature of the census clanked with all the weight of European fears of declining birthrates, the colonial purification and rationalization of religion was also partly tied up with such homegrown movements. Spirit mediums and occultism might be winning converts in urbane Europe, but they must not be allowed to distort the "true" practice of Buddhism. In their prescriptions for the true shape of that Buddhism, those scholars active in the late nineteenth and early twentieth century, such as Rhys Davids and Louis Finot, were, in a spirit of inadvertent narcissism, reading the "Buddhist" cultures and societies they encountered through the filter of their own, unarticulated ideals of a religious utopia.

Against the intellectual backdrop of their time, their emphasis on the "scientific" and "rational" potential of Buddhism marked an essentially egalitarian impulse: by charting and scripting the history of Buddhism, they hoped to earn for it acceptance as a religion on a theological par with Christianity. The scapegoat of these scholarly pursuits was Hinduism, disparaged by Orientalist scholarship as irrational, densely material, and overly ritualistic. The corollary emphasis of Buddhism as spiritual saw its emergence, in European mind-sets, as the "thinking man's religion." Its characterization as a serene and abstract religion with an emphasis on meditation and separation—in mind, spirit, and lifestyle—from earthly cares may have cohered with the conceptions and identifications of monks, but not with the broad lay public in most Southeast Asian Theravadan societies.

The school of Buddhist studies that emerged in Europe during the early nineteenth century found its initial inspiration in India and remained dominated by Indologists, such as Finot, well into the 1900s. The Buddhism that concerned this first wave of European scholars was, argues Donald Lopez, "an historical projection, derived exclusively from manuscripts and blockprints."[27] The British army might later sequester the Rosetta Stone, but it was a French soldier-turned-savant who stole Britain's thunder in Indian scholarship. When English troops captured Pondichéry in 1761, Abraham-Hyacinthe Anquetil-Duperron walked away with some two hundred Persian and Sanskrit manuscripts, which he took back to Paris. Here began France's *renaissance orientale*.[28] The publication of later French works on India sparked a culture war, leading England's first Sanskritist, William "Oriental" Jones, to establish the Asiatic Society in London in 1784, so that "the activity of the French in the same pursuits may not be superior to ours."[29] Competition was followed by cooperation, and in 1837 a British scholar, Brian Houghton Hodgson, sent eighty-eight Sanskrit texts, followed by some Tibetan texts acquired in Kathmandu, to the Collège de France. Here, the philologist Eugène Burnouf (1801–1852), working in Sanskrit, Pali, and Tibetan—languages that would form the basis of Suzanne Karpelès' training some eighty years later—began to document the origins of Buddhism and the evolution of the Buddhist doctrine.[30] Closely tied to eighteenth- and nineteenth-century attempts to reconstruct a classical period for India, this textual reification of Buddhism was exemplified by Burnouf's seminal work *l'Introduction à l'histoire du buddhisme indien* (Paris: Imprimerie Royal, 1844).[31]

Eleven years before publication of Burnouf's book, in 1833, Prince Mongkut was ordained as a monk. Already exposed, through European advisers and tutors at the royal court, to Western discourses, he went on to found the Thommayuth sect in Siam. The founding impetus and subsequent identification of the "reformist" sect commonly hailed as a radical and enlightened movement was not an issue of doctrinal interpretations but of correct clerical practice. Where Burnouf and others labored to trace the correct contours of a history of Oriental religion, Mongkut found "a pristine source for his reforms in the Pâli scriptures."[32] Mongkut's prescriptions were deep-seated convictions developed over years of observance and practice. By the time of the widespread adoption of Buddhism in Siam and Cambodia, in the twelfth to thirteenth centuries, a corpus of texts and commentaries had evolved. Mongkut's aims were to inject new moral rigor into the *sangha* through a scriptural revival and to demystify Buddhism by purifying it of practices that deviated from the spirit and letter of these received scriptures. Ritual recitations of the much loved Jataka tales were a first casualty of his campaign; the Thommayuth maintained that merit could not accrue from such "farcical" renderings of the Maha Jataka, and that its embellishment for heightened entertainment value was a travesty of the "true words" of the Buddha.[33]

In 1853, a Thommayuth sect modelled on Mongkut's movement was established in King Ang Duong's kingdom by a Khmer monk named Pan (1824–1894), who had trained with Mongkut. In Cambodge as in Siam, the Thommayuth advocated a purist approach to Buddhist doctrine, its scriptural elaboration and its ritual application.[34] Whereas the Mahanikay recited Pali texts with Khmer pronunciation and incorporated vernacular Buddhist literature into their repertoire, the Thommayuth recited Pali texts without Khmer pronunciation, and also rejected most popular Buddhist literature as impure and unorthodox.[35] Although radical, these ideas had little impact outside elite enclaves. The Thommayuth sect remained the preserve of the royalty: Ang Duong's sons, the future kings Norodom and Sisowath, were both ordained there.

Meanwhile, in Europe, the scriptural bias of Buddhist studies focused on the pursuit of master texts and their documentation and retrieval for imperial scholarly institutes. Concerned that such texts were collecting dust rather than fresh scholarship, the Pali Text Society established by Thomas Williams Rhys Davids in 1881 vowed to render accessible the Buddhist manuscripts housed in the libraries and universities of Europe. Critically for the later development of Buddhism in the French Protectorate, Rhys Davids promoted the Pali canon as the original, "true" Buddhism, later corrupted by Mahayana distortions. The texts which he, Mongkut, and others accepted as canonical originated in Ceylon, where, in the first century AD, the Buddhist king Vattagamini had the teachings of the Buddha inscribed on palm-leaf manuscripts in Pali, a North Indian vernacular related to Sanskrit, which the Buddha was believed to have used as the medium for his teachings. This recognition by Western scholars of these texts as *the* authentic, Buddhist canon encouraged further cleavage and differentiation between the Theravada school and any "accretions," whether in script or practice, that could be traced not only to animism, Hinduism, or Brahminism but also to the "Sanskrit"-based Mahayana school. At its worst, Rhys Davids maintained, that deviation had transformed proper practice into Tibetan "Lamaism," a religion he deemed "antagonistic to the primitive system of Buddhism."[36]

It was this sanitized, doctrinal interpretation of Buddhism that was taken up by the leading advocate of national Sinhalese Buddhism, Anaganika Dhammapala (1864–1933), who was partly influenced by his own close involvement with the Buddhist Theosophical Society, established in Ceylon in the early 1880s.[37] The first print-

ing press controlled by Sinahalese Buddhists was established in 1862, and in 1885 a
catalogue of temple libraries of Ceylon was produced, and Pali verses on the Vinaya
followed. In 1891, the year after Finot joined the Bibliothèque Nationale, a French
socialist and feminist named Alexandra David-Néel joined Dhammapala in Ceylon
and went on to establish the first European branch of his newly formed Maha Bodhi
society.

As an archivist and paleontologist, Finot's interests took a more bookish bent
when he joined the Bibliothèque nationale in Paris in 1890. Here, he studied Sanskrit with Sylvain Levi. He received his diploma in 1894, and four years later became
director of the Archaeological Mission to Indochina established by Doumer. But
bohemians and bibliophiles were not the only French citizens with a vested interest in the state of religion in Ceylon. In 1884, a French intelligence agent stationed
in Pondichéry filed a lengthy report on Ceylonese Buddhism to Jules Ferry, France's
minister of the colonies, in which he noted the presence of Cambodian monks in the
orbit of Dhammapala's elder, the Venerable Sienangala Theno. "It is here," wrote a
M. Deloncle, that "Burma, Siam, Cambodge, Annam and southern China . . . send
homage, tributes of gifts." Deloncle described Theno's Vidyodaya Parivena college as
"the grand seminary of Siamese and Cambodian monks," sent by their kingdoms to
learn through readings of sacred books. Conversant with French and English, Theno
was a corresponding member of the Parisian Society of Anthropology and had recruited Chulalongkorn and the prime minister of Burma to the Theosophical Society. He had campaigned against "the cult of the White Elephant" so deeply rooted in
Burma, Siam, and Cambodge, considered Buddhism not as a religion but as a "system of moral philosophy," and, holding up Ceylon as an example to the world, had
set himself the task of "liberating human thought everywhere." The Venerable Theno
was extremely critical of "the gross rites, superstitious practices, and occult methods"
that were turning Mahayana Buddhism in Tibet, Nepal, Bhutan, and central China
into a close cousin of Shamanism. Moreover, letters he had received from Burma,
Siam, and Cambodge, as well as news from Reuters, had made him deeply concerned
about France's "action in Cambodge," fearing both the influence of Mahayana Annam, which had only a "very inexact notion of Buddhism," and the spread of Christianity in these countries.[38]

IMPRINTING MODERNITY: THE "ILLUSION OF WRITING"
AND THE CONFUSION OF COPYING

In Cambodia, as elsewhere in Theravadan Southeast Asia, the spiritual dimension to writing was reinforced by the sharp distinction between written and spoken
language. Centuries of linguistic evolution had resulted in the exclusion of vernacular Khmer from written documents. By the nineteenth century, literary Khmer was a
sophisticated mix of Sanskrit, Pali, and the High Language, including royal vocabulary. These distinctions were underscored by the use of an elaborate Khmer script,

aksa mul, for royal and religious announcements, and the use of a plainer script, *aksa chrieng,* for daily official correspondence.[39]Khmer religious manuscripts, much like the illuminated manuscripts produced in the monasteries of medieval Europe, were highly potent objects of religious significance, which acquired a value beyond the words contained therein.

Manuscripts also possessed their own distinct visual appeal, and their production carried its own aesthetic. The art of writing and reading was associated with particular gestures and the proper arrangements of forms, and the divine essence of sacred manuscripts was intimately bound up with the material and corporeal: the scent of ink, the feel of palm leaf, the sound of a stylus making its mark, its pressure between the fingers. Khmer verse was composed with a distinct ear for metronome and the resonation between syllables, the way these traveled on the air. In one sense, these forms existed, in their oral lives, as free-floating forms, unattached to paper. But in another sense, the fact and form of Khmer inscriptions translated these sounds into an elegant symphony that enriched manuscripts with meanings, associations, and an aesthetic appeal far beyond the term "text." Whether carved in stone, inked on bamboo leaf, inscribed with ink or chalk on stiff, feltlike card, or penned on the imitation silk banners distributed in Battambang by Sisowath on the retrocession of the western provinces from Siam, these written materials, like other indigenous art forms, lacked a dimension that would be popularized by print media and European artistic practice. They were not simply black-and-white. Even in cardboard form, they lacked the thinness and flatness of pages in the modern newspaper or book.

Following the casting of the first Khmer typographic characters in Paris in 1877, the late nineteenth century saw a rapid proliferation of printed works in Khmer, using lithography and typography—first in Saigon, then in Paris, Hong Kong, Hanoi, and Singapore.[40] In September 1885, Governor of Cochinchina Thomson wrote to the representative of France in Cambodge, Badens, stressing the colonial administration's strategic and political "interest [in] the prompt creation of a Cambodian printing press in the Protectorate" so as to "enlighten the population as to the intentions of the French government . . . win over the sympathies of Cambodians, and combat seditious incitements." Thomson anticipated a particularly vast and fertile audience for such Khmer print propaganda in the pupils of *vat* schools.[41] By January 1886, Badens was placing urgent orders in Saigon for gutta percha and other materials for the protectorate's new printing press.[42] In 1893, the Protectorate Printing Press expanded and relocated into majestic premises in the administrative and symbolic heart of the protectorate, at the foot of Vat Pnum.[43] By 1902, a second printing press had been established in Phnom Penh.[44] In 1904, Son Diep wrote an excited letter to Auguste Pavie, informing him that a Khmer printer, the Kambujavarokas Press, would soon be established in Phnom Penh for the publication of *satras,* laws, and regulations.[45]

By this juncture, the Parisian publishing house Plon et Nourrit was cranking out various Khmer texts on history, geography, and grammar as well as a French–Khmer and Khmer–French dictionary, and a number of *chhap* and verse-novels. Once the preserve of an elite corps of scribes in the cultural sanctums of palace and pagoda, the sacred *aksa mul* script and the pedestrian *chrieng* script were now sold by the kilo in Paris. One company, Deberny, claimed that their printing blocks created "a complete illusion of Cambodian writing," and charged extra for *aksa mul*.[46] This very act of valuation would ultimately devalue the magical aura of the written word. But the cultural repercussions of print production did not stop there.

Although Khmer scribes were hailed by the French scholar-official Adhémard Leclère in one late-ninteenth-century study, as "translators" less inclined than Siamese or Burmese "adaptors" to embroider on the "original" text, both the idea of a mechanical, soulless copy and its form were new to Cambodians.[47] Oral forms of transmitting knowledge and mores were a significant aspect of Buddhist tradition.[48] Ceremonies, temple restoration, and religious ritual sustained in practice across the centuries in precolonial Cambodia were all means whereby people were, in Chandler's analysis, continually reliving, repeating, or "restoring" what was past—in ceremonial terms, in adages, and in the agricultural cycle. But these practices were not a simple copying or reproduction of past events, any more than one Buddhist manuscript was a copy of another. Rather, they were a performance of the past in the present. Modernity's emphasis on purity and authenticity interpreted changes from any original in the negative and carried its own damning lexicon. In his 1878 French–Khmer dictionary, Aymonier noted the tendency of Khmer words of Sanskrit or Pali origin to deviate from the original. "Often they have been altered, disfigured, cor-

FIGURE 5. "A Monk in Cambodia." *Die Katholischen Missionen: Illustrierte Monatschrift,* January 1911.

rupted, or even, in Cambodian, have acquired a sense quite different from their original meaning."[49]

In this conception, all changes from an original declared to be of historic or ancient value, such as the artistry of Angkor, entailed disfigurement and corruption. Consider RSC Huyn de Verneville's dismissal, in 1895, of religious manuscripts found by Faraut as "poorly transcribed copies of originals."[50] Describing the devotion of Cambodians listening to a Buddhist birth story in the late 1890s, Leclère wrote of how they savored each syllable as if "*it really was* the life of the Master, the Teacher . . . that they were hearing."[51] Similarly, Félix Gaspard Faraut declared his reluctance to translate and publish a treatise on Cambodian astronomy because "the authentic works used by the ancient Khmers no longer exist," and all that could be found were "incomplete, poorly transcribed copies" containing errors.[52] Whereas European scholars and officials, like their counterparts in Bali studied by Margaret Wiener, focused on the poverty of translations, the "technological incapacity" of scribes, and the historical inaccuracy of different manuscripts, Cambodians valued the wealth of merit contained within *satras* and related to them as scriptures whose performance infused them with divine aura.[53]

The notion of producing a "perfect" replica and its twin, the notion of a "corrupted" text, were both products of the "fixity of print."[54] In Theravadan Buddhist culture, manuscripts were likely never thought of as copies in the modern sense of a facsimile, as each one was a unique product of particular craftsmanship whose creation had been marked by ritual and steeped in merit, and whose veracity as a "true" manuscript resided more in the attention to proper observance of merit-based rituals of production than in the mechanical aspects of syllabic imitation. Europeans in search of "pure" religious texts in South and Southeast Asia were prone to bemoan the infidelity of scribes. This obsession with scriptural integrity and its verification led colonial scholars of Buddhism to view native interpreters with both trust and suspicion, as holders of valuable information and potential distorters of the "true" scriptures.[55]

Shortly after the establishment of French rule, the hunt began for Khmer works of history, morals, science, and literature. The accounts of such scriptural reconnaissance missions exuded much the same zeal as those of expeditions to explore and demarcate Cambodge's physical boundaries and its monumental topography. The naval lieutenant Doudart de Lagrée pioneered this work in 1863, but despite a crash course in Khmer and his friendship with the king, which gave him "free entry everywhere," his search only yielded a few *satras*.[56] In 1875 the French engineer and fluent Khmer speaker Félix Gaspard Faraut (1846–1911) conducted extensive research in temples and the palaces of the king, queen mother, and obbareach (second king). Faraut collected some hundred manuscripts, mostly poems of Indian origin and Buddhist myths. When France's National Library showed an interest in collecting a body of Khmer literature four years later, M. Sylvestre, a senior administrator in Cochinchina, visited Cambodge on the library's behalf and commissioned Faraut to build a collection.[57]

Faraut's year-long trawl of temples yielded slim pickings. Apart from religious *satras* in Pali, the only other texts he found were those for *vat* schools—presumably, *chbap*. The kingdom's written documents were jealously guarded by mandarins, highly revered old monks, or the king himself.[58] These failures do not indicate a textual dearth in Cambodge so much as the reluctance of Khmer custodians both to yield control over religious texts and to expose sacred manuscripts to profane handling. The relationship between knowledge, power, and secrecy in precolonial Khmer society was exemplified by the false windows of the "libraries" of the Angkor period, which were small buildings, built apart from the main temple complex, possibly for divine readers looking down from Mount Mehru.[59] More akin to the collections of medieval monasteries than the public libraries of nineteenth-century Europe, the "libraries" attached to Khmer temples existed as repositories for ritual implements and manuscripts.[60] By the beginning of the nineteenth century, Hansen writes, a number of noteworthy collections of manuscripts had been formed, suggesting a strong indigenous emphasis on the import of acquiring and copying texts. Presumably, the bias of European scholars led them to ignore or overlook such collections.[61] In the apparent absence or ready accessibility of an "authentic" body of Khmer Buddhist literature, scholar-officials began to pen their own tomes. Among Leclère's many works on Cambodian culture were the first European study of Buddhism in Cambodge, *Le bouddhisme au Cambodge* (Buddhism in Cambodge, 1899) and a collection of sacred texts entitled *Livres sacrés* (Sacred books, 1906). The latter included a translation of *Préas Pathama Sampothian,* a Khmer version of a text that existed in Thai, the *Pathama-Sambodhikatha.*[62]

This valorization of texts as historical documents differed sharply from longstanding indigenous ways of relating to religious manuscripts, a relationship illuminated by Nancy Florida in her study of colonial Java. Florida stresses that the vast majority of such texts were written to be read aloud and redefines literacy in the context of nineteenth-century Java to incorporate the act and art of listening, through which the unlettered public became highly conversant with literature, and temple audiences could acquire merit.[63] Like Javanese performative prose, Khmer versions of the Jataka tales lent themselves well to oratory and were probably considered as texts for oral delivery rather than silent scrutiny.[64] Cambodians went to the monastery on holy days *(tngai sul),* which fell on the eighth and fifteenth days of the waxing and waning moon, to "receive the holy precepts" *(som sul),* sometimes staying all day to hear a sermon and recitation of scriptures by the monks.[65] In his account of two recitals of the *Préas Pathama Sampothian* on such a holy day, Leclère describes how the audience savored, "with utter reverence and in absolute silence" the "high, clear, almost singsong" voice of a monk who delivered each word with the apparent conviction that "the Khmer letters have another value when they reproduce a word of the holy language."[66]

Leclère introduced his study of Cambodian Buddhism with the disclaimer that it was an investigation of "what Buddhist doctrine has become among the masses of the people, and what place it occupies in their conscience." This unorthodox approach, his interest in popular opinions and vernacular sources, and his lack of a formal Orientalist training rankled with several of his peers.[67] In 1895, RSC Huyn de Vernéville delivered a stinging condemnation of Leclère's professional abilities, lampooning him as a charlatan.[68] These criticisms were later echoed by Coedès and Finot in their reviews of Leclère's work.[69] But few could deny the pioneering nature of that work. It remains the only comprehensive study of Buddhism from the colonial period that sought to understand Buddhist practices in their own right, including the presence of *neak-ta,* rather than measuring such beliefs against an idealized Buddhist orthodoxy.[70]

More commonly, French accounts of religion stressed the need to "purge" Cambodge of superstitious practices; a range of figures from healers to astrologers were treated with a similar invective to that reserved for such social ills as gambling.[71] The colonial consolidation of the reformist section in the Mahanikay, coupled with the increasingly close embrace of the Thommayuth by successive monarchs, saw the near total occlusion of positive references to supernatural practice in studies and representations of Cambodian religions. Typical was a 1903 article in the EFEO bulletin, possibly authored by Finot, describing a ceremony conducted by King Norodom in February 1903 as a hodgepodge of "semiprofane, semireligious rituals." Incorporating fireworks, dances, the distribution of gifts, a lottery, a banquet, the pardoning of criminals, and the freeing of animals, the ceremony marked the transfer of the ashes of Norodom's parents, King Ang Duong and Queen Pen, to the newly built Vat Preah Keo in the palace grounds. The author condemned the lavish temple as a monument to bad taste "as far removed from tradition as it is devoid of originality."[72] This division of ritual into profane and sacred, and the dismissal of Norodom's construction as inauthentic, reflected contemporary European preoccupations with religious authenticity and national specificity. Such conceptions billed Buddhism, as popularly practiced in a holistic sense, as a narcotic mix of quackery and degeneration, unworthy of reification as a "national religion."[73]

THOMMAYUTH

In 1867, when Norodom moved to the new capital of Phnom Penh, he sponsored construction of a Thommayuth temple, Vat Botum Vaddey, adjacent to the palace, conferred the title of Samdec Preah Sokhun on Maha Pan, and invited him to take up residence at the new temple, which subsequently became the center of Thommayuth activities in Cambodia.[74] Mongkut's theological reform was accompanied by a restructuring of the *sangha* from scattered, autonomous clusters of monks into a "unified structure paralleling the structure of government," presaging the formation of a national *sangha* in Siam.[75] Perhaps following his cue, in 1880, according to Leclère, Norodom also created a national *sangha* and immediately gave dual "national" legitimacy to the two sects by appointing the most senior Mahanikay monk, Venerable Tieng (1848–1913), to the newly created post of supreme patriarch (*sang-*

hareach), of patriarch, and promoting the Thommayuth monk Preah Sokhun Pann to the second-highest rung of his new structure.[76] This technical assertion of Mahanikay ascendancy belied the Thommayuth's steady consolidation of power in elite circles.

By the turn of the century, the Thommayuth were firmly ensconced as the moral guardians of Khmer royalty. Future kings and princes all observed Thommayuth rites.[77] These distinctions were embodied in deportment—the Mahanikay suspended their alms bowls from their shoulders, while the Thommayuth carried alms bowls in their hands—and in dress—Thommayuth novices covered both shoulders, while Mahanikay novices kept one shoulder bare. Colonial manipulation of strategic alliances with the Thommayuth and Mahanikay would fundamentally alter the balance of power between the two sects. The Thommayuth commitment to rationalism, and their pledge to restore the objectivity of Buddhism, opened up mutual intellectual ground between the sect and European savants. Thommayuth pagodas were concentrated in Phnom Penh and provincial towns, roughly paralleling the parameters of colonial settlements. This blend of urban bias, royal affiliations, and modernist aspirations encouraged the Thommayuth's designation of Mahanikay as both "rural" and "retrograde," and fostered a sense of allegiance between French government officials and the Thommayuth.[78] The Thommayuth "never hesitate to put their influence at our disposal when asked," reported one Sûreté officer in a retrospective overview of *sangha*–administration relations several decades later.[79]

Mongkut's establishment of a Pali Institute at Vat Mahathat in 1890 consolidated Bangkok's reputation as the nucleus of Theravadan Buddhist studies in mainland Southeast Asia. Three years later, Mongkut's son Prince Vajiranana founded an institute for higher Dhamma and Pali studies at Norodom and Sisowath's former haunt, Vat Borvornnivet.[80]

But the Thommayuth were only a small part of the larger picture. Mahanikay monks had long traveled to Siam in search of scriptures, to practice healing arts, and to visit holy sites. These traditions of learning and pilgrimage had fostered intellectual synergy between Cambodian monks and those in Siam and the growth of a community of Cambodian monks in Sri Lanka.[81] Talented monks from within the Mahanikay regularly traveled to Siam in search of scholarship, and there many stayed in the Mahanikay temples served by those Mahanikay monks chastised by Mongkut and the Thommayuth with malpractice or misinterpretation. During their long stays, they acquired Siamese language as well as Pali scholarship. Appointed supreme patriarch in 1883, Tieng, who had come to King Ang Duong's attention at the age of eight, had completed his entire training in Buddhist scriptures at a Mahanikay Monastery in Bangkok, where he was ordained at the age of twenty-one. Although the Thommayuth was the preferred sect for royal ordination, as supreme patriarch, Tieng was called upon by King Norodom, and subsequently King Sisowath, to perform at numerous ceremonies, to preside over the transfer of Buddhist relics from Phnom Penh to a Mahanikay temple in Kompong Luong, and to organize temple construction. Fluent in Pali, Sanskrit, Khmer, and, presumably, Thai, Tieng had initiated some Pali translations of Buddhist scriptures and, with Sisowath's approval, announced his own declaration of support for a Pali translation program.[82] Exposure to Siam may have encouraged the reformist leanings of the respected scholar of Buddhism Preah Maha Vimaladhamma Thaong (1862–1927). Born in Phnom Penh and affiliated with Vat Ounaloum, Thaong travelled to Siam in 1903 to make a collection of manuscripts.[83] During Norodom's reign, it was commonplace for devout members of the *sangha* and secular literati to go to Siam, which "had organized study properly and had many institutes of learning and numerous Pali manuscripts."[84] In Battambang, the government of Siam subsidized education at three pagodas and had also organized a school of Pali and Sanskrit.[85] Each year a senior monk from Bangkok visited Battambang to oversee examinations, and students who successfully completed them were allowed to continue their education in Bangkok.[86]

While Deloncle saw Ceylon as the Rome of Theravada Buddhism, officials in Indochina focused on Bangkok. The paramount status of the king of Siam as the guardian of Buddhism in mid- to late-nineteenth-century "Indo-Chine" was noted by de Carné.[87] In 1902, the protectorate's perception of Siam as a hive of British subterfuge was given a new, Khmer dimension with the installation of the exiled Francophobic contender for the Cambodian throne, Prince Norodom Yukanthor (1860–1934), in Bangkok. Schooled in Sanskrit and Pali and conversant with Thai, Lao, and Burmese as well as French,[88] Yukanthor, who remained a prime Sûreté suspect for spates of popular unrest in Cambodge until his death, maintained close links with members of the Siamese and Khmer *sangha* throughout his exile.[89] Ever mindful of the political liability of such connections, the French Protectorate sought to attenuate links between Siam and Cambodia. A critical area in which the Thommayuth differed from the Mahanikay was in their emphasis on Siamese and Pali as the correct languages of Buddhism, and in their adoption of print production.

By establishing competing facilities for the study of Buddhism in Cambodge, and particularly by promoting the parallel study of Khmer and Pali and expanding the dissemination of Khmer tracts and Khmer language education in the protectorate, the French administration paved the way for a later emphasis by reformists from within Cambodia on the Khmerization of Buddhist practice. Sisowath's own backing for this policy was reflected in his announcement that France was occupying Battambang "for the greater glory of the Buddhist religion," produced in Khmer on sumptuous tracts of imitation royal silk for distribution to Cambodian administrators in the region.[90] The next step in this direction was the creation of an *école de Pali* at Angkor in 1909. "As the Pali language has been revered in Cambodia since antiquity, and as Pali is the language of the Tripitaka which contains the Bhuddha's *dhamma* and *vinaya*," the school's founders decided, "it is indispensable to advocate the study of Pali so that monks and laypeople can fathom the depths of the teachings and precepts of our master . . . [the] Buddha." Learning Pali was also crucial to the development and enrichment of its language and literature, the document continued, and for the "uplifting of the moral and intellectual level of our subjects." While the scope and content of the ordinance indicates a high degree of Khmer agency, the inclusion of the ending colonial cliché points to the protectorate's involvement.[91]

In the early 1900s, the protectorate made token concessions to local demands for instruction in Pali, appointing a teacher of Sanskrit and Pali at the École du Protectorat.[92] But not until the retrocession of Battambang, Siem Reap, and Sisophon in 1907 did the protectorate begin to make a concerted effort to compete with Siam as a center of Buddhist learning. The establishment of new Pali schools under colonial rule strengthened reform elements within the Mahanikay by providing tuition in such subjects as science and geography and by creating an institutional framework in which they could distill the essence of Buddhist teachings and articulate the correct Vinaya through advanced studies. At the same time, the schools allowed them to consolidate a skills base to rival, and in some cases surpass, their elders within the Mahanikay through mastery of Buddhist scriptures as well as Sanskrit and Pali.

By giving the Mahanikay access to the higher learning that many Thommayuth monks considered their prerogative, French scholars and colonial institutes stymied the monopolization of Cambodge's "national" religion, Buddhism, by a sect they identified as Siamese in origin and orientation. They also steered what had started out as a movement concerned with "orthopraxy," a term coined by Frits Staal to denote "a religious emphasis on correct practice," toward a protonationalist movement. As in Ceylon, the European provision and official support of Pali education was a critical facet of this project.

Established by royal ordinance on 13 August 1909, the protectorate's first School of Pali was opened to great fanfare by Sisowath and GGI Klobukowski, who had been promoted to GGI in 1908 after twenty-five years service in Indochina, in the course of which time he had become a "personal friend" of Sisowath's.[93] The aim of the school, enthused Klobukowski in his opening speech, was to give Cambodge the center of high learning it lacked, so as "to forge a new link between the promising present of the Khmer people and the well-documented grandeur of their moving past."[94] The then Royal Commissaire to Battambang, a Mahanikay traditionalist, claimed some years later to have conceived the school in order to "arrest Siam's spiritual and political invasion . . . [of] Cambodia [and] the hegemony of the Thai race in Indochina."[95] Another source credits Supreme Patriarch Tieng, former head of the Mahanikay Vat Ounaloum, with the initiative.[96]

Each school was to have two directors, a Mahanikay or Thommayuth representative nominated by the king and a secular figure chosen from among the palace scholars, and would employ both monks and lay teachers. Both schools at Phnom Penh and at Angkor would be open to star pupils from among the *samnar* and *bhikku* in the capital and provinces. To further sever scholastic dependence on Siam, the "royal service" would reproduce Pali scriptures "more meticulous than any Bangkok production," either on palm leaves or by printing. Finally, the ordinance forbade Khmers to study in Siam.[97]

The ordinance also appealed to royalty, ministers, mandarins, and all subjects to donate funds to the school for the greater good of the Buddhist religion.[98] In the apparent absence of such charity, the Cambodian Sub-Committee of the Society of Angkor assumed financial responsibility for the School of Pali, and heaved a transparent sigh of relief when the school's closure in 1910 allowed the society to return its full attention and resources to its founding aim of restoring Ankor.[99] It is not clear why the school closed. The Society of Angkor's account, and a later report in the *BEFEO*, point to both a shortfall in funding and insufficient student enrollments. The reluctance of monks to nominate students for a school that was both outside of their control and associated with the French administration may have been a factor. Competition from and loyalty towards superior, established schools in Battambang and Bangkok may also have been among the unnamed factors behind Finot's assertion some years later that the school had been "doomed to failure."[100]

Where the Angkor initiative failed, plans for the capital succeeded. Envisaged as a "sort of grand central seminary," the School of Pali was founded in Phnom Penh in 1914, to provide Cambodge's clerical elite with the religious education they had habitually sought in Bangkok and to further the Indianist ambitions of the EFEO.[101] Located in two pavilions of the Vat Preah Keo in the royal palace, the school had sixty students, came under the patronage of the EFEO, the jurisdiction of the Ministry of Public Education, and the RSC.[102] As director of the school, the fifty-three-year-old Preah Maha Vimaladhamma Thaong, renowned for his mastery of Pali and extensive knowledge of Buddhist texts, shaped a syllabus that reflected "his liberal and enlightened spirit" and "allowed the first rays of European science into the Cambodian clergy."[103] That beam of rationalist light in a syllabus otherwise exclusively devoted to the study of Pali texts was a mandatory weekly lesson in the "French and Thai alphabet . . . Pali texts in Siamese translation and . . . the Latin transcription system used in European editions," which the protectorate only managed to include in the curriculum due to Thaong's support.[104] Described at the time by the EFEO as "the very tenuous thread linking the School of Pali to Western science," this small window on the Western world was heralded by the EFEO as a happy portent for the "intellectual development of the Cambodian people."[105]

The expanded syllabus also had strategic import. In 1914, the protectorate proclaimed new travel restrictions prohibiting the *sangha* from visiting Siam for language studies unless they could "justify the acquisition of broader knowledge than that taught at the School of Pali." The EFEO hoped that the school's location in a "town replete with facilities for study," its practical organization, and stringent controls would ensure its success and foster increasing confidence in the "methods and results of French Indology."[106] In 1913, the governor of Ceylon, Sir Robert Chalmers, a keen proponent of Pali literature, had urged Sinhalese Buddhists to follow the example of Burma and Siam. Under Mongkut, Siam had taken the lead in issuing printed yellow-bound volumes of the Tripitaka, he urged: it was now time for Ceylon to follow suit with the production of the Tripitaka in Sinhalese characters, worthy of Sinhalese traditions of Pali scholarship.[107] Like the Sinhalese-Pali print revival currently under way in Ceylon, Cambodge's new School of Pali would have important ramifications for the development of Buddhist nationalism. As counselor and organizer of the school, Finot, who spent the next twenty years alternating between scholarly positions in Paris and permanent or acting appointments as director of the EFEO, played a critical role in fostering the intellectual leanings of Cambodian monks and so shaping a modern clerical elite. He donated a small library to the school, compiled a commentary on the Tripitaka, and taught Sanskrit and the history of Buddhism to several key figures in the monastic reform movement.[108] His principal protégés were Nath and Tath.[109]

Like Prince Mongkut and Dhammapala, Nath and Tath sought to divest Buddhist text and practice of the accretions of Khmer popular culture, promoting a return to the "pure" dhamma as elaborated in the code of conduct, or *vinaya*. Together with colonial scholars, these members of the *sangha* would apply a microscopic eye to Buddhist scriptures and practice, aiming to disentangle strands of custom and belief into pure and corrupted, Khmer and non-Khmer, secular and religious, and Buddhist and superstitious categories.[110]

REFORMING THE MAHANIKAY FROM WITHIN: CHUON NATH AND HUOT TATH

In 1912, three years after the establishment of the Pali school at Angkor, the twenty-year-old Huot Tath was ordained by Supreme Patriarch Tieng at Vat Ounaloum, the chief Mahanikay temple in Phnom Penh. Here he met Chuon Nath, who had been ordained as a *bhikku* in 1904, at Wat Beddi Breus in a district of Kandal Province. Nath had completed a year's Pali studies at Vat Ounaloum and had returned to finish his diploma.[111] Tath and Nath also had an Indian connection, having learned Sanskrit from an Indian peddler who sold peanuts at the temple and who taught them the *devanagari* in the sand with a stick. This thirst for knowledge of other languages and cultures outside the standard domain of Mahanikay teachings also impelled Tath and Nath to pore over French books behind closed doors in their monks' quarters. That they had to conceal these encounters with both the language of colonialism and the modern book indicates that, even as late as the 1910s, when civil servants had founded the Committee for French Education and ministers were patronizing the Angkor Society, there remained a pronounced tension between these Francophone worlds of secular government and the monastic domain. As Tath later recalled in his memoirs, "at that time any monk who studied French was criticized."

Supreme Patriarch Tieng passed away in October 1913, and the following year King Sisowath appointed Kae Uk Supreme Patriarch (Mahasanghareach).[112] The next few years saw a battle of words and wits between the more conservative Kae Uk and the reformists Nath, Tath, and a third reformist monk, Em Sou. The crux of this conflict was Nath and Tath's push to reform monastic practice according to a strict interpretation of the Buddhist precepts, or *vinaya*. This agenda was shared by some members of the royal family, one of whom offered to sponsor a daily sermon on the *vinaya* throughout the Buddhist lent (*uesaa*). Kae selected Nath, Tath, and Em Sou (1891–1939) to deliver the sermons. In a radical departure from the traditional rote recital of scriptures, Nath, Tath, and Sou composed sermons explaining the *vinaya*, so as to enlighten their fellow monks. The sermons attracted huge crowds and stimulated lively debate, much to the chagrin of traditionalist elders, who complained to Kae. The sermons were abruptly terminated, but not before they had launched the reform movement within the Mahanikay. Monks began to observe the scriptures in a new way.

This was at first an underground movement. With the exception of Nath, Tath, and Sou, monks did not dare to reveal their interest in the *vinaya* precepts for fear of upsetting their superiors. Working together, often late at night, Nath, Tath, and Sou pored over manuscripts and, in Tath's later version of events "distilled their true essence," each making extracts and annotations in their own books. In the meantime, they continued to debate and preach in their daily discussions with other monks. Their ideas gradually percolated through Mahanikay temples in the capital and beyond.

The reformist monks antagonized members of the Mahanikay far beyond Vat Ounaloum, and particularly in the provinces of Kompong Cham, Svay Rieng, and Prey Veng. These areas of central and southeastern Cambodge had remained isolated from the ideas propagated via the Siamese Thommayuth movement and its Cambodian successor, which was predominantly concentrated in the western provinces. Nath and Tath rejected the populist pollution of received accounts of the lives of Buddha in such mainstays of Mahanikay tradition as the Jataka tales; they advocated a levelling of the monastic hierarchy, arguing that novices *(samner)* should cover their shoulders like *bhikku,* and that *bhikku* should go into retreat during the Buddhist lent like *samner;* they advocated preaching in both Pali and Khmer, and they argued that the purpose of sermons should be to provoke reflection and enhance understanding of the *vinaya.* The royal sponsorship of the Thommayuth presented a conundrum to scholars and officials in the French Protectorate. Its textual bias corresponded with that of European Buddhology, but the group had been influenced by intellectual developments in Sri Lanka and closer to home in Siam, both of which were feared as theatres of British influence. This genealogy, coupled with the Thommayuth's orientation towards Bangkok as the primary seat of Buddhist learning, presented a quandary to savants and administrators seeking to establish an authentic, Khmer religion and to use it as a strategic bulwark against political and cultural subversion from Siam, Ceylon, and also Vietnam. This dilemma was resolved by fostering reformist elements within the Mahanikay sect, which shared both the rationalist objectives of the Thommayuth and the protectorate's preoccupations with constructing a geocultural body of Cambodge. Like the Thommayuth movement, Chuon Nath and Huot Tath's reform movement interpreted correct Buddhist practice as that outlined in the Vinaya, or that section of the Tripitaka (Three Baskets of the Buddhist canon) concerned with doctrinal practice rather than intellectual interpretation.

Whereas differences between the Thommayuth and Mahanikay revolved around issues of orthopraxy,[113] Nath and Tath's movement assumed a more probing, socially engaged dimension. It was this latter emphasis on the importance of adequate reflection and interpretation of the scriptures that must have provided a refreshing alternative, to the more open-minded of their pupils as well as their lay sponsors, from a seemingly obsessive attention to such material dimensions of practice as the correct way of wearing a robe or carrying an alms bowl. But to conservative monks it was precisely their transgression of prescribed modes of dress and chanting and their attachment to such modern media as the printed book that most rankled. In their concerns for "authenticity," and their attachment to the correct and mechanical copies made possible by printing, such programs of Buddhist scriptural reform and European scholarship devalued those Buddhist manuscripts whose sacrality, in the minds of many monks and laity, lay as much in their form as in their content. Unsurprisingly, they sparked fierce antagonism.

Alarmed at these proposals for reform, a number of Mahanikay monks petitioned King Sisowath, who summoned Tath and Nath to a meeting at the palace along with the complainants. At the meeting, Chuon Nath allegedly mounted an eloquent defense of the reformist interpretations of the *vinaya,* demonstrating his bilingual Pali–Khmer mastery of scriptures, treatises, and commentaries, and emphasizing the value of study:

> Your Majesty, all these matters are written clearly in the *vinaya* scriptures, but in our country it seems that these matters of *vinaya* have completely vanished, because war was frequently breaking out in our country of old, causing the destruction and loss of scriptures and commentaries and precepts, which have almost vanished, and some of the scribes and scholars in our country died, and some were taken away by enemy countries. . . . It's only just recently, now that our country's peaceful and calm, that some of the scriptures and precepts have returned, and those who study them continue to study hard, . . . In this time, those who study are once again beginning to have a little knowledge. . . . [114]

Sisowath was allegedly so impressed by Nath's erudition that he dismissed the petitions and awarded Nath a prize in recognition of his learning. But the dispute was far from settled in the minds of traditionalist monks.

SHIFTING THE VERNACULAR REGISTER

While Dhammapala had promoted his Sinhalese vernacular Buddhism in opposition to centuries of imperial Christianization, Chuon Nath and Huot Tath, in concert with the French Protectorate, forged their vision of Buddhism in opposition to that in Siam. This was not a doctrinal opposition but an ethnolinguist construction. While the Thommakay embraced modernist notions of pure practice, its defining parameters were not so much doctrinal as national. Their movement shared much of its doctrinal emphasis on correct practice and its rejection of popular, animist, and Brahministic beliefs with the Thommayuth movement founded by Mongkut. Its nationality lay both in its linguistic form, the use of vernacular Khmer as a tool of transmission, and in its designated constituency—ethnic Khmers. Quoting Norodom Sihanouk, Huot Tath would later stress that there was no "old" *dhamma* and no "new" *dhamma,* but only one *dhamma:* "What is known as the new Dhamma was just the diligent purification of Buddhism to free it from erroneous beliefs. It was about understanding the origins, and about the wrong traditions, but it was not about reforming Buddhism. In truth, it was only about returning Buddhism to its good, proper, and original source."[115]

The act of "returning" the contemporary state of Buddhism to a pristine origin, however, necessarily involved the reform of local, contemporary Buddhist practice. As a deputy minister of religion explained it in an intervention during a meeting with King Sisowath in the early 1910s, it was not that they wanted monks to stop telling the Maha Jataka story, but rather to edit out such choice embellishments as "[the Brahmin beggar] Jujuk guzzled up all his rice and soup along with the pan they were in, and then his belly burst open with such a deafening roar that even the elephants in the stable panicked." Such ad-libbing had no place, in Huot Tath and Chuon Nath's view, both because it was a distortion of the "words of the Lord Buddha" and because this merrymaking distracted people from listening to the Dhamma in a spirit of serious reflection. Rather than employ vernacular Khmer for such irreverent sorties, it should be used in another way: to explain the *Vinaya* to the people. "Those people who stuck to the old traditions," wrote Huot Tath, "had always recited the Dhamma in Pali" without necessarily understanding it themselves, let alone enlightening their audience as to its content. Their movement, by contrast, "called anyone who recited the Dhamma in Pali and then translated it into the national language *(piesaa-jiet)* a New Dhamma-ite." Their use of the national language, Huot Tath later maintained, was purely explicative—to ensure that people gained a clear understanding of correct practice.[116]

But the very notion of a "national language" was as much a product of modernity as that of the national religion Nath and Tath's reform project would help to delineate. There was neither time nor room on historicism's tightrope walk from national decline to national greatness for the intricate hierarchies of popular Buddhist cosmology, with their broad, galactic spread and its interplay with the spirit world.[117] In her work on Khmer thought worlds in transition in the colonial period, Anne Hansen has shown how an either/or binary gradually became incorporated into the moral ordering of things presented by the highly erudite poet In, notably in his injection of usage of geographically and locally specific terms that differentiated between humans, not only on the basis of different degrees of morality, but on that of different points of origin, juxtaposing *jiet-mennuh-yeung* (people of our kind), where the Khmer was implicit and emphasized in locally framed stories, with peoples, notably *jiet-barangseh* (used specifically for French, and generically for westerners).[118] The ability and eagerness of Nath, Tath, and others to think in religious, national, and ethnic categories was in part a legacy of In, and new *neak-cheh-doeng* such as Son Diep and Thiounn, who negotiated the period of turbulent intellectual and social change by brokering a subtle shift in the meaning of *sasana* and *jiet,* which would prove to be essential terms in forging a nationalist vocabulary capable of differentiating Khmer from non-Khmer.

As discussed in the Introduction, *jiet* appeared in early Khmer texts not as a label for race or nation but as a moral and cosmological term whose meanings were intricately tied up with its Pali root *jati*.[119] Aymonier and Son Diep's 1878 Khmer–French dictionary, renders the Khmer term as "birth, existence, generation, natural; flavor, essence," which, in certain compounds, could also indicate sex, or a gender group.[120] This usage resonates with the term *jati* as used in India. Although translated as "caste" by Orientalists, Debjani Ganguly writes, *jati* far exceeded "the secular, sociological category of caste in European thought."[121] Ronald Inden and McKim Marriott interpret the semantic sweep of *jati* as indicative of the absence, in the South Asian view of generic order, of the "exclusively differentiating, branching, taxonomic pattern" common to Linnean assumptions. Instead, "sex genera, language genera, occupational genera and kinship genera may and typically do intersect and interact in complex ways."[122] The Thai counterpart of *jati*—*chat*—carried similar resonances of birth groups and blood ties.[123] During the late nineteenth and early twentieth century, Khmer Buddhist literati educated in Siam would have been exposed to the gradual evolution of *chat* to a word denoting "the shared linguistic and cultural traits that make up a nationality."[124] King Vajiravudh (r. 1910–1925) expanded the national dimensions of *chat* with his promotion of a civic trinity of "*chat* (the nation conceived in terms of both territory and people); *satsana* (the specifically religious dimension, identified primarily with Buddhism); and the *mahaksat* (the king or monarchy)," as defined by Frank Reynolds.[125] If we enrich this territorial definition of *chat* with Craig Reynolds' interpretation of *chat* as a "cultural community," we are perhaps closer to understanding the use of *jiet* by Siamese-educated *sangha* in early-twentieth-century Cambodge.[126] During the first decades of the twentieth century, *jiet* was increasingly deployed in Khmer Buddhist texts as a term inflected with geographic and ethnic specificity, a shrinkage in semantic range roughly paralleling the constriction of the French term *race* from its broad early-nineteenth-century constellation of meanings to the newly emerging Linnean notion of race as a monolithic, singular, and impermeable construct.

Vajiravudh's tripartite formula marked "the emergence of the nation as an independent entity with a position of equality (and perhaps even pre-eminence) vis-à-vis Buddhism *(satsana)*."[127] The 1878 Khmer–French dictionary prepared by Aymonier and Son Diep defines *sasana* and its root, *sas,* as "religion, race" and "nationality," but indicates clear overlap between these two, as in its rendering of *sah-barang* (French *sah*) for Christianity.[128] Both the terms *sasana* and *chat* had long been in use, and it was not solely shifts in the individual registers of *sas* and *jiet* that signaled a new era, as their linkage into a compound that conflated the horizons of a race, people, and belief system. Alhtough these processes were in train, Chuon Nath and Huot Tath's movement was a long way from becoming a *sasana-jiet.*

A significant area of convergence between the European mission to identify a "Cambodian religion" and the quest by reformist monks to free contemporary Buddhist practice from what they saw as indigenous malpractice was in their entertainment of modern visions of time. In Khmer cosmologies, the past was very much in the present, in that those phenomena which defied prediction, such as natural disasters and war, were linked in peoples' minds both with what was wild and, perhaps more fuzzily, as Chandler argues, "with immoral, unremembered behaviour in the past," while high rank was thought to derive from meritorious behavior in another life. These were, as Chandler writes, unverifiable pasts—pasts that could only be diagnosed by present circumstance.[129] Moreover, in their "historically charged interpretation of the present," Hansen argues, "Buddhist assumptions about history went beyond the conception that the past was the model of a better, more righteous world," viewing the past instead as "a template for what the future would become as sentient beings cycled from Buddha era to Buddha era."[130] These conceptions of the past were probably more closely grounded in sites, shrines, statues, and places of worship than in the "royal chronicles" and textual accounts. In Theravadan Southeast Asia, animism contributed to this layering of past and present: ancestral spirits inhabited forests as *neak-ta* living in the land, defying the rationalist partitioning of life and death. Highly localized, the *neak-ta* comprised a key strand of place-based identifications and ancestral orientations to a more immediate past than that embodied in Angkor. Like all ancestral figures, Forest argues, the *neak-ta* was not the eruption of some lapse of logic, but part of a rational discourse that allowed individuals to relate to their immediate environment and to the past.[131] European conceptions of linear history were a reversal of such indigenous approaches and required the deciphering of the past and its verification—through texts and documents—in order to understand the present.

PUBLISH OR PERISH

The eruption of peasant protests in early 1916 would temporarily strengthen the traditionalists' hand with the French Protectorate. Capitalizing on establishment fears of further unrest, and doubtless galvanized into action by a widening and deepening secular intrusion into *vat* education, traditionalists in the *sangha* persuaded the king, with the protectorate's blessing, to crack down on breaches of tradition within the *sangha*. Issued on 2 October 1918, Royal Ordinance No. 71 recognized the Mahanikay and Thommayuth as the only two lawful Cambodian sects, prohibited monks from teaching reforms or spreading new, nonauthorised religious theories, and prohibited novices and monks in the Mahanikay and Thommayuth sects from any practices that deviated from the traditions established in the time of the now deceased religious leaders Tieng and Pann.[132] It specifically forbade monks, lay preceptors, and Buddhists in or out of government office from "teaching reforms themselves, or designating delegates to explain or teach to monks and believers the observance of reforms which they might have brought about to the Buddhist rites and precepts traditionally followed in the sect to which they belong." Anyone wanting to teach any Buddhist precepts other than those traditionally observed in their sect must first submit them to the Ministry of the Interior, who must then pass them to the Council of Ministers for rexamination and submit them to the king for his final approval, and anyone who failed to comply with the ordinance would be disciplined by a "competent religious assembly."[133] According to Huot Tath, this latter ruling merely whet the appetites of leading reformist monks and their protégés. Tath alleges that the ban proved ineffective, and that while few novices or monks openly violated it, many monks continued their quest to establish the "true practices" in private.

Shortly after the ordinance was issued, Chuon Nath and Huot Tath completed their compilation of two books on the *vinaya*, which they took to Minister of Education Ponn, requesting permission to publish. Ponn gave them a warm reception and intimated there would be no problems. Only a year earlier, Ponn had bought twenty-seven books on the protectorate account for distribution to prizewinning students at the École de Pali.[134] However, a week later, the ministry officially rebutted the request and ruled that:

> The Council of Ministers will not allow *bhikku* or *samnar* to study *Vinaya Paade'mook* or *Kathen-kanake* inscribed in paper books. . . . [It] will only allow the study of the *vinaya* [inscribed] on palm-leaf manuscripts. Any *vinaya* in a paper book like this is considered New Vinaya *(vinaya tmae)*, which is different from the tradition in the time of Supreme Patriarch.[135]

The contrast between this view of the sacred significance of writing materials and the response of Nath, Tath, and their supporters—that "palm-leaf or paper books were only materials. . . . There was no difference between them"—reveals the huge gap between traditionalist perceptions and rationalist prescriptions. According to Tath, the message from the ministry triggered a flurry of clandestine copying, lithography, and circulation of Nath's book by monks and novices. An informant reported these events to the Ministry of Religion, which subsequently summoned Nath for several days' interrogation and ordered the confiscation of all such copies. The affair soon blew over, due to the assistance of Minister of War and Education Ponn.[136]

Later that year, RSC Baudoin intervened to allow the publication of *Samnar vinaya* (Vinaya for novices) against the wishes of the traditionalist religious authorities. Huot Tath authored the book shortly after Chuon Nath's confrontation with the Ministry of Religion and, seeking safety in numbers, asked Em Sou and Chuon Nath to put their names to it. The monks then gave the book to a sympathetic official, Keth, who wanted to print it for distribution at a ceremony for his parents.[137] When Supreme Patriarch Kae Uk refused permission to publish, Keth—an alumnus of the École cambodgienne in Paris—sought, and obtained, permission from the RSC. He then hired the Albert Portail printing press, and had five thousand copies printed for circulation among the monks, keeping only a few copies for his own use. Subsequent attempts by senior monks to ban the book and have Nath, Tath, and Oum expelled from Vat Ounaloum for their violation of Royal Ordinance 71 failed, partly because both Sisowath and his son Prince Monivong supported their bookish enterprise. Despite the best efforts of the "old" Mahanikay to obstruct the youthful pursuit of knowledge, "they couldn't stop progress," wrote Tath. "Books for study and practice were being churned out," and

> [Although] all monks and laypeople considered this a time of danger for Buddhism, or an immoral era, it was [also] a time of the flowering of Buddhism in the Mahanikay sect, [when] all those who liked studying strove hard and spared no effort in their quest for knowledge. As for their detractors, their ardent quest to stir up trouble was fruitless. On the contrary, more and more people studied and wanted to know. And there were more and more books on Vinaya for Buddhists to study.[138]

Traditionalist suspicion of the Pali School was also reflected in the Royal Ordinance No. 71 of 1918.[139] By 1919, French was taught thrice weekly at the École de Pali.[140] In 1922, the École de Pali was renamed the École supérieure de Pali (ESP) and installed in new, custom-built premises. As part of this restructuring, the ESP was financially aligned with the Royal Treasury and brought under the intellectual supervision of the EFEO, so as to ensure its appropriate "technical direction." The director of the ESP was to report to the EFEO annually, and to consult with the EFEO on all projects that might change the organization, educational activities, and programs of the school.[141] Finot's protégé George Coedès played a key advisory role in RSC Baudoin's establishment of the school.[142] Unlike its predecessor, the ESP would teach "not just Buddhism" but also Sanskrit and Pali; French; Cambodian history, trisected into the pre-Angkorean, Angkorean, and post-Angkorean ages; Khmer language; sacred and secular Khmer literature; the political, religious, and archaeological history of Cambodia; and the geography of East Asia and the Indochinese peninsula. "Principles of Buddhist theology" and "the general history of Buddhism" came last on this list, and "elements of modern science" was offered as an optional course.[143] The renovation of the school and syllabus may well have been espoused by the school's director Thaong, whose reformist opinions were evidenced in his authorship of several practical works dedicated to the explanation of the Vinaya.[144]

Perhaps partly at the behest of Coedès, who was then curator of the National Library of Siam (1918–1926), the revamped school also assumed a new role as a repository of literary culture, which would "research, classify, and conserve all works, documents, and texts bearing on Buddhist history, literature, and theology." To this end, a library was designed in the new school buildings for the receipt and conservation of all printed works and manuscripts concerning Pali, Sanskrit, Buddhism, and Khmer religious literature.[145] The year 1922 also saw the construction of Cambodge's first public library. The Central Library of Cambodge, built in Phnom Penh to house the library of the RSC, comprised a reference library and a lending library, each of which held about five thousand books, mostly in French.[146] As we shall see in subsequent chapters, these libraries, in conjunction with a proliferation of print media later in that decade, would further fracture the monastic monopoly on knowledge while cementing notions of a single Khmer cultural collectivity.

In tandem with this increased cultural role for the school, the new ordinance sought to insert the school more fully into nation-state structures by reserving a quota of colonial posts for its graduates as *vat* school inspectors, teachers at the ESP, Khmer-language teachers in secular colleges and schools, and Pali-language teachers in temples.[147] A special teaching grant was also established to encourage all monks and *achar*s who, upon graduating from the school and returning to religious life, offered regular French lessons in *vats*.[148] In 1922, Finot met with Baudoin and impressed upon him the importance of including Pali and Sanskrit in secondary and elementary school curricula in Cambodge, stressing in particular the need to expand knowledge of Sanskrit. On Finot's advice, Baudoin asked Director Thaong to select two monks versed in Pali to study Sanskrit with Finot at the EFEO. Later that year, Nath and Tath set sail for Hanoi. A hint of pathos surrounds Tath's later description of their send-off, which drew only a handful of novices, monks who were friends, and one dignitary, Keth. Poetic license, sentiment, and the passage of nearly fifty years all may have clouded Tath's recollection of events. But his account indicates clearly that the two young monks were guided not just by religious conviction but by a firm sense of national mission as the potential guardians of Khmer culture.[149]

Led by Chuon Nath and Huot Tath, the reformists within the Mahanikay offered something of a compromise between the "frivolity" and elaborate rituals of Mahanikay and the austerity and rigour of Thommayuth. Although they discredited Mahanikay performances of the Jataka, they offered uneducated laity a different kind of theatre through which the public could engage with their new Buddhism, namely the nation. The notion of the nation as a geographic and ethnolinguistic zone was incorporated into the Thommakay school through their emphasis on the national language and their acceptance of such "rational" teaching tools as maps.

CONCLUSION

The valorization of a "real" Cambodian Buddhism as a textual religion, and the attendant marginalization of the panoply of animist, Brahmin, and Hindu beliefs suffusing popular religious practice, carried through to colonial imagery. While poetry and prose romanticized monks as mystic and enigmatic, the photographs accompanying articles on Cambodge commonly stressed monastic literacy. A 1911 German missionary magazine (fig. 5) and a 1928 *National Geographic* offer similar clichés. Monks are shown posing with clocks and kettles, reading from *satras* and books to quiet children, seated up on a European chair, feet resting on a tapestry carpet.

In the late 1920s, the *National Geographic* magazine ran a series of pictures by the French photographer Gervais Courtellement showing a monk seated on a "prayer-chair" poring over palm-leaf manuscripts. The monk first appears in a chair shaped like a small deer, which has been erected on a floral rug spread out in the same garden setting. The brilliant hues of the chair, possibly one of those stored at the Royal Library and mentioned by Karpelès in correspondence that same year, are offset by a luxuriant tropical garden. "A Cambodian priest reads one of his country's classics," reads the caption. Another photo shows monks in worship at an ornate, gilded pulpit, possibly at Vat Preah Keo or Vat Botum Vaddey. In startling contrast to these images is another shot, equally posed, on what appears to be the main walkway to Angkor. A barefoot man carries a large spray of wildflowers. His white, orange, yellow, purple, and sepia strips of cloth are reminiscent of robes arranged around spirited statues in offering. "This demented Buddhist priest has convinced himself that he is lord of all he surveys at the ruined capital of the Khmers." The antithesis of the bookish priests shown earlier, he conjoins the heretic and the lunatic in a figure whose eclectic dress and effects signal a range of possibilities and practices beyond the margins of "his country's classics" and thus embrace and debase a panoply of beliefs marked as "superstitions." Diagnosed in his mixing of myth and history, Angkorean eras and Buddhist beliefs, his delirium becomes more than a case of mistaken identity. To the European observer, as well as, no doubt, to secular literati such as Thiounn et al., he is the perfect personification of cultural dementia: a vision of the nation—and native—in negative.

By the late 1920s, when this image appeared, popular religion had been edited out of the photographic, literary, and scholarly records of Cambodian Buddhism to the extent that it was increasingly rejected by Cambodian intellectuals, from secular figures such as Thiounn to monastic reformists such as Nath. The colonial separation of Buddhism from the supernatural, and the attempt to remodel and validate beliefs through Western-derived methodologies, had as profound an impact on Cambodian intellectuals as it did on the British-educated Sinhalese elite.[150]

Through their engagement with the EFEO and the Royal Library in the 1920s, both monks developed a more socially engaged sense of Buddhism, which had more in common with that developed by the Sinhalese monk Anagarika Dhammapala (1864–1933) and the reformist Buddhism of the Thai monk Buddhadasa (1906–1993) than with that espoused by Mongkut and the Thommayuth. While Thiounn and Son Diep actively embraced and promoted a bounded Khmer national culture, and saw in technical progress, from printing presses to communication routes, a secure future for their own political careers and the development of the Khmer "race," neither envisaged a role for young lay Cambodians or monks beyond the production and consumption of Buddhist texts in modern printed form and the introduction of colonial school curricula to lay communities through the inclusion of maps and other modern teaching tools in Khmer monasteries.

In Cambodge, high colonialism and its attendant secularization and modernization, like the more cataclysmic cycles of mass violence wracking the late twentieth century, steered faith outward, away from the inner workings of the soul and towards the "commotions" of "the polity, the state, and that complex argument we call culture."[151] The notions of a national culture and a national language were mutually constitutive of Nath and Tath's reform project. Colonialism coined the categories of public and private, indigenous and European, spiritual and secular domains. But the cross-cultural crossings, trespasses, and collisions also fostered multiple crossings between those spheres, allowing for the engagement of what Geertz calls the "inner workings of the soul" with the mundane theatres of secularism's godless time. As Nath and Tath's story shows, there was no single way of life but plural possibilities of maneuver and traffic between the domains of French scholarship, the royal court, printing press, and palm leaf. Shades of this duality, and the resistance of the Buddhist reform movement in Cambodia to categorization as a single unitary ideology, are reflected in the two names for the reform movement: Thommakay, with its implicit emphasis on intellectual activity and rethinking of the dhamma, and Mahanikay Tmae, with its implicit emphasis on a fusion between the popular practices of religious faith and the modern *(tmae)*. These monastic narratives of modernity were not untroubled songs of praise for colonialism's disenchanting impulse. Here it is perhaps more helpful to think in terms of Ashis Nandy's distinction between religion-as-ideology and religion-as-faith, where ideology means that which is elaborated externally and promulgated for a political purpose as a cross-national or national identifier, and faith denotes those inner reflections and feelings inscribed in daily practice in a way of life that is "non-monolithic and operationally plural."[152] This was no partition.

The life worlds of Chuon Nath, Huot Tath, and others were deeply spiritual, and just as, in their youth, each studied French books behind closed doors in Phnom Penh's chief Mahanikay monastery, so each would open some doors to colonialism's modernizing project and close others. Questions of ideology and matters of faith are intimately intertwined and can be jointly mobilized. In becoming a thinker, one does not stop being a believer. The colonial period, as Hansen has convincingly demonstrated, called forth multiple responses to modernity.[153] Chuon Nath and Huot Tath acted not only as intellectual intermediaries between Europeans and Khmers, and spiritual brokers between tradition and modernity. We can also see them as mediators between different temporalities—that inhabited by the poet Suttantaprija In, and that to be inhabited by Lon Nol and Saloth Sar. In its delineation of a "Khmer nation," Chuon Nath and Huot Tath's movement was critical. Their fusion of the modern and the Khmer with Buddhism, and their denigration of popular, noncanonical religious practices as diabolic impurities, contributed to the codification of a new "superstition," that of the Khmer nation *(jiet kmae)*. This transformation of religion and its subsequent politicization were intimately interwoven with another significant thrust of colonial reform: the desacralization of Angkor Vat.

5 | Violent Lives

Disengaging Angkor, 1907–1916

If stones have fallen from the building
Sir has them reset in the original position.
Sir Monsieur Commaille, from France,
Takes cement and paints it on like paper as reinforcement.
Wherever moss grows thick enough to block your view
Sir has it swept out clean.

Penned by the distinguished poet Oknya Suttantaprija In (1859–1924) in his verse *Journey to Angkor Vat (Nirieh Nokor Vat)*, commemorating King Sisowath's visit to Angkor in 1909, the above description of French conservation is serene and orderly.[1] We see the newly appointed curator to Angkor, Jean Commaille, portrayed as poetry in motion, diligently restoring order, seemliness, and cleanliness. But the serenity of the above scene was undercut by ripples of violence, culminating in the curator's brutal gang murder on his own journey to Angkor Thom in 1916. Three years after the establishment of the protectorate, the pioneer of conservation of France's national monuments, Viollet-le-Duc, had written: "To restore a building is not to maintain it, to repair it, or remake it, but to reestablish it in a state of completeness that can never have existed at a given moment."[2] It was in the search for such an impossibly perfect pristine moment that French savants set about dismantling the dynamic site of worship Angkor had become, so that they might resurrect it as it existed in the European romantic imagination. With each act of sweeping and tidying, and each chapter of Angkor's disengagement from the jungle, colonial curators were also, often unwittingly, disengaging the temples and associated statuary from indigenous belief systems.

Besieged by unfettered jungle growth ranging from the powerful roots of massive banyan trees to rampant lianas, Angkor was the antithesis of the pastoral landscape celebrated in the literary and artistic tradition of *la douce France* (sweet France), with its regulated rivers, vineyards, and orchards. While colonial explorers were confronting Angkor's chaotic mixture of ancient relic and jungle mayhem, the forests of Fontainebleau, like their counterparts in Germany, were being rearranged and organized into a romantic woodland hike.[3] As one young delegate from the Quai d'Orsay described this disjuncture between European woodland and Angkorean wilderness, "Before these grand debris of the past, one is struck by admiration, but emotion is lacking. . . . The remains of a ruined monastery in the heart of a German forest, or the scaly walls of a deserted chateau . . . move more deeply."[4] Bringing Angkor into the cultural landscape of greater France would require cultivating the spirit of *la douce France* at Angkor. From the early 1900s, archaeologist and administration joined forces to convert Angkor into parkland that would appeal to European tourists and coincide with French notions of monumental space.

These notions of space and its configuration differed dramatically from indigenous visions. In Khmer cosmology, the forest was the preserve of *yeak,* demons; it was an unregulated space, but also a deeply spiritual place. Trees were shelters for and repositories of ancestral spirits, or *neak-ta.* The vast Angkor complex's very engulfment in this haunted terrain largely protected it from the predators whose greed would dismember it on its "rescue" from forest undergrowth.[5] Indigenous initiatives in small-scale clearing of the immediate surrounds of Angkor Vat and Angkor Thom (Bayon) dated to at least the 1870s, when monks around Angkor cleared away plant life, wild grasses, and "to honor the new governor of the province," had felled some trees obstructing the views of Angkor Thom.[6] Despite such actions, Delaporte noted in 1880, the French Protectorate faced a challenge in overcoming the "superstitious beliefs of the natives" and mobilizing indigenous labor on a larger scale to arrest the "invasions of exuberant vegetation."[7] In its very approach to space, the colonial project to deforest and demarcate Angkor would thus represent another strand in the temple's secularization, through its disengagement from the surrounding landscape and its conversion into "Angkor Park."

The protectorate's conservation agenda was dictated not only by a need to conquer the land through the production of aesthetically pleasing, bounded parklands and to compartmentalize time itself into periods of Angkorean glory, post-Angkorean decay, and colonial regeneration. It was also shaped by scholarly, museological, and strategic ambitions to partition what had, by the turn of the century, become referred to as "Cambodian religion" *(sasana kmae)* into Buddhism (associated with present practice) and Hinduism (associated with Angkor). These in turn were intimately tied up with the modern preoccupation with the "real."

AUTHENTICATING AND DESACRALIZING ANGKOR

The need to fashion and fix a material culture for Cambodge was itself bound up with the process of colonial travel, circuits of knowledge and exchange, and modern print media, which collectively ensured that travel to and through the French Protectorate would always remain what James Clifford has termed an "imperfect equivalent." In other words, the experience of European travellers in Cambodge, like their counterparts elsewhere, was destined to remain a realm of anticipation in which "the real" never quite matched the images purveyed by Parisian exhibitions, French travel journals, or colonial novels. In his work on colonial representations of the Middle East, Timothy Mitchell has shown how the nineteenth-century emphasis on spectacle ensured that representations of the "real" Orient became widely accepted as arbiters of authenticity.[8] In this hierarchy of the real, the plaster casts and molds that produced the replicas of Angkorean bas-reliefs and statues from the temples acquired a particular status as means capable of reproducing "real" models of Angkor that were "true" in scale and dimension and manufactured on site. What was obviously unreal thus gained an imprimatur of authenticity. Eighteenth-century material representations of both European and other worlds, from dollhouses to colonial dioramas that may still be seen in Amsterdam's Rijksmuseum, had seen a preoccupation with miniaturization, where intricate craftsmanship and the ability to scale things down took pride of place.

In contrast, the nineteenth century was the century of the simulacrum, where a premium was placed on the draughtsman, the cartographer, the surveyor, the stenographer, and the photographer, whose craft was precisely not the creation of a fantasy world—whether through the miniaturization of relics, tableaux, or artifacts—but the *re-creation* of the real. The ramifications of this ascendance of "the real" went far beyond print shop and darkroom. The asymmetries of imperial travel and the colonial exhibitionary complex—which saw millions of Europeans witnessing re-creations of "Cambodge" and other colonies in Paris, London, and elsewhere, while only an elite trickle of tourists was witnessing Angkor in situ—meant that almost all travellers to Cambodge, whether colonial officials or private tourists, were travelling with Cambodge "in mind" and with expectations of what constituted the "authentic" against which colonial archaeologists, museologists, and administrators were obliged to compete. Conservation, colonial archaeology, and tourism thus constituted a double-edged threat to indigenous sites: on the one hand, European audiences and events demanded an offshore traffic in cultural icons and "authentic relics"; on the other, the traffic of tourists to Cambodge placed an onus on local administrators to bend and shape the landscape to coincide with the colonial aesthetic, even when this meant the removal of monks and the rearrangement of sacred artifacts.

Sensitivity to conservation's violent underbelly shaped King Norodom's response to Raffegaud's request in 1891 to remove pieces of sacred statuary from temples of the Angkor era for transport to Paris. As we have seen, Norodom consented to Raffegeaud making casts and drawings, and offered to provide paid guides. But he also stressed that "since antiquity, Cambodian laws and customs under all reigns to this day have never permitted the abduction of pieces of religious sculpture. The Cambodian people set great store by these laws and customs. To allow the removal of statues of monumental stone from the Cambodians would be tantamount to destroying the Khmer religion." Apologizing for his inability to help further, the king stressed that it was impossible "to contravene the laws and customs [of Cambodia], or to attack the Cambodian religion."[9]

In the nineteenth century, the Khmer term for religion *sasana* communicated the sense of a realm of being and belonging, not of a tightly bound entity, a fluidity reflected in its own range of meanings. Although Cambodge's majority religion was Buddhism, *sasana* embraced a range of the sacred without regard for denominational divides, including animist practices and beliefs in ancestral spirits, which coexisted with Buddhist precepts and preachings, and a veneration for certain Hindu figures, notably Vishnu and Shiva. It was most likely in this sense that Norodom used the term "Cambodian religion," rendered in French by his interpreter, Thiounn, as *"la religion cambodgienne"* in the above quoted letter from Norodom to the RSC. Now in his thirteenth year of colonial service, Thiounn enjoyed the confidence of Norodom, who may have dictated or paraphrased the letter for immediate translation into French, rather than first having it committed to writing in Khmer. Whatever the case, Thiounn's choice of phrasing reflects his own cross-cultural fluency and his position at both the social interstices of Cambodian/French power blocs and the temporal nexus between the old order and the new. He is able to name something as "the Cambodian religion," but one senses that it is governed by a territoriality—a swathe of land and people joined in common observance of shared beliefs—rather than a religious or sectarian specificity.

What is clear from Norodom's response, as mediated by Thiounn, is that the ancient temples enjoyed strong contemporary relevance as powerful sites of belief, and that "the Cambodian religion" could not precisely be distilled to a particular object. It was in this sense that the removal of a part from the whole, through its categorization and display, was tantamount to destroying the whole. Norodom's assertion of the strength of local antipathy to the dislocation of Khmer temples and statuary from indigenous circuits of exchange is corroborated by oral history accounts of local vigilantes who murdered Sophan Ket, a Khmer native of Battambang, in the nineteenth century, because they were incensed by his intention to abolish the Ta Prohm temple in Siem Reap and transfer it in toto to the king of Siam, who had offered to promote Ket to the position of deputy governor of Battambang in exchange for a replica of an Angkorean temple. Folklore relates that Sophan Ket had hardly begun the work when villagers killed him, cut open his stomach, filled it with grass, and placed his penis in his mouth as a symbol of his limitless greed.[10]

The disjuncture between European and Khmer notions of exchange can be seen in an early-twentieth-century encounter between a Buddhist monk and a European official as related by Dr. Pannetier, a seasoned observer of Cambodge and outspoken critic of many protectorate polices. The European asked the head monk to entrust to his care an ancient statuette of Buddha, famed in the region for its powers. A Khmer interpreter explained that the European wanted to borrow it to protect him from malevolent forest spirits, and the European donated twenty piastres to the temple. To the head monk, the loan of the statue and the gift of the money were separate transactions, each an independent act of faith. The monk patiently awaited return of the statue, but when, three years later, it had still not reappeared, he asked Pannetier how they could retrieve the figure, expressing genuine concern that some mishap had befallen the European. Pannetier fudged a reply, but saw in his mind's eye: "the indifferent traveller, disappearing into the distance in the gently swaying cradle of his elephant sedan, the bells of his forest convoy softly clinking, no doubt harboring some unkind contempt for the venal and impious [Khmer] race."[11] Disparaging the ability of indigenous monks from the monastery in the grounds of Angkor to "conserve" the temples in 1901, a French student related how a "Siamese" monk had presented him with a sculpted pillar from a temple window in exchange for a pocket mirror.[12] Two years earlier, a British police inspector in Siem Reap noted the use of "debris carted down from the ruins of Angkor Wat" in a fortified enclosure surrounding the house of the governor of Siem Reap.[13]

A similar approach to ancient stones was noted in the early 1900s by members of the EFEO, who reported that "everywhere monks are demolishing the ruins to use them as materials to repair their monasteries." Noting the difficulty of suppressing such "ravages," Finot proposed two circulars, one to be issued by the Supreme Patriarch calling upon monks not to take their building materials from old temples, and one to be issued by the administration to indigenous officials inviting them to take full responsibility for guaranteeing integrity of the monuments.[14] On the face of it these reports, and allusions within French literature to ancient sacred artifacts being passed on to European visitors by monks, contradict Norodom's objections to the removal of sacred statuary as being an attack on Cambodian religion that would not be tolerated by the people. Although apocryphal, such stories indicate that there was a hierarchy of the sacred which contravened the antiquarian's assignation of a flat historic value to all relics from a particular period of time. To a monk, relics were valued, not for their age, but for the sacred properties that were their birthright or the particular powers they had accrued since their creation. The pillar from a window frame allegedly traded by a monk at Angkor for a pocket mirror in Challaye's account, as well as the antique temple components used by monks in the renovation or building of monasteries in Groslier's report, were naturally of lesser spiritual value than the Buddhist statue purloined in Pannetier's story.

What appears to have provoked Norodom's and In's responses is not the act of removal of a statue or a temple component per se, but the agents and aim of its removal, its destination and destiny. Plans by Delaporte and others to remove statuary from Cambodge to Paris, apogee and heart of world civilization, where, in the European view, they would benefit from the safe climate of museums, far from the onslaught of tropical vegetation and from the secular adoration of a French public, centered on the physical preservation of objects. Both Raffegaud's and Commaille's projects involved the extraction of religious statues and structures from local circuits of merit and power, and their conversion to a very different currency as objects valued primarily for their historical, aesthetic, and scientific interest, and thus denuded, by their relocation in Metropolitan museums and Parisian pastiches of pagodas, of other divine properties.

Museology was another critical site of cultural production driving the dissection of Cambodian religion into authentic and corrupted strands. The desire to catalogue, conserve, and map world religions was encapsulated in such institutions as the Musée Guimet, a museum of religion established in Paris in 1889.

THE MUSÉE GUIMET

The European objectification of Buddhism was not purely textual. It also enjoyed a significant plastic dimension, signaled in France by the appearance of a hall dedicated to the religions of the Far East at the 1878 Exposition universelle in Paris, not far from Louis Delaporte's Angkor display. The wealthy Lyonnais industrialist Émile Guimet (1836–1918), a collector of Oriental antiquities who had recently returned from a government-funded trip to research the religions of India, Japan, and China, was so impressed by this exhibit that he established his own Musée des religions in Lyon the following year.[15] It was opened by Minister of Public Education Jules Ferry. A champion of the role of museums as vehicles for public education, Ferry would have fully endorsed Guimet's aim to "spread knowledge of Oriental civilisations and to facilitate religious studies, through sacred images and religious objects."[16] The following decade, lured by the prospect of acquiring colonial administrator Étienne Aymonier's (1844–1929) collection of "religious sculptures, divinities, and religious objects from Cambodia" and hoping to realize his long-term goal of centralizing all objects of religious interest from Asia under one roof, Guimet moved his museum to the capital.[17] Opened to great fanfare by the president of the Republic in November 1889, to coincide with that year's Exposition universelle, the Musée Guimet was dedicated primarily to "religious objects of Asian origin, and especially from India and Indochina."[18] To clarify the context of each object, the Musée Guimet began to sponsor research on religion in Cambodge, Tibet, China, Japan, Java, Siam, and Burma.[19] The museum was not just an assembly of objects, declared a turn-of-the-century guide. It was, above all, "a collection of ideas. Each vitrine represents a dogma, a belief, a sect."[20]

Each vitrine, of course, represented more than that. These empty display cases were the cultural equivalent of Joseph Conrad's "white patches" waiting to be filled. In tandem with the insistence of scholars to locate, date, and translate religious texts, institutions such as the Guimet telegraphed a desire from the Métropole to the colonies. In other words, like the subtle power of the map described by Thongchai Winichakul, the vitrines not only came to represent "a dogma, a belief, a sect" but *anticipated* the compartmentalization and categorization of complex belief systems into "Asian religions."[21] Once filled, such vitrines stripped indigenous religions of their performative content, reducing them to mere representations.

Such displays underwrote another aspect of the cataloguing impulse of libraries and Orientalist scholarship, and that was the division, opposition, and contrast of Hinduism and Buddhism into two temporal planes and two oppositional categories. As Charles Hallisey has noted, one way in which nineteenth-century Orientalism pointed up the contrast between Buddhism and Hinduism was by emphasizing the relative prominence of ritual in the latter. This division was tied up with "an Orientalist contempt for Hindu religiousness, in which Hindu social activity was belittled as inherently irrational and politically ineffective." In a direct mirror image of the direction of French scholarship in Cambodge, which extracted Angkor from the past

FIGURE 6. The Musée Guimet, Paris. *L'Illustration,* 1889.

to emphasize the absence of such activity in the present, Orientalists in India saw the recovery of Buddhism as the salvation of "a rational and practical aspect of India's past, but one that was now absent from the present."[22]

In 1900, for example, a special exhibition of religious objects in a replica of the Royal Pagoda atop the Vat Pnum in the 1900 Paris exhibition, put together by administrators in Indochina, defied Guimet's neat classificatory grid in its syncretic mix of Buddhist and Brahmin figures, statues, vases for holding incense, *brûle-parfums,* altar tables, models of temples, decorated and perfumed candles, fans, jeweled crosses, and "objects from all the different cults in Indochina."[23] The appointment of Louis Finot as director of the newly formed EFEO in 1901, and the commitment of both individual and institution to classify and catalogue, would contract the space for such messy juxtapositions. When Vietnamese and Cambodians dared to gather a similar array of artifacts at Caodai houses of worship some twenty-five years later, they faced ridicule, demolition orders, and imprisonment.

The drive to define, compartmentalize, and "purify" Khmer religion was not confined to Metropolitan display cases, but also spilled into the built environment in Cambodge. In Theravada Buddhism, the erection of new buildings rather than the patching up of old structures was a principal means of acquiring *kammic* merit for lay sponsors. Skill in temple architecture was also a prized attribute of monks. This partly explains why the temples of Angkor continued to function as sites of worship while yet remaining in what Europeans deemed a state of physical neglect, despite missions, visitations, and sponsorship of restorations of parts of the complex by Khmer monarchs in the seventeenth century.[24] King Ang Duong (1847–1860) made a significant contribution to, and in some cases personally supervised, the construction and restoration of Buddhist temples, along with wealthy lay patrons who saw their dedications as an investment in a meritorious future.[25]

Those monks who heeded the protectorate's admonitions, in the early 1900s, to cease patching up their monasteries with parts from antique temples, and turned instead to new suppliers for the upkeep or construction of temples, were berated for violating the template of "original Khmerness." Bemoaning the replacement of finely detailed woodwork by cement in Cambodian monasteries, and the production of commercial molds that enabled the multiple replication of the columns and decorative details of a particular monastery, arts administrator Groslier issued a ringing condemnation of the emergence of "serial pagodas."[26] Finot, an avid supporter of the Guimet museum who shared Groslier's distaste for cement temples, was to play a leading role in fostering such notions of authenticity.

RE-HINDUIZING ANGKOR

"Under the central tower [of Angkor Vat] was a very mediocre statue of Buddha," the French missionary Bouillevaux had written, "said to have been donated by the king of Siam. Cambodians also pay tribute to several other statues of Indian divinities, more or less damaged. The poor idolators come, on holy days, to prostrate themselves before these monsters and burn incense sticks at their feet, while the bonzes chant their Pali prayers. These pagan priests no longer live in the galleries of the old temple; they reside in spindly wood cabins on stilts, right next to the superb monument. . . ."[27] Bouillevaux's account highlighted two facets of Angkor's integration into contemporary life that would emerge as key sources of anxiety from the 1900s onward. One was the presence of Buddhist statuary—donated by a Siamese monarch, no less—in what was popularly promoted as a Hindu temple; the other the juxtaposition of contemporary monks' dwellings and the ancient ruins.

The inaugural corps of EFEO savants either had come to Angkor via India, like Finot and Foucher, as trained Indologists or, like Delaporte, had visited India subsequent to their involvement with Angkor. But even savants who did not specialize in India, such as C.-E. Maître, the professor of Japanese studies who succeeded Foucher as director of the EFEO in 1907, saw the cultural heritage of Indochina as purely derivative from the "two great civilizations of this part of the world, the Hindu and the Chinese." Cambodge, Maître continued, had received "all [its] religion and civilization from India" and, as such, did not merit study in itself.[28] As one visitor to Angkor had remarked in 1903, the EFEO was exploring the temples in order to ascertain "whether Cambodge represents, and to what extent it could represent, the part of India in Indochina."[29] This Hindic orientation was formalized in 1909 through an archaeological cooperation treaty drawn by Dufour, in his capacity as permanent secretary of the Indochinese Committee of Antiquities, between the EFEO and India.[30] On site, the Hindu framing of Cambodge encouraged Angkor's new guardians not only to relocate members of the *sangha* but also to take down and remove Buddhist statues that had been erected in the temple in its centuries' long conversion to a site of Buddhist worship. The desire to create France's "India" also shaped local conservation agendas. The enormous temple complex of which Angkor was part contained several Buddhist sanctuaries, but by the 1920s, reported one eminent Siamese visitor to Angkor, none were "so well cleared and restored" as Angkor Vat, "a Hindu monument of the Vishnaite cult."[31]

Angkor's Hinduization was a mirror image of events transpiring in late-nineteenth-century Ceylon. In 1873, two years after an envious French commissioner had ordered a copy of the cast of the Sanchi Tope displayed by British India at the London International Exhibiton, King Mindon of Burma gifted a gilded Buddha statue to the Bodhgaya temple in Ceylon. In 1886, while Fabre, Delaporte, and others were busy planning for the 1889 Exposition universelle in Paris, and French administrators marvelling at such symbols of India as the Gwalior gateway on display at Kensington for the 1886 Colonial and National Exhibition, a British journalist-cum-Orientalist, Edwin Arnold, sparked off what would become an international campaign to rid the Mahabodhi temple at Bodhgaya of Hindu *mahants*.[32] When visiting Bodhgaya in search of Mindon's Buddha, the celebrated author of the *Light of Asia*—which recounted Buddha's life in verse and had won Arnold the Order of the White Elephant from King Chulalongkorn—was outraged to find there a stone lingam, the symbol of Shiva. Worse still, under the Bodhi tree in the temple grounds, Hindu worshippers were making offerings of cakes, with the full blessing of a *mahant*. Citing the Buddhist statues and bas-reliefs piled in broken disarray in the temple grounds as evidence of governmental and Hindu neglect, Arnold began lobbying to oust the Hindus from the temple and transfer it to Buddhist control. In 1891, his campaign was taken up by Anagarika Dhammapala and became integral to Dhammapala's popularization of a Sinhalese Buddhist national religion. With Dhammapala's sponsorship, and the support of the thirteenth Dalai Lama of Tibet, the Maha Bodhi Society was established to protect and conserve the ruins, making Mahabodhi temple a cause célèbre among Indologists and antiquarians.[33]

In Cambodge, the process of Hinduizing Angkor Vat developed in tandem with the delineation of Khmer Buddhism as the national religion. The presence of Buddhist statues and the practice of Buddhist worship at Angkor presented unwelcome challenges to colonial desires to compartmentalize Cambodge both vertically, through time, and horizontally, through the categorization of religion. A key goal in this partitioning was the political and cultural severing of Cambodge from Siam, with which it had enjoyed a centuries' long traffic of knowledge, manuscripts, and other ritual objects both within the Buddhist sphere and between royalty. One of the first acts of "conservation" at Angkor Vat was the removal of Buddhist icons that had been erected around the central tower, obstructing its doorways.[34]

Suttantaprija In's *Journey to Angkor* bears witness to this act of disestablishment. In's long verse narrative begins with a description of his journey by river to Angkor. His first experience on arriving at the temple complex is colonial ceremony. As part of the entourage of the governor of Siem Reap, In witnesses a ceremony jointly orchestrated by King Sisowath and the colonial administrations to celebrate the recent retrocession of Battambang, Siem Reap, and Sisophon. Shortly after arriving at Angkor, and after a brief description of the splendid dais set up for King Sisowath and the French podium where "Mister Big Governor from Saigon," the GGI, is enthusiastically attending to his duties, In slips off to "the European house" to examine Commaille's work. From here on, his account steers us in a reverse direction to the linear logic celebrated in colonial conservation narratives. The European's dual presence and distance resonates in the names In assigns them, "Sir Mr Commaille, from France" and "Mr. Big Governor from Saigon," but the only people encountered by In once he departs from the scene are the agents of their grandiose schemes:

> Coolies are hired as labor
> Chopping wood and hauling stone slabs to and fro
> . . . . seeing our Khmer race as coolies,
> I am overcome with pity for the Khmer race, dirt poor,
> Working as coolies for somebody else's money.
> I watch their bodies, frail and flat-bellied
> Hair thick with dust and grime, stinking like otters.[35]

The coolies' dishevelled misery is thrown into sharp relief by the backdrop of Angkor itself, the theme of whose past glory resonates throughout In's long verse, his reference to Monsieur's obsessive attention to cleanliness and order, and by the unrecorded fact of In's own attire. In was a snappy dresser, joining hat and silver-topped cane to a wraparound length of silk *sampot*. A waist-length, close-fitting mandarin-collared jacket would probably have completed his outfit.[36] In's coolies were absent from French coverage of the gala, and from most published accounts of Angkor's conservation.[37] Indeed, many such reports appear to attribute no less a magical hand to the French than to Indra in Angkor's apparent auto-reconstruction under colonial direction. But coolies, the use of their labor, the effects of their conscription on local agricultural practice, and the lingering resentment at perceived unjust calls on the local population's time all figure strongly in Commaille's private correspondence.

Journeying with In through Angkor, we sense that we are walking against the grain of colonial time. We travel from high ceremony to a sketch encompassing the mundane minutiae (clearing away moss) and quasi-divine ambition (restoring stones to their "original position") of Commaille's conservation project and its subjugation of Khmer labor, until finally our journey stops at the entrance to the central tower. Here, through In's eyes, we see the full force of conservation's silent and sectarian violence:

> Doorways opened onto [the central tower] from four directions, they had been
> closed off
> And shut tight, preventing entry.
> The building was decorated with standing statues,
> Posted on all floors in all four directions.
> Scattered fragments of gold and silver, and broken limbs,
> And objects of essence,
> Were inside the courtyard,
> Out of the menacing grasp of thieves and enemies of Buddha.
> Sir Monsieur Commaille, the Chief of Works,
> Had the statue of Buddha cut out of the southern gateway,
> Uprooted from the gateway and taken out.
> [Then] he had the crushed statue removed from the courtyard.
> I could see that they had cut the door-statue away,
> And broken its neck, the statue was smashed beyond all recognition,
> It worried me, that they had destroyed the statue.
> The time of the religion of the door-deity was over.
> All the other three door-deities were well preserved.
> They hadn't been handled like the southern statue,
> Oh, the southern statue from that day forward,
> His body was eliminated, he had reached the shore of Nirvana. . . .[38]

During the following decade, colonial attempts to re-Indianize Angkor would see the quarantining of scores of such Buddhist icons in a designated space that became known as the Mille Bouddha (thousand Buddha) gallery.[39] The year of In's visit to Angkor also saw Commaille's relocation of various monastery buildings established within the wall of Angkor Vat to the west of the temple, where they would not disrupt the frontal view.[40] Those monks who had been the chief curators of the temple complex long before the EFEO was founded were cleared off the land in 1909, as their presence immediately in front of the temple was considered an eyesore.[41] A primary motive for the removal was the colonial aesthetics of tourism, which demanded the rearrangement of indigenous sites to correspond to European expectations.

This exercise was in keeping with the museumization of sacred monuments as "regalia for a secular colonial state" in train elsewhere in Southeast Asia, for instance at Burma's Pagan and the Dutch East Indies' Borobodur where, as Anderson has noted, monuments were "to be kept empty of people, except for perambulatory tourists," and pilgrimages discouraged.[42] But in Cambodge's case more subtle considerations were at stake that would have deep implications for Angkor's reconfiguration as a lodestone of the Khmer nation. In sequence with European artistic depictions and exhibition displays of Angkor, this local surgery was another step in the reduction of the vast temple complex of Angkor to a particular view. If, as Viollet-le-Duc suggested, restoration was a self-defeating exercise, then the landscape at least could be manipulated and framed so as to form a view reproducing that impossibly perfect moment of the past that Angkor had now become. Creation of that view required the forced absenteeism of precisely those contemporary Cambodians on whose "coolie" labor and monetary donations the restoration project utterly depended.

From the establishment of the EFEO in 1901 and Angkor's subsequent territorial recovery through the retrocession of the provinces of Siem Reap to Cambodge in 1907 through to the early 1940s, the myth of vanishing was largely supplanted by the theme of cultural, archaeological, and theological recovery. Implicated here was also the recovery of beforeness, of authenticity and purity, through scholarship and the retrieval of physical objects from texts to sculptures. However, embroiled as it was with the development of Angkor as the monument to Khmerness, this phase of the colonial aesthetic also accentuated notions of loss. As Roland Barthes has written, "monuments suppress at one stroke the reality of the land and of its people, in that they account for nothing of the present," so that "[w]hat is to be seen is . . . constantly in the process of vanishing." Like the Blue Guide described by Barthes, symbols such as Angkor Vat become "the very opposite of what [they] advertise, an agent of blindness."[43] Angkor's magnificence, and its choice as the central point of reference for Cambodge, ensured that the Cambodians themselves were, in the eyes of European observers and true to Barthes' maxim, constantly in the process of vanishing. Indeed, it was on seeing Angkor in its new, landscaped form that European visitors as late as the 1930s reflected that the Khmers had either vanished or were inexorably sliding towards disappearance.[44]

For Angkor to retain its integrity as ancient view not only necessitated the removal of contemporary indigenous structures from it, but the removal of Angkor, or elements of it, from Buddhist monasteries. The removal of an ancient temple plinth to furnish a contemporary monastery not only violated European notions of historicity by fragmenting and interleaving different eras, it also disrupted the notion of "Khmer Buddhism" as a singular and contemporary category.

THE ANGKOR SOCIETY

Increasingly intertwined with tourism, colonial archaeology allowed the Protectorate of Cambodge and its counterparts throughout Empire to pose as the gatekeepers of tradition through the incorporation of ancient, sacred spaces into the colonial map, as reflected in the marking of tourist, educational, and other maps with images of Angkor, the Bayon, and other ruins. But monumental archaeology was rarely a self-conscious project on the part of either European or native administrators, most of whom remained oblivious of its deeply political nature.[45] Like the museographer described by Claude Lévi-Strauss, the French curators of Angkor in Cambodge and the Métropole would have had the texture, form, and smell of Khmer antiquities ingrained into their consciousness through their daily handling of objects.[46] Archaeology had not yet come into its own as a discipline in Europe, and most curators came to Angkor trained as engineers or architects. They were motivated by neither profit nor politics, but by a romantic and often deeply personal fascination with Angkor, a professional curiosity and a genuine belief that Cambodge might indeed "disappear." These yearnings are reflected in the mandate of the Société d'Angkor pour la conservation des monuments anciens d'Indochine (Angkor Society for the Conservation of Ancient Monuments of Indochina), founded in Paris in 1907 at the instigation of Delaporte, Finot, Doumer, and others.[47] King Sisowath headed the list of the society's one hundred and more founding patrons, which united such regulars on the metropolitan and colonial Cambodge circuit as George and Hippolyte Coedès, Emile Guimet, Admiral de Jonquières, Auguste Pavie, and the novelist Pierre Mille with such Parisian socialites as Prince Roland Bonaparte and Auguste Rodin in its aim to advance "the conservation and study of monuments in Indochina."[48] Its program, less concise, reflected the romantic motivations of its founders: "Angkor ranks alongside the Parthenon, Luxor, and the Taj Mahal, as one of the architectural wonders of the world. France, the trustee of these treasures, has a duty to conserve them. . . . It will not be said that Angkor suffered more from the indifference of its new owners than from the wounds of time and past depredations."[49]

The burden of duty extended beyond Angkor to Cambodge and the Cambodians: it became France's duty to preserve Cambodge and the Cambodians—but for whom? Angkor was not a distant forefather of European heritage. Rather, as we have seen, its connections to French consciousness were worked out in the immediate, in the here and now of the colonial encounter, as a key to the security of France's colonial authority and to the dangers of decay within France itself. Stressing the urgency of protecting the temples from further damage by "the ravages of time, climate, and nature," the society's mandate stressed the need for private fund-raising initiatives to supplement local budgets.[50] By October 1907, the society had won the official approval of the Ministry of Public Education and the strong backing of the EFEO, which recognized its value as a showcase for the EFEO's achievements, as a vehicle for raising awareness of Cambodge's archaeological riches in France, and as a potential catalyst for a flow of tourists towards Angkor.[51] The mystique of Angkor popularized in journals, books, museums, and expositions had already secured the temple a niche on the itineraries of a slowly expanding pool of wealthy tourists from the Métropole.[52] Later that year, a Cambodian chapter of the Angkor Society was founded in Phnom Penh by Félix Faraut, who had developed a keen interest in Khmer monuments, literature, and astronomy since first accompanying Delaporte on his earliest archaeological mission to Angkor.[53] The society enjoyed the active support of key Khmer ministers.[54] Its creation coincided with Chulalongkorn's founding of the Antiquarian Society of Siam.[55]

In November 1907 the EFEO sent Lunet de Lajonquière on a new mission to Cambodge to "make an inventory of the archaeological riches of our new territory . . . [and] to study the organization of a department of Cambodian antiquities."[56] Earlier that year, Lajonquière had argued that "the very life of the Cambodian nationality" depended on France's ability to return the ruins of Angkor, and he had also noted, but not described, "regrettable acts of vandalism."[57] De Lajonquière's comprehensive survey of Cambodge's monuments proved a milestone in Western scholarship on Angkor.[58] Claiming that "neither Java nor the Indies possesses such a perfect and considerable archaeological ensemble," de Lajonquière subsequently summarized the EFEO's task as improving tourist access and accommodation, and assuring conservation. In 1907, more than two hundred people visited Angkor, and several leading travel agencies began including the temple in their world tours. To improve tourist access and facilities, de Lajonquière recommended building a new road and a new guesthouse. The EFEO adopted his proposal. Modelled on similar constructions in British India, this "comfortable bungalow, with 10 rooms, 14 beds, a drawing room and a large dining room" was built at the entrance of the temple.[59] Proximity to Angkor Vat allowed guests of this *Salaa d'Angkor* to view the shifting hues of the ruins by day and night.[60]

In July 1908 Angkor gained its first European curator, a skilled draughtsman, Jean Commaille (1868–1916). The son of a soldier, born in Marseille, and trained at military school, Commaille decided against attending the St. Cyr military academy. Trading his military colors for a painter's palette, he trained as an artist. Financial need led him back to his father's vocation: in 1896 he signed up for the Foreign Legion and was posted to Cambodge as chief guard of the Cambodian militia. On his release from these duties in 1898, he found work with the Civil Service in Phnom Penh. His first visit to Angkor was in 1899, and in 1900, on the creation of the EFEO, he was appointed to it and assigned the task of establishing the Musée du Saigon.[61] On his move to Angkor, Commaille and his wife lived in a traditional wooden house on stilts close to Angkor Vat. Less smitten than her husband with their "quasi-ascetic" existence, his wife had a piano installed in their home. Symbolically, the floor gave out under its weight and, soon after, their marriage collapsed. Commaille remained alone, distracting himself with making watercolors and sketches of Angkor, which he passed around among colleagues, hoping to use them as illustrations for a monograph, a project upon which he had set his mind since arriving at the temples.[62]

Over the next eight years, he authored and cowrote six books and articles, including a 1912 guide to the temples.[63]

Under Commaille's direction, and with funds collected from villagers across Cambodge via the Society of Angkor, physical restoration of the temples began.[64] By May 1909, the Cambodian public had become the Angkor Society's major donors.[65] Appealing to individuals to "preserve the glory of the Khmer people" enshrined in Angkor, "for the reputation of Cambodge and its inhabitants," the society printed a Khmer-language circular inviting further donations.[66] At a meeting of the society in August 1909, Deputy Minister of Justice Douch stressed the importance of Angkor's restoration for the Cambodian people.[67]

Those European curators of Angkorean culture who had not been schooled in Indian arts—Henri Parmentier, Henri Marchal, George Trouvé, and Maurice Glaize—approached the temples and their conservation as trained architects who had worked in the colonial public works administration.[68] Through the prism of European architecture, and in the wake of the Gothic revivalism led by Viollet-le-Duc and others, numerous comparisons were made between the style and function of Khmer temples and Roman and Gothic cathedrals. One turn-of-the-century publication described Angkor Vat and Angkor Thom as "something like the Louvre, combined with the Tuileries and finished off with the Pantheon, Notre-Dame, and St. Sulpice . . . but with a little more harmony."[69] Commaille asserted that Angkor Vat's bas-reliefs played the same role as the stained-glass windows of French cathedrals. Such comparisons were sometimes tainted with implicit allegations of cultural superiority, as in one journalist's assertion that the monks and natives on pilgrimage to Angkor who spent hours studying the bas-reliefs were often unable to penetrate their meaning.[70] Until the 1930s, the prevailing assumption was that the temples had served a similar function as French cathedrals.[71]

By December 1909, Commaille had supervised clearance of the overgrowth from the facade of Angkor Vat and the inner courtyards.[72] Earlier that year, a young scholar named George Groslier (1887–1945) had arrived in Cambodge on a mission funded by the Ministry of Education and Fine Arts to research Khmer customs and monuments.[73] Born in Phnom Penh where his father, George-Antoine, had served as chancellor to the RSC and headmaster of the École franco-cambodgienne, the young Groslier had been sent to France to round off his own education, majoring in arts and the classics.[74]

By 1910, working under the auspices of the EFEO and tapping the expanding reservoir of knowledge about the monuments, the budding Indologist George Coedès had established the common genealogy of the Khmer Empire and contemporary Cambodians. Coedès' scholarship shattered the myth that the Khmer race had been extinguished by the forces of degeneration and natural selection. However, the fusion of Khmer and Angkor in the public imagination was far from complete in 1909. Records of the Angkor Society reveal a concerted effort to incorporate non-Khmer communities into the restoration project and indicate a sense of inclusion and participation in Angkor regardless of ethnic background. In December 1909, at a meeting of the Cambodian Committee of the Society of Angkor, Petillot appointed Chinese, Cham, and Vietnamese representatives as committee members, following a recommendation by the Cambodian minister of arts and culture, Alexis Chhun, a Cambodian of Portuguese ancestry. Noting that contributions from Cambodians alone had more than doubled the society's takings during the past year, President Jeannerat assured the new Chinese, Vietnamese, and Cham members that their communities had not been excluded from the society's previous ventures on account of any racism. Nor did the society appeal to them now on financial grounds, he continued, but simply because

> we firmly believe that all religious people must be moved by the same emotions to rescue the marvellous monuments, where your ancestors adored their gods, from ruin. We want all inhabitants of Cambodia, without distinction of origin, without the irritating questions of race, to be able to help us by their offerings, however small, to our conservation work, and all, in a common and religious effort, to contribute, for the greater glory of the country, to reviving the splendors of the monuments. . . .[75]

Here, the compass of religion was expanded to transcend questions of race, and the temples become the heritage of all inhabitants of Cambodia, without distinction of origin. This act of inclusion, apparently motivated by the desire to tap both donations and labor from Chinese and Vietnamese communities, was short-lived. During the next decade, those "irritating questions of race" came back to haunt the view of Angkor.

Recording the minutes of this meeting was a nineteen-year-old Roland Meyer (b. 1889), a low-ranking clerk who had arrived in Cambodge in 1908 after a short stint with GGI Paul Beau's cabinet in Saigon. Meyer's minutes are free of personal marginalia, but his later writings show that he, like many other colonial scholar-officials, did not share this constructive vision of multiethnic participation in Cambodge's heritage and culture. Instead, Chinese and Vietnamese were billed in his works and those of many others as swamping, flooding, greedy races intent on eradicating Cambodge. This heightened vision of Cambodge's cultural purity was fired in part by the disjunction between the banalities of colonial society in Saigon and the exotic expectations forged by Meyer's vision of the Cambodian dancers at Marseille and his exposure to Loti and others, which cinched his resolve to seek out "the apotheosis of the kingdoms of rajahs and golden pagodas."[76] His involvement in the society meshed with his burning ambition to be the first "Frenchman of Asia" to "write the book of Angkor," and he would increasingly channel his desires to conserve Cambodge from vanishing into the written word.[77] In April 1910, the RSC appointed the architect Henri Marchal, inspector of civil buildings in Phnom Penh, as assistant curator of the Musée Khmer.[78] When Marchal returned to France on temporary sick leave the following year, Meyer replaced him.[79] Now in his third year of writing a fictionalized account of his Cambodge experiences, Meyer supplemented his museum duties with his continuing collection of information from Cambodian city dwellers and peasants, whose revelations "daily enriched [his] treasury of knowledge, inspiring one by one the pages of [his] great book which will sing of the beauties of the old Khmer country."[80]

The Angkor Society met again in January 1910. Sisowath's recent issue of a royal circular had attracted substantial donations to the temple's upkeep from Cambodians across the protectorate.[81] These funds were allocated to clearing the grand stairway of Angkor Vat and erecting balustrades alongside the stairway, so creating a "majestic entry to the monument" that won high praise from the EFEO.[82] On 22 March 1911, the society met again under President M. Ch. Gravelle, director of the Bank of Indochina in Phnom Penh.[83] Founder of the Society for the Protection of Children in Cambodge, Gravelle's horror of racial or cultural hybridization was reflected in his denunciation of the deracinated, déclassée women spawned by miscegenation.[84] While these views sat oddly beside Gravelle's own marriage to a Cambodian woman, they resonated with themes that would emerge in the writings of Meyer, Groslier, and another member of the Angkor Society, Paul Collard. Like many of his contemporaries, Collard, mayor of Phnom Penh, subscribed to the belief that the Khmers were part of Hindu civilization and members of the great "Aryan family" who should be cocooned from other cultures. He later praised the protectorate for having re-animated a "vanished civilization" and claimed personal credit for assisting in the Khmer "butterfly's" emergence from its chrysalis.[85] Such bold claims, and their implicit suggestions of Cambodian passivity, fly in the face of society records.

During 1910, Cambodians had once again been the society's major donors, contributing over half of the funds dedicated to the conservation of Angkor in 1911. While financial resources were donated with apparent enthusiasm, physical labor was not so easily recruited, and it may be that the collection of donations was presented to villagers as an alternative to manual labor, as occurred in the corvée system. A series of correspondence from 1909 to 1910 revealed difficulties in obtaining labor and warned of the "excessive burden" the Angkor conservation project imposed on the population of Siem Reap. The EFEO had sought alternatives to local conscription, including a proposal tabled to the Résident supérieur in 1908 for the engagement of fifty Chinese coolies to be taken from the colonial prison population, or unemployed Asiatics from the pepper plantation in Takeo. The RSC rejected the request, claiming that such measures would jeapordize general security. Following up the matter two years later, GGI Beau argued that while "the introduction to Siemreap of a small group of individuals of suspect morality could present some inconveniences, the constant requisitions to which local inhabitants are subjected are of the type that might provoke, in the long term, an 'initiation' and discontent with the potential for far graver serious political consequences." Besides, Angkor's year-round monopoly on a large number of natives of Siem Reap employed in the management of the ruins meant that other services, such as communication routes, were deprived of adequate coolie labor for their maintenance. The GGI asked for advice as to what "type of manual labor, Cambodian, Asiatic, or Malay, would . . . be most suited to recruit for

Angkor," and warned against conscripting coolies from the local population, especially in the rainy season, when such conscription would drain work in the fields.[86] In subsequent correspondence Parmentier communicated Commaille's own opposition to recruiting coolies from Phnom Penh for fear that such men of base morals might upset the beautiful moral equilibrium of the countryside, and in particular that they might prey on tourists.[87]

The roads whose maintenance was now endangered by the skewed ratio of coolie labor at Angkor had been laid to assist tourist and administrative access to the temples. The ancient roads of the city of Angkor had spread out in straight lines from the central hub of Angkor Vat to the surrounding temples. The foundations of these roads remained intact in the early twentieth century, but were crisscrossed by new paths and tracks.[88] In 1909, a year after duc du Montpensier had started a vogue in driving from Saigon to Angkor, careening up the stairway to Angkor Vat in his automobile, GGI Klobukowski officially launched new access routes opening up Angkor to "savants, artists, and tourists" come rain or shine, by land or water.[89]

By 1910, growing European interest in Angkor had catalyzed the creation of a Department of Colonial Tourism in France, and the protectorate granted a monopoly on tourism in Angkor to the Compagnie des messageries fluviales de Cochinchine.[90] Tourists were beginning to emerge as donors to the upkeep of "Angkor Park" via a newly installed donations box. However, their combined offerings in 1910 paled beside the donations solicited by the Society of Angkor in Paris and channeled to Cambodge by its treasurer, Pierre Guesde. But these mostly European offerings, from a society that now claimed the celebrated sculptor Auguste Rodin among its members, totaled less than half of contributions from Cambodians.[91] Guesde, a former administrator in Cambodge, where he had married a Khmer, and organizer of the Indochina section at the 1906 exposition in Marseille, would later shape Cambodge's apparition at the 1931 Exposition coloniale internationale in Paris. As we have seen, Angkor formed a central motif of works by his novelist and poet daughter, Nelly Pierrette Guesde (1898–1969), who wrote under her Khmer name, Makhâli Phal.

On an April afternoon in 1916, seven years after the absent figure of "Sir Mr Commaille, from France" had become intertwined, in the mind and writings of In, with the uneasy presence of "Khmer coolies," Commaille set off from his house in Siem Reap, taking with him the weekly pay of the coolies employed on the works at Angkor Thom. He never arrived at his destination. On Kilometre 49, one of the new colonial roads, he was shot in the stomach. Had he continued on or turned back, he might have survived, but Commaille stopped his car to confront his attacker. On stepping down, he tumbled to the ground, and a group of five or six armed men rushed upon him. Commaille's driver, Ngac, who had stayed in the car, drove off to get help. Badly injured by rifle shots and knife blows to his head, Commaille was lucid to the last. Announcing that "death was not sad," he died with his eyes wide open. M. Belou, the chief forest guard, closed them. He was placed in a hardwood coffin and buried near the administrative post, near the Bayon temple. In an uncanny echo of In's description of an abandoned and entombed statue whose broken body the poet equated with Buddha's release from this world, Commaille was buried in a small tomb near the Bayon, his grave marked by a stupa-style tombstone. In the days following his death, an administrator in Siem Reap found what was Commaille's last piece of work, a report drafted to the EFEO on that fateful afternoon urgently requesting an installment of 1,000 piastres to pay his staff for the week of 24 to 29 April, without which he would have to suspend work on the disengagement of Phimeanakas.[92] Commaille's death brought another figure into the archival spotlight. That October, in Marseille, his widow received a pension of 1,875 francs.

Colonial documents described the murder as an "isolated act of purely financial motive," an interpretation that legitimated a wave of recrimination and repression in surrounding districts.[93] Three suspects were condemned to death and executed in Phnom Penh, while his servant was given an eighteen-month prison sentence for fleeing the scene of the crime.[94] Commaille's murder, of course, was far from an isolated incident, but was deeply embedded in a system of injustice and forced labor. He was a casualty of a colonial regime that by 1916 had exacted a punitive toll on Cambodians through corvée labor schemes. Across the country, contemporary Cambodians angrily reasserted themselves into the view of Cambodge through mass protests. Rudely awakened from their romantic imaginings, colonial administrators were forced to look at Cambodge in a new light.

But Commaille left behind a curiously durable legacy. In just under a decade, he had sculpted a particular image of Angkor onto the landscape and overseen the physical partitioning of contemporary Buddhist practice and an antiquarianized Hinduism in situ. He had also witnessed massive indigenous participation in Angkor's renovation through coolie labor that was in part funded by financial donations from the local populace. These activities, and the role played by elite Khmers in the Angkor Society, are ample testimony to indigenous engagement, both voluntary and involuntary, in Angkor's conservation. The momentum of colonial mythmaking, however, had already cast France and the French as Angkor's sole rescuers and financiers. The deaths of Carpaux and Commaille, and the burial of their remains at the temple sites, carried this synergy to a deeper material and spiritual level through the enshrinement of men who were at once martyrs to and ancestors of European cultural intervention at the temples, and subtly heightened the sacredness of the site to European savants. During the next decade, the conservation of Angkor proceeded apace, and the field of French curatorial efforts extended from physical monuments to cultural practices. Guided by the same assumptions about the artistic genius of Angkor's builders, cultural policies now turned to the conservation of Cambodge's contemporary arts.

6 | Copy Rites

Angkor and the Art of Authenticity

"What is a nation?" asked a Khmer contributor to the scouting magazine *Servir,* writing under the pseudonym Yuvan Boraan (Ancient Youth) in 1942. "A nation is all things that are Khmer, . . . the territory on which Khmers live, . . . the conservation of our handicrafts, ancient customs," and the sites holding the bones of the ancient ancestors of "our Khmer race."[1] The writer's pen name echoed the central oxymoron of modern nationalisms, which claim both the youthfulness of a nation-in-formation and its purported rootedness in antiquity, a bipolarity reflected in the author's exhortation to his readers to worship both ancient ancestral bones and new national flags. A key example of this bipolarity is the compound *Altneuland,* coined some thirty years earlier by the Zionist Theodore Herzl to designate the as yet unformed Jewish nation-state and translated into Hebrew as *Tel Aviv* (spring ruins), a name subsequently given concrete formation in the sprawling modern metropolis of Israel's largest city. Although tallying with this and other nationalist nomenclature globally, the Khmer writer's contradictory signature also encapsulated tensions specific to the colonial encounter, particularly marked in Cambodge, where youth and antiquity, variously interpreted as present and past, West and East, new and old, modern and traditional, progress and backwardness, were in constant tension. Culture was to become fixed in its colonial status in Cambodge as in the French Africa, analyzed by Frantz Fanon as both "present and mummified."[2] These tensions, like the name Yuvan Boraan, were natural precursors to Saloth Sar's imaginings of the Khmer nation and to his identification as Kmae daem.

The colonial injunction to contemporary Cambodians was to detach themselves from the past and to live in the modern in a way that would allow presentation of Angkor and other monuments as antiquity. This was linear identity without linear progression. There was no gradual laying of milestones from then to now, as occurred in the marking of national historical time and space in the heritage movements of France, Britain, Germany, and elsewhere. There was only an Angkorean ancestral then and a colonial now, with a yawning abyss in between. Like the figures erased from Mouhot's sketches of Angkorean monuments and the monasteries removed from the frontal approach to Angkor, contemporary Cambodians disturbed the European view of Cambodge. Refashioning the contemporary Cambodian into a modern national subject—the subject of a colonial protectorate, of a disempowered Khmer kingdom, of the twentieth century—required the bisection of past and present. The split space designated for the Khmer in this colonial vista was as the vanished, absent or lacking in the present, and as the ancestral Khmer suspended at the peak of Khmer time.

In 1959, Saloth Sar's future foreign secretary, Khieu Samphan, submitted his doctoral thesis in economics to the University of Paris, arguing that "the decline of handicrafts" in Cambodge exemplified the economic damage wrought by colonial intervention. Cheap goods supplied by French businesses, Khieu argued, had "prompted the decline of much of the national craft sector," with the result that, in postcolonial Cambodia, "national crafts are fading away and dying."[3] Unknowingly or not, both Khieu Samphan and "Yuvan Boraan" were articulating the thoughts and fears of a colonial administrator who exerted a significant and lasting influence on Cambodian arts, George Groslier (1889–1945). From 1918 to 1942, Groslier had shaped his career as a rescue mission and established institutions, principally an art school and museum, which he described as a life raft to save Cambodge's national arts from vanishing. While Groslier focused on luxury, elite goods, and Khieu on such crafts as silk weaving, tinware, pottery, and basket weaving, both shared the core assumption that a nation, and its life span, has a material dimension in artistic production.

THE BIRTH AND ETERNALLY IMMINENT DEATH OF "NATIONAL ARTS AND CRAFTS" IN CAMBODGE

In precolonial Cambodia, objects such as luxurious *sampots* (lengths of handwoven, hand-dyed silk) and sumptuous silver fretwork functioned as key material signs of prestige. These portable tokens of individual power and status, associated with ritual, ceremony, and gift giving, were treated not just as "symbols of merit, but as proof and manifestations of it."[4] Like the regalia in island Southeast Asia, such objects were probably perceived "not as causes of a person's prestige, but as the signs or by-products of his or her potency."[5] In embodying such potency, objects such as the king's sword *(preah khan)* at once encoded and helped to decipher a hierarchical order. As such, they were integral to those indigenous sociopolitical hierarchies described by Hansen as "deeply engrained cultural metaphors employed in religious and cosmological schemas."[6] But were such ritual effects, as Chandler argues, important in forming a notion of what Cambodia "was"? Yes, if we take "Cambodia" to constitute a set of hierarchical arrangements, in other words a domain of power relations where possession of, the power to commission, or the ability to produce such ceremonial objects were not seen as national skills framed by political boundaries, but as sociocultural transactions determined by one's rank in society. By marking such objects as "national" and fixing them in a bounded geocultural sphere, colonialism transformed ritual objects into signs that no longer purely indicated individual, royal, or divine *potency* but instead emblematized national *potential*—a potential increasingly tied up, in the European imagination, with a nation's longevity and territoriality. This location of Cambodge in material artifacts rather than in the complex skein of hierarchical relations sketched by Chandler and Hansen proved the diagnosis that the Khmer civilization had indeed "disappeared," and might do so again without due protection. "The ancient Khmer civilization vanished long ago," wrote two Khmerophiles engaged in collecting Cambodian music and songs for posterity in the early 1920s.[7]

Similar transformations of the local and practiced to the national and studied occurred in Java and Burma, where colonial conservation and arts education simultaneously germinated notions of a bounded "national" art and the prospect of its vanishing. The impulse to name indigenous crafts and styles as national was intensified by Cambodge's inclusion in the world exhibitionary complex and the pressure exerted on Cambodian kings and ministers to muster ornaments and devise displays that would signify Cambodge to the world. Silverware was one of the examples of Khmer art that Delaporte shipped to France in 1882 for museum and exhibition display.[8] In 1887, a French government minister had indicated that the exhibition of "samples of Khmer art such as sculptures, paintings, and bronzes" might best further the government's efforts "to develop the Republic's influence overseas."[9] Bronze statues were among the prizewinning Cambodge exhibits at Anvers.[10]

However, Cambodge's incorporation into the global economy did not bring about a complete decline in indigenous artistic production. The loss felt most keenly by colonial administrators, who consorted predominantly with high-status Cambodians or experienced Cambodge as an artistic entity in exhibition displays, was the decreased availability of such refined products as sumptuous silk *sampots* and silverwork, whose widespread production had attracted the admiration of one delegate of the French Ministry of Public Education on a visit to Cambodge in 1893.[11] By the turn of the century, wealthy Cambodians who were the traditional patrons of the arts had developed a taste for Western luxury goods, partly as badges of status with which they could negotiate their place in the new colonial order by simultaneously demonstrating their power and purchasing prestige, and partly, we can presume, out of a fascination with the novel range of colors, forms, and styles represented in this occidental exotic. The appreciation of imported goods in royal quarters was noted by Henri Mouhot in 1860 and Bouillevaux before him.[12] A colonial atlas produced in the early 1900s documented the desire of wealthy Cambodians for Victorian tasseled furniture, British shooting sticks, French wallets, and diamond-encrusted bowler hats.[13] The last was a much commented upon accessory of Sisowath's on his 1906 visit to Marseille, while the sporting of other French attire by princes and artisans in France from the late 1880s through the 1920s bitterly disappointed European expectations of Khmer authenticity.[14]

As Western accoutrements began to displace indigenous adornments and ceremonial objects as status symbols, indigenous production of the latter diminished. In British Burma and the Dutch East Indies, the supply of cheap manufactures and the withdrawal of indigenous elite patronage had had similar ramifications for artistic production.[15] Lower down the social scale, although the weaving of cloth *sampots* and the manufacture of rush baskets were inevitably affected by the importation of cheap and readily available substitutes, production nevertheless continued. As Muan has demonstrated, the crafting of silver betel boxes and other such labor-intensive and expensive artifacts did not cease, but simply became less visible. In Cambodian rural society, with its seasonal, rice-growing rhythms, filigree silverware and other such artistic objects were typically made not by full-time professional artisans but by multiskilled individuals, who made their living by farming and produced pieces on commission. Because such objects came to be seen as "national" crafts whose manufacture was increasingly perceived as a national skill, and because the practitioners of such skills remained invisible in the protectorate's meagre official records, a panic cry arose. The nation was perceived to be dying along with its crafts. It was above all the decline in items that could be conspicuously associated with "Cambodge" that attracted the concern of the protectorate's new wave of cultural conservationists.

Their agenda differed from those of the first generation of colonizers, from Delaporte to Doumer, many of whom saw no vestiges of "Khmer" civilization around them and brusquely declared that culture and civilization dead. By the late 1900s, enough of an idea of Cambodge had been circulated in museums, expositions, and texts to have imparted a strong sense of the existence of Cambodge to France's cosmopolitan elite. Displays of Angkorean artifacts in Metropolitan museums, cultural pavilions in colonial expositions, the circulation of images and ideas of Cambodge in news media and travel literature, and the interweaving of Angkorean tropes into Phnom Penh's built environment gave the rubric of Cambodge a coherency, immediacy, and visibility that the first wave of explorers had not experienced. Arriving at this juncture in the making of Cambodge, Meyer, Groslier, Marchal, and others were caught in a conundrum. On the one hand, they could point to Cambodian culture. On the other, they were faced with a disappearance of many of those "signs" which had constituted Cambodge at museums and expositions where they had first encountered it. Often, the notion of disappearance and vanishing was an exaggerated response premised on the incompatibility of merging two styles and the undesirability of hybridity, whether it were art fashioned from a fusion of ancient and modern style, or from a mixture of European and Asian influences, or Cambodian and other Asian forms, such as Vietnamese.

The retrocession of Angkor and adjoining temples to Cambodge under the treaty of 1907 led to new emphasis on the state and whereabouts of artists. On his reconnaissance mission to Angkor and surrounds in 1907, Lunet de Lajonquière, finding the only signs of artistic production a few women weaving *sampots,* a few jewelers, and some pleasing carpentry, remarked that "we are far . . . from those who built Angkor" and cited this absence of identifiable art in close proximity to the temples as further proof of "the sudden and until now unexplained disappearance of the artistic sentiment brought into this country by the Kambudjas."[16]

George Maspéro, author of the first synoptic history of Angkor, founded Indochina's first colonial school of arts, the Bien-Hoa School, in Cochinchina in 1907. That year also saw the establishment of a palace workshop in Phnom Penh, whose output allegedly comprised souvenirs for visitors to the Musée khmer.[17] In 1912, the

Royal School of Decorative Arts was established as an adjunct to the workshop. King Sisowath's agency and initiative in establishing this artistic conservation effort are unclear. His attendance at the Marseille exposition in 1906 would have honed his awareness of European interest in Oriental ornament. The retrocession of Angkor in 1907 might have stimulated Sisowath's appetite to reclaim cultural terrain. An indication of the import Sisowath attached to this venture was his assignment of his son Prince Monivong as the manager of the palace "jewelry shop" on his return from St. Maixent Military Academy in France, where he had enrolled in 1907.[18] The establishment of a fine arts department by King Vajiravudh in Siam in 1912 illuminates a growing interest on the part of indigenous leaders in the region to define and conserve their artistic heritage.[19] Colonial support for expanded art education, as reflected in the founding of the Gia-Dinh School of Applied Arts in Cochinchina the same year, might also have played a part.[20]

In Cambodge, however, the establishment of school and workshop did little to stem the decline of luxury arts. The increasing "Europeanization" of Khmer art and architecture proceeded apace, horrifying Groslier, Meyer, and Marchal. In 1913, Groslier voiced his concerns about the imminent demise of Cambodian court dance in a beautifully produced book, published in Paris with a foreword by the minister of public education.[21] While Meyer channeled his dismay into the pages of his secret project, Marchal drew public attention to the neglect of Cambodge's native crafts in 1913.[22] The announcement in Paris of a new law on historic monuments in December 1913, and the parallel application of conservation legislation in Indochina, strengthened his cause.[23] In 1914, the French Ministry of Public Education funded new research directed by Groslier on the Angkor ruins.[24] In 1915 the Angkor Society proposed that the French Protectorate establish a school to foster traditional arts and crafts so as to protect them from extinction.[25] The society was perhaps also anxious to establish a means of artistic production to meet the demand for souvenirs fuelled by a fivefold increase in tourists to Cambodge since the turn of the century. The palace workshop's output had steadily declined, and by 1917, the attached school had only ten pupils.[26]

In 1916, Marchal was appointed to succeed Commaille as curator of Angkor, a position that gave his mission added clout.[27] The following year, on Groslier's return from war service, GGI Sarraut entrusted him with the portfolio of art education in Cambodge, seeing in Groslier a potential solution to the "crisis" in native arts.[28] Published the previous year, Groslier's book À l'ombre d'Angkor: Notes et impressions sur les temples inconnus d'ancien Cambodge had stressed the tenacity of Cambodian artistic tradition.[29] Now, perhaps propelled by a heightened sense of mortality after experiencing the vast carnage of World War I, Groslier rose vigorously to his new responsibilities. Those arts he had only years ago described as "immortal"[30] now seemed to Groslier to be on the verge of vanishing. He would devote the rest of his life to the conservation and containment of Cambodge's artistic tradition.[31] GGI Albert Sarraut, a leading advocate of associationist policies, believed that the future of colonial rule lay, not in assimilating cultures, but in "understanding [them] so that they may evolve, under our tutelage, in the framework of their civilization."[32] RSC Baudoin was instrumental in translating those associationist goals into a new arts education and museum policy for Cambodge. This sudden elevation of artistic education to a central concern of colonial government was linked to another, far deeper crisis of control.

The mass peasant protests that convulsed Cambodge in 1916 highlighted three major failings of French rule.[33] First was the protectorate's extraordinary lack of knowledge about the actual lives and contemporary aspirations of Cambodians, a failure stemming from a lack of interface at the grass roots and from French administrators' inability, through ignorance, lack of will, or the daily mechanics of distance, to penetrate indigenous communications systems at the village and district levels.[34] This ignorance also resulted from the protectorate's obsession with history as opposed to ethnography, which had long superseded history as the primary modality of colonial knowledge in British India. Whereas the latter had emerged as an "ethnographic state" by the late 1850s, Cambodge still remained very much a "museological state" by the 1910s, with the vast majority of state resources for research being devoted to history, archaeology, and museology, either via the EFEO or as grants to scholars.[35] This bias was reflected in the dearth of census reports for Cambodge. Second, the protests had revealed the near-complete diminishment of "white prestige" in Cambodge, pointing to the need to assert the impression of French authority.[36] Third, in subjecting the Cambodian populace to such a severe tax and corvée regime, France had breached its mandate to protect the population. It was now imperative, reported the GGI after visiting Cambodge, to raise France's profile and to shore up the image of its protective powers in the eyes of Cambodians.[37] As highly visible monuments of France's investment in Cambodge's culture, the proposed Museum and Arts School promised to realize both these goals.[38]

Baudoin and Groslier moved quickly to create a new artisanate. In July 1917, Baudoin instructed Residents throughout Cambodge to organize a census of artisans.[39] One hundred and thirty artisans were found in an estimated population of 1.5 million. However, most were no longer practicing, finding farming more profitable.[40] Great difficulties were encountered in rediscovering disappearing techniques.[41] A royal ordinance and GGI decree issued in December 1917 officially transformed the Royal School and adjoining workshops into a school of Cambodian arts, and in 1918 a plaque reading "École des arts cambodgiens" was erected on an old building of the Royal Palace.[42] Within three weeks of opening, the school had attracted over one hundred pupils. Demand for places was high.[43] In its first year, the school received 150,000 piastres from the administration. To facilitate the organization of conservation, and "to popularize Khmer art in all its manifestations," a Cambodian Department of Fine Arts was established on Baudoin's initiative in December 1919 with a portfolio covering historical monuments and ancient ruins, the Musée khmer, the École des arts cambodgiens, and tourism.[44]

Groslier blamed Cambodge's artistic collapse on both the nebulous demons of decadence and the stark dictates of market forces. His scheme centered on replacing the former patrons of Cambodian art—the wealthy elite who had once sponsored local artisans and now invested in foreign manufactures—with a new clientele: tourists and colonials. By rekindling the demand for Cambodian artifacts, he hoped to feed the embers of what he saw as an innate and eternal Khmer artistic potential. His moral project stretched far beyond classroom and corporation: to Groslier, art was the key to bringing "the Cambodian" out of "his apathy, his indifference" and thus galvanizing national energy.[45] Maintaining that "the Cambodian artisan has the same mentality as in the times of Suryavarman II," Groslier saw the art school as a rescue mission to protect, not only Khmer art and workmanship, but the very essence of Cambodge, from a slow and painful death.[46] In order to reanimate the spirit of Suryavarman II, Groslier's curriculum focused exclusively on the reproduction of ancient art forms and artifacts, so as to distill "drops of pure blood" from contemporary Khmer art, which Groslier saw as having become bastardized by over fifty years of Western influence.[47]

But the greatest artistry that Groslier recognized in contemporary Cambodians was their gift for copying. Recognition of this skill was also the root of his greatest fear for Cambodge's artistic future. So talented were the Cambodians as copyists that they copied indiscriminately, daring to reject ancestral patterns and to apply their gifts to non-Khmer objects, styles, and influences. It was precisely this talent for copying that led Groslier to insist so strongly on what he defined as a Khmer template, and on the need to steer Cambodge's new generation of artists away from their "decadent path" as copyists of the European and back onto ancestral tracks.[48] As Muan demonstrates in her brilliant study of the arts school, Groslier's key legacy was a "particular frame of copying" that still haunts visual production.[49] Of particular note was the "exclusively two-dimensional foundation of the curriculum," which ensured that students only ever drew directly from diagrams and patterns modelled on Khmer ornamentation, so as to acquire mastery of production of the decorative object. But this was no wholesale reproduction of Angkor. Quite rightly, Groslier rejected claims that his school was "simply teaching students to be copyists of the past." Instead, he was teaching his students to be copyists of the colonial conception of Khmerness.

ANGKOR IN VIEW

Colonialism's most compelling narratives were often visual, not purely textual. Even written versions of the past increasingly relied on images to convey those ways of life and art whose exoticism and distance simultaneously fired the metropolitan consumer's passion to read on and denied him the power, based on his own experience and the limits of European languages, to visualize that other world. It was an illustration, not the prose, that had engraved Angkor so clearly on the memory of the great travel writer Loti after his boyhood encounter with Cambodge in a colonial journal. Meyer was propelled to Indochine on the wings of a visual feast, a Cambodian dancer's tableau at Marseille. Fournerau's watercolors of Angkor, and not text messages, set the grand doyen of Angkor's conservation, Marchal, on his Angkor-bound trajectory. As the Indochinese volume of an early-twentieth-century encylopedia of images put it:

> THE IMAGE IS QUEEN. We are living in the century of photography. In papers, journals, magazines, it is images which first inform us, at a glance, of the events of the day, scientific discoveries as well as artistic novelties. The text only comes afterwards.
>
> BECAUSE TIME IS SHORT. In our era of the rat race, everyone, absorbed in his business, has no time to spare. To understand even a short article takes long minutes. A few seconds is all it takes to look at a drawing, a sketch, a photograph, and grasp its evocative meaning.[50]

European modes of copying and of print production, as well as image production, from daguerreotypes to photographs, expanded ways of seeing and means of representing the world. But the flip side of this proliferation of new media was the introduction of a new, restrictive spectrum congruent with the linear divisions of time and the sharp distinctions between racial, cultural, and territorial entities or clusters, which transformed the world as seen to kodachrome. The ability to see in black-and-white is an acquired art. Such linear, black-and-white imaging was not unknown in the region and had a particularly strong history in China, Japan, and Vietnam. But it is likely that most indigenous inhabitants of nineteenth- and early-twentieth-century Cambodians, like students encountered by the Reverend James in late-nineteenth-century Siam, had to learn to see in black-and-white. This grounding was only one facet of a much larger colonial process of teaching Cambodians how to see their world, how to see themselves in it, and how to reproduce what they were trained to see in text, images, and the plastic arts.

In an essay on the distinctions between history and anthropology, Clifford Geertz has remarked that " '[w]e' means something different, and so does 'they,' to those looking back than it does to those looking sideways." When "we" look back with a historian's gaze, Geertz argues, the "other" appears to us as ancestral; "we" constitutes a juncture in a cultural genealogy and "here" is heritage.[51] This description of the historical imagination holds true in part. When a French "we" looks back to a French (metropolitan) past, then ancestors do indeed function as the other, validating "our" (French) existence in the here and now. But what happens when the "we" becomes disrupted by colonialism? When a French we looked back in Cambodge, or a British we looked back in India, the we was split across time, place, and race. The other appeared, not as ancestral in an incorporative sense, but as a juncture in an other cultural genealogy. This was not solely because colonial accounts tended not to use the term "we" or "our" except where referring to the French, as in the formulation it is our (French) duty to preserve Angkor for the world; it was also because the very business of looking possessed its own colonial etiquette.

It was the business—a duty—of Cambodians to be observed, not to observe. Under the controversial 1884 convention, the "native" couldn't go out without a lantern after nine at night. From then until at least the 1900s, the crime of remaining invisible by moving in a dark space out of sight, unmarked by a blaze of light, incurred a hefty fine or corvée time. Bhabha has described landscape in all its recurrent metaphors, as "the inscape of national identity," emphasizing both the "question of social visibility," and "the power of the eye, to naturalize the rhetoric of national affiliation and its forms of collective expression."[52] But in Cambodge, ways of seeing Angkor were closely orchestrated. Cambodians might be featured as parts of Angkor in replicas of Angkor at international exhibitions. Angkor could be shrunk, molded, cleaned, reproduced by Europeans, but within this scheme Cambodians themselves were to retain the function of ornament to the grand European view, either by their absence—as the vanished Khmer—or through their presence—as contemporary evidence of the great distance they had fallen, in time and glory, from that past. Here was the crux of colonial identifications, one that still haunts contemporary Cambodian nationalisms. To be an authentic Khmer was to be a copyist. To be an authentic Khmer was to have vanished.

In his textual analysis of writing and repetition, Bhabha has described the desire to emerge as "authentic" through mimicry as "the final irony of partial representation."[53] In Cambodge, as Muan has shown, modes of mimicry were acutely circumscribed. Cambodians themselves were denied access to a larger view: instead, while Europeans operated within the grand vista of Angkor, Cambodian teachers and students at the school were charged with mimicking their ancestors through the repetition of Khmer motifs and ornamental fragments, whose authenticity was vetted by Groslier. From the founding of the Cambodian School of Arts in 1918 until Groslier's death in 1945, this curriculum had no room for life classes or landscape, only for instruction in the serial still lifes of history. Painting Angkor was a preserve of the French.[54] This prospectus differed markedly from that of the École des beaux arts d'Indochine, founded in 1924 by Sarraut's successor, GGI Merlin. Rejecting the "servile imitation of the past" and condemning their products as "pastiche[s] of vanished eras," the École des beaux arts sought instead to channel the artistic aspirations of young Asians into new directions, and students at Hanoi were taken on trips to ancient ruins to learn the "European" art of monumental landscapes.[55] In Phnom Penh the reverse held true; Angkor was, Muan writes, off-limits for total reproduction by the natives, and Cambodians who bypassed Groslier and tried their hand at landscape were berated as bad artists.[56]

Groslier's insistence on the proper place for Cambodian artists was not purely the product of Orientalist imaginings. Like a latter-day Ruskin, his distaste for artistic degeneracy tallied with a commitment to providing vocational training, and he envisioned the School of Cambodian Arts as a cog in a larger machine of cultural and government institutions—school, museum, retail outlets, and tourism departments—that would harmonize the needs of artists and clientele by training a vocational, economically viable artisanate.[57] This utilitarian view was shared by some Cambodians. In 1919, Minister of War and Education Ponn lobbied for a school place for Kong, an impoverished carpenter recently returned from military service in France, so that he could "earn his keep in the future."[58] Trade between the artisans and their tourist clientele was conducted through Corporations cambodgiennes, first conceived by Groslier in 1918.[59] A GGI decree of 9 August 1922 mandated the director of Cambodian arts "to direct and develop groups of free artisans with a view to maintaining the artistic traditions of Cambodia."[60] These artists' guilds were Groslier's answer to the virtual absence of Khmer shopkeepers in Cambodia.[61]

The following August, the GGI decreed the establishment in Phnom Penh of "a museum of art, history, and archaeology." Named the Albert Sarraut Museum, this would foster "the artistic renaissance among Cambodian artisans and provid[e] a local collection of Cambodian antiquities for tourists."[62] Perturbed by the entry of the contemporary into this antiquarian arena, the director of the EFEO recommended quarantining recent objects of artistic interest from archaeological finds and ancient ruins by the creation of three separate displays.[63] Groslier's objective to constitute an "exclusively Cambodian milieu" through the school syllabus was reflected in its architecture, modelled on a palace that once stood on the Elephant Terrace at Angkor Thom.[64] Echoes of Angkor were particularly apparent in the elaborate doors and shutters, carved by Cambodian craftsmen and students.[65] A marked departure from the tawdry Indochinoiserie of existing colonial buildings, and a deviation from Groslier's own condemnation of the aesthetic perils of miscegenation, the red brick, tile, and terra-cotta buildings allied the elegance of contemporary Buddhist monasteries with Angkorean ornament.[66] Groslier described the museum, opened in 1920, as "a living envelope, a contemporary work" enclosing the arts of the past, and later credited it with rescuing everything it had collected since 1920 from "certain and irreversible disappearance."[67] Under Groslier's direction, and equipped with a small library, the museum rapidly developed into an excellent resource for both scholars and tourists.[68] In 1922, the museum launched the journal *Arts et Archéologie Khmers.*[69]

The year 1922 also saw the first Parisian print run of Meyer's novel *Saramani: Une danseuse cambodgienne,* first published in 1919 in Saigon. According to Meyer's memoirs, publication of *Saramani* aroused a furor, not least due to its blanket condemnation of the conduct and attitudes of French colonial civil servants, who closed administrative ranks against him leading to his prompt transfer to Laos, where he continued his campaign, in a new location, for the rebuilding of ruins and a discovery of past traditions.[70] Meyer's arrogant portrayal of his thinly disguised literary alter ego, Komlah (Khmer for bachelor), as "the only one of his race to have penetrated the mystery of [the Khmer's] millennial domain," can have done little to enhance his popularity with such scholar-officials as Groslier, Finot, and the Orientalist establishment. But his juxtaposition of Khmer nobility with the "horrific plague of [Western] civilization that is wreaking a global trail of ugliness, vice, and suffering," would have struck a chord with other Khmerophiles. Like the Marseille exposition that had first fired his passion for Cambodge, Meyer's novel conflated woman, Angkor, and nation.[71] A similar dynamic shaped representations of Cambodge at the Marseille Exposition coloniale of 1922, which would provide the first major European market entry for products from Groslier's school.[72]

The Marseille exhibition was conceived as a "living history of our colonization," and its centerpiece was a "formidable palace of Angkor" designed to symbolize "the general synthesis of our efforts" in Indochina.[73] Structured from casts and molds of Delaporte's collection at the Trocadero, the 1922 Angkor was a vast improvement on the pastiches of 1889, 1900, and 1906, and managed to evoke something of the symmetry and grace of the original, leaving powerful and lasting impressions on visitors.[74] Replicas of bas-reliefs lined the inside, and rectangular ponds simulated the original moat. Inside the shell of Angkor, Laos, Cochinchina, Annam, Tonkin, and Cambodge were all on display.[75] The Angkor pavilion provided the perfect venue for a series of colonial career seminars, at which crowds of schoolchildren attended lectures on Khmer civilization.[76] Nearby, a local confectioner reproduced Angkor Vat in chocolate.[77] During the exposition, the Cambodian dance corps performed on the steps of the Angkor pavilion. Decked out in Oriental robes, Rodin's friend the American celebrity Loïe Fuller performed alongside the Cambodian dancers on at least one occasion.[78]

Sales at the Marseille exposition revealed a sizeable European clientele for Indochinese arts and crafts, some of which were produced at on-site workshops. The Marseille exposition had barely closed when the Ministry of Colonies informed GGI Merlin of another "exceptional opportunity for colonial propaganda"—the Exposition internationale des arts decoratifs, scheduled for 1925—and expressed a strong

FIGURE 7. Angkor in Marseilles, 1922. From *Exposition Nationale Coloniale de Marseille* (Marseille: Commiassariat General de l'Exposition, 1922). Courtesy of the Chamber of Commerce, Marseille.

desire for an Indochina exhibit in which each protectorate or colony would stress the "unique character" of its "local art." Groslier was appointed to oversee Cambodge's participation and to illuminate France's guardianship of "the aesthetic heritage of those races placed under our tutelage" and the "veritable renaissance of all indigenous arts."[79] The architect Gabriel Blanche, who would oversee Angkor's largest ever replica in Paris in 1931, was commissioned to design the Indochina pavilion.[80]

A postwar vogue in Oriental art would ensure the continued expansion of Groslier's initiative. "Khmer art is increasingly becoming the [most] fashionable Oriental art," wrote Victor Goloubew in 1927, predicting that Khmer jewellery would soon be on sale in Parisian boutiques. After the Marseille exhibition, he declared "Cambodian sampots are being bought and worn, and they are even making them in Paris and Lyon," while the costumes of Cambodian dancers are "regular accessories in our theatre and cinema studios."[81] The school, which numbered 165 students in 1922, expanded with the establishment of two annexes in Kompong Chhnang and Pursat in 1924. A late 1920s general survey on education in Indochina singled out the School of Fine Arts as proof that "artistic education was of the greatest interest for Indochina," pointed to the economic importance of Indochinese artists, and declared the school an appropriate model for Laos and Annam.[82] In 1929, output of the Corporations cambodgiennes had reached 4,434 items.[83] But Groslier's most important target market remained European residents of Indochina, and international tourists en route to or from Angkor.

TOURISM AND ANGKOR

By the 1920s, the ancient city of Angkor had become officially known as "Angkor Park" (parc d'Angkor), reflecting the landscaping and mapping of the temples into a designated tourist zone.[84] A troupe of Cambodian dancers performed scenes from the Ramayana at the Grand Hotel and in the Angkor temple.[85] "Cars now drive right up to the temple doors, telegraph wires touch its walls, and hotels are built within view of its towers," wrote Groslier of the changes wrought by the tourist trade.[86] In 1928, a luxury hotel was built at Angkor. At the EFEO's insistence, it was set at a distance from the ruins, so as not to detract from their grandeur.[87] As hotels went up, huts came down. Hoping to maximize Angkor's value as a public space, a GGI decree of 21 May 1930 revised the boundaries of Angkor Park to incorporate the western Baray, allowing the EFEO to dispose of more native dwellings. "Thanks to this expansion, recorded that year's bulletin, "we can tear down the unsightly *paillotes* [wooden houses on stilts] built during the last years and disfiguring access to the temple."[88] Attempts to marshal Angkor's spirituality for particular purposes were not entirely successful, however, and local practices persisted. Visiting Angkor in the late 1920s, a British travel writer found a small Buddhist community living within the great enclosure, their "apology for a monastery a mushroom growth of wood or matting which seems to cringe to the great ruin now in the keeping of the state. The monks and students wander round making offerings to the Buddha of the tower, his satellites and to another group on a lower level."[89] Further, pilgrims from Burma and elsewhere left their twentieth-century traces on the temple in the form of unofficial inscriptions recording visits and donations, as well as acts of filial piety, in Burmese and Chinese.

Angkor also had its share of regional tourism and diplomatic visitors. In 1921, King Vajiravudh's brother Prince Paribatra Nakhorn Sawan toured Angkor Vat and Angkor Thom, guided by the EFEO acting curator of Angkor, Charles Batteur.[90] In 1924, Mongkut's son Prince Damrong Rajanubhab travelled to Angkor, where he was received by an EFEO delegation that included a young Indologist named Suzanne Karpelès. He published his impressions in a book entitled *Nirat Nakhon Wat* (Journey to Angkor Vat).[91] From the 1920s, the Royal Siamese Railways ran tours from Bangkok through Angkor and Phnom Penh to Saigon, "the Paris of the East."[92] Between November 1928 and November 1929, the Hôtel des ruines d'Angkor hosted ninety-nine French visitors and twenty-four Annamese but only ten Cambodians. Improved transport facilities and a new vogue in travel literature in Annam led the women's daily *Phu Nu Tan Van* to organize Annamese excursions to Angkor Vat in the late 1920s.[93] Most travellers completed the 560-kilometer journey by car and boat from Saigon to Angkor in one day.[94] This is probably how Finot travelled with the monks Chuon Nath and Huot Tath on his various excursions to Angkor in the mid-1920s. "Whenever Finot visited Angkor on a tour of inspection," Tath recalled, "he took me with him to study Sanskrit in his offices at Angkor Vat."[95]

More intrepid visitors deliberately avoided the "wide, convenient, and practical road to Angkor, comparable to the roads of France," travelling instead by the narrow path across the jungle in search of kudos and wild game.[96] In 1929, an air route linking Saigon and Angkor, until then used only for mail and commerce, was first used for purely touristic purposes.[97] Travelling west in 1932, a two-hour car journey brought tourists from Angkor to the Siamese border, from which an "excellent and comfortable" train carried them to Bangkok.[98] In 1933, the sixty-five-bedroom Grand Hotel was opened in Siem Reap, offering visitors "modern comfort" and "good French cuisine"; its rooms were filled by an Angkor tourist office in Saigon's rue Catinat.[99] By the 1930s, American, English, and other European tourists to Angkor far outnumbered French visitors.[100] "So few French people know the joy that is Indochina, or the treasures of Angkor," lamented one Parisian representative of Thomas Cook who visited the temples in 1934.[101]

By retailing substitutes for original statues and trinkets in the form of authenticated Khmer art at a sales stand at Angkor, Groslier hoped to stem the desecration of the temples by European tourists.[102] Ten years after the new art school opened, the writer Harry Hervey remarked on the proliferation of ornamental metalwork and Buddhist trinkets to be found in Phnom Penh, while two decades later Norman Lewis wryly applauded the booming trade in silver filigree cigarette cases and powder compacts.[103] But the output of Groslier's arts school did not entirely satisfy tourist demands for "real" souvenirs. During the 1920s, the same passion for Orientalism also escalated the demand for Angkorean antiquities.

TRAFFICKING ANGKOR

While lessening indigenous demand for local crafts, Cambodge's incorporation into the global capital economy had created a network for the trafficking of native antiquities that would steadily deplete the country's ancient relics. The populariza-tion of Khmer culture through European museums, a growing tourist trade, an ex-panding international art market linking elite circles in Siam with prospective buy-ers as far afield as the United States, and improved communication routes to Angkor, all created a lucrative market for objects of antiquity.[104] Numerous individuals in Indochina—usually enterprising dealers or colonial administrators—continued to send to the European market articles that had been "discovered" in the jungle or pro-cured from natives living near important archaeological sites.[105] The rapid growth of tourism to Indochina in the aftermath of World War I increased the theft of antiqui-ties, while the desire on the part of some Europeans to leave their imprint on Angkor sparked a wave of graffiti on the ancient stones.[106]

Authorities in Indochina, after repeated proddings from the EFEO, made in-termittent and halfhearted attempts to curb such traffic. However, most provincial officials looked the other way. Not until the boundaries of Greater France's *patrimoine* were violated by the appearance of several specimens of antique Khmer statuary in American museums was the GGI prompted to take action. In 1922, an article in the *Revue Archéologique* bemoaned the "emigration" of a total of eight masterpieces of Angkorean art to the United States and the recent acquisition of one such piece by the Fogg Museum.[107] The reaction of the Indochinese academic establishment was swift. The following year Finot, director of the EFEO in Hanoi, wrote to the GGI submitting a proposal from members of the Commission of Antiquities and the di-rector of Cambodian arts (Groslier), who believed that "the ability to acquire travel souvenirs would be greatly appreciated by tourists, without causing the least archae-ological damage, as long as the necessary precautions were taken to prevent any ill-considered transfer."[108] Later that month, RSC Baudoin signed an *arrêté* allowing the sale of objects from historic monuments, with a certain proviso: the objects must be without scientific or artistic interest. Spiritual significance, it seemed, did not merit consideration. The curator of the Angkor temple complex and the director of Cambo-dian arts would draw up a register of objects for sale, which must then be sold only through the Musée Albert Sarraut. All revenue would go to the EFEO to be invested in work on Angkor.[109]

Such measures did little to satisfy the appetite of a twenty-three-year-old An-dré Malraux, who was arrested for pilfering crateloads of statuary from Banteay Srey temple in 1923. Indeed, the GGI's creation of a special commission in August 1923 to study and tighten regulations to preserve the historical and archaeological remains of the peninsula may well have precipitated his quest. Earlier in the 1920s, Prince Damrong was implicated in a scheme concocted by Malraux to sell Thai statuary to a US private collector for some US$50,000. By 1924, at the estimation of one Parisian antiques dealer, severed heads of Angkorean statuary "much less beautiful" than those purloined by Malraux had a market value of approximately 40,000 francs. At Kompong Chhnang, Groslier himself intercepted the riverboat taking Malraux and his wife, their friend Chevasson, and crateloads of bas-reliefs and statues to Phnom Penh. Malraux pleaded not guilty in the ensuing trial, claiming that he had only taken goods from "abandoned property." In the witness box stood Parmentier, now head of the Archaeological Service, condemning the act, but so impressed by Malraux's mastery of that scuptural surgery first practiced by Delaporte that he praised the young writer's dexterity with "picks and stone saws." Malraux claimed in his defense that he had planned to donate any superior pieces to the Musée Guimet.[110] Soon after being charged and fined, Malraux began work on a fictional account of the episode, *La voie royale* (The royal way).

Published in 1929, *La voie royale* depicts Cambodge as a "land of decay . . . a land possessed and tamed to humble uses, its ancient hymns, like its temples, fallen on evil days: of all dead lands most dead." As he hacks his way through the jungle on his mission to dismember Khmer monuments, the young Claude feels himself "disintegrating like the world around him." The most vivid descriptions in the work are not of the temple ruins but of the jungle, where "every thought grew turbid, decomposed."[111] Despite having stood on opposite sides of the law, Groslier and Malraux clearly shared similar preoccupations with degeneration. While Groslier's own writings, numerous travel writers, and the propaganda of colonial exhibitions celebrated the success of his attempt to reverse the flow of degeneration through his artistic revival, others painted a different picture, recognizing the strength of indigenous resistance.

Goloubew alleged that the modernist aspirations of Cambodians had doomed Groslier's campaign from the start, while Finot, aware of the difficulties of defending "an art steeped in legend and pious traditions from the venal attacks of a nihilist epoch," also judged Groslier's experiment an overall failure marked by several fleeting successes.[112] Twenty years after Groslier's appointment as director of the arts in Cambodge, a graduate of the Arts School named Say highlighted the divergence between the romantic prescriptions of Groslier and the actual aspirations of contemporary Cambodians. In a column in *Nagaravatta* in 1937, Say congratulated the protectorate for having established the art school and museum to "save the arts of the pure Khmer," "preserve Khmer antiques for the future," and display Khmer arts to foreign visitors. Yet a sense of frustration permeates Say's commentary, indicating that his own artistic inclinations had been hampered by precisely that exclusively Cambodian milieu which Groslier had created to free each artist's inner Suryavarman. In its very act of "saving the Khmer nation," Say suggested, the School of Fine Arts had inhibited the development of Cambodge's national economy. Some graduates of the school went on to work in the Albert Sarraut Museum or elsewhere in the administration. Yet those who made a living from selling their wares in markets in Phnom Penh and the provinces, Saigon, and Paris, often only earned a tiny margin, their stultified works increasingly eclipsed by the modern adaptations of their Chinese and Vietnamese counterparts. While Groslier's school had provided a lifeboat for Khmer traditional arts, only schooling in modern methods could provide a lifeline to Khmer artisans, Say implied.[113] A different critique was leveled at the arts school by Henri Marchal, who lambasted the market supply of "standardized models of bronze dancers," which were neither "Cambodian nor European," as the outcome of a rage for souveniring that was supported by some French established in Cambodge, and that even Groslier's arts school was powerless to resist, leaving the Cambodian artist no way to fight this commercial current.[114]

Say's subversive assessment made little headway in French colonial propaganda, which continued to extol the School of Cambodian Arts, focusing instead on the school's international success. From 1930 to 1940, the Corporations cambodgiennes displayed their output in ninety international exhibitions, mostly in French provinces, but also in Algeria, San Francisco, Prague, and Milan.[115] A silversmith who had graduated from the school in 1922, Minh Moll won several awards for his work at regional and international exhibitions, established his own business, and won fame among Europeans in Cambodge for his work in "all Cambodian Styles: Local, Angkor-Wat, Modern and de Luxe," achievements that one French newspaper saw as proof of the Cambodian elite's unequivocal desire to "collaborate with the French government."[116]

But French administrators and journalists were not the only ones to smother the voice of Say and others like him who, trained in the Arts School, yearned to experiment with new technologies and to fuse their knowledge with techniques from different eras or cultures. Although for Say the tensions between this restrictive proscription and the yearnings of twentieth-century Cambodians, fed by their experiences of travel, of things outside the "Khmer" mold, were hard to reconcile; outside of the arts world, national arts and crafts were the one area in which secular nationalists, religious reformists, and pro-democracy and pro-monarchy activists came together in their vision of a material realm of Khmerness. By allowing the "essence" of Khmerness to be distilled and frozen in the plastic arts, these nationalists could direct their efforts towards movement and development to political arenas while promoting "tradition" in arts and crafts as an unyielding yardstick of Khmer cultural superiority, and one that could compete with the perceived economic superiority and business skills of the Vietnamese and Chinese.

REBUILDING ANGKOR IN SIEM REAP, MARSEILLE, AND PARIS

In the early 1920s, the scholar Victor Goloubew documented influences from Java, Champa, and China in Khmer art, and identified the work of Chinese artisans in the sixteenth-century renovation of the eastern wing of Angkor Vat.[117] But by this point Cambodge had secured its place in elite indigenous and European imaginations as a specifically Khmer monument. Conferment of its architectural ancestry on "the Khmers" did not detract from the contemporary belief of most Europeans that the Khmers of the day could not have built Angkor. This evaluation persisted throughout the 1930s, despite the fact that the rebuilding of Angkor was carried out largely by Cambodian coolies. But the official reconstruction of Angkor, like the view of Angkor, on-site and in its offshore replications, remained the preserve of the French. The logic ran that Cambodians were artists because they built Angkor, but that only the French were capable of *rebuilding* Angkor. Its subtext was acknowledgment, in academic circles, that the Khmers were excellent artists but bad builders. This reasoning would not change until the 1940s.

Since its inception, the Angkor conservation program had proceeded under the broad mantle of "renovation." Its focus was on the perfecting of Angkor Park, on the extraction of contemporary dwellings, the choreography of national ceremony, the "cleaning up," deforesting, and strengthening of the principal monuments in the temple complex. Actual reconstruction, however, was considered taboo, and the ruins were fixed in place by concrete props and iron buffers.[118] Meanwhile, the EFEO's rebuilding of Angkor continued, encouraged by GGI Pasquier, who saw archaeological enterprise as valuable tourist bait.[119] Expanded excavations, new scholarship, and tighter collaboration with the Archeologische Dienst (AD) in Java brought fresh revelations. Building on Goloubew's research of the previous decade, Marchal further elaborated the multiple foreign cultural influences in Khmer art.[120] Links with Thai scholarship were also tightened.[121] During the 1930s, scholars discerned that the temples of Angkor "were not public spaces, like the temples of classical antiquity or our cathedrals," but were "mausoleums, funerary temples, each one doubtless holding the human remains of a king."[122] In 1931, commencing at Banteay Serei, under Coedès' new directorship and following a series of visits to the AD, the EFEO officially adopted anastylosis, a technique involving the dismantling and subsequent reconstruction of ancient sites.[123] The same year, another opportunity presented itself for Angkor's rebuilding, at the Exposition coloniale internationale in Paris.

Issued in Hanoi, the general directives for Indochina's participation in the 1931 exposition conceived a general exhibit to demonstrate the scope and potential of colonial activity in Indochina, and to mount local displays that would communicate to the public the "Indochinese reality" by broadcasting "real" images of France in Asia.[124] The apotheosis of this window on the real was the largest ever re-creation of Angkor Vat. Costing 12.5 million francs, it was built to disappear.

The commissioner general of the exposition had first mooted a permanent replica of Angkor Vat in 1926, but his plans were promptly quashed by the EFEO, which objected that his proposed pavilion would misrepresent the great Khmer temple. As well as being an inaccurate and culturally insensitive undertaking, such a replica would be downright dangerous, claimed the director of the EFEO. Built in the tropics, Angkor was structurally ill-suited to the European climate, and replicating the technical faults of Angkor's architects in reinforced concrete was a recipe for rapid disintegration. Moreover, the basement, entries, and other features of the planned exhibition hall would betray the spirit of this sublime monument, fusing a mockery of a Khmer temple with stairs from a Loire château. Despite these technical reservations, the EFEO welcomed the idea of a large Angkor pavilion as an excellent promotional device for France, empire, and the EFEO, and approved the plan, but only on condition that Angkor be built to disappear.

Two eminent Parisian architects, Charles and Gabriel Blanche (father and son), were assigned to reproduce Angkor. During the 1920s, the Blanches had supervised the cleaning and recording of over eight hundred temple sites at Angkor and, assisted by a sculptor, had immortalized numerous bas-reliefs and structural features of the temples in plaster cast for future replication.[125] On their return to France, the Blanches mapped out the entire Indochina section to reproduce the spatial arrangement of Angkor. A causeway ran from the gates of Angkor to the edge of the Daumesnil lake. Pavilions were arranged on either side, correlating with the temple's monasteries and libraries. *Nagas* and lions flanked the walkways. At night, art deco lighting illuminated the temple towers and steps in reds, greens, and yellows. This reconstruction was symbolic of the belief, now firmly established in French academic and administrative circles, that colonial intervention in Cambodian culture had led to the country's "reincarnation."[126] It also reflected the place of architecture as a major keystone of the sophistication of an indigenous civilization.[127] But most important in terms of its development as a national site, the Parisian palladium represented the most brazen attempt so far to further Angkor Vat's secularization. This was also reflected in the "logo-ization" and commercialization of Angkor in the Parisian press, where the temple's silhouette was used to launch safari suits, pith helmets, refrigerators, travel clocks, and package tours.[128]

The temple's transplantation to metropolitan soil, and its integration into a larger historical and geographical theme park, were nothing new. And, from a curatorial point of view, as Marchal might have argued, it was infinitely preferable to display "Khmer idols" in the context of the temple where they had once sat, in the center of a sanctuary dedicated to them, however artificial, than "isolated in a museum gallery."[129] Angkor's exaggerated presence in the Métropole's political and cultural heartland represented an unequivocal assertion of France's place as the rightful guardian of this colonial heirloom. Most important, it presented the French, not the Cambodians, as the only people capable of rebuilding Angkor here and now, in the present. Unprecedented in size and scope, this symbolic incorporation of Angkor into France's *patrimoine* was reinforced by exhibition literature. As accompanying propaganda made clear, Angkor's builders (like the French) had dominated Indochina. Stealthily, unwittingly perhaps, the French were now presenting themselves as Angkor's rightful inheritors, and Paris as the consummate sanctuary for its divinities. Describing contemporary Khmers as "timid debris" and Angkor as the symbol of a "dead civilization," which it was France's duty to revive, Claude Farrère declared France the "legitimate heir of this ancient Khmer civilization."[130] This binary of past and present resonated in the juxtaposition of the temple to reconstructed Cambodian wooden houses, which provided a powerful architectural foil to the Angkor extravaganza.[131]

An integral part of the Blanches' design for the Indochina exhibitionary complex, these "humble native houses," "evocative of bush and swampland," provided the stage for "whole families, rushed over from Cambodge, Laos, or Tonkin." Half-naked waxwork natives provided the finishing touches to one such structure, labelled "Cambodian rural household."[132] The use of an identical, neighboring *paillote* as the pavilion for Indochina's wildlife underscored the implicit assumption of the natives' animal nature.[133] Here was the raw material, the simple native whom France had saved from degeneration, but who still needed the benefits of French economic regeneration and moral uplifting. What better material to communicate the assumed qualities of native docility, malleability, and immobility than wax? Those who doubted Khmer latent potential need only look to a symbol of ancestral glory in Angkor. Between the Blanches' bipolar world of ancient glory and native stasis, a separate Cambodge pavilion, designed by Groslier and closely modelled on his arts school, represented the contemporary phase of French colonial renewal. The souvenir shops and workshops organized by Groslier in the arts section of the Indochina exhibit testified to the success of French efforts to unleash this Angkorean atavism, demonstrating the poignancy and importance of the *mission civilisatrice*.

In addition to proclaiming France's dominance in Indochina, and the vigor and valor of France's conservation efforts vis-à-vis the stasis of indigenous races, Angkor acted as a crucial signifier of Khmer difference. France's projection of Angkor Vat as the key emblem of Indochina fostered Khmer national pride and aroused Vietnamese indignation. Vietnamese employees of the EFEO later claimed that they and many other Vietnamese had deeply resented the constant glorification of Angkor in colonial exhibitions.[134] By depicting each of the five separate constituents of Indochina as crystalline, discrete structures, the exhibition organizers implicitly emphasized the need for the umbrella of French control, without which these distinct cultures would degenerate into a morass of violence and destruction. This message was particularly aimed at Annam, the site of violent anticolonial protest in recent years. Indochina's independence would result in the "massacre or enslavement of all Cambodians," wrote the novelist Claude Farrère, describing communist chants of "Indochina for the Indochinese" as a Soviet plot to extinguish the Khmer nation that France had saved from destruction.[135] The exposition was not only an attempt to create a new identity for *"la France des cinq continents."*[136] It was also designed to give tangible form to the colonial fiction of five unique, racially and culturally distinct countries of Indochina, depicted as the five flowers *(cinq fleurs)* of Indochina in scholar-official Jean Marquet's novel of that name, by emphasizing the individual "geographic, ethnic, political, and moral personality" of Indochina's constituent countries.[137] On the threshold of a vital, formative decade in the crystallization of Cambodian nationalism, the 1931 exposition gave millions of visitors a few months of phantasmagoria. But on the close of the exhibition, in a reversal of the French trope, Angkor was reduced to rubble and drifting dust clouds. While Angkor had vanished, the notion of the Kmae daem had gained increasing momentum.

Ironically, by the 1930s, when French savants had discovered that the temples of Angkor had historically never been "public spaces," colonial reconstructions of the temple complex and the political choreography of cultural ceremony had irrevocably restructured Angkor as an arena of national, public space. The colonial drive to return Angkor to a state of past perfection ensured that what was billed as a rehabilitation was in fact a re-creation. In film, literature, art, architecture, and archaeology, Angkor was remade as both the embodiment of Khmer national essence and an irretrievable, unachievable, and impossible moment of cultural perfection. Suspended in space and time as an idée fixe, embodied in the replications of Angkor, the image of the Kmae daem epitomized the logic of colonial conversion.

Through a curious process of copying and replication, of imitation, and, ultimately, of anticipation, the credentials of the "Original Khmer" were simultaneously invented and validated in textual, material, and visual fields. But this was no simple facsimile of the past. In Cambodge, mimicry anticipates rather than repeats: what was mimicked was precisely that which Viollet-le-Duc and other conservators in nineteenth-century Europe declared an impossibility to reconfigure—a void. To many Cambodians, attempts at this blind copying of Angkor were perplexing. When, in the 1930s, a Russian dancer visiting Cambodge attempted to copy the gestures of *apsaras* inscribed on Angkor's bas-reliefs, she encountered complete puzzlement on the part of her Khmer audience.[138] When Cambodians applied their alleged atavistic powers of mimicry to the contemporary and Western, they met with unequivocal derision. Cambodians wearing Western hats were scorned and lampooned in European writings, and Cambodian women adopting European modes of dress stimulated particular angst. The menace of mimicry, Bhaba writes, is its double vision and its power to articulate "those disturbances of cultural, racial and historical difference that menace the artistic demand of colonial authority."[139]

In 1940, Muan writes, when an entrepreneur named Say developed a stamping machine for embossing silver boxes, buckles, and earrings, Groslier declared that his "dangerous" invention should be thrown away, and the inventor shot. Groslier's production of the visual logic of seriality described by Anderson relied, not on modern technologies of mass reproduction, but on what Muan describes as "exquisite handmade . . . identical multiples."[140] Handmade or not, the very fact of their serial production offended purists like Henri Marchal, who saw these plastic translations of the two-dimensional ornament at which Cambodians excelled as "bastard productions" that were "neither Cambodian nor European."[141] These artifacts also operated as "semiotic illusions" whose seriality helped to construct the ideal of a bounded national aesthetic, so producing what Michael Herzfeld describes as " iconicities of national culture."[142]

The colonial cultivation of a school of artists taught to reproduce Angkorean motifs at once emphasized the inability of Cambodians to attempt the grander scheme and revealed the reluctance of their "protectors" to equip them with training in architecture. What the school did succeed in producing was the illusion of an atavistic memory chain linking the Cambodians of the 1930s and 1940s to the builders of Angkor Vat as members of the same production line. Where Lunet de Lajonquière had remarked, in 1907, on how far (in time) "we" (Europeans resident in Cambodge) were from the builders of Angkor, European visitors to Cambodge during the 1930s and 1940s, encouraged to visit the arts school as part of the standard itinerary, felt that they were witnessing a cultural continuum. Visiting Vichy Indochina in 1942, one Frenchwoman was amply rewarded in Phnom Penh in her quest to *"retrouver le passé dans le présent."*[143]

> How true it is that Cambodge, under a frail modern veneer, remains true to its antique tradition. . . . Young Cambodians work with the tools of their ancestors. Borrowing their motifs from the stones of Angkor, thus linking the present to the past, they chisel designs as delicate as lace on silver, copper, wood, stone. . . . The design is better imprinted in their memory than on paper. Here is the real Cambodge: the artisan. . . . By nature, Khmers are neither farmers, nor functionaries, nor merchants. They are essentially artisans. . . .[144]

CONCLUSION

During the first decades of colonial rule, it was primarily European scholars, administrators, and visitors who related to Angkor as national monument. Indeed, the apparent lack of interest displayed by Norodom Yukanthor vis-à-vis the Cambodge exhibit at the 1900 exposition, by Son Diep and others towards the Cambodge pavilion at the 1906 exposition, and by early-twentieth-century students in France during their compulsory museum visits indicates that this way of seeing and relating to Angkor as icon was not yet in place. For the Khmer poet In, writing in 1909, Angkor was a source of veneration and fascination, and a site of royal and religious ceremony, but was far from being a sign of the modern Khmer nation. The lack of Khmer print media and literature on Angkor during the following two decades make it impossible to chart the precise trajectory of Angkor's consolidation in the Khmer imagination as a national icon. What is clear is that by the 1930s the process was already in motion, and Angkor was increasingly held up as a model of national potential and a sign of Khmer racial supremacy. While the Blanche brothers were erecting their Angkor palladium in Paris, a 1931 article in the Khmer newspaper *Kampuchea Bodemien* preached the virtues of national revival through scholarly application. "Our ancestors were not stupid," the article continued, "they were as knowledgeable as the European race is today, that's why they built Angkor Vat, to leave as a legacy for us . . . so that we can study and so that other nations won't look down on us."[145]

Writing in, and of, Cambodia at the cusp of the new millennium, Muan concluded her intricate analysis of the colonial legacy with the observation that the model and the copy—as well as the procedure taught for its multiplication—seemed to have become a form of identity, a "Cambodian" way of making art.[146] Muan's astute insight invites a more sinister twist to the notion of Cambodian as copyist. The model and the copy had emerged as forms of identity not only in the art world; the very art of copying had become a central pillar of Cambodian national identity as defined by Europeans. When a "true Khmer," a Kmae daem, becomes one who is innately gifted as a copyist, his claim to authenticity hinges on his ability to copy. Those who create, like Say with his stamping machine, like the Mahanikay with their poetic license and eclectic practices, like the monks who worship Buddhist idols at the Hindu temple of Angkor, stepping out of their true ancestral, Angkorean time, have failed in some way to be Khmer, since being Khmer requires copying. But it is not enough just to be a copyist; what makes one a real Khmer is one's ability to copy things that are really Khmer.

A Khmer who copies a European by sporting European clothes or mastering French is déclassé, hybrid, inauthentic. And, since the Khmers are pronounced from the 1860s onward as a vanished race, since their artisans, as late as the 1910s, are denounced as dying out, since their monks are denounced as degenerate, parasitic, and unaware of the true words of Buddha, since the "real" Khmer no longer exist, they must be created: the authentic model must be found on which these innately skilled copyists can model themselves. If the authentic model is not to be found, then Buddhism in Cambodge, which has never been practiced as a nationally bounded religion but spread west into Siam and east into Cochinchina, risks becoming inauthentic and non-Khmer. The search for such authenticity, by Khmers and Europeans, shaped the reform of Buddhism in Cambodge and the development of a national religion, or *sasana-jiet.*

7 | Secularizing the *Sangha*, 1900–1935

Outside the rarefied domain of Buddhist studies, colonial perceptions of the *sangha* were colored by a deeper ambivalence than that shaping the scholarly mistrust of erratic scribes and inaccurate scriptures. In the 1860s, the entrepreneur L. Faucheur felt nothing short of repulsion for Cambodge's ubiquitous monks whom he nicknamed *talapoins* (small, yellowish monkeys), with their shaved heads, yellow costumes, begging bowls, and hypocrisy, their ducklike walk and mendacity. Gradually, however, his feelings changed to admiration for the monks' immersion in religion, dedication to children's education, and observation of religious discipline.[1] Others clung to their initial negative impressions. "I don't like it one bit when I see those yellow rags bustling about near the coolies," declares Barnot, a railway engineer in Henry Daguerches' novel *Le Kilomètre 83,* published in 1913 but loosely based on the author's tour of Battambang as a director of artillery for Cochinchina in 1908–1909. "It was a pretty astute observation," ruminates Barnot's partner. "Some shifty 'yellow rag' lay in ambush behind nine out of every ten obstacles confronting our rails."[2] In a later poem, "The Monk of Angkor" (Le bonze d'Angkor), Daguerches merges ignorance and enigma in the figure of a lone monk whose "shapeless robes" signify his detachment from desire and disdain for life, a detachment which also explains his failure to "decipher [either] the hollow architecture" or its bas-reliefs.[3] "Disdain for the devoted crowd" distinguishes the monk in Maurice Olivient's poem "Le bonze," also published in 1918.[4] These literary characterizations of Khmer monks as alternately venerable, mystical, arrogant, ignorant, and rebellious reflected the administration's ambivalent attitude towards the *sangha,* whose powerful status jarred with larger colonial projects of subjugation.[5]

But these perceptions did not stop there. Increasingly, such literary metaphors informed policy as well as prose and verse. Much like the veil, which aroused complex feelings of fascination and discomfort over its power to obstruct the business of bodily surveillance in the Middle East, monastic robes were an intense irritant to the colonizing eye. *Loques jaunes,* the disparaging colonial epithet for the *sangha,* assumed powers of disguise and deception, their veiling function most commonly associated with issues of criminal shelter and tax evasion.[6] Equally frustrating to the modern bureaucrat was the minute and concealed shape of the *chhaya* which each monk carried on his person as a mark of his ordination. Under Mahanikay practice, upon ordination a lay preceptor or elder monk would transcribe the *chhaya* on a long sliver cut from a palm leaf. This would then be rolled into a tiny ball threaded on cotton, encased in gum, and "threaded on to prayer beads, in such a way that it could not be opened."[7] No less galling to the agents of colonial order were the *sangha*'s immunity from prosecution and the moral injunction whereby "no monk may make a complaint against anyone," which effectively debarred monks from becoming colonial informants.[8] A disgruntled RSC Baudoin reported how this rigorously observed precept was a godsend to "troublemakers," who "ask to *prendre le froc* or dress in yellow robes without ordination, and escape police enquiries by taking shelter in pagodas."[9] Surveillance of the Thommayuth and Mahanikay sects was made easier by the identifiable differences in dress. Indeed, it was in their confusion of these distinctions that Nath and Tath drew some of the most trenchant criticisms from more conservative members of the *sangha* and government.[10]

The tax-free status of monks also rankled, and many colonial administrators likely shared the sentiments of Ch. Lemire, who described "the excessive number of monks [as] a deadweight that continues to weigh heavily on revenues in Siam, as in Cambodge and Laos.[11] The sheer size of the *sangha,* its resistance to administrative reforms, its close ties with monks and monasteries in Siam, and its conspicuous influence over a deeply reverent population fostered increasing unease among colonial administrators. By the early twentieth century, recognition of the *sangha*'s value as a pillar of the status quo, and appreciation for the reverence in which monks were held by the population, was commonly tempered by fear of their potential to turn that power against the protectorate, dislike of their "arrogance," and contempt for their "laziness" or "ignorance." At the root of these mixed feelings was a deep anxiety over the *sangha*'s existence on the margins of the secular world in a spiritual corridor which allowed monks to elude state control.

The Buddhist polities of Southeast Asia merged *sangha,* kingship, and polity in a constellation of interdependent and overlapping roles and expectations whose ideological fulcrum consisted of the three jewels of Buddhism: the Buddha, dhamma, and *sangha.* This trilogy is reflected in one precolonial version of the Cambodian Bansavatar (Chronicles), which tells how Ketumala (Jayavarman II), son of the god Indra and Queen Dharavati, "was permitted to see heaven and was taught by Indra how to protect Buddhism and make Cambodia prosperous."[12] As living embodiment of the dhamma, the king (dhammaraja, or righteous ruler) acted as mediator between social disorder and order, and had a moral obligation to protect the *sangha,* which mediated between this fettered world and the state of deliverance.[13] In turn, a virtuous society ministered to the *sangha.*[14] Monks earned supreme respect as the "living embodiments and spiritual generators of Buddhism."[15] Both the welfare of the state and the welfare of the *sangha*—as reflected in the number and opulence of functioning monasteries, the strictness of monastic practice, and the demonstration of clerical erudition and scholarship in the scriptures—were seen as evidences of a king's meritoriousness and his right to rule.[16]

The symbiotic relationship between *sdic* (king), *srok* (district), and *sangha* (monastic community) was underpinned by traditions of land ownership whereby the temple and monastery belonged not to the monks but to the village and ultimately to the king, who owned all land in Cambodia.[17] The conceptualization of the king as the protector and nurturer of the *sangha,* and the linkage of sovereignty to Buddhist patronage, was complicated by the energetic sponsorship of scholarship by the Kingdom of Siam, as reflected in the continued devotion to effigies of Siamese kings among Khmer communities in Cochinchina in the 1920s.

Despite these distinctions, there was fluidity between the *vat* and village life. In precolonial Cambodia as in Siam, the *sangha* offered one of the few paths to power outside of birthright. On leaving the *sangha,* highly trained monks could gain access to positions of great power in the secular world.[18] Membership in the *sangha* was open to males from all social strata, and completion of at least one Buddhist lent in a *vat* was tantamount to a male rite of passage in Cambodian society.[19] Popularly known as *uesaa* (Khmer for wet season), this three-month period typically encompassed a grounding in personal discipline, basic teachings of Buddha, and memorization of a few Pali texts.[20] A complex code of linguistic and ritual etiquette governed interaction between laity and monks, whose ethereal status was reinforced by separate living quarters, exemption from taxation and conscription, and the prohibition of physical contact with women.[21] The only restrictions on monastic mobility were during the *uesaa,* when monks were forbidden to leave their temple other than for exceptional reasons such as family illness or death. Monks traveled in search of scriptures and to practice healing arts, as well as to make pilgrimage to holy sites. The mobility of the *sangha* simultaneously defied colonial stereotypes of the passive, immobile Cambodian and threatened to destabilize the very structure of the protectorate. Long part of a peripatetic, Theravadan community extending from Sri Lanka, Burma, and Siam in the west to Sipsongbanna and the Shan states in the northwest, Cambodian monks were a natural focus of colonial efforts to curtail movement across Cambodge's borders.

Another dimension of this eclecticism was regional diversity. Nineteenth-century Cambodge possessed, in the words of Leclère, "no church, no national *sangha*" but a multitude of *sangha* whose primary geographic locus of identity was the village, district, or provincial center where their *vat* was located, and not the nation.[22] In addition to their much vaunted role as centers of education, curators of Buddhist scriptures, and diffusers of a socially binding culture, monasteries also tied isolated districts into a loosely knit conglomeration of *sroks* at whose apex stood the Buddhist monarch, in whom temporal power was invested.[23] Equilibrium between these diverse spheres of spirituality, status, and duties was maintained without rigid institutional structures.

From the turn of the century onward, the protectorate increasingly began to regard the *sangha* with suspicion as an arena beyond its bureaucratic ken and introduced legislation in education, taxation, and travel restrictions aimed at separating the *sangha* in Cambodge from that in Siam and placing the *sangha* under direct state control. These hardening attitudes were shaped by the millenarian movements of the late nineteenth century, Doumer's drive to centralize and standardize government procedures during his term in office from 1897 to 1902, and the 1905 Separation of Powers Act in France. The latter, legal bifurcation of church and state in the Métropole set in motion a new compartmentalization of religion in Cambodge. The two main targets for this intervention were temple schools, long situated within monasteries and controlled by the *sangha,* and the monastic body, which, as an embodiment of Buddha's teachings, represented a particularly complex and quasi-sacred site of cosmic power.

By bringing monks under the jurisdiction of colonial courts and issuing them with identity cards, the colonial administration partially eroded the cosmic aura that had long formed a wellspring of the *sangha's* moral authority. Educational reforms promoted the incorporation of modern, secular subjects into temple school curricula. New restrictions on travel to Siam attempted to restrict the *sangha's* movement to a sphere cohering with such bounded, cartographic notions and contributed to the crystallization of a *sasana-jiet* by aligning monastic mobility with the geopolitical boundaries of Cambodge. The adoption of Khmer as a national curricular language and its promulgation through schoolbooks among minority ethnic groups in Cambodge such as Thais, and among Khmer communities in Cochinchina, transported these notions into an ethnolinguistic community oriented away from Siam and towards a Khmer cosmos within the colonial construct of Indochina.

Linking these policies was the insertion of the state into the web of relationships between the *sdic, sangha,* and the *srok,* a territorial rather than political concept referring to the immediate locality of a temple and village. By bringing temple schools under state control and making monks targets of Sûreté surveillance, the protectorate upset the equilibrium that had previously governed the *sdic–sangha–srok* trilogy. In their rejection of animism and other practices as superstition, these policies also privileged Buddhism as Cambodge's national religion, and so dovetailed with the cultural and scholarly projects considered earlier in this book. Alongside Chuon Nath and Huot Tath's development of a Khmer national Buddhism, these administrative measures created space for a new mantra which came to be promoted by the Cambodian monarchy, namely the slogan "Nation, Religion, King." Adapted from the jingoistic Edwardian formula "God, Nation, King" by King Rama VI (1910–1921) into the Thai *chat-sasana-phra maha'kesat* (nation-religion-monarch), the slogan appears to have first entered Khmer usage in the 1930s.

A significant aspect of these interventions was the official promulgation of an ethnolinguistic, Khmer nation through primary and temple school programs involving the state's training of monk and lay Khmer language teachers. Colonial intervention in the management and curriculum of *vat* schools saw the creation of a corps of professional teacher-monks. These programs dovetailed with the prescriptions for monastic reform and higher Pali education considered earlier, paving the way for the consolidation of a vernacular Khmer nation, the promulgation of a *piesaa-jiet,* and for its conflation with a *sasana-jiet,* or national religion.

IDENTITY CHARADES: TAXING
AND CARDING THE *SANGHA*

The ascension to the throne of King Sisowath in 1904 ushered in a new era of active collaboration with French policy-makers. There was no sweeping act to match that which shook France in 1905. Instead, the separation of *sangha* from an increasingly regulated *srok,* and the de facto replacement of the figure of the *sdic* with that of the colonial state, was an insidious and incremental process. The year 1907 saw the finessing of plans for the overhaul of Cambodge's politico-territorial organization, designed to remap administrative circuits of power and zones of French governance by fragmenting Cambodge into a series of *khums,* or communes. Devised by Thiounn, the initial blueprint for this territorial reform sought to harness the long-standing synergy between *sangha, srok,* and *sdic* by including, in a proposed body of councilors attached to the *khum,* a religious adviser *(preah dhammakar)* who would not only control the temples and monitor monks entering and leaving temples but also conduct ceremonies. Significantly, he would "arrang[e] ceremonial materials" to praise the village *neak-ta.* As has been well documented elsewhere, these *neak-ta* played a critical role as boundary markers between the cultivated world of the *srok* and the wilder world of the *priy,* or forest. Thiounn's vision clashed with the separation of church and state, and, in a stunning example of the "fiction" of the royal administration, the *preah dhammakar* and all mention of religious or spiritual roles vanished from the pursuant 1908 royal ordinance on territorial administration. In law if not in practice, the role of the *neak-ta* as the demarcator and regulator of boundaries was henceforth replaced by the modern bureaucratic genie of the state.[24]

This was perhaps the last time that Cambodian bureaucrats in the protectorate would attempt to include the *neak-ta* in a policy paper. Colonial administrators feared the *neak-ta* more as a backward-dragging superstition than as any real challenge to state authority. However, popular and deep-seated beliefs in the powers of a *neak-ta,* vested in a *srok,* naturally militated against the formation of national identifications, not least because, as Leclère noted, some of the most popular *neak-ta* were those who protected *sroks* from meddling mandarins.[25]

The incorporation of Siamese zones of influence into Cambodge under the Franco-Siamese Treaty of 1907 heightened the protectorate's concern to control and monitor the traffic of monks to and from Siam, and to erect a clear, cultural boundary around Cambodge to match the newly determined border. The bifurcation of *srok* and *sangha* was reinforced by a royal ordinance of 1907, which attempted to tighten control of monks through identity cards issued in the guise of tax-exemption certificates.[26] The measure sparked immediate protest among monks, who saw it as a step towards future imposition of taxes. Efforts to distribute the new cards to monks in Kompong Chhnang triggered a fresh wave of complaints. Members of the Council of Ministers remained almost as intransigent as the country's two heads of sects in their opposition to the policy, and the ordinance remained a dead letter.[27] But other means were found to cream state revenue from acts of religious observance. On 25

December 1907, the protectorate set a levy of 1.5 piastres on Khmer funeral processions in Phnom Penh, with an extra charge for firecrackers.[28]

By 1916 there were approximately thirty thousand monks spread among 2,505 pagodas, 21 of which were in Phnom Penh.[29] Only five years after the 1911 revolution in China, at a time when Europe was plunged in the carnage of the First World War, and on the eve of the Russian Revolution, the explosion of mass peasant protests in Cambodge in 1916 focused fresh attention on the threat and promise of the *sangha* as a vehicle for mobilizing popular opinion.[30] Long-held suspicions of Siam as an outpost of British nefariousness were further complicated by the anti-German sentiment fuelled by World War One.[31] Colonial paranoia fostered speculation about German backing of Yukanthor, whose hand was seen behind the 1916 uprisings. In the thick of the 1916 protests, a group of Buddhist monks quit their studies in Bangkok to support Yukanthor's claims to the throne, only to find that their training in martial arts and consumption of herbal medicine did not render them invincible to the Sûreté.[32] When the Résident of Kampot accused a monk recently returned from Siam of "wanting to stir up trouble" in February 1916, the RSC ordered him to "seize [the monk] by whatever means."[33] The following month, several monks sent to Cambodge by Yukanthor were arrested at the Siamese frontier.[34] These incidents compounded long-standing colonial fears about both Yukanthor's hold over the *sangha* and the political liability of religious education in Siam, leading Baudoin to instruct administrators throughout Cambodge to "keep a particularly close watch on the monks who travel around the country and make periodic stays in Siam, and to maintain a general surveillance of monasteries."[35] Legislation was promptly introduced prohibiting monks from preparing special medicines or training in martial arts.[36] But there were more than strategic objectives guiding such directives. The mobility of cross-border monks and others denaturalized the geographic and political structure of the colony.[37] As Anderson and others have noted, mobility across ethnic and geographic boundaries was often infuriating to colonial administrators and scholars, whose duty, as determined by government and the fashionable paradigms in the late-nineteenth- and early-twentieth-century academic communities of Europe was to catalogue, compartmentalize, and map boundaries.

A month after filing his report on Yukanthor's suspected machinations to the GGI, and barely a week after Sisowath had defused the mass demonstrations, Baudoin secured the king's signature on a new royal ordinance (18 March 1916) restricting the mobility of monks and obliging them to carry identity cards. Novices were henceforth required to carry proof of their "morality" by way of a "certificate of good living," issued by the village chief. *Bhikku* would carry printed ordination certificates, in lieu of the miniscule and inaccessible *chhaya* described earlier.[38] Novices were to carry a printed certificate of their status, and all monks were forbidden to travel within Indochina without an *exeat,* or to leave the country without a passport. These certificates were to be issued not by monks or lay preceptors, but by village chiefs, whose secular roles had been newly defined in the earlier noted 1908 ordinance on territorial administration. The requirement to bear such documents, a Cambodian minister of the interior later reasoned, was so that people of bad faith, capable of cooperating with troublemakers or crooks, could no longer shelter in ecclesiastical robes, and also to facilitate the control of monks, allowing the punishment of individuals hiding under religious robes. After this measure, wrongdoers would have no further recourse to this "means of disguise."[39]

The onus on monks to carry good-behavior bonds must have particularly rankled beside the appalling conduct of some colonial administrators. In 1915, lessons and worship at Vat Thlok Chreou in Muk-Kompoul were disrupted by a French surveyor, who occupied a *salaa* next to the temple for seven weeks along with his wife and children, and while there killed chickens and drank wine, leading the head monk to protest strongly against his presence.[40] Meyer provides anecdotal evidence of similar acts of cultural insensitivity.[41] The new ordinance obliged the *achar* to inform village chiefs of any journeys made by the monks at their *vat,* and of all visits by monks from outside Cambodge, within three days of their arrival. Any visiting monks without passports or travel permits faced instant deportation. The *achar,* traditional medium between laity and the spirit world, now assumed a new role as the interface between *sangha* and state. The role of village chief as issuer of certificates of good conduct further expanded secular control over the *sangha.* Such measures, reasoned Baudoin, not only "filled an important administrative gap, but met an urgent necessity in view of the political machinations from abroad that seek to rally the most influential element to their cause."[42] As anticolonial sentiment and the French fear of communism grew, monks—and temple schools—increasingly emerged as much needed allies and valuable conduits of influence.

LANGUAGE AND RATIONALISM: REEDUCATING *SANGHA* AND LAITY

Whereas Paul Doumer had focused on the systematization of colonial administration, his successor, Paul Beau, made indigenous education a priority. Temple schools rapidly emerged as a focus of these efforts. The "moral, social, and educational centre" of Khmer villages, *vats* were virtually the exclusive means of schooling in rural areas.[43] Here, as in Siam, Laos, and Burma, monks taught village boys reading, writing, and manual arts as well as the fundamentals of Buddhism.[44] Prior to colonial rule, didactic moral poems *(chbap)* functioned as the principal "textbooks" in Cambodia. Designed to be read aloud and memorized rather than studied silently and copied for future reference, the *chbap* held a moral message and social instruction for laity of all strata.[45] They were accessible in written form only to monks or to relatively well-to-do literati.[46] In 1903, François Fontaine, the acting director of the École franco-cambodgienne in Phnom Penh, had stressed the value of temples as effective places for expanding notions of French education suited to the Cambodian mentality and noted that the Protectorate Printing Press was preparing Khmer-language pamphlets along these lines.[47]

Launched in 1904, Beau's reform campaign saw the establishment of "Indigenous Committees for the Improvement of Education" across Indochina.[48] Recognizing the need to reform Cambodian education so as to "spread knowledge of the French language and to give a more practical slant to schooling," and under the specific instructions of the GGI, the RSC created a Commission to Study the Reorganisation of Education in Cambodge on 15 November 1904.[49] Prince Sutharot, Palace Minister Thiounn, and a Mahanikay designate from Vat Ounaloum sat on the committee alongside seven French members, including the entrepreneurial Vandelet. The commission was tasked with devising a "program for teaching the history of the country" and legal knowledge; and with studying the provision of special courses for careers in the arts, administration, law, commerce and industry. The absence of a Thommayuth delegate contrasted with the prominent involvement of Thommayuth monks in the secularization of national education inaugurated by King Chulalongkorn (1868–1910) in Siam, perhaps indicating the sect's resistance to yielding monastic control over *vat* education to colonial administrators.[50]

By March 1905, the commission had returned a comprehensive report, recommending the dual promotion of French language and basic science, and the maintenance of *vat* school education to teach Khmer reading, writing, and moral and religious principles. It also included a wish list of Khmer textbooks—ranging from the Khmer alphabet, volumes of *chbap* and moral lessons, and a concise history of Cambodge, to a Buddhist primer—for publication by the protectorate.[51] In a recommendation that revealed the fluidity between *sangha* and *srok* in Cambodian conceptions, the commission suggested a four-year term for pupils at *vat* schools, from the ages of eight to twelve, which would enable them to become novice monks *(samnar)* and to combine their studies with Buddhist worship. At the age of twelve, these pupils would enter a provincial school, where they would spend two years learning French, written and spoken Khmer, arithmetic, and national history. The committee also suggested establishing teacher-training centers for monks in *vat* schools.[52] In July, RSC Jules Morel, who had so carefully noted his lack of bias towards French-speaking officials in his correspondence with King Sisowath over Son Diep's appointment, made a separate set of recommendations for educational reform to the GGI. Instead of Khmer textbooks and traditional materials, he stressed the need to replace Cambodge's "sterile and outdated moral education" with "practical knowledge and modern science." He rejected the commission's idea of a royal ordinance encouraging children to attend *vat* schools, arguing that it would be better to convince parents to send their children to the protectorate's secular schools.[53] Promoting himself as a champion of progress, Morel stressed that the diffusion of French in Cambodge had been greatly neglected, and suggested that previous administrators had steered clear of schooling natives in European ideas and practices for fear that they might encourage the "dawn of national sentiment" by "loosening the bonds of tradition."[54] This tension between prescriptions for Khmer education and the promotion of French-language schooling would long dog protectorate policy-makers and practitioners in the field of education, and would be replicated in splits among Cambodians be-

tween advocates of Khmer cultural and educational projects and champions of a fully
French secular schooling.

Closely following Morel's replacement in 1906 by RSC Lamothe, who emerged
as an energetic devotee of educational reform, the retrocession of the western provinces in 1907 provided further stimulus to the protectorate's active championing of
vat school reform.[55] "Now begun, the [educational improvements] will not stop, and
in the near future we will be able to oppose a solid rampart of Khmers and Lao to
the infiltration of Anglicized Thais," commented the editor of the *Bulletin du Comité de l'Asie Française,* contrasting Cambodge's previous inertia with the resolute
engagement of its "rival nation," Siam, in Western civilization.[56] Comprising one-
fifth (36,000 sq. km) of Cambodge's territory and containing one-sixth (250,000) of
Cambodge's total population in 1907, Battambang would be the center of colonial
attempts to create such a rampart.[57] Since the launch of Chulalongkorn's program to
reform, standardize, and nationalize *vat* education in 1884, about thirty temples in
Battambang, Siem Reap, and Sisophon had modernized.[58] As part of this process,
the Siamese government had deployed Thai monks trained in "modern methods" in
Bangkok to teach in Battambang's three principal *vats,* and posted specially trained
Khmer teachers to teach Thai in Battambang, Sisophon, and Siemreap.[59] These trajectories formed part of a larger turn-of-the-century schema to knit center and periphery together through educational exchange, principally through Thommayuth
channels, whereby promising monastic scholars in Siam's northeastern regions were
brought to Bangkok for advanced Pali studies and sent back after a few years, so as to
bring the far Lao- and Khmer-speaking provinces into the Siamese nation-state.[60]

In some colonial quarters, the more radical means of linguistic unification
through romanization was proposed. In his 1903 report on education, Fontaine also
recommended the development of a system for the romanization of Khmer, independent of *quoc ngu,* to make written Khmer more intelligible and easier to learn for the
"natives."[61] Shortly after Fontaine's report, Louis Finot devised the first efficient romanization scheme for Khmer, leading the administrator Guillaume Monod (1907)
to recommend the romanization of the entire Khmer language along the lines of *quoc
ngu.*[62] Monod's proposal was perhaps influenced by the recent retrocession to Cambodge of Battambang, Sisophon, and Siem Reap, where the depth and breadth of
Siamese influence in these provinces was felt in many domains, among them the use
of Thai. It was during a tour of these provinces that, in 1908, Lunet de Lajonquière
declared the creation of public opinion in Cambodge an impossibility, as "neither
books nor journals, nor even almanacs of any sort circulate in the interior" and "the
majority of Cambodians have not yet [embraced] the idea of unity in the kingdom."[63]
Printed Khmer circulars were one step towards building such ideas of national unity.
By 1909 the Council of Ministers was communicating its legislation to district chiefs
throughout Cambodge in circulars printed in the official *chrieng* script.[64] Perhaps
owing to the perceived success of such efforts, no further proposals for national romanization appear to have been raised or given serious consideration until the 1940s,

although, as we have seen, the system of Latin transcription was incorporated in the syllabus of the School of Pali in Phnom Penh in 1915.

The first practical step towards secularizing *vat* schools was made by François Baudoin, who had won special commendation for his service to "Public Education" as the protectorate's delegate to the Marseille exposition of 1906, and went on to prove an energetic shaper of Cambodge through his backing of numerous cultural policies from the mid-1910s to the 1920s, as R.S.C.[65] In 1908, now entering his third decade of service in Cambodge and recently promoted to Résident of Kompong Cham, Baudoin appointed a number of lay supervisors to teach elementary French and Khmer at *vat* schools outside the hours devoted to religious education.[66] However, Baudoin's reforms remained an isolated initiative. Not until 1911 did the protectorate launch an overhaul of elementary native education through a royal ordinance. A belated concession to the recommendations of the 1905 commission, the ordinance made attendance at *vat* schools obligatory from the age of eight, and made secular subjects compulsory at *vat* schools.[67] To mitigate the *sangha*'s fear of losing control, the ordinance specified that the *sangha* would be in charge of organizing education. In a direct challenge to the widespread instruction in Thai in the western provinces, it made Khmer-language lessons mandatory at all *vat* schools.[68] In an apparently related move in 1912, the Kambujavarokas printing press in Phnom Penh produced the entire series of *chbap* whose publication had been recommended by the 1905 commission as teaching manuals for *vat* schools.[69] The following year, "with a view to raising the moral and intellectual level of the Cambodian people," the French administration created two inspectorates of *vat* schools, one for each sect.[70]

A number of monitors were subsequently deployed throughout Cambodge to educate monks about the new reforms and to monitor the application of the 1911 royal ordinance. Some met with strong resistance. In January 1914 one monk appointed as inspector of Thommayuth *vat* schools in Kompong Chhnang found monks in one district ignorant of the administration's reforms. Pointing to the presence of "bad people" who were inciting the inhabitants of the kingdom to disobey the administration's orders, Yen reported that the administration's textbooks were not being used, and that many temples in the area had not created schools conforming to its demands.[71] Grievance at this accelerated state participation was likely to have been compounded by the fact that these inspectors were visiting from the capital and threatened to weaken the local, regional autonomy long enjoyed by the *sangha*. Mey, a monk appointed to inspect Mahanikay *vat* schools in Samrongtong, Kandal-Stung, Phnom Penh, and Kong-bisey from October to December 1914, instructed a number of *vat* schools to implement the reforms, instructing monks to teach Pali, Sanskrit, Khmer, and arithmetic, and advising them to let the students follow their own personal abilities and inclinations.[72] Such advice was a radical departure from the strict hierarchical and traditional modes of instruction invoked by the *chbap*, which stated that the *kru* "bestowed, recited and commanded: the student listened, memorized and obeyed."[73]

No less radical was a recommendation by Cambodian Minister of War and Education Ponn to the RSC the following year. Noting the lack of Khmer-language teachers in the Mahanikay temple Vat Ounaloum, Ponn advocated instituting a monthly state salary for *vat* teachers at both Ounaloum and the Thommayuth temple of Vat Botum-Vaddey so that these could serve as "models" piloting the new educational reforms. "Teachers must have a monthly salary to buy food and clothes," petitioned Ponn, reasoning that expanded teaching duties prevented monks from attending to such traditional fund-raising functions as reciting prayers at ceremonies.[74] Ponn's recommendation breached tradition by bringing the state into a network of transactions traditionally involving *sangha* and their constituency and regulated by the search for and generation of merit. Ponn's insistence on the importance of having regular Khmer-language instruction in temples would also have buttressed the linguistically framed projects of Nath and Tath.

Colonial administrators interpreted acts of resistance to such measures as marks of excess or lack. "Jealously guarding their prerogatives and especially their influence," monks were naturally reluctant to promote Western education and any metaphysical principles that could ultimately "ruin their authority," reported Baudoin in March 1916. He recommended training monitors in the protectorate's schools, so as to "leave monks free to follow their vocation and to entrust the mass dissemination of modern ideas to schoolteachers trained by us, and . . . impregnated with our ideas and our spirit."[75] Recalling his success in introducing lay teachers to *vat* schools in Kompong Cham, he recommended that elementary French should be taught in *vats* throughout Cambodge by specially trained lay instructors, who would work alongside Buddhist monks while spearheading "a secular . . . mission of civilization and of progress," using French as their medium of instruction, and preparing their best pupils to move directly from *vat* to state schools.[76] Baudoin further recommended placing *vat* schools under the control of the Department of Education.[77] The following month, Russier returned a report on education that blamed the failure of the 1911 reforms on the low calibre of Cambodge's *sangha,* who were "lazy, formal, proud, [and] poorly educated." These monks had been inadequately prepared for the mission, which ideally required prior professional training.[78] Later that year, Ponn appointed a number of lay teachers, on annual, renewable contracts and funded by the French administration, to the principal *vats* in Phnom Penh and surrounding areas. In the provinces, such teachers were chosen by the chief monks of temples, and were generally monks. In 1919, Ponn sent a monk of the rank of Preahphootivong, a title conferred by the king and usually indicating responsibility for Buddhist studies, on a mission of inspection to Kompong Thom, providing him with two coolies to carry 197 books to be disseminated among *vat* schools. The new restrictions on the mobility of *sangha* under the 1918 royal ordinance meant that Ponn had to apply to the administration to grant the team the necessary travel permits.[79]

However, the *sangha* in Battambang remained resistant to colonial intervention in education. In 1919, Ponn endeavored to arrange for a team of inspectors to visit *vat* schools in Battambang, which had escaped inspection since the province's annexation in 1907. Ponn's initiative was roundly rebuffed by the Résident of Battambang, who declared that there were not yet any modernized *vat* schools there, but that he was currently opening twelve, which would be operative by the end of 1920 at the earliest.[80]

Meanwhile, European cartography took its place alongside Buddhist cosmography through the introduction of maps and geography lessons into *vat* schools.[81] In 1919, Ponn requested fifteen of the "newly printed, large, Khmer-language maps of Cambodia that show the mountains and all zones *(damboun)*, provinces, and *khum*" as teaching aids to replace the "little maps" then being used for geography lessons in Phnom Penh's temple schools.[82] Khmer-language "Physical and Political Maps of Cambodia and Politics" were duly supplied by the Ministry of Public Education.[83] Unlike the precolonial list maps that had described Cambodia as a series of toponyms, these modern maps enabled a visualization of the territorial dimensions of a nation as a distinct, bounded entity, providing nascent forms of nationalism with what one scholar has described as "carefully guarded spaces of cultural intimacy."[84] In Cambodge as elsewhere, maps brought a new way not only of relating to one's own territory but of visualizing and compartmentalizing the peoples who had long lived in close proximity to the Khmer kingdom, entangled in war and confrontation as in peace and cultural exchange. It mattered not whether Cambodge's grand cartographer, Auguste Pavie, and his successors rendered Siam, Annam, or Laos in pink, green, or white. What mattered was that modern mapping technology irrevocably converted these countries, and their inhabitants, into Cambodge's cartographic *others*.[85]

RENOVATING EDUCATION, 1924–1935

Throughout the protectorate, attempts to reform education were tempered by the concern within the colonial administration that, while Buddhist education was unscientific and thus incapable of training Cambodians to participate fully in the colonial economy, it was in temples that Cambodians acquired the "piety" and "honesty" widely attributed to them in colonial accounts. From the 1920s onward, the protectorate revamped its earlier, halfhearted campaign to reform temple education in ways that would reconcile the twin aims of modernizing native minds and conserving native morals.

The catchwords of this new campaign were the "renovation of traditional education" and "renovated *vat* schools." Introduced on a local, experimental basis in 1924, the scheme was launched nationwide in 1925 and gathered increasing momentum during the next ten years. The new system instituted certificates for students who had attended *vat* schools from the age of six to nine. By giving "young peasants in poor and isolated regions" access to state schools and French-language education, these diplomas were designed to augment rural participation in the colonial state.[86] The costs of disenfranchisement had been made abundantly clear in 1925 when a

French Résident Bardez was murdered, along with his clerk and an interpreter while on tax collection duties, by a group of Cambodian villagers. In their defense the lawyer argued, "to colonize is not only to give natives roads . . . but also schools."[87] But the equation of benefaction with the provision of education was overly simplistic. To some monks, the so-called renovation of traditional education would appear to be an egregious act of moral trespass.

In a move that would have alarmed and angered many monks, religious education was removed from the official *vat* school curriculum, which was now reduced to Khmer writing and reading, arithmetic, rudimentary "national history," and geography.[88] Arithmetic would enable Cambodians to hold their own against Chinese creditors; history would teach the Cambodian "the reasons for his decadence, the efforts made by France to liberate him from . . . his dangerous neighbors and to reconstitute for him a Khmer country."[89] Training schools (*écoles d'application*) were established to train monks in French methods of education for the renovated *vat* schools, and Khmer school manuals were produced by the Direction of Public Education in Hanoi.[90] In 1927, the veteran educationalist Henri Gourdon, Honorary Inspector of Public Education in Indochina, proposed the continued modernization of temple schools in Cambodge and Laos.[91] The following year, *Srok Khmer* published a verse by a regular contributor named Oknya Sann encouraging Cambodians to send their children to the new schools:

> Don't delay, do as the world is doing today:
> Study to the point of saturation, get a diploma from the administration.
> Don't wait for the village chief to tell you the rules,
> When your child turns six, send the kid to school.
> The administration has built no end of places,
> And provided books and blackboards, to put you through your paces;
> There are desks and chairs, and window blinds too,
> So you'll be sitting pretty, and the heat won't make you stew.
> And when school's been and gone, you'll have a foreign tongue,
> The teacher uses French and Khmer, so learn your share:
> Do as the big government says: it has organized education
> For our ignorant Khmer nation.
> There's even a Royal Proclamation.
> So don't wait any more, or you'll be breaking the law.[92]

In May 1928, the Ministry of War and Education launched a new series of Khmer-language school manuals.[93] Support for renovated *vat* schools continued to strengthen in Kampot during 1928, where the "loyal collaboration" of the head monk and teacher of the scriptures of Vat Ang Sophi in Kompong Trach facilitated the establishment of a new *école d'application* catering to eighty-three novices and eighteen teacher-monks from *vats* in eight districts and communes.[94] But monks in the western and eastern provinces were less receptive.[95] Although the Résident of Kompong Thom noted the strong enthusiasm for *vat* school reforms among chief monks, the statistics tell a different story.[96] Of the fifty-three renovated *vat* schools established by 1931, forty-seven were in Kampot. Battambang, Pursat, and Prey Veng each had only one renovated school, and Kompong Chhnang had three.[97] The establishment of an inspectorate of *écoles d'application* on 16 December 1930 signalled an escalation of French efforts to secularize *vat* schools.[98] By 1935, five hundred renovated *vat* schools had been established.

The political agenda behind this new push was the outbreak of violent antico-lonial protests in Cochinchina and Tonkin in 1930, the contemporaneous resurgence in Caodai support, and a general atmosphere of discontent exacerbated by the Great Depression. Stressing the rapid spread of "intrigues, plotting, and pernicious ideas" in the "hotbeds" of Annam and Tonkin, the former GGI and current president of the republic, Doumer, pointed to Cochinchine and Cambodge as the next potential weak links in Indochina and hinted at the "whiff of the bad thoughts and bad intentions sprouting there."[99] Several years after Doumer aired his fears, the strategic agenda of *vat* school reform was elucidated by a colonial administrator:

> in Cochinchine, in Annam, and in Tonkin, subversive propaganda had yielded red and bitter fruits. The signs were that the apostles of the wicked would begin to infiltrate Cambodge. The docility and naïveté of the Khmer people might easily provide the wicked shepherds with overly malleable material. But how to stop the flood? The rural population is scattered over areas too vast and too poor to warrant the installation of indigenous administrative officials who could maintain perma-nent contact with them. . . . But we remembered, opportunely, the respect of the masses for monks; their confidence in their words. The monks lived in the most re-mote districts. Defenders of royal authority, which had always protected them, the monks were qualified to become the militant adversaries against the spreaders of disorder. . . . Their moral level had evidently declined with the drop in Khmer gran-deur. But why not try to raise them up?[100]

In 1931, a new inspectorate of renovated *vat* schools was established, and Louis Manipaud was appointed as a "technical adviser to help create a monastic teach-ing corps."[101] The new post alarmed both the Thommayuth and Mahanikay sects, which saw it as a move to bring *vat* schools under complete colonial control.[102] The *vat* school's use of Khmer as the official and exclusive langue of instruction earned the contempt of the Thommayuth, who prided themselves on their literacy in Thai. This was not just abstract linguistic snobbery, however. By the 1930s, the religious, educational, and printing projects of the protectorate were all working to consolidate a linguistically inscribed Khmer nation.

Soon after his appointment, Manipaud created a team of Khmer-speaking French inspectors to monitor adherence to the official syllabus.[103] At least one Cambodian welcomed these developments. Writing in 1931, a school inspector in Pursat de-scribed the average *vat* schoolteacher as a poorly educated, barely literate monk whose lack of teaching skills was compounded by a lopsided knowledge of the Khmer lan-guage. Most monks, the inspector complained, were versed only in the "elaborate *aksa-mul* script used in religious texts and *satras,* far removed from the *chrieng* script for everyday affairs," and therefore "of no use . . . in modern life."[104] As we have seen, the *chrieng* script was the simpler form used for official correspondence, print media, and in the Khmer-language publications of the Royal Library and the Buddhist Institute.

To counter such moves, in 1930 a Siamese monk tried to establish courses in religious education in Thommayuth temples in Phnom Penh and Battambang, and to train lay preachers to spread "Siamese religion" in the provinces. The failure of his efforts was presumably tied to the success of the Buddhist Institute in curbing travel by Thommayuth monks to Siam and curtailing Siamese influence in Cambodge.[105] The overthrow of the absolute monarchy in Siam in 1932, and the death of the Thommayuth's Bangkok-based patron Prince Norodom Yukanthor in June 1934, would further attenuate links between the Siamese and Khmer *sangha*.[106] A new program to "Khmerize" Thai-speaking communities through monk emissaries would further secure the western boundaries of Cambodge's *sasana-jiet.*

In a report of 1934, Manipaud stressed the political advantages of establishing renovated *vat* schools in areas where ethnic Khmers formed a minority, including the Gulf of Siam, Battambang, and Pursat. In Siem Reap and Battambang, conflict still simmered between overzealous preachers from the Thommakay and the long-established Thommayuth, jeopardizing plans for renovated *vat* schools.[107] But Manipaud could point to the success of pilot projects among Siamese and Lao settlements along the Mongkol-Borey River, where Khmer had been taught to non-Khmer-speaking monks so that they could teach it to their pupils.[108] Action was now needed in the Gulf of Siam, where Thai was the language of administration and where, for political ends, the systematic diffusion of Khmer was urgently required. In preparation for such a "Khmerization" program, Manipaud had already identified some monks who would be willing to travel to Kah-kong as "missionaries" and teachers.[109] The following year, two monks trained at the *école d'application* at Vat Ang Sophi in Kampot were sent to Kah-kong to found a school to teach the "national language" (Khmer) to the Thai-speaking Cambodian population. Their proselytizing mission, noted one administrator, "was less a Buddhist enterprise than a specifically Khmer [enterprise]."[110] Stressing the urgency of such Khmerization, Manipaud proposed that the Council for the Perfection of Franco-Indigenous Education research ways of embracing other non-Khmer minorities in the protectorate's education programs.[111] These activities at the grass roots correlated with Nath and Tath's promotion of Khmer vernacular publications and bilingual Khmer-Pali editions of Buddhist texts. The reform of the Mahanikay, the establishment of the Pali School, the renovation of *vat* education, and the publication of Khmer manuals were all critical facets of this development.

Impressed by the success of *vat* schools in Cambodge, Director of Education Henri Gourdon recommended establishing Franco-Khmer schools to serve Cochinchina's 300,000-strong Khmer population, so that ethnic Khmers could receive Franco-Khmer, as opposed to Franco-Annamite, diplomas. Special schools were established in Cochinchina for Cambodians who had, in the words of one French administrator writing in the 1930s, "resisted assimilation by their Annamite conquerors and had jealously preserved their morals and their native character," in part through maintaining temple education for the moral and religious instruction of young boys.[112] The Khmer language was introduced into the official currriculum and a certificate of Cambodian studies instituted.[113] In a direct replica of the system in Cambodge, access to these new Franco-Khmer schools could be gained by satisfactory attendance at a renovated *vat* school. The Khmer population of Cochinchina was estimated at 320,000 in 1931, with 3,900 Khmer pupils enrolled at an estimated 229 *vat* schools.[114] This system of Franco-Khmer elementary education would help to reorient the scholastic and professional sights of ethnic Khmers in Cochinchina away from Saigon and Hanoi and towards Phnom Penh, providing fertile ground for the cultivation of Khmer nationalists.[115] In Cochinchina, the campaign to modernize *vat* schools entailed the provision of equipment, "rational teaching tools," and professional training to monk teachers.[116]

By 1934, with the exception of continued friction in the western provinces, Manipaud noted a general harmony between Buddhist monks and secular officials in the field of education, identified growing popular support for such schools, and alleged that donations to temples were increasingly tied to the provision of satisfactory schooling.[117] This vision of harmony belied the emergence of renovated *vat* schools as a major bone of contention among both Cambodian and European secular elites. While some favored full-scale secularization of education, others supported reform within the traditional framework. Predictably, the strongest Cambodian detractors of *vat* schools were the graduates of colonial and French secular schools.[118] One such urbane Cambodian was Areno Iukanthor, an alumnus of the Paul Bert School in Hanoi, who had rounded off his education in France and who argued that the promotion of traditional education was designed "to keep us in ignorance."[119] Debates on native education also polarized the French administration. In 1933, the head of the Education Department of Cambodge declared that Cambodge lagged behind the rest of Indochina in its schooling and warned that the prioritization of *vat* school reform could jeopardize indigenous interest and enrollments in secular schools.[120] The veteran colonial administrator Dr. Pannetier shared this opinion.[121] When a frustrated Manipaud threatened to resign in 1934 unless he was shown due "moral and material support," a Council for Perfecting Traditional Education in Cambodge was promptly convened, comprising Manipaud, the Mahanikay and Thommayuth chiefs, the minister of public education, and the minister of the interior and religion.[122] But despite the GGI's and RSC's attendance at the opening ceremony of the 500th renovated *vat* school in 1935, colonial opposition to *vat* schools persisted. In 1934, for example, the mayor of Phnom Penh, M. Lambert, rejected a request for financing for new *vat* schools on the ground that there was no use for such establishments in a capital replete with secular schools.[123] Jean Dorsenne's *Sous le soleil des bonzes* (In the *bonzes'* sun), published in 1934, gives us some insight into the European perceptions of Buddhism that shaped such views.

Set in early 1930s Cambodge, Dorsenne's novel constructs a dichotomy of Orient and Occident through the lens of religion. In a brief flirtation with Buddhism, Jacques Damien, Dorsenne's filibustering, hard-living French protagonist, finds some fleeting comfort. However, reality soon supersedes his romantic fantasy of the Orient, and he recognizes the "egotism" of the *sangha,* whose Buddhist faith is incompatible with his Western soul. Jacques' journey is paralleled by that of his Cambodian servant, Mao, who also fails to find salvation in Buddhism. Out of loyalty to Jacques, Mao commits a dreadful crime and then takes refuge in a *vat,* where the "Buddhist" emphasis on individual deliverance and the absence of such "Christian" virtues as forgiveness reduce him to a shadow of his former self. He develops epilepsy and is sent by the monks to a French doctor, to whom Mao confesses all. The doctor then takes him to a Catholic priest, whom he deems "the only doctor" for Mao's tormented soul. Enervated and emaciated by Buddhism, expiated by Catholicism, but still shackled by the Buddhist belief in "retribution," Mao becomes a skeletal ascetic and dies in the forests of Siem Reap.[124] We do not know how Dorsenne's novel was received in the colonial administration, nor how widely it was read. However his juxtaposition of a dynamic, redeeming European culture of mutual help with a Buddhism characterized by individual passivity and moral paralysis, provides some clues as to the mindset of French opponents of *vat* school reform.

Dorsenne's portrait of a monk, and those considered earlier in this chapter, existed alongside more respectful descriptions of cultural and religious distinction, as in the poetry of Mary Gerny-Marchal. Alongside the intellectual curiosity and textual passions of Buddhologists and museologists considered earlier in this book, the crass stereotypes produced by some colonial writers, and the administration's strategic evaluation of monks discussed here, there was emerging in Europe a new interest in Buddhism that stood somewhere between the esoteric approaches of the Buddhologists and the romantic fantasies of Dorsennes, and was reflected in the foundation in France of a society named les Amis du bouddhisme in 1929.[125]

In the early 1920s, a female newcomer to the male-dominated EFEO would arrive in Cambodia and pave the way for a broadening of the conceptual corridor between "East" and "West" through her energetic promotion of several cultural projects and institutions centered on Khmer Buddhism. Building on the gains made by *vat* schools in Cambodge and Cochinchina in promoting Khmer-language education, the printing projects promoted by Nath and Tath, and the School of Pali, her projects would create a dialogue between the protectorate and members of the *sangha* through a range of cultural institutions; their effect was partly to augment the protectorate's moral authority by extending its scope of cultural custodianship from the "national" monuments of Angkor to a national Buddhist heritage, and so implicitly to shore up the protectorate's "right" to rule in ways traditionally associated with Khmer kingship. Like Manipaud, she recognized the potential of Khmer vernacular education and publications to translate imaginings of a Khmer Buddhist nation from a zone of belief and practice into an ethnolinguistic domain. Her name was Suzanne Karpelès.

8 | Holy Trinity

Chuon Nath, Huot Tath, and Suzanne Karpelès

It is the first time Cambodian monks have gathered in Paris in such numbers. They are seated in the inner hall of a temple, where barefoot men and women also sit, dwarfed by a statue of Buddha in beatific pose. Their heads are bowed and palms joined in a *samp'ea,* a gesture of respect that European onlookers will readily translate as prayer. A row of bowls laden with fruits and other offerings separates them from some thirty men, women, and children seated on a rush mat. The women wear crocheted lace tops and silk *sampots,* the men a mixture of checkered *sampots,* the cotton scarves known as *kramas,* and crisp white jackets. Garlands of flowers encircle the sleek black topknots of several girls in the audience—topknots referred to by Thiounn in an early piece he wrote for the *Revue Indochinoise* on the haircutting ceremony, topknots whose passing from urban Cambodge is mourned in several colonial accounts. A fresco from the Ramayana stretches across one wall, its scenery punctuated by a window overlooking twisted tree trunks and Lake Daumesnil. Drifting through this window, over the tiled rooftops of nearby Vietnamese temples and Angkorean towers, sounds vary daily. On Tuesday it might be a Vietnamese marching band; on Wednesday, Cambodian musicians striking up a tune for the Ramayana procession. Over it all comes the boisterous hum of the crowd, the occasional hollering of a lost child, and, on and off, solemn moments of silence, the sound of a car engine, the slam of a door, and official speeches followed by rapturous applause. There is never a whisper or a fidget from the Cambodians. In their place they stay, partitioned by space and design from Annam, Tonkin, and Cochinchina. Ropes cordon them off from the curious crowd. They have been assembled here to represent Cambodge's national religion. They are made of wax.

Like many other displays at the dazzling Exposition coloniale of 1931, the neatly bounded scene of waxworks at worship belied a far more complex reality on the ground. *Le Cambodge: Intérieur de temple Bouddhiste,* reads the caption.[1] But in Cambodge, tensions within Cambodge's *sangha* are now rife, sparked in part by clashes between the purification campaigns led by Nath, Tath, and other reformists within the Mahanikay and the apparent aspirations among sections of the laity and the *sangha* for the perpetuation and expansion of a more physical, bodily participation in religion, with the retention of supernatural elements. Since 1927, the establishment of a dynamic, pantheistic, transborder religious movement in the form of the Caodai

FIGURE 8. *Le Cambodge: intérieur de temple Bouddhiste*. J. Trillat, *L'exposition coloniale de Paris,* Librairie des Arts Decoratifs, 1931, Plate 15.

presented an alternative religion to which thousands of Cambodians began to turn. The Caodai embraced a pan-temporal pantheon, situating modern figures—Charlie Chaplin, Victor Hugo, and Joan of Arc—whose name and imagery had circulated in French Indochina, alongside Jesus Christ and Sakyamuni. Part of the attraction, and subversive potential, of the movement resided in its regional character. While the leadership of Cambodge's *sangha* objected to the Caodai movement's heterodoxy, nationalists objected to its pan-ethnic character, and colonial administrators were chiefly concerned about the movement as *precisely* that: large movements of people across Cambodge's cultural and territorial borders. Next to such challenges to European authority and colonial boundaries, the freeze-frame of Cambodian Buddhists at the 1931 exhibition was a more accurate depiction of elite visions of Buddhism-as-national-religion than the contemporary scene.

The display of the Parisian tableau roughly marked the first anniversary of a new forum in Cambodge, the Indigenous Institute for the Study of Buddhism of the Little Vehicle. Established by government decree in January 1930 and inaugurated to full ceremony that May, the institute's mandate was the study of Theravadan Buddhism among the populations of Laos and Cambodge, and among Khmer communities in Cochinchina. Its council included delegates of Lao and Cambodian royalty and the French administrations in Laos, Cambodge, and Cochinchina. But its positioning in the Royal Library, inclusion of the director of the École supérieure de Pali (ESP) on its council, and the appointment of Karpelès as its secretary ensured a strong focus on Cambodge. This impressive array of councilors and the institute's broad sweep conjured notions of a large and glamorous enterprise. But from the outset, the institute's staff counted only one accountant, six clerks, a driver, and a secretary, and its early years were dogged by budgetary restrictions, resentment by officials in Cochinchina at perceived intrusion in non-Cambodian affairs, and a miserly GGI who clearly did not attach the enormous Indochina-wide strategic importance commonly imputed to the institute. Rather, it was the combined energies and talents of a few core staff, coupled with popular engagement with its innovative outreach projects, that created the illusion of a massive enterprise, proving that Nath, Tath, and their colleagues were worlds apart from the still-life Buddhists presented at the exhibition. From 1922 to 1931, first as students of the EFEO in Hanoi and later on fieldwork and monitoring missions in Kampuchea Kraom, these leaders of the reform movement used modern technologies—from book buses to radio—to broadcast their vision. These journeys moved away from the Siam-centric pathways of the nineteenth-century Buddhist community. In Hanoi, Nath and Tath had begun to make comparisons between Vietnamese city life and that in Cambodge. Their tours of Khmer communities in Cochinchina shifted their focus from the questions of scriptural interpretation and practice that had preoccupied them in the 1910s and early 1920s to issues of ethnolinguistic identification and representation.

"After we left Phnom Penh [in 1922]," wrote Huot Tath in his memoirs, "some monks and lay people . . . spoke out against us and said, 'Those two monks have disappeared to Hanoi, perhaps they'll never come back, the administration has got rid of them.'"[2] However, the appearance of a new European scholar at the EFEO in Hanoi early the following year would ultimately put paid to any hopes of Tath and Nath disappearing as forces in Cambodian Buddhism. Her name was Suzanne Karpelès, and she would emerge as the protectorate's leading *khmèrofille.*

SUZANNE KARPELÈS (1890–1968)

In 1898, a year after Chuon Nath became a novice at Vat Pol Yat temple, a young Suzanne Karpelès (1890–1968) was probably biting her lip as she surveyed the imposing Lycée Molière on her first day at school. Adapting to the "cold mists" of Paris and the regimentation of French education was not easy for Suzanne and her two sisters, who nursed a nostalgia for the warmth, light, scents, and freedom of their former "tropical garden." But their friends, and two excellent teachers in history and philosophy, helped them "to understand the Occident." Born into a wealthy bourgeois family in Paris, Suzanne's first encounters with the Orient were in India, where her Hungarian-Jewish father took his family on long and frequent business trips. By the time she turned eight, one friend recalled after her death, she had spent more time in the Indies than in France.

Infused with "the spiritual, religious, and social values of the Orient," and equally fascinated by the Western sciences she had learned at school, the bright and ambitious Karpelès applied to the École des langues orientales of the École des hautes études pratiques in Paris, "in the hope of linking the two civilizations" through a better understanding of their techniques and, above all, their "religious sentiments." Here, she studied Sanskrit, Pali, Tibetan, and Nepalese and Tibetan religion with Finot, Sylvain Lévi (1863–1935), and Alfred Foucher (1865–1952), former director of the EFEO. She proved a brilliant student; but a sense of duty led her to abandon her studies in midstream, on the outbreak of the First World War. At twenty-four she became an ambulance driver, rescuing the wounded from the front lines and assisting in the evacuations of hospitals under fire. After the war, in 1918, her organizational flair became apparent when she and other "Orientalists" founded the Association of the Friends of the East, at the Musée Guimet. The following year, she published a remarkable annotated translation of an important religious text in Sanskrit and Tibetan, "one hundred stanzas in honor of Boddhisatva Lokecvara," in the prestigious *Journal Asiatique,* and in 1922 she became the first woman to graduate with a degree in Oriental languages from the École des hautes études pratiques in Paris.[3]

But these academic achievements alone were not enough to secure a place for a woman in the EFEO. In a biographical sketch prepared for a woman's radio program in Paris, Karpelès later recounted how it was her military service as an ambulance driver in the First World War, and the veteran credentials this gave her, that bought her entry into what was, until this point, a very male club. Her age was also against her: she had turned thirty, the maximum age for "titularization." Reluctantly, the members of the institute in Paris, on which the EFEO depended, accepted her as a temporary member. In 1922, the first woman to join the EFEO, she set sail for Indochina on a three-year contract.[4]

Karpelès arrived in Hanoi on 1 January 1923.[5] Her first project was to collate a Pali text from Ceylon with a Khmer manuscript, work that probably brought her into contact with Nath and Tath, who continued as visiting scholars at the EFEO, under Finot's supervision, in 1923. The next two decades would see the "bright,

FIGURE 9. Suzanne Karpelès. Courtesy of the Buddhist Institute, Phnom Penh.

វិទ្យាស្ថានពុទ្ធសាសន

pleasant, and sometimes caustic" Karpelès divert her energies from an academic ca-reer marked by "brilliant beginnings" to the cultural conservation of Cambodge.[6] Karpelès moved to Phnom Penh in 1925, and did not leave Cambodge until 1941, when she moved to Sri Lanka, and then on to the French colony of Pondicherry.[7]

Photographs reveal Karpelès to have been an austere, self-contained, and unpre-tentious woman. Her long shift dresses of Indian fabric, an echo of her Pondicherry origins, were more a tribute to indigenous style than to French fashion. Studied por-traits of her with a perfume pomade, or powdering her nose, or applying lipstick while gazing into a mirror reveal her to be very much a woman of her time. But these were perhaps her only obvious concessions to contemporary norms of feminin-ity. Her commitment to her career, her independent existence as a woman without husband or children, the uncluttered interior of her Phnom Penh abode, all violated the bourgeois conventionality of prescribed lives for women in the colonies. There were no signs here of that paragon of French colonial femininity trumpeted in colo-nial propaganda, whose *mission domesticatrice* was to create a quiet corner of France as homemaker to the masculine forgers of empire. In some senses, however, Suzanne's was a nurturing role. She devoted sixteen years in Cambodge to the establishment and management of several key cultural institutes and journals, all keenly oriented towards the purification and salvation of Khmer Buddhism from degeneration and "foreign" contamination. She got to know, and visited, the mothers and other family figures of her protégés, and vested the political passion of a pacifist, as well as the emotional energy of a mentor figure, in a widening circle of French-educated or EFEO-trained Cambodians and monks, while creating a role for young female college students in her activities. Although teaching was recognized as an acceptable and, by the 1920s, desirable career for women, Karpelès surpassed all expectations, and she was perhaps the only woman in Indochina to have attained her status within the administration.

In the Cambodge of the 1920s, Karpelès would have run across some of the several thousands of Indians of French nationality, originating from Pondicherry and employed as civil servants, alongside lesser numbers of Indians from Madras, Bombay, Gujerati, and Bengal, engaged in commerce and credit, textile trade, banking and moneylending.[8]

Karpelès played a critical role in bridging these domains, and in mapping the boundaries of a *sasana-jiet* for Cambodge. As director of the Royal Library (1925–1941) and the founder of the Buddhist Institute (1930–1941), and as chief publications officer for the École supérieure de pali, she engineered and oversaw an institutional framework for the documentation and codification of a specifically "Khmer" Buddhist tradition that helped to secure the ascendance of the reformist faction in the *sangha*. In 1926, she established the first Khmer-language journal, the Buddhist review *Kambuja Surya,* which would long outlive both the protectorate and Karpelès. This journal and the numerous works on Cambodian history, culture, and religion published by the Royal Library and the Buddhist Institute would consolidate the transition from a scribal to a print culture in Cambodge. They also provided vital arenas for the formulation and circulation of emerging ideas about Buddhism and nation, allowing Finot, Tath, Karpelès, and Nath to translate their beliefs and ideas about the true and proper shape of Khmer Buddhism into a coherent body of thought and literature that, by the 1930s, had emerged as the authentic, national model of Khmer Buddhism.

By incorporating the ethnic Khmer population of the western provinces of Cochinchina, known variously as Khmer Kraom and Kampuchea Kraom, into the Buddhist Institute's field of activities through preaching tours by reformist monks and the dissemination of publications, Karpelès also encouraged the crystallization of an ethnically discrete rubric of nation. Karpelès' Jewish origin may have influenced her empathy towards these Khmer Kraom communities, marginalized within French Cochinchina within whose new borders they had been arbitrarily included since 1873. Attending university in Paris in the immediate aftermath of World War I, she may well have been sensitized to emerging notions of "national minorities" when this concept was first given legal coinage by the League of Nations and the plight of Europe's various minority peoples, particularly those straddling borderlands, elicited much public and political attention. Ironically, having devoted her career in Cambodge to creating space for a religious movement, she fell victim to Vichy anti-Semitic legislation.

One testament to the power of Karpelès' persona was the reverence in which Cambodian monks held her, as evidenced not only by their entrusting sacred relics and manuscripts to her protection, but by their preference for dealing directly with her on all manner of issues and bypassing the French administration.[9] Thus, while her projects in Cambodge dovetailed with the broader strategic goals of the French administration in Indochina, they were launched at her own instigation, and most were probably informed not only by her academic knowledge but by her dialogue with Nath, Tath, and other Cambodians. Although motivated by the Khmerophilia that colored the amateur scholastic pursuits of her antecedent Adhémard Leclère, the directions of her later life indicate that her ambitions may also have been of a more spiritual nature, and that she found succour in religious movements outside the Judaeo-Christian tradition. Shortly before her death in 1968, the chief guru of the Sri Aurobindo Ashram, which she had joined in the 1950s, described Karpelès as having been a "Buddhist" on her arrival in Pondicherry.

But Karpelès' influence reached far wider than Cambodge. In the same way that Tath and Nath acted as cross-cultural intermediaries, an interface between modernity and its methods and the Mahanikay, so Karpelès acted as a broker of Buddhist knowledge between Cambodge and France, and thus contributed to the global spread of Buddhism. She was an active member of the first French Buddhist Association, les Amis du bouddhisme. This small society, founded by the wealthy expatriate American Grace Constant Lounsbery (1876–1964) in Paris in 1929, launched its own journal, *La Pensée Bouddhique*.[10] In 1931, Karpelès lectured to the International Congress of Orientalists in Leiden on Buddhist Studies in Laos and Cambodge.[11] After leaving Cambodge, she continued with the French explication and translation of Buddhist texts at the Sri Aurobindo Ashram. Some thirty years after her death, U Thitinyana, a Burmese monk in France, wrote that Karpelès would "always be remembered in Theravada countries for having initiated, supervised, and brought to completion the printing of the Theravada Tripitaka, both in Pali and in the Khmer language."[12] Today, Buddhism is recognized as France's sixth official religion. Although its acceptance as such is in large part due to the voices and presence of those Buddhists from Asia who have made France their home in the postcolonial world, figures such as Karpelès also deserve a place in the processes which, over time, raised understanding and awareness of Buddhism in France.

Karpelès' projects not only cemented the conceptual contours of a *sasana-jiet*. Through provincial tours, book buses, excursions to Cochinchina, involvement in journal issues and cultural seminars, the Royal Library and the Institute gave their staff opportunities for mobility, autonomy, and freedom of association and expression unmatched by other colonial departments in Cambodge, facilitating the emergence of an actual community of scholars and *sangha*. Karpelès' commitment to freeing a "degenerated" Cambodian Buddhism from impure superstitions and the reification of a *sasana-jiet* cohered with the continuation of the protectorate's policy of isolating the *sangha* from foreign contagion.[13] With the emergence of the Caodai movement, feared as a potential vehicle of anticolonial sentiment and reviled as a challenge to the paradigm of a *sasana-jiet,* the focus of this quarantining of Khmer Buddhism shifted from Siam and the western provinces to Cambodge's eastern border. Alarm at the possible repercussions of the pan-ethnic harmony of the Caodai saw the administrations of Cochinchina and Cambodge, and the GGI, divert attention to the Khmer Kraom as a key constituent in the creation of a transnational, Indochinese, Khmer Buddhist cosmos, and grant strong backing and unusual autonomy to Karpelès', Nath's and Tath's border-crossing activities among Cochinchina's Khmer Kraom communities.

THE ROYAL LIBRARY AND THE ÉCOLE SUPÉRIEURE DE PALI

During their first year in Hanoi, Nath, and Tath complained to Finot of the restrictions on publishing and circulating Buddhist texts in Cambodge. Finot subsequently persuaded RSC Baudoin to authorize the École supérieure de Pali to publish books, and to appoint a French administrator to control the printing and dissemination of the ESP's publications.[14] In late 1922, after completing ten months of study in Sanskrit, Nath, and Tath returned to Phnom Penh to escape the Hanoi winter. They resumed studies with Finot early the next year, moving to a dormitory within the EFEO compound. After a further several months of Sanskrit, courses in deciphering ancient Khmer inscriptions, and the geography and history of Buddhism in India and China, Tath and Nath returned to Phnom Penh in late 1923.[15] In May 1924, at Finot's request, Huot Tath was appointed teacher of Sanskrit at the École supérieure de Pali.[16] Chuon Nath was later made deputy director of the school.[17] During their second sojourn in Hanoi, Finot's protégés had experienced the beginnings of a national and political consciousness later described by Tath as an "awakening."[18] On Sundays, the two monks downed their books and toured the rural hinterland of Hanoi, comparing peasant life in Vietnam and Cambodge, and analyzing differences between the two societies.[19]

In August 1924, a royal ordinance established a commission to study and propose measures, "conforming to Buddhist tradition, to give monasteries an organization, and the clergy a statute, that would maintain the glory of the religion of our ancestors, assure peace in the kingdom and the prosperity of our people." The minister of religions was president of the commission, which included the heads of the Thommayuth and the Mahanikay, the director of the ESP Thaong, and Palace Minister Thiounn.[20] That year, Karpelès published French translations of six Pali tales from the *Dhammopadatthakatha* in the *Revue Indochinoise.* Her research on this manuscript had led her across the textual terrain of Ceylon, Cambodge, and Siam, and through an institutional maze spanning the EFEO in Hanoi, where she would have met with Finot, Nath, and Tath, and the National Library in Bangkok, where she worked under the guidance of its chief curators, Coedès and the Siamese historian Prince Damrong, and produced an inventory of all the library's Thai manuscripts. This circumnavigation of Cambodge in her quest to translate a Khmer manuscript may well have led Karpelès to identify the need for a new cultural institution in Cambodge and, no doubt inspired by what she saw in Siam, she began to lobby for the establishment of a national library in Cambodge.[21]

Her proposal received prompt backing from RSC François Baudoin, who saw the spectre of Khmer vanishing in the "evolution" and westernization of Cambodians. A royal ordinance of 15 January 1925 established the Royal Library to research, collect, conserve, and reproduce ancient manuscripts scattered in temples and homes. By centralizing this literary legacy and reproducing it in modern publications, the library could maintain the study of classical Khmer language, preserve an ancient civilization, and "safeguard Cambodge's past as its intellectual future," declared Baudoin.[22] Impressed by Karpelès "erudite zeal and energy," Finot appointed her as director.[23] By "centralizing and translating all sacred texts" and "allowing monks to consult them without the need to visit Bangkok," the protectorate and its security services hoped that the library, together with the École supérieure de Pali, would "curb emigration and check Siamese influence."[24]

To Palace Minister Thiounn, the establishment of the Royal Library was the perfect opportunity to bring his own writing projects to book. In March he forwarded his three bilingual volumes, two on the Cambodian Reamker, and one on the life of Buddha, to Karpelès for consideration. In her letter of May 1926, detailing her decision not to publish and her failure to find a publisher on a trip back to France, Karpelès—who was herself on the verge of publishing an article on the Ramayana in Siam—curtly noted that Thiounn's Ramayana was "illustrated after the Siamese style." Returning all three works to the RSC, Karpelès explained that she had already told Thiounn that

> nowadays, the French public, an amateur in Oriental matters, are perfectly acquainted with the life of Buddha (see the editions by Payot, Piazza, Bossard, Abeille d'or, Leroux, etc.) and has read, in translation from Sanskrit, the Ramayana either in whole or in part (editions Maisonneuve, Bossard Michaud, etc). What this public now wants are illustrations with "local colour" . . . if we could publish a folder of the illustrations from the two works, that would be the best solution. Each engraving, in black-and-white and in colour, would be published with the Khmer text, with the French translation. The great advantage in proceeding this way is that the publications would, at the same time, serve the [interests of] the French public and the Cambodian public.

However, Karpelès continued, the minister of the palace was opposed to this view. Had he changed his mind?[25] No, he had not. Thiounn was furious at the suggestion that these works were worthy of anything less than full bookish production, and at the idea that anyone should tamper with his text. On 22 May 1926, the chief of the second bureau wrote to the RSC, arguing that the Cambodian version of the Ramayana created by Thiounn was of local interest, due to the "very probable inexistence of a complete manuscript of the Reamker in Cambodge" while numerous French and Khmer editions carried "the life of the Buddha," making its publication of little current interest. Thiounn's resistance to editorial intervention in the text or form of his magnum opus indicates that these publications never eventuated.

Later that year, Karpelès published "An Episode of the Siamese Ramayana." Arguing that "European authors working on Siamese literature have never undertaken a special study of Ramakien," she asked, "What diverse influences and local traditions could have transformed Valmiki's opus into a grand dramatic and national poem?" King Rama VI had studied these issues in his work *The Sources of the Siamese Ramayana,* but it was to be regretted, she argued, that such an erudite scholar had not extended the scope of his study beyond his kingdom, and that he omitted any mention of the Cambodian version, "older sister of the Siamese editions."[26]

We have seen how, in its formative years, the protectorate capitalized on the spiritual potency of the Vat Pnum by establishing its political offices there and financing its renovation and landscaping in ways that intimately allied this sacred site to French power and prestige. From the 1920s to 1940s, Karpelès' projects would also cement Phnom Penh's status as a religious capital by centralizing spiritually potent manuscripts, relics, and texts in its cultural institutions, allowing the protectorate to claim the role traditionally played by the monarchy as the supporter of the *sangha.* While ancient statues and texts flowed from various locales to the ESP library and the Royal Library, the modern texts produced in the Buddhist Institute were dispersed outward from the colonial capital throughout Cambodge, highlighting the colonial capital's function as a center of cultural exchange and allowing the protectorate some measure of participation in indigenous systems of merit.

As director of the Royal Library, Karpelès oversaw the production of secular texts, including a series of Khmer folktales and history books, and the religious publications of the École supérieure de Pali.[27] We glean something of the production process involved from the Buddhist Institute's publication of Louis Finot's *Le Bouddhisme, son origine, son évolution* (The origin and evolution of Buddhism), which Finot had written at the request of Nath and Tath, and which was subsequently translated by Choum Mao, a talented clerk at the Royal Library.[28] Karpelès' two largest projects were the production of a Khmer–Pali bilingual edition of the Tripitaka and the creation of a Cambodian dictionary. The dictionary project was resurrected by Sisowath, Karpelès, Nath, and the director of the ESP, Thaong, in 1926 after an earlier attempt, initiated in 1915 by Finot, had been deadlocked in a battle between reformists and conservatives that partly related to the weight and status to be accorded words in the Battambang and Siem Reap dialects.[29] The library distributed its output through "bookstores" that offered the public "books and engravings suited to national tastes, at modest prices."[30] It established four such outlets in 1927, and between 1927 and 1930, close to 60,000 volumes and 52,000 engravings were sold.[31] We get a feel for one such outlet from a letter Karpelès wrote to Palace Minister Thiounn in 1928. Noting a brisk trade in Siamese publications in Battambang on a recent visit, she commended the Royal Library's local depot there. In three months, it had sold several hundred Khmer volumes, convincing Karpelès that it could boost sales further if it made an attractive display of the library's pictures and books, instead of piling them up behind other merchandise. She had subsequently organized some display cases and was delighted to note on visiting Vat Pichharam that her guidelines had been followed by one teacher's exemplary display of books and manuscripts. At Vat de Poveal, she found the library "a model workroom, clean, calm, and well ordered," with "classes well run, and an admirable attitude on the part of the monks," and she had later been impressed on a visit to Pursat. Declaring the temple an honor to Cambodians and to the Buddhist clergy, she suggested that a letter of appreciation signed by the king be sent to the chief of Vat de Poveal.[32]

With provincial sales more than double those in the capital, the library invested in a mobile book distribution service to accelerate and expand rural access to its publications.[33] By 1930, fifty-seven provincial depots had been opened around the country, and the library's "book bus" toured each province monthly. Those who did not want to buy were free to browse through the library collections, which included both "ancient and modern" manuscripts in Khmer, Siamese, Burmese, and French, and "the political, artistic, and religious chronicles of Buddhist countries in southern Indochina," a geographic orbit that included the Khmer Kraom.[34] In 1928, the Royal Library received over five thousand readers, two-thirds of them monks.[35] "Popular curiosity fills the Library with the bare-footed every Sunday," noted the journalist Guy de Pourtalès in 1930.[36]

In addition to circulating images and ideas, the Royal Library centralized Khmer Buddhist material and literary culture, leading one visitor to describe it as a "museum of books and manuscripts." This was not a solely top-down process. Delegations of monks travelled to Phnom Penh from the provinces to donate Buddhist works and ritual objects for safekeeping in the library. De Pourtalès witnessed firsthand Karpelès' success in winning the confidence of monks from "the entire region" and in interesting Cambodians in her work, causing their gifts and books to "spontaneously accrue" in the Royal Library.[37] In 1928, for example, a group of senior monks from Kompong Cham donated antique objects and 233 manuscripts to the library.[38] Rare or decrepit manuscripts were copied on palm leaf by hired monks and scribes. As Hansen writes, the hurried execution of these mass-produced manuscripts, shorn of ritual, "undermined, rather than bolstered" traditional processes of manuscript production.[39] Here were more examples, within colonialism's cultural project, of salaried transactions that would assist in the alignment of *sangha,* state, and nation. These manuscripts, together with ritual writing objects and several pieces of statuary, were later transferred to a small museum at the School of Pali. Marvelling at the exquisite beauty of the museum's calligraphy in black and gold, seals, engravings, lacquerware, poetry, and history, one French visitor in the early 1940s dwelt on the potential of these objects to "reawaken in the Khmer soul love and pride in the past, and to stimulate [the Khmer soul] for the future."[40]

As well as printing and preserving Buddhist texts, the library stimulated reflection on the state of religion and the shape of the nation through a series of seminars launched in 1927, including a lecture by Inspector of Education Henri Gourdon on the "intellectual state of Cambodge." In 1930, Coedès invited Kram Ngoy (1865–

1936), a highly gifted balladeer of considerable local renown, to perform before Karpelès, Khmer monks, and literati at the Royal Library so that they might record in writing his oral repertoire.[41] Karpelès subsequently published a collection of his ballads.[42] Attended by average audiences of 250 monks and laypeople in their first year, these functions provided valuable forums for the identification of a national Khmer culture and bridged both *sangha* and secular worlds.[43] The seminar series continued into the late 1930s, bringing together institute and library staff, *sangha* and *neak-cheh-doeng,* and French Orientalists, and included a lecture by Paul Lévy, director of the EFEO's newly created Department of Ethnography and future director of the EFEO, on the "national characters" of Asia.[44]

In 1927, the year in which a standard Khmer orthography for the Cambodian dictionary was finally agreed upon, two people who had contributed to the conservation and edification of a Khmer national Buddhism passed away. First was Finot's protégé Thaong, director of the ESP, who had played a leading role in the Dictionary Commission. Second was Sisowath. In a letter to the reformist prince Norodom Phanuvong, written shortly after this double loss, Finot noted how he first had come to Cambodge some thirty years before, and how, on each of his returns, he was delighted to discover anew that Cambodge "has not disappeared."[45] The deaths of Thaong and Sisowath, also corresponded with the beginning of a new era of Khmer print production in Cambodge ensuring that neither the notion of Cambodge, nor the ethnolinguistic nation that Cambodge was becoming, would "disappear."

As one Cambodian lamented in 1927, unlike their bookish Siamese and Annamite counterparts, many of whom were prolific poets and writers, Cambodian officials had produced no studies or memoirs for over seventy years. Their intellectual and literary level was "nil," and even a travelogue was beyond their ken.[46] This was an exaggeration, but it was true that secular officials were more prone to write in French than Khmer, and that French works were more likely to make it into print. Karpelès' experimentation with Khmer print media corrected this imbalance, creating new opportunities for indigenous expression. Cambodge's first Khmer-language journal, *Kambuja Surya* (Cambodia sun) a monthly embracing articles on Buddhism, social and cultural events, folktales, and Cambodian history, appeared in 1926. Its flavor was serious, scholarly, literary, and documentary. Articles ranged from a series of historic articles on Angkor by Finot to reports by Nath and Tath on their tours of Cochinchina, to Suttantaprija In's *Journey to Angkor* and a Khmer summary of Zhou Daguan's thirteenth-century text.[47] In 1927, the *Société anonyme d'édition et de publicité indochinoises* launched a second Khmer periodical, *Srok khmer.*[48] Compiled by a group of French and Khmer staff and printed in Phnom Penh, this was the local edition of the Indochinese monthly *Extrême-Asie,* and its circulation reached two thousand in its first year. Like *Kambuja surya,* it was written in vernacular Khmer and published in *chrieng* script, but its tone was lighter, its language simpler, and its topics more accessible, practical, and pedestrian. The pilot issue promised advice on manual labor and farming, lessons on child care and writing, Buddhist stories and poetry, as well as news about France, Indochina, and Cambodge.[49] It urged interested readers to submit their own letters and stories, and offered subscription discounts to schools and temples.[50] By 1931 *Srok khmer* had acquired a Cambodian director, commenced weekly production, adopted a newspaper format, and begun to print photos and to sell advertising space.[51] With the three central towers of Angkor Vat as its logo, its banner and layout would provide the blueprint for the later nationalist newspaper *Nagaravatta*.

These two Khmer journals constituted significant steps towards establishing a "reading public" among Khmer residents of Cambodge. The profanity of the medium—modern print—and the vernacular language of the articles dispensed, in principle, with the need for a monk to interpret and disseminate the written word. The establishment of a commercial contract between producer and subscriber, and the journal's open invitation to readers to become its writers, represented an unprecedented leveling of the cultural hierarchy in Cambodge. It was this, rather than the actual quality of the journal, which probably led observers such as Guillaume Monod and Areno Iukanthor to condemn *Srok khmer* as the dumping ground for erroneous articles of "primary-school standard" on Cambodian culture written by Western "ignoramuses" translated clumsily into Khmer.[52]

The Khmer-language newspaper *Kampuchea bodemien* (Cambodian news), was established in 1931, and the short-lived *Ratri tngai sau* (Saturday night) in 1935. Seeking new subscribers, editorials stressed the value of newspapers as educational tools that, by making Cambodians *sivilai* (civilized), would help the development of the Khmer nation. But modern print media was far from creating a direct contract with a Cambodian reading public, and its scope for cultivation of a broad "imagined community" outside of elite enclaves was partly dependent on monks, who continued to act as information brokers in provincial and rural Cambodge. Here, *vats* or village *salaas* served as the key interface between secular and monastic, "ignorant" and "knowing" worlds, and the term *sdap gazaet* (listening to newspapers) was still used in the early 1930s to describe how *Kampuchea bodemien* was heard, not read, by most village residents. During holy days and after sermons, monks would enlighten their constituency about recent events in such invisible, but increasingly imaginable, geographic and political locations as the Khmer nation, the French colony of Indochina, Paris, and the world. Audiences who had once gathered to acquire merit now lingered to learn about current affairs and the state of the nation.[53]

Days before Sisowath's death, GGI Pasquier had sent an urgent despatch to the minister of colonies in Paris arguing that Monivong's accession was in France's best interests, not least because Monivong was a "real Khmer" who felt no attraction for Siam and would be ready to help France create a national army should France elect to pursue "racial politics" in Indochina, pitting Cambodians against the Vietnamese. He was also the Mahanikay's preferred candidate, and, presumably because he was less intelligent than other candidates for the throne, he was more "disposed to follow the directions of the French administration." The year following Monivong's accession to the throne saw the appointment of Lvi Em (1879–1957) as the new director of the École supérieure de Pali.[54] Few would have disputed the view of one of his contemporaries that Lvi Em was "Phnom Penh's best educated monk," "very capable and extremely popular." His erudition and appetite for learning earned him the respect and admiration of Nath, Tath, and the reformists, and also ensured his standing among those older Mahanikay monks who had "learned Pali under the old system, with a strong sense of religious vocation," and who distained the secular ambitions of the young students at the ESP. If due care was not given to supporting the Mahanikay's educational development, the former royal commissioner to Battambang argued presciently in a letter to the RSC soon after Lvi Em's appointment, a class of malcontents would emerge. He recommended reform of the school, as its pupils were "fleeing" from Mahanikay Buddhism instead of strengthening it, a trend that threatened to destroy Cambodge's "moral security" and to leave the country ripe for revolt. Unlike the Thommayuth, who were "Siamese partisans," and the Thommakay, the dissident faction nurtured by Thaong, the Mahanikay was intrinsic to Cambodge, enjoyed mass popular support, and was therefore the protectorate's best ally against revolution.[55] In recognition of Em's value to the protectorate, he was decorated as a Chevalier du Légion d'Honneur in 1934.

By 1927, the protectorate had brought the *sangha* under the jurisdiction of ordinary courts, thereby partially succeeding in eroding the Theravadin transcendence of common law that had once so irked colonial administrators. Shortly after his appointment as director of the ESP, Em allegedly voiced concern at the increase he had witnessed over the past fourteen years in complaints from monks, forbidden under traditional Theravadan law.[56] In July 1928, the policy linking the École supérieure de Pali to the civil service through a quota of posts for graduates, was revoked by royal ordinance.[57] Two days later, Monivong issued a new ordinance reserving the school exclusively for members of the *sangha*.[58] Traditionalist concerns that students were entering the school purely for the purposes of self-advancement in secular life may well have catalyzed these changes.[59] But of far greater concern was the role of the ESP in creating converts to the "new Mahanikay." The effects of the 1918 Ordinance No. 71 in bringing about initial peace and harmony were increasingly offset by those monks within the Mahanikay who, having acquired new learning through their study of the Vinaya books and various other works, began again to behave "contrarily to their capacity as Mahanikay," so creating new discord. In the 1920s and 1930s, as in the 1910s, the clash of opinions revolved around the reformists' translation of certain rules in Pali into Khmer, their transmission to the broader population, and the incantation of their pre-meal prayers in honor of the Buddha loudly and in unison. By contrast, "partisans of the old way" of doing things only recited the rules in Pali without feeling the need to know their meaning and recited their preprandial prayers very quietly. As described by Monivong's minister of the interior in 1937, "the new Mahanikay are also very numerous and exist in every province, and since the creation of the ESP, parents interested in the education of their sons have sent them to Phnom Penh for their studies. They then return to their village, where each monitor teaches a number of students and, as a result, these new Mahanikay have emerged as a very significant group."[60] Instigated by Monivong after consultation with the RSC, the Council of Ministers, and the heads of the Mahanikay and Thommayuth sects, the royal edict of 17 September 1929 was issued to reinforce and remind monks of the 1918 ordinance and was aimed specifically at reformists in the Mahanikay. "Certain monks, lay preceptors, and laity of the Mahanikay sect are making completely individual innovations, and are then teaching these nonconformist rules to other monks, lay preceptors, and laity in certain temples in the provinces." The new regulation formally prohibited any innovations contrary to Ordinance No. 71 of 1918 and added to the sanctions listed there the threat of recourse to "the Cambodian penal code."[61] As a follower and supporter of the Thommayuth, Monivong saw more to fear in the "new Mahanikay," whose adaptation of their robes as well as ritual and intellectual approaches threatened to blur boundaries between them and the Thommayuth, than in the "old Mahanikay." But there was another issue driving these measures to strengthen the traditional practices in the Mahanikay, and that concerned the spread of a new religion to Cambodge from Cochinchina.

THE CAODAI MOVEMENT

Founded in 1925 in Ha Tien in Cochinchina and popularly known as the Caodai, the Dai Dao Tam Ky Pho Do (the Great Way of the Third Era of Salvation) was an eclectic mix of Buddhism, Taoism, Confucianism, Catholicism, séance, and ceremony. Its syncretistic pantheon included Jesus Christ, Joan of Arc, Sakyamuni, and Victor Hugo, reflecting the cross-cultural background of its founders, who included retired colonial officials and wealthy landlords. This deification of European figures was "not a tactical cover," writes David Marr, "but a transcultural reference with political content" that asserted parity between colonizer and colonized.[62] Elaborate festivals and messianic promises won a following of hundreds of thousands of southern Vietnamese landlords and peasants, while a prolific Caodai press spread the movement among urban intellectuals.[63]

Earlier in the 1920s, nationalist rumblings in Vietnam had heightened French vigilance against threats of subversion in Cambodge. In 1924, despite noting the mostly "excellent morale" of Cambodians, RSC Baudoin had stressed the need to maintain "constant surveillance" of Cambodian officials.[64] The triple murder of the French Résident of Kompong Chhnang, his interpreter, and his bodyguard while they were on tax-collection duty in 1925 triggered an escalation of this surveillance. Nineteen villagers were imprisoned by nightfall for what appears to have been a spontaneous attack, motivated by deep resentment of a tax regime for which peasants could discern little returns and catalyzed by the trio's truculence.[65] Announcing the Phnom Penh court's guilty verdict in December 1925, the general attorney ascribed the crime to a "mass movement," thus giving rare public recognition to popular misgivings about colonial rule.[66] Over the next two years, the conversion of thousands of Cambodians from the eastern provinces to Caodai would compound colonial fears of mass action and subversion, adding impetus to the protectorate's policy to bolster Buddhism as a geocultural divide.

The establishment of a "Holy City" in 1927 just outside the city of Tayninh, mere miles from the Cambodian border, heightened this symbolic threat of a movement that threatened to erode racial, national, and religious boundaries Whereas both the protectorate and Mahanikay conservatives had seen the Thommayuth as a potential vehicle of Siamese influence, many French and Khmer administrators feared Caodaism as a Vietnamese ruse to lure Khmer believers from their "national" religion. The sheer scale of the movement, which captured the imaginations of tens of thousands of Cambodians and led to mass pilgrimages across the border to Tayninh, frightened both Khmer and French rulers and the leadership of all factions of the *sangha*. While the French saw their rule under threat, the newly installed King Monivong feared the erosion of loyalty to the royal house of Sisowath, not least because of connections between the movement and Prince Norodom Yukanthor. King, colonizer, and *sangha* therefore joined forces to repress and discredit the sect.

However, it would be oversimplistic to categorize all resistance to the movement as merely strategic or entirely manipulated by colonial control. Mahanikay conservatives were likely to have rejected the Caodai as a heretical blend of nontraditional influences, while Mahanikay reformists and Thommayuth rationalists would have shared doctrinal reservations and purist objections to the new sect. Secular *neak-cheh-doeng,* who campaigned against Caodaism as a "non-national" religion in Khmer media in the late 1930s, also framed their disdain in terms of its irrationality and superstitious practices. These attitudes tally with the "rationalist" agendas of secular intellectuals elsewhere in Asia at this time, notably the Kuomintang antisuperstition movements of 1927 to 1930.[67]

On 23 May 1927, the heads of Mahanikay and Thommayuth and the minister of religion issued a circular condemning and penalizing visits to Caodai sites of worship.[68] A week later, noting that the Cambodian population was still untainted by the nationalist and revolutionary propaganda evident elsewhere, RSC Baudoin reported that "Caodaism alone warrants our attention, because of its probable collusion with anti-French groups in Cochinchina."[69] In his report, Baudoin ridiculed Caodai publicity about miracles occurring at Tayninh Pagoda as a device to impress the "naïve and credulous Cambodians" in the frontier provinces, and prescribed a counteroffensive of surveillance and preventive measures to combat Caodai propaganda.[70] Within months, Baudoin was trumpeting the success of this initiative, claiming that peasants were increasingly reluctant to place their trust or money in the Caodai sect. Instead, the Caodai were targeting young, urban *évolués,* mostly Annamite secretaries, accountants, and telegraphers.[71]

This was wishful thinking. Ignoring the orders of their provincial governors, an estimated eight thousand Cambodians from Prey Veng and Svay Rieng travelled secretly to Tayninh for the Caodaist festival of 7–9 November 1927.[72] Despite this massive pilgrimage by entire families and Buddhist monks, the RSC refused to accept that these Cambodians were responsible for their own actions, claiming that they had not the slightest idea why they went. "We heard that there was an omnipotent being here who would alleviate our moral and physical misfortunes, reduce our taxes, give land to the poor and cure all sicknesses. We came because we are miserable, and we believe in the all-powerful one," wrote the RSC, speaking for the eight thousand.[73] Despite the lack of incident, the French administration took "necessary steps" to "ward off danger."[74] The danger to which Baudoin was alluding was not that of riot or rampage—the chief of police, who monitored the festival, was impressed by the exemplary conduct and absolute calm of the Cambodians present.[75] Rather, it was the danger of cross-cultural contamination and the contingent crystallization of transnational, anticolonial sentiment.

From the outset, the French administration suspected the Caodai movement of having a master plan involving the conquest of Cambodians and considered Tayninh a strategic hub from which the movement would radiate out into Kompong Cham, Kratie, Svay Rieng, and Prey Veng provinces through Cochinchinese proselytizers. Caodai propaganda was deemed similarly adroit: a mixture of pan-doctrinal liberalism and "a remarkable exploitation of the incurable Khmer mysticism."[76] The appeal of Caodai to Cambodians was increased with the addition of Poukombo, the rebel monk who had lived on in popular memory at Ba Pnum since 1867, to its pantheon. "Nothing was neglected," noted the RSC in 1930, "that could move the simple or stir up crowds, neither the commentaries that had arisen, in interested circles, about Monivong's accession to the throne, nor Siam's ancient prestige, nor superstitions and local legends, nor the ancient belief of the Cambodian people that, one day, a miraculous personage would end their misery. A complete arsenal of marvels was set to work; the most esoteric practices merging with vulgar wizardry, arcane formulas, and flasks of magic water to cure all ills; an equestrian statue of Sakyamuni was pulled loose and swivelled around to face Phnom Penh."[77] Peasants stockpiled salt and food in preparation for trouble, and a medium predicted political strife fomented by Siam, and the advent of a new king.[78]

Colonial administrators blamed the success of Caodaism on the cunning of its organizers and the gullibility of Cambodians. What they failed to examine or to acknowledge were the socioeconomic factors propelling a sizeable number of disillusioned Cambodians towards a new moral leadership. Within the context of earlier millenarian movements in Cambodia, Caodai's mass appeal was an index of peasant disorientation. Rural converts may have equated the sect's promise of salvation with the prospect of the regeneration of the Cambodian state.[79] One Cambodian opponent of the movement acknowledged that monks and laity were drawn to the sect by the need for consolation.[80] Another explained the movement and the emergence of other "heretical" sects as results of the social dislocation brought about by colonial intervention and warned that, despite traditional Khmer antipathy towards the Annamites, "an abnormal feeling now exists in the population" favoring the spread of Caodaism.[81] Resentment of the modernist onslaught on the "impure" layers of superstition and tradition that held meaning for many Mahanikay monks and adherents, and the Caodai's embrace of elaborate ritual and other populist practices, may also have enhanced the new sect's appeal for the Mahanikay clergy and constituency in the eastern provinces. The identification of the reformist and Thommayuth movements with the colonial capital, and the various centralizing tendencies of colonialism and its commercial and cultural projects, may have encouraged the flow of laity and monks from Svay Rieng and Prey Veng to Tayninh as a means of expressing or attempting to create a different form of regional autonomy.

In addition to flouting Cambodge's colonial border controls, this massive unauthorized human traffic challenged the geocultural constructs so carefully orchestrated by decades of French rule. Months after Pasquier had dispatched his secret missive celebrating Monivong's potential as a "race politics" warrior capable of pitting Cambodians against Vietnamese, Caodai leaders declared to a large mixed audience at Tayninh that their new religion aimed to vanquish the "traditional animosities" that had kept Cambodians and Annamites divided for so long.[82] The French response was swift. Using monks and Khmer administrators as their mouthpieces, the protectorate warned Cambodians that pilgrimages to Tayninh violated both the Buddhist faith and royal authority. Border surveillance was stepped up and legal sanctions applied as further efforts to stem the Caodai tide.[83]

Like the French administration and the Buddhist establishment, the reigning house of Sisowath saw Caodaism as a threat to its power. When a group of Cambodians at Tayninh challenged Monivong's right to the throne while Norodom's descendant Yukanthor still lived, a Caodai leader replied that "better times will surely come and the culprits will be punished."[84] No doubt shaken by the number of Cambodian pilgrims to Tayninh, and concerned about news of forthcoming rallies for Prince Yukanthor, Monivong issued another royal proclamation on 31 December 1927. Posted in all temples and district offices in the frontier provinces, the notice reminded Cambodians of their duties to their king and the fundamental truths of the Buddhist faith, denounced Caodaism as a doctrine created by Annamites who were more interested in exploiting the naïveté of Cambodians than in assuring their happiness, and reaffirmed Monivong's right to the throne.[85] Six weeks later, Monivong issued another royal ordinance, warning his subjects against engaging in disloyal activities condemned by the Buddhist faith and penalizing practice of nonrecognized religions in Cambodia.[86] This measure, wrote the RSC, "closed the first stage of Caodai development in Cambodia, namely intensive propaganda in Cambodian milieux."[87]

These steps appear to have had immediate effect. Although Caodaist activity continued in Annamite communities in Svay Rieng and Prey Veng, these passed without public incident, while Caodai propagandists steered clear of Khmers. However, behind this calm facade the Caodaists were reorganizing. Early 1929 saw a rapid resurgence of Khmer pilgrimages to Tayninh, perhaps triggered by the deprivations of the Great Depression.[88] Economic incentives certainly featured in a new barrage of Caodaist "tracts and harangues," which "promised converts the advent of a quasi-Edenic era, free from taxes and rid of the French."[89] Although the 1929 pilgrimages paled in scale beside the mass exodus of 1927, the protectorate reacted sternly, taking police measures to squelch what it saw as "dangerous propaganda." On 10 April 1929, King Monivong wrote to the RSC, imploring the protectorate to honor its pledge to help him maintain social peace in Cambodia, which was now compromised. The Cambodian authorities and people, Monivong continued, found it hard to understand why the Annamites, guests in Cambodge who openly proselytyzed for the Caodai, could celebrate the forbidden religion with total impunity while subjects of the kingdom faced severe penalties.[90] Despite such misgivings, the monarchy and the administration agreed upon a policy of tolerance, so as not to create martyrs of Annamite Caodaists. The religion would remain unauthorized and under close surveillance; but it would be tolerated, provided there was no proselytizing, no public ceremonies, and no new temples.[91]

Cambodge was not alone in fearing Caodai. In 1929, an article in the *Bulletin du Comité d'Asie Française* likened the Caodai to a large political organization and focused attention on its eight departments—which included justice, labor, agriculture, education, and external affairs. Depicting its devotees as brainwashed dupes who could easily be whipped up into an explosion of fanaticism, the Saigon newspaper *l'Impartial* warned of the incalculable repercussions should Caodaism trade its purely philosophical and religious character for a political orientation. With its passionate clientele, cellular structure, and "army of disciplined believers," the Caodai was a machine in waiting for Moscow's command. As such, it was not the repression of religion but a colonial "duty" to keep their activities under close surveillance and to ensure that such activities remained confined to the spiritual.[92]

In 1930, exasperated by the Caodaists' tenacious disregard for the law and alarmed by the coinciding of renewed Caodai activity in February with violent revolutionary protests in Tonkin and Cochinchina, the protectorate adopted a more aggressive policy of repression.[93] In April 1930, the RSC reported that Caodaists in Takeo, Phnom Penh, and Svay Rieng had "abandoned their earlier reserve" and were holding large meetings, ceremonies, and fund-raising benefits and constructing new buildings.[94] He called for watertight surveillance.[95] The suspected involvement of communist activists from Chaudoc in a flurry of Caodai meetings in Takeo, Kandal, and Prey Veng led to a further clampdown in August.[96] Provincial governors were henceforth to ban all Caodai ceremonies. Force was to be used as a last resort. All Residents were to inform the RSC of the identity of any Caodai proselytizers, who would be instantly deported.[97] In September 1930, Sûreté agents infiltrated a Phnom Penh meeting of over a hundred Annamite Caodaists, arrested ninety-six participants, and imprisoned Le Van Bay, the director of the Caodai Association in Cambodge.[98]

Although publicly legitimated as a policy to conserve Buddhism, the protectorate's suppression of Caodaism in Cambodge had clear political objectives.[99] First was the desire to preserve "Cambodian loyalism" and to recognize and protect this "admirable example" in an increasingly volatile Indochina.[100] A second, related goal, enunciated by the GGI at a meeting of the Great Economic Council in Hanoi in December 1931, was to stymie a sect perceived as a "fearful force" open to manipulation by "skilful agitators" who could use it to spread "revolutionary ideas."[101] A bureaucratic chain magnified these fears, embracing the offices of the RSC, the Phnom Penh Sûreté, and the GGI in a circular trail of espionage and reportage.[102]

In November 1931, the public prosecutor in Phnom Penh found Le Van Bay guilty of violating legal restrictions on the freedom of association and announced the dissolution of the Caodai Association of Cambodge. The Saigon appeals court upheld the ruling.[103] Le Van Bay was fined, released, and confined to Cochinchina, his movements closely monitored.[104] Outside the colonial capitals, in Cambodge's eastern provinces of Prey Veng and Svay Rieng, Caodai activities and clandestine border crossings continued. When some two hundred Cambodians attended Caodai Christmas festivities in Tayninh in 1931, the RSC declared "the need to educate the Cambodian constantly and to protect him from his own weakness."[105]

The year 1933 witnessed a fresh surge in Caodai activity. In June, French police discovered two important covert Caodai propaganda centers in the provinces of Kandal and Kratie.[106] Close surveillance of illegal Caodai meetings in August resulted in the arrest of at least eighteen Caodaists in Phnom Penh.[107] A protectorate court action against the Caodai sect's unauthorized construction of seven buildings, and its illicit establishment of two secret schools, coincided with the discovery of forty issues of the revolutionary journal *L'Aurore Malgache* at the home of a Caodai leader.[108] The year closed with another police raid on a secret Caodai gathering in Phnom Penh.[109] By 1935, at least in the eyes of the Sûreté, Caodaism was on the wane in France and Cambodge, if only in the capital and central provinces. The report noted a recent memorial ceremony held for Victor Hugo at the Caodai temple in Phnom Penh as the watershed in Caodai's local fortunes. Attended by some five hundred people, this "ridiculous ceremony," the report claimed, had "ridiculed the sect in the eyes of intelligent natives" and generated a slew of scathing commentaries in the Cochinchina and Cambodge press.[110] Despite isolated incidents, such as the arrest of a Khmer Caodai missionary in June 1936 and the defrocking of a Mahanikay monk from Prey Veng as punishment for attending a Caodai temple in Tayninh, the RSC was satisfied that Caodaism no longer constituted a threat to public order.[111]

But Caodai was not the only religion to win new converts. In the 1930s, a number of movements emerged in Vietnam to revive and modernize Buddhist activities, alongside a growing interest in both Theravada meditiation methods and the Pali canon. The attractions of the Buddhist reform movement at Vat Ounaloum changed the life of one Vietnamese veterinary doctor, Le Van Giang, whose chance encounter with Chuon Nath in Phnom Penh in the 1930s led him to ordination as a Theravada Buddhist monk at Vat Ounaloum and later to establish the first Theravada temple for Vietnamese Buddhists, which was later visited by Chuon Nath. The catalyst for Le Van Giang's reorientation had been a French translation of the Noble Eightfold Path; he went on to translate parts of the Pali canon, and to teach the Buddhist dhamma, in quoc ngu.[112] For all these projects, he would have found inspiration in the Buddhist Institute.

THE TRIPITAKA COMMISSION AND THE BUDDHIST INSTITUTE

In 1929, Coedès was appointed director of the EFEO and moved from Bangkok to Hanoi.[113] His appointment signalled a new form of response to the Caodai movement through the vigorous promotion and institutionalization of Khmer Buddhism, both in Cambodge and among Khmer Kraom communities in Cochinchina. The year of Coedès' appointment, a Tripitaka Commission was established in Cambodge, and Karpelès coordinated an intense phase of colonial and Khmer monastic activity in Cochinchina, including visits by herself, temple tours by Tath, and a visit by GGI Pasquier, whom we last met as the eloquent champion of distinct racial and cultural milieux at Marseille in 1906.[114] On 14 December, Royal Ordinance No. 106 established the commission for editing the text of the Tripitaka. Headed by Lvi Em, director of the ESP, assisted by Em Sou (1891–1939), a monk from Ounaloum who was posted to the Royal Library, the commission was otherwise composed entirely of monks from Phnom Penh's chief temples. It was to meet in a place decided upon by the president in order to study the text of the Tripitaka with the goal of printing all its eighty-four thousand verses in a complete bilingual edition of the Pali canon, to be printed, in Khmer characters (aksa Chrieng) and on paper, in the ordinary form of a book.[115] This project represented a resounding victory for Nath, Tath, and other Mahanikay reformists.

A month later, their cause was further strengthened with the establishment of the Buddhist Institute. In late 1929, Karpelès proposed the creation of such an institute, and the following January an arrêté gave her proposal legal life.[116] The Institut indigène d'études bouddhiques de petit véhicule (Indigenous Institute for the Study of Buddhism of the Little Vehicle) opened at the Royal Library in Phnom Penh on 12 May 1930.[117] King Monivong, King Sisavong Vong of Laos, the GGI, and Coedès presided over the opening ceremony.[118] Addressing some two thousand monks from Cambodge, Cochinchina, and Laos, Monivong described the institute as "a house of Franco-Buddhist friendship" where the French elite would offer "intelligent understanding" to the intellectual elites of Laos and Cambodia.[119] Karpelès' appointment as secretary of the institute heralded a new chapter in her project to divest Cambodian Buddhism of corrupting influences.[120] The institute's founding mandate was to conduct research about Cambodian Buddhism so as to rescue it from "degeneration." This mission had both scriptural and material dimensions, as reflected in the Editorial Commission of Buddhist Scriptures in Khmer and a more abstract, geopolitical agenda. Centered in Phnom Penh, the Buddhist Institute would strengthen perceptions of Cambodge as the heartland of Theravadan Buddhism in French Indochina and reorient the Khmer sangha away from Siam and towards Indochina.[121] Studying (and so magnifying) "minor differences" between Cambodian practices and those in Siam was one means of severing the sangha's links with Siam.[122] Strengthening links between monks in Cambodia and Laos through the creation of the Buddhist Institute of Laos was another.[123] But it was above all through raising Khmer Buddhist consciousness in and between the Khmer Kraom communities of Cochinchina that Karpelès hoped to combat the lure of heterodox religions.

In 1931, Karpelès defined the Buddhist Institute's zone of action as Cambodge, Laos, and "a large part of the provinces of Southwest Cochinchina, where more than 200,000 souls who have remained deeply Cambodian and profoundly attached to the land of their birth, continue their fervent practice of Buddhist precepts despite a number of obstacles."[124] The Buddhist Institute, Karpelès declared, was "helping them to conserve the pious heritage of their ancestors" and generating moral support by "establishing a constant liaison between them and their brothers in Cambodge."[125] That year, thirty monks trained at Phnom Penh's École supérieure de Pali were dispatched to *vat* schools in Cochinchina.[126] The Royal Library's book bus also ensured the dissemination of Khmer-language publications to Cochinchina, while fundraising campaigns allowed Khmer Kraom participation in the Tripitaka project.[127]

In 1932, Karpelès emerged as a passionate defender of the cultural and religious rights of ethnic Khmers in Cochinchina. Touring Tayninh in 1932, she found that the situation for Khmers had improved since 1928 but regretted that "an Annamite is teaching Khmer to the Khmer children": this was a "dangerous" precedent that risked compromising the goal set by the administration for "uplifting" the Khmer population. She recommended restricting all such education to monks. In Travinh, she found that the Khmer secretary in the Bureau of Inspection could not read, write, or speak his mother tongue fluently, and that Khmers had to pay between one to twenty piastres for the right to cremate the deceased. In Baclieu, where Son Diep had trained some sixty years earlier, she found much to praise; and in Soc Trang, Son Diep's former administrative haunt, there was a notable advance in Khmer education. In sum, Karpelès recommended the translation of all official circulars for these regions into Khmer as well as French and quoc ngu. She noted the joy and astonishment of the Khmer population in seeing, for the first time, the head of the province accompanying her to various pagodas for the donation, in the GGI's name, of the first Khmer edition of the Tripitaka.

However, Karpelès added that, whatever measures the administration took, and all it might do in the future to "give back this ethnic Khmer group its national vitality," would not be viable unless it attended to strengthening the Buddhist monkhood, "the nerve center of Khmer society." In her version, France, or at least the protectorate of Cambodge, became a protector par excellence, while Vietnam assumed the role of colonizer. "The Annamites, absolute colonizers that they were, well understood that the surest means to fragment Khmer society right down to its deepest roots" was to suppress the *sangha,* and it was clear at that point in time that the Buddhist monkhood in Cochinchina was far from fully supportive of the administration. Referring to the papal annointment of Catholic bishops in France, Karpelès suggested that the Buddhist clergy in Cochinchina could receive their nominations from the king of Cambodge or his minister of religion. In this way, she argued, the Buddhist church of Indochina could be unified; and, after all, this institution was the best guarantee the French administration had, in Indochina, against all "that which is opposed to order and to discipline."[128]

One argument for the government's investment in such projects was the notion that strengthening the Khmer Kraom's religious foundations would innoculate them against revolution as well as against the Caodai. From a scholarly perspective, the communities were of research interest, and Karpelès' conservation project was dictated by a genuine concern for their potential disappearance and assimilation to Annamite culture. As Cambodge itself seemed less and less likely to disappear as a result of its demographic development and the consolidation of colonial rule, the narrative of the "vanishing Khmer" was displaced onto the Khmer Kraom.

When Résident Supérieur of Laos Bosc recognized Karpelès' "fervent zeal, tireless energy, and profound knowledge of Orientalist scholarship" and described her as "the soul of the renovation of Buddhist studies" in Indochina, he was expressing the views of many.[129] At the same function, Tath applauded Karpelès' dedication and her zealous work on behalf of Buddhism.[130] Soon after the Tripitaka commission began its Khmer translation of the Pali canon,[131] the Venerable Narada from Ceylon visited Indochina, bringing cuttings from the Bodhi tree to plant in monasteries. Throughout this time, Karpelès also maintained connections with the Mahabodhi society and its journal. Speaking at the Buddhist Institute in Laos in 1931, Nath stressed the duty of the government and the king to protect the Tripitaka, and the *sangha*'s duty to study it.[132] In August 1931, *Srok Khmer* heralded the printing of the Tripitaka in Khmer and Pali as "a matter of interest for all 'true' Khmers, that is, those who love their country (*srok*) and race (*jiet*) and have a strong belief in Buddha," which would alert neighboring countries to Cambodge's superior stature as a world-famous center of Buddhism rivaling Burma, Siam, and Sri Lanka.[133] Four months later, two thousand monks gathered in the royal palace to witness the presentation of the final manuscript of the first volume of the Tripitaka to the visiting minister of colonies, Paul Reynaud.[134] In a commemorative verse dedicated to Suzanne Karpelès, "who loves my country," Makhali Phâl linked this achievement to the building of Angkor, praising the "children of the people of Angkor, the children of the great Khmer people" who had risen up to resuscitate the Buddhist scriptures.[135]

But not all Cambodians or Europeans shared these sentiments. In 1932, internal colonial reports began to register strong antipathy to the Buddhist Institute among certain sections of the *sangha,* most notably among the Thommayuth sect, and especially in the western provinces.[136] Many Thommayuth monks were actively obstructing the diffusion of the Royal Library's "works of popularization" in their key zones of influence, namely Battambang, Siem Reap, and Sisophon.[137] These works included a Pali-language manual composed by Nath, which Coedès acclaimed as a remarkable, modern, and practical educational tool for Pali studies in Cambodia.[138] Noting the Thommayuth's intellectual superiority complex and keen sense of independence, a Sûreté report of July 1932 attributed the sect's opposition to the Royal Library and École supérieure de Pali to concerns that the "primitive" Mahanikay sect could now acquire learning hither to considered a Thommayuth prerogative. These fears were well-grounded, according to the report, which alleged that the Mahanikay had begun to outshine the Thommayuth in erudition. The Thommayuth also feared the political repercussions of what they saw as strong protectorate support for the reformists, and were particularly incensed by what they saw as official colonial approval for the replacement of the Thommayuth head monk of Battambang by a Thommakay stalwart.

From 1930 onward, the French administration authorized the Buddhist Institute to dispatch monks to preach the Buddhist doctrine in all *résidences* of Cambodge. This proselytizing role would have a number of far-reaching consequences. The strong institutional and logistical backing afforded Nath, Tath, and their colleagues accelerated the ascendancy of the reformist faction, alienating the Thommayuth from the Buddhist Institute. The opening of hundreds of preparatory Pali schools in *vats* across Cambodge in the early 1930s also strengthened the hand of Nath and Tath's reform movement, whose virtual eclipse of the once stronger Thommayuth sect was reflected in its new nomenclature.[139] Increasingly, the Mahanikay-tmae was known simply as the Thommakay.[140]

The protectorate's official sanction and restitution of monastic rights of movement to the Thommakay and all those monks associated with the secularization of education was not welcomed by all colonial officials. In 1933, the Résident of Kompong Thom warned against the disruptive influence and "uncontrolled proselytizing" of the new Thommakay sect, both in his province and beyond. Detecting plotting by high-ranking Khmer functionaries and the Buddhist Institute, he urged the RSC to encourage the Thommakay to show greater discretion and modesty. To defuse tensions, King Monivong toured the provinces in July 1933, emphasized the "sacrifices" made by the protectorate to renew Buddhism, and urged members of the *sangha* to forget their differences and focus on the moral education of the masses.[141] The following year, the RSC sternly condemned factionalism among the *sangha* in a speech addressed to senior monks and students at the École supérieure de Pali.[142] Thommakay provocations and "incidents" subsequently abated, but by 1938, the ascendance of the reformists was reflected in the election of Nath and Tath's fellow thinker, Em Sou, to Supreme Patriarch and chief of the Mahanikay order.[143]

Other key detractors of the Buddhist Institute existed among the European and Cambodian critics of the temple-school renovation program. Such members of the Francophone elite and royalty resented Karpelès' crusade as an obstacle to the whole-hearted adoption of French education systems.[144] Prince Areno Iukanthor, for example, mocked Karpelès and condemned France's *mission civilisatrice* as an exoticist attempt to structure a traditional culture that would lock Cambodge in the past.[145] Ironically, it was precisely by recruiting the graduates of colonial schools that Karpelès facilitated the crystallization of modern nationalism in Cambodge where, as elsewhere in Asia, the "stirrings of religious reform and the effort to rehabilitate the dignity of the traditional religious culture" became politicized through the alliance of key religious leaders with a modern intelligentsia.[146]

During the 1930s, perhaps to engage the Khmer Kraom elite with her visions for a trans-border Theravadan community, Karpelès drafted a number of Khmer Kraom from Cochinchina into her project to reanimate Cambodian Buddhism and culture.[147] The most prominent such recruit was Son Ngoc Thanh (1908–1977).

Born in Cochinchina, where he had attended *vat* school before joining the French secondary-school system, Thanh completed his baccalaureat and started, but did not finish, a law degree in Paris and Montpellier before joining the Royal Library as a clerk in 1933.[148] The official relegation of animist and Brahmanistic popular beliefs from the sphere of religion to that of superstition was accelerated from 1934 onward through the establishment of the Commission on Cambodian Mores and Customs at the Buddhist Institute. It was as if the institute, in a quasi-superstitious move of its own, had opened up a new locker into which to place, and finally put the lid on, all those spirits, ghosts, and *diables* (as one translator referred to the malicious spirits known as *arak-ta*) that had been disenfranchised by its institutionalization of a new, national, and rational Khmer Buddhism. The commission reflected a new commitment on the part of the EFEO to study contemporary ethnology. In 1935, Thanh was promoted to a post within the Buddhist Institute where he worked on the Mores and Customs Commission.[149] From these offices he launched Cambodge's first overtly political newspaper, *Nagaravatta,* and established Cambodge's first school alumni association, the Association des amis du Lycée Sisowath, both of which would prove critical forums for the expression and crystallization of nationalist sentiment during the next decade.

Son Ngoc Thanh was also involved in a program administered by the Buddhist Institute to provide moral instruction to soldiers in the Cambodian militia and to Cambodge's colonial troops. Selected by Son Ngoc Thanh, monks who were "strongly nationalist, good talkers, and skilled in persuading the soldiers, using the Buddhist style of enlightenment, to love their country," made monthly visits to barracks in Cambodge and to Khmer Kraom soldiers in Chaudoc. After each session, Thanh's recruits would write an official report for the Buddhist Institute but file another report to Thanh, naming any soldiers they had identified as likely recruits for the "nationalist struggle to chase out the French."[150]

Nagaravatta encouraged a similar campaign of Buddhist education among the lay population and demonized the Caodai as a dangerous cultural contaminant antithetical to the realization of a Khmer, Buddhist nation. Despite a marked decline in Caodai activities, blatant preparations for the inauguration of a new temple in Phnom Penh in 1937 sparked an indignant article in *Nagaravatta*.[151] By prohibiting Khmers from practicing Caodai religion in Tayninh, the protectorate had effectively encouraged the Caodai to "invade Cambodge" and to consolidate a powerful physical presence and erect temples next to which official bans carried little weight. In September 1937, *Nagaravatta* printed the royal ordinance outlawing Caodaism and endorsing Buddhism as the only true and proper Khmer religion.[152] The paper escalated its campaign against Caodaism later the following year. An article entitled "Cao Dai Religion Invades Buddhism" defined Buddhism as the pure and proper religion that had existed in Cambodge for centuries and berated Khmers for allowing "Yuon (Vietnamese) to control your ideas and even Buddhism," warning that if Khmers did not snap out of their stupidity, Khmer *vats* might all be taken over by the Caodai sect. Focusing on Svay Rieng Province, it blamed the mass appeal of Caodaism on the naïveté of the Cambodian population and their complete ignorance of "the essence of Buddhism," on the province's proximity to Vietnam, and on district chiefs who thought "Caodai is strong and clever and really has the power to heal and save people." The article alleged that Caodaists from Cochinchina were living all over Svay Rieng and urged the administration to strengthen their prohibition by completely banning Cambodians from watching or listening to Caodai ceremonies or sermons and confiscating all Caodai propaganda books and pamphlets. It also recommended a campaign to propagate Buddhism in the more ignorant districts to educate Cambodians in the precepts of "their original religion" *(sasana-daem)* by organizing knowledgeable Buddhist scholars—like the Indian sages who had once spread Buddhism in Cambodia—to preach morals and spread enlightenment.[153]

Although *Nagaravatta* supported the reform movements, it blamed the feuding between the Thommayuth and the Thommakay for fracturing Cambodge's Buddhist unity and allowing Caodaism to gain a foothold. Warning that such factionalism could lead to the decline of Buddhism, the paper urged its readers not to worry about who was a Thommayuth, a Thommakay, or an old-school Mahanikay, but just to think of themselves as the Khmer race *(jiet kmae)* who were all united in one Buddhism and made merit with Buddhist monks in (the name of) Buddhism.[154] In early 1938, a *Nagaravatta* editorial called for harmony between the Mahanikay and Thommayuth sects and their supporters, and touted the slogan "One nation, one religion." Real Khmer lovers of nation would not love just one sect but both, the writer declared, exhorting readers to embrace all Khmer Buddhist factions as one. However, the article implicitly endorsed the reformist movement in the *sangha,* urging its readers to "reform your ideas and discard the prejudices of olden times, when we were stupid and didn't understand about ideas."[155]

By the late 1930s, the unintended effects of these religiocultural projects began to arouse deep concern among the upper tiers of the Khmer administration, as in the offices of the French administration. By stopping the flow of Thai Buddhist monks and materials to Cambodge, and vice versa, the cultural investments of the 1920s and 1930s had created a new arena for the flow of ideas within and between the Khmer *sangha* and laity in Cambodge and Cochinchina, with potentially destabilizing effects. As bastions of tradition, the *sangha* had long been upheld by French administrators as the best cordon sanitaire against a feared communist flux and, equally, against the feared ramifications of the pan-ethnic, trans-boundary Caodai movement that emerged in Cochinchina in the mid-1920s. But as a fluid, youthful movement committed to the energetic spread of ideas, and one whose adepts enjoyed a high degree of movement as well as public association and moral authority over both disaffected lay publics and such constituencies as the Cambodian militia, the Thommakay, or Mahanikay Tmae, had lost this simple inoculating effect against either Communism or Caodaism. Its fluidity, experimentation, and influence over a newly educated monastic and secular youth had taken the refined cultural projects of Son Diep, Pavie, Thiounn, et al. to a larger and more restless audience. A Khmer "national religion" had been successfully created, with the necessary leadership, Khmer

FIGURE 10. Image of Ven. Chuon Nath. Courtesy of National Archives of Cambodia.

vernacular texts, and virtual deification of the conceptual apparatus of a modern Khmer nation. But this was no longer a neat museum exhibit. The Thommakay had become suffused with, and espoused, a vibrant, infectious, and potentially rebellious nationalist spirit.

From 1937 onward, the avowedly anti-intellectual and anti-Semitic RSC Thibaudeau began trading notes with Thiounn and other key Cambodian figures who, in the previous decade, had been active committee members and supporters of the Royal Library and Buddhist Institute through whose offices Nath, Tath and their cause thrived. Nath and Tath's movement had gotten out of hand. While official critiques focused on the clashes it had caused between the two main sects, the Thommayuth and the Mahanikay, the real cause for alarm simmered in the subtext: the movement itself had grown through its appeal to youth. It consisted of young, inexperienced monks who were impressionable, argumentative, and arrogant. In addition to teaching Sanskrit and Pali and assisting in such literary projects as the publication of the Khmer–Pali Tripitaka, Chuon Nath and Huot Tath began to develop a more socially oriented engagement with Buddhism through such exercises as preaching tours to Cambodian militia in Cochinchina and fieldtrips with Suzanne Karpelès to Khmer communities in Cochinchina. In 1939, a Buddhist association (*Putthik samakum kampujie roat*) was established to spread knowledge of Buddhism in Cambodge. Although religious in orientation, it was modeled on a wave of new, secular associations known in Khmer as "solidarity groups" (*krum samaki*).[156]

9 | Traffic

Setting Khmerism in Motion, 1935–1945

"An aging mind, a used soul can find refuge in religion. . . . But a mind, a soul of tender years is anchored in passion." Or so was "the opinion of the students of the Lycée Sisowath, in the years leading up to the Second World War." "All these youngsters thought, perhaps wrongly and not quite fairly, that adults oppressed their mind and soul, and would even go as far as poisoning their pleasure. Rightly or wrongly, once they have an idea in their head, adolescents waste no time in doing everything in their power to "make it happen." Pain and hope alternate in the "intelligent mind" of Tikeavuth, a twenty-year-old student at the Lycée Sisowath and chief protagonist of the celebrated novel *Mealea duong chet* (Garland of the heart), written in the early 1950s by a former Sisowath alumnus, Nou Hach. Tikeavuth loves modern languages and excels in English, French, and Khmer. A fan of French poetry, he prefers new works, like André Gide's *La porte étroite* or Vaudoyer's *La bien-aimée,* to the old masters. He has no taste for science, physics, and mathematics. But he can hold his own on politics, film, and literature. A boarder, he spends his Sunday afternoons at the cinema.[1] The restless spirit of youth, experimentation, rejection of the old and embracing of the new, intertwined with the sense of being shaped by another culture and language, which pervade Nou Hach's work, also infused Cambodge's nationalisms from 1935 to 1945. This decade paved the way for the perpetuation of "Cambodge" as a concept and the collapse of the political construct of the French Protectorate. The youthful zeitgeist of these ten tumultuous years simmered in the pages of the newspaper *Nagaravatta* and in a number of new youth, school, travel, and professional associations.

Rising anticolonial sentiment jostled with deepening acceptance, among a burgeoning youth culture as well as the established politicocultural elite, of the colonial dictum that the way forward for Cambodge was a "return," through the Angkorean past, to a glorious future. Newspapers, novelists, students, reformist monks, young civil servants, and the networks in which they moved allowed the crystallization of a lasting, Khmer vernacular language of nationalism, which included calls for a "Cambodia for the Cambodians" outside of the Indochinese matrix.[2] Founded in 1936, the newspaper *Nagaravatta,* named after Angkor Vat, was pivotal in forging and disseminating this language and its visions beyond urban enclaves, often through the role of monks who read it out loud to rural audiences. New secular organizations, dubbed *krum samaki* (solidarity groups) helped to translate the rhetoric of print into the lived experience of Cambodian students and civil servants in the capital and provinces. Culture had become overtly politicized. A protest march by the most active *krum samaki,* the Association of Friends and Alumni of the Lycée Sisowath (AFALS), in 1936 was followed in 1942 by mass demonstrations by the *sangha* in the center of Phnom Penh, when thousands of Thommakay, Thommayuth, and Mahanikay monks made a rare display of anticolonial unity. The crowds were brutally dispersed, together with long-fostered illusions of a colonialism without clashes, under whose image the ghosts of more brutal clashes—those witnessed by Thiounn and Son Diep in the 1880s—had long lain buried.

This tumultuous decade was sharply imprinted by political vicissitudes in the Métropole. The 1936 electoral victory of le Front populaire (the Popular Front), led by France's first Jewish prime minister, Leon Blum, expanded the public sphere at home and abroad through its liberalization of press restrictions, while providing a fillip to such homegrown internationalist movements as the Auberges de jeunesse (youth hostels) by legislating the first paid vacations for the workforce.[3] This period of liberalization was short-lived. The Nazi–Soviet pact of August 1939 exacerbated a split in the Popular Front between the Communist Party and the rest of the left. In 1939, laws enacted against the French Communist Party were applied in the colonies, targeting such "seditious" elements as the left-wing and nationalist parties.[4] The establishment of the Vichy government the following year ushered in five years of stringent censorship in Indochina. In June 1940, the Government of Indochina swore its allegiance to Marshal Pétain and his Vichy regime, thus winning the dubious distinction of being the only "Vichy in the tropics" to outlive the fall of Pétain's command by several months.[5] Under Decoux's tutelage, the cosmopolitan Auberges de jeunesse was sidelined for patriotic scout groups that translated Vichy prescriptions for the role of youth and the celebration of antiquity into a Khmer nation with a strong monarchic, authoritarian orientation.[6] Reverberations of Vichy policy in Cambodge saw heightened surveillance not only of Cambodians but also of Europeans, particularly those of Jewish origin or cosmopolitan aspirations. Karpelès came under intense scrutiny. Peppered with contempt for senior French administrators, her letters fired the wrath of RSC Thibaudeau, who launched a vitriolic behind-the-scenes campaign to remove her from office on the grounds of her Jewishness, her gender, and her internationalist identifications. Established as bulwarks against cultural contagion and political subversion from Siam and Cochinchina, the Buddhist Institute and the École supérieure de Pali were now eyed as hotbeds of civic and political unrest, and as brakes on the modernization and Vichyization of the "Cambodian mind." The artist and romanticist Groslier, architect of an artistically defined and contained Cambodge tied to a vision of purity, ancestral repetition, and consummate replication, met a brutal end in 1945 at the hands of the Japanese police. A road was named after him in Phnom Penh, inscribing him into a cityscape whose gestures to Angkorean monument and architecture he had favored over its "westernization."[7] Karpelès, by contrast, was temporarily scrubbed from official memory.[8]

Although the departure of Karpelès and the death of Groslier prefigured the partial transfer of power and cultural custodianship to Cambodians, this process was also curbed by Vichy's "cleansing" of established Cambodian interlocutors from the political landscape. Premier Thiounn, his formidable influence feared as a potential blockage to French plans to place the teenaged Norodom Sihanouk on the throne, was forced into early retirement in 1941, by which time the perks of office had translated into a fat portfolio of land deeds. His retirement signalled the twilight of the first generation of secular literati and the ascendance of a fully formed *neak-cheh-doeng* who were decidedly less Francophile, and markedly less pro-monarchy, than Thiounn, Son Diep, et al. *Nagaravatta* was closed down in 1942 and replaced by the blander *Kampuchea,* a mouthpiece for Vichy propaganda. Long-standing plans to romanize Khmer gathered momentum, while new projects and prizes promoted French literary forms in a bid to "modernize" the "Cambodian mind." Vichy maintained a bizarre equilibrium between such modernizing projects and the cult of Angkor, managing the tensions inherent in these oscillations between modernity and antiquity through its promotion of King Norodom Sihanouk. From the time of his nomination for the throne as a teenager in 1941, colonial propaganda portrayed Sihanouk as Jayavarman the Boy Scout, a future-facing icon of the burgeoning Vichy youth movement and a backward-looking mascot of Angkorean ancestry.

Just as Doudart-de-Lagrée's 1863 assessment of Cambodians as a malleable menagerie of childish monkeys, had been proved dramatically wrong by Norodom I's subsequent attempts at coalition building with Siam, so latter-day assumptions that the newly incumbent monarch could be tailored to suit Vichy myths backfired when Sihanouk argued for, and won, national independence in 1953. Once again, as in 1916, the French Protectorate had fallen victim to its own image making, and this in an era when the power of the image was more consciously manipulated than at any prior time by European policy-makers.[9] Vichy repression could not contain the emerging realization, in Cambodge as elsewhere in Asia, of the fragility of European power. Growing indigenous aspirations for autonomy were stimulated by Japan's ascent. In 1945, Son Ngoc Thanh was installed as prime minister of Cambodge, with Japanese support. One month after his inauguration, allied military action forced Japan's retreat from Indochina and the collapse of Vichy rule, and the end of his stint in office. While internal personal constellations of political power changed, the cult of Angkor as the seat of the Khmer nation remained. By 1945, Angkor Vat had moved irreversibly from its position as an object of antiquarian curiosity on the geographic fringes of Cambodge, and its subsequent cultivation as an objet d'art in the rarefied curriculum of Groslier's school, to a highly charged political icon whose currency as a national symbol within Cambodge was heightened by its ready acceptance and salience outside the protectorate, due to its already existing place in European and regional imaginations.

CULTURES OF NATIONALISM

By the mid-1930s, the glorification of Angkor, the privileging of a *sasenaa-jiet,* the cultivation of a national style in architecture as well as dress, and the exultation of a national character in the *kmae-daem* had resulted in a reified notion of Khmer national culture on which there was general consensus in elite circles. What was disputed was the political translation of this cultural content to the foundations of a modern nation-state. Was Cambodge intrinsically royal and Francophone, as younger members of both royal houses such as Prince Sisowath Monireth and Prince Norodom Iukanthor argued, or should it be anticolonial and republican, as Son Ngoc Thanh and the editor of *Nagaravatta,* Pach Cheoun, contended? Should its culture be allowed to adapt, as many of the "Nagaravattistes" and members of the Lycée Sisowath alumni argued, to allow for the emergence of a nationally inflected, vernacular cultural sphere embracing modern Khmer novels, theater, and dance, or should Cambodian culture remain suspended as a "classical" enterprise, an isolated bubble of "national character" that might decorate but must not be allowed to pollute, and certainly not to hold back, the full modernization of schools, offices, and dress after the European model?

At stake here was also a contention of ownership of Angkor's past, and its future. In the nineteenth century imagery of Angkor had circulated in coins minted under Ang Duong, and in 1900 Prince Norodom Iukanthor had used an embossed silver seal of Angkor on his personal notepaper. The incorporation of Angkor into the letterhead of *Nagaravatta* signalled not only its transition from religious to secular icon but a more complex trajectory from royal property to an arena of national pride and participation. Until the 1885 convention, the Cambodian sovereign was the undisputed owner of all land in his kingdom. Although Angkor still lay "outside" that kingdom, its symbolic usage, and its continued place on the itineraries of queens and kings in the region, indicates that it occupied a special place in the mind maps of sovereigns as a reservoir and symbol of past power. While members of the lay public and monks used and resided in the temple grounds, and their meritorious deeds as participants in ceremonies were sponsored by wealthy patrons, this appears to have been a small and predominantly local constituency. In asserting itself as the custodian of Angkor for "global civilization" and, through the Angkor Society, the creation of Angkor Park and the propagation and replication of its imagery, the protectorate had broadened the horizons of the transmission of Angkor and had provided people across the country with an active role in Angkor—voluntary or involuntary—as coolies, donors, architects, artists, sculptors, and students. In so doing, it had laid the ground for a new dispute of ownership over the Angkorean heritage that would engage Cambodian politicians for decades to come.

In France and its colonies, royalist and republican schools of nationalism adopted diverse iconology, exemplified by the split imagery of Joan of Arc as the favorite of the right wing and Marianne as the sobriquet of the Republic. In Cambodge, competing nationalisms centered on a single image—Angkor—and, while most of the country's future political leadership by now shared the view that the temple was a national monument of a racially pure Khmer origin, they differed as to its political purchase. Was Angkor a royal symbol, embodying the greatness of past emperors and the potential of royal regeneration, a potential literally embodied in the remains of Suryavarman II? Or was it a public symbol and sign of *national* potential, evidence of the great skills and labors of those common people, enslaved to royalty, who built it?

Like the founders of the Young Men's Buddhist Association in Rangoon (1906) and their near contemporaries in the Union of Malay Youth (1938), the founders of *Nagaravatta* and the new wave of *krum samaki* had acquired a complete "column" of colonial education.[10] But the French maintenance of the monarchy in Cambodge had created a category of royalty that did not exist in Burma, where the monarchy had been exiled in 1885, or in Malaya—namely, those princes whom the protectorate had sponsored to attend lycées and military academies in France and Indochina. Such figures championed an odd mixture of authoritarianism, militarism, monarchism, and traditionalism, combining Angkorean symbolism with the notion that Cambodians were intrinsically good, naïve, and ignorant. Exponents of this school held that common Cambodians should be consigned to what Chakrabarty aptly calls the "waiting room" of history as people unfit for self-rule. Some also maintained that existing French rulers were imposters who should make way for the return of a new, improved monarchy. These included Prince Monireth, whose preferred pen name was Kmae Botraa (Son of the Khmers), and Prince Areno Iukanthor, the son of the exiled Norodom Iukanthor.[11] While Monireth invoked RSC Sylvestre's ire by publishing his poems in *La presse indochinoise* in the 1930s, Iukanthor outraged the GGI with his book *Destin d'empire* (1935), a rambling diatribe against a corrupt French administration.[12] Although the book discredited Iukanthor's rival contender for the throne, Sisowath Monivong, it championed the monarchy as an institution and explicitly condemned republican civil servants. "In Asia and in Africa, [bolshevism] calls itself nationalist," argued Iukanthor, calling for "a monarchist colonial program."[13] His concerns foreshadowed a central rift in the contending nationalisms that would color Cambodian politics through and after the transition to Independence, pitting the advocates of paternalism and autocratic rule, such as Monireth and Sihanouk, against the proponents of democracy and popular participation, such as Son Ngoc Thanh and Prince Yuthevong.[14] Although both schools of thought championed Buddhism as the national religion and Angkor as the avatar of the nation, they differed in the ways in which they interpreted and mobilized these fields of belonging.

The new generation of *neak-cheh-doeng* stressed the need for Cambodge to experiment, adapt, and modernize, and to move away from the notion of Cambodians as copyists towards one of Cambodians as builders by promoting the development of modern cultural forms through adaptation and innovation, sometimes as a means of competing, in cultural production, with neighboring countries. *Nagaravatta* aired some of the frustration felt by Cambodians at the constricting template of colonial arts education and expressed aspirations of those wishing to experiment with modernity.[15] The more conservative school, however, harnessed colonial narratives of past grandeur to a royalist vision and shared Groslier's view of artistic tradition as contemporary Cambodge's national heirloom. By enlisting the semiology of Angkor as evidence of the greatness of Suryavarman II and Jayavarman VII, and therefore of the innate potential of the Khmer monarchy, figures such as Monireth, Iukanthor, and Sihanouk stepped more readily into the space the protectorate had carved out for itself as guardian and protector of an innocent, passive, pious, and highly dependent people. These were not exclusive categories, however, and some forged a nationalism combining elements of both of these main schools.[16]

Ironically, while many European savants and colonial officials emphasized Angkor as an indicator of past superiority vis-à-vis other regional "races," notably Annamites, those who favored innovation often phrased their arguments for change by stressing the need to compete with the cultural productions of Vietnam and China. This discourse was particularly marked among those who could best make these comparisons, notably Khmer Kraom such as Son Ngoc Thanh and Pach Cheoun. Unlike Son Diep, they had, or claimed, no royal connections or patrons. Both had served or studied in the Métropole, and both were presumably proficient not only in Khmer and French but also in quoc ngu. As subjects of Cochinchina, they moved in a legal buffer zone, being at once on the receiving end of special Khmer educational programs and subject to the jurisdiction of Vietnamese, not Khmer, courts. They are likely to have taken a central part in debates that raged among Annamese, Cambodian, and Lao contributors to the French-language media from 1934 onward, and probably fired some of the leading sallies in a war of words calling for a Cambodia for the Cambodians, and for the liberation of Cambodge from Indochine. We can only guess at the psychological effects of these cross-currents of official geographic and identity discourses, but in many respects the contemporary climate in Cochinchina must have resembled Anderson's evocative metaphor of the "darkroom" of nationalism, where the trilingual fluency of such young intellectuals would have heightened their anomie and, perhaps, reinforced their desire to carve out a cohesive ethnic space for themselves "as" Khmers, with the cultural credentials of "pure-Khmer-ness" *(kmae-sot)*. Son Ngoc Thanh and Pach Cheoun's promulgation of an ethnically homogeneous but territorially elastic vision of the Khmer nation allowed for the incorporation of Khmer Kraom in Cochinchina as well as ethnic Khmers in Siam into their visions for the nation. Although this debate was sparked by concern over Annamese immigration and legal rights and distinctions affecting both Vietnamese and Chinese in Cambodge, the ideas of nation espoused by contributors to the 1930s debate were always primarily framed with reference to language, literature, and culture, and only secondarily with legal issues. "To whom does Cambodia belong?" asked Khemeravanich (Khmer commerce) in August 1934. In a nationalization program for "foreigners" in Cambodge, he insisted that, first, "all denizens in Cambodge had to learn to speak Khmer," as language would precipitate Khmerization; second, he suggested "a chair in Cambodian literature in order to improve and enrich the Khmer language," and only third demanded "Khmer legal jurisdiction over all Annamese." Similarly, in 1937, a Khmer nationalist named I.K (possibly standing for Ieuv Kaoes) pled for mandatory Khmer-language instruction in all public and private schools. While calling for a halt in Annamese immigration to Cambodge, Khemeravanich argued that ethnic Vietnamese could become "Cambodian" because "Cambodge belongs to all of its members without racial or religious distinctions." This argument would have cut little ice with opponents of the Caodai sect, but here the Khmer language becomes the defining instrument of national identification. In a statement that would have alarmed Sylvestre as much as his successor Thibaudeau, I.K. linked this conceptual, Khmer nation to the territiorial integrity of a separate Khmer state: the Indochinese union was detrimental to "our national future," he argued. Echoing these sentiments, Khmerak Bottra postulated, Cambodge is certainly not a province, but a "veritable country with its own national *patrimoine*." [17]

THE *NAGARAVATTISTES:* MEDIATING ANGKOR AND "KHMERISM," 1935–1941

Khmer Issarak historiography pinpoints 1935 as the starting date for nationalist struggle, when "Son Ngoc Thanh, together with the Cambodian elite, began to seek Independence for Cambodia and to fight openly against the French" through such vehicles as the Association of Sisowath Alumni and *Nagaravatta*.[18] From its launching in 1936 until its closure by colonial authorities in 1942, *Nagaravatta* provided a forum for editors, journalists, members of the *sangha,* civil servants, artists, and others to articulate their visions of a Khmer nation. Son Ngoc Thanh's chief sidekick in these ventures was a Khmer Kraom named Pach Choeun, who had served as an interpreter for Khmer troops in France during World War I and had since established his own business in Phnom Penh.[19] Established under the patronage of Norodom Sihanouk's father, Prince Norodom Suramarit, *Nagaravatta* fast became Cambodge's best-selling newspaper.[20] This was partly due to the energetic efforts of Pach Choeun, who doubled as a travelling salesman in the provinces, broadcasting *Nagaravatta*'s nationalist message at *vats* and government offices.[21]

The paper's provocative articles questioning French policies, and its use of such symbols as Judge Rabbit, an arbiter of justice in Cambodian folklore, also struck a popular chord. "When {*Nagaravatta*} had been out for a while, the Khmer people, who used to be fast asleep and deadly scared of the French, started to open their eyes, to wake up, to like their nation," wrote Bunchan Mul in his postcolonial memoirs. Claiming that all Cambodian officials despised the Khmer script, Mul described the bulk of *Nagaravatta*'s readers as the products of *vat* schools, poor people, and workers who could not read the French-language newspapers. In a reversal of Nath and Tath's hiding of French books, officials in the administration who wanted to read *Nagaravatta,* wrote Mul, would hide it inside the pages of their French newspapers. He maintained this was out of linguistic snobbery, but it may equally have reflected the newspaper's reputation as subversive.[22] As Mul well knew, most of *Nagaravatta*'s articles were written by Cambodian products of the colonial school system; it was because they were tied to their office jobs, or working for the administration and unable to write using their real names, that Pach Cheoun, a businessman, fronted the paper and did all the legwork of marketing it in the provinces. Written by bureaucrats, many of the articles were directed at the products of colonial schools. Indeed, this elitist slant led one incensed reader from Svay Rieng to complain about *Nagaravatta*'s preoccupation with the salaries of colonial civil servants, when most Cambodians were working the fields for scant return.[23] But it soon attracted a broader readership.

Although precedents for *Nagaravatta* existed in the journals of the Royal Library, its founders are also likely to have been inspired by the quoc ngu newspapers *Công Luân, Diên Tin,* and *Saigon*. Printed in Cochinchina, they each had a weekly Cambodge page, were present in the reading rooms of the Cambodian civil service associations, and their growing circulation attracted Sûreté concern. An additional template existed in the fiercely irreverent *Le Khmer*.[24] In July 1935, under a directive of the new government of the Popular Front, the GGI lifted colonial censorship restrictions, unleashing an explosion in the writing, printing, and dissemination of quoc ngu materials in Vietnam.[25] Despite these concessions to press freedom, *Nagaravatta* was subject to the same close scrutiny as the French, Chinese, quoc ngu, and Thai journals then available in Cambodge, all of which were monitored by the Sûreté through its Bureau du Contrôle de la Presse (Office of Media Control). Of most concern to the protectorate was the French media, and particularly the avant-garde *Le Khmer,* whose "disruptive influence" and "ridicule" of French authority was identified by Sylvestre, in 1935, as a critical factor behind the growing disaffection of indigenous officials and educated youth.[26] In addition to such official screening, *Nagaravatta*'s contents were regulated by the self-censorship of its authors and editors, and in that sense its articles should be read as the surface wrappings of a nationalist movement whose debates probably went far deeper in private conversations. Despite these limitations, though, the paper offers a valuable window into key debates among Khmer intellectuals in the 1930s, and was probably the most successful among the protectorate's Khmer-language publications in soliciting and printing letters and opinion pieces from a range of Cambodians.

Nagaravatta's editors defined it as "the newspaper belonging to the Khmer nation," and extended the horizons of this "national" readership from the Cambodian capital and provinces to embrace "our brothers" scattered in Cochinchina and Siam.[27] It was probably Pach Cheon, who in a 1938 editorial described the newspaper's mission as to "persuad[e] the Khmer race, it's blood brother, to march forward in progress, to work hard, to study with all its strength, so as to embarrass other neighboring races, who have already developed."[28] A common undercurrent to this discourse was a deeper matrix of comparison in which writers for *Nagaravatta* compared Khmer society and "national character" to those of the Vietnamese and Chinese. The derogatory term "Yuon" was commonly used to denote Vietnamese, and Vietnam was depicted as an erstwhile invader with an appetite for swallowing Khmers and Cambodia. Responding to an editorial by "Achar Kuy," which had suggested that Cambodians should learn from the Chinese and Vietnamese, a reader who "had read *Nagaravatta* for many days and months now" worried that Khmers were "too shy" to learn from the Chinese and Vietnamese, implying that in this respect Khmers were their own worst enemy. Using the example of students in school being afraid to ask the teacher if they did not understand something as they were afraid of being looked down upon, he suggested that it was this same fear that was holding Khmers back from acquiring knowledge.[29] Echoing these sentiments, a later reader asked, "If Vietnamese look down on Khmers, what do the French think?"[30]

However, there were two areas in which *Nagaravatta* remained staunchly against adaptation to a Vietnamese model and insistent upon Khmer cultural superiority, and that was in the area of religion and its writings about Angkor Vat, both of which domains became inextricably intertwined with developing debates on racial superiority and cultural specificity, and with the growth of an ideology first coined by Pach Cheoun in 1938, which would later be elaborated upon by Lon Nol—"Khmerism" *(kmae-niyum).*

DEBATING KHMERISM *(KMAE-NIYUM)*

Explaining why the newspaper had chosen the name *Nagaravatta,* an editorial in September 1938 identified it with "Khmerism" *(kmae-niyum).* Stressing Angkor's unique status, the writer claimed that Angkor had been erected "to demonstrate the great power of the Khmers in the world, both to the West and to neighboring countries (like Tonkin)." Not only did Angkor attract visitors from all over the world, including America, Europe, Africa, and elsewhere, but the imagery of Angkor had spread across the globe. Echoing the theme of regional cultural competition, one writer stressed Angkor's central place on the Khmer national flag and emphasized its role as an instrument for demonstrating Khmer greatness to the world.[31] Another writer urged the Khmer nation *(khemera jiet)* to visit the temples at least once, because it was the heritage and handiwork of the Khmer race *(puc kmae),* and urged those who had already seen it to reflect upon it deeply and recognize how high the Khmer nation had once been, and how low it had now fallen.

Indicating that this colonial trope had not permeated deeply throughout Cambodge beyond *neak-cheh-doeng* circles, the writer expressed his sadness over Khmer visitors to the temples who dismissed Angkor as just a pile of old stones and compared such reactions to those of the Cambodians referred to in early French accounts, who "didn't know or recognize the beautiful and valuable things that their ancestors had bequeathed to them." In a now familiar refrain, he urged readers to "take great pride in the Khmer temples of the Khmer nation *(jiet).*[32] In 1930, perhaps reflecting his own detachment from emerging debates within *neak-cheh-doeng* circles, the French priest Guesdon had translated the word *jiet* as "existence . . . generation . . . avatar, taste, essence" in his French–Cambodian dictionary, only slightly expanding upon the meanings recorded by Aymonier and Son Diep some fifty years earlier.[33] Depending on the context, *jiet* could be construed to mean race or nation. By this juncture, *sasana* was still being used to encompass religion, race, and ethnicity, and its root, *sah,* was rendered in Guesdon's 1930 Cambodian–French dictionary as "order, commandment, precept, discipline, religion, race, caste."[34] Heder and Ledgerwood have interpreted this semantic overlap as reflective of a worldview wherein in-groups and out-groups were defined by perceived religious distinctions, as opposed to skin color.[35] However, during the 1930s, skin color began to feature in *Nagaravatta*'s race discourse.

In addition to European racial ideology, burgeoning nationalist movements and media in India, China, Annam, Tonkin, Cochinchina, and Siam were given widening currency to such notions. Key here was Sun Yat-Sen's promotion, in China and among overseas Chinese, of the idea of "yellow" race as a unifying identification embracing Chinese, Vietnamese, and others against the oppressive, colonizing "white" races of Europe, and the juxtaposition of this yellow race against the lower "brown" races of Cambodia and the Philippines.[36] By the late 1930s, some Cambodians had apparently begun to adapt such notions alongside Metropolitan discourses such as that expounded by Louis Jacolliot, whose theory of the "Aryan" race was at this juncture being adapted by Adolf Hitler as theoretical ballast for his holocaustic vision of a Jew-free world.[37]

In 1938, a self-styled "Son of the Khmers" drew upon such theories to construct a variation on the Chinese theme, arguing that Cambodians and French shared the same Aryan racial roots and belonged to a different race than the "yellow" people of Japan, China, and Vietnam. Describing the Khmer nation (*jiet kmae*) as a good race (*puc laa),* Son of the Khmers explained that the blood of the Khmers came from "Klung" (Indians), which was already mixed with European blood, meaning that Khmers were blood relations of the French, and that this explained why Khmers were big and strong, in contrast to Asian stock.[38] But this racial difference was not only located in the Khmer physique; it was also identified with the huge temples of Angkor, whose stones and building took on an almost machismo quality in some writing, and whose locality allowed Khmers simultaneously to claim the common "Aryan" genealogy mooted by a number of French writers in the 1920s and early 1930s, and to claim for Cambodge a cultural specificity.

The 1930s also saw the emergence of nationalist prescriptions for "modern" cultural performances and representations of Cambodge, which diverged from the exoticist formulae of the protectorate and the elaborate theater of court dance and comprised both vernacular novels and modern drama. Both these genres were sponsored by AFALS, while *Nagaravatta* printed outside contributions and its own opinions on Cambodian dance and art, some of which indicate how fraught this domain for the performance of a nation became and illuminate the frustrations of those writers, artisans, and actors who wanted to experiment and improve upon the patterns of tradition.

Emphasizing a growing appetite among Khmers for reading stories, and noting popular enthusiasm for the newspaper, a group of readers writing to *Nagaravatta* from the province of Kompong Cham in 1938 asked the paper to establish an association for printing such moral treatises as *Katalok* and *Katatho,* so that the Khmer *jiet* would "definitely progress and not disappear." Without *Nagaravatta,* the writers continued, "our country *(srok-yeung)* would certainly be as dark as night, and would definitely be destroyed."[39] A few months previously an article had hinted at the dangers of such cultural forgetting. Asking readers, "Have [we] all forgotten our birthnation?" an anonymous author, who fused monument and race in the term *puc-nokorvat* (Angkor Vat race) pledged to correct the amnesia of anyone who had "forgotten" how Angkor was built.[40]

In its reporting on modern Khmer theater, *Nagaravatta* also encouraged a vision of an inclusive and progressive national culture, more closely allied to the concerns and lifestyles of the French-educated secular elite than were the lengthy performances of court dance associated with political tradition, and especially the monarchy. This debate was not restricted to *Nagaravatta,* as indicated by a 1936 article by a Vietnamese in *Le Khmer* who spoke of his excitement on discovering "new spectacles" in Cambodian theater, including an aria apparently "borrowed from . . . Cambodians from Cochinchina," which were a welcome break from the archaic costumes and classical gestures of court performances.[41] The debate resurfaced in the mid-1940s, when a master of "old Khmer theater" wrote a letter to *Nagaravatta* stressing the value of traditional theater as a medium of moral education.[42] While conceding "that *lkaon* [a stylized form of dramatic dance] is useful . . . as a school" in its reply, *Nagaravatta* depicted *lkaon* as a theater of the absurd, bereft of all but bad morals, including stories that lampooned monks and told of princes who sold or killed their wives or children.[43] An article published soon after the establishment of Vichy used the fact that "Cambodian theaters are continuing to give their regular performances" to emphasize the existence of a state of normality and to show how all Cambodians, from intellectuals to peasants, continued to go about their daily business.[44] The next month, an article on Khmer theater stressed the number of modern Khmer performances, critiquing aspects of them—including a tendency to break into other languages while speaking Khmer, leaving audiences in the dark—and hoping for the modernization and improvement of "Khmer theater" *(lkaon kmae).*[45]

In a similar vein, *Nagaravatta* saw an indispensable place for both the Buddhist Institute and the Royal Library in conserving Khmer culture and aligning Khmer Buddhism with modernity, describing the library as "the heart of Srok Khmer," a place rich in Khmer customs and social mores and a "meeting place for Khmer scholars who disseminate these precepts to the Khmer nation."[46] The paper welcomed Karpelès' projects—the mobile book bus, a new globe she installed in the institute, her broadcasting of music from Buddhist countries, and the launch of a Buddhist Institute radio program—as her ways of bringing "modernity to Cambodge."[47]

This dual attachment to a body of cultural "tradition" and recognition of room for improvement, ran parallel to a renunciation of political traditions. A 1938 article in *Nagaravatta* condemned the continuation of old paths to power whereby people exploited personal connections, and not the formal educational qualifications established by colonial schools, to access rank and wealth.[48] Exasperated by the emphasis on following in ancestral footsteps and adhering to ancestral norms, the writer blamed "Khmer tradition" for leaving the country "as stunted as a monkey's bottom."[49] Another 1930s writer, who styled himself Son of the Khmers, condemned the Khmer culture of obedience for miring Cambodians in a rigid social hierarchy through subservience and fear.[50] A group of writers from Kompong Cham submitted the following views on the matter:

> Our country has only one real leader but it's like two leaders. It's too difficult for us to act free and happy and developed if we are afraid to go and find the "owners" *(look-mjah)* to decide things for us because we don't know who we should go and see first; it's like ghosts with a big family tree, when Blue-Vase walks in she says Prince Pundit *(samdec-preahkru)* did it, but then when Prince Pundit makes his entrance he says it's all Lady Hotcoals' doing. This country's not much different from this fairy clan; if we are sick and get well they say they've cured us, but if on the other hand we die, they deny [responsibility].[51]

Such critiques mirrored the beginnings of a nationalist ideology that would on the one hand hold on to and magnify the geocultural body of Cambodge shaped by the colonial encounter while on the other hand rejecting autocratic modes of governance in favor of a European-style meritocracy and democracy. Their clever ambiguity—was the "real leader" the French or the Cambodian administration?—allowed them to escape the Sûreté's ire.

In addition to its cultural and political prescriptions for the Khmer nation, *Nagaravatta* espoused a form of economic nationalism, often with an ethnic bias. An early "Saturday report" by columnist Achar Kuy asked, "Why is the Khmer nation poor?" and held up the success of businesses in Cochinchina as an example that Cambodians could ignore at their peril.[52] Another pointed to the thrift and industry of the Chinese as a model, and designated not racial characteristics but their "social conventions" as the reason behind the financial success of penniless immigrants from China who established their own shops and businesses within one or two decades.[53] During the late 1930s, these concepts gained a new means of circulation in the form of Cambodge's first *krum samaki,* or solidarity groups.

ORGANIZING KHMERISM: ALUMNI, *AJISTES,* AND SCOUTS

Unlike their earliest known predecessor in Cambodge, the Mutual Education Society founded in 1905, the *krum samaki* of the 1930s enjoyed a broad and predominantly Khmer management structure and membership base. Ranging from provincial business associations for the promotion of Khmer trade to a national network of judges, these groups offered many of their members their first experience of belonging to an extrafamilial group outside the *sangha* and a new sense of organizational autonomy, which generated a palpable sense of power and pride, as reflected in many related letters and articles published in *Nagaravatta*.[54] While not all secular associations were nationalist—a prime example being the Friendship Association of Khmer Judges—most were national in membership, branch activity, and orientation.[55] Aided by the protectorate's expanding system of roads and railways, and by the *krum sama-ki*'s own erection of clubhouses and hostels, the *krum samaki* fostered new activities of people—whether to visit national sites, as did the Youth Hostelling Association and the Cambodian Scout Group; or to stage and watch "national" plays in Phnom Penh and the provinces, as did the Association of Friends and Alumni of the Lycée Sisowath; or to inaugurate provincial branches and discuss national networks. By fostering contacts and a kindred spirit among the nascent class of *neak-cheh-doeng,* these groups stretched the parameters of the newly emerging public cultural sphere in ways that translated the sense of imagined collectivity and imagined community described by Shils and Anderson into a new experience of both national space and *l'idée national.*

A local model for the new groups existed in the Association amicale du personnel indigène des résidences du Cambodge, established in 1932 or earlier. By 1938, perhaps reflecting the preference of Cambodians for the new *krum samaki,* key leadership positions in the association that had been held by Cambodians in 1932 were entirely filled by Vietnamese, and the association changed its name from an *indigène* (native) association to an *indochinois* (Indochinese) association.[56] But the most obvious models for the *krum samaki* were in interwar France, whose proliferation of royalist "old boys" *(anciens élèves)* clubs at Catholic schools and republican Freemason clubs, whose rank and file were poorly paid schoolteachers and civil servants, may well have inspired Son Ngoc Thanh during his legal training, and Prince Monireth during his training at the St. Cyr military academy, to set up similar networks in Cambodge. In their thinking and later activities, Son Ngoc Thanh and Monireth reflected the intellectual divisions of interwar France, torn between the virulently nationalist, anti-Semitic, and antidemocratic platform of the Action française and the republican, participatory nationalism espoused by such groups as the Freemasons.[57] These contesting nationalisms were mirrored in the agendas of the Métropole's two major youth groups: the youth hostelling association (Auberges de jeunesse) and the scout movement, both of which expanded in 1930s France, as youth movements did in Mussolini's Italy and Hitler's Germany.[58]

Son Ngoc Thanh, who had enrolled at law school in early 1930s France, adapted the French models of the *anciens élèves* clubs and the *auberges de jeunesse* to his Cambodian support base, whose social profile resembled that of the Freemasons. Travelling to France, he would have already had "solidarity" on his lips and in his mind as one of a string of buzzwords circulating in the quoc ngu and French media in early 1920s Vietnam.[59] Prince Monireth, like Prince Iukanthor and such technocrats as RSC

Thibaudeau, subscribed to a blend of Maurassisme in their disparagement of lawyers and intellectuals as unfit to rule and their emphasis on military stature. Founded by Prince Monireth, supported by King Monivong and the RSC, and joined by Prince Sihanouk, the Cambodian scout movement enjoyed the strong backing of both monarchy and protectorate, and grew particularly active during the Vichy regime.[60] The transference and adaptation of these foreign models of social cohesion and national contestation into Cambodge was accelerated by the 1936 electoral victory of le Front populaire (the Popular Front), a coalition of left-wing parties that began planning colonial reforms under Leon Blum, and that also lent new impetus to youth groups.[61]

First noted in a Sûreté report of 1934–1935, scout groups in Cambodge created new travel networks centered on camps and outdoor hikes designed to build national character through exposure to the great outdoors and national sites.[62] The movement described itself as a "solidarity group" that aimed to teach Khmers to love the nation (jiet) and the country (nokor). True to its founder and chief, Prince Monireth, it espoused strong ties to military, royal, and colonial authority.[63] Its corralling by Francophile royalists, and its synergy with Vichy projects, presented few problems to the authorities.

Modelled on the Auberges de jeunesse, Cambodge's first youth hostel association (yuvsalaa) was launched in 1938 at the Royal Library[64] to encourage Cambodian students to visit such sites as Angkor Vat at little cost.[65] Its first provincial hostels were established in Kampot and Takeo, and in December 1938 Yuvsalaa announced plans for a new Siem Reap hostel and a future focus on "ancient sites."[66] By uniting Cambodians from different provinces in a secular setting in celebration of national sites of natural beauty such as Bokor, or of antiquity such as Angkor, these groups enabled their members to experience national space in a new way.

This traffic did not stop at the boundaries of each krum samaki, nor did these secular groups operate on a purely secular plane. Plural membership facilitated the flow of ideas across and between different groups, while Nagaravatta acted as a noticeboard for many krum samaki activites. The establishment of the Buddhist Association in 1939 generated further exchange of ideas between temple and clubhouse. The ESP prize-giving ceremony held in the Royal Library in March 1942 neatly illustrates this cross-weaving of religious and secular. Nagaravatta and AFALS sponsored the prizes for the school's best pupils, and the ceremony was attended by the secretary of the Buddhist Insititute, the director of the ESP, and designates of the Buddhist Association, Lycée Sisowath alumni, Nagaravatta, the Mahanikay, the Thommayuth, the king, the RSC, monks, and laypeople. Pivotal to this interface were intellectuals who straddled several institutional domains, such as the novelist Nou Hach, and the writer Gnok Them (1903–1974). Schooled in Battambang and Thailand, Gnok Them joined the Tripitaka Commission in the 1930s, defrocked in 1936, and became editor of Kambuja Surya in 1938. His first novel, Pisac snaehaa (The love demon), published by the Buddhist Institute in 1942, was set in the Lycée Sisowath.[67]

THE LYCÉE SISOWATH

"Sunday! In the East, dawn stains the horizon purple. The Lycée Sisowath is still calm before wake-up time, but some rustlings can be heard here and there in one of the dormitories. . . . A moment later, the concierge shatters the blue haze of dawn with a roll of the drum. Strident cries ring out like Chinese firecrackers . . . armed with galoshes, some students wage war on the bugs, crushing last night's blood-sucking enemies against the slats of their beds. . . . Other boys, a *krama* wrapped around the waist, are busy collecting their laundry. . . . " So opens *Garland of the Heart (Mealea doung chet)* by Sisowath alumni Nou Hach (1916–1975), who entered the Collège Sisowath in 1932 and graduated from the Lycée in 1939.[68]

The hand behind the establishment of the Lycée Sisowath in 1935 was that of RSC Sylvestre, veteran administrator and author of "How To Be a Khmer Civil Servant." "Old Cambodians saw a near future where all the posts in the French administration would be occupied by . . . graduates of the Lycée Sisowath," who would help administrators increase "their understanding of the true Khmer soul," commented an editorial in *Le Khmer*.[69] By 1940, the Lycée, which enjoyed the same status and a similar curriculum to the existing *lycées* in Saigon and Hanoi but taught in Khmer and French, had an intake of five hundred, more than double that of the Collège Sisowath's 1930 enrollments. Most of its students were from the Francophile Khmer aristocracy, the new secular elite, Sino-Khmer and Chinese merchants, and high-ranking Vietnamese administrators. An ethnic quota system led to a steady increase in the proportion of native Khmer students, and after 1940 the great bulk of Khmer-speaking adolescents who achieved a solid French education in Indochina did so in Phnom Penh.[70]

The Lycée's contribution to the uniting of young minds was not purely intellectual. Its classrooms and dormitories, largely insulated from Sûreté surveillance and removed from the watchful eyes of family or community elders, offered Cambodian youth a rare freedom of association and discussion, and helped to forge a sense of connection that was far from imagined in its physical immediacy. This sense of cohesion was first given political vent in May 1936, when RSC Sylvestre issued a circular ordering all Cambodian students at the new *lycée* aged twenty and above to pay the same poll tax as their peers in Vietnam, hoping to net a total 3,000 piastres in revenue from the school. Arguing that the protectorate's own failure to provide decent schooling had inevitably delayed their secondary education through no fault of their own, and that a comparison with Vietnam was therefore invalid, students rallied in protest and asked the RSC to raise the age limit to twenty-four years. The first protest involved boarding students who separated from a school outing and did not return to the *lycée*.[71] Among the striking students was Nou Hach, and possibly Pach Choeun.[72] Subsequently, a group of students who left Phnom Penh to seek an audience with King Monivong at Oudong were stopped en route and detained for two days by the Sûreté. But the protests were successful. His hand forced by the intervention of King Monivong and the director of education, Sylvestre waived the tax.[73]

In his monthly report to the GGI, Sylvestre blamed the "most evolved Cambodian milieux" for the strikes, and stressed the "disturbing . . . political evolution" of the Cambodian elite.[74]

Nagaravatta dated the founding of the Sisowath Alumni Association to late 1934 or early 1935 and implied that Son Ngoc Thanh had founded it to further Khmer progress.[75] The Sûreté described its organizers as "pretty active, evolved Cambodians, with a rebellious temperament," and identified it as the most dangerous of those "associations, sports clubs, boy-scouts, etc." being established by Cambodians to "round off their social and intellectual development."[76] Perhaps to keep AFALS on its side, the colonial administration contributed to its running costs. However, AFALS rapidly became financially independent, earning enough money to hire new premises and to start a fund for needy students from membership subscriptions from Phnom Penh and the provinces, and from various fund-raising benefits.[77]

In June 1937, probably in a bid to weaken Son Ngoc Thanh's organizational clout and his popularity in the capital, the French administration transferred him from the Buddhist Institute to a post as prosecutor at the provincial court in Pursat. *Nagaravatta* mourned the loss of this Khmer Kraom who knew Khmer language, literature, customs, and culture even better than some "real" Khmers *(kmae-sot),* and condemned his relocation to this remote posting as a deliberate ploy to deprive the capital of a valuable spokesperson for Cambodian culture.[78] This definition of a *kmae-sot* as something that a Khmer Kraom was not innately but could aspire to, emphasized the territorialization of the concept of a Khmer nation as an area demarcated by Cambodge's colonial borders, implying that "real" Khmers must be born and acculturated within these new borders. In a similar vein, a 1937 obituary for Sylvestre in *Nagaravatta* likened his grip on the administration and customs of Cambodge to that of a "pure Khmer" *(kmae-sot).* Such statements implied that Kmae-sot-ness and a "true Khmer soul" consisted of a cultural condition that could be acquired through appropriate education and familiarization.

Far from weakening Son Ngoc Thanh's hold or nipping nationalism in the bud, his transfer expedited the creation of an interprovincial AFALS network. In May 1937, soon after Thanh's relocation, a new branch opened in Pursat.[79] An AFALS delegation from Phnom Penh attended the launching by its president, provincial governor Nhek Thioulong, and spent two days in Pursat discussing plans to open branches in all provinces.[80] Months later, Pach Cheoun attended the opening of a new Ministers' Clubhouse founded by the governor of Siem Reap as a meeting place for Khmer and Vietnamese administrators to discuss "matters of progress."[81] By December 1938, the provincial branches of AFALS had all expressed interest in setting up guesthouses in the chief provincial towns so that provincial members could meet together in their free time and organize events to "increase solidarity."[82]

This was a two-way traffic. AFALS events in Phnom Penh brought members from the provinces to the capital to "meet face to face, increasing strong feelings of friendship and solidarity, and morale for the future."[83] In this spirit, in November 1938 the Sisowath Alumni Association and *Nagaravatta* announced plans for a party to celebrate the outcome of a "big conference" in Hanoi, where Khmer delegates had protested plans by the GGI to transfer Vietnamese to live in Cambodge and argued against granting property rights to Vietnamese immigrants.[84] Advertised in *Nagaravatta,* the party was open to all who "love Cambodge"—Khmer and French, men and women, from all social strata and all provinces, in and outside of government office—and aimed to fête the delegates, Khmer ministers, the RSC and senior French administrators, in order to demonstrate that "we Khmers are all very loyal."[85] Nineteen thirty-eight was a year of tightening repression in Indochina and, perhaps alarmed at the political slant to the proposed gathering, the RSC cancelled it at the last minute.[86] Perplexingly, this non-event would prove a watershed in Khmer nationalism. Within days of posting the announcement, *Nagaravatta* had received over six hundred acceptances from people across the country, many of whom were not members of AFALS, but were willing to travel to Phnom Penh and pay the 3 riel ticket price.[87] On Friday and Saturday, busloads of prospective party-goers, male and female, young and old, drove in from the provinces. This groundswell took *Nagaravatta* by surprise. "Before, we did not know our own strength; we have only just seen it clearly," stated an editorial, which expressed delight at the massive response and pledged that *Nagaravatta* would now work even harder for the nation.[88] A group of *Nagaravatta* readers from Kompong Cham wrote a joint letter to the paper to register their anger over the money and time they had lost in traveling to the non-event. However, their disgruntlement was a thin disguise for their euphoria at the wakening of Khmer nationalism, and they concluded by expressing their wholehearted support for *Nagaravatta* and urging the paper to continue working to help the *jiet.*[89]

One way in which AFALS helped to nurture a national culture was through the staging of plays and the sponsorship of Khmer-language novels about Cambodge. In 1937, AFALS staged the first of a series of fund-raising plays. *Manuss gam damn puon (Les quatres bossus)* was the work of the budding Cambodian playwright and novelist Rim Kin (1911–1959), who began writing Khmer prose, poetry, and plays while a student at the Lycée Sisowath "so as no longer to feel ashamed in front of foreigners," namely, his fellow Vietnamese students and the Vietnamese writers whose books flooded the Phnom Penh market.[90] In February 1938, Rim Kin joined other "gifted actors" on stage in Kompong Cham for a performance of French and Khmer plays at a well-attended AFALS benefit and reunion.[91] The following month, AFALS, Phnom Penh branch, travelled to Kampot to stage a repeat performance.[92] AFALS also subsidized publication of Rim Kin's first novel.

In July 1937, a lead article in *Nagaravatta* exhorted Khmers to show greater solidarity and urged them to build granaries modelled on an initiative of Nhek Thioulong's administration in Pursat. By building a communal granary for Cambodian farmers and advising them on fluctuations in rice prices and when to sell, Nhek Thioulong had cut Chinese middlemen out of the rural credit economy, allowing the profits to accrue directly to farmers.[93] In early 1939, a "Khmer national solidarity group" *(krum samaki jiet kmae)* in Kratie Province established a refreshments stall called "Khmer nation" *(jiet-khemara),* owned by Khmers. Provincial Governor Khim

Tit applauded the association as proof that "our Khmer nation can also have the same ideas of business cooperation as the Chinese and Vietnamese," and *Nagaravatta* reported increasing numbers of Khmers in other provinces going into business.[94]

In Cambodge, Pétain and his Indochinese representative, Admiral Decoux, found a staunch supporter in the conservative, anti-Semitic, and anti-internationalist RSC Thibaudeau. Thibaudeau's animosity towards Karpelès was partly fuelled by his Vichyesque disdain for idle intellectuals, which was readily apparent in October 1939. In an address at the inauguration of the School of Industry in Phnom Penh, whose intake of Khmer students had increased in leaps and bounds since the school's creation in 1939, he took issue with the notion that Cambodians had an incurable aversion to physical effort. Far from it: "The race whose muscular force built up Angkor's mountains of stone and which, today, continues to raise rice and fields of wheat with their bare hands, has shown that it is just as capable of physical effort as any other race." Spoiled by nature, the Cambodian should guard against a "softening euphoria" and instead work "to retrieve the traditional virtues of his ancestors: valiant effort, the joy of producing, constructing, and creating." In light of such atavistic gifts, and the beck of green fields, "pseudo-intellectual professions" were nothing short of "pernicious."[95]

Under the cover of new Vichy legislation restricting the occupations open to Jews and women, and acting in concert with the Sûreté, the governor-general, and Karpelès' erstwhile mentor George Coedès, Thibaudeau engineered Karpelès' removal from Indochina, partly to better expose the activities of Cambodge's own "pseudo-intellectuals." But Karpelès' expulsion and a wave of other repressive measures came too late to stem the tide of nationalist sentiment among those Cambodians once seen as the future of the protectorate by administrators such as Pavie and now feared by Thibaudeau and others as the key to its collapse: those very *évolués* whose cultivation had inspired Pavie's École cambodgienne in 1888. Recognition of this new elite's political strength impelled Thibaudeau, in 1939 and 1940, to communicate proposals by figures such as Monireth for Cambodge's pseudosovereign status as a separate Khmer nation-state within Indochina to Governors-General Catroux and Decoux.[96] Whereas Karpelès had been his bête-noire, the educator and champion of renovated temple-school reform, Manipaud, was Thibaudeau's model functionary. Manipaud dedicated his Khmer-language primer to Thibaudeau in "grateful homage" and was Thibaudeau's preferred candidate to replace Karpelès as head of the Buddhist Institute.[97]

SPACING THE NATION

While the colonial construct of Cambodge gained a "reality effect" from such trajectories, "Indochina" remained an abstraction for the average Cambodian, as was reflected in the Khmer translation of the word, coined not from the existing words for India *(klung)* and China *(cen)* but from a syllabic string void of referents to existing

Khmer cosmologies or place-names—*in-do-sin*. In the late nineteenth century, this abstract concept of "Indochine" had been made legal tender through the homogenizing currency of the colonial Piastre, whose "Indochine" banknotes, printed in Paris, replaced a plethora of local currencies and carried images of Indochina dominated by singular or combined visions of its constituent countries.[98] But for most Cambodians, Indochine remained just such a decorative, surface concept, and, in *Nagaravatta* and other forums, the protectorates and colonies of Tonkin, Annam, and Cochinchina were still commonly lumped together as, simply, *"yuon* country" *(nokor-yuon* or *srok-yuon),* a term emphasizing not geographic integration but racial differentiation.[99] This dual usage indicated a parallel, colonial geography that did not replace but rather coexisted with indigenous cosmologies. The nebulousness of "Indochine" was reinforced by most Cambodians' lack of practical experience of this greater colonial space.

Although the educational or career journeys of Khmer and Kampuchea Kraom may have encompassed Hanoi, Saigon, or even Paris, their sphere of identity as shaped in *Nagaravatta* and other forums of expression was largely refracted back to Cambodge.[100] Anderson has noted how the career paths of colonial functionaries engineered the "subtle, half-concealed transformation, step by step, of the colonial-state into the national-state, a transformation made possible not only by a solid continuity of personnel, but by the established skein of journeys through which each state was experienced by its functionaries."[101] Anecdotal evidence suggests that travel within Indochina and outside of Cambodge encouraged a reverse pattern of identification, exaggerating the external expressions of Khmerness, as in the gesture of Lon Nol who, when attending college in Saigon in the 1930s, insisted on wearing a checkered *sampot* instead of the standard-issue white colonial uniform, as a demonstration of difference.[102]

Whereas Vietnamese bureaucrats tended to relate to the larger construct of Indochine, Cambodge's secular elite identified themselves primarily as members of a distinctly Khmer cosmos. The territorial dimensions of that cosmos were defined in the late 1930s in the Khmer newspaper *Nagaravatta* through such compounds and neologisms as *mattophum* (motherland), *srok kluen* (one's country), *srok kmae* (Khmer country), *nokor yeung* (our city/kingdom), and *srok yeung* (our district/country).[103] The urban bias of colonial transport and communication systems partly explains why, outside Phnom Penh and elite circles, local identities persisted. So did the preference for proximate, provincial positions of power as opposed to the invisible seats of power outside of a person's birthplace and kinship ring. In 1941, *Nagaravatta* chastised the common antipathy of Cambodians to travelling far from their birthplace, reporting that many who passed the civil service exams refused appointments outside their hometowns *(srok kamnaet).*[104] The dangers of venturing far from home on administrative postings also haunted the first Cambodian novel, *Sophat,* written by Rim Kin in 1938 and published in Saigon in 1942 to wide acclaim.[105] This centripetal tendency and the locally based identities of provincial and rural Cambodians provided a striking contrast with the centrifugal, Indochina orientations of Annamese civil servants, who experienced the colonial construct of Indochine as "a functional concept and space" through postings to all five parts of the Indochinese union.[106]

From around 1935, scoutism, previously concentrated in private Catholic schools in Vietnam, began to take off within the state school system, with large colleges and the French *lycées* setting up their own scout groups.[107] In August 1934, to great ceremony, King Monivong and the Vietnamese president of the Scout Federation of Cochinchina conferred the title of Supreme Chief of the Éclaireurs du Cambodge on Prince Monireth. The following year, the national director of the Éclaireurs de France visited Indochina, while scouting's local kudos gained lustre from a marathon publicity stunt in 1938, when two champions of France's scout movement, Roger Drapier and Guy de Larigaudie, arrived in Saigon by car, so ending a two-year road trip. In 1937, the Indochinese Federation of Scouts was created.[108]

In inculcating team spirit and the discipline of daily group maneuvers, scout groups offered fertile training and recruitment grounds for nationalists and communists, and also familiarized their members with the geographies and communication routes of Indochina.[109] In contrast to Anglo-Saxon cultures and countries, sports and youth movements were outside the mainstream in France.[110] Pacifist desires to prevent the carnage of another world war, by heightening international amity and solidarity among youth through travel and cross-cultural hospitality, had stimulated the birth of the *auberge de jeunesse* (youth hostel) movement in interwar France. In Vichy Indochina, this genealogy was tainted with suspicions of subversion.

The first *auberge de jeunesse* was established near Paris in 1925 to ensure that "we will never again see" the horrors of war.[111] That year, the Chamber of Deputies voted for a draft law giving workers fifteen days of paid leave; the law was put aside, but on 20 June 1936 became the first law to achieve a unanimous vote under Leon Blum's new Popular Front government. Leisure, previously seen as the preserve of the rich, was now made a national right. Members of the Auberge de jeunesse (AJ) became known as *ajistes*. Their theme song celebrated travel, love, and friendship. A 1938 handbook gave them a more precise political identity, comparing each hostel to a "little republic." Being a "good *ajiste*" meant doing your share of collective labor.[112]

It was in this spirit of pacifism and popular socialism, and perhaps as an antidote to the authoritarianism with which she connected Cambodge's burgeoning scout movement, that Karpelès launched the Cambodian chapter of the AJ. Although he later used its activities as ballast in his campaign against Karpelès, Thibaudeau warmed to the practical thrust of this initiative and encouraged it, hoping it would "lead Cambodian youth to travel, and so broaden the mind."[113] Prince Sutharot became its honorary president. Hostels were established in Kep and near Wat Damnak, in Siem Reap, and excursions were organized by bus. Its logo showed a sailboat and bicycles passing a *salaa* from which flew a Cambodian flag and a tricolour, against a rural backdrop. Despite Thibaudeau's concerns, the AJ continued to operate until 1940. Visiting Phnom Penh that year, a sailor and active *ajiste* from France was impressed by the talented membership and organizational flair of the *Yuvsalistes* in Cambodge, although he apparently found the physical effort to which Thibaudeau had referred somewhat lacking, and recommended less bus travel and more cycling, camping, and backpacking.[114] By November 1939, the movement counted close to two hundred members. Karpelès had recently launched a series of Khmer-language children's books, one of which was titled *Means of Travel in Srok Kmae—in Fact and Legend*.[115] In addition to outings, the AJ produced plays, and it was the pacifist and internationalist nature of one such production that sparked the brisk train of events leading to Karpelès' ouster.

Over two weeks in December 1939, during the Tang Toc festivities staged for the king's birthday, a play in French entitled *Among the Young,* promoting the AJ movement, was staged by seven Cambodians and five Vietnamese. Plans were to stage an official performance at the town hall, featuring a Khmer play entitled *Indra's Bored (Indra s'ennuie)* by Kim Hak, a civil servant in Phnom Penh. The play tells of Indra's descent to Cambodge, and his realization, on visiting the *auberge de jeunesse* near Vat Damnak in Siem Reap, that paradise is in fact on earth. Dancing a fox-trot to music composed by an Annamese and words by a Cambodian civil servant, performers sang the *ajiste*'s road song, a "Travel Invitation." The lyrics celebrated youth hostels in Kep, a hostel for women on Mount Bokor, and Angkor:

> If you want to ensconce yourself
> In the great past,
> Come to Angkor,
> Kingdom of folklore.

Travel is beautiful, proclaimed a second verse, but alas, requires money; the *Yuvsala* has opened up travel to the poor. In the second act, Indra visits Angkor and learns of the Gallery of Mille Bouddhas, where Cambodians come annually to make offerings. Later, near Vat Damnak, he finds young men and young women properly dressed, singing and playing music, and exclaims that you cannot find any *auberge de jeunesse* in paradise.[116] Accompanying performances included Lao dances, and American dances by Vietamese *yuvsalistes.* As if this international mélange wasn't enough to get Thibaudeau's whiskers bristling, parts of the proposed play were downright subversive. Indra was not only multilingual but antiwar. Hearing tearful prayers rise above the terrifying noises of war, he vowed to stop these "scandalous games." Worse still, Indra spoke Thai, and in one of the plays, allusion was made to a trip to Thailand. Alarmed on both counts, the GGI suggested that both plays be banned.[117] Rather than approach Karpelès directly, Thibeaudea scribbled a secret note to the Phnom Penh police chief, asking for changes to be made to *Among the Young,* playing at the Buddhist Institute. "Certain passages are of a completely pacifist nature, and moreover, all belligerents are treated on an equal footing"; this was doubly damaging in that the plays were aimed at youth.[118] Another play by Kim Hak was allowed to go on, in a censored version, while *Parmi les jeunes,* suspected of being coauthored by Karpelès, was pulled. Unabashed, Karpelès staged two film showings the following January as well as a ceremony for the promotion of Mr. Tan Mau, a long-standing clerk and translator for *Kampuja Surya.* Sutharot and Thiounn both attended, and Thibaudeau noted with concern that Karpelès had dared to give an off-the-cuff talk to the fifty assembled, after a congratulatory speech by Thiounn in Tan Mau's honor.[119] The following month, Karpelès gave Thibaudeau advance notice of an archaeological excursion to Kompong Cham and news of one *yuvsaliste* who had been "mobilized," presumably for action along the Thai border.[120]

In contrast to the Third Republic, which vigorously promoted centralization, Vichy encouraged the deepening of local attachments through a revival of provincial folk culture.[121] While galvanizing its youth to carry the torch of France's future, the Vichy regime also sought to resuscitate visions of past grandeur through a new pantheon of national heroes and heroines and a revisionist history glorifying the monarchy.[122] Decoux adapted this formula to Indochina, establishing a "highly erudite cultural team," headed by Coedès, to stimulate Lao, Cambodian, and Vietnamese nationalisms in the Indochinese federation, in order to defuse the counternationalisms fanned both by regional contenders for influence in Indochina, notably Japan and Siam, and by Vietnamese revolutionaries.[123] The French choreographers of these particular patriotisms also scripted a rich array of ceremonies from school yards to national spaces such as Vat Pnum and Angkor, designed to shore up the sovereignty of France throughout Indochina.[124] Cambodge's Vichy pantheon as fashioned through the French-censored Khmer media included Joan of Arc, the Trung sisters who had led a Vietnamese rebellion against China in the second century, Jayavarman VII, and Klang Moeung, a sixteenth-century Khmer general alleged to have mobilized an army of ghosts to defend the Khmer kingdom against invading troops from Siam.[125] In only the previous decade, a similarly eclectic line-up had earned the Caodai ridicule and typecasting as a deceitful cult, but now that these icons had been pressed into the service of the French government, they were treated with solemn devotion in media, monuments, and marches.[126] The centerpiece of this motley crew was Jayavarman VII.

JAYAVARMAN THE BOY SCOUT: VICHY DISCOURSES OF NATIONALISM

In September 1941, the Vichy government, unable to reinforce its military position in Indochina, signed agreements with Tokyo putting Indochinese territory and resources at the discretion of Japan and allowing Japan to station troops in Indochina.[127] After fierce fighting, Phibul Songkram's government in Thailand soon regained Battambang and Sisophon, but Cambodge retained Siem Reap. The EFEO continued its work at Angkor, giving the temple complex renewed importance as a rare monument to France's now visibly fading powers of protection.[128] France's defeat at home by Germany, and in Indochina by Japan, exposed the fragility of both Metropolitan might and colonial power, forfeiting France the right to protect Indochina in indigenous eyes.[129] Until 1945, the Japanese were content to use Indochina as a base for military action in Southeast Asia, and as a source of food and raw materials.

Vichy officials remained in nominal control of the country. These shifting alliances coincided with changes in Cambodge's leadership. After the death of King Sisowath Monivong in 1941, the Cambodian throne devolved to the Norodom branch of the royal family with the accession of the teenage Norodom Sihanouk, a graduate of Saigon's Lycée Chasseloup-Laubat.

In Indochina, Vichy ideology was interpreted for native consumption by the autocratic workaholic vice admiral Jean Decoux. To implement Vichy's heavily gendered youth policy, which prioritized the resuscitation of national "virility" by "remasculiniz[ing] the male body, and viriliz[ing] elites," and relied heavily on the ethos and applications of "scoutism," Decoux appointed the energetic naval captain Maurice Ducoroy to head his new General Commissariat for Physical Education, Sports, and Youth.[130] From the time of his appointment, Sihanouk was held up as an icon of Vichy youth ideals, winning high praise from Decoux for his eager participation in youth movements.[131]

Media, meetings, and marches promoted Angkor and the Khmer kings of yore as the embodiments of Cambodge's past grandeur and future promise. During his first meeting with Sihanouk, Decoux praised the new king as a living symbol of "the historic glory of the Khmers."[132] Decoux joined Sihanouk in royal tours around the Cambodian countryside and into Vietnam.[133] Interestingly, Decoux's rhetoric was rife with allusions to architecture and monuments: France's colonial universities became "monuments of influence and penetration," and Hanoi University a "temple of culture."[134] King, Khmer, and past grandeur were knit together through such events as the 1941 youth march from Hanoi to Angkor, where Sihanouk lit an "Indochinese torch."[135] Scout rallies and youth camps at Angkor and other ancient sites were one means of inculcating this double-edged formula of youthful zeal and ancient glory, as demonstrated by a scout trip to Oudong to visit the stupas containing the ashes of past kings and to encourage youth "to meditate . . . on the marches of a glorious past" while pledging to look "resolutely to the future."[136] Similarly, at training schools for Vichy youth monitors at Angkor, aspiring leaders of the Indochinese youth movement promised to "raise the grandeur of their country" by cultivating heroism.[137]

The war with Thailand along Cambodge's western border, and Thai propaganda claiming Angkor as part of Thai heritage, heightened Angkor's symbolic potential as both a fortress of the "Khmer soul" and a testament to colonialism's benign intentions. In November 1940, a writer who signed himself "Kampuputra" (Son of the Khmers) took issue with recent Thai claims that the Khmers who had built Angkor had vanished and been replaced by Thais.[138] In March 1941, la Jeunesse franco-indochinoise (Franco-Indochinese Youth) launched the monthly *Ralliement.* Its militant pilot issue floated the dream of "dying like our elders, somewhere along the Siamese frontier, for Indochine, for the Empire, for immortal and eternal France."[139] At an organized demonstration in early November 1941, some ten to fifteen thousand people marched through Phnom Penh, hoisting French and Cambodian flags and banners proclaiming, "Angkor belongs to Khmers!" and "Long live Cambodge! Khmers! We want to remain Khmers!"[140] Several members of the Khmer scout movement enlisted in the war to fight Thailand, and December 1941 saw the launch of a Khmer scouting manual named *Servir,* which posted news of trips to historic national sites and boasted about the Khmers' ancient and royal lineage.[141] The EFEO's conservation activities at Angkor continued despite the air bombardment of Siem Reap and hostilities with Thailand, providing France a fig leaf of moral authority.[142] In November 1942 Sihanouk visited Angkor, demonstrating his interest in the reconstruction of the monuments.[143]

These indigenous debates on Angkor paved the way for the temple's symbolic transition, in the 1940s, from a symbol of France's power to make Cambodge anew to proof of Cambodians' capacity for nation building. This act of claiming Angkor for Khmers by Khmers, during a period when France's own power as a protector was visibly weakened, helped to change Angkor's symbolic value. "It has been said again and again and again," stated RSC Gaultier in 1943, "that Cambodians are artists, because there is Angkor . . . let us simply change our viewpoint and say . . . if the Cambodians built Angkor, then that proves first and foremost that they can be builders."[144] Banner slogans and editorials in *Kampuchea* promoted the same theme.[145] Despite their political differences, Son Ngoc Thanh espoused the same pantheon of nation as his royalist rivals. "Khmers, show yourself worthy of your race, worthy children of the builders of Angkor," he declared in a letter written from his Japanese exile in July 1943.[146]

ARRESTING NATIONALISM: THE MONASTIC
PROTESTS OF 1942 AND THEIR AFTERMATH

In the cultural struggle to gain and retain indigenous allegiance, Vichy Indochina was quick to recognize the significance of the Buddhist Institute. On 3 July 1940, in an apparent attempt to reinforce Indochina's geocultural boundaries and boost the immunity of the *sangha* to overtures from Siam, Decoux issued a decree confirming the Cambodian Buddhist Institute's responsibility for directing and coordinating studies of Theravada Buddhism in Indochina, and especially in Cambodge and Laos.[147] In Nazi Germany, Buddhism was tolerated, and Buddhists were regarded as harmless "pacifists and eccentrics."[148] In Vichy Indochina, however, Decoux's administration sought to prevent Japan from stimulating anticolonial nationalism through cooptation of the *sangha* through such organizations as the Buddhist associations. Japan also protected Caodai leaders and those of various other Buddhist organizations in Vietnam.[149] Despite these strategic goals, and the tolerance of Buddhism in an increasingly intolerant and anti-Semitic Europe, within one year of the establishment of Vichy, the protectorate had alienated leading figures in the *sangha.*

Since taking office in 1936, the year in which Hitler's troops took up their positions on the left bank of the Rhine, Thibaudeau, in tandem with the chief of police and assisted by the underhand maneuvers of Thiounn, launched a campaign against Karpelès. Thibaudeau et al. were careful not to sack her for her Jewishness but for her gender. Repeatedly Thibaudeau and the police chief, as well as reports apparently drafted by Thiounn, stressed that she had no place in a religious milieu almost exclusively closed to woman. Numerous monks, apparently, disagreed; frequently, they sought out Karpelès to intervene in even the most sacred of matters, such as the cremation of Em Sou, rather than dealing directly with the RSC. It was the fact that she actually had higher status among monks than he who, in his own interpretation of Buddhist and bureaucratic lore, should have been far more highly sought after, which irked Thibaudeau. Strict censorship brought with it acute embarrassment: while Thibaudeau fumed at the carefully typed transcripts of Karpelès' letters to her mother, others may have chuckled at her descriptions of his buffoonery. On 21 August, Thibaudeau wrote a note for his file: given her "sex, her political and personal ideas" he stressed the desirability of moving Mlle K., a permanent member of the EFEO, to another job as soon as circumstances permit her replacement in Cambodge.[150] Her internationalism, pacificism, cosmopolitanism, and her, to him, bizarre possession of supposedly masculine attributes (confidence, arrogance, extreme intelligence) tallied with other unorthodox aspects of her behavior—from her spinster status to her camaraderie with Khmer monks to her quasi-native dress—all of which flouted Vichy's rigid gender ideology.

Days of police time were spent in monitoring and translating Karpelès' correspondence, drawing up lists of her family, background, addresses in France, and contacts. These ranged from a White Russian Buddhist monk in Ceylon, a sailor and would-be founder of the *auberges de jeunesse* in Saigon; a Khmer monk from Cochinchina, now in Battambang, seeking her help to evade a military draft; the president of the Society of the Friends of Buddhism in Paris; a Thai feminist and radio journalist; a peripatetic French doctor and student of Dharma; and the president of the International League of Women in New Zealand. A steady stream of postcards and letters, in French, English, and Pali, from Sweden, New Zealand, Ceylon, Constantinople, and elsewhere, were proof positive to Thibaudeau and his police chief of a "European" (not French) identity, international tendencies, and an "almost masculine intelligence." Karpelès' mother and sister had traveled to Sweden "in exile," not knowing when they could return to France; there they attended Catholic mass while also maintaining Jewish candlesticks at home, and their letters made occasional mention of Israel. To mother and sisters, war waged by any side was heinous, but Hitler in particular was an evil, and *Mein Kampf* dangerous. When, in a letter to her mother, Karpelès described herself as "a child of Israel," the chief of police instantly wrote to RSC Thibaudeau. "This *demoiselle-fonctionnaire*," he griped, "is now playing the part of one 'persecuted' by the local authority; she's chosen easy ground, and is proving a talented performer." "If the administration wants to annoy me," she had written to her mother, and "if the Résuper makes it clear . . . that I, like all children of Israel, are highly *antipathique* to him, there is one thing they cannot take away from me: the gentle feelings I have each time I see the Cambodian monks from the Buddhist Institute and the joy I feel, seeing their admiration before our book stands. . . . No-one can take this precious and encouraging thing from me."[151]

The file on her international correspondence thickened: "I have heard they are not yet reading our mail," she wrote to her mother in late 1939, "but only newspapers." Dr. Migot, who had visited Cambodge in the late 1930s and witnessed the cremation of Mahanikay Supreme Patriarch Em Sou, which was, tellingly, coordinated by Karpelès, asked after the "enemies of the Buddhist Institute." He named no names, but Karpelès had earlier recounted a brush with the "cunning Thiounn," who had sidled up to her, happy enough to claim credit for a successful event but who on all other fronts "wanted to suffocate the Buddhist Institute." To Karpelès, the success of Em Sou's cremation, and its reaffirmation of her standing in the eyes of monks, was proof that "In spite of everything that's being done to stifle" the Buddhist Institute, it is "living and developing, and has shown up in all their dazzling dementia all those imbeciles, demonstrating the bad faith of those meddling authorities." Chuon Nath's brother, Nouth, saw this clearly enough: "Everyone wants Mademoiselle to do something which no man in her place could have done, and now that cunning Thiounn wants to show people that he and the Buddhist Institute are as one, so as to better stifle our development?" Such people had their sights set on one thing only: their own role, and if they could suppress the institute while going about it, so much the better. The institute "doesn't steal from the people and is helping them to rise above the mud under which people want to suffocate them." As for the RSC and his minions, they were clueless imbeciles who knew next to nothing about the people they were governing. While Karpelès was getting monks to pray for peace instead of victory, Thibaudeau, at the cremation of Em Sou, asked all to observe a minute's silence for France's fighters.[152] Attended by two thousand monks, the cremation filled Karpelès with nostalgia, reminding her of the inauguration of the Buddhist Institute and allowing her to momentarily forget the "anti-Buddhist" time in which she was now living.[153]

With the collusion of George Coedès, Karpelès was sacked in late 1941, under a Vichy law of 11 October 1940 stipulating early retirement for women in the administration. In March 1941, Coedès wrote to his protégé. "My dear friend," he began. "I learned of your retirement and your imminent departure through a word from M. Thanh [Son Ngoc Thanh]." Feigning near-complete ignorance of the moves that had led to her ousting, Coedès offered her his assurance that he would watch over the "beautiful work you have accomplished in Cambodge" to soften her pain at leaving a country to which she had given so much.[154] A month earlier, Coedès, himself of Jewish descent, had added four decisive words to her personnel file: NON PROPOSÉE (*pour l'avancement*) (not recommended for promotion). Agreeing with Thibaudeau that it had been a mistake to appoint a woman to this post, while highlighting her remarkable achievements, he suggested that, under the "decree of 11 October 1940," Karpelès could now be "retired."[155] In a cover letter to the director of personnel in Hanoi, Coedès suggested she be replaced by Pierre Dupont, who was picking up some Khmer and Thai and had completed some studies in Buddhism. "From the political point of view, he is the complete opposite of Mlle S.K.," Coedès continued. "While his attachment to the Buddhist Institute would officially be a purely scholarly one, he would no doubt be capable of effectively conducting a certain secret activity conforming to the needs of the politics of the Protectorate." In other words, he could be relied upon to spy on the natives.[156] Karpelès was notified of the decision in a letter from Thibaudeau dated 4 March 1941. "I have the honor to inform you," Thibaudeau began, "that the governor-general has decided to propose your retirement to the department according to article 8 of the law of 11 October 1940 on the employ of female personnel within the administration." Karpelès was granted passage to France, where others who shared her Jewish surname were selected for transport to death camps. "Seven million Jews have been exterminated," wrote Duras, the writer born as Marguerite Donnadieu, who had also spent time in Cambodge and was now in France. "In Paris, people don't talk about the Jews yet." Karpelès' departure ushered in a new era of close scrutiny of the Buddhist Institute, doubly tainted by its founder's Jewish credentials and the politicization of her protégés. Academic qualifications alone could not win her replacement Pierre Dupont the respect of and rapport with the Khmer that Karpelès had cultivated over close to twenty years.

"Without you at the Buddhist Institute," wrote Son Ngoc Thanh to Karpelès in 1947, "on the grounds of a simple suspicion, mass arrests were made among your staff, without the slightest explanation. The monk Hem-Chieu was arrested and immediately defrocked (he died in Paolo Condor), without anyone knowing why; Nuon-Duong was arrested and his house turned upside down, but nothing was found; all personnel were threatened with arrest from one moment to the next. . . . It was this extraordinary police brutality which led me to abandon my family and my children, to leave my country, for Japan." "It was these events of 1942," recounted Son Ngoc Tanh, "concocted by the police, that threw me squarely into politics, in spite of myself." Now it was France, not Vietnam or Siam, that threatened to make Cambodge disappear: "I took this road," Son Ngoc Thanh explained, "out of the duty that I must fulfill towards my Khmer country (ma Patrie Khmere), [which was] in danger."[157]

The protectorate closed down Nagaravatta, hoping to win over its readership of some five thousand to the official newspaper, Kampuchea, which Desjardins, head of the Information, Press, and Propaganda Department, saw as a means of inculcating new values in a "monkhood and people [who] live in another century." Reluctant to admit the real reasons for Nagaravatta's appeal, Desjardins attributed its success to "entertaining gossip" and "satirical tittle tattle."[158] Strict censure, bland content, and association with the administration ensured that Kampuchea never achieved Nagaravatta's mass appeal. Neither government subsidies to expand readership rates nor its blatant poaching of such Nagaravatta hallmarks as the "Judge Rabbit" column could boost Kampuchea's circulation, which barely reached 1,700 in 1943, indicating a stubborn resistance among the bulk of former Nagaravatta subscribers to switch allegiance or patronize a brazenly colonial production. When subscriptions dropped again the next year, Desjardins did not blame the dullness or bias of its content or the politics of such indigenous rejection, but the ignorance of the "Cambodian masses," for whom, he concluded, newspapers remained "inessential"; meanwhile RSC Gaultier blamed the lack of desire for journals on the Cambodian elite's "intellectual tor-por."[159] Another reading of the figures and format of *Nagaravatta* indicates that Cam-bodians were enthusiastic consumers of news stories, but that information pure and simple was not popular, and it was even less so when wrapped in the unmistakeable language of protectorate propaganda. While, like all totalitarian governments, the protectorate placed an understandable premium on "information," for most Cambo-dians the kind of information purveyed in official newspapers was not only dull but largely irrelevant or, like the stories in *Kampuchea*—printed in Khmer—advertising the romanization campaign, downright offensive and insensitive.

Plans to romanize Khmer had gained momentum in the wake of the rapid secu-larization of education in the 1930s, and there are indications that some Cambodians supported the argument that romanization alone was capable of bringing widespread literacy to Cambodge.[160] In the late 1930s, Coedès devised a new system of Khmer romanization, which was promoted vigorously during the first years of the Vichy regime together with the Gregorian calendar as twin planks in a move to perfect the modernization and secularization of Cambodian education and administration. Throughout the 1940s, *Kampuchea* ran numerous articles stressing the advantages of romanization for promoting national literacy.[161] One such article ridiculed a boy who had spent too long in *vats* and could speak only in religious language.[162] In 1943, the protectorate heralded the second and final volume of the Cambodian dictionary as a boon to the romanization campaign and decreed the new romanized script compul-sory in all administrative correspondence.[163] In January 1944, a class in Cambodian romanization opened in the head Thommayuth temple, Botum Vaddey.[164] Later that year, Gaultier sponsored publication of a hundred-page *Lexique cambodgien romanisé* (Lexicon of romanized Cambodian), which was heralded by Desjardins as a simple yet effective tool for "the reconstruction of Cambodge and profound renovation of Cambodian thought."[165]

However, both because the reforms threatened the high status of traditional ed-ucators and because *Nagaravatta* and the works of the reformist monks had aroused strong consciousness of *piesaa-kmae* as a national langue, or *piesaa-jiet,* the proposed romanization provoked widespread condemnation.[166] The most prominent opponents of the campaign were Achar Hem Chieu, a teacher at the École supérieure de Pali, and Achar Nuon Duong, a graduate of the school. On 18 July 1942, the Sûreté ar-rested Achar Hem Chieu and Nuon Duong for preaching anti-French sermons to Khmer troops. Here, the epithet of *"loques jaunes"* came back to haunt the protector-ate, for it was not just the fact of arrest but the act of arresting Achar Hem Chieu in his robes that galvanized extraordinary feeling among the monks, triggering a pan-denominational demonstration of several thousand of them, including an estimated five hundred monks from the Thommakay sect, mainly from Vat Ounaloum and Vat Langka. This peaceful expression of outrage was promptly quashed with truckloads of baton-wielding Sûreté, leading many monks to wield their parasols in response. The subsequent internment and exile of key agitators, including Pach Cheoun, broke the backbone of the nationalist movement.

The protests also prompted a crackdown on the École supérieure de Pali, which *Nagaravatta* had identified in 1941 as a "school for the nation *(jiet)*." In December 1942, Thibaudeau's like-minded replacement RSC Gaultier openly accused the Buddhist Institute of breaching its mandate and catalyzing the July demonstrations by espousing political sympathies in its texts.[167] The following April, Desjardins accused the institute of crossing the boundary between religion and politics, harboring an "anti-French minority"—the Thommakay—and spreading Thommakay influence in Cambodge via its publications.[168] Later that year, Gaultier identified the "modernist" students of the École supérieure de Pali as prime participants in the July 1942 protests, warned that the school was rapidly becoming a third "modernist" sect, and reminded Karpelès' successor as secretary of the school, Pierre Dupont, that the Mahanikay and Thommayuth were the only two sects recognized by the Ministry of Culture. Monks attached to either the institute or the ESP were henceforth banned from preaching.[169]

In Vichy more than ever before, Khmer culture became seen as a germane ground for the fomenting of nationalist sentiment by an administration that had operated largely on the assumption that culture and politics were antonyms. By conserving Khmer language and literature, *Nagaravatta* wrote in 1941, the ESP and its graduates would "defend the Khmer country against destruction," and without them, "Khmer writing and religion would go to rack and ruin and eventually disappear." Several months later, *Kampuchea* claimed that the protectorate's publications and modernization of education had led to a disappearance of a different sort, namely the erosion of the traditional "awe of writing" among "boys and girls in the city and country."[170]

Partly in retaliation for the Buddhist Institute's failure to translate any "French masterpiece" into Khmer, the Department of Information pruned its publications and cut back its paper rations. By promoting Buddhist precepts antithetical to the protectorate's values of "action, enterprise, ambition . . . , [and] the love of profit," reported RSC Gaultier in 1943, the Buddhist Institute's projects to conserve tradition had undermined the protectorate's efforts to "awaken Cambodge," left it stewing "in the contemplation of its past and its traditions," and failed to instill the remotest desire for "intellectual awakening" among the Cambodian masses. Cambodge was still the least literate country in Indochina.[171] While Desjardins accused the institute of producing "lifeless" works of no use "in forming the Cambodian spirit," RSC Gaultier blamed this mass inertia on the esoteric and inaccessible nature of institute literature, condemned its channels of distribution—*vats*—as incapable of awakening "creativity" or "intellectual curiosity," defined the Buddhist Institute's primary role as publication of the Tripitaka and teaching materials, and warned that "indulgent works on high religious culture and linguistic, ethnographic, and historical culture must remain its last priority."[172]

Chuon Nath acquiesced to Decoux's choreography of nation and was appointed to write the words and music of Cambodge's first national anthem in 1942.[173] But he played a double game. While assisting with such official projects, he and Huot Tath maintained covert contacts with Son Ngoc Thanh during his years in Japan.[174] Their support for Son Ngoc Thanh's anticolonial struggle may well have been intensified by the protectorate's expulsion of Karpelès and its interference with the activities of the Buddhist Institute and the ESP. Resentment over the protectorate's brusque and brutal treatment of the demonstrating *sangha* was deepened by the death in captivity of Achar Hem Chieu. Son Ngoc Thanh and Pach Choeun increasingly came to be seen by monks and a now silenced but still extant Sisowath Alumni Association as offering both an alternative, nonroyal locus of leadership and a viable alternative to French control.[175] From Japan, Son Ngoc Thanh petitioned for Cambodian independence and formed "The Khmer Nationalist Party for the Independence of Cambodge," comprising "Cambodian monks and laity, Cambodians living in ceded territories and former Khmer territories, Cambodians from Cochinchina," and excluding "the king, the council of ministers, the royal family, and pro-French functionnaries." Its core group were what Thanh described as "the Nagaravattistes" and included Huot Tath and Chuon Nath, as well as several regulars on the *krum samaki* circuit.[176]

Hoping to inspire popular participation in the protectorate's printing projects, Desjardins launched a literary contest sponsored by the French administration and King Sihanouk, which offered prizes for Khmer novels, songs, poetry, and translations of French works in Khmer script or romanized script.[177] Two years later, RSC Gaultier approved the formation of the Aymonier Association to promote Franco-Cambodian rapprochement through French and Khmer periodicals, translations, and works on Cambodge.[178] From 1 January 1944, the Aymonier Association assumed responsibility for Radio-Bulletin, *Kampuchea,* and the literary contests.[179] Son Sann, who would serve as finance minister to Sihanouk in the 1960s and as leader of the Buddhist Liberal Democratic Party during the 1980s and 1990s, cut his political teeth on the Directing Committee of the association in the early 1940s, as did Khieu Ponnary.[180] Celebrated in *Kampuchea* as the first Cambodian woman to complete her baccalaureat, Khieu Ponnary later went on to become "Hanoi Rose" as a broadcaster on communist radio during the Vietnam War, but became better known as a Khmer Rouge leader and the future confidante and wife of Saloth Sar. In 1944, Saloth Sar enrolled in the Collège Sihanouk and worked his way into the periphery of AFALS through his friendship with Kim Trang, a Khmer Kraom scholarship student at the Lycée Sisowath who became highly active in the alumni association and rallied its members to form a new lobby group called the Liberation of Cambodia from French Colonialism.[181] Kim Trang married Khieu Ponnary's sister, Khieu Thirith, and would later gain fame as Ieng Sary, foreign minister of Democratic Kampuchea.

In the summer of 1944, Pétain's regime in France collapsed under the weight of domestic resistance and allied assault. In Indochina, Vichy continued: Decoux stood firm, maintaining the appearance of authority, for ideological and strategic reasons, in the face of increasing Japanese demands.[182] On 9 March 1945, Japanese military forces moved to disarm all French units and to intern French officials throughout Indochina. In a brutal end to an inspired and creative life, Groslier, an avid wireless enthusiast, was arrested and tortured to death by the Kempetei on suspicion of espionage.[183] Within a week, Sihanouk had annulled the 1863 Treaty of Protectorate, abrogated the decrees of 1943 and 1944 enforcing romanization and the Gregorian calendar, and proclaimed Cambodge's place in the Greater East Asian Co-Prosperity Sphere headed by Japan. The next month, following lobbying by monks and other supporters, King Sihanouk pressured Japan for Son Ngoc Thanh's return. Thanh arrived in Phnom Penh in May 1945 and was promptly named foreign minister. In August, he was appointed prime minister and tasked with forming a new government. Two months later, Khim Tith, his former colleague from the *krum samaki* and *Nagaravatta* era, travelled to Hanoi and denounced him to the Allied forces. On 15 October, General Leclerc and two officers arrived in Phnom Penh to arrest Son Ngoc Thanh. Found guilty of spying for the Japanese, Thanh was sentenced by a Saigon court to twenty years' emprisonment.[184] He was released after seventeen months and, with the assistance of the French government, was resettled in France with his two wives and seven children. General Decoux was removed from office and, despite his energetic, offshore advancement of Pétain's ideals, survived the turbulent and often violent anticollaborationist campaigns that gripped France over the next few years.[185]

The harmony between the monarchy and Son Ngoc Thanh's nationalist movement proved equally short-lived. The high rank subsequently conferred on Khim Tith by Sihanouk indicates his complicity or design in this abrupt end to Son Ngoc Thanh's political career. In 1947, the Cambodian cabinet adopted a constitution closely modelled on that of France. Sihanouk adopted a policy of negotiating independence from the French. Within the negotiating theater, the shape of Khmer nationalism—and the desire by leading founders of the *krum samaki* such as Nhet Thiouloung, as well as nationalists such as Son Ngoc Thanh, to dispense with the rubric of an Indochina federation as it had emerged from Vichy rule—became a critical theme and would remain so throughout postcolonial conflicts and politics. In meetings with the French to bring Cambodge back into the colonial orbit after Japan's defeat, Nhet Thiouloung made pitches against an Indochinese federation and for a national, not federal, citizenship, while a later negotiator, Chan Nak, argued that "Cambodge is an autonomous state that does not have a place in the Indochinese Union." Cambodge no longer wanted to have to contribute its money and wealth to Annam, explained Prince Monireth: "We must be able to live by ourselves, to live by our own means, instead of contributing these means to the Annamites." As Khy Panra and Goscha have demonstrated, it would take four more years before France created associated states along the national lines desired by Monireth and others.[186] If nationalism had "finally begun" in legal terms, as Goscha convincingly argues, its intellectual underpinnings were a rough consensus, shared by scoutists and *ajistes* and established by the late 1930s, about the sacrosanct nature of Khmer *patrimoine*. Quibbles over genealogy mattered little: fusing Monireth's and Thiouloung's stances at the negotiating table was an ethnonational pride and commitment to the geocultural body of a Khmer nation that had been foreshadowed in the writings and translations of Son Diep and Thiounn, and in the later educational programs of Chuon Nath, Huot Tath, Groslier, Son Ngoc Thanh, and Karpelès.

"I love my Khmer country *(patrie khmère),*" Son Ngoc Thanh wrote to Karpelès from France in 1947. But still, even after spending seventeen months in a colonial prison, he professed "a debt of gratitude to France," not only personally, but for "the good works France has done for Cambodge and in the Khmer provinces of Cochinchina." It was apparently a source of personal satisfaction and professional pride that he had fulfilled his duty to his country as a Cambodian, while remaining loyal, grateful, and worthy of France. Now he considered his career in politics finished and wanted nothing more than to return to the lands of his ancestors, in Travinh.[187] This was either posturing or wishful thinking. Together with another Khmer Kraom, Son Ngoc Minh, Son Ngoc Thanh mobilized a small army of freedom fighters known as Khmer Issarak (Free Khmer). The French administration made various concessions to political freedoms, including allowing Cambodge's first elections for the National Assembly in 1947. Among the propaganda accumulated by the Sûreté was one testament to the enduring linkage of Son Ngoc Thanh's nationalist movement and Suzanne Karpelès. A cartoon shows Karpelès, who was not especially tall, towering over a diminutive Son Ngoc Thanh: the Khmer caption reads, "In the Protectorate, Son Ngoc Thanh sheltered in the shadow of Madame Karpelès' skirts." A bespectacled Thanh in suit and tie is later depicted riding in comfort, with beer and cigarettes, in a train in Japan, leading the monks' demonstration (billed not as the "umbrella war," as it was later trivialized by King Sihanouk, but as "monks speaking out and demonstrating") in Phnom Penh and being arrested for the demonstration. A fifth panel depicts emaciated prisoners serving a four-year term in prison; the sixth depicts Son Ngoc Thanh being flown to Japan; the seventh, his swearing in as prime minister under the Japanese and Cambodian flags. The pamphlet also shows Son Ngoc Thanh facing a crowd of people with a Japanese soldier standing by, and mentions the coolie labor and forced conscription under the Japanese, with an apparently sarcastic statement about the wonderful accomplishments Son Ngoc Thanh achieved for Independence.[188]

Cambodian nationalism was never a single "movement," but a travelogue of diverse itineraries, the constellation and intersection of myriad journeys by individuals who—separately and collectively, through soliloquies and in dialogue—coined ideas of the modern Khmer nation and, through their travels, reports, and engagement with the *krum samaki,* gave these ideas national currency in an ethnically framed cosmos. The Lycée Sisowath alumni, the now defunct *ajistes,* various *krum samaki,* the offices of *Nagaravatta,* the Royal Library, and the Buddhist Institute, all had established personal networks of nationalists that would ultimately carry the concept of "Cambodge" as an ethnolinguistic, religious, and geocultural entity into the era of political party formation after the fall of Vichy in 1945. Cambodge did not achieve technical independence from France until 1953, gaining full independence in 1954. But in many respects the bifurcation of modern Cambodian history into colonial and postcolonial is an optical illusion. Long after the dismantlement of the protectorate of Cambodge, the conceptual rubric of Cambodge established during ninety years of colonial rule continued to haunt and shape the country's political landscape.

10 Past Colonial?

On 9 November 1953, France granted full independence to Cambodge, an act marked by the closure of colonial departments and functions operating in Cambodge and the withdrawal of colonial military troops. While this political and military withdrawal was relatively straightforward, cultural disengagement was far more complex. The symbiotic, indigenous–European cultural legacy of the French Protectorate was already indelibly marked in the sculpting of a Khmer national style and character in religious, museological, and artistic areas. There was therefore no need to indulge in an "official" handover of many colonial tropes and cultural visions of the Khmer nation articulated in the colonial era, specifically with regard to Angkor, Kmae-daem-ness, and Buddhism, which were sustained and reframed in nationalist propaganda, both in this transitional era and in postcolonial Cambodia.

A dominant notion of Khmer nationhood had developed under colonial rule through synthesis, graft, and borrowing, as a bricolage of ideas and influences that crystallized around the monuments of Angkor. The splintered nature of nationalisms and the multiplicity of identity choices available to Cambodians problematized the notion of a single national psyche or monolithic national culture. As we have seen, visitors to Angkor in the 1930s, when the inculcation and transmission of colonial ideas extended into schoolroom, exhibition hall, scout group, youth club, and news and print media, differed in their responses. To some Angkor was a pile of stones; to others it was the incarnation of Khmer ancestral achievement and contemporary potential; but both are primed responses, loaded with the disappointment or realization of expectations. One way in which we can understand this legacy and its ramifications is as a "temple complex," where "complex" refers at once to the physical constellation of Angkor and to a group of associated ideas or impressions. On one level we can read colonialism's legacy not as the recovery of memory but as the creation of "false" or induced memories.

In her forthcoming book on caste and postcolonial consciousness, Debjani Ganguly contrasts the legitimating and overtly sovereign "homogeneous discourses of cultural nationalism" produced in metropolitan, postwar India with the "palpably heterogeneous ways in which postcolonial histories and identities have been imagined and constructed."[1] The sinews of Khmer cultural nationalism developed by the French Protectorate's intellectual elite were one of many possibilities for imagining and performing the nation. In focusing on their story, and containing it within

Metropolitan–colonial contours, this book has elided the paths of resistance travelled by monastic leaders of millenarian movements and has sidelined the impact of the major, broader political movements of communism. The Angkorean narrative of cultural homogeneity that emerged as a unifying thread among colonial, communist, intellectual, indigenous, and European narratives was not some "sleight of sight," nor a strategic gambit.[2] Outwardly homogeneous and single-stranded, this was a multi-stranded narrative, cross-woven with allusions to ancestral brilliance, contemporary decadence, ancient statecraft, modernity, Buddhist cosmology, and cross-cultural synergy. Depending on who utilized them, and for what purposes, these threads slackened and tightened, from Thiounn's ribbons of self-congratulation and mutual flattery to Son Ngoc Thanh's tense noose around France's neck.

In billing such figures as cross-cultural interlocutors, we must apply the same anthropological scrutiny to those within the French imperial complex who acted as brokers between cultures, albeit from a different starting point and power base. The life journeys and intellectual circuits of Mouhot, Delaporte, Commaille, Karpelès, Groslier, and Finot, whose sites of birth and burial spanned Laos, Marseille, Paris, Pondicherry, and Phnom Penh, were anything but homogeneous. These European narrators were neither selfless beacons of light, as cast in colonial propaganda, nor the narcissistic couturiers of national culture sketched by Said, Cohn, and others. They were vectors of change whose passage to and through Cambodge left traces on that country's cultural topography while delineating the contours of a new, national cosmology. But theirs is less than half the story. It was Son Diep, Thiounn Sambath, Suttantaprija In, Chuon Nath, Huot Tath, Son Ngoc Thanh, Pach Cheoun, Nou Hach, and others whose energies and intellects created a traction with such European personalities, igniting subtle shifts in indigenous philosophies. Without these Cambodian figures, the projects and trajectories of Karpelès et al. would have left different traces. These Cambodians were not dragged by their heels and "dragooned into the colonial project." And while colonial scholars and record keepers may have been driven by a "need to know," catalogue, and transcribe, figures from Son Diep to Son Ngoc Thanh were equally compelled by a need to *tell*. We see this impetus to transmit in Son Diep's and Nou Hach's scripting of travelogues and novels set in France and such Franco-Khmer milieux as the Lycée Sisowath. Whereas Son Diep hoped "to inform the public for posterity" (Son Diep, 1902), Nou Hach's description of life in late 1930s and early 1940s, first published after the fall of Sihanouk in 1972, performed the function of a witness to history, for history. Chuon Nath and Huot Tath's publications outlining the proper path to enlightenment, and their lectures to audiences in Cochinchina warning Khmer communities of the dangers of extinction, were equally driven, not by a dry response to colonial requests to fill the blank pages of some ledger marked "Cambodge," but by a passion to transmit not only what they had heard, learned, and seen, but their ideas.

These men's excitement at new opportunities, keen intellects, pursuit of new knowledge forms, mastery of newly available technologies—such as printing and map reading—forged meaningful conversations with those few Europeans who had made an effort to understand their language and their culture. Poised at the interstices of the colonial encounter, on the seam lines of political and cultural change, these figures evinced an enthusiasm for their new "protectors" that ran deeper than propaganda. Thiounn's overtly sycophantic gestures to "reciprocal trust and fecund cooperation" were fuelled not purely by his own political ambition but by a broader intellectual wanderlust. Working closely with Pavie to quell an insurrection, Thiounn's and Son Diep's eyes were wide open to the double-edged rapier of military and cultural power. Like Son Diep, Thiounn likely accommodated his own accommodation with the protectorate as proof that he was a person of merit and wisdom: one whose *kusala* and *punnya* allowed him to travel to France.[3]

As indicated by the protests of the 1940s, even those individuals most willing to embrace and converse with colonial methodologies and technologies were ultimately insulted and angered by colonialism's repressive machinery. But by the 1940s, figures like Son Ngoc Thanh could simultaneously repudiate colonialism as politically obsolete and champion the need for Cambodian independence and choose from colonialism's mixed bag of legacies. In carrying colonialism's iconicities, notably that of Angkor, as well as the notion of Buddhism as a neatly framed national religion, forward into an independent future, these Cambodians were not adopting colonial ideology but transmuting it and adapting it to their own political purposes and agendas. Just as they had exercised their own choices and initiatives in entering into dialogues with Europeans, and concluding those dialogues with the display of anger and protests when it appeared they could go no further, so these savvy interlocutors ultimately defied colonialism's characterizations. These were no blind copyists, but discriminating intellectuals. Whether motivated by personal ambition like Thiounn Sambath, by religious conviction like Chuon Nath and Huot Tath, or by political prescriptions like Son Ngoc Thanh, these individuals in many respects held considerable power over their European colleagues through their possession of and access to indigenous knowledge, skills, and networks that rendered Finot, Groslier, Karpelès, et al. their cultural dependents.

Khmer Issarak tracts distributed in 1947 along the Vietnam border declared that "the Cambodian race, Cambodian blood and Cambodian nationality are all the children of his majesty Jayavarman, the builder of Angkor Thom and Angkor Vat. Rise up, open your eyes, get back onto the proper path."[4] The central assumptions of these tracts were far from revolutionary and were shared by Cambodge's minister of education. In a 1947 article outlining the government's education policy, Princess Ping-Péang Yukanthor, now minister of education, painted a picture of past grandeur to preach the dangers of decline in the fashion of Mouhot and his successors. "The world renown of Kampuchea has made the country the envy of its neighbors," she wrote. In the Angkor era, the Khmer race had reached "a higher stage" than anyone else, but the "Khmer nation" grew arrogant, neglected national defense, and dwindled in size and stature. The Khmer people "lost the notion of national consciousness" although, deep down, they kept "the memories of their glorious past." Under the French, Yukanthor continued, the "Khmer embryo developed and took on a new personality." A new pride in the past was kindled, imbuing the Khmer with the desire to preserve all those "ancestral traditions which gave him his own personality."[5]

Here, history becomes tautology: Yukanthor at once reifies the Khmer personality and fixes it in the Angkorean era and ancestral traditions, and credits the protectorate with allowing Khmers to develop a "new" personality, where "new" refers, not to the primordial Khmer soul or ancestral tradition, but to its *restoration*. The rebuilding of the Khmer "national character" follows a similar path to the reconstruction of Angkor and of Buddhism in colonial rule.

For all its horrors of hybridity, colonialism was always necessarily a process of mixing. Attempts to purify and constrain by keeping races or cultures apart cast a smokescreen around a fundamental contradiction of colonialism, namely, its complete dependency on hybridity—on the acquisition of the colonial language by indigenes, on the mastery of "modern" methods in science and the arts, and on the adoption of certain facets of European hygiene and medicine. A varied vocabulary was forged to reconcile colonial antipathy to mixing with this dependence syndrome: *métissage* was to be frowned upon, both as miscegenation and as cultural pollution, both of which were read, in colonial discourses, as sexual acts, not least because those aspects of indigenous arts and cultures—cloth, weaving, ornament, art—were commonly equated with the invocation of the colonized as "feminine" while the West and its influences were seen as "masculine" and "modern." At times, this masculinity was located in the so-called modern European woman, who was depicted as the antithesis of the presumedly primordial, feminine colonized woman and was derided in Groslier's novels and in the writings of many colonials, as in the writings of contemporary modern romantics such as D. H. Lawrence, for her shrill, manly ways and her power to erode and erase "traditional" femininity. As a site of building, construction, a project of mass labor designed by King Suryavarman, and one that became the scene of much male coolie labor under conservation projects directed by European males, Angkor Vat was indisputably a "masculine" site, one used by writers for the newspaper *Nagaravatta* to symbolize assumed racial difference between the Khmers (big and strong) and "yellow" races; by Lon Nol as evidence of Cambodia's warrior heritage; and by Pol Pot to galvanize proletarian potential. To feminize Angkor would have been to undermine the protectorate's projects of rebuilding and resurrection: Angkor thus became the locus for a masculine, national identity, and the seat of the Kmae daem.

Assumptions about the feminine and malleable aspects of indigenous society and culture, those eternal tropes of colonialism, were literally lifted from Angkor's walls and bas-reliefs: the *apsaras, thevadas,* or Khmer dancers were to represent Cambodge's potential for domestication and operate as a theater of Khmer national and racial purity. As we have seen, this dance, or *lkaon kmae,* was open to modernization, in the same way that a minority of elite Cambodian females—such as Khieu Ponnary—were admitted to secular colonial schools. In early discourses of nation authored by such women, as Kate Frieson has shown, women sought a space outside the confines of the home, scorning "uncivilized" customs that prohibited education for girls, while arguing for female participation in the nation on familial grounds, in a maternal role.[6] Central to these arguments was the discourse of *sivilai,* which figured so prominently in the writings of male nationalists. This split gendering of nationalisms was reflected in the pen names adopted by male writers. "Son of the Khmers," "Original Khmer," "Ancient Youth," and other such names were associated, not with the procreation of the nation, but with its construction and location at Angkor, while women writers declared their identification with spiritual mediums and dancers, *apsaras* and *thevadas,* through such nom de plumes as Obaphabal Devi (Happy Goddess) and Devada (Keov Thevada). Fictionalized in Roland Meyer's *Saramani: Une danseuse cambodgienne,* the figure of la cambodgienne as Thevada offered women a place as intermediaries between the world of man, whose concerns were with the concrete edification of a nation-state, and the spiritual space for women who, in the same way that Devada hovered above this mortal world, were expected to transcend politics and focus their energies on the spiritual and private domain of the home. By the late 1940s, this national paragon of femininity had come to incorporate elements of Vichy ideology.

Corporeal manifestations of the nation took on a similarly gendered character under colonialism. In the late nineteenth century, Cambodian women in the town had worn shortly cropped hair and had worn their *sampots* as trousers in an almost, but not quite, identical fashion to men. This apparent convergence of male and female styles in hair and wear had troubled colonial efforts to define a national style that was also gendered. By the late 1940s, consensus had been reached in much writing that the "national" garb for women that was considered both *sivilai* and sufficiently "feminine" was a *sampot* worn as a long skirt *(sampot samloy)* and bobbed hair, while men were encouraged to wear trousers or shorts in place of the tucked and folded *sampot* that had been the standard mode of dress for Cambodian males at the outset of the colonial encounter. These distinctions, and discourses about them, mirrored notions that man's place was in the office and the public domain, as a builder of nation (where trousers gave him enhanced mobility), and woman's role was as the nation's homemaker, caregiver, mother, and daughter.

The emphasis on gender differentiation tallied with other concerns about the cleavage between and clear delineation of distinct types, races, and cultures. The horror of slippage across class and cultural divides was reflected in late-nineteenth-century preoccupations with the state of being déclassés, a term commonly applied to Cambodians educated in Paris, or to Cambodian women who had cohabited with European men, and that was associated with the acquisition of the French language by Cambodian women or the mixing of European clothing and cloths with "traditional" wear and local produce. To some extent, we can view these déclassés as symbolic of policies of assimilation. In the 1900s, these policies gave way to those of association introduced by Governor-General Albert Sarraut, and the protégés of this new cultural politics became known as *évolués.*

Évolués implied the development of, say, a Cambodian within the confines of his Cambodian-ness, as simply having evolved into a better and more modern Cambodian. This was to be a controlled hybridity, where men like Groslier, who insisted on keeping themselves as French as possible not least by dining *en plein pique-nique* in the middle of the jungle, would teach Cambodians how to be, and remain, Khmer. Despite the European insistence on keeping the milieu *propre,* in its senses of clean, proper, and appropriate, colonial officials were inevitably forced or chose to adapt to a plethora of differences in living, etiquette, diet, and dress that were geographically and culturally marked. Precisely because the maintenance of a distinct milieu was so patently a fiction, an enormous premium came to be placed on acts of symbol and ritual, on both the representation of the nation and its performance. In such assertions of identity, audience was all-important. When Buddhist monks wore imported cloth as robes, or commissioned new temple buildings in cement from Chinese firms in Saigon, or displayed Christian sculptures in their places of worship, they apparently did not suffer a crisis of identity, or feel any more or less Cambodian, or any more or less Buddhist. But their cross-cultural experiments kindled unease in their European audience. To Groslier and others, they appeared less Cambodian, their authenticity horribly diluted by modernity, and their national distinction threatened by external contamination.

In a rare allusion to the synergy of colonial exchange, Princess Yukanthor, writing in 1947, referred to a "half-occidental, half-oriental" culture in colonialism. Such references would soon fade altogether from the Cambodian historiography of the colonial period, which developed a binary reading of history. With the rare exception of Huot Tath's memoir, published in 1969, which records a dialogue between himself, Chuon Nath, and the French administration, and casts Louis Finot and Suzanne Karpelès as the supporters of Khmer Buddhism, Cambodian accounts of the colonial period tended to screen such episodes of cooperation from the record. But even the most radical writers could not escape the "temple complex."

The EFEO echoed these inflated views of Cambodge's importance to the world. "It is through France that Cambodge, surprised by the world's admiration, became conscious of its ancestors, genius founders of marvels comparable to the Taj Mahal, the Parthenon, or the Pyramids." Likewise, it was through the EFEO, declared a 1948 EFEO publication, that "the modern Khmer perceives proudly that he is in fact the *real* kinsman of Kambuj, mythical ancestor to the breed of the Kambujas, a race of builders and keen artists." The book compared Jayavarman VII to his French contemporary, a trope that Sihanouk would later adapt.[7] Angkor was repeatedly used to shore up the legitimacy of the monarchy in popular literature: the strong implication was that Sihanouk's crusade toward independence would lead Cambodge to a time of Angkorean grandeur.[8] Although the agents of transfer of such tropes remained an elite nucleus of Cambodians who were conversant with both French systems of education and the Khmer vernacular, a number of whom originated from Kampuchea Kraom in western Cochinchina, these visions of nation and their claiming, reframing, and distortion by successive political regimes would have a lasting, and in some instances tragic, impact on millions of Khmers, Chams, Vietnamese, and Chinese in Cambodia, particularly in the Lon Nol era and in Democratic Kampuchea.

Khmer oral histories and myths of origin continued, and continue today, to locate Angkor in a supernatural cosmos outside the tight reins of European historical schemes. However, the colonial era, and in particular the archaeological revolution pioneered by the EFEO, forged a new past for Cambodge. In the popular imagination, Angkor still lives on as a powerful site of memory, a magical space for whose power and allure science has no answers. But colonial rule indelibly stained the mystery of Angkor's making and meaning, repackaging old lore into a new story of *national* glory, *national* neglect, *national* decline, and *national* renaissance. Exhumed and invested with this new historic significance, the temples of Angkor would in time be used by Cambodian leaders, from Sihanouk to Pol Pot, to bolster political claims to national legitimacy.

The cultural core of the Khmer nation invoked by modern politicians and intellectuals as the vital fabric of Cambodian identity and the key to national survival is not some primordial given but in many respects the outcome of the colonial encounter. Nationalism, whatever its ideological framework, is never a purely political entity, but is intimately bound up with notions of cultural identity. The years between Mouhot's discovery of Angkor in 1860 and the short-lived premiership of Son Ngoc Thanh in 1945 witnessed a complex series of cross-cultural encounters that irrevocably shaped the physical environment and the conceptual contours of the modern Cambodian nation. European imaginings and indigenous perceptions of what constituted a Cambodian identity, or the quintessence of Cambodge, converged on a set configuration of cultural totems. While archaeological, academic, and museological projects ensured the identification and preservation of these icons, the political, educational, infrastructural, and cartographic activities of the French Protectorate translated the paradigm of Cambodge into the administrative reality of a colonial nation-state.

For the majority of Cambodians, the French Protectorate did not bring about a universal, homogenizing compression of time and space. Instead, it introduced a parallel realm with its own sense of time, its own lines of authority, and its own skein of power relations. This parallel realm was inscribed onto the Cambodian landscape through the laying of telegraph poles, boundary markers, and the creation of new administrative districts. The challenge to the protectorate was to harness this traffic and harmonize these parallel zones of influence, practice, intellectual activity, and geographical movement. That it appeared to do so was largely a matter of illusion.

The interface between these coexisting realms were the new, secular literati, like Thiounn and Son Diep, trained in the modern secular schools and modernized temple schools, whose curricula were fashioned to produce good modern citizens and obedient colonial subjects by inculcating a strict sense of where Cambodians stood in relation to other French colonized peoples, in relation to passages of their past, and, most important, in relation to their future. It was through this elite interface—what Clifford has called the cultural interlocutors, those complex individuals made to speak for "cultural" knowledge—that the French Protectorate sought to inculcate modernity and an appreciation and faith not only in Western secularized governance but also in the superiority of French civilization.

While secular *neak-cheh-doeng* and those working within colonialism's knowledge projects, whether as researchers, journalists, or schoolteachers, helped to mediate these other worlds, assisting with the creation, translation, and dissemination of national narratives of space and history through maps and articles, the *sangha* helped to locate these narratives within a Buddhist framework. Linking these exercises was the celebration of Khmer as a "national language." In these arenas the Khmer nation/*jiet-kmae/sasana-kmae* was read, performed, articulated, and practiced. Although eighteenth- and nineteenth-century incursions by Siam and Vietnam had wreaked incalculable loss and damage to human life and material culture, this period of instability had not, apparently, destabilized the underlying conceptions of Buddhist cosmology within that mass of land and people commonly identified, through such characteristics as language, familial, social, and aesthetic practice, as Khmer. Rather, violent episodes were accommodated and interpreted within normative poems and oral history, whose retelling of these events in what has been widely acknowledged as a Khmer moral vocabulary and Buddhist cosmology ensured the partial reclamation and reconquest of these periods of cultural subjugation and territorial fragmentation. Although dismissed as nonhistory, and labelled as "folklore," "fairytale," or under the broader rubric of the mores and customs of Cambodia, alternative readings of the past—oral history, legend, normative poems, and song—persisted in the daily lives of most Cambodians. Colonialism's writing of a linear history for Cambodia, then, acted as a parallel text: it could coexist with, but did not seriously threaten, other readings of time and space through which Cambodians made sense of their world.

In postcolonial Cambodia, acquisition through formal education of the status of *neak-cheh-doeng* has persisted as a qualification to rule across the political spectrum,[9] assuring the longevity of individuals and families borne to prominence in the protectorate. Democratic Kampuchea leaders Thiounn Prasith, Thiounn Thioenn, and Thiounn Mumm are direct descendants of Thiounn.[10] The history of postcolonial governments and political movements in Cambodia, as elsewhere, has been riddled with contesting ideological claims for national legitimacy. Precursors to this factionalism exist in the rival democratic and royalist prescriptions for the Cambodian nation that emerged in the late 1930s, and in the previous century's fragmentation of the Cambodian elite into supporters of established ways of governance and collaborators with the French administration. By the 1930s, however, notions of a "national culture" had emerged that both served as a common ground linking these two camps, and whose reification and territorialization as a grounded, geocultural body of the Khmer "nation" also constituted the site on which future contests for political legitimacy would be fought. Precisely because Angkor had emerged as *the* signature of Khmerness, it would be claimed by all political parties in postcolonial Cambodia, and used to stake claims to sovereignty and moral legitimacy, in ways that echoed colonial propaganda.

Although ethnically inflexible in that it was commonly invoked to represent a "Khmer" lineage and heritage, Angkor's political uses were manifold. Sihanouk adopted it as a symbol of royal glory and of the greatness of his ancestor, claiming direct descent lines from Jayavarman VII and comparing his Sangkum Reastr Niyum regime with the Angkorean era and likening himself to Jayavarman, who had "regained national independence."[11] Like Paul Doumer, he saw Angkor as a tool for educating youth, as reflected in one 1959 youth magazine, which declared that "we Khmers used Angkor to educate Cambodian youths in the glory of their ancestors, a highly skilled, strong, prosperous, and famous people, with a grand future, and our glorious heritage is concrete proof of [our ancestors'] tremendous . . . artistry and culture," adding that Cambodian youth must now follow in these ancestral footsteps by building the motherland.[12]

In the rewriting of Cambodian nationalist scripts during successive decades, the conceptual and cultural legacy of Nath and Tath remained writ large. In 1947, Sihanouk styled himself the Great Buddhist King (*dhammika mahareach*) in the constitution and, after Independence, he defined the guiding ideology of the Sangkum Reastr Niyum (People's Socialist Community) as Buddhist socialism, and stressed its continuity with "the religious traditions of our national existence."[13] In 1946, three of Thiounn's grandsons—Thiounn Thieunn, Thiounn Thioum, and Thiounn Mumm—arrived in France and roomed at the Indochina Pavilion in the Cité universitaire in Paris. Here, along with four other students, Thiounn's grandsons founded a Metropolitan mirror of the Lycée Sisowath Association, the Association des étudiants khmers (AEK), whose goal was to encourage "the desire to know and to help each other."[14] "We were full of enthusiasm," one of its founding members affirmed, and "we wanted to show the French authorities that we were capable people." AEK had its own bulletin, *Khemara Nisset* (Khmer student), with articles on national reconstruction, history, art, India, and China. What appealed to its readers was its "nationalist spirit," and it advocated independence. The earliest split in the Cambodian student movement in Paris occurred in 1951, prompted by questions of material culture and national ceremony.

The Khmer New Year was coming up. Since 1949, the AEK had decided to celebrate the Khmer New Year outside of the Indochina Pavilion because it was built in a Vietnamese style. "It [was] a cultural problem. The national problem is instinctively linked to cultural problem," reasoned Ong Thong Heoung. But in 1951, the AEK's representative on the committee of the Indochina Pavilion bowed to pressure from the French minister of colonies and agreed to organize festivities within the Indochina Pavilion. Internal divisions were magnified by two recent arrivals from Cambodge: Saloth Sar and Ieng Sary.[15] Two years later, the French government dissolved the AEK, but it continued to function more or less normally until 1954, the year in which Cambodge gained independence, under the label *groupe folklorique*. Its president, the hugely talented Vann Molyvann, returned to Cambodge in the 1950s and was assigned to build the Independence monument, which he first conceived as a sort of *arc de triomphe*: tellingly, it was constructed over an old canal and a bridge known as *spean kounkat* (*pont métis,* or mixed-race bridge) and drew on both this reservoir of French monumental framing, the Banteay Srey temple, and on the work of a French goldsmith who fashioned parts of the interior. But more than architectural styles were migrating.

Since 1951, the Cambodian community in France had been split into right, left, and moderate factions. The left organized a Marxist-Leninist club (*cercle*), with the support of the Parti communiste français. This clandestine, closed group was dedicated to reading the works of Marx, Lenin, Engels, and Stalin. Its founding members were linguistic nationalist Keng Vannsak, champion of the first Khmer typewriter, Khieu Samphan, Hou Yuon, Ieng Sary, Saloth Sar, Thiounn Mumm, and another of Thiounn's grandsons, Thiounn Prasit. On 26 November 1956, a Union of Khmer Students was formed, uniting such leftists as Khieu Samphan, who succeeded Ieng Sary as chief of the Marxist-Leninist club in 1956 and was considered an honest nationalist, and Ieng Sary, valued as a good organizer and timekeeper. While Saloth Sar was a discreet student, whose stay in Paris passed unnoticed, the club's members viewed its influential organizer, Thiounn Mumm, as part of Cambodia's "living national heritage."

Meanwhile, in the Cambodia of the 1950s, Sihanouk's Sangkum Reastr Niyum regime was redefining the ethnic dimensions of Khmer national heritage. The Sihanoukian Khmer embraced Cham and Malay Muslims as "Kmae-Islam" and subsumed the various hill tribes as "Kmae-Leou" (literally meaning, upland Khmer) but excluded Vietnamese and Chinese—an exclusion reiterated in a law passed in 1959 that made assimilation to Khmer customs, morals, and traditions a condition of eligibility for citizenship, and adherence to the credos of "Khmerism" espoused in official journals during the Sangkum Reastr Niyum.[16] "The Khmer race is as eternal as stone," went the National Anthem, correlating with official statements that Angkor was a mirror and repository of "the Khmer soul."[17] These sentiments were translated into the built environment. Angkorean motifs were a major feature of a new school of national architecture championed by Vann Molyvann and reached their epitome in the Independence Monument erected in central Phnom Penh in 1963, which re-created the Prasat Khmer, the central sanctuary of ancient Khmer temples.[18] Whereas ancient Prasat housed the souls of kings and deities, this new monument housed the "Khmer soul," symbolizing the perpetuity of a nation.[19] Sihanouk's regime proved less eternal; in 1970, he was overthrown in a coup, and the American-backed Lon Nol was installed as president of the Khmer Republic.

Lon Nol interpreted Angkor's bas-reliefs as evidence of a Khmer warrior culture and readapted the colonial "descent into decadence" trope to depict the monarchy as intrinsically corrupt and regressive.[20] Cartoons and other propaganda showing Vietnamese military assaults on Angkor and its deities bolstered Lon Nol's equation of the Vietnamese, communists, and "nonbelievers" (whom he referred to as *tmil*). The notion of Buddhism as a *sasana-jiet* was integral to Lon Nol's ideology. Achar Hem Chieu's ashes were returned to Phnom Penh with great ceremony in 1972, and a Buddhist inscription was engraved on a monument to the republic built outside the Royal

Palace.[21] In circa 1970, the republic also produced a mass memorial to Chuon Nath in the form of a commemorative stamp that depicted him as a man of learning, ringed by an aura of brightness symbolizing both his own lucidity and the forces of enlightenment, against a dark background. The stamp's epitaph to Nath—Grand Renovator of the National Language—conveyed a message that conflated the Khmer Republic, the Cambodian nation, Buddhism (Khmer Buddhism), and language—"national language"—while simultaneously eliminating space not only for non-Khmers but for Khmers of a particular type: kings and queen.

As reflected in the canonization of Chuon Nath as the renovator of the national language, Lon Nol's republic also placed a premium on linguistic nationalism and invested heavily in philological and linguistic research projects designed to demonstrate the purity of Khmers and to emphasize the regime's Angkorean lineage. Purification of the nation would not only involve the expulsion of the monarchy and violence against Vietnamese in particular, but also the closure of non–Khmer-language spheres, such as Chinese schools and newspapers. Such decisions were often rationalized as actions against "communism," but this totalizing conflation of race and anti-regime politics belied a more complex array of factors centering on the government's conceptualization of the Khmer nation. Lon Nol stressed the supremacy of the Khmer race and its distinctness from Vietnamese or Chinese residents of Cambodia and introduced a new constitutional definition of Khmers as those, living in or outside of Cambodia, who possessed "Khmer blood, Khmer traditions, Khmer culture, Khmer language and who were born on the territory that is the heritage of our Khmer ancestors."[22] This ethnocentric vision of nation was given a theoretical framework with Lon Nol's invention of the doctrine of "Neo-Khmerism." "The prefix 'neo' . . . symbolizes the journey towards the future. The word 'Khmerism' reminds of the bonds of past history," providing for the "self-identification and instituting a factor of continuity that will ensure the safeguarding of the Khmer people. For there is one Khmer culture of its own, separated clearly from other cultures . . . [and] more than 2,000 years old." From now on, claimed a leading republican journal in 1974, there were no more "Khmer Kraom, Khmer Kandal, Khmer Islam, Khmer Leou, Lao Khmer, or Siam Khmer. . . . There are only Khmer," adding that all those who fitted these descriptions and were on Cambodian territory could acquire citizenship immediately.[23]

The DK took these conceptualizations further, through its draconian enforcement of standards of Khmerness in language, dress, and other areas. In its own bizarre "renovation" of Khmer language, it introduced a number of new terms while abolishing others and forced the use of Khmer on the entire population, inflicting often tragic penalties and mass punishment upon those who violated the prescribed *sound* of the Khmer nation—a sound whose ideal blend of Khmer vernacular and socialist terminology was exemplified in the aptly named *Voice of Democratic Kampuchea* radio program—by speaking Chinese or other non-Khmer dialects. This insistence on Khmer language may be seen as part of Bhaba's earlier mentioned notion of the authoritarian regime's need for narrative, whereby the Khmer Rouge set themselves up as the custodians of written culture and the macabre inducement of historical texts at Tuol Sleng provided the regime with its own "inscriptions," like those at Angkor. Despite its pledge to erase "all vestiges of the old regime . . . and wipe out old habits," Democratic Kampuchea also perpetuated the legacy of Cambodge, clinging to Angkor as a national monument to "original Khmerdom" and a symbol of the racially pure nation to which it aspired. It was also used as a monument to the productive potential of Cambodians, and the despotic potential of the monarchy, to say nothing of the symbol of a vast irrigation scheme that DK proposed as a path to "Independence mastery." It employed allusions to Angkor to galvanize that Khmer productive potential and to distance the regime from the decadent king, for whose "pleasure" these "original Khmers" had toiled.[24] While the colonial map of Cambodge was reworked into a series of numbered zones, Angkor's significance was reflected in the naming of one such zone as Angkor–Siem Reap and its inclusion in the itinerary of state visits from China and elsewhere. Angkor was prominently featured on the flag, and was conjured in revolutionary songs, which urged Cambodian soldiers to "defend . . . the heritage of our ancestors, precious and good."[25]

Finally, in its bid to establish a pure, non-corrupt Cambodian culture, the regime relied heavily on the symbolism of dress, scrambling together the masculinist nationalism of Angkor and the rhetoric of the Thevada in the reconstructed female body. Their baggy black jackets designed to disguise or negate their femininity, women in DK sported bobbed haircuts reminiscent of those favored by late 1940s nationalist writers such as Khieu Ponnary, and the *sampot,* developed in colonial rule as national costume was enforced wear for women, as a national dress and instrument of Khmerization. Trousers—which had once been the standard wear for Cambodians in rural and urban areas, worn as the *sampot chong k'ben,* and commonly worn by urban and rural Chinese and Vietnamese women and men—were now banned on the ground that they were un-Khmer. The construction of the Khmer peasant entailed the enforcement of prescribed "womanly, Khmer" garb.

Less than a decade after the passing of Chuon Nath and Suzanne Karpelès, who died as Bharatidi in Pondichéry in 1968, Huot Tath is believed to have perished during Democratic Kampuchea (1975–1978), a regime whose eagerness to fast-forward linear history wrought havoc and destruction upon monks and their institutions. This was nation *as* religion, and history *as* disenchantment, taken to their most fearful conclusion. In place of the national anthem penned by Chuon Nath in 1942, new songs, including a bloody national anthem, and tracts, were scripted. Religion was not separated from politics: it was simply abolished. A constitutional ban on "reactionary religion" gave legal definition to the physical destruction and desecration of the country's *vats,* mosques, temples, and churches, the forced defrocking of virtually the entire *sangha,* and the execution of thousands of monks.[26]

The DK also sought to secure a place in history through unrealized plans for revolutionary monuments representing the postcolonial equivalent of Stoler's "blueprints of distress." Disparaging the Independence Monument as a curio for elite spectators, DK rhetoric urged Cambodians to "build their own independence monuments" by building dikes and digging canals.[27] While much of Phnom Penh lay deserted and in neglect, Saloth Sar, who would undoubtedly have visited the Vat Pnum during his adolescence in Phnom Penh, dreamed of a revolutionary monument to complete the nightmare that this capital city had become. Artists at Tuol Sleng were commissioned to design a suitable sculpture, and came up with a Maoesque ensemble of anonymous, weapon-wielding people led by Pol Pot, right hand stretched skyward and left arm grasping a copy of the red book. The designated site for the monument was Vat Pnum, but before the DK could implement plans to destroy the hilltop temple and replace it with the monument, the Vietnamese invaded and the regime fell.[28]

Where are these figures today? Chuon Nath is widely iconized in Cambodian temples, and in 1999 a ceremony and conference commemorating the thirtieth year of his death was celebrated in the Buddhist Institute, at Vat Ounaloum. The institute has now moved to an attractive building, designed by the Cambodian architect with a grace and symmetry that would have earned Groslier's praise, next to the concrete monstrosity of the Naga Casino, financed by Malay investors, whose driveway boasts a garish mural of Angkor Vat. The EFEO now maintains a presence at Vat Ounaloum.

Today, the Vat Pnum has once again been restored in ways that speak to multiple categories of belonging more than to its 1900 designation as a "national pagoda." A large clock adorns the base of the hill, and Sisowath, gouged out of Theodore Rivière's statue during the DK, has been replaced. In addition to the Buddhist temple crowning the hill, a Chinese temple to the deity Bentougong, widely revered in Kampot and elsewhere in Cambodia by Chinese as well as Khmer, sits farther down the hillside. New replicas of the replicas of Angkorean steles have been cast. Surrounding the base of the hill are new cement lampposts, their ornate castings reminiscent of colonial pasts and Parisian streets. Motorbikes, cyclos, *tuk-tuks,* and minibuses skirt the base, travelling at a range of speeds and in different directions. The zoo is no longer, but an elephant circles the foot of the hill and gibbons play and scavenge for food around the balustrades.

Not far away, along a road named for Christopher Howes, the British victim of a Khmer Rouge kidnapping, sits the Lycée René Descartes, half of its original campus taken over by an Institute of Management, where the preferred medium of instruction is English, and whose students, mostly the children of the elite, boast a more dazzling array of new Japanese cars than the medley of motorbikes, cherokee jeeps, *tuk-tuks,* and cyclos vying for space outside the Lycée. Opposite is the National Library, and behind it the National Archives, whose extensive documentary and photographic holdings eclipse the National Museum's recent treatment of *"Le passé au Cambodge":* the museum's one concession to modern history are two dismal boards of tattered and badly dubbed photos. Elsewhere, the museum captions still bear the names of Groslier and his later successor, Jean Boisselier. A staircase away, out of public view in the museum's carefully tended library, the sombre, leather-clad spines of books on wall-to-wall shelves speak of a deeper, more complex history. Here, the collected volumes of Eugène Viollet-le-Duc rub spines with an original guide to the 1900 Exposition universelle in Paris, A. Sylvestre's "How To Be a Khmer Civil Servant" (1920), the annals of the Musée Guimet, and countless other volumes. Downstairs, in a sculpture gallery, French, English, and Khmer sayings encircle sixteenth- and eighteenth-century bronze and copper statues. "You should abandon origins," reads one, near to a Buddha of "Unknown origin/*Provenance inconnue.*" For Cambodians, however, the museum remains a deeply spirited place; Cambodian staff at the museum, students, and pilgrims journey here to make offerings to images imbued with particular spiritual powers.[29]

Across town, a newly built Buddhist Institute, funded largely by Japanese and German aid, sits in the shade of the monstrous multistory Naga casino, whose driveway sports the obligatory Angkor Vat mural. Host to the Tripitaka Commission, the Mores and Customs Commission, and Kampuja Surya, the Buddhist Institute is a fragile monument to the cultural and intellectual activity of the 1930s and 1940s.

The closest thing to a modern history museum, hugely popular with Cambodians as well as Thai and Chinese tourists but largely scorned by Europeans as kitschy and inauthentic, is the Cambodian Cultural Village in Siem Reap. Financed by an overseas Chinese bank, the Canadia Investment Bank, the village exhibits waxworks of Zhou Daguan, Kram Ngoy, Chuon Nath, and well-known singers and film stars from the 1950s to 1970s. Kram Ngoy's selected Khmer ballads, first recorded and compiled for printing by Suzanne Karpelès, are on sale alongside Chinese guides to Angkor. Among the miniature monuments arrayed outdoors, the village boasts a meticulous replica of Groslier's arts school and museum, as well as Hébrard's New Market (whose renovation, in Phnom Penh, was contracted to a French firm in 2004) and, in an echo of the 1900 exposition, a miniature of the Vat Pnum. The only Caucasian face in this complex, other than the occasional tourists, is the waxwork of a "blue beret," a United Nations soldier flirting with a miniskirted call girl outside a brothel.

In 2003, French was dropped as the official second language of Cambodia, and the children of the new elite are more likely to be found at Northbridge International School or the British International School of Phnom Penh than at the Lycée René Descartes. Next to the *lycée* is a vast building site, the former grounds of the Club Sportif, now razed to the ground to make way for the new American embassy. English and Chinese are preferred to French as a second language, but the streets still bear the name *rue*. There is no longer a rue Groslier, and there has never been a rue Karpelès, but Nehru, Mao Zedong, and Tito figure in the urban legends provided on city maps. The palace and the arts school still grace the skyline. These are no empty monuments to the protectorate, but living testament to the vibrancy of a world where traces of the colonial encounter merge with echoes of past tragedies and the regeneration of diverse communities, among them Chinese, Cham, and Vietnamese. This activity has also regenerated echoes of colonial concerns about the disappearing Khmer, while the rapid depletion of sculptures and statuary from Angkor has focused international attention on the maintenance of the temples. In turn, colonial experience and diasporic movements have collectively embroidered "Indo-chic" into the cultural vernacular of contemporary France, as evident in such every-day sights as restaurants, monuments, museums, and the *bobo* (bourgeois-bohemian) merchandising of the exotic.

Fifty years after the collapse of French colonialism, signs of France are every-where in Cambodia's chief cities, from lurid Alain Delon cigarette advertisements whose English slogans boast of "a taste of France," to shops, hotels, opticians, phar-macies, tailors, and restaurants named after the Eiffel Tower, the Arc de Triomphe, and the Champs Elysée. By inscribing such imagery upon the quotidian urban land-scape of postcolonial Cambodia, the people of the Cambodian diaspora have inter-twined the semiology of their former colonizer with contemporary reconstruction. In these streets, as Ong Thong Hoeung writes, the perpetrators of Pol Pot's genocide circle freely, rubbing shoulders with their former victims. "All dictators represent themselves as defenders of national sovereignty," writes Ong Thong Hoeung. "But experience shows that, often, when one shelters behind his own sovereignty, his own culture, or his own tradition, an injustice is in the making."[30]

NOTES

ABBREVIATIONS

ACCIM	Archives de la Chambre de Commerce et d'Industrie, Marseille
BCAF	Bulletin du Comité de l'Asie française
BEFEO	*Bulletin de l'École française d'Extrême Orient*
BSEI	*Bulletin de la Société d'études indochinoises*
CAOM	Centre des Archives d'Outre Mer
CARAN	Centre d'acceuil et de recherche des Archives Nationales, Paris
IHI	*L'Indochine: Hebdomadaire illustré*
JAS	*Journal of Asian Studies*
JSEAH	*Journal of South East Asian History*
JSS	*Journal of the Siam Society*
NV	*Nagaravatta*
OIORC	Office of the India and Oriental Records Collection

INTRODUCTION: ORIGINATIONS

1. *Khemara Niset* (Khmer student), no. 14, August 1952; Kiernan, *How Pol Pot Came to Power,* 121.

2. Maurice Blanchot, *The Writing of the Disaster,* trans. Ann Smock (Lincoln: University of Nebraska Press, 1995), 42–47; Kerwin Lee Klein, "On the Emergence of Memory in Historical Discourse," *Representations* 69 (Winter 2000): 141; Locard, "Khmer Rouge Gulag," 1.

3. See Chandler, *Brother Number One;* Locard, "Khmer Rouge Gulag."

4. Chandler, *Brother Number One.*

5. There was no evidence of money, either, in the Angkorean era. A variety of currencies were in circulation when the French established the protectorate. These were homogenized into the piastre.

6. Herzfeld, *Cultural Intimacy,* 59.

7. 29 February 1988. Anonymous cover letter attached to an English translation of "What Is the Virtue, the Quality, the Reality and the Responsibility of Democratic Kampuchea in the Past, Present and Future?" (unpublished MS). I am grateful to Teri Caraway for sharing this document with me at Cornell in 1991.

8. Chakrabarty, *Provincializing Europe,* 44.

9. Stephen Heder, cited in David Chandler, *Voices from S-21,* 50.

10. Chandler, *Voices from S-21,* 50, 109.

11. Bhabha, *Location of Culture,* 98; Derrida, "Living on: border lines," in Derrida, de Man, Miller, Bloom, and Hartman, eds., *Deconstruction and Criticism,* 87.

12. Chandler, *Voices from S-21,* 14.

13. Evans and Rowley, *Red Brotherhood at War,* 20–21; Um, "Brotherhood of the Pure," 361.

14. See, e.g., Chandler, *Tragedy of Cambodian History,* 12–13; Kiernan, *How Pol Pot Came to Power,* 21–23; Osborne, *Sihanouk,* 28–29; Vickery, *Kampuchea,* 8; Evans and Rowley, *Red Brotherhood at War,* 20–21.

15. See Ben Kiernan and Chanthou Boua, "The Umbrella War of 1942 by Bunchan Mul," in Kiernan and Boua, eds., *Peasants and Politics in Kampuchea, 1942–1981,* 115–126.

16. Bhabha, *Nation and Narration,* 1–7.

17. Artaud, *Messages révolutionnaires,* 6.

18. Kohn, *Idea of Nationalism,* 18–20, 329–331.

19. Hutchinson, *Dynamics of Cultural Nationalism,* 12–13.

20. Chatterjee, *The Nation and Its Fragments,* 121.

21. Kapferer, *Legends of People, Myths of State,* 97; Anderson, *Imagined Communities,* 6.

22. Todorov, *On Human Diversity,* 174–175.

23. Hobsbawm, *Nations and Nationalism since 1780,* 12; Miroslav Hroch, *Social Preconditions of National Revival in Europe* (Cambridge: Cambridge University Press, 1985).

24. Chandler, *History of Cambodia,* 89.

25. Sinha, *Colonial Masculinity,* 22; Chatterjee, *The Nation and Its Fragments,* 95–98.

26. Barnett, "Cambodia Will Never Disappear," 101–103, 105–107.

27. Burton, *Burdens of History,* 36; Stoler, *Race and the Education of Desire,* 12.

28. Frances Gouda and J. Clancy-Smith, "Introduction," in Clancy-Smith and Gouda, eds., *Domesticating the Empire,* 1–3; Norindr, *Phantasmatic Indochina,* 3.

29. For an excellent analysis of the influence of Chinese cosmology and intellectual traffic on Cambodia's modern development, see Népote "Les nouveaux Sino-Khmers acculturés: Un milieu social perturbateur?" *Péninsule* 30, no. 1 (1995): 133–154.

30. Smail, "On the Possibility of an Autonomous History of Modern Southeast Asia," in Sears, ed., *Autonomous Histories, Particular Truths,* 61.

31. Chandler, *Tragedy of Cambodian History,* 12–13.

32. Barbara Harlow, "Introduction," in Alloula, *Colonial Harem,* xvii–xviii.

33. Bunchan Mul, *Kuk Noyobay* (Political prison); trans. Chantou Boua, in Kiernan and Boua, *Peasants and Politics,* 115–117.

34. David Chandler, "Cambodian Palace Chronicles (Rajabangsavatar), 1927–1949," in Chandler, *Facing the Cambodian Past,* 200–203.

35. In particular, as Ashley Thompson notes, Western historians of Cambodia have focused their attention principally on two phases of history: the Angkor era and Democratic Kampuchea. See Thompson, "Changing Perspectives, after Angkor," in Jessup and Zephir, eds., *Sculpture of Angkor and Ancient Cambodia,* 22.

36. Corfield, *The Khmers Stand Up,* 2; Um, "Brotherhood of the Pure," 18.

37. Kiernan, *How Pol Pot Came to Power,* xiii, xiv.

38. Judy L. Ledgerwood, "Politics and Gender, 144.

39. Chandler, *History of Cambodia,* 2.

40. "In the sunset of dissolution," writes Milan Kundera, "everything is illuminated by the aura of nostalgia, even the guillotine" (*The Unbearable Lightness of Being* [London: Faber and Faber, 1990], 4).

41. Winichakul, *Siam Mapped.*

42. Thion, "Remodelling Broken Images," in Guidieri, Pellizzi, and Tambiah, eds., *Ethnicities and Nations,* 251.

43. Jan Nederveen Pieterse and Bhikhu Parekh, "Shifting Imaginaries: Decoloniza-tion, Internal Decolonization, Postcoloniality," in Pieterse and Parekh, eds., *Decolonization of Imagination,* 2; Sinha, *Colonial Masculinity,* 22; Aijaz Ahmad, *In Theory: Classes, Nations, Literature* (London: Verso, 1994).

44. Thomas, *Colonialism's Culture,* 26.

45. Clifford, *Routes,* 10.

46. Milner, *Invention of Politics in Colonial Malaya,* 1–2, 282.

47. Renan, *Qu'est-ce qu'une nation?* 26–29.

48. Ernest Renan, *Future of Science* (1848; Boston: Roberts Brothers, 1891), 228; Re-nan, *Mélanges d'histoire et des voyages,* xii, xiii, 28–75, 509, 513.

49. Jules Michelet, *History of France,* trans. Walter K. Kelly (London: Chapman and Hall, 1844), 74.

50. See Hansen, "Ways of the World."

51. Aymonier, *Le Cambodge: Tome I,* 56.

52. Osborne, *French Presence in Cochinchina and Cambodia,* 182; Um, "Brotherhood of the Pure," 19.

53. Hansen, "Religion and Identity in Turn-of-the-century Cambodia."

54. Weber, *France,* 130; Tzvetan Todorov, *On Human Diversity,* 90–170.

55. See Duara, *Rescuing History from the Nation,* 36.

56. Iukanthor, *Destin d'empire,* 131–137.

57. Lowenthal, *The Past Is a Foreign Country,* xvi.

58. Milner, *Invention of Politics,* 70.

59. Chatterjee, *The Nation and Its Fragments,* 95.

60. Barnett, "Cambodia Will Never Disappear," 102; Chandler, *History of Cambo-dia,* 89.

61. Shils, "Intellectuals in the Political Development of the New States," 342–344.

62. Kmae Botra, "Kmae pneak kluen-dongkluen ning baek pneik pleu haey niw?" (Have Khmers woken up, gained consciousness, and become enlightened yet or not?), *Nagaravatta,* 15 January 1938, 1–3.

63. Milner, *Invention of Politics,* 51, 67–69.

64. Stephen Heder and Judy Ledgerwood, "Introduction," in Heder and Ledger-wood, eds., *Propaganda, Politics and Violence in Cambodia,* 21.

65. Achar Kuy, "Ompi yoobal kmae ning yoobal sasana date dael mok niw srok kmae" (About Khmer opinions and the opinions of other races {sasana} who come to live in Cambodia), *Nagaravatta,* 22 May 1937, 1; Nokorvat Botra Seeliekar, "Boriyiey Tngai Sau" (Saturday report), *Nagaravatta,* 5 June 1937, 1.

66. Elizabeth Becker, *When the War Was Over,* 50.

67. Milner, *Invention of Politics,* 282.

68. Hustvedt, *What I Loved,* 152.

69. Timothy Mitchell, "Annals of the Archive: Ethnographic Notes on the Sources of History," in Axel, ed., *From the Margins,* 47–48.

70. Ann Laura Stoler, "Developing Historical Negatives: Race and the (Modernist) Visions of a Colonial State," in Axel, ed., *From the Margins,* 156–158, 180.

71. Anderson, *Imagined Communities,* 228.

72. Norindr, *Phantasmatic Indochina,* 2.

73. Christopher Goscha, "Beyond the Colonizer and the Colonized: Intra-Asian De-

bates and the Complexities of Legal Identity in French Colonial Indochina" (paper presented at the Southeast Asia Studies Seminar Program, Yale Center for International and Area Studies, Yale University, 7 April 2004).

CHAPTER 1: THE TEMPLE COMPLEX

1. C. Lavollée, "Le Tour du Monde," *Revue des deux mondes* (Paris, 1889), 906–917.

2. Charles Mouhot, "Preface," in Mouhot, *Travels in Siam, Cambodia, and Laos, 1858–1860,* 15.

3. "Exposé de la situation de l'Empire," *Revue Maritime* (janvier–février 1863), 13; (janvier 1863), 166.

4. Vice-Amiral Bonard, "Angcor en Septembre 1862," *Revue Maritime et Coloniale* (fevrier 1863), 244–247.

5. V. Saint-Martin, "Revue geographique 1863," in *Tour du Monde* 4 (1863): 424. Following the international fanfare accorded Mouhot's discovery of Angkor in 1860, the missionary Bouillevaux complained bitterly that he had reported his own sighting of Angkor years previously. Bouillevaux's account, first published in 1851, had dismissed Angkor as "pagan temples—the work of idolators." See C.-E. Bouillevaux, *L'Annam et le Cambodge* (Paris: V. Palmé, 1874); Ponder, *Cambodian Glory,* 91.

6. Lavollée, "Le Tour du Monde," 906–917; Henri Mouhot, *Travels in Indo-China, Siam, Cambodia and Laos* (London: John Murray, 1864), 275. This vision of Cambodge as France's India was later elaborated by numerous colonial and Metropolitan scholar-officials, and is a theme I develop in Edwards, "Taj Angkor: Enshrining l'Inde in le Cambodge."

7. Mohout, *Travels in Siam:* see the introduction by Michael Smithies, xvi.

8. Barnett, "Cambodia Will Never Disappear," 101–125.

9. F. Garnier, *Voyage d'exploration en Indo-Chine* (Paris: Hachette, 1885), 12.

10. Anderson, *Imagined Communities,* 181n33.

11. Mouhot's original sketches are reproduced in his *Diary: Travels in the Central Parts of Siam, Cambodia, and Laos during the Years 1858–1861,* plates VI–VIII.

12. Léon Garnier, *Notice sur Francis Garnier* (Paris: Imprimerie Émile Martinet, 1882), ix–xiii.

13. See especially the engravings in Louis Delaporte, *Voyage au Cambodge,* 157, 190–191, 206–207, and 268–269, all of which show Angkor in an imagined, perfect past.

14. Anderson, *Language and Power,* 181.

15. Bussagli, *Oriental Architecture,* 174.

16. Mannika, *Angkor Wat,* 6–7.

17. Anderson, *Language and Power,* 22–23, 28–30.

18. French, "Hierarchies of Value at Angkor Vat," 4.

19. Swearer, *Buddhist World of Southeast Asia,* 19–20.

20. Mannika, *Angkor Wat,* passim; Schwartzberg, "Introduction to Southeast Asian Cartography," 693; Bruno Dagens, *Angkor: La forêt de pierre,* 172.

21. Private correspondence with Ashley Thompson, 17 April 1998.

22. Thompson, "Changing Perspectives," 22–32; 23–24.

23. Saveros Lewitz, "Les inscriptions modernes d'Angkor Wat," *Journal Asiatique* no. 260 (1972): 1–2, 107–129; Dagens, *Angkor,* 172.

24. Ai Khme and Ly Theam Teng, "Outline of the Development of Khmer Lit-

erature," *New Cambodge Monthly,* 3rd year, no. 19 (May–September 1972): 46; Jacobs, *The Traditional Literature of Cambodia,* 32–33; Saveros Pou, "Note sur le date du poème d'Angkor Vat," *Journal Asiatique* no. 263 (1975): 119–124; J. Moura, 1882–1883 "'Le poème de Nocor Vat' par Pang, traduit du cambodgien," *Bulletin de la Société Académique Indochinoise de France* 2, no. 2 (1882–1883): 197–203.

25. V. Goloubew, "Mélanges sur le Cambodge ancien (Section III: Artisans Chinois à Angkor Vat)," *BEFEO* 24 (1924): 513–519.

26. David Chandler, "An Eighteenth Century Inscription from Angkor Wat," in Chandler, *Facing the Cambodian Past,* 15–24; Lewitz, "Les inscriptions modernes."

27. Osborne, "History and Kingship in Contemporary Cambodia," 1–14.

28. C.-E. Bouillevaux, *L'Annam et le Cambodge: Voyages et notices historiques* (Paris: Victor Palmé, 1874).

29. Moura, *Le Royaume du Cambodge,* 128.

30. Lieutenant Ibos, "The Rights of France in Siam" (Hanoi: F-H. Schneider, 1900), 197.

31. Ibid., 197.

32. Rémusat, *L'Art khmer,* 10; Michael Brand, "Khmer Sculpture: From Monument to Museum," in *The Age of Angkor: Treasures from the National Museum of Cambodia,* exh. cat. (Canberra: Australian National Gallery, 1992), 25.

33. Teston and Percheron, *L'Indochine moderne,* 691.

34. Henri Marchal, "Des influences étrangères dans l'art et la civilisation khmères," *BSEIS* 11, no. 2 (1936): 9–10; Edwards and Chan Sambath, "Ethnic Chinese in Cambodia," in W. Collins, ed., *Ethnic Groups in Cambodia* (Phnom Penh: Preas Sihanouk Raj Academy, 1997), 55 and appendices B and D.

35. Dagens, *Angkor,* 20–21.

36. Charles Keyes, "The Case of the Purloined Lintel: The Politics of a Khmer shrine as a Thai National Treasure," in Reynolds, *National Identity and Its Defenders,* 264–265.

37. Goloubew, "Mélanges sur le Cambodge ancient," 519. W. Willmott has linked these sculptures to the consolidation of a Chinese community in Phnom Penh during the early seventeenth century. Willmott, "The Chinese in Cambodia," 20.

38. Dagens, *Angkor,* 21.

39. Princess Ping-Péang Yukanthor, "Souvenirs de mon première voyage à Angkor," *France-Asie* 2, no. 16 (15 July 1947): 644–652.

40. L. de Lajonquière, *Inventaire descriptif des Monuments du Cambodge,* 182, 199. E. Aymonier, *Le Cambodge: Tome III,* 32–33, 55. In 1997, Lam Pheak and So Chheng, two students at the Royal University of Fine Arts, recorded current versions of the legend at Ta Nei, but found nothing at Ta Prohm. I am grateful to their former supervisor, Ashley Thompson, for this information.

41. Keyes, "Case of the Purloined Lintel," 264–265.

42. Thomson, *The Straits of Malacca, Siam and Indo-China,* 135.

43. Dagens, *Angkor,* 20–21.

44. Lefebvre, *Production of Space,* 222.

45. L. M. de Carné, "Exploration du Mekong. I. Les ruines d'Angcor et les rapides du Khon," *Revue des Deux Mondes,* 1 March 1869, 179.

46. Lemire, *L'Indochine,* 221.

47. Brossard, *Colonies françaises,* 432.

48. See, e.g., J. Campbell, "Notes on the Antiquities, Natural History, of Cambodia, Compiled from Manuscripts of the Late E. F. J. Forrest, Esq., and from Information Derived from the Rev. Dr. House, etc.," *Journal of the Royal Geographic Society* 30 (1859): 186; Vincent F. Vincent, "The Wonderful Ruins of Cambodia," *Journal of American Geographic Society of New York* 10 (1878): 234.

49. Bouillevaux, *Voyage dans L'Indo-Chine 1848–1856,* 172.

50. Mouhot, *Travels in Siam, Cambodia and Laos 1858–1860,* 279.

51. Garnier, *Voyage d'exploration,* 27.

52. G. Monod, *Le Cambodgien,* 89.

53. See *L'Air d'Angkor,* in Charles Regismanset, "Chansons cambodgiennes," *BSEI* 1 no. 5 (1923): 45.

54. David P. Chandler, "The Tragedy of Cambodian History," *Pacific Affairs* 52, no. 3 (Fall 1979). His emphasis.

55. Osborne, "History and Kingship in Contemporary Cambodia," 1–14.

56. David Chandler, "Folk Memories of the Decline of Angkor in Nineteenth-Century Cambodia: The Legend of the Leper King," *Journal of the Siam Society* 67, pt. 1 (January 1979): 54.

57. Thompson, "Myth of the Saviour," 13.

58. Malleret, *Le cinquantenaire de l'École française d'Extrême-Orient,* 34.

59. Charles Saumarez Smith, "Museums, Artefacts and Meanings," in Vergo, ed., *The New Museology,* 8.

60. C. S. Smith, "Museums, Artefacts and Meanings," 6–7; see Dominique Poulot, *Musée, Nation, Patrimoine, 1789–1815,* 11–36 and 79–81, on the development of French notions of *patrimoine* and the establishment of a heritage movement in late-eighteenth-century France. See André Chastel, "La notion de patrimoine," in Nora, ed., *Les lieux de mémoire,* 416–445. See also Richard Tarnas, *The Passion of the Western Mind* (London: Pimlico, 1991), 79, 448; and Daniel J. Boorstin, *The Discoverers: A History of Man's Search to Know His World and Himself* (New York: Vintage Books, 1985), 604.

61. Duncan, *Civilizing Rituals,* 21–27.

62. Ames, *Cannibal Tours and Glass Boxes,* 22.

63. See Poulot, *Musée, Nation, Patrimoine,* 20; L. Theis, "Guizot," "Guizot et les institutions de la mémoire," in P. Nora, ed., *Les lieux de mémoire,* 575–576; Chastel, "Le notion de patrimoine," 443; Chatterjee, *The Nation and Its Fragments,* 95.

64. Theis, "Guizot," "Guizot et les institutions de la mémoire," in P. Nora, ed., *Les lieux de mémoire,* 575; Lowenthal, *The Past Is a Foreign Country,* xvi.

65. Chastel, "Le notion de patrimoine," 424.

66. Theis, "Guizot," 574.

67. Chastel, "Le notion de patrimoine," 419, 443.

68. Bruno Foucart, "Viollet-le-Duc et la restauration," and Dominique Poulot, "Alexandre Lenoir et les monuments français," in P. Nora, ed., *Les lieux de mémoire,* 618–649; 521; Alexander, *Museums in Motion,* 83.

69. N. Oulebsir, "La découverte des monuments de l'Algérie: Les missions d'Amable Ravoisié et d'Edmond Duthoit (1840–1880)," in Pierre R. Baduel, ed., *Figures de l'Orientalisme en architecture* (Aix-en-Provence: Édisud, 1994), 59.

70. Lowenthal, *The Past Is a Foreign Country,* 412.

71. W. S. Gilbert and A. S. Sullivan, *The Mikado* (1885), act 2.

72. Weber, *France: Fin de siècle,* 9–26, 215; Wright, *Politics of Design,* 33.

73. Said, *Culture and Imperialism,* 171.

74. C. S. Smith, "Museums, Artefacts and Meanings," 19.

75. Chastel, "Le notion de patrimoine," 429.

76. On the role of colonial displays in fashioning British national identity, see Coombs, *Reinventing Africa,* 63–83, 85–106, 187–213. On the influence of expositions on French national identity, see Norindr, *Phantasmatic Indochina,* 14–33; and for insights into the nexus between Dutch national identity and representations of the Dutch East Indies at colonial expositions, see Frances Gouda, *Dutch Culture Overseas,* 194–236.

77. Alphonse Esquiros, a journalist reporting on the 1862 event, as quoted by Mary E. Daly, "London 1862: International Exhibition of 1862," in Findling and Peele, eds., *Historical Dictionary of World's Fairs and Expositions, 1851–1988,* 27.

78. Arthur Chandler, "Paris 1867: Exposition Universelle," in Findling and Peele, *Historical Dictionary.*

79. Poirier, *Les Expositions Internationales du XIXe siècle,* 84–85.

80. Hoffenberg, *An Empire on Display,* 5. However, during Sisowath's reign, the exhibitionary mode was integrated into capital life as a "traditional" means of marking the king's birthday, and was later used to great effect by King Sihanouk. See Muan, "Citing Angkor," 128–141.

81. Michael Rowlands, "The Politics of Identity in Archaeology," in George C. Bond and Angela Gillian, eds., *Social Construction of the Past,* 134.

82. Oulebsir, "La découverte des monuments de l'Algérie," 59; Wright, *Politics of Design,* 78–79.

83. Norindr, *Phantasmatic Indochina,* 90–91. As Norindr notes, this argument is echoed today in UNESCO's endeavor to declare the temples of Angkor part of the *patrimoine mondiale* (world heritage).

84. Barnett has traced the strongly cultural focus of French colonial practice to psychological and political imperatives to fill this credibility gap. See Barnett, "Cambodia Will Never Disappear," 101–125. See also Greenfield, *The Return of Cultural Treasures,* 108–109. Duncan, *Civilizing Rituals,* 33.

85. Said, *Orientalism,* 169.

86. Marcel Dubois, "Preface," in *Empire colonial de la France: L'Indochine* (Paris: Librairie Coloniale Augustin Challamel, n.d.), ix.

87. Norindr, *Phantasmatic Indochina,* 4.

88. Loti, *Un pèlerin d'Angkor,* 4–5, 221–223.

89. Loti's Angkor also apparently featured in the childhood readings of Roland Meyer and the Cochinchina-born Marguerite Duras. See M. Duras, *The Sea Wall* (New York: Farrar, Strauss and Giroux, 1985), 17; R. Meyer, *Komlah,* 17; R. Meyer, *Le Propos,* 43.

90. *Courrier de Saigon,* 5 August 1865.

91. Léon Garnier, *Notice sur Francis Garnier* (Paris: Imprimerie Émile Martinet, 1882), ix–xiii; Garnier, *Voyage d'exploration en Indochine,* 1–2, 35.

92. Vercel, *Le fleuve,* 29–30; Louis Delaporte, "Rapport fait au Ministre de la Marine et des colonies et au Ministre de l'Instruction Publique, des cultes et des beaux arts, par M. Louis Delaporte, sur la mission scientifique aux ruines des monuments khmers de l'ancien Cambodge," *Journal Officiel de la Republique Française* 6, no. 90 (1874): 251.

93. Duprés, "Voyage au Cambodge: Suite," *Revue Maritime et Coloniale,* in papers of Jean Bouault, Teacher of History and Geography at Lycée Chasseloup-Laubat, Centre des Archives d'Outre Mer (hereafter CAOM) FPAPC4.

94. Centre d'acceuil et de recherche des Archives Nationales, Paris (hereafter CARAN), F21 4489 3a, "Notes relatives aux ruines Khmers du Cambodge" (n.d., unsigned), 5–8.

95. CARAN, F21 4489 3a, Ministère de l'Instruction Publique, des cultes et des beaux arts, Direction de Beaux Arts, Arrêté 7 May 1873.

96. CARAN, F21 4489, Delaporte to Minister of Public Education, 24 May 1873.

97. CARAN, F21 4489 3a, Delaporte to Minister of Public Education, 16 May 1873, 1–2.

98. Louis Delaporte, "Rapport fait au Ministre de la Marine et des colonies," 2517.

99. Louis Delaporte "Rapport fait au Ministre de la Marine et des colonies et au Ministre de l'Instruction Publique, des cultes et des beaux arts par M. Delaporte (suite et fin)" in *Journal Officiel de la Republique Française* 6, no 91 (2 April 1874): 2546.

100. Ibid., 2547–2548.

101. CARAN, F21 4489 3a, Sec Gen de l'Administration des Beaux Arts, Ministry of Public Education and Fine Arts to M. Sous-Secretaire d'Etat (n.d.).

102. George Coedès, *Les collections archéologiques du Musée National de Bangkok* (Paris and Brussells: Van Oest, 1928), 8.

103. CARAN, F 21 4489 3a, Directeur de Personnel, Ministry of Marine and Colonies to Ministry of Public Education, 26 July 1877.

104. CARAN, F21 4489 3a, Arrêté, Ministry of Public Education, Religion and Fine Arts, Paris, 10 November 1876.

105. CARAN, F 21 4489 3a, Directeur de Personnel, Ministry of Marine and Colonies to Ministry of Public Education, 26 July 1877.

106. The Third Republic's expenditure on acquisitions has been estimated at roughly one-third that of London's National Gallery. Staff salaries were negligible, so most curators were amateurs, often part-time. Zeldin, *History of French Passions,* 451–452.

107. "Les Colonies Françaises," *l'Illustration,* 15 June 1878, 399; *l'Illustration,* 21 September 1878, 186; Col. Duhousset, "Exposition ethnographique des missions scientifiques au Palais de l'Industrie," *l'Illustration,* 19 January 1878, 39. Jean-François Champollion (1790–1832) was the first scholar to decipher Egyptian hieroglyphs, initially working from copies and casts of the Rosetta Stone. See Vercoutter, *The Search for Ancient Egypt,* 90–95.

108. *L'Illustration,* 21 September 1878, 186–187.

109. E. Monod, *L'exposition universelle de 1889,* 291.

110. Hoffenberg, *Empire on Display,* xix.

111. See picture in Delaporte, *Voyage an Cambodge,* 243; see "Les missions scientifiques," *l'Illustration,* 14 September 1878.

112. CARAN, F21 4489 2, Jules Ferry Arrêté, 29 November 1879; Ministry of Public Works to Minister of Public Education, 30 June 1879; Chef du Bureau des Travaux historiques et des sociétés savants to Sous-Secrétaire d'État des Beaux Arts, 24 May 1879; Sous-Secrétaire d'État des Beaux Arts to Minister of Public Education and Fine Arts, 20 June 1879; Sous-Secrétaire d'État to Minister of Public Education and Fine Arts, 20 June 1879.

113. CARAN, F21 4489 3a, Delaporte to M. Sec Gen, 21 August 1881; Jules Ferry, Minister of Public Education and Fine Arts, Arrêté 8 September 1881, Delaporte to Minister of Public Education, 16 May 1882, Paris.

114. CAOM, INDO GGI 12504, Charles Thomson Avis: Gouverneur Général de la Cochinchine, circular addressed to Director of Interior, Chiefs of Administration and Departments, President of Colonial Council, President of Chamber of Commerce, Administrators of Arondissements, Representative p.i. of Protectorate of Cambodia (n.d).

115. CAOM, INDO GGI 12504, F. Faure, Under-Secretary of State for Marines and Colonies, to Governor General of Cochinchina, 20 June 1884, 1–4.

116. CAOM, INDO GGI 12680, Governor of Cochinchina Begin to Repr. Gen. Badens, 14 November 1885; Representative General in Cambodia Badens to Governor of Cochinchina Begin, 9 November 1885.

117. Bouinais and Paulus, *L'Indochine française contemporaine,* 460.

118. CARAN, F21 4489 3a, Myre de Vilers, Governor of Cochinchina to Minister of Public Education, 10 November 1887, 1–2.

119. CARAN, F21 4489 3c, Ministère de l'Instruction Publique et Beaux Arts Arrêté, 31 January 1889; CARAN, F21 4489 2, Delaporte to Directeur des Travaux d'Art, Direction des Beaux Arts, 27 May 1889.

120. CAOM, INDO GGI 23194, Louis Henrique, Special Commissaire for Exposition Coloniale 1889, Sous-Secrétaire d'État, Min. of Marine and Colonies Paris to GGI Saigon, 7 December 1888.

121. L. Marc, "La Pagode d'Angkor," *l'Illustration,* 5 October 1889, 280.

122. See picture in *l'Illustration,* 5 October 1889, 273. This transformation of place of worship to exhibition hall found a precedent in the erection of a full-size Gothic cathedral at the 1867 Paris exhibition. See A. Chandler, "Paris 1867: Exposition Universelle," in Findling and Pelle, eds., *Historical Dictionary,* 27.

123. CAOM, INDO GGI 23194, Fabre to Résident General, 30 September 1887, 3.

124. Schneider, *Empire for the Masses,* 141, 177.

125. Richer, *Histoire de la restauration,* 20.

126. Bernard Heitz, "Les aventuriers du royaume perdu," in Thierry Leclère, ed., *Les sourires d'Angkor,* 34.

127. *La Republique Française,* 26 July 1890.

128. CARAN, F 21 4470 3, Conservateur du Musée Guimet Hackin to M. le Directeur, 29 June 1927.

129. CARAN, F21 4489 3d, Delaporte to Directeur des Travaux d'Arts, 26 July 1886, 7; CAOM, INDO GGI 23194, Résident General Piquet to Governor of Cochinchina, 25 April 1887.

130. CAOM, INDO GGI 23794, Sous-Secretaire d'État des Colonies Eugène Étienne to GGI Paris, 16 April 1890.

131. CAOM, INDO GGI 23794, RSC to GGI, 6 February 1891.

132. CAOM, INDO GGI 23794, Raffegeaud to GGI, 23 March 1891; CAOM, INDO GGI 23794, Inspecteur, Service des Bâtiments Civils, Direction des Travaux Publics, report dated 31 October 1891; CARAN, F21 4470 3, Note pour M. le Ministre, Direction du Sec, 1ˢᵗ Bureau, Ministry of Public Education and Fine Arts, 17 June 1891.

133. CARAN, F21 4470 3, Minister of Foreign Affairs to M. Rambaud, Minister of Public Education (Direction des Beaux Arts), 12 September 1897.

134. Doumer, *L'Indochine française* 268, 290; J. Campbell "Notes on the Antiquities" (n. 48), 186; F. Vincent "The Wonderful Ruins of Cambodia," 242–244; W. S. Maugham, *The Gentleman in the Parlour: A Record of a Journey from Rangoon to Haiphong* (London: William Heinemann Ltd., 1930), 220–221. See V. Savage, *Western Impressions of Nature and Landscape,* 317–318.

135. Wright, *Politics of Design,* 21.

136. See Janet Horne, "In Pursuit of Greater France: Visions of Empire among Musée Social Reformers," in Julia Clancy-Smith and Frances Gouda, eds., *Domesticating the Empire: Race, Gender and Family Life in French and Dutch Colonialism* (Charlottesville: University of Virginia Press, 1998), 21–42.

137. Doumer, *L'Indochine française,* 270; Paul Levy, "L'École française d'Extrême-Orient," in *France-Asie: Revue Mensuelle de Culture Franco-Asiatique* (Imprimerie de l'Union, Saigon), 15 June 1947, 52.

138. "Le dégagement de Sambor Prei-Kuk," *Extrême-Asie,* no. 36 (June 1929), 536.

139. M. Petit, ed., *Les colonies françaises: Petite encyclopédie coloniale* (Paris: Larousse, 1903), 456.

140. Anderson, *Imagined Communities,* 179–180n30.

141. Paul Levy, "L'École française d'Extrême-Orient," *France-Asie* 15 (15 June 1947): 523.

142. Doumer, *L'Indochine française* 270–274.

143. Carpeaux, *Les ruines d'Angkor,* 227.

144. CARAN, F21 4042, Cabinet du Ministre d'Instruction Public et des Beaux Arts to Directeur, Direction des Beaux Arts Paris, 10 July 1901; Directeur of Beaux Arts to Jean Ajalbert, 20 July 1901.

145. CAOM, INDO GGI 16922, Société d'Angkor pour la conservation des monuments anciens de l'Indo-Chine Statutes.

146. Levy, "L'École française d'Extrême-Orient."

147. MS2966, Coedès Collection, National Library of Australia.

148. CAOM, INDO GGI 23789, EFEO to GGI Paris, 10 August 1902.

149. CAOM, INDO GGI 23789, Foucher to GGI Paris, 10 August 1902; GGI to Foucher, Directeur adjoint, EFEO, 19 September 1902.

150. Wright, *Politics of Design,* 194, 360.

151. Schneider, *Empire for the Masses,* 177, 180. Category Number VII, Colonization encompassed three subcategories: Methods of Colonization; Colonial Buildings and Implements; Special Products Suitable for Export to Colonies.

152. "L'Exposition de L'Indochine," in *l'Illustration,* 1 September 1900, 134–135; W. Brown, "Paris 1900: Exposition universelle," in Findling and Perle, eds., *Historical Dictionary,* 155.

153. Pierre Nicolas, "Notices sur L'Indochine," in Charles-Roux, *Colonies et pays de protectorates,* 3; "L'Exposition de l'Indochine," *l'Illustration,* 1 September 1900, 135.

154. "M. Loubet dans la grotte du pnom cambodgienne," *l'Illustration,* 9 June 1900, 372.

155. Iukanthor, *Destin d'empire,* 86–88. The silver, raised circular seal containing Angkor Vat's three towers can be seen on copies of Yukanthor's correspondence in the CAOM.

156. Loti, *Un pèlerin d'Angkor.*

157. M. Klobukowski, *Discours à l'ouverture de la session ordinaire du Conseil supérieur le 27 novembre 1909* (Saigon: Imprimerie Commerciale Marcellin, 1909).

158. Barnett, "Cambodia Will Never Disappear," 117. Maspéro dedicated his work to his father. In one example of Franco-British collaboration, Gaston Maspéro became the director of the Department of Antiquities in Egypt and was tangentially involved in developments leading to the discovery of the tomb of Tutankhamun in 1920. Howard Carter and A. C. Mace, *The Discovery of the Tomb of Tutankhamen* (New York: Dover, 1977), 30, 76.

159. Ibid.

160. J.-L. Brunet, *L'Exposition de Hanoï en 1902* (Paris: Les actualités diplomatiques et coloniales, Septembre 1902), 17–18.

161. *Le Musée Guimet à Paris,* 10 May 1904 (Paris/Chartres: Imprimerie Dubard).

162. CAOM, INDO GGI 2576, Sarin, Paris to M. Vatt, instituteur à Triton, 12 December 1911: "Each Thursday we're taken on an excursion, accompanied by a professor, either to the museum, or around Paris. . . ."

163. *BEFEO* 7 (1907): 422.

164. CAOM, INDO GGI 16916, Protectorate of Cambodge Arrêté, 1 December 1905.

165. Peleggi, *The Politics of Ruins and the Business of Nostalgia,* 4, and 4n32.

166. Archives de la Chambre de Commerce et d'Industrie, Marseille (hereafter ACCIM), MK6 1 42 D. Heckel, Directeur, Musée et Institut Coloniale de Marseille, to the Marseille Chamber of Commerce, 20 July 1903.

167. Schneider, *Empire for the Masses,* 194; J. Chailly-Bert, *Quinzaine Coloniale,* 25 April 1900; ACCIM, MK6 1 42, D. Heckel, Directeur, Musée et Institut Coloniale de Marseille, letter to Marseille Chamber of Commerce, 20 July 1903.

168. ACCIM, MK6 1 42, J. Charles-Roux, President, Congres Colonial de 1906, circular letter and brochure advertising Congress, Paris, 1 January 1906, 2–4.

169. Schneider, *Empire for the Masses,* 132, 154.

170. CAOM, INDO GGI 5881, Commissaire-Général de l'Indo-Chine M. Baille, Report to Governor General of Indochina, 31 December 1905, 2–4.

171. Ibid.

172. CAOM, INDO GGI 6507 RSC to GGI, Telegram No. 240, 18 April 1902.

173. Gervais-Courtellemont, "Les danseuses du roi du Cambodge," *l'Illustration,* 2 June 1906, 344.

174. "Une soirée de danses au Théatre de verdure," *l'Illustration,* 21 July 1906, 48.

175. Gervais-Courtellement, "Les danseuses du roi du Cambodge," 344.

176. G. Bois, "Le sculpteur Rodin et les danseuses cambodgiennes," *l'Illustration,* 28 July 1906, 65.

177. R. Meyer, *Komlah,* 14.

CHAPTER 2: URBAN LEGEND

1. Phal, *The Young Concubine* 172, 238. This novel was first published in Paris by Albin Michel as *La favorite des dix ans.*

2. NLA, Coedès MS 2986, Makhali Phal to Coedès, 28 April 1958.

3. Malcolm McLaren sings, "I often go to Paris to live yesterday tomorrow," in his song "Walking with Satie" on the album *Paris* (World Attractions Limited, BMG Entertainment, 1994).

4. Wright, *Politics of Design,* 303.

5. James T. Clifford, *Routes: Travel and Translation in the Late Twentieth Century* (Cambridge, MA: Harvard University Press, 1997).

6. See Ana María Alonso, "The Politics of Space, Time and Substance: State Formation, Nationalism and Ethnicity," *Annual Review of Anthropology* 23 (1994): 379–405. For more on domestic planning in Cambodge and Burma, see Penny Edwards, "On Home Ground: Settling Land and Domesticating Difference in the 'Non-Settler' Colonies of Burma and Cambodia," *Journal of Colonialism and Colonial History* 4, Issue 4 (December 2003). http://muse.jhu.edu/journals/journal_of_colonialism_and_colonial_history/v004/4.3

7. James Scott, *Seeing Like a State: How Certain Schemes to Improve the Human Condition Have Failed* (New Haven, CT: Yale University Press, 1998), 55–56; René Descartes, *Discourse on Method,* trans. Donald A. Cress (Indianapolis: Hackett, 1980), 6.

8. Milton Osborne, *Prince of Light, Prince of Darkness* (Sydney: Allen and Unwin, 1994), 16.

9. Jaques Népote, "Les nouveaux Sino-Khmers acculturés: Un milieu social perterbateur?" *Péninsule* 30, no. 1 (1995): 149.

10. Lamant, "La création d'une capitale," in Lafont, ed., *Péninsule indochinoise,* 69.

11. King, *Urbanism, Colonialism and the World Economy,* 29.

12. Igout, *Phnom Penh,* 37.

13. James Scott, *Seeing Like a State* (New Haven, CT: Yale University Press, 1998), 62.

14. Lamant, "La création d'une capitale," 71.

15. Wheatley, *Nagara and Commandery,* 123.

16. Dumarçay (trans. and ed. Michael Smithies), *Palaces of Southeast Asia,* 44.

17. CAOM, FM INDO 11058, M. Martin, Entreposeur to Chef de Cabinet du Gouverneur, 9 December 1884, 5.

18. P. le Faucheur, *Lettre sur le Cambodge,* 5–6; see *Courrier de Saïgon,* June 1864.

19. CAOM, FM INDO NF 828, Minister of Marine and Colonies to Dupré, Governor General of Cochinchina, 10 August 1872, 2. The decoration was timed to coincide with France's decoration of King Mongkut of Siam.

20. CAOM, FP 8 APC 4, Cornelier to Representative of French Protectorate in Cambodia, 26 March 1870; Dupré to Representative of French Protectorate in Cambodia, 11 July 1873 and 26 January 1873.

21. CAOM, FM INDO NF 829 Contre-Amiral Dupré Gouverneur et Commandant en Chef du Cochinchine to Minister of Marine and Colonies, 13 August 1873; *Arrangement conclu entre S.M. le Roi du Cambodge et M. le Contre-Amiral Dupré, Gouverneur et Commandant en Chef du Cochinchine,* 13 July 1873; Minister of Foreign Affairs to Minister of Marine and Colonies, 6 November 1873; CAOM, FP 8 APC 4, Dupré to King of Cambodia, 12 July 1873.

22. Pierre Pasquier, "Rapport sur l'Indochine," in Compte rendu des travaux du Congrès colonial de Marseille, Tome II (Marseille, 1906), 535.

23. Wright, "Tradition in the Service of Modernity," 292.

24. Chandler, "From 'Cambodge' to 'Kampuchea,'" 37.

25. Lewis, *A Dragon Apparent,* 289.

26. *Foire Exposition de Saigon: Pavilion de l'Histoire, La Cochinchine dans le Passé* (Saigon: A.I.L.I, 1942), Item 511.

27. Reddi, *History of the Cambodian Independence Movement,* 101.

28. The population of the palace ranged from 5,000 to 10,000 during the protectorate.

29. CAOM, INDO GGI 13276, Moura to Admiral Cornulier-Lucinière, Governor of Cochinchine, 15 February 1870; Lamant, "La création d'une capitale," 72–73.

30. Le Faucheur, *Lettre sur le Cambodge,* 34.

31. CAOM, INDO GGI 11740, Décision relative à l'organisation politique et administrative du Cambodge, 27 Oct 1884 (Saigon: Imprimerie Coloniale, 1885).

32. Anon., "Le Cambodge en 1893," *Revue Indochinoise* 1, no. 2 (September 1893): 174.

33. E. Lagrillière-Beauclerc, *Au Cambodge et Annam: Voyage Pittoresque* (Paris: La librairie mondiale, 1900), 24, 30.

34. Lamant, "La création d'une capitale," 95–97; Albert Sarraut, *La mise en valeur des colonies françaises,* 104.

35. Wright, *Politics of Design,* 55.

36. Muan, "Citing Angkor," 36, NAC, No. 23706, 12 April 1912, Sisowath to GGI Sarraut; competition brochure, NAC, No. 23706.

37. Muan, "Citing Angkor," 37; E. Ménétrier, "Les fêtes du Tang-Tok à Phnom Penh" *RII,* October 1912, 341.

38. See Hoffenberg, *Empire on Display,* 230–231.

39. CARAN, F21 4489 3a, Séance de Commission d'Organisation de la Section Coloniale Française, minutes of meeting, 11 November 1887.

40. J.-L. de Lanessan, "Participation de la Tunisie a l'Exposition internationale de 1889," *Le Progrès Colonial, Journal de Colonies,* 15 December 1886, 2, CARAN, F12 3760 Arrêt 17 May 1886; letter from Minister of Foreign Affairs to M. Édouard Lockroy, Minister of Commerce and Industry, Paris, 28 May 1886.

41. CAOM, INDO GGI 23194, Resident General Piquet to Governor of Cochinchina, 25 April 1887, CARAN, F12 3760, 19 September 1887, Filippine, Governor of Cochinchina to Minister of Marine and Colonies.

42. CAOM, INDO GGI 23194, Resident General of Cambodge to Governor of Cochinchina, 12 August 1887.

43. CAOM, INDO GGI 23194, Sous-Secrétaire de Ministère de Marine et Colonies Étienne to Governor of Cochinchina, 1 July 1887, 2.

44. CAOM, INDO GGI 23194, Resident General of Cambodge to GGI, 29 July 1888, 15–16.

45. CAOM, INDO GGI 23194 17, Resident General of Cambodge to Governor of Cochinchina, Oct 1887; Governor of Cochinchina to Resident General, 4 August 1887, Confidential.

46. CAOM, INDO GGI 23194, Fabre to Resident General, 30 Sept. 1887. This file includes a copy of Fabre's plans for the Cambodge pavilion.

47. CAOM, INDO GGI 23194, GGI to Ministry of Marine and Colonies, Paris, 3 August 1888.

48. Falasca-Zamponi, *Fascist Spectacle,* 17; Mosse, *Nationalization of the Masses,* 46, Wright, *Politics of Design,* 40–41.

49. Henrique, *Les colonies françaises,* 124.

50. "Le Cambodge en 1893."

51. Ajalbert, *Ces phénomènes, artisans de l'Empire* (Paris: Édouard Aubanel, 1941), 162–174.

52. "Le Cambodge en 1893," 175–176.

53. Gervais-Courtellemont, Vandelet, et al., *L'Indochine,* 61. (Librairie de Paris Firmin-Didot et Cie, n.d. [ca. 1902]).

54. Tissandier, *Cambodge et Java,* 4.

55. Agostini, *Au Cambodge,* 13–14.

56. Nicolas, *Notices sur l'Indochine,* 158–159.

57. Anon., "Le Cambodge en 1893," 178.

58. Gervais-Cortellement, Vandelet, et al., *L'Indochine,* 55.

59. For more on this, see Edwards, "Womanizing Indochina."

60. Nicolas, *Notices sur l'Indochine,* 16.

61. "M. Loubet dans la grotte du pnom cambodgienne," *l'Illustration,* 9 June 1900, 372.

62. CAOM, INDO GGI 8443, Alexandre Marcel and Louis Dumoulin to GGI (n.d.), 1.

63. Pinet, *Ornement de la durée,* 8.

64. Muan, "Citing Angkor," 35; NAC, RSC No. 4651.

65. Gerny-Marchal, "Sur le Phnom," in *Enthousiasmes recueillements et poèmes khmèrs,* 38–39.

66. Lagrillière-Beauclerc, *À travers L'Indochine,* 134.

67. Harry, *L'Indochine,* 87.

68. R. Meyer, *Saramani,* see especially pp. 23, 24, 25, 36.

69. Private communication with Dipesh Chakrabarty, Canberra, November 2001.

70. Anderson, *Spectre of Comparisons,* 62.

71. Rivière, who designed the Monument à la France built in Hanoi in 1908, stayed in Cambodge in April 1908 together with his assistants Beau and Nache to conduct research; CAOM, INDO GGI 16924, RSC Luce to GGI, 9 April 1910; GGI to Luce, 20 May 1910.

72. CAOM, INDO GGI 16920, Ministry of Colonies to GGI, 18 Sept. 1908; GGI to RSC, 21 September 1908; RSC to GGI, 22 September 1908.

73. "L'inauguration d'un monument commémoratif royal au Cambodge," *Bulletin du Comité de l'Asie Française,* no. 97 (Avril 1909): 171–173.

74. Brossard, *Colonies françaises,* 431.

75. National Archives of Cambodia (hereafter NAC), RSC 455, RSC Phnom Penh, 26 October 1917, "Circulaire No. 82: Des constructions diverses."

76. Ibid., 1–2.

77. NAC, RSC 455, RSC Baudoin, "Circulaire no. 64: Des constructions de style Cambodgien," Phnom Penh, 12 August 1918, 1–2.

78. NAC, RSC 455: G. Groslier to the RSC, 2 October 1917; Groslier to RSC, 14 June 1918; 25 June 1918; 2 August 1918.

79. NAC, RSC 4191, Thiounn, *Allocution,* 4.

80. Henrique, *Les colonies françaises,* 124.

81. Agostini, *Au Cambodge,* 11.

82. Eric Hobsbawm, "Mass Producing Traditions: Europe, 1870–1914," in Hobsbawm and Ranger, eds., *Invention of Tradition,* 271.

83. CAOM, INDO GGI 10044, Representat du Cambodge to Governor of Cochinchina, 15 July 1885.

84. Le Myre de Vilers, "Préface," in Rondet-Saint, *Choses de l'Indochine contemporaine,* xli.

85. CAOM, INDO GGI 2189, *Budget urbain de la ville de Phnom Penh exercice 1902* (Phnom Penh: Imprimerie du Protectorat, 1901), chap. 5, p. 8, chap. 6, p. 14.

86. Agostini, *Au Cambodge,* 11.

87. Ibid.

88. A. Raquez, "Les fêtes de Pnom-Penh," *RI,* no. 264 (9 November 1903): 1017, 1019.

89. Osborne, *French Presence,* 257. See Wright, "Tradition in the Service of Modernity, 291–316; see p. 292 for an analysis of a similar cultural strategy adopted by the French Résident-Général in Morocco to buttress the installation of French favorite Sultan Moulay-Yussef in 1912.

90. CAOM, FM INDO GGI 65502, RSC Rapport, Third Trimester, 1923, 25 October 1923, 6.

91. Ibid., INDO GGI 65502, RSC Rapport politique 1922, Third trimester, 31 October 1922, 3. CAOM, INDO GGI 65503, RSC Baudoin Rapport, Third Trimester, 1924, 29 November 1924, 2.

92. CAOM, INDO GGI 2189, GGI Beau and RSC Luce Arrêté 25 December 1907, Municipal taxes for Phnom Penh. The new fees were 1.50 piastres for the Tet festival, 1 for a cremation with music, and an extra 1.50 for fireworks.

93. Ajalbert, *Ces phénomènes,* 166–167.

94. C. Meyer, *La vie quotidienne,* 139.

95. AOM, INDO GGI 23798, Letter from Résident Général de la Republique Française au Cambodge Champeaux, Phnom Penh, to GGI, Saigon, 28 March 1888, 1–7.

96. See Edwards, "Womanizing Indochina," for a more detailed treatment of this theme.

97. Gervais-Courtellemont et al., *L'Indochine,* 61.

98. Pierre Pasquier, "Rapport sur l'Indochine," *Compte rendu des travaux du Congrès colonial de Marseille, Vol. II* (Marseille, 1906), 533.

99. Ann Laura Stoler, "Sexual Affronts and Racial Frontiers: European Identities and the Politics of Exclusion in Colonial Southeast Asia," *Comparative Studies in Society and History* 34 (1992): 517, 535–536.

100. Wright, *Politics of Design,* 17–19.

101. Lamant, "La création d'une capitale," 68.

102. Le Myre de Vilers, *Les institutions civiles,* 3, 7.

103. "Le Cambodge en 1893," *RI* 1, no. 2 (September 1893): 173.

104. Henrique, *Les colonies françaises,* 124, 137.

105. Chandler, *History of Cambodia,* 80, 89, 100.

106. Marcel Ner, "Les musulmans de l'Indochine Française," *BEFEO* 41 (1941): 165, 169, 192.

107. Igout, *Phnom Penh,* 6–7.

108. Forest, *Le Cambodge,* 435.

109. "Le Cambodge en 1893," *Revue Indo-Chinoise Illustrée* 1, no. 2 (September 1893): 176.

110. Gervais-Courtellemont et al., *L'Indochine*, 66.

111. CAOM, INDO GGI 12359, Arrêté, 19 November 1884. The penalties for going out without a torch were a fine or a month's labor.

112. E. Lagrillière-Beauclerc, *À travers l'Indochine*, 134; C. Meyer, *La vie quotidienne*, 116; Groslier, *Eaux et lumières*, 80.

113. *Annuaire du Cambodge*, 1905, cited in C. Meyer, *La vie quotidienne*, 140.

114. "Au Cambodge," *BCAF* 2, no. 12 (March 1902): 127. Paul Bergue, "L'habitation européenne au Cambodge," *RII* 7 (15 April 1905), 490–498.

115. NAC, RSC 25728, M. Collard, Mayor of Phnom Penh to M. Christian, 13 May 1907.

116. NAC, RSC 32858, "Situations journalières d'effectif des ouvriers employés aux jardin du Protectorat, 1905."

117. NAC, RSC 24127, L'Administrateur des Services Civils de l'Indochine Résident Maire de Phnom Penh à Monsieur le Résident Supérieur de la République Française au Cambodge, Phnom Penh, 14 October 1914.

118. NAC, RSC 24127, "Travaux d'assainissement de la ville de Phnom Penh," 2.

119. NAC, RSC24127, "Notes Relatifs aux Projets de Remblais de la ville de Phnom Penh pour l'année 1915," 18 December 1914.

120. Rondet-Saint, *Choses de l'Indochine contemporaine*, 125.

121. See, e.g., Groslier, *Le retour à L'Argile*.

122. R. Meyer, *Komlah*, 98–99.

123. Albert de Pouvourville, "Une lettre de l'Indochine," in Pouvourville, *L'heure silencieuse*, 141–142.

124. Chandler, *History of Cambodia*, 156.

125. Lycanne, "Ce que je pense de mon roi," *L'Action Indochinois*, 23 August 1928, 2.

126. Chandler, *Brother Number One*, 15. See also Kiernan, *How Pol Pot Came to Power*, 27.

127. Durtain, *Dieux blancs, hommes jaunes*.

128. Tricon and Bellan, *Chansons cambodgiennes*, 75.

129. Bunchan Mul, *Kuk Noyobay* (Political prison) (Phnom Penh, 1971), 8.

130. Franck, *East of Siam*, 34.

131. Groslier, *Eaux et lumières*, 80.

132. Igout, *Phnom Penh*, 12.

133. NAC, RSC 12450, Thibaudeau to M. le Résident-Maire de la Ville, 18 October 1937. Condemning the poor road access to the market, Thibaudeau predicted the "deplorable effect" of the new market and its potential to disrupt the harmony of the new quarter, and insisted on the prompt creation of a Commission d'Urbanisme to avoid future such mistakes.

134. "Recensement de Phnom Penh," *Le Khmer*, 3 August 1936, 2.

135. Groslier, *Eaux et lumières*, 80.

136. Robert J. Casey, "Four Faces of Siva: The Mystery of Angkor," *The National Geographic Magazine*, September 1928, 323.

137. Ennis, "The French Administration and Problems in Indochina," 2.

138. See François Ponchaud, "Social Change in the Vortex of Revolution," in Karl Jackson, ed., *Cambodia: 1975–1978* (Princeton, NJ: Princeton University Press, 1989), 154–159.

139. Lefebvre, *The Production of Space,* 220.

140. Groslier, *Eaux et lumières,* 80.

141. "Ompi keehastan riecka roboh muntri kmae" (About the administrative offices of Khmer ministers), *Nagaravatta,* 13 November 1937, 1–3.

142. Phal, *The Young Concubine,* 168.

CHAPTER 3: *LES FIDÈLES CAMBODGIENS* AND *LES KHMÈROPHILES*

1. Khing, "Le voyage de l'envoyé Cambodgien Son Diep à Paris en 1900," 370–378.

2. Nicolas, *Notices sur l'Indochine,* 15.

3. CAOM, FP APC 461. The Europeans are identified as Lefevre and Pontalis.

4. Thiounn, Secrétaire Général du Counseil des Ministres du Cambodge, to M. Pavie, Phnom Penh, 20 December 1899, CAOM, FP APC 461; "The History of Samdech Thiounn," *Nagaravatta,* 27 September 1941, 1–2.

5. *Echo,* 15 September 1941.

6. CAOM, FP APC 461, Son Diep, Tri-Phu of Soctrang, to Auguste Pavie, 15 May 1904.

7. CAOM, FM INDO NF 581, Thiounn to RSC, 15 November 1900.

8. NAC, RSC 25097, "Komnat jun bodemien (Information form)" (n.d.); "Secdey joos jumpuk" (undated manuscript), État des Services, Phnom Penh, 22 September 1905. Dr. Hahn, Klobukowski, and Mr. Luce were also present.

9. NAC, RSC 25097, Son Diep—Personnel File.

10. Thiounn was born in Srok Longvek, Kompong Kralach, Kompong Cham Province. CAOM, FM INDO NF 581, Thiounn to RSC, 15 November 1900.

11. On Taw Sein Ko, see Edwards, "Re-locating the Interlocutor"; on Mukharji, see Hoffenberg, *Empire on Display,* 50, 52–56, 60–62, 100, 111–113, 255–256.

12. Osborne, "History and Kingship in Contemporary Cambodia," 14.

13. Chandler, "Songs at the Edge of the Forest," 79.

14. Ponchaud, "Social Change," 155.

15. Robert Headly et al., *Cambodian-English Dictionary* (Washington, DC: Catholic University of America Press, 1977), 534–535.

16. Saveros Pou, "L'Offrande des mérites dans la tradition Khmère," *Journal Asiatique* 282, no. 2 (1994): 394–401. Pou cites, among others, an eighth-century inscription by a princess who, in adding stones to an image of Siva she had erected with her husband, hoped to increase "her own merits" (punya-upacayam).

17. David P. Chandler, "Normative Poems *(chbap)* and Pre-colonial Cambodian Society," in Chandler, *Facing the Cambodian Past,* 49. Chandler, *History of Cambodia,* 121.

18. "Bonhae-neakta" (Procession of the spirits), *Nagaravatta,* 19 February 1938, 1; see also Ebihara, "Social Organization in Sixteenth and Seventeenth Century Cambodia," 284.

19. Ebihara, "Interrelations between Buddhism and Social Systems in Cambodian Peasant Culture," 177.

20. Ebihara "Social Organization in Sixteenth and Seventeenth Century Cambodia," 284.

21. Robert Headly et al., *Cambodian-English Dictionary,* 534–535. The poet In describes a district chief's house as samsak in *Niries Nokor,* 44.

22. Chandler, "Normative Poems *(chbap)* and Pre-colonial Cambodian Society," 49; Chandler, *History of Cambodia,* 121.

23. May Ebihara, "Social Organization in Sixteenth and Seventeenth Century Cambodia," 284.

24. Kate Frieson, "Women, Power and the State" (paper presented at Monash University Conference, "Cambodia: Power, Myth and Memory" 1996), 5; Anderson, *Language and Power,* 43.

25. Cohn, *Colonialism and Its Forms of Knowledge,* 1; Foucault, *Power/Knowledge,* 104–105, 125–126.

26. Max Weber, *On Charisma and Institution Building,* 69–70; Foucault, *Power/Knowledge,* 156.

27. Paul Alduy, "La naissance du nationalisme outre-mer," in *Principles and Methods of Colonial Administration* (London: Butterworth Science Publications, 1950), 126.

28. Ponchaud, "Social Change," 155.

29. Ian Mabbett and David Chandler, *The Khmers* (Boulder, CO: Westview Press, 1996). Chou Ta-kuan (Zhou Daguan), *The Customs of Cambodia* (Bangkok: The Siam Society, 1992), 9.

30. Mak Pheoun, "L'Introduction de la Chronique Royale du Cambodge du lettre Nong," *BEFEO* 67 (1980): 144.

31. Népote and Khing, "Literature and Society in Modern Cambodia," 61.

32. Ebihara, "Social Organization in Sixteenth and Seventeenth Century Cambodia," 284.

33. Chandler, *History of Cambodia,* 122; Chandler, "Songs at the Edge of the Forest," 78.

34. Heder, "Cambodia's Democratic Transition to Neo-authoritarianism," 425.

35. Mabbett and Chandler, *The Khmers,* 161.

36. Louis de Carné, *Travels in Indo-China and the French Empire,* 3.

37. Moura, *Le royaume du Cambodge* (Paris: Librairie de la Société Asiatique, 1883), 367.

38. Chandler, "Normative Poems *(chbap)* and Pre-colonial Cambodian Society," 50.

39. Alexander Woodside, "Medieval Vietnam and Cambodia," *JSEAS* 15, no. 2 (September 1984): 319.

40. Chou Ta-kuan, *Customs of Cambodia,* 9.

41. Vickery, *Kampuchea,* 51.

42. Letter from Doudart de Lagrée cited in C. Meyer, *La vie quotidienne,* 110.

43. Khing, *Écrivains et expressions littéraires,* 45.

44. Weber, *On Charisma and Institution Building,* 68, 74–76.

45. Girardet, *L'idée coloniale en France,* 53–57.

46. Zeldin, *France 1848–1945,* 223–233. Between 1870 and 1940, France had 108 ministries. This compares with 44 ministries in England in almost twice the time, between 1801 and 1937, with an average tenure of three years and one month.

47. CAOM, INDO RSC 466, Minister of War and Education Ponn to RSC, 11 February 1915.

48. CAOM, INDO RSC 466, Khun Sneha Neayok Chiy to Minister of War and Education Ponn, 5 January 1915; Minister of War and Education Ponn to RSC, 25 March 1915; Minister of War and Education Ponn to RSC, 19 January 1915; Men to Minister of War and Education Ponn, 4 January 1915; to Minister of War and Education Ponn, 7 January 1915; Khun Thipolsen Néang to Minister of War and Education Ponn, 12 December 1914.

49. NAC, RSC 25097, "État de Service, 1873–1905," 4.

50. Gellner, *Encounters with Nationalism,* viii, 39.

51. A. D. Smith, "Ethnic Election and Cultural Identity," 9–25; Hoffenberg, "Introduction," in *Empire on Display.*

52. CAOM, INDO GGI 1220, Representat du Protectorat du Cambodge to Governor of Cochinchina Charles Thomson, 26 August 1884, 7 June 1885, 24 June 1885; Governor of Cochinchina Charles Thomson to Representat du Protectorat du Cambodge, 29 August 1884, 12 June 1885, 29 April 1885.

53. CAOM, INDO GGI 12232, Governor of Cochinchina to Representat du Protectorat du Cambodge, 29 April 1885, 1–2.

54. CAOM FP 46 APC 1, Minutes of the Meeting of the Commission etc., 1; CAOM, GI INDO 1226, Gov. de la Cochinchine General Begin "Decide," 24 August 1885.

55. CAOM, INDO GGI 12685, Res. Gen. Cam to GGI, 11 June 1883. They were not the first Cambodians to receive a Parisian education. In 1883, the protectorate had sponsored a Cambodian named Khun to attend the Lycée St. Louis in recognition of his brother Chhun's long service in the French administration. Chhun almost certainly referred to Alexis Chhun, of part Portuguese ancestry and one of Cambodge's small Catholic minority, who began work for the French as an interpreter at the age of thirteen, by 1878 was principal interpreter, and in 1886 was appointed to the judiciary. See Osborne, *French Presence,* 246.

56. Mme Auguste Pavie, "Souvenirs," *Indochine française* 4 (31 May 1947), 73.

57. CAOM, FM APC 46 1, *Commission Instituée pour determiner les conditions de l'établissement à Paris de la mission des jeunes cambodgiennes,* Première Séance, 17 February 1886, 2, 4.

58. CAOM, INDO GGI 10062, Badens to Begin, 10 April 1886.

59. CAOM, GGI INDO 12226, *Liste nominative des jeunes Cambodgiens susceptibles d'être envoyés en France.*

60. CAOM, FM APC 46 1 *Commission Instituée pour determiner les conditions de l'établissement à Paris de la mission des jeunes cambodgiennes,* Première Séance, 17 February 1886, 7.

61. CAOM, INDO GGI 10070, Lt.-Col. Badens, Commandant supérieur des troupes au Cambodge, acting Résident General, to GGI General Bégin, 2 April 1886 1; CAOM, INDO GGI 12225, Résident Général du Cambodge to Gouverneur de la Cochinchine, 3 February 1887.

62. CAOM, INDO GGI 23798, Letter from Résident Général de la Republique Française au Cambodge Champeaux, Phnom Penh, to GGI, Saigon, 28 March 1888, 1–7.

63. CAOM, INDO GGI 23798, Résident Général Champeaux to GGI, 20 July 1888, 1–7.

64. CAOM, INDO GGI 12227, Prof. Brégéger, Collège d'Adran Saigon to Governor of Cochinchine, 24 August 1885; Penne, Interpreter in Khmer and Vietnamese at the

Court of Appeal in Saigon to Governor of Cochinchina, 1 October 1886; RSC Piquet to Governor of Cochinchine, 10 July 1887.

65. CAOM, INDO GGI 12227, Penne to GGI, Paris, 10 August 1887, 1–2. The original letter was written in Quoc Ngu, indicating that Penne was Khmer Kraom from Cochinchina.

66. CAOM, INDO GGI 23798 RSC to GGI, 8 August 1889, 1.

67. CAOM, INDO RSC 466, Letter from Minister of War and Education Ponn to RSC, 23 September 1919. Ponn's father was Oknya Metrey Phuton.

68. Girardet, *L'idée coloniale en France,* 121. See Zeldin, *History of French Passions,* 931.

69. CAOM, INDO GGI 5870, Fontaine 1903, 4–5.

70. CAOM, INDO GGI 1579 RSC Arrêté, 15 November 1904 . See also Gervais-Courtellement et al., *Empire colonial de la France,* 67.

71. CAOM, INDO GGI 5870, RSC Lamothe Phnom Penh to GGI, "Rapport sur l'enseignment au Cambodge en 1904," Phnom Penh, 26 July 1904, 3.

72. Ibid., "Rapport sur l'enseignment au Cambodge en 1904," 3; GGI Beau, "La situation," 11.

73. See Edwards, "Propa-Gender: Marianne, Joan of Arc and the Export of French Gender Ideology to Colonial Cambodia."

74. CAOM, INDO GGI 2576, Thiounn to RSC, 9 July 1907.

75. Ibid., RSC Paul Luce to Fourés, 25 June 1910.

76. Ibid., Sarin, Paris, to M. Watt, instituteur à Triton, 12 December 1911.

77. Ibid., RSC Ernest Outrey to GGI 6 December 1912.

78. Ibid., GGI's Delegate, Office Colonial in Paris, to RSC Baudoin, 7 July 1914; GGI to Thiounn, 9 July 1914.

79. CAOM, INDO GGI 2716, RSC to GGI, 14 October 1918.

80. Teston and Percheron, *L'Indochine moderne,* 193.

81. *Kraoy moroneahphiep ney look Silveastra* (After the death of Sylvestre), *Nagaravatta,* 15 May 1937, 1–3.

82. J. Norre, Administrateur des services civils 1923, "Les carrières administratives en Indochine," *L'Orientation Professionelle: Revue d'études et de documentation sur toutes les professions,* no. 49–50 (August–September 1923): 1; CAOM, FM INDO NF 873, Gouvernement Général de l'Indochine Agence Économique, *Renseignements sur les emplois privés ou administratifs en Indo-Chine,* 1–2.

83. CAOM, INDO GGI 2716, Directeur de l'Instruction Publique en Indochine to GGI, 22 November 1921.

84. CAOM INDO RSC 304, Humbert-Hesse, Director of Primary Education, "Rapport General sur l'Enseignement au Cambodge," 10 January 1923, 31.

85. Teston and Perchon, *L'Indochine moderne,* 193.

86. CAOM, INDO GGI 65502, RSC L'Helgoualch Report, 4th Trimester 1923, 24 January 1924, 12–17.

87. CAOM, INDO GGI 11804, Mayor of Municipality of Phnom Penh to Representat du France en Cambodge Fourés, 1–4.

88. Ibid. See numerous stationery orders dated 1886.

89. CAOM, INDO GGI 12224, "Certificate of birth," 25 September 1880.

90. Ibid., Fred Thomas-Caraman to Governor of Cochinchine, 20 May 1885; Repre-

sentative of France in Cambodge Aymonier to Governor General Bégin, 28 August 1885; Resident General Piquet to Gov. of Cochinchine, 28 September 1886; Saigon Cabinet to Res.-Gen. in Phnom Penh, 14 October 1886.

91. CAOM, INDO GGI 10062, Badens to Bégin, 17 April 1886. Badens instituted surveillance of all people coming from Prince Sivutha to Phnom Penh to intercept letters.

92. CAOM, INDO GGI 10053, Résident du Cambodge to Governor of Cochinchine, n.d.

93. Doumer, *L'Indochine.*

94. Report de M. Doumer to the Superior Council of Indochina, extraordinary session, 1902 cited in "Réforme de l'administration locale du Cambodge," in *Bulletin du Comité de l'Asie Française* 8, no. 1 (October 1908): 413.

95. Doumer, *L'Indochine* 253–254; J. Meyer et al., *Histoire de la France coloniale,* 697–699.

96. Zeldin, *History of French Passions,* 938.

97. CAOM, INDO GGI 24210, RSC to GGI, 16 November 1897; GGI to Ministry of Colonies, 24 November 1897.

98. Leclère, *Les codes cambodgiens: Tome I* (Paris: Ernest Leroux, 1898), frontispiece.

99. "Réforme de l'administration locale du Cambodge," in *Bulletin du Comité de l'Asie Française* 8, no. 1 (October 1908): 413; Osborne, *French Presence,* 238–239; Pannetier, *Notes cambodgiennes,* 95–96.

100. Bhabha, *Location of Culture,* 93; David Malouf, *Remembering Babylon* (New York: Pantheon Books, 1993).

101. Leclère, *Les codes cambodgiens: Tome I,* viii–ix, xi, xix.

102. Barnett, "Cambodia Will Never Disappear," 107, 114, 117, 119, 121.

103. Serge Thion, "Remodelling Broken Images, 251.

104. Lunet de Lajonquière, "Les provinces récouvrées du Cambodge," *BCAF* 7, no. 74 (May 1907): 160.

105. Ennis, *"The French Administration and Problems in Indochina,"* 136–137; A. Smith, "Ethnic Sources of Nationalism," 51.

106. J. Derrida, "Living on: Border Lines," in Derrida et al., eds., *Deconstruction and Criticism* 87; cited in Bhabha, *Location of Culture,* 98.

107. Bhabha, *Location of Culture,* 99.

108. Népote and Khing, "Literature and Society in Modern Cambodia," 56–81; see 75n21.

109. Aymonier, *Textes khmers: Première série* (Saigon, 1878).

110. Aymonier, "Foreword," *Dictionnaire Khmer–Français* (Saigon, 1878).

111. Son Diep's and Aymonier's contemporary, the entrepreneur P. le Faucheur, showed keen sensitivity to this issue, stressing that the Khmer term for esclave (slave) is very far, in Cambodge, from the meaning of the word as Europeans then understood it. See le Faucheur, *Lettre sur le Cambodge,* 8–9.

112. Aymonier, *Dictionnaire Khmer–Français,* 385.

113. Khing Hoc Dy, *Le voyage de l'envoyé cambodgien Son Diep à Paris en 1900,* 370.

114. Originally four pages of official news, Gia Dinh expanded its cultural and literary content in 1869 and became bimonthly. See Neil Jamieson, *Understanding Vietnam* (Berkeley: University of California Press, 1995), 68.

115. Pavie, *A la conquête des coeurs,* 46–47.

116. "A nos lecteurs," *Revue Indochinoise Illustrée* 1, no. 1 (1893): 1–2.

117. CAOM, GGI 24210, GGI to RSC, 29 January 1895.

118. Mohandas K. Gandhi, *An Autobiography, or The story of my experiments with the truth* (Ahmedabad: Navajivan Publishing House, 2001), 65–66. Gandhi had a "fair recollection" of the Eiffel tower, where he dined on the first floor "just for the satisfaction of being able to say that I had had my lunch at a great height." He appreciated its novelty value, but found "no real art" or "real beauty" about the tower, and his account lacks the wonder and enthusiasm of Son Diep's later encounter. Gandhi puts the year as 1890, but it must have been 1889 or 1900.

119. Khing, *Le voyage de l'envoyé cambodgien,* 374, 380.

120. Jacobs, *The Traditional Literature,* 10.

121. A. Pavie, *Contes du Cambodge* (Paris: Éditions Sudestasie, 1988), 22–24.

122. CAOM, FP APC 46 1, Thiounn, Secrétaire Général du Counseil des Ministres du Cambodge, to M. Pavie, Phnom Penh, 20 December 1899.

123. Auguste Pavie, *Contes populaires du Cambodge, du Laos et du Siam. Collection des contes et chansons populaires* (Paris: Leroux, 1903).

124. Thiounn, "Cérémonie du transfert de la salle Moha Moutt," "Cérémonie de la remise des Titres Royaux," in *RII* no. 2 (30 July 1904): 79–81; Thiounn, "Cérémonial cambodgien concernant la prise de fonctions des mandarins nouvellement promus," *RII* no. 50 (31 January 1907): 71–75.

125. NAC, RSC 4191, "Allocution de S. E. L'Oknha Vèang Thiounn, Ministre du Palais Royal, des Finances et des Beaux Arts du Cambodge, à la ceremonie de la pose de la première Pierre du Palais intérieur de Sa Majesté le Roi du Cambodge a Phnom Penh," le vendredi 13 août 1920.

126. CAOM, FM INDO NF 581, Thiounn to RSC, 15 November 1900.

127. In 1916, the exiled Prince Mayura accused Thiounn of corruption. In 1967, Sihanouk accused Thiounn of "dipping his fingers in the palace treasury" so that he might commit the apparently greater sin of raising his children "as princes." See CAOM, FM INDO NF/22, Mayura, 12 October 1916; *Les paroles de Samdech Preah Norodom Sihanouk* (Phnom Penh Ministry of Information: Oct.-Dec. 1967), 811; Kiernan, *How Pol Pot Came to Power,* 29; *Bulletin Administratif du Cambodge* (1902), 135.

128. A. Raquez, "Les fêtes de Phnom Penh," in *RII,* 9 November 1903, 1017–1018.

129. CAOM, INDO GGI 2597, Société d'enseignement mutual des Cambodgiens—statuts et Règlements, Phnom Penh, 1905, 1, 3–4, 7; 2597 Kethe, President du Conseil d'Administration, Société d'Enseignment mutuel des Cambodgiens, Phnom Penh, to GGI, Saigon, 7 March 1905; Société d'Enseignement mutuel des Cambodgiens, Réunion du Comité de patronage, 23 mars 1905 1, 3–4. Nearly 150 Cambodians, mostly civil servants, enrolled for the society's free French tuition.

130. Osborne, *French Presence,* 255.

131. GGI Paul Beau, "La Situation de l'Indochine: Discours de M. Beau au conseil supérieure, le 11 decembre 1905," *BCAF,* 11.

132. CAOM, FP APC 46 1, Son Diep, Tri-Phu of Soctrang, to Auguste Pavie, 15 May 1904.

133. NAC, RSC 25097, M. Jules Morel, RSC, to King Sisowath, 3 May 1905.

134. CAOM, INDORSC 466, Protectorat Français du Cambodge Administration Indigène, *Bulletin Individuel de Notes de Personnel Indigènes,* 1901, 1904.

135. CAOM, INDO RSC 466, Protectorat du Cambodge, *Bulletin Individuel de Notes,* 1908.

136. CAOM, INDO GGI 2576, RSC Jules Morel Phnom Penh to GGI, 30 March 1905.

137. Girbat et al., *Les colonies françaises au début du XXe siècle,* 69–70.

138. Pierre Pasquier, "Rapport sur l'Indochine," in *Compte rendu des travaux du Congrès colonial de Marseille, Tome II* (Marseille, 1906), 526.

139. NAC, RSC 25097, Rapport de l'Oknha Oudom Réach Kech, secrétaire général, adressé a sa majesté le Roi, n.d.

140. Ibid., 2–3.

141. CAOM, INDO GGI 5881, Captain Chan, Officer d'Ordonnance du GGI, Report to GGI, 1 July 1906, 8–11. The delegation included 10 delegates from the provinces, 69 dancers and concubines, 12 musicians, 5 guardians, 2 jewellers, and 1 doctor.

142. CAOM, INDO GGI 5881, Captain Chan, Officer d'Ordonnance du GGI, Report to GGI, 1 July 1906, 8–11; Thiounn to RSC, 30 March 1907; *Guide officiel de l'Exposition Coloniale de Marseille* (Marseille, 1906), 158; "L'Exposition Coloniale de Marseille," in *L'Illustration,* 7 April 1906.

143. CAOM, INDO GGI 5881, Captain Chan, Officer d'Ordonnance du GGI, Report to GGI, 1 July 1906, 8–11.

144. *Rodin et l'Extrême-Orient Musée Rodin 4 avril–2 juillet 1979* (Paris, Musée Rodin, 1979), see "Le Cambodge dans le dessin de Rodin," 97.

145. "Un Ministre Cambodgien," *L'Illustration,* 21 July 1906, 48.

146. CAOM, INDO GGI 5881, Thiounn to RSC, 30 March 1907; CAOM, INDO GGI 2576, Thiounn to RSC, 9 July 1907.

147. CAOM, INDO GGI 2576 Sisowath to RSC, 7 April 1909.

148. NAC, RSC 25097, Son Diep to RSC, 19 July 1919 (Traduction).

149. Ibid., minute: RSC Baudoin to Son Diep, 21 July 1919.

150. Ibid., "Son Diep." This sheet of paper lists Son Diep's starting salary, from 1873 to 1882, as 1,200 francs. It then veered from 480 to 720 piastres from 1899 to 1904. For the four-year period from June 1904 to 1 January 1908, no salary is recorded. CAOM, INDO GGI 5880, Cabinet du Roi Sisowath to GGI Roume, 27 February 1915.

151. NAC, RSC 25097, Ordonnance Royale, 15 April 1922. Son Diep and Prince Suphanovuong each received 800 piastres' salary and 1,500 in allowances.

152. NAC, RSC 27548, Arrêté, 21 Decembre 1928.

153. NAC, RSC 9890, Thiounn, Ministre du Palais Royal, to RSC, 26 May 1924.

154. Ibid., "Très urgent," Le Délégué, 30 December 1924.

155. Ibid., Thiounn, Conseil des Ministres, to RSC, Leik. 158, 14 June 1923.

156. Ibid., G. Van Oest to M. le Directeur de l'Agence économique de l'Indochine, Paris, 13 October 1923.

157. Ibid., "Très urgent," Le Délégué, 30 December 1924.

158. Franck, *East of Siam,* 84–85.

159. Kiernan, *How Pol Pot Came to Power,* 29; Charles Meyer, *Derrière le sourire Khmer* (Paris: Librairie Plon, 1971), 109. Meyer notes Monivong's opposition to the marriage of Thiounn's daughter, Rosette Poc Hell, to his son Sisowath Monireth.

160. Vickery, *Kampuchea,* 5.

161. The *"cheh"* in *neak-cheh-doeng* implies a sense of innateness, while *"doeng"* can only be acquired; hence Stephen Heder's rendering as "person with know-how and

knowledge." See Heder, "Cambodia's Democratic Transition to Neoauthoritarianism," 425.

162. Tani E. Barlow, "Theorizing Woman: *Funü, Guojia, Jiating* (Chinese woman, Chinese state, Chinese family)," in Zito and Barlow, eds., *Body, Subject and Power in China,* 253–280. See especially 261–262.

163. Shils, "Intellectuals in the Political Development of the New States," 330–331, 349.

164. Bruce Kapferer, *Legends of People, Myths of State,* 1–2.

165. *Kampuja Surya,* no. 7 (1927): 7–10.

166. S. E. Thiounn, Ministre du Palais, "Les dix Jatakas et le Pathamma Sambodhi," *Kampuchea Surya,* no. 6 (1927): 7, 8.

167. Samdach Chaufea Thiounn, *Danses cambodgiennes* (Phnom Penh: Bibliothèque Royale du Cambodge, 1931).

168. Judith Jacobs, "The Deliberate Use of Foreign Vocabulary by the Khmer," in Hobart and Taylor, eds., *Context, Meaning and Power,* 117; David P. Chandler, "The Duties of the Corps of Royal Scribes: An Undated Manuscript from the Colonial Era," in Chandler, *Facing the Cambodian Past,* 164.

169. Kapferer, *Legends of People, Myths of State,* 96.

170. Thion, "Remodelling Broken Images."

171. Mabbett and Chandler, *The Khmers,* 225.

172. NAC, RSC 25097, L'Administrateur des Services Civils Résident Maire de la Ville de Phnom Penh à M. le Délégué du Protectorat auprès du Gouvernment Cambodgien, 16 April 1934. Marginalia records that the rifle and permit were returned on 24 April.

173. NAC, RSC 25097 Cérémonie de l'Incinération; "Liste des participants au convoi funèbre de Son Excellence le Samdach Préa Pothisal Réach pour son entrée dans la Pavillon crématoire le mercredi 18 Avril 1934."

174. NAC, RSC 25097.

175. Ibid., Bulletin de soit communiqué: Objet de l'Affaire Demande de secours en date du 17 Aout formulé par Mme Veuve Son Diep: No. 289-DGC du 1-9-37. The document is signed by Hoareau, Monsieur le Délégué du Protectorat au près du Gouvernment Cambodgien.

176. "Domning ompi preas riec banyalay krong Pnum Pen" (News from the Royal Library in Phnom Penh), *Nagaravatta,* 22 November 1937, 1.

177. Kiernan, *How Pol Pot Came to Power,* 29. Thiounn Hol had four sons—Prasith, Thioeunn, Mumm, and Chum. He married Bunchhan Moly, sister of Lon Nol's future Minister of Cults, Bunchan Mul, the author of *Kuk noyobay.*

178. "Provat niy samdec Thiounn" (A history of Samdec Thiounn), *Nagaravatta,* 27 September 1941, 1–2. This article appears to be based on a tribute to Thiounn published in the *Echo du Cambodge,* 15 September 1941.

CHAPTER 4: COLONIALISM AND ITS DEMERITS

1. C. Reynolds, "Buddhist Cosmography in Thai History," 212.

2. Charles F. Keyes, "Communist Revolution and the Buddhist Past in Cambodia," in Keyes et al., eds., *Asian Visions of Authority,* 47–48.

3. See Huot Tath, *Kalyanamit roboh knom kii Samdec Sanghareach Chuon Nath* (My

soul mate Venerable Samdec Sanghareach Chuon Nath) (Phnom Penh: Buddhist Institute, 1993), 10. I am indebted to John Marston for alerting me to this publication and sharing his copy with me.

4. Hansen, "Khmer Identity and Theravada Buddhism," in Marston and Guthrie, *History, Buddhism, and New Religious Movements,* 47–50.

5. NAC, RSC 2369, Minister of Religion K. Chea, *Rapport d'ensemble sur la religion Bouddhique au Cambodge.*

6. Porée-Maspéro, "Notes sur les particularités du culte chez les Cambodgiens," 619–620.

7. Ibid., 620. Keyes, "Communist Revolution," 46.

8. Ibid., 44–45.

9. See Craig Reynolds, "Buddhist Cosmography in Thai History," 204, 207, for a discussion of similar developments in Siam.

10. Hang Chan Sophea, "Stec Gamlan and Yay Deb: Worshipping Kings and Queens in Cambodia Today," in Marston and Guthrie, *History, Buddhism, and New Religious Movements,* 113.

11. Didier Bertrand, "A Medium Possession Practice and Its Relationship with Cambodian Buddhism: The Gru Parami," in Marston and Guthrie *History, Buddhism, and New Religious Movements,* 150.

12. Ang Choulean, *Mennus ning dae* (Phnom Penh: Reyum, 2002), 1–3. Bertrand, "A Medium Possession Practice," 160.

13. Peter A. Jackson, *Buddhadāsa.*

14. Forest, *Le Cambodge et la colonisation française,* 96.

15. Jackson, *Buddhadāsa,* 307–310.

16. Leclère, *Le bouddhisme,* 390–393.

17. Pou, "*L'offrande des merites dans la tradition khmère,*" *Journal d'Asie* 282, no. 2 (1994): 405.

18. Charles Keyes, *The Golden Peninsula: Culture and Adaptation in Mainland Southeast Asia* (Honolulu: University of Hawai'i Press, 1995), 89–90, 94.

19. Taylor, *Forest Monks and the Nation-State,* 64–65, 74.

20. Jacobs, *Traditional Literature of Cambodia,* 50.

21. David Chandler, "An Eighteenth Century Inscription at Angkor Vat," in Chandler, *Facing Cambodia's Past,* 21, 24.

22. On the sanctity of writing in Burma, see Mendelson, *Sangha and State in Burma,* 154–155.

23. Khing Hoc Dy, *Écrivains et expressions littéraires du Cambodge au XXème siècle* (Paris: L'Harmattan, 1993), 2.

24. Swearer *Buddhist World of Southeast Asia,* 18.

25. Hansen "Ways of the World" (1999), 74–75.

26. Lopez, *Curators of the Buddha,* 12.

27. Ibid., 7.

28. Charles Allen, *The Buddha and the Sahibs,* 44–45.

29. Ibid., 57.

30. Ibid., 196.

31. Baumann, "Global Buddhism," www.globalbuddhism.org, vol. 2 (2001), pp. 1–43.

32. Jackson, *Buddhadāsa,* 37.

33. Huot Tath, *Kalyamit roboh knom,* 17.

34. Ishii, *Sangha, State and Society,* 154–156; Keyes, "Communist Revolution," 46; Lester, *Theravada Buddhism in Southeast Asia,* 95.

35. Ebihara, "Interrelations between Buddhism and Social Systems in Cambodian Peasant Culture," 176.

36. Allen, *Buddha and the Sahibs,* 240–242.

37. Jackson, *Buddhadāsa,* 47.

38. Archives of the Quai d'Orsay, M.D. Asie, vol. 51 (Birmanie 3), 1883–1885. M. Deloncle, Rédacteur au Ministère des Affaires Étrangères, à M. Jules Ferry, 7 July 1884, Columbo, pp. 89, 90, 91, 92 of microfilm. I am most grateful to the University Historical Research Centre, Yangon, for allowing me access to their microform copy of these records.

39. Fonds Provencaux 5551, Bibliothèque Municipal de Marseille, *Fonderie Typographique Deberny & Cie Caractères Quôc-Ngu (Annamites)—Caractères Khmêr (Cambodgiens),* 1906, 2; Jacobs, "The Deliberate Use of Foreign Vocabulary," in Hobart and Taylor, eds., *Context, Meaning and Power,* 117.

40. Népote and Khing, "Literature and Society in Modern Cambodia," 61.

41. CAOM, INDO GGI 11804, Governor, Saigon to Representative of Cambodge, 5 September 1885; CAOM, INDO GGI 11804, Badens to Mssieurs Guilland and Martinon, 16 January 1886.

42. Henrique, *Les colonies françaises,* 153; CAOM, INDO GGI 11804, Badens to Mssieurs Guilland and Martinon, 16 January 1886.

43. "Le Cambodge en 1893," in *RII* 1, no. 1 (1893): 179; see also Igout, *Phnom Penh Then and Now,* 51.

44. Gervais-Courtellemont et al., *Empire colonial de la France,* 67.

45. CAOM, FP APC 46 1 (File 5), Son Diep to Auguste Pavie, 13 May 1904. See also Jacobs, *Traditional Literature of Cambodia,* 10.

46. Fonds Provencaux 5551, Bibliothèque Municipal de Marseille, *Caractères Quôc-Ngu (Annamites)—Caractères Khmêr (Cambodgiens)* (Marseille: Fonderie Typographique Deberny & Cie, 1906), 2.

47. A. Leclère, *Livres sacres* (Paris: E. Leroux, 1906), 9.

48. Hansen, "Ways of the World," 100.

49. E. Aymonier, "Foreword," *Dictionnaire khmêr–français* (Saigon, 1878).

50. CAOM, GGI 24210, RSC Huyn de Vernéville to GGI, 30 March 1895, 1–6.

51. See Charles Hallisey, "Roads Taken and Not Taken in the Study of Theravada Buddhism," in Lopez, *Curators of the Buddha,* 52.

52. Faraut, *Astronomie cambodgienne,* i.

53. Wiener, *Invisible Realms,* 84–85.

54. David Lowenthal, *The Past Is a Foreign Country* (Cambridge: Cambridge University Press, 1985).

55. Lopez, *Curators of the Buddha,* 3.

56. CAOM, GGI 24210, RSC Huyn de Vernéville to GGI, 30 March 1895, 1–6; Andre Migot, *Les Khmers: Des origines d'Angkor au Cambodge d'aujourd'hui* (Paris: Le livre contemporaine, 1960), 303.

57. CAOM, GGI 24210 RSC Huyn de Vernéville to GGI, 30 March 1895, 3.

58. Ibid., 1–6.

59. Marston, "Cambodia 1991–94," 10. As Marston notes, these false windows also protected the contents from sun and rain.

60. Georges Coedès, "Études cambodgiennes VI: Des édicules appelés bibliothèques," *BEFEO* 22 (1922): 405–406; Mannika, *Angkor Vat,* 98–106.

61. Groslier, *Recherches sur les Cambodgiens,* 7; Anne Hansen, "Ways of the World," 79.

62. Hallisey, "Roads Taken and Not Taken," Lopez, *Curators of the Buddha,* 41. Porée-Maspéro, "Notes sur les particularités du culte," 619. A. Leclère, *Livres sacres,* 9.

63. Florida, *Writing the Past, Inscribing the Future,* 11–12.

64. Jacobs, "Deliberate Use of Foreign Vocabulary by the Khmer," 117–119; Marston, *"Cambodia 1991–1994,"* 14.

65. Ebihara, "Interrelations between Buddhism and Social Systems in Cambodia," 177.

66. See Hallisey, "Roads Taken and not Taken," 52.

67. See ibid., 50.

68. CAOM, GGI 24210, RSC Huyn de Vernéville to GGI, 30 March 1895.

69. Finot, *BEFEO* 7 (1907): 384–385; Coedès, *BEFEO* 14 (1914): 45–54.

70. Forest, *Le culte des génies,* 5.

71. Bouinais and Paulus, *L'Indochine française contemporaine,* 523.

72. "Cambodge," *BEFEO* 3 (1903): 368.

73. Forest, *Le culte des génies,* 7.

74. R. Lingat, "History of Wat Pavaraniveca" *Journal of the Siam Society* 26, no. 1 (1933): 102.

75. Kirsch, "Modernizing Implications," 60–61.

76. A. Leclère, *Le bouddhisme au Cambodge,* 122.

77. CAOM, FM INDO NF 570, RSC Baudoin to GGI A.s. de la surveillance des bonzes au Cambodge, Phnom Penh, 2 April 1916, 1–9.

78. Bizot, *Le figuier à cinq branches,* 9.

79. CAOM, FM INDO, GGI 65539 Sûreté Phnom Penh, Sectes Réligieuses du Cambodge, 20 July 1936, 1.

80. Lester, *Theravada Buddhism in Southeast Asia,* 114–115.

81. CAOM, FM INDO, GGI 65547 Illisible to RSC, Phnom Penh, 15 December 1927.

82. Li Sovar, Preariecjivapravat Samdec Preah Mahsanghariec Nil Tieng Kannah Mahanikay (The holy life of his Holiness the Supreme Patriarch Nil Tieng of the Mahanikay Sect) Phnom Penh: Buddhist Institute, 2004. I am grateful to Chor Chanthyda, Ang Sokreoun, Hom Samnom, Than Bunly, and Hok Meng for their translation of this book.

83. Louis Finot, "Maha Vimaladhamma," *BEFEO* 27 (1927): 523.

84. "Preahriecietibay niy Samdecpreahmasangriec Sangniyuk" (Speech by the Venerable Supreme Patriarch and Chief of Monks), *Kampuja Surya* 1, no 7 (July 1927): 10.

85. P. De la Brosse, "Dans les provinces cambodgiennes rétrocédées," *RII,* 2nd sem. (1907): 1152.

86. Tauch Chhuong, *Battambang during the time of the Lord Governor,* trans. Hin Sithan, Carol Mortland, and Judy Ledgerwood (Phnom Penh: CEDORECK, 1994), 101.

87. De Carné, *Travels in Indo-China and the Chinese Empire,* 24.

88. Iukanthor, *Destin,* 83–85.

89. King Norodom's nephew Yukanthor had been exiled from Cambodge by Norodom on the advice of the RSC and GGI in 1900 after his public outburst against court corruption and colonial ineptitude during his visit to the Exposition Universelle in Paris. Osborne, *French Presence,* 237, 238, 241–246, 345; Tully, *Cambodia under the Tricolour,* 226–227.

90. De la Brosse, "Dans les provinces cambodgiennes," 1152.

91. "École de pali d'Angkor," *BEFEO* 9 (1909): 824. The meeting was attended by monks, court ministers, and administrators schooled in Pali.

92. *BEFEO* 3 (1903): 768. The Pali lessons proved popular with Khmer, Chinese, and Annamite students; *BEFEO* 9 (1909): 820.

93. CAOM, FM INDO NF 580, speech by Sisowath on king's 69th birthday, 25 August 1908; "Preahriecietibay niy samdecpreahmahasangriec" (Speech by the Venerable Supreme Patriarch), *Kambuja Surya,* no. 7 (1927): 12–13.

94. A. Klubokowski, *Discours prononcé par M. A. Klobukowski Gouverneur Général de l'Indochine à l'ouverture de la session ordinaire du Conseil Supérieure le 27 novembre 1909* (Saigon: Imprimerie Commerciale Marcellin Rey, 1909), 26.

95. CAOM, INDO GGI 65547, PNP "Illisible," 15 December 1927, to Résident Supérieur. The only file copy of this communication is an official translation, which notes that the signature on the original Khmer document was illegible *(signe illisible).* The author identifies himself as former royal commissioner to Battambang who first demanded the creation of the Pali School at Angkor.

96. E. Flaugergues, "La mort du chef suprème des bonzes," *RII* (1914), 175–182.

97. "École de pali d'Angkor," *BEFEO* 9 (1909): 825.

98. Ibid., 827.

99. "La section de Phnom Penh de la Société d'Angkor," *BEFEO* 11 (1911): 252–253.

100. *BEFEO* 14 (1914): 95.

101. "École supérieure de pāli," *BEFEO* 35 (1935): 463; "École de pāli (Phnom Penh)," *BEFEO* 14 (1914): 95.

102. *BEFEO* 14 (1914): 95.

103. Louis Finot, "Maha Vimaladhamma," *BEFEO* 27 (1927): 523.

104. "École de pāli (Phnom Penh)," *BEFEO* 14 (1914): 95–96.

105. Finot, "Maha Vimaladhamma," 523. Finot claimed that it was largely due to Thaong's support that the protectorate was able to introduce Sanskrit into the school.

106. CAOM, FM INDO NF 570, RSC Baudoin to GGI A.s. de la surveillance des bonzes au Cambodge, Phnom Penh, 2 April 1916, 1–9.

107. G. P. Malalasekera, *The Pali Literature of Ceylon* (Kandy: Sri Lanka, 1994), 304–306.

108. Victor Goloubew, "Nécrologie: In memoriam," *BEFEO* 35 (1935): 528.

109. Charles Keyes, "Communist Revolution, and the Buddhist Past in Cambodia," in Keyes et al., *Asian Visions of Authority,* 47–48.

110. Forest, *Le Cambodge et la colonisation française,* 45, 79.

111. Trinh Hoanh, "Biography of Samdech Preah Sanghareach Gana Mahanikay Chuon Nat," trans. Phlong Pisith, in *Bulletin of the Students of the Department of Archaeology,* no. 3 (July 2004): 18.

112. Li Sovar, "Preariec Jivatprovat Samdec Preah Maha Sanghariec Nil Tieng," 6.

113. Frits Staal, *Exploring Mysticism* (London: Penguin Books, 1975), 72; Jackson, *Buddhadāsa*, 20.

114. Tath, *Kalyanamit roboh knom,* 17–18.

115. Sihanouk to Chuon Nath, 28 May 1967, cited in Tath, *Kalyanamit roboh knom,* 12–13.

116. Tath, *Kalyanamit roboh knom,* 41.

117. Anne Hansen, private communication, 21 October 1998.

118. Hansen, "Khmer Identity and Theravada Buddhism," in Marston and Guthrie, eds., *History, Buddhism, and New Religious Movements in Cambodia,* 57.

119. Anne Hansen, private communication, 21 October 1998.

120. Aymonier, *Dictionnaire français-cambodgien.*

121. Ganguly, "Hierarchy and Its Discontents," 17.

122. Ronald Inden and McKim Marriott, "Towards an Ethnosociology of South Asian Caste Systems," 230. See Ganguly, passim, for a wonderfully rich discussion of the (mis)interpretations of caste in British India.

123. Charles Keyes, "Towards a New Formulation of the Concept of Ethnic Group," 206.

124. Craig Reynolds, "Introduction," in C. Reynolds, ed., *National Identity and Its Defenders,* 23–24.

125. F. E. Reynolds, "Civic Religion and National Community in Thailand," 274.

126. C. Reynolds, "Introduction," 24.

127. F. E. Reynolds, "Civic Religion and National Community in Thailand," 274.

128. NLA Coedes Collection, E. Aymonier, "Preface," *Dictionnaire khmer-français.*

129. Chandler, "Songs at the Edge of the Forest."

130. Hansen, "Khmer Identity and Theravada Buddhism," in Marston and Guthrie, *History, Buddhism, and New Religious Movements,* 49; see also Ashley Thompson, "The Future of Cambodia's Past: A Messianic Middle-Period Cambodian Royal Cult" in ibid., 13–39.

131. Forest, *Le culte des génies,* 68.

132. CAOM, INDO GGI 65502, RSC to GGI, 3 June 1927; Tath *Kalyanamit roboh knom;* see also Keyes, "Communist Revolution," 47–48.

133. NAC, RSC 23609, Box 2791, Ordonnance Royale No. 71, 2 octobre 1918.

134. CAOM, INDO RSC 466, Ponn to RSC, 23 February 1917.

135. Tath, *Kalyanamit roboh knom,* 22.

136. Ibid., 23–25.

137. An alumnus of the Class of 1885 of the École cambodgienne, Oknya Keth was the founder of the Cambodian Mutual Education Society in 1905. By 1917 he had become Inspector of Legal Affairs and Cambodian Administration.

138. Tath*, Kalyanamit roboh knom,* 17, 30–32.

139. NAC, RSC 23609, Box 2791, No. 71, 2 octobre 1918, Ordonnance Royale.

140. CAOM, INDO RSC 466, Ponn to RSC, 4 August 1919.

141. NAC, RSC 23609, Box 2791, Ordonnance Royale No. 62; Réorganisation de l'École de pâli du Cambodge, Ordonnance Royale No. 21.

142. "École supérieure de pâli," *BEFEO* 35 (1935): 463.

143. "Cambodge," *BEFEO* 22 (1922): 428.

144. Finot, "Maha Vimaladhamma," *BEFEO* 27 (1927): 523; CAOM, INDO GGI 65547, Phnom Penh, 15 December 1927, to RSC.

145. *BEFEO* 22 (1922): 428.

146. Lévi, ed., *Indochine,* 197–198.

147. Ghosh, *A History of Cambodia from the Earliest Times to the End of the French Protectorate,* 196; *Sasanaa Kiw Dae luk loy Preahputsasanaa* (Cao Daism invades Buddhism), *Nagaravatta,* 4 June 1938, 1–2.

148. "École de Pâli (Phnom Penh)," *BEFEO* 22 (1922): 434.

149. Tath, *Kalyanamit roboh knom,* 42–43.

150. Jackson, *Buddhadāsa,* 61; Forest, *Le culte des génies,* 5–6.

151. Geertz, *Available Light,* 170.

152. Ashis Nandy, "The Politics of Secularism and the Recovery of Religious Tolerance," in *Mirrors of Violence: Communities, Riots and Survivors in South Asia,* ed. Veena Das (Delhi: Oxford University Press, 1990), 69–93.

153. Hansen, "Ways of the World."

CHAPTER 5: VIOLENT LIVES

1. Oknya Suttantaprija In, "Nirieh Nokor Vat (Un pélerinage à Angkor en 1909)," *Kampuja Surya* (1934): 5–53.

2. To maintain integrity, and to be true to history, Viollet-le-Duc reasoned, any restoration must honor the discontinuity of times and styles necessarily encompassed in most of those large, ancient, regal, and ecclesiastical buildings now catalogued as "historic monuments." His principle was to restore "each building or each part of a building . . . in the style belonging to it, not solely in its appearance, but in its structure." Viollet-le-Duc, "Restauration," *Dictionnaire raisonné,* tome 8 (Paris, 1866), cited in Bruno Foucart "Viollet-le-Duc et la Restauration," in Nora, *Les lieux de mémoires,* 622.

3. Louis Delaporte, "Rapport fait au Ministre de la marine et des colonies et au Ministre de l'instruction publique, des cultes et des beaux arts, par M. Louis Delaporte, sur la mission scientifique aux ruines des monuments khmers de l'ancien Cambodge," *Journal Officiel de la Republique Française* 6, no. 90 (1874): 2516; Schama, *Landscape and Memory,* 15, 17, 163–165; Knight, *Robin Hood,* 153–273; see also Mosse, *Nationalization of the Masses,* 41.

4. Louis de Carné, "Impressions d'Asie," *Anthologie franco-indochinoise Tome I* (Hanoi: Imprimerie Mac-Dinh-Tu, 1928), 31.

5. "Testimony of Ouk Samith," in Debré, *Cambodge,* 50.

6. Delaporte, *Voyage au Cambodge,* 255.

7. Ibid., 252.

8. See Timothy Mitchell, "Orientalism and the Exhibitionary Order," in Nicholas Dirks, ed., *Colonialism and Culture* (Ann Arbor: University of Michigan Press, 1992).

9. CAOM, INDO GGI 23794, S.M. le Roi du Cambodge Norodom to RSC, 2 February 1891. According to the RSC, despite his overt objections, the king privately informed the RSC that he would turn a blind eye to the removal of artistic objects, but only on condition that no complaints were raised by Cambodians. See CAOM, INDO GGI 23794, RSC to GGI, 6 February 1891.

10. Princess Ping-Péang Yukanthor, "Souvenirs de mon première voyage à Angkor," *France-Asie* 2, no 16 (15 July 1947): 652. Khmer guides told this story to Princess Ping-Péang Yukanthor (1892–1969) during her visit to Angkor in 1909. They showed her the scene of the crime, and the piles of stones "stacked up close to the wall like charcoal bricks in a warehouse."

11. Pannetier, *Notes cambodgiennes,* 154–156.

12. Félicien Challaye, "Angkor," *La Revue de Paris* 29, no. 8 (15 April 1922): 787; A. Raquez, "Les boursiers de voyage de l'Université de Paris," *RII,* no. 7 (15 October 1904): 236–251.

13. British Library Office of Indian and Oriental Records, (OIORC) MSS Euro F111 397 SIAM, Confidential 325 (April 1), Section 1, No. 1. Report by Mr Black on the Town and Province of Chantaboon, and the French Occupation, 8.

14. NAC, File No. 14613, May 13, 1902, Director of EFEO Finot to RS, Cambodge [No. 14613].

15. Émile Guimet, *Le jubilé du Musée Guimet: 25eme anniversaire de sa fondation* 1879–1904 (Paris: Ernest Leroux, 1904), i, xvii.

16. Keiko Omoto, "Émile Guimet et le Musée des religions," in *Musée national des arts asiatiques Guimet* (Paris: Beaux Arts, 1993), 9–10.

17. Jean François Jarrige, "Angkor et dix siècles d'art khmer" (introduction), in *Angkor et dix siècles d'art khmer* (Paris: Édition de la Réunion des musées nationaux, 1997), xxi.

18. CARAN, F 214471, "Project d'installation à Paris du Musée Guimet," *Bulletin Municipal Officiel de la Ville de Paris* 4, no. 76 (17 March 1885): 574–577; CARAN, F214470 3, E. Guimet, Directeur, Musée Guimet, to Minister of Public Education, 12 November 1889.

19. Ibid.

20. *Le Musée Guimet à Paris,* 10 May 1904 (Paris: Chartres: Imprimerie Dubard).

21. Winichakul, *Siam Mapped,* 114, 310.

22. Charles Hallisey, "Roads Taken and Not Taken in the Study of Theravada Buddhism," in Lopez, *Curators of the Buddha,* 46.

23. Nicolas, *Notices sur L'Indo-Chine,* 10.

24. Ashley Thompson, "Text and Temple: The Memorialization of Angkor Vat," paper presented at the annual meeting of the Association of Asian Studies, 1999.

25. Jean Moura, Le Royaume du Cambodge, 2: 4, 135–136; Mouhot, *Travels in Siam, Cambodia, and Laos,* 202; Hansen, "Ways of the World," 72–73. Chandler, *Songs at the Edge of the Forest,* 60, 70.

26. Muan, "Citing Angkor," 22–23.

27. C.-E. Bouillevaux, *L'Annam et le Cambodge: Voyages et notices historiques* (Paris: Victor Palmé, 1874).

28. C.-E. Maître, 1907, cited in Maspéro, ed., *Un empire colonial français,* 113; "EFEO," *BCAF* 7, no. 70 (January 1907): 30.

29. Salaun, *L'Indochine,* 100.

30. In 1918, and from 1922 to 1925, Dufour went on mission to India, where he negotiated an archaeological convention. See Dufour's curriculum vitae, on file at the National Library of Australia, Coedès MS2966.

31. Prince Damrong, "Angkor from a Siamese Point of View," in Damrong, *Miscellaneous Articles,* 99.

32. Hoffenberg, *Empire on Display* 153. Commissioned from some one thousand stonemasons by the local government and arts schools, the Gwalior gateway was designed to assemble diverse regional styles in one massive slab and to signpost an "authentic and original India."

33. Allen, *The Buddha and the Sahibs,* 243, 250–251.

34. Dagens, *Angkor,* 172–173.

35. In *Nirieh Nokor Vat,* 69–70.

36. Jacobs, *Traditional Literature,* 70.

37. "Cambodge," *BEFEO* 9 (1909): 827.

38. In, *Nirieh Nokor Vat,* 86–88.

39. Dagens, *Angkor,* 173.

40. NAC, No. 15197, Société d'Angkor, Procès verbal de l'assemblée general, 12 March 1910.

41. *BEFEO* 9 (1909): 828; *BEFEO* 10 (1910): 268.

42. Anderson, *Imagined Communities,* 182.

43. Barthes, *Mythologies,* 75–77.

44. Gas-Faucher, *En sampan sur les lacs du Cambodge et à Angkor,* 87.

45. Anderson, *Imagined Communities,* 181–182.

46. Claude Lévi-Strauss, "The place of anthropology in the structural sciences and the problems raised in teaching it," in his *Structural Anthropology,* 375.

47. "Cambodge," *BEFEO* 7 (1907): 422.

48. Article 2 of "Statutes of Society of Angkor," *BEFEO* 7 (1907): 209–210; "Société d'Angkor pour la conservation des monuments anciens de l'Indochine: Statuts," *BCAF* 8, no. 88 (July 1908): 284–285.

49. "Programme of Society of Angkor," *BEFEO* 7 (1907): 210.

50. Ibid.

51. CAOM, INDO GGI 16920, GGI to Ministry of Colonies, 11 October 1907. Letter from M. Maître, Acting Director of EFEO, to M. Jeannerat, Administrator of Kandal, *BEFEO* 7 (1907): 422. Maître stressed the role of similar conservation societies in generating tourist traffic to Luxor.

52. Etienne Richet, "Heures d'Asie: Le Cambodge et les ruines d'Angkor," *Bulletin de la Société Royale de Geographie d'Anvers* 28 (1904): 324.

53. Cl. E. Maitre, "Nécrologie: F. G. Faraut," *BEFEO* 11 (1911): 253.

54. "Cambodge," *BEFEO* 7 (1907): 423.

55. Peleggi, *The Politics of Ruins,* 4.

56. "Cambodge," *BEFEO* 8 (1908): 419.

57. Lunet de Lajonquière, "Les provinces récouvrées du Cambodge," *BCAF* 7, 74 (May 1907), 161.

58. Michael Brand, "Khmer Sculpture: From Monument to Museum," in *The Age of Angkor: Treasures from the National Museum of Cambodge,* exh. cat. (Australian National Gallery, Canberra, 1992), 25; see also Général L. de Beylié, *Les ruines d'Angkor,* 12.

59. "Cambodge," *BEFEO* 8 (1908): 419–420.

60. Félicien Challaye, "Angkor," *La Revue de Paris* 29, no. 8, 15 April 1922, 787.

61. EFEO, *Chercheurs d'Asie,* 107–110.

62. This tragiccomic anecdote appears in the letters of Henri Marchal, as quoted in Richer, *Histoire de la restauration,* 24.

63. J. Commaille, *Guide aux ruines d'Angkor* (Paris: Hachette, 1912). For a complete list of his publications, see EFEO, *Chercheurs d'Asie,* 111–112.

64. CAOM, INDO GGI 16926, GGI Arrêté, n.d., to take effect from 1 July 1908; *BEFEO,* no. 1-2 (January–June 1908): 284; Beylié, *Les ruines d'Angkor,* 12.

65. CAOM, INDO GGI 16922, Petillot to RSC, 22 May 1909.

66. Ibid., Circular sent to all villages in Khmer script, Phnom Penh (n.d.) [1909].

67. CAOM, INDO GGI 16922, Minutes of Meeting of Cambodian Sub Committee, Society of Angkor, 13 August 1909, 2.

68. Dagens, *Angkor,* 88.

69. M. Petit, ed., *Les colonies françaises,* 351.

70. François de Tessan, "Les aspects intimes et pittoresques de l'Indochine," *l'Illustration,* 21 October 1922, 387.

71. G. Coedès, "Angkor: Les travaux de l'EFEO," *IHI,* 3 October 1940, vi.

72. CAOM, INDO GGI 16922, Compte rendu de la Séance du Comité cambodgien de la Société d'Angkor, 21 Dec. 1909.

73. L. Forestier, "George Groslier: Prix de littérature coloniale 1929 'Le retour à l'argile'" *Extrême-Asie,* no. 38 (August 1929): 602.

74. CAOM, INDO GGI 2397, Antoine-George Groslier, Administrateur du 4e classe des services civils, Commissaire du gouvernement adjoint à Luang-Prabang, to GGI, 25 June 1906, and to GGI, 10 July 1906.

75. CAOM, INDO GGI 16922 Compte rendu de la Séance du Comité cambodgien de la Société d'Angkor, 21 Dec. 1909.

76. R. Meyer, *Komlah,* 20.

77. R. Meyer, *Le propos du Vieux Colonial,* 43; Meyer, *Komlah,* 17.

78. CAOM, INDO GGI 17000, RSC to GGI, 12 April 1910. Marchal was appointed to replace Petillot.

79. *BEFEO* 11 (1911): 252–253.

80. R. Meyer, *Komlah,* 32.

81. CAOM, INDO GGI 17000, RSC Luce to GGI, 22 March 1910.

82. *BEFEO* 10 (1910): 268.

83. *BEFEO* 11 (1911): 252–253. This meeting was attended by Faraut and Chhun, treasurer of the Angkor Society, graduate of the École cambodgienne in Paris, and Secretary of the Angkor Society Keth (first secretary of the Council of Ministers), who would go on to sponsor the first publication of reformist monks Chuon Nath and Huot Tath.

84. M. Ch. Gravelle, "Les métis et l'oeuvre de la protection de l'enfance au Cambodge," *Revue Indochinoise* 21, no. 1 (January 1913): 32.

85. Collard, *Cambodge et Cambodgiens,* viii, 4–6, 137–138.

86. NAC, RSC 15197, 11 August 1910, letter GGI to RSC.

87. NAC, RSC 15197, 31 August 1910, Director EFEO Parmentier to GGI.

88. Groslier, *À l'ombre d'Angkor,* 153–154. Groslier describes the road from Angkor Vat to Banteay Chma.

89. De Beylié, *Les ruines d'Angkor.* See dedication on frontispiece, and 28; Dagens, *Angkor,* 84–85.

90. CAOM, INDO GGI 16926, Contract between M. Breucq, Commissaire Délegué du RSC à Battambang et Compagnie des messageries fluviales de Cochinchine, signed 10 June 1910, approved by RSC, 27 July 1910; *Exposition universelle et internationale Bruxelles 1910: Section coloniale française,* 44.

91. The society had raised over 4,000 piastres for 1910, including 2,440 piastres from native donations—approximately one-third of which was raised in Battambang—and 400 piastres from tourist contributions to the collection box at the Angkor Vat bungalow. The Paris Society of Angkor had contributed another 1,500 francs. *BEFEO* 11 (1911): 252.

92. NAC, RSC 14689, May 16, 1916, letter to RSC from Siem Reap. The description of the tombstone and burial site is taken from EFEO, *Chercheurs d'Asie,* 109.

93. J. Tully, "Cambodia in Sisowath's Reign," 234–236.

94. Details of the sentence are taken from EFEO, *Chercheurs d'Asie,* 109.

CHAPTER 6: COPY RITES

1. Yuvan Boraan, "Ompi Phithi Banghout Tungcay"(About the flag-raising ceremony), *Servir,* no. 3 (February 1942).

2. F. Fanon, *Toward the African Revolution,* trans. H. Chevalier (London: Pelican, 1967), 44.

3. Khieu Samphan, *L'Economie du Cambodge et ses problemes d'industrialisation,* trans. Laura Summers, submitted for the doctorat in economics, University of Paris, 1959 (Ithaca, NY: Cornell University Monographs on Southeast Asia).

4. Chandler, "Songs at the Edge of the Forest," 67.

5. Shelly Errington, "Recasting Sex, Gender and Power," in Atkinson and Errington, eds., *Power and Difference,* 43.

6. Hansen, "Khmer Identity and Theravada Buddhism," in Marston and Guthrie, *History, Buddhism, and New Religious Movements,* 49.

7. Tricon and Bellan, *Chansons cambodgiennes,* i.

8. CARAN, F21 4489 3a, Delaporte to Minister of Public Education, 16 May 1882.

9. CAOM, INDO GGI 12504, F. Faure, Under-Secretary of State for Marines and Colonies, to Governor General of Cochinchina, 20 June 1884, 1–4.

10. Ibid., Exposition of Anvers List of Awards: Cambodge (n.d.).

11. A. Tissandier, *Cambodge et Java,* 7.

12. Henri Mouhot, cited in Lewis, *A Dragon Apparent,* 212–213.

13. See *Atlas coloniale: L'Indochine française,* 191; Lewis, *A Dragon Apparent,* 211.

14. Edwards, "Restyling Colonial Cambodia, 1860–1945."

15. J. Furnivall, *Colonial Policy and Practice,* 229–231.

16. Lunet de Lajonquière, "Les provinces récouvrées du Cambodge," *BCAF* 7, no. 74 (May 1907): 155–162, 160.

17. See Ponder, *Cambodian Glory,* 171.

18. CAOM, INDO GGI 2576, Thiounn to RSC, 9 July 1907. See CAOM, INDO NF 22, for Mayura's comments (writing under a pseudonym) to M. L'Inspecteur Général des Colonies, 12 October 1916, 2.

19. The recently crowned King Vajiravudh (Rama VI of Siam, r. 1910–1925), promoter of a royalist brand of nationalism, established the fine arts department in 1912. Peleggi, *Politics of Ruins,* 4.

20. Teston et Percheron, *L'Indochine moderne,* 710.

21. George Groslier, *Danseuses cambodgiennes anciennes et modernes* (Paris: Augustin Challamel, 1913).

22. Ponder, *Cambodian Glory,* 171. Long after his cremation and Cambodian funeral, Cambodians still remembered him as "the stone doctor." Mao Kusumo, *Cambodge: Cahiers Intimes, Tome 2* (Grenoble: Librairie de l'Université, 1985), 556.

23. The new French law governed the disposal of art treasures by defining "protected property" and effectively precluded national museums from either disposing of

their treasures or making any cultural returns. See Greenfield, *Return of Cultural Treasures,* 109, on the law in France, and Wright, *Politics of Design,* 44, 194, on the passage of historic preservation legislation in Indochina the same year.

24. Groslier, À *l'ombre d'Angkor;* see frontispiece.

25. Ponder, *Cambodian Glory,* 171. Ponder actually refers to a "Society of Friends of Angkor" in his account, but is almost certainly referring to the Angkor Society.

26. Teston and Percheron, *L'Indochine moderne,* 713.

27. G. Coedès, "Angkor: Les Travaux de l'EFEO," i–viii. See Tully, "Cambodia in Sisowath's Reign," 234–236.

28. George Groslier, "Les arts indigènes au Cambodge," in *L'Indochine française: Recueil de notices rédigées à l'occasion du Xe Congrès de la Far Eastern Association of Tropical Medicine Hanoi (Tonkin) 24–30 November 1938* (Hanoi: Imprimerie G. Taupin, 1938), 161.

29. Groslier, À *l'ombre d'Angkor,* frontispiece, 31.

30. Ibid., 31.

31. Groslier died in 1945 after an interrogation by Japanese police. See Dagens, *Angkor,* 96.

32. Albert Sarraut, *La mise en valeur des colonies françaises,* 104.

33. CAOM, INDO NF 570, GGI to Minister of Colonies, Paris, 31 March 1916; Sarraut, "Événements du Cambodge en janvier et février 1916," 48.

34. Tully, "Cambodia in Sisowath's Reign," 226.

35. Nicholas B. Dirks, "Annals of the Archive: Ethnographic Notes on the Sources of History," in Axel, *From the Margins,* 56.

36. CAOM, INDO NF 28, RSC Report to GGI, 29 January 1916, 13.

37. Sarraut, "Événements du Cambodge," 40, 44–45.

38. Baudoin, "Le nouveau statut du personnel de l'administration indigène au Cambodge," *RII* 1918, 105–123.

39. Ibid., 105–123; *Les arts indigènes au Cambodge* (Publication du Gouvernement Générale de l'Indochine à l'occasion de l'exposition internationale des arts et technique de Paris en 1937), cited in Fillieux, *Merveilleux Cambodge,* 218; Groslier, "Les arts indigènes au Cambodge," 164.

40. Thirty-two practicing artisans lived in Phnom Penh, excluding the twenty artisans at the palace workshops.

41. Teston et Percheron, *L'Indochine moderne,* 714.

42. George Groslier, "La convalescence des arts Cambodgiens," *Revue Indochinoise,* First Semester (1991): 872.

43. Ponder, *Cambodian Glory,* 90.

44. CAOM, INDO, GGI 16926, RSC to GGI, 9 August 1918, 15–16. Corporations cambodgiennes, *Les Corporations cambodgiennes* (Phnom Penh: Imprimerie Henry, 1942), 51.

45. Groslier, "La convalescence des arts cambodgiens," 871.

46. De Pourtalès, *Nous, à qui rien n'appartient,* 116.

47. Groslier, "La convalescence des arts cambodgiens," 161.

48. Muan, "Citing Angkor," 19.

49. Ibid., 62.

50. NLA, Coe Pam 8, *Encyclopédie par l'image: Indochine française* (Librairie Hachette) (n.d.).

51. Geertz, *Available Light,* 132–133.

52. Bhabha, *Location of Culture,* 143.

53. Ibid., 88.

54. Muan, "Citing Angkor," 186, 190, 191.

55. Teston and Percheron, *L'Indochine moderne,* 717–718; Wright, *Politics of Design,* 225–226.

56. Muan, "Citing Angkor," 185–186, 190–191.

57. Corporations cambodgiennes, *Corporations cambodgiennes,* 39.

58. CAOM, INDO RSC 466, Letters from Minister of War and Public Education Ponn to the RSC, 25 February 1919 and 4 March 1919.

59. Groslier, "La convalescence des arts cambodgiennes," 872.

60. Corporations cambodgiennes, *Les Corporations cambodgiennes.*

61. Groslier, "La tradition cambodgienne," 465; *Corporations cambodgiennes,* 51. Sales proceeds went to the Khmer artisans.

62. Ponder, *Cambodian Glory,* 170–171.

63. CAOM, INDO, GGI 16926, Director EFEO to GGI , 5 July 1919, 4–5.

64. Teston and Percheron, *L'Indochine moderne,* 714.

65. Ponder, *Cambodian Glory,* 171–172.

66. Dagens, *Angkor,* 96; Bleackley, *A Tour in Southeast Asia,* 60–61.

67. Groslier "Les arts indigènes au Cambodge," 168–169.

68. Victor Goloubew, "Nécrologie: In memoriam" (obituary for Louis Finot), *BEFEO* 35 (1935): 527.

69. Ibid., 169; CARAN, F21/4489/3c, Louis Delaporte to Ministère de l'Instruction Publique et Beaux Arts, 29 September 1924, 2.

70. R. Meyer, *Komlah,* 33, 102–104, 246–247; and Goscha, *Vietnam or Indochina?* 60–61.

71. For discussions of Meyer's novel, see Edwards, "Womanizing Indochina," and Srilata Ravi, "Exotic Reminiscchces: The Feminine Other in French Fiction in Southeast Asia," *French Cultural Studies* 11, no. 1 (2000): 53–74.

72. CAOM, INDO GGI 46483, GGI to Commissariat Général de l'Indochine, Commissariat Exposition Coloniale, 26 May 1923.

73. Commissariat Général de l'Exposition National Coloniale de Marseille, *Exposition national coloniale de Marseille* (Marseille, 1922) 9, 10; see also Teston and Percheron, *L'Indochine moderne,* 831.

74. L. Vernet, "Un visiteur de 11 ans à l'Exposition coloniale de Marseille," in *Orient des Provencaux,* 100.

75. L. Naudeau, "L'Exposition coloniale de Marseille," *l'Illustration,* 21 October 1922, 371–373.

76. *Le petit marseillais édition de l'Exposition coloniale* 18 November 1922, 1. Félicien Challaye, "Angkor," *La Revue de Paris* 24, no. 8, 15 April 1922, p. 787.

77. Vernet, "Un visiteur de 11 ans à l'Exposition coloniale de Marseille," 100.

78. Vieille Charité, *Orient des Provencaux,* 55, 102; Pinet, *Ornement de la durée,* 2–3,18.

79. CAOM, INDO GGI 46483, GGI Merlin to RSC, 20 October 1923.

80. CAOM, INDO GGI 46483, GGI to Ministry of Colonies, telegraph, 2 December 1923.

81. Victor Goloubew, "Avant-Propos," in Marchal, *Costumes et parures khmèrs,* x.

82. CAOM, INDO NF 259, Dossier 2226, Report by H. Gourdon, 21.

83. *Les Corporations cambodgiennes,* 51.

84. Bleackley, *Tour in Southern Asia,* 65.

85. Challaye, "Angkor," 810–811.

86. Groslier, *Angkor,* 2.

87. Wright, *Politics of Design,* 196.

88. *BEFEO* 30 (1930): 215.

89. Rachel Wheatcroft, *Siam and Cambodia in Pen and Pastel with Excursions to China and Burmah* (London: Constable, 1928), 55.

90. Jeanne Beausoleil, ed., *À l'ombre d'Angkor: Le Cambodge années vingt* (Paris: VILO, 1992), 29, 152. Batteur was a temporary replacement for Henri Marchal during his home leave from Sept. 1920 to Jan. 1922.

91. Charles Keyes, "The Case of the Purloined Lintel," in C. Reynolds, *National Identity,* 266–267.

92. "Angkor-Siam: Un promenade inoubliable," *Extrême-Asie: Revue Indochinoise Illustrée,* no. 42 (December 1929), Advertising Supplement.

93. Goscha, *Vietnam or Indochina?* 40.

94. "L'Inauguration du tourisme aérien en Indochine," *Extrême-Asie: Revue Indochinoise Illustrée,* no. 35 (May 1929), 1.

95. Tath, *Kalyanamit roboh knom,* translated excerpt in Edwards, "Cambodge" (PhD diss.) 406.

96. Recouly, *À travers L'Indochine,* 321.

97. Nathan Fernand *L'Indochine* (Paris, 1939), 3.

98. Recouly, *À travers L'Indochine,* 337.

99. See the numerous advertisements placed throughout A. Messner, ed., *Angkor: Conférence de M. Victor. Goloubew sur les récentes fouilles d'Angkor (au Musée Louis Finot à Hanoi, le 16 Avril 1934).*

100. Recouly, *À travers L'Indochine,* 336.

101. Ribardière, "Siemreap 20 October 1934," in Messner, *Angkor,* 24.

102. Dagens, *Angkor,* 96; Teston and Percheron, *L'Indochine moderne,* 716–717.

103. Hervey, *Travels in Indochina,* 105–108; Lewis, *A Dragon Apparent,* 220.

104. Walter G. Langlois, *André Malraux,* 8.

105. Pannetier, *Notes cambodgiennes,* 154–156.

106. Henry de Lachevrotière, "Le vol des bas-reliefs d'Angkor," *l'Impartial,* 22 July 1924, 1; see also Dagens, *Angkor,* 100.

107. See Norindr, *Phantasmatic Indochina,* 82.

108. CAOM, INDO 16938, Louis Finot, Director EFEO Hanoi, to GGI, 2 February 1923.

109. CAOM, INDO GGI 16938, Arrêté 14 February 1923.

110. Malraux was helped by fourteen Annamite and Cambodian servants and drivers. Langlois, *André Malraux,* 8, 23, 35, 232n17.

111. A. Malraux, *The Royal Way* (New York: Harrison Smith and Robert Haas, 1935), 71, 99–100.

112. Goloubew, "Nécrologie: In memoriam," 527.

113. Say, "Kar Racana" (Art), *Nagaravatta,* 20 February 1937, 1.

114. Marchal, *Le décor et la sculpture khmers,* 118.

115. *Les Corporations cambodgiennes,* 53–54.

116. "Minh-Moll: Orfèvre diplomé de l'École des arts cambodgiens," *Le Khmer,* 20 November 1936, 11.

117. Goloubew, "Mélanges sur le Cambodge ancient," 513–519; Teston and Percheron, *L'Indochine moderne,* 691.

118. Dagens, *Angkor,* 105, 108.

119. Speech by Pierre Pasquier at the inauguration of the Louis Finot Museum in Hanoi, November 30, 1932, *BEFEO* 33 (1933): 481.

120. Henri Marchal, "Des influences étrangères dans l'art et la civilisation khmères," *BSEIS* 11, no. 2 (1936): 9–10.

121. Coedès, "L'EFEO: Méthodes modernes et orientation nouvelle," 2.

122. Coedès "Angkor," vi.

123. Ibid., ii; Anthony Reid, "Who Made Southeast Asia," *The Asia-Pacific Magazine* 9/10 (1998): 62–67.

124. Commissariat de l'Indo-Chine, *Directives générales* (Hanoi: Imprimerie d'Extrême Orient, 1929), 2.

125. Wright, *Politics of Design,* 194.

126. Maspéro, *Un empire colonial français,* 2: 442.

127. Émile Bayard, *L'Art de reconnaître les styles coloniaux de la France* (Paris: Garnier, 1931), 2; see Norindr, *Phantasmatic Indochina,* 24–25, 27.

128. *L'Illustration,* 23 May 1931, Annoncés LXXVII and LXXII.

129. Marchal, *Le décor et la sculpture khmers,* 54.

130. C. Farrère, "Angkor et l'Indochine," *Exposition coloniale internationale de Paris 1931* (Paris: l'Illustration, 1931). Farrère was a former colonial civil servant famed for a fictionalized version of his Indochina years entitled, tellingly, *Les civilisés,* which won the prestigious Prix Goncourt. Claude Farrère, *Les civilisés* (Paris: Flammarion, 1905).

131. "Les pavillons de la chasse et de la pêche indochinoise," *l'Illustration,* 27 June 1931, 313.

132. Teston and Percheron, *L'Indochine moderne,* 831.

133. "Les pavillons de la chasse," 313.

134. Private communication with Esta S. Ungar, University of Western Australia, July 1996.

135. Farrère, "Angkor et l'Indochine."

136. Norindr, *Phantastmatic Indochina,* 27.

137. Robert de Beauplan, "Les Palais d'Indochine," *Exposition coloniale internationale de Paris 1931* (Paris: l'Illustration, 1931). Jean Marquet, *Les Cinq Fleurs: L'Indochine expliquée* (The Five Flowers: Indochina explained) (Hanoi: Direction de l'Instruction Publique en Indochine, 1928). See Goscha, *Vietnam or Indochina?* 33–35.

138. "Ompi robam niw munti preah riec banyalaay" (About the dance at the Royal Library), *Nagaravatta,* 22 January 1938, 1.

139. Bhabha, *Location of Culture,* 88, 91.

140. Muan, "Citing Angkor," 125–127.

141. Marchal, *Le décor et la sculpture khmers,* 118.

142. Herzfeld, *Cultural Intimacy,* 31.

143. Mlle A. de Rotalier, *Comme les jours passent,* 249.

144. Ibid., 252–253.

145. *"Secday romluk dal ah kounchiw aoy uesaa rien sout"* (A reminder to all grandchildren to study hard), *Kampuchea Bodemien,* 2 May 1931, 1.

146. Muan, "Citing Angkor," 368, 369.

CHAPTER 7: SECULARIZING THE *SANGHA,* 1900–1935

1. Faucheur, *Lettre sur le Cambodge,* 14.

2. Daguerches, *Le Kilomètre 83,* 323–325.

3. Henri Daguerches, "Le bonze d'Angkor," *RII* 18, no. 11 (1918): 360.

4. Maurice Olivient, "Le bonze," *RII* 18, no. 7 (1918): 71–72.

5. Lopez, *Curators of the Buddha,* 3.

6. Jean-Philippe Geley, "Postface," in Daguerches, *Le Kilomètre 83,* 24–25.

7. NAC, RSC 23609, Box 2791, K. Chéa, le Ministre de l'Intérieur, "Note sur l'Institut Bouddhique au Cambodge" (28 June 1937), 10.

8. CAOM, FM INDO NF 570, RSC Baudoin to GGI, A.s. de la surveillance des bonzes au Cambodge Phnom Penh, 2 April 1916, 1–9.

9. Ibid.

10. CAOM, FM INDO GGI 65539, Sûreté Phnom Penh Sectes Réligieuses du Cambodge, 20 July 1936, 1.

11. Ch. Lemire, "Recensement au Siam en 1904," *BCAF* 6, no. 58 (January 1906): 35.

12. Jacobs, *Traditional Literature,* 46.

13. See, e.g., S. J. Tambiah, "Sangha and Polity in Modern Thailand: An Overview," in B. L. Smith, ed., *Religion and Legitimation of Power in Thailand, Laos and Burma,* 111–133.

14. Tambiah, *Buddhist Saints of the Forest,* 7; Taylor, *Forest Monks and the Nation-State,* 217–218; Lester, *Theravada Buddhism in Southeast Asia,* 3.

15. Ebihara, "Interrelations between Buddhism and Social Systems in Cambodia," 177.

16. P. Jackson, *Buddhism, Legitimation and Conflict,* 11–12.

17. A. Leclère, *Le bouddhisme au Cambodge,* 398.

18. Forest, *Le culte des génies,* 1992, 96.

19. Kirsch, "Modernizing Implications of Nineteenth Century Reforms in the Thai Sangha," 559.

20. A. Leclère, *Le Bouddhisme au Cambodge;* CAOM, FM INDO NF 570, RSC to GGI, 2 April 1916, 2–3.

21. Ebihara, "Interrelations between Buddhism and Social Systems in Cambodian Peasant Culture," 178.

22. Ibid.

23. A. Leclère, *Le bouddhisme au Cambodge,* 390–393.

24. Sreang, "The Cambodian Khum from 1879 to 1919," 28; NAC, RSC 12808, la proposition de la premier ministre cambodgien, le 5 août 1907.

25. A. Leclère, *Le bouddhisme au Cambodge,* 154.

26. A royal ordinance of 29 October 1907 officially sanctioned monks' tax-free status and stipulated that "permanent identity cards" would be handed out to them free of charge. CAOM, INDO GGI 2162, Ordonnance Royale du 29 octobre 1907.

27. CAOM, FM INDO NF 570, Baudoin to GGI, 2 April 1916, 4–5.

28. CAOM, INDO GGI 2189, GGI Beau and RSC Luce Arrêté, 25 December 1907, Municipal taxes for Phnom Penh. The new fees were 1.50 piastres for the Tet festival, 1.00 for a cremation with music, and an extra 1.50 for fireworks.

29. CAOM, FM INDO NF 570, RSC Baudoin to GGI, A.s. de la surveillance des bonzes au Cambodge Phnom Penh, 2 April 1916, 3–4.

30. Doumer, *L'Indochine française* 1.

31. Tully, *Cambodia in Sisowath's Reign,* 226–227; Franck, *East of Siam,* 28–29.

32. Forest, *Le Cambodge,* 395.

33. CAOM, FM INDO NF 28, RSC Confidential Report on Yukanthor, 16 February 1916, 12.

34. Tully, *Cambodia in Sisowath's Reign,* 227.

35. CAOM, FM INDO NF 570, GGI to Minister of Colonies, 2 May 1916.

36. Forest, *Le Cambodge,* 147.

37. Ana Maria Alonso, "The Politics of Space, Time and Substance: State Formation, Nationalism and Ethnicity," *Annual Review of Anthropology* 23 (1994): 379–405.

38. CAOM, FM INDO NF 570, RSC to GGI, A.s. de surveillance des bonzes.

39. NAC, RSC 23609, Box 2791, K. Chea, le Ministre de l'Intérieur, "Note sur l'Institut Bouddhique au Cambodge" (28 June 1937), 10.

40. The topographer turned a deaf ear to the various pleas of the head monk, who referred the matter to the Council of Ministers. Minister of War and Education Ponn took up the case in a letter to the RSC, asking that M. Duvar move out of the *salaa.* CAOM, INDO RSC 466, Dossier 39, Minister of War and Education Ponn to RSC, 20 July 1915.

41. R. Meyer, *Komlah,* 94–95.

42. CAOM, FM INDO NF 570, RSC to GGI, A.s. de surveillance des bonzes, 5–6.

43. Leclère, *Le bouddhisme au Cambodge,* 390–393; Ebihara, "Interrelations between Buddhism and Social Systems in Cambodian Peasant Culture," 183.

44. Lester, *Theravada Buddhism in Southeast Asia* 114–115.

45. David Chandler, "Normative Poems *(chbap)* and Precolonial Cambodian Society," in Chandler, *Facing the Cambodian Past* 55; Jacobs, *Traditional Literature,* 28–32.

46. Chandler, "Normative Poems," 55.

47. CAOM, INDO, GGI 5870, F. Fontaine, "Instruction publique. Cambodge" n.d. (ca. 1903), 23.

48. "Asie Française," *BCAF* 6, no. 64 (July 1906): 278–280.

49. CAOM, INDO GGI 1579, RSC Arrêté, 15 November 1904.

50. Chulalongkorn appointed his brother Prince Wachiryan, head of the Thammayut in Siam, to oversee implementation of his educational reforms, which merged Buddhist precepts with the modern curriculum and initially used *vat* schools and monk teachers. See Kirsch, "Modernizing Implications," 60.

51. CAOM, INDO GGI 2598, RSC Jules Morel Phnom Penh to GGI, 17 March 1905.

52. Ibid., 4–5; an annotated version of these recommendations appears as "La réorganisation de l'enseignement au Cambodge," in *BCAF* 5, no. 51 (June 1905): 258–259.

53. Ibid.

54. CAOM, INDO GGI 2598, RSC Morel Report to GGI, 20 July 1905, 3.

55. *BCAF* (1907): 475.

56. Ibid.

57. Morizon, *Monographie du Cambodge,* 179.

58. Forest, *Le Cambodge,* 158–159.

59. P. de la Brosse, "Dans les provinces Cambodgiennes rétrocédées," *RII,* 2nd semester (1907): 1240; see also Tauch Chhuong, *Battambang,* 100–103.

60. Taylor, *Forest Monks,* 19, 45, 53–55, 147. The Thommayuth reform movement was established in Laos in 1888, and soon afterward Lao monks from the Thommayuth order began bringing back gifted pupils from Bangkok to serve as career administrators and educationists in Laos.

61. CAOM, INDO, GGI 5870, F. Fontaine, "Instruction publique. Cambodge," n.d. (ca. 1903), 23.

62. G. H. Monod, "L'orthographie dite "Quoc-Ngu" appliquée au Cambodgien," *RII* 2nd Semester 1907, 1172–1177. *BEFEO* 8 (1908): 316.

63. Lunet de Lajonquière, "La rétrocession des provinces cambodgiennes," *BCAF* 8, no. 87 (1908): 227–228.

64. CAOM, INDO RSC 466, Royaume du Cambodge Conseil des Ministres No. 102, *Preahkorana jie ommcah jiwit le drungpreahreach anunyat prumpong Satra,* 21 October 1909.

65. CAOM, INDO GGI 5881, M. Baille, Inspecteur de Services Civiles d' Indo-Chine et Commissaire Générale de l'Indochine à l'exposition de Marseilles, Proposals for Chevalier de la Légion d'Honneur, 30 September 1906.

66. Teston and Percheron, *L'Indochine moderne,* 182–183.

67. CAOM, INDO GGI 2702, RSC to GGI, 24 March 1916, 2.

68. Morizon, *Monographie du Cambodge,* 180–181.

69. Jacobs, *Traditional Literature of Cambodia,* 10.

70. CAOM, INDO RSC 304, *Note sur les Écoles des pagodes: Renseignements fournis par SE le Ministre de l'instruction publique au Cambodge,* 18.

71. CAOM, INDO RSC 466, Report from Prea Vimol Methea Charey Yen, Inspector of Thommayut Schools, to Resident of Kompong Chhnang, 1 January 1914. Yen reported that he had given Chau Attikear Or from Trabek Pagoda a good dressing down in front of the governor of Kompong Leng, to teach him the rules.

72. CAOM, INDO RSC 466, Letter from Ponn Chakrey, Minister of War and Public Education, to the RSC, 11 February 1915.

73. Chandler, "Normative Poems" (n. 45), 45–60.

74. CAOM, INDO RSC 466, Letter from Minister of War and Education Ponn to RSC, 31 August 1915.

75. CAOM, INDO GGI 2702, RSC to GGI, 24 March 1916, Inspection des Écoles du Cambodge, 3.

76. Ibid., 6.

77. Ibid., 7, 18.

78. CAOM, FM INDO NF 570, RSC Baudoin to GGI, A.s. de la surveillance des bonzes au Cambodge, Phnom Penh, 2 April 1916, 3–4.

79. CAOM, INDO RSC 466, Letter from Ponn, Minister of War and Public Education, to Chief of the Second Bureau in Phnom Penh (n.d.).

80. CAOM, INDO RSC 466, Letter from Minister of War and Public Education Ponn to RSC, 29 October 1919; Letter from Résident of Battambang to Minister of War and Education, 4 November 1919.

81. CAOM, INDO RSC 466, Letter from Ponn, Minister of War and Public Education, to RSC, 29 January 1919.

82. Ibid.

83. CAOM, INDO RSC 466, Note from RSC to Ponn, November 1919.

84. Herzfeld, *Cultural Intimacy*, 13.

85. Benvenisti, *Sacred Landscape*, 55.

86. Porée and Maspéro, *Moeurs et coutumes des Khmèrs*, 183.

87. "Revue de la presse locale: Après l'Affaire Bardez" and "La suite de l'Affaire Bardez," *L'Indochine enchaînée*, no. 15 (1925/1926): 4.

88. Grauclaude, *Le réveil du peuple khmer*, 6.

89. Teston and Percheron, *L'Indochine moderne*, 182–183.

90. Porée and Maspéro, *Moeurs et coutumes des Khmers*, 183.

91. CAOM, INDO NF 259, Dossier 2226, Report by Gourdon, 39–40.

92. Oknya Sann, "Benyuel bi aoy koun coul rien salaa" (Explaining about sending children to school to study), *Srok Khmer*, no. 7 (January 1928): 3–5.

93. "Secdey jun damneng ompi siewpiew bothhum vicie khemara piesaa" (Information about Khmer-language educational books), *Srok Khmer*, no. 11 (May 1928): 3.

94. CAOM, INDO RSC 648, Richomme, Résident of Kampot, Extrait du Rapport politique, 3e trimester, Kampot, 15 September 1928, 2. This was the École d'application d'Ang Sophi, in Khum Kanthor (Canthor Commune).

95. CAOM, INDO RSC 648, Extrait du Rapport politique, 4th Trimestre 1928, Résident du Prey Veng, "Instruction Publique," 2.

96. CAOM, INDO RSC 648, Extrait du Rapport annuel, June 1927–June 1928, Kompong Thom, 27 August 1928, 4.

97. Morizon, *Monographie du Cambodge*, 182. Higher figures, but no provincial breakdown, are given in another 1931 publication, which records 58 schools and 2,775 pupils. Teston and Percheron, *L'Indochine moderne*, 184.

98. CAOM, INDO RSC 269, RSC Lavit to Chef Local du Service de l'Enseignement à Phnom Penh, 12 November 1931, 1–2.

99. Doumer, "Avant propos, 1930," to *L'Indochine française (souvenirs)*, 1.

100. Le Grauclaude, *Le Reveil du peuple khmer*, 17–18.

101. CAOM, INDO RSC 269, Louis Manipaud, le Délégué de SM à l'Enseignment Traditionnel, Rapport annuel 1933–34: Enseignement Traditionnel Renové, 9. CAOM, INDO RSC 269, RSC Lavit to Chef Local du Service de l'Enseignement à Phnom Penh, 12 Nov. 1931, 1–2.

102. CAOM, INDO RSC 269, RSC Lavit to Chef Local du Service de l'Enseignement à Phnom Penh, 12 November 1931, 1.

103. CAOM, INDO RSC 269, Louis Manipaud, le Délégué de SM à l'Enseignment Traditionnel, Rapport annuel 1933–34: Enseignement Traditionnel Renové, 9.

104. CAOM, INDO RSC 269, L'Inspecteur Indigène de l'enseignement primaire, Kampot, *Au sujet de la substitution des caractères latins aux caractères cambodgiens*.

105. CAOM, INDO GGI 65539, Sûreté Phnom Penh, "Sectes réligieuses du Cambodge," 20 July 1933, 2.

106. Norodom Yukanthor died on 27 June 1934, aged seventy-four. His funeral was attended by the "finest flowers of the ancient court of HM Chulalongkorn." Iukanthor, *Destin d'empire,* 83.

107. CAOM, INDO RSC 269, le Délégué de SM à l'Enseignment Traditionnel, Rapport annuel 1933–34: Enseignement Traditionnel Renové, 19.

108. CAOM, INDO RSC 269, Louis Manipaud, le Délégué de SM à l'Enseignment Traditionnel, Rapport annuel 1933–34: Enseignement Traditionnel Renové, 20.

109. Ibid.

110. Le Grauclaude, *Le reveil du peuple khmer,* 19.

111. CAOM, INDO RSC 269, Louis Manipaud to M. Richomme, Phnom Penh, 31 January 1934, 1–4.

112. Schools were also set up for other ethnic groups, including Chams. Grauclaude, *Le réveil du peuple khmer,* 98.

113. Teston and Percheron, *L'Indochine moderne,* 181.

114. Gastaldy, *La Cochinchine,* 98, 101.

115. Stephen Heder, "The Khmer Krom Reaction to its Decline and the Emergence of Son Ngoc Thanh" (unpublished ms, n.d.); Anderson, *Imagined Communities,* 128–129.

116. Gastaldy, *La Cochinchine,* 99.

117. CAOM, INDO RSC 269, le Délégué de SM a l'Enseignment Traditionnel, Rapport annuel 1933–34: Enseignement Traditionnel Renové, 19.

118. Porée and Maspéro, *Moeurs et coutumes des Khmers,* 183.

119. Iukanthor *Destin d'Empire,* 131.

120. CAOM, INDO RSC 269, Chef Local du Service de l'Enseigenement to RSC, 20 September 1933.

121. Iukanthor, *Destin d'empire,* 131. Iukanthor cites a letter from Pannetier in Phnom Penh, dated 18 January 1934.

122. CAOM, INDO RSC 269, Louis Manipaud to M. Richomme, Phnom Penh, 31 January 1934, 1–2, Arrêté of 14 February 1934. AOM, INDO GGI 1579, RSC Arrêté, 15 November 1904.

123. "Demande de crédit, pour la construction d'Écoles de Pagode à Phnom Penh," *Le Khmer,* 28 December 1935, 2.

124. Dorsenne, *Sous le soleil des bonzes,* 147, 151, 196–197, 206, 210, 213.

125. Baumann, "Global Buddhism."

CHAPTER 8: HOLY TRINITY

1. "Le Cambodge, intérieur de temple bouddhiste"(Cliché Chevojon), in J. Trillat, *L'Exposition coloniale de Paris* (Paris: Librairie des Arts Decoratifs, 1931), plate 15.

2. Tath, *Kalyanamit roboh knom,* 43.

3. Dr. G. Montreuil-Strauss, "Suzanne Karpelès (1890–1968)," *Femmes Médecins* (Juin 1969), 203–211. I am very grateful to Marie-Paule Ha for sharing this article with me.

4. NAC, RSC 4182, untitled, n.d. typed manuscript, read in conjunction with a letter from Mlle Puech, Paris, to Karpelès, 26 February 1940, 1.

5. *BEFEO* 22 (1922): 444.

6. Jean Filliozat, "Suzanne Karpelès," *BEFEO* 56 (1969): 1–3.

7. Ibid., 2.

8. Dreyfus, *Le Cambodge économique,* 21.

9. Conversation with Anne Hansen, 28 March 2003. Hansen's comments were based on her extensive reading of EFEO documentation in Paris relating to Karpelès.

10. U Thitinyana, *Buddhism in France,* 1.

11. Rhys David Collection RDJ/22, Suzanne Karpelès, Lecture on Buddhist Studies in Laos and Cambodia, 1931, given at the International Congress of Orientalists, Leiden, 10 September 1931.

12. U Thitinyana, *Buddhism in France,* 1.

13. Teston and Percheron, *Indochine moderne,* 184.

14. Tath, *Kalyanamit,* 51–53. "From that time on," wrote Tath, "the ESP could organize the printing of Pali books for study and other books."

15. Ibid., 47.

16. The post was formalized in May 1925. Ibid., 53.

17. Victor Goloubew, "Nécrologie: In memoriam," *BEFEO* 35 (1935): 528.

18. Ibid., 48.

19. Ibid.

20. NAC, File 23609, Box 2791, Extrait au receuil des actes du Gouvernement Cambodgien (1920–1925), 50: Ordonnance Royale, 4 août 1924.

21. Filliozat, "Suzanne Karpelès," 1.

22. CAOM, INDO GGI 65502, RSC Report, First Trimester 1925, 17 April 1925, 5–6.

23. Goloubew, "Nécrologie: In memoriam," 528.

24. CAOM, INDO GGI 65539, Sûreté, Phnom Penh, "Sectes réligieuses au Cambodge," 20 July 1933, 2.

25. NAC, RSC 9089, Mme. S. Karpelès, Le Conservateur de la Bibliothèque royale, to M. le Chef du 2e Bureau de la Résidence Supérieure, 4 May 1926.

26. S. Karpelès, "Un episode du Ramayana siamois," Extrait des études asiatiques, publiées a l'occasion du 25e anniversaire de l'EFEO (Hanoi-Haiphong: Imprimerie d'Extrême-Orient, 1926), 315–316.

27. "Bibliothèque royale du Cambodge," *BEFEO* 30 (1930): 212. "École supérieure de pâli," *BEFEO* 35 (1935): 464.

28. "École supérieure de pâli," *BEFEO* 35 (1935): 464. Three "years later, a Lao edition was published by the Buddhist Institute.

29. Louis Finot, "Maha Vimaladhamma," *BEFEO* 27 (1927): 523.

30. Teston and Percheron, *Indochine moderne,* 338.

31. "Bibliothèque Royale du Cambodge," *BEFEO* 30 (1930): 212.

32. NAC, RSC 26355, S. Karpelès, La Conservateur de la Bibliothèque Royale, to S.E. Monsieur le Ministre du Palais, 20 June 1928.

33. "Bibliothèque royale du Cambodge," *BEFEO* 30 (1930): 526.

34. Sylvain Lévi, *Indochine,* 197–198; Guy de Pourtalés, *Nous à qui rien n'appartient* (Paris: Flammarion, 1931), 113.

35. Sylvain Lévi, *Indochine* 197–198. The same year 9,500 readers visited the central library, which housed mostly European works.

36. De Pourtalès, *Nous à qui rien n'appartient,* 113.

37. Ibid.

38. Choum Mau, "Remise solenelle des dons à la Bibliothèque royale par la délégation de la province de Kompong Cham," *Kambuja Surya* 2, no. 3 (1928): 115.

39. Hansen, "Ways of the World," 104.

40. De Rotalier, *Commes les jours passent,* 252–253.

41. Jacobs, *Traditional Literature,* 75. The library subsequently recorded a number of Ngoy's ballads, some of which were published in *Kambuja Surya.*

42. Private communication with Jacques Népote, Phnom Penh, September 2004.

43. "Bibliothèque royale du Cambodge," *BEFEO* 27 (1927): 492.

44. "Sicdey koab prasae roboh neak srey kramom Karbeylaeh jie saka niyuk niy Preah Riec Banyalaay" (The goodness of Miss Karpelès, head of the Royal Library), *Nagaravatta,* 9 April 1938, 2; "Ompi Robam niw munti Preah Riec Banyalaay" (About the dance at the Royal Library), *Nagaravatta,* 22 January 1938, 1.

45. Letter from Finot to Norodom Phanuvong, *Kambuja Surya* 2, no. 4 (1928).

46. CAOM, INDO GGI 65547, "Illegible" to RSC.

47. "Ompi prasat borann niw srok kmae" (About ancient temples in Cambodia), *Kambuja Surya,* 5–9. See Jacobs, *Traditional Literature,* 214–217, for an index of the chief *chbap,* Jataka, folktales, and legends published in *Kambuja Suriya* during the protectorate. L. Finot, "Origine d'Angkor: Traduit en cambodgien par M. Choum Mau," *Kambuja Surya* 2, no. 3 (1928): 43–52; no. 4 103–114; no. 5; no. 6.

48. *Société anonyme d'édition et de publicité indochinoises: Les Éditions d'Extrême Asie: Extrait des statuts 1928* (Phnom Penh: Imp, S.E.K., n.d.), 1.

49. "Why You Should Read Srok Khmer," in *Srok Khmer,* no. 1 (July 1927), 1.

50. Ibid.; *Srok Khmer,* 29 December 1928, 1. The header lists annual subscription rates as 5 piastres, or 3 piastres for schools and temples.

51. The director was Sann Yuneerong, possibly the Oknya Sann who contributed poems, essays, and occasional editorials to the journal.

52. Iukanthor, *Au seuil du narthex khmère,* 419.

53. Mem Soth, "Athibay ompi kar mien proyaoc thom dal bandarie kmae deang-ah knie" (An article about the great benefit for all the Khmer people), *Kampuchea Bodemien,* 24 March 1931.

54. CAOM, FM INDO NF 578, GGI Pasquier, Secret note to the Minister of Colonies concerning the devolution of the Cambodian throne, 3 August 1927, 6.

55. CAOM, INDO GGI 65547, "Illegible" *(Signé Illisible),* Phnom Penh, 15 December 1927, to Résident Supérieur, 2, 5.

56. Ibid., 4.

57. Ghosh, *History of Cambodia,* 196.

58. Ibid.

59. CAOM, INDO GGI 65547, "Illegible," Phnom Penh, 15 December 1927, to RSC, 2, 5, 8–9.

60. NAC, RSC 23609, Box 2791, "Rapport d'Ensemble sur la religion Bouddhique au Cambodge," Ministre de l'Intérieur K. Chea, 28 June 1937, 13.

61. Ibid., Conseil des Ministres Édit Royal: Observance des règles Bouddhiques, 17 septembre 1929.

62. Marr, *Vietnamese Tradition on Trial,* 303–304, 306.

63. Ibid., 51–52.

64. CAOM, INDO GGI 65502, RSC Baudoin Rapport Politique, Troisième Trimestre, 28 November 1924, 3.

65. Bleackley, *A Tour in Southern Asia,* chap. 6, pp. 45–54.

66. The Phnom Penh court sentenced one of the villagers to death, four to life, others to hard labor, one juvenile to a penitentiary. There were five acquittals. "La suite de l'affaire Bardez," in *L'Indochine enchaînée,* no. 15 (1925/1926): 4; for a fuller treatment, see Chandler, "Assassination of *résident* Bardez," in Chandler, *Facing the Cambodian Past,* 139–158.

67. Duara, *Rescuing History from the Nation,* 99–110.

68. CAOM, INDO GGI 65547, Chief of Police, Cambodge, to RSC, 25 November 1927, 3.

69. CAOM, INDO GGI 65502, RSC to GGI, 3 June 1927.

70. Ibid.

71. Ibid., RSC to GGI, 1 October 1927.

72. CAOM, INDO GGI 65547, Chief of Police Cambodia to RSC, 25 November 1927, 3–4.

73. Ibid., RSC to GGI, 2 August 1930, 3.

74. Ibid., RSC to GGI, 2 August 1930, 3.

75. Ibid., Chief of Police to RSC, November 1927.

76. Ibid., RSC to GGI, 2 August 1930, 2.

77. Ibid., 3.

78. Ibid., 2.

79. Osborne, "Peasant Politics," 242.

80. "Sasanaa Kiw Dae luk loy Preahputsasanaa" (Cao Daism invades Buddhism), *Nagaravatta,* 4 June 1938, 1–2.

81. CAOM, INDO GGI 65547, "Illegible" to RSC, Phnom Penh, 15 December 1927, 2.

82. Khy Phanra, "Les origines du Caodaisme au Cambodge, 1926–1940," *Mondes Asiatiques* 3 (Automne 1975): 321.

83. CAOM INDO, GGI 65547, RSC to GGI, 2 August 1930, 3.

84. Kiernan, *How Pol Pot Came to Power,* 5–7.

85. CAOM, INDO GGI 65547, RSC to GGI, 2 August 1930, Confidential Report, 4.

86. Ibid.; CAOM, INDO GGI 65547, RSC to GGI, 9 January 1932, 1.

87. CAOM, INDO GGI 65547, RSC to GGI, 2 August 1930, 4.

88. The bankruptcies of Chinese rice traders in 1928–1929 may well have led a number of Chinese moneylenders to call in their debts.

89. CAOM, INDO GGI 65547, RSC to GGI, 2 August 1930, 5.

90. Ibid., 5–6.

91. Ibid., 5.

92. Colonel Duboc, *L'Indochine contemporaine* (Paris: Charles-Lavauzelle et Cie, 1932), 28–30.

93. CAOM, INDO GGI 65547, RSC to GGI, 2 August 1930, Confidential Report, 6.

94. Ibid., 6. In Phnom Penh, Le Van Bay staged a fund-raising benefit to finance a new Caodai temple. Caodaists in Svay Rieng constructed a new religious building under cover of night. See also CAOM, INDO GGI 65547, RSC Political Report, 1 April 1930, 1–2.

95. Ibid.

96. Ibid., 7. One suspect, named Chim, was arrested.

97. CAOM, INDO GGI 65547, RSC to GGI, 2 August 1930, Confidential Report, 8.

98. Ibid., RSC to GGI, 28 September 1930, 1–2.

99. Ibid., Réunion du Grand Conseil Économique, 9 December 1931, 1–2. "We are armed!" warned the RSC in December 1931, defining the protectorate's policy as "respecting the will of our protégé the king, who has prohibited Caodaism."

100. CAOM, INDO GGI 65547, RSC to GGI, 28 September 1930, 1–2.

101. Ibid.

102. CAOM, INDO RSC 227, Administrateur des Services Civils Siem Reap to RSC, 16 October 1930; Service de la Sûreté, Chief of Local Police, 29 March 1940; see also CAOM, INDO GGI 65547, Charles Desfrançois, Commissaire Spécial, to Chief of Local Police, Phnom Penh, 20 May 1931, 1–4. Non-Catholic Christian missionaries and evangelical groups, such as the Assemblies of God, were also kept under close surveillance. Although the Treaty of Protectorate of 1863 authorized only Catholics to teach and preach, the protectorate had pressured Monivong to issue a royal ordinance allowing French Protestants freedom to practice in 1930, presumably also in the belief that Protestant converts were preferable to communist converts.

103. CAOM, INDO GGI 65547, Avocat General Lafrique to Public Prosecutor at Court of Appeal, Saigon, 23 November 1931.

104. Ibid., RSC Political Report, June, 13 July 1932, 2. In October 1932, the RSC reported that Le Van Bay was campaigning to win over French public opinion via press campaigns in France, arguing for freedom of religion. See ibid., RSC Political Report, October 1932, 1.

105. Ibid., RSC to GGI, 9 January 1932, 1.

106. Ibid., Pujol, Chief of Police, to RSC, 9 June 1933.

107. Ibid., Inspector Pain to Commissaire Chef de la Section d'Information Politique, Phnom Penh, 18 August 1933.

108. Ibid., Political Report for October 1933, 14 November 1933, 1. The report referred to one girls' school and one boys' school with about thirty pupils each.

109. Ibid., M. Nadaud to Chief of Police, Phnom Penh, n.d.; Chief of Police, Phnom Penh, to RSC, 15 December 1933.

110. CAOM, INDO GGI 65453, Service de la Sûreté Protectorat du Cambodge, Rapport Annual d'Information Politique, 1 June 1934–31 May 1935, 33, 35.

111. CAOM, INDO GGI 65502, RSC Political Report for June 1936 and RSC Political Report for October 1936.

112. Dhammaduta: The Theravada Bhikkhu Sangha in Vietnam, http://www.quantrum.com.my/duta/vietnam.htm (accessed 8 April 2002).

113. Jean Filliozat, "Notice sur la vie et les travaux de M. George Coedès (1886–1969)," BEFEO 57 (1970): 2.

114. See, for example, Tath, "Tournée d'inspection dans les pagodes cambodgiennes du Sud-ouest de la Cochinchine," Kambuja Surya 2 (1929): 39–62; Tath, "Suite et fin," Kambuja Suriya 2, nos. 9 and 10. Srok Khmer 3, no. 27 (September 1929): 2.

115. NAC, RSC 23609, Box 2791, Ordonnance Royale No. 106, Institution d'une Commission chargée d'éditer le texte de la Triple-Corbeille.

116. Jean Filliozat, "Suzanne Karpelès," BEFEO 56 (1969): 1–3.

117. "Bibliothèque royale du Cambodge," *BEFEO* 30 (1930): 212.

118. *BEFEO* 30 (1930): 185; Teston and Percheron, *L'Indochine moderne*, 338.

119. Ibid.

120. *BEFEO* 30 (1930): 190. Becker, *When the War Was Over*, 55.

121. Becker, *When the War Was Over*, 55; Chandler, *Tragedy of Cambodian History*, 18.

122. Ghosh, *History of Cambodia*, 198–199.

123. R. Meyer, *Indochine française*, 33; Teston and Percheron, *Indochine moderne*, 338–339.

124. "Rapport du Secrétaire de l'Institut," *BEFEO* 31 (1931): 337–338.

125. Ibid.

126. Marquet, *La France mondiale au XXe siècle*, 157.

127. "Rapport du Secretaire de l'Institut," *BEFEO* 31 (1931): 337–338; 2,500 piastres were raised towards printing costs. "Discours du venerable Nath, representant du clergé cambodgien," *BEFEO* 31(1931): 339–340.

128. NAC, RSC 23608, Suzanne Karpelès le Secretaire de l'Institut Bouddhique à M. le Gouverneur de la Cochinchine, 28 septembre 1932.

129. "Discours du Résident Supérieur," *BEFEO* 31 (1931): 336–337. Résident Supérieur Bosc applauded her dedication, her "fervent zeal, her tireless energy, a profound knowledge of Oriental scholarship."

130. "Discours du venerable Nath, representant du clergé cambodgien," *BEFEO* 31 (1931): 339–340.

131. Khing, *Écrivains et expressions littéraires du Cambodge au XXème siècle*, 55; Jacobs, *Traditional Literature of Cambodia*, 76–77. Gnok Them (1903–1974), who had completed a monastic education in his native Battambang and Pali studies in Thailand, returned to Phnom Penh from Bangkok to work for the Tripitaka Commission.

132. "Discours du venerable Nath, représentant du clergé cambodgien," *BEFEO* 31 (1931): 339–340.

133. "Ompi bahphum trey-bi-ta-ka" (About printing the Tripitaka), *Srok Khmer*, 21 August 1931, 1.

134. "Le voyage ministeriel en Extrême-Orient," *l'Illustration*, 21 November 1931, 364.

135. Makhali Phal, *Chant de Paix: Poème au peuple khmèr pour saluer l'édition cambodgienne du Vinaya Pitaka, la première corbeille du canon Bouddhique* (Song of Peace: Poem to the Khmer people to salute the first Cambodian edition of the Vinaya Pitaka, the First Basket of the Buddhist canon) (Phnom Penh: Institut bouddhique, n.d, ca. 1932). The dedication appears on the frontispiece.

136. CAOM, INDO RSC 321, Annual Report of Résident of Siem Reap (1 June 1931–31 May 1932), 3, 13.

137. CAOM, INDO GGI 65539, Sûreté Phnom Penh, "Sectes Religieuses du Cambodge," 20 July 1933, 2.

138. "École supérieure de pâli," *BEFEO* 35 (1935): 463.

139. Marcello Zago, "Contemporary Khmer Buddhism," in H. Dumoulin, ed., *Buddhism in the Modern World* (New York: Collier Macmillan, 1975), 109–119.

140. The "Thommakay" sect that emerged in 1920s and 1930s Cambodge should not be confused with its Thai namesake, the Thammakay or Dhammakaya sect, now

based at the Vat Pra Thammakaay temple near Bangkok and founded on the teachings and meditation methods of a former abbot, Sot Jantharaso (1884–1959), popularly known as Luang Phor Sot. Jackson, *Thai Buddhism, Legitimation and Conflict,* 199–221.

141. CAOM, FM INDO NF 577, RSC Sylvestre, Confidential Report to GGI no 499-SPK, Entitled *Voyage de SM Monivong dans les Provinces de son Royaume,* 18 July 1933, 2.

142. CAOM, INDO RSC 269, Résident of Kompong Thom, Rapport d'Ensemble for school year 1932–1933, Enseignement Traditionnel, 24–25. CAOM, INDO RSC 269, Annual Report 1933–1934, Enseignement Traditionnel renové, 18–19.

143. Coedès, "Dictionnaire cambodgien," BEFEO 38 (1938): 314–321; Kiernan, *How Pol Pot Came to Power,* 4.

144. Iukanthor, *Au seuil du narthex khmère,* 419, 428.

145. Ibid., 278; Iukanthor, *Destin d'empire,* 83–88.

146. Shils, "Intellectuals in the Political Development of the New States," 342–344.

147. Becker, *When the War Was Over,* 50–51. These "Khmer Krom" immigrants became the most ardent nationalists in subsequent years, favored by the CIA and Lon Nol's Khmer republic.

148. "Provatgar ney rieckarkmae" (History of the Khmer administration), *Nagaravatta,* 26 June 1937, 1–3, 2.

149. Chandler, *Tragedy of Cambodian History,* 18. Chandler suggests that Thanh was secretary of the Buddhist Institute, but this post was held by Karpelès until 1941.

150. Bunchan Mul, "The Umbrella War," in Kiernan and Boua, *Peasants and Politics,* 117–119. The red-boot army were the (French-sponsored) fighting soldiers who wore red bands around their stomachs and legs and red berets. The black-boot army wore black bands and black berets; their task was to look after the country "like police."

151. "Ompi sasana kiwdae" (About the Caodai religion), *Nagaravatta,* 29 May 1937, 1–3.

152. "Krong Kampucheathepdey," *Nagaravatta,* 18 September 1937, 2–3.

153. "Sasana Kiw Dae luk loy Preahputsasana" (Cao Daism invades Buddhism), *Nagaravatta,* 4 June 1938, 1–2.

154. *Nagaravatta,* 10 July 1937, 1.

155. "Boriya tngai siw Thommayuth ning Mohanikay" (Saturday report: Thommayuth and Mahanikay), *Nagaravatta,* 29 January 1938, 1.

156. "Secdey jun domning ompi put samakum" (News about the Buddhist Association), *Nagaravatta,* 21 January 1939, 1; "Secdey camraen niy puthika samakum" (The growth of the Buddhist Association) *Nagaravatta,* 29 July 1939, 1.

CHAPTER 9: TRAFFIC: SETTING KHMERISM IN MOTION, 1935–1945

1. Nou Hach, *Ma guirlande, mon amour* (Mala Duongcet), trans. Gérard Groussin (Paris: Cedoreck, 1988), 6, 12, 14. On Nou Hach's life, see Khing Hok Dy, "Notes de lecture," *Seksa Khmer* 6 (1983): 171–173.

2. For an original and comprehensive discussion of Khmer nationalist commentaries in the Indochinese French press of the 1930s, see C. Goscha, "Beyond the 'Colonizer' and the 'Colonized'" (paper presented at the Southeast Asia Studies Seminar Program, Yale Center for International and Area Studies, Yale University, 7 April 2004).

3. Brocheux, *Mekong Delta,* 179; Hall, *Youth of Vichy France,* 187.

4. Brocheux, *Mekong Delta,* 182.

5. Eric Jennings, *Vichy in the Tropics: Pétain's National Revolution in Madagascar, Guadeloupe and Indochina, 1940–1944* (Stanford, CA: Stanford University Press, 2002).

6. Jacques Lamasse, "Les mouvements de jeunes," *L'Avenir du Tonkin,* 10 April 1941, 3.

7. Muan, "Citing Angkor," 184–185.

8. See Malleret, *Le cinquantenaire de l'École française d'Extrême-Orient,* 32–37. Karpelès' name does not feature once in this tribute to the EFEO's achievements in Cambodge.

9. Falasca-Zamponi, *Fascist Spectacle;* Mosse, *Nationalization of the Masses,* passim.

10. Porée and Maspéro, *Moeurs et coutumes des Khmèrs,* 183. Anderson, *Imagined Communities,* 118–119; Cady, *History of Modern Burma,* 178–180.

11. Iukanthor, *Destin d'empire,* 128ff., re a letter he had received from the palace, 7 December 1934.

12. CAOM, INDO NF 568, GGI to Minister of Colonies, 3 October 1935; Direction politique 3. Bureau ministère de colonies to Iukanthor, 8 November 1935; CAOM, INDO NF 569, Deputy Director of the Marseille Colonial Department of the Ministry of Colonies to Princess Ping-Péang Yukanthor Institutrice Principale, H.Q de l'Enseignement Primaire en Indochine Paris (n.d.).

13. Correspondence between Iukanthor and M. Dominique Delhaye, Royalist Senator of Anjor, September 1927, reprinted in Iukanthor, *Destin d'empire,* 71–73.

14. Although Sûreté reports noted that the antimonarchist coup in Siam of 1932 had had no repercussions in Cambodia, the coup may have catalyzed this cleavage by encouraging frightened royalists to cling tighter to the raft of colonial power.

15. On the creation of a "national dress" for Cambodge, see Edwards, "Restyling Colonial Cambodia."

16. Such as the royalist and Francophile governor of Kampot Khim Tit, who was ranked as one of Cambodge's early nationalists by Son Ngoc Thanh; Kiernan, *How Pol Pot Came to Power,* 20–21, 50–51; Chandler, *Tragedy of Cambodian History.* Khim Tit was appointed defense minister 1945 and founded the National Union Party circa 1947. The Lycée Sisowath Alumni Association also supplied a core membership, including Sim Var and Nou Hach, to the Democratic Party established by Prince Sisowath Yuthevong in April 1946. See Chandler, *Tragedy of Cambodian History,* 30.

17. The arguments of "Khmervanich" and "I.K" were identified and analzyed by C. Goscha, "Beyond the 'Colonizer' and the 'Colonized'" (paper, Southest Asia Studies Seminar Program, Yale University, 7 April 2004); Khemerak Bottra, "Cambodge aux Cambodgiens et Cambodgiens pour le Cambodge," *La Presse Indochinoise,* no. 490 (18–19 August 1934): 6; Khmervanich, "A qui devrait appartenir le Cambodge?" *La Presse Indochinoise,* no. 491 (26 August 1934): 6.; I.K., "Réponse à l'aimable M. Vu Dinh Da: 'L'immigration annamite au Cambodge,'" *La Presse Indochinoise* (2 September 1937), 4.

18. Son Ngoc Thanh Papers, *Tale traitre: Sihanouk et un simple cambodgien libre (Khmer-Sérei): Lequel des deux est traitre à la Nation Khmère?,* 1 (n.d.)

19. Pach Choeun, "Secdey jun damnong" (News announcement), *Nagaravatta* 7 (January 1939): 1–2.

20. Osborne, *Sihanouk,* 29–32. Suramarit allegedly enjoyed reading *Nagaravatta.* "Ompi kimnit roboh Nuon Sou" (About Nuon Sou's ideas), *Nagaravatta,* 30 July 1938, 1.

21. Occasional issues of *Nagaravatta* featured photographs of staff members, such as Pach Cheoun and Sim Var, informing readers that they would be coming soon to a province near them, selling *Nagaravatta*. See *Nagaravatta,* 18 September 1937, 1.

22. See Bunchan Mul, *Kuk Noyobay* (Phnom Penh, 1971); and "The Umbrella War of 1942," trans. in Kiernan and Boua, *Peasants and Politics in Kampuchea 1942–1981,* 116–117.

23. "Knom Svay Rieng" (I, Svay Rieng), *Nagaravatta,* 9 July 1938, 1–2.

24. CAOM, INDO GGI 65453, Service de la Sûreté, Rapport annuel d'information politique, 1 June 1934–31 May 1935, 3; Association amicale du personnel indigène des résidences du Cambodge, Procés-verbal de l'assemblée générale du 10 janvier 1932, 10.

25. Marr, *Vietnamese Tradition on Trial,* 45–49, 178–180; Zeldin, *History of French Passions,* 1075.

26. CAOM, INDO GGI 65453, Protectorat du Cambodge, Service de la Sûreté, Rapport annuel d'information politique, 1 June 1934–31 May 1935, 44–46; CAOM, INDO GGI 65502, RSC Rapport politique, Mai 1936, 6 June 1936, 1.

27. Sim Var, "Kar joapliengphesac ney krumsamakum jiet kemara niw kaet kracheh (Going to a party of the Khmer Nation Solidarity Group in Kratie), *Nagaravatta,* 4 February 1939, 2.

28. "Jietkmae kandae camraen daoy samakitho" (The Khmer race continues to progress through solidarity), *Nagaravatta,* 22 January 1938, 1.

29. "A Response to Achar Kuoy" (Piekchlay protnaa neak Achar Kuoy), *Nagaravatta,* 15 May 1937, 1.

30. "Nokor Vat jie dom tmaa thom thom" (Angkor Vat is a huge stone structure), *Nagaravatta,* 3 September 1938, 1–2.

31. Ibid.

32. Khemara Botraa (Son of the Khmers), "Sicdey klaac nyonyoet roboh jiet khemara" (The fearfulness of the Khmer nation), *Nagaravatta,* 12 February 1938, 2–3.

33. Guesdon, *Dictionnaire cambodgien-français, première partie,* 517.

34. Ibid., 1738–1739.

35. Stephen Heder and Judy Ledgerwood, "Introduction," in Heder and Ledgerwood, eds., *Propaganda, Politics and Violence in Cambodia,* 21.

36. See Edwards, "Time Travels," 258.

37. I am grateful to Jyoti Mohan of the University of Maryland for bringing this to my attention.

38. Khemara Botraa (Son of the Khmers), "The fearfulness of the Khmer nation," *Nagaravatta,* 12 February 1938, 2–3.

39. "Yeung baan tutuel sambot mouy chbap bi neakmeulkasaet yeung mouy krum niw kompong cham douc mien kaangkraoy nih" (We've received the following letter from a group of our readers in Kompong Cham), *Nagaravatta,* 17 December 1938, 1–3.

40. "Satmeeomciw plicjiet kamnaet kluen" (The whole family's forgotten their birthrace) *Nagaravatta,* 10 September 1938, 1.

41. D.V.C., "Le théâtre cambodgien vu par un Annamite!" *Le Khmer,* 11 January 1936, 2.

42. Taukey Kuem, "Dear Editors," *Nagaravatta,* 8 June 1940, 1.

43. Taukey Kuem, "Part Two," *Nagaravatta,* 15 June 1940, 4.

44. CAOM, INDO GGI 65415, Traduction résumé "La rumeur publique" (Pikey Cacamaraom), 20 July 1940.

45. "Ompi lkaon kmae" (About Khmer theater), *Nagaravatta,* 14 August 1940, 1, 2.

46. "Ompi vittyu niw preahreach banyalay niw Pnum Pen" (About the radio at the Royal Library in Phnom Penh), *Nagaravatta,* 12 June 1937, 1.

47. Yukanthor, *Au seuil du narthex khmère,* 419. (About the Radio at the Royal Library in Phnom Penh) *Nagaravatta,* 12 June 1937, 1.

48. "Bonhae-neakda" (Procession of the spirits), *Nagaravatta,* 19 February 1938, 1.

49. Ibid.

50. Kmae Botra (Khmer son), "Secdey klaac nyonyoet roboh kmae" (The fear of Khmers), *Nagaravatta,* 19 March 1938, 1–2.

51. "Sambot muoy chbap bi kompongcham" (Letter from Kompong Cham), *Nagaravatta,* 17 December 1938, 1–3.

52. 'Haet-away baan-chie kmae kraa?' (Why are khmers poor?), *Nagaravatta,* 27 March 1937, 1.

53. "Education is the strength of the nation" (Pol-seksaa jie kamlang-roboh-jiet), *Nagaravatta* 1, no. 23 (Saturday, 5 June 1937): 1.

54. Chandler makes this important point with reference to the youth groups that emerged in Cambodge during the 1940s. See Chandler, *History of Cambodia,* 165.

55. Sim Var, "Kar joapliengphesac ney krumsamakum jiet kemara niw kaet kracheh (Going to a party of the Khmer Nation Solidarity Group in Kratie), *Nagaravatta,* 4 February 1939, 2.

56. Association amicale du personnel indigène des résidences du Cambodge, "Procés-verbal de l'assemblée générale du 15 janvier 1933," 7, and Association amicale personnel indochinois des résidence du Cambodge, "Procés-verbal de l'assemblée générale du 19 février 1938," 17, cited in Goscha, *Vietnam or Indochina?* 29–30.

57. Ibid.

58. Johnson, *Modern Times,* 145–146.

59. Goscha, "Beyond the 'Colonizer' and the 'Colonized'" (paper, Southest Asia Studies Seminar Program, Yale University, 7 April 2004): "'Organization,' 'unity,' and 'solidarity' became the buzzwords in the press in 1919 and 1920, on the lips of every nationalist and dominating the titles of their editorials."

60. Pukkrum Kayritti (The scout group), "Krum Kayritti niw Krong Kampuchea" (The scout group in Cambodia), *Nagaravatta,* 11 June 1938, 2–3.

61. Brocheux, *Mekong Delta,* 179, W. D. Hall, *Youth of Vichy France,* 187.

62. CAOM, INDO GGI 65453, Service de la Sûreté, Rapport annuel d'information politique, 1 June 1934–31 May 1935, 3.

63. *Nagaravatta,* 20 March 1937, 1; "Krum Kayritti niw Srok Kambujie" (The Scout Group in Cambodia), *Nagaravatta,* 11 June 1938, 1; "Yeung baan tutuel sombot tvay preahporchaymonkul mouy ombi pukkrumkayrithi doucmien secdaykaankraom nih" (We have received the following letter of blessing about the Scout Group), *Nagaravatta,* 24 April 1937, 1–2. The language used in this letter indicates that the author is royalty.

64. Ploang Dei, "Yuvsalaa" (Youth hostels), *Nagaravatta,* 24 December 1938, 2.

65. Monsieur le President du Yuvsala, "Yuvsalaa" (Youth hostels), *Nagaravatta,* 10 September 1938.

66. Dei, "Yuvsalaa," *Nagaravatta,* 24 December 1938, 2.

67. "Pithhi caekrongvan a'thik-a—thom dal seh Sala Pali Joankpueh," (Magnificent prize-giving ceremony for the students of the École supérieure de Pali) *Nagaravatta* 14

(March 1942): 1–2; Népote and Khing, "Literature and Society in Modern Cambodia," 55; Jacobs, *The Traditional Literature of Cambodia,* 76–77.

68. Khing *Écrivains et expressions littéraires,* 32, 51–53.

69. "Une irréparable faute politique," *Le Khmer,* 18 May 1936, 1.

70. Stephen Heder, "The Khmer Krom Reaction to Its Decline," 2–3; Anderson, *Imagined Communities,* 128–129.

71. "Une irréparable faute politique," 1.

72. Incident as remembered by Nou Hach's widow, Rem Tan, and son Vinit Nou, interviewed together with son Voravid Nou, 3 March 1998, Sydney. "Une irréparable faute politique," 1.

73. CAOM, FM INDO NF577, Marius Moutet to the Direction des Affaires Politiques, Cabinet du Ministre, Minister of Colonies, Note No. 932, 25 June 1936.

74. CAOM, INDO GGI 65502, RSC Rapport politique Mai 1936, 6 June 1936, 1.

75. "Provatgar ney rieckarkmae" (History of the Khmer administration), *Nagaravatta,* 26 June 1937, 1–3. "Krum samakum sessanuseh cah knong sala bangrien kouleeh ru lisee preah sisowath" (The friendship association of former students of the Collège or Lycée Sisowath), *Nagaravatta* 6 March 1937, 1.

76. CAOM, INDO GGI 65453, Service de la Sûreté, Rapport annuel d'information politique, 1 June 1934–31 May 1935, 3.

77. "Krum samakum sessanuseh cah knong sala bangrien kouleeh ru lisee preah sisowath" (Association of old students from the School, Collège or Lycée Sisowath), *Nagaravatta,* 6 March 1937, 1.

78. "Provatgar ney rieckarkmae," *Nagaravatta,* 26 June 1937, 1–3.

79. "Ompi Damnae bi Pnumpenh tiw leeng Poothisat niy Krum jumnum 'Puk mit cah niy sala sisowath'" (About the journey by the Sisowath Alumni Association to Pursat), *Nagaravatta,* 22 May 1937, 1.

80. Ibid., 2.

81. "Bonn samphooth keehstan kanlaeng samakum pukmuntry niw siemreap" (Opening ceremony for the Ministers Club of Siem Reap), *Nagaravatta,* 7 August 1937, 2.

82. "Komnut kat haet ney krumsamakimit kaljumnum bi tngai bi deesem 1938" (Report of the meeting of the Solidarity Association on 2 December 1938), *Nagaravatta,* 24 December 1938, 1–2. The venerable Moni-ou, chief of Vat Svay Popae, had offered great support to friends and alumni of the Lycée Sisowath as well as a monk named Sajun, a skilled healer, who had offered 20 percent discount on consultations to all members of the alumni association.

83. "Jietkmae kandae camraen daoy samakitho" (The Khmer race continues to progress through solidarity), *Nagaravatta,* 22 January 1938, 1; 136 members attended the 1938 event.

84. "Secdae Jundamnang" (Announcement), *Nagaravatta,* 26 November 1938.

85. Ibid.

86. Brocheux, *Mekong Delta,* 182.

87. "Komnut kat haet ney krumsamakimitkaljumnum bi tngai bi deesem" 1938 (Report of the meeting of the Solidarity Association on 2 December 1938), *Nagaravatta,* 24 December 1938, 1–2.

88. Secdae dreeta haeyning soumtooh compueh dal sampounjiet kmae dael coul lieng (Delighted, but sorry to all those Khmer allies who showed up for the party), *Nagaravatta,* 10 December 1938, 1.

89. "Satmeeomciw plicjiet kamnaet kluen" (The whole family's forgotten their birthrace), *Nagaravatta,* 10 September 1938.

90. "Jietkmae kandae camraen daoy samakitho" (The Khmer race continues to progress through solidarity), *Nagaravatta,* 22 January 1938, 1. J. Népote and Khing Hoc Dy, *Samapheavi de Rim Kin* (Phnom Penh: Angkor, 2005), 7–11.

91. "Ompi Kar wenmitknie ney krumsamaki mitsehcau ney witilaysisowath" (Reunion of the AFALS), *Nagaravatta,* 12 February 1938, 1–2.

92. "Karsamdaengmitphiep hangcnet ney seh cah salaa sisowath" (Expression of close-knit friendship of Sisowath alumni), *Nagaravatta,* 2 April 1938, 1. Four busloads went to Bokor.

93. Achar Kuy, "Ompi robiep bangkaet samakum baan daoy ngiey" (How to set up associations easily), *Nagaravatta,* 17 July 1937, 1. Similar agricultural collectives, also called *krumsamaki,* were established during the People's Republic of Kampuchea in the 1980s. Eva Mysliwiec, *Punishing the Poor: The International Isolation of Kampuchea* (Oxford: Oxfam, 1987), 28. I am grateful to Sue Downie for drawing my attention to this parallel.

94. Sim Var, "Kar joapliengphesac ney krumsamakum jiet kemara niw kaet kracheh (Going to a party of the Khmer Nation Solidarity Group in Kratie), *Nagaravatta,* 4 February 1939, 2.

95. "Discours prononcé par M. le Résident Supérieur Thibaudeau" (21 octobre 1939), in *L'Inauguration de l'École pratique d'industrie à Phnom Penh, 21 octobre 1939* (Phnom Penh: Imprimerie Albert Portail, n.d.).

96. Goscha, "Beyond the 'Colonizer' and the 'Colonized'" (paper, Southest Asia Studies Seminar Program, Yale University, 7 April 2004).

97. Manipaud also presented a copy to Coedès, with his own penned dedication; National Library of Australia, Coedès 508. L. Manipaud, with Khem-Penn and Chin-Soth, *Cours de langue cambodgienne: Cours élémentaire* (publisher and date not listed in this copy).

98. Edward Brown, *Cochin-China and My Experience of It,* 20. A. Bouinais and A. Paulus, *L'Indochine française contemporaine,* 574–575. Pierre de la Brosse, "La territoire de Battambang: Notes économiques," *Revue Indochinoise,* 2nd semestre (1907): 1329.

99. See, for example, the Tonkin travelogue "Bi krong kampujie tiw dal Tongking" (From Cambodge to Tonkin), *Nagaravatta,* 17 July 1940, 1.

100. Anderson, *Imagined Communities,* 129–130.

101. Ibid., 114.

102. Private communication, with Han Sereykan, Sydney, 1998.

103. Kmae Botra, "Kmae pneak kluen-dongkluen ning baek pneik pleu haey niw?" (Have Khmers woken up, gained consciousness, and become enlightened yet or not?), *Nagaravatta,* 15 January 1938, 1–3.

104. "Khmer refuse to go far from their homes."

105. The novel relates the story of a young Thai-Khmer orphan seduced by M. Suon, the district chief posted to her native town of Sisophon. Suon is subsequently promoted and relocated to his hometown of Phnom Penh, whereafter his abandoned lover bears a son, Sophat, before dying of grief.

106. Anderson, *Imagined Communities,* 114, 129–130; Goscha, *Vietnam or Indochina?* See especially 13–95, 24–30, 33–36.

107. Anne Raffin, "The Integration of Difference in French Indochina during World War Two: Organizations and Ideology Concerning Youth," *Theory and Society* 31, no. 3 (2002): 121–140.

108. Agathe Larcher-Goscha, "Sports, colonialisme et identités nationales: premières approches du « corps à corps colonial » en Indochine (1918–1945)," in Nicolas Bancel, Daniel Denis, and Youssef Fates, *De l'Indochine à Algérie* (Paris : Éditions la Découverte, 2003), 27.

109. Ibid., 28.

110. Bancel, Denis, and Fates, "Introduction," in ibid., 7–8.

111. Marc Boyer, *L'invention du tourisme* (Paris: Gallimard, 1996), 103.

112. Ibid., 97, 100.

113. NAC, RSC 17380, RSC Thibaudeau—n.d.

114. NAC, RSC 4182, M. Dusserre-Telmont Alain, Saigon 9 mars 1940 to "Chers amis yuvasalistes."

115. NAC, RSC 4182 Karpelès, Phnom Penh, to J. Buhot, France, 5 novembre 1939.

116. NAC, RSC 17380 *Parmi les jeunes,* scenes II, III.

117. NAC, RSC 17380 Thibaudeau to Inspecteur de Police, Hanoi, 5 December 1939; 8 January 1940 GGI to RSC.

118. NAC, RSC 17380 Thibaudeau, SECRET to M. le Chef local des Services de Police, 7 December 1939.

119. NAC, RSC 17380 Sûreté to RSC, 16 janvier 1940.

120. NAC, RSC 17380 SK, President du Conseil de l'Administration, Auberges Cambodgiennes de la Jeunesse, to RSC, 2 February 1940.

121. Hall, *Youth of Vichy France,* 220–223.

122. Ibid., 219.

123. Amiral Decoux, "Preface," in Maurice Ducoroy, *Ma trahison en Indochine* (Paris: Les Éditions Internationales, 1949), 110. Goscha, *Vietnam or Indochina?* 80.

124. Hall, *Youth of Vichy France,* 15.

125. Teri Shaffer Yamada, "The Spirit Cult of Klang Moeung in Long Beach, California," paper presented at the Annual Meeting of the Association of Asian Studies, Washington DC, 27–30 March 1998; Pierre Andelle, "Folklore et légendes du Cambodge: Le génie Khléang-Muoeung," *Indochine Hebdomadaire Illustrée* 1, no. 11 (21 November 1940): 5–7.

126. Yamada, "Spirit Cult of Klang Moeung"; Andelle, "Folklore et légendes du Cambodge," 5–7. Klang Moeung is the center of a cult that continues to this day in Cambodia and Khmer communities overseas.

127. Dieter Brötel, "Imperialist Domination in Vietnam and Cambodia: A Long-Term View," in Wolfgang Mommsen and Osterhammel, eds., *Imperialism and After,* 176.

128. Brocheux, *Mekong Delta,* 182.

129. Ellen J. Hammer, "The Emergence of Vietnam" (unpublished ms, New York International Secretariat, Institute of Pacific Relations, June 1947), 5.

130. Muel-Dreyfus, *Vichy et l'éternel féminin* 283–285.

131. "Cambodge: Le Vice Amiral d'escadre Jean Decoux Gouverneur General d'Indochine rend visite au nouveau souverain," *L'avenir du Tonkin,* 5 Jne 1941, 1.

132. Ibid.

133. Goscha, *Vietnam or Indochina?* 80.

134. NLA, Coedès Collection, J. Decoux, "Discours de l'Amiral Decoux," in *Séance solennelle de rentrée de l'université Hanoi, le decembre 1940* (Hanoi: Imprimerie Trung-Bac Tan-Van, n.d. [1940]), 19, 20.

135. Ducoroy, *Ma trahison en Indochine,* 119.

136. "Rallye," *Servir,* no. 3 (February 1942): 27. In a hint of the factionalism that would dog Cambodian politics for decades, the author continued, "we will forge the clear and balanced future of our wishes through constant effort, a daily battle with ourselves and with others."

137. Capitaine Vaziaga, "Les écoles de cadres de jeunesse," *IHI,* 1 July 1943, 7–8.

138. "Kampuputra," *IHI* 1, no. 9 (7 November 1940): 7–8. Prince Yuthevong (1913–1947) wrote under this pen name in Khmer democratic journals from 1945 to 1946. However, it is unlikely he was the author of this article. At the time of publication, Yuthevong was studying at the Faculty of Sciences in Montpellier, France, where he was awarded a PhD in physical sciences in 1941. See Chandler, *Tragedy of Cambodian History,* 109; Corfield, *Khmers Stand Up,* 22.

139. "Le Vice Amiral d'escadre Jean Decoux Gouverneur General d'Indochine" (reprinted from *Ralliement*), in *L'avenir du Tonkin,* 18 March 1941, 1.

140. "Une manifestation populaire: Le Cambodge manifeste ses sentiments de loyalisme et de fidelité au Roi et à la France," *L'Echo du Cambodge,* 6 November 1940; see also "Le trois novembre a Phnom Penh," *IHI* 1, no. 11 (November 1940): III.

141. Baloo, editorial, *Servir,* 1 Dec 1941, 1.

142. See, for example, "Ompi karjuesjuel prasat boran kmae" (About the restoration of ancient Khmer temples), *Kampuchea,* 2 February 1943, 1.

143. "Cambodge," *BEFEO* 42 (1942): 223.

144. Interview du RSC Gaultier par Radio Saigon, *IHI* 4, no. 153 (5 August 1943): 13.

145. *Kampuchea,* 20 July 1944, 1; 2 Feb. 1945, 1.

146. Son Ngoc Thanh Papers, Channa 3, 25 July 1943, Son Ngoc Thanh, Tokyo, to Sin-You or Ros-Yoeun, Battambang.

147. CAOM, INDO RSC 464, GGI Arrêté, 3 July 1940, Article (1).

148. Baumann, "Global Buddhism."

149. Nicholas Tarling, *A Sudden Rampage,* 212–213.

150. Paul Mus Collection, Lyon: Notes du Résident Supérieur au Cambodge Thibaudeau, Phnom Penh, 21 août 1940. I am indebted to Christopher Goscha for sharing this and other materials from the papers of Paul Mus.

151. NAC, RSC 4182 Karpelès to her mother, 25 1 [January] 1940.

152. NAC, RSC 4182 SK to her mother, Sweden, 10 novembre 1939.

153. NAC, RSC 4182 SK to M. J. Buhot, France, 5 novembre 1929.

154. Paul Mus Collection, Lyon, G. Coedès to S.K., Hanoi, 15 March 1941.

155. Paul Mus Collection, Lyon, Notes de G. Coedès, 12 février 1941.

156. Paul Mus Collection, Lyon, Note de G. Coedès, No/D.C. 11/33 Confidentiel. Hanoi 9.4.41 Le Directeur de l'ÉFEO a M. le Directeur du Personnel Gt. Gl. Hanoi.

157. Paul Mus Collection, Lyon, Son Ngoc Thanh, to Mademoiselle Karpelès, 15 April 1947.

158. CAOM, INDO RSC 464, Desjardins to Secretary General of Buddhist Institute Dupont, 23 April 1943.

159. Ibid., RSC Gaultier to Dupont, Secretary General of Buddhist Institute, 22 June 1943, 6; J. Desjardins Chef du Service Local d'Information de la Propagande et de la Presse, to RSC, 25 April 1944, 1.

160. CAOM, INDO RSC 269, Résident of Pursat to RSC, 15 September 1932; L'inspecteur indigène de l'enseignement primaire, Kampot, 29 September 1932, *Au sujet de la substitution de caractères latins aux caractères cambodgiens.*

161. CAOM, INDO RSC 654 "Prolung Aksasastra" (Literary contest), *Kampuchea* 2 (6 March 1945): 1–2; *Kampuchea* 11 (14 Nov. 1944).

162. Kim Hak, *Kampuchea* (10 October 1944).

163. CAOM, INDO RSC 464, Report from Pierre Dupont to RSC, 1 September 1943.

164. *Kampuchea,* 11 January 1944. This indication of Thommayuth support for the romanization campaign perhaps stems from the sect's reputed disdain for the Khmer script as inferior to Pali or Thai.

165. CAOM, INDO RSC 303, Chef Local du Service de L'IPP, article on "Lexique Cambodgien Romanisé," 1 June 1944, for diffusion in *Radio Bulletin.*

166. Keyes, "Communist Revolution," 49; Chandler, *History of Cambodia,* 170.

167. CAOM, INDO RSC 464, Letter from RSC to Secretary General of Buddhist Institute, 18 December 1942.

168. Ibid., M. Desjardins Chef de la Service Local d'Information de la Propagande et de la Presse to RSC, 22 April 1943.

169. Ibid., RSC to Secretary General of the Buddhist Institute, 22 June 1943, 2, 3, 5, 8.

170. *Kampuchea,* 28 July 1941, 1.

171. CAOM, INDO RSC 464, M. Desjardins Chef de la Service Local d'Information de la Propagande et de la Presse to RSC, 22 April 1943, 3.

172. Ibid., Desjardins to Secretary General of the Buddhist Institute Dupont, 23 April 1943; RSC to Secretary General of the Buddhist Institute, 22 June 1943, 2, 3, 5, 8.

173. Harris, "Buddhism in Extremis."

174. Son Ngoc Thanh Papers, Son Ngoc Thanh, Letter from Tokyo, 22 February 1943.

175. Osborne, *Sihanouk,* 30–32.

176. Son Ngoc Thanh Papers, Channa 2, g., "Le parti nationaliste Khmer pour l'independence du Cambodge"; u.d. letter (circa September 1942) to Japanese emperor; Tokyo, Letters, 2, Son Ngoc Thanh, 26 April 1943.

177. "Prolung Aksasastra" (Literary contest), *Kampuchea,* 6 March 1945, 1–2.

178. CAOM, INDO RSC 303, Statuts Association Aymonier, 30 March 1944.

179. Ibid., Sûreté Intérieure Annexe à l'envoi, no. 54-IP du 8 janvier 1944.

180. Ibid., *Extrait du registre des délibérations* (n.d.), Association Aymonier, Extrait du Registre des Délibérations, 15 December 1943.

181. Becker, *When the War Was Over,* 68.

182. Jean-Pierre Gomane, "La jeunesse indochinoise française et "indigène" sous l'administration Decoux," in Nicolas Bancel, Daniel Denis, and Youssef Fates, eds., *De l'Indochine à l'Algérie* (Paris: Éditions la Découverte, 2003), 56.

183. Richer, *Histoire de la restauration,* 34.

184. Charles Meyer, *Derrière la sourière khmère* (Paris: Plon, 1971), 111–117.

185. Jean-Pierre Gomane, "La jeunesse indochinoise française et «indigène» sous l'administration Decoux," in Bancel, Denis, and Fates, *De l'Indochine à l'Algérie,* 56.

186. Goscha, "Beyond the 'Colonizer' and the 'Colonized'" (paper, Southeast Asia Studies Seminar Program, Yale University, 7 April 2004).

187. Paul Mus Collection, Lyon, Son Ngoc Thanh, Vence to Mademoiselle Karpelès, New Delhi, 15 April 1947.

188. NAC, RSC 9273. John Marston kindly brought this cartoon to my attention.

CHAPTER 10: PAST COLONIAL?

1. Ganguly, "Hierarchy and Its Discontents," 17.

2. Anita Callaway, "Sleight of Sight," Visiting Scholars Program, Centre for Cross-Cultural Research, Australian National University, 2001.

3. Khing Hoc Dy, "Le voyage de l'envoyé cambodgien Son Diêp à Paris en 1900," 378, 380.

4. Chandler, *Tragedy of Cambodian History,* 34.

5. Princess Ping-péang Yukanthor, "Les aspirations du Cambodge," *France-Asie Revue Mensuelle de Culture Franco-Asiatique,* no. 11 (15 February 1947): 34–36.

6. Frieson, "Sentimental Education," 14.

7. Claeys, *Angkor,* 1–5. "It is interesting to note that this king was a contemporary of our French sovereign Philip-Augustus," writes Claeys of Jayavarman VII.

8. Illustration to Nouth-Onn, "Les Rivals," in *Cambodge: Revue Illustrée Khmère,* no. 3 (July 1953): 49.

9. Heder, "Cambodia's Democratic Transition to Neoauthoritarianism," 425–429.

10. Kiernan, *How Pol Pot Came to Power,* 29–30; Chandler, *History of Cambodia,* 188, on Thiounn Mumm, 214, on Thiounn Thioenn; Chandler, *Tragedy of Cambodian History,* 53–55, 206–207, on Thiounn Mumm, and 52, 55, 206, 309, on Thiounn Prasith.

11. Norodom Sihanouk, *La monarchie cambodgienne,* 1.

12. "Bonleu jiet" (Light of the nation), *Tohsanaawiday Santephiep* (Peace Magazine) 1, no. 1 (1 August 1959), 22–23.

13. Harris, "Buddhism in Extremis," 13; Marcello Zago, "Contemporary Khmer Buddhism," in Dumoulin, ed., *Buddhism in the Modern World,* 112.

14. Ong Thoung Heoung, *J'ai cru aux Khmers rouges* (Paris: Buchet Chastel, 2004), 1.

15. Ibid., 18.

16. Ny Bunheang, "I here do swear," *Kambuja* 3, no. 33 (15 December 1967): 157; Fillieux, *Merveilleux Cambodge,* 178.

17. "Hymne National Khmer," *Cambodge Revue Illustrée Khmer,* 1 January 1954, 30–31; Office National du Tourisme, *Cambodia* 1, no. 2 (n.d.), 55.

18. San Sarin, "To Create in the Khmer Vision," *New Cambodge* 2, no. 12 (July 1971): 42–56.

19. San Sarin, "The Khmers and Their Independence Monument," *New Cambodge* 1, no. 8 (December 1970): 40.

20. "Phnom Penh," *Khmer Republic* 1, no. 3 (March 1972): 35.

21. Harris, "Buddhism in Extremis," 17.

22. "We Are Khmers," *Khmer Republic* 1 (September 1971): 25–29.

23. *Kmae Satiranaroat* (Khmer Republic) 1, no. 5 (14 September 1974): 3. General

Lon Nol, "De notre race" (Extrait du Centre d'Instruction des Forces Armées Nationales Khmères), in *Bulletin Mensuel edité par le Comité chargé de suivre l'évolution de l'esprit et des idées de la Republique Khmère,* issue no. 1 (December 1970).

24. David Chandler, Ben Kiernan, and Muy Hung Lim, *Early Phases of Liberation in Northwestern Cambodia,* 11.

25. "In one hand holding a gun, in the other hand a hoe, defending and building the motherland"; trans. John Marston, in J. Marston, "Khmer Rouge Songs" (unpublished MSS, 1990). This song is almost identical in parts to a popular song in the Chinese Cultural Revolution.

26. Chandler, "The Constitution of Democratic Kampuchea," 513.

27. Chandler, Kiernan, and Lim, *Early Phases of Liberation in Northwestern Cambodia,* 11.

28. Chandler, *Voices from S-21,* 40.

29. Hang Chansophea, "Stec Ganlan and Yay Deb: Worshipping Kings and Queens in Cambodia Today," in Marston and Guthrie, eds., *History, Buddhism, and New Religious Movements,* 113–126.

30. Ong Thong Heoung, *J'ai cru aux Khmers rouges,* 264.

GLOSSARY

Note: Fr = French, Kh = Khmer, P = Pali, S = Sanskrit, Th = Thai

achar (Kh). Lay preceptor; wise man; honorific for a former Buddhist monk

ajiste (Fr). Member of the Auberges de jeunesse

aksa (Kh). Writing, script

aksa chrieng (Kh). Oblique style of Khmer script

aksa mul (Kh). Rounded style of Khmer script

angkaa (Kh). (1) Organization; (2) in Democratic Kampuchea (1975–1978), used to refer to the regime

anitcang (Th; P *anicca*). Buddhist law of impermanence

apsara (Kh). Celestial nymph, heavenly dancer

arak-ta (Kh). Malignant spirit

Arrêté (Fr). Ministerial, government, or local decree

ashram (S *āsrama*). Hermitage or place of retreat for a religious group

atman (Kh; S *ātman,* self, soul; P *attā*). Soul, spirit

auberge de jeunesse (Fr). Youth hostel

Auberges de jeunesse (Fr). Youth hostel organization

bangsaa (Malay). Race, lineage

barang (Kh; Th *farang;* Hindustani *ferenghi*). French; European

bikkhu (Kh). Fully ordained monk, a member of the Buddhist *sangha*

bon-amnaac (Kh). Power, authority

bon-kathen (Kh). Kathen festival marking the end of the Buddhist lent

bon (Kh; P *punnya;* S *punya,* rendered as *punnya* (good) in the Saveros Pou transliteration system; Th *bun;* Burmese *phon;* note also possible linkages with Fr *bon* and English *boon*). Goodness; meritorious deed; rank, grade; promotion; festival; a kind of auspicious, purifying power or quality

bon-sak (Kh). Honor, merit, dignity, promotion, rank

borann (Kh). Ancient, old

botraa (Kh). Son

Brahma. The first god of the Hindu triad; the creator of the universe

Brahmin. Priest; one of the highest or priestly caste among the Hindus

Buddha (P, S). Awakened, thus the enlightened one who has attained nirvana; title for Gotama or Sakyamuni Buddha, the historical founder of Buddhism

cakkavattin (P). Universal monarch

Caodai. The Heavenly Way; a pan-denominational religious movement established in 1927 in southern Vietnam

chau-atthika (Kh). Abbot

chau-krum (Kh). Judge

chayya (Kh). Identity card of a *bikkhu*. Until the early twentieth century, *chayya* denoted an ordination record inscribed on a sliver of palm leaf that was then rolled up into a ball, set with glue, and threaded onto prayer beads.

chbap (Kh). law, norm, normative poem

congaï (Fr colonial usage in Indochina). Concubine

corvée (Fr). Forced labor

déclassé(e)s (Fr). Fallen ones; people who have dropped in social status

Deva (Kh; S *deva,* a shining one, a god). God, gods

devanagari (S town script of the gods). The character in which Sanskrit is usually written and printed

deva-raja (Kh, S). God-king; can also mean god(s) of kings

dhamma (P; S dharma; the Pali form is preferred by the Theravada school). "That which is right," thus the ordained duties; in Buddhism, the eternal law of the universe as discovered and preached by Gotama Buddha; the theory and practice of the Buddhist doctrine

Dhammapada (P). The most famous scripture in the Pali canon; the path or the way of the Buddha's dhamma

domboun (Kh). District, zone, area

écoles d'application (Fr). Teacher training schools

Exposition universelle (Fr). Universal exhibition; world's fair

Gotama (P; S Gautama). The Buddha, known to Theravadan Buddhists as Siddhatha Gotama (ca. 484–404 BCE) and to Mahayana Buddhists as Sākyamuni (sage of the Sakyans)

L'imaginaire français (Fr). Literally, the French imagination. Used here to denote a broad repertoire of cultural constructs associated in popular imaginings with French national and imperial identity

intérieur (Fr). Home, foyer; hinterland; interior

Jataka (S). A nativity. Birth stories of the Buddha, collected in a work of the Theravada canon, which narrate the lives of Gotama Buddha before he attained enlightenment

jiet (Kh; P *jati;* S *jata,* birth or rebirth). A group to which one belongs by birth; in the early- to mid-twentieth century, *jiet* came to denote race, nation, national

kamma (Kh; P *karma,* S *kharma,* act). The conception of the quality of actions whose benign or malign motivations and dimensions determine the future condition of all sentient beings

Kampuchea Kraom. Area of the lower Mekong delta in southern Vietnam that was once attached to the Khmer empire and was incorporated into Cochinchina

kathen-kanthake. Book about the Kathen ceremony

khemerah (Kh). Khmer

khlum (Kh). Monastic dress

Khmer Kraom (Kh). Ethnic Khmer living in Kampuchea Kraom

Khmèrophile (Fr colonial). An afficionado of Cambodge

khum (Kh). Commune

kinnari (Kh). Mythical creature half-woman, half-bird

kluen (Kh). Self

Kmae daem (Kh). Original Khmer (literally, Khmer before)

krama (Kh). Checkered cotton piece of cloth used as headscarf, loincloth, or sampot

kru (Kh). Teacher, guru

krum (Kh). Group

krum samaki (Kh). Solidarity group

kusala (Kh; *kusala*). Wholesome, skillful; morally wholesome or profitable

lama (Tibetan). Religious teacher in Tibet; hence "Lamaism"

lingam (S). The Hindu phallas, a symbol of Shiva

lkaon (Kh). Theater, performance

loques jaunes (Fr colonial). yellow rags; colonial epithet for monks

maha (Kh). Great. An honorific for monks and kings. *Maha* was used to denote the masses *(maha-jun)* in Democratic Kampuchea.

Maha Bodhi (Kh). The Great Bodhi, the tree under which Gotama attained enlightenment at Bodh Gaya in India. Maha Bodhi also became the namesake of the Sri Lankan Buddhist revival movement, centered on the Maha Bodhi temple at Bodh Gaya, which was allegedly built on the site of a cutting from the original Maha Bodhi tree.

Maha jat (Kh, pronounced *maha jiet;* see also *Mahavesantarajatak:* Th *Maha ch'at;* S *Mahat,* great, *jata,* born). The great nativity; one of the best-known and most popular of the Jataka, which tells the story of how Buddha Gotama gave away his child, wife, and elephant

mahaksat (Kh; Th *maha'kesat*). King

Maitreya (S; P *metteya*). Loving One, last of the five great bodhisattvas and the future Buddha to come

Mahanikay (Kh). "The Great Division (Sect)," the older and larger of the two official orders of Theravada Buddhism in Cambodia

Mahanikay-cah (Kh). Old Mahanikay, term used by reformists to describe those with a more traditional orientation in the Mahanikay

Mahanikay-tmae (Kh). New Mahanikay term coined in the 1920s or 1930s to denote the reformist school of monks within the Mahanikay. This sect was also known as the Thommakay.

Mahant. Hindu chief priest

Mahavesantarajatak (P; pronounced *mahavasanta jietok* in Khmer). A very popular Jataka tale. See also *Maha jat*

Mahayana (S great vehicle or path). The northern schools of Buddhism now found in China, Vietnam, Japan, Korea, Mongolia, and Tibet that seek enlightenment for all humanity, embrace many methods for attaining it, and identify with Sanskrit as opposed to Pali script and scriptures

mandala (S). (1) Symbolic representation of the universe as perceived in Buddhist cosmology. (2) A model used by Stanley Tambiah and other scholars to conceptualize the configuration of political power in Theravada Southeast Asia, whereby different polities are connected to a symbolic center

mattophum (Kh). Motherland

mee-kon (Kh). Chief Buddhist monk of a province

métis (m.), *métisse* (f.) (Fr). Person of mixed descent

Métropole (Fr). The metropole; in colonial contexts, used to refer to France

mission civilisatrice (Fr). Civilizing mission

naga (Kh). A divine serpent; mythical serpent, often with seven or nine cobra heads, and protective powers

Nagaravatta (S *nagaran,* town, temple). Angkor Vat; also the name of a Khmer newspaper, 1936–1941

neak (Kh). Classifier for person

neak-cheh-doeng (Kh). Intellectual, savant; person with knowledge and know-how

neak-mien-bon (Kh). Person who has merit

neak mien sak samboat (Kh). Person who has both merit and riches

neak-sel (Kh). Person of virtue. (P and S *sīla:* precept, moral practice, moral conduct, moral principles)

neak-ta (Kh). Spirit, tutelary god; ancestral spirit

Nikay (Kh; Th Nikai). an order of Theravada Buddhism

nirvana (S *nirvāna;* P *nibbana*). Salvation, the complete and permanent extinction of suffering; the only state in Buddhism that is eternal, or timeless

nokor (Kh; S *nagara*). City

nokor vat (Kh; S. *nagaravatta*). Temple city; Angkor Vat

obbareach (Kh). Heir apparent; crown prince

oknya (Kh). Noble; title traditionally bestowed by the king

ordonnance (F). Edict

paillote (F). Thatched hut of wood, matting, or bamboo, usually on stilts

Pali. Sacred language, derived from Sanskrit, in which the Pali canon is written

pannya (Kh). Wisdom; liberating insight into reality

patrimoine (Fr). Heritage, patrimony

phnom (Kh). Mountain, hill; toponym

piastre (Fr; Italian, *piastra,* a leaf of metal). A coin; unit of currency used in French colonies, also in Mexico

piesaa (Kh). Language

piesaa-jiet (Kh). National language

pnum (Kh). Village

prasat (Kh). Temple; tower

preah (Kh). Honorific used for monks, royalty; also for royal objects and holy scriptures

preah khan (Kh). Sacred sword, possession of which denotes true kingship

preah sokhun (Kh). Chief of the Thommayuth sect

priy (Kh). Forest; wild

pteah lveeng (Kh). Narrow, storied brick buildings commonly known as "shop-houses." Similar structures appeared elsewhere in late-nineteenth-century urban Southeast Asia, where they were commonly associated with Chinese communities.

puc (Kh). Race

punnya. See *bon*

putthika samakum kampujie roat (Kh). Buddhist association of Cambodia

quoc ngu (Ch *guo-yu,* national language). Romanized script introduced by missionaries to Vietnam

Reamker (Kh). Cambodian version of the Ramayana

Résidence (Fr). Residence; offices of the protectorate in chief provincial towns

Résidence supérieure (Fr). the headquarters of the protectorate in Phnom Penh

Résident (Fr). Title of the protectorate's chief administrator in each province

Résident supérieur (Fr). Title of France's chief administrator in the protectorate

riel (Kh). Unit of currency

sah (Kh, root of *sasana*). Racial or religious group

sah-barang (Kh). Literally, Western race/religion; translated as "Christianity" in one nineteenth-century French–Khmer dictionary

sak (Kh; P *sakti*). Power

saksam (Kh). Power that is deserved

Sakyamuni. Mahayana Buddhist appellation for Siddhata Gotama

salaa (Kh; S *sāla*). (1) Shelter built along roadsides in most Cambodian villages and in temple grounds to offer shade and rest to travellers and pilgrims, and to house visitors and host ceremonies. (2) Short for *salaa-rien* (hall of study), school

samaki (Kh). solidarity, unity, togetherness

samdecpreah mahasangreac (Kh). Full honorific title for the supreme patriarch, chief of the Mahanikay

samdecpreah potvisal reac (Kh). Honorific title for particularly learned monks

samnar (Kh; P *sāmanera;* S *sramana,* renunciant). A novice who keeps the precepts but has not yet achieved full ordination to the rank of *bhikku*

samp'ea (Kh). Gesture of respect and greeting, with upright palms joined together

sampot (Kh). A length of cloth, commonly worn as an ankle-length, wraparound skirt for informal wear and in the house

sampot chong k'ben (Kh). An older style of wearing the *sampot,* still used on ceremonial occasions and worn by men and women with different variations, the *sampot* is pulled back between the legs and tucked into a waistband, forming baggy culottes.

sampot samloy (Kh). A more formal, stitched version of the *sampot* worn and tailored as a three-quarter-length or ankle-length skirt

samsak (Kh). Deserving of power

samsara (Kh). Universal cycle of birth, death, and rebirth caused by ignorance and craving, and escaped only by achieving nirvana

sangha (Kh; P *sangha;* S *samgha*). Monastic community

sanghareach (Kh). Supreme patriarch and chief of the Mahanikay sect

sangkum (Kh). Society; a neologism probably coined in the 1930s

Sanskrit. Indo-European language in which the earliest religious texts of Vedic Hinduism were written, giving rise to many of the languages of Southeast Asia, as well as Pali *sasana* (Kh; P *sāsanā*). (1) Buddhist teaching; a term used to denote Buddhism as a religion. (2) In nineteenth- and early-twentieth-century Cambodia, the word was also used to denote race. (3) With qualifiers, it is used to denote other non-Buddhist religions.

sasana pritikirya (Kh). Democratic Kampuchea term meaning reactionary religion

satra (Kh; S *sutra,* P *sutta*). (1) Thread used to tie beads, thus Buddhist scripture as derived from Gotama Buddha's teachings, usually dealing with doctrine; (2) used to denote ancient palm-leaf manuscript, as distinct from modern books or print media

sdic (Kh). King

Shiva. The destroyer Shiva, god from the Hindu triad whose destructive powers transform reality into novel forms

siwpiw (Kh). Modern book, as distinct from a *satra* or *chbap*

som sul (Kh). Ask for the precepts

sot (Kh). Pure

spean (Kh). Bridge

srok (Kh). District

stupa (S *stûpa*). Domed monument or tumulus containing relics of Buddhist saints, royalty

Surêté (Fr). Criminal investigation department; colonial police

surya (Kh). Sun

Theravada (P, doctrine or path of the elders). The "Southern school" of Buddhism—preserved in Ceylon/Sri Lanka and predominant in Burma, Cambodia, Thailand, and Laos—that is based on the teaching of the Pali canon

Thevada (Kh; S *devada*). Celestial being; a generic female divinity who communicates between heaven and earth

Thommakay (Kh). Dhamma-ist: the reform school of Buddhist monks

Thommayuth (Kh). Literally, "those adhering strongly to the Dhamma"; one of the two official orders of Theravada Buddhism in Cambodia, modelled after the Thammayuth in Siam

tngai sul (Kh). Holy day

Traiphum (Th). Map of the Three Worlds

Tripitaka (S; Kh *trae-bee-tok;* P *tipitaka*). Literally, three baskets: the earliest collection of Buddhist texts. Relating to Buddha's teachings, monasticism, and scholasticism, they are also known as the Pali canon. These have become the canonical Theravada scriptures and incorporate the Vinayapitaka (the rules and precepts governing monastic life), the Suttapitaka (discourses of the Buddha on the doctrine [Dhamma]), and the Abidhammapitaka (scholarly treatises analyzing material taken from the *suttas*).

uesaa (Kh; S *vassa*). Rainy season, the Buddhist Lent

Vat Botum Vaddey. The chief Thommayuth temple in Cambodia

Vat Preah Keo. Thommayuth temple in the grounds of the Royal Palace

Vat Ounaloum. The chief Mahanikay temple in Cambodia

Vat Pnum (literally, temple toponym). The toponym, with temple and stupas, that is Phnom Penh's oldest landmark

viel men (Kh). Field north of the Royal Palace in Phnom Penh, used for ritual ceremonies

Vinaya (Kh, S, P). The code of monastic discipline as set down in the Vinayapitaka. See Tripitaka.

Vinaya Paade'mook (Kh). Writings on the Vinaya, title of a book

Vipassanā (P, literally, insight, intuitive vision). Insight meditation, a form of meditation aiming for liberating insight into reality, also used for Satipatthāna, the Theravada system of developing "right mindfulness"

Vishnu (S). The Preserver. Embodiment of the cosmic principle that holds reality in existence, Vishnu is one of the trinity of gods (together with Brahma and Shiva) in the basic pantheon of Hinduism as developed in the Vedic literature.

yeak (Kh; S *yaksa;* P *yakkha,* genie, demon). Giant, devil; derogatory Khmer term for Europeans in the colonial period

yeung (Kh). We, our

yuon (Kh). Derogatory term for Vietnamese

yuvan (Kh). Youth

zhishifenzi (Chinese). Intellectual

BIBLIOGRAPHY

PRINCIPAL ARCHIVES AND LIBRARIES VISITED

ACCIM   Archives de la Chambre de Commerce et d'Industrie (Marseille)
CAOM   Centre des Archives d'Outre-Mer (Aix-en-Provence)
CARAN   Centre d'acceuil et de recherche des Archives Nationales (Paris)
FPM   Fonds provençaux (Marseille)
NAC   National Archives of Cambodia, Phnom Penh
NLA   National Library of Australia. Of especial value here are the George Coedès and the Gordon Hannington Luce Collections.
NLA/MS   NLA, Manuscripts Collection
OIORC   Oriental and India Office Records Collection, British Library (London)
UHRC   Universities Historical Research Centre, Yangon, Myanmar

ADDITIONAL LIBRARIES VISITED

Bibliothèque Municipale, Marseille
Bibliothèque Nationale, Paris
Fisher Research Library, Sydney
Library of the Centre Culturel Français, Phnom Penh
Library of the EFEO, Vat Ounaloum, Phnom Penh
Library of the National Museum, Phnom Penh
Menzies Library, Australian National University, Canberra
Monash University Library, Clayton, Victoria
National Library of Cambodia, Phnom Penh

PRINCIPAL WORKS CONSULTED

Age of Angkor: Treasures from the National Museum of Cambodia. Canberra: Australian National Gallery, 1992.

Agostini, Jules. *Au Cambodge.* Paris: Plon Nourrit, 1898.

Ahmad, Aijaz. *In Theory: Classes, Nations, Literatures.* London: Verso, 1994.

Ajalbert, J. *Ces phénomènes, artisans de l'Empire.* Paris: Édouard Aubanel, 1941.

Ajalbert, Jean. *L'Indochine en peril.* Paris: Stock, 1906.

———. *Mauvaises débuts de la politique d'association.* Limoges: Imprimerie P. Dumont, 1906.

Alexander, Edward P. *Museums in Motion: An Introduction to the History and Function of Museums.* Nashville: AASLH Press, 1995.

Allen, Charles. *The Buddha and the Sahibs.* London: John Murray, 2002.

Alloula, Malek. *The Colonial Harem.* Minneapolis: University of Minnesota Press, 1995.

Ames, Michael M. *Cannibal Tours and Glass Boxes: The Anthropology of Museums.* Vancouver: University of British Columbia Press, 1992.

Anderson, Benedict. *Imagined Communities: The Origins and Spread of Nationalism.* London: Verso, 1991.

————. *Language and Power: Exploring Political Cultures in Indonesia.* Ithaca, NY: Cornell University Press, 1990.

————. *The Spectre of Comparisons: Nationalism, Southeast Asia and the World.* London: Verso, 1998.

Angkor et dix siècles d'art khmer. Exh. cat. Paris: Édition de la Réunion des musées nationaux, 1997.

Anthologie franco-indochinoise tome I. Hanoi: Imprimerie Mac-Dinh-Tu, 1928.

Arnaud, Adrien. *Exposition coloniale.* Marseille: Barlatier, 1919.

Artaud, Antonin. *Messages révolutionnaires.* Paris: Gallimard, 1971.

Atkinson, Jane, and Shelly Errington, eds. *Power and Difference: Gender in Island Southeast Asia.* Stanford, CA: Stanford University Press, 1990.

Axel, Brian K., ed. *From the Margins: Historical Anthropology and Its Futures.* Durham and London: Duke University Press, 2002.

Aymonier, E. *Le Cambodge: Tome I.* Paris: Ernest Leroux, 1901.

————. *Le Cambodge: Tome III. Le groupe de l'Angkor et leur histoire.* Paris: E. Leroux, 1904.

————. *Cours de Cambodgien.* Saigon, 1875.

————. *Dictionnaire franco–cambodgien.* Saigon, 1874.

————. *Dictionnaire khmer–français.* Saigon, 1878.

————. *Géographie du Cambodge.* Paris: E. Leroux, 1876.

————. *Textes khmers: Première série.* Saigon, 1878.

Barnett, Anthony. "Cambodia Will Never Disappear." *New Left Review* 180 (March/April 1990): 101–126.

Barthes, Roland. *Mythologies.* London: Vintage, 2000.

Baudel, Pierre R., ed. *Figures de l'Orientalisme en architecture.* Aix-en-Provence: Édisud, 1994.

Baumann, Martin. "Global Buddhism: Developmental Periods, Regional Histories, and a New Analytical Perspective." *The Journal of Global Buddhism* 2 (2001): 1–43. (www. globalbuddhism.org).

Becker, Elizabeth. *When the War Was Over: The Voices of Cambodia's Revolution and Its People.* New York: Simon and Schuster, 1986.

Benvenisti, Meron. *Sacred Landscape: The Buried History of the Holy Land since 1948.* Trans. Maxine Kaufman-Lacusta. Berkeley: University of California Press, 2002.

Beylié, Général L. de. *Les ruines d'Angkor: Notice illustrée de 16 gravures.* Paris: Ernest Leroux, 1909.

Bhabha, Homi. *The Location of Culture.* London: Routledge, 1994.

————. *The Nation and Narration.* London: Routledge, 1990.

Bizot, François. *Le figuier à cinq branches, recherche sur le bouddhisme khmer.* Paris: Publications EFEO, 1976.

Bleackley, Horace. *A Tour in Southern Asia (Indo-China, Malaya, Java, Sumatra and Ceylon 1925–1926).* London: Bodley Head, n.d.

Bond, George C., and Angela Gillian, eds. *Social Construction of the Past.* London: Routledge, 1994.

Bouillevaux, C.-E. *L'Annam et le Cambodge: Voyages et notices historiques.* Paris: Victor Palmé, 1874.

————. *Voyage dans L'Indo-Chine 1848–1856.* Paris: Librairie de Victor Palmé, 1858.

Bouinais and A. Paulus. *L'Indochine française contemporaine: Cochinchine, Cambodge, Tonkin, Annam.* Paris: Challamel Ainé, 1885.

———. *Le royaume du Cambodge.* Paris: Berger-Levrault, 1884.

Brocheux, P. *The Mekong Delta: Ecology, Economy and Revolution 1860–1960.* University of Wisconsin–Madison Center of Southeast Asian Studies, Monograph No. 12. 1995.

Brossard, P. *Colonies françaises: Asie.* Paris: E. Flammarion, n.d.; ca. 1905.

Brown, Edward. *Cochin-China and My Experience of It: A Seaman's Narrative of His Adventures and Sufferings during a Captivity among Chinese Pirates and afterwards during a Journey on Foot across That Country in the Years 1857–58.* London: Charles Westerton, 1861.

Burton, Antoinette. *The Burdens of History: British Feminists, Indian Women, and Imperial Culture, 1865–1915.* Chapel Hill: University of North Carolina Press, 1994.

Bussagli, Mario. *Oriental Architecture.* New York: Harry N. Abrams, n.d.

Cady, John. *A History of Modern Burma.* Ithaca, NY: Cornell University Press, 1958.

Carné, Louis de. *Travels in Indo-China and the French Empire.* Paris, 1872.

Carpeaux, Charles. *Les ruines d'Angkor.* Paris: A. Challamel, 1908.

Chafer, T., and A. Sackur, eds. *Promoting the Colonial Empire: Propaganda and Visions of Empire in France.* Basingstoke: Palgrave, 2002.

Chakrabarty, Dipesh. *Provincializing Europe: Postcolonial Thought and Historical Difference.* Princeton, NY: Princeton University Press, 2000.

Chandler, David P. *Brother Number One: A Political Biography of Pol Pot.* Boulder, CO: Westview Press, 1992.

———. *Facing the Cambodian Past: Selected Essays 1971–1994.* Chiang Mai: Silkworm Books, 1996.

———. "From 'Cambodge' to 'Kampuchea': State and Revolution in Cambodia, 1863–1979." *Thesis Eleven,* no. 50 (August 1997).

———. *A History of Cambodia.* Boulder, CO: Westview Press, 1983.

———. "Songs at the Edge of the Forest: Perceptions of Order in Three Cambodian Texts." In *Moral Order and the Question of Change: Essays on Southeast Asian Thought,* ed. David K. Wyatt and Alexander Woodside, 53–77. New Haven, CT: Yale University Southeast Asia Studies Monograph Series No. 24, 1982.

———. "The Tragedy of Cambodian History." *Pacific Affairs* 52, no. 3 (Fall 1979).

———. *The Tragedy of Cambodian History.* New Haven, CT: Yale, 1992.

———. *Voices from S-21: Terror and History in Pol Pot's Secret Prison.* Sydney: Allen and Unwin, 2000.

Chandler, David, Ben Kiernan, and Muy Hung Lim. *Early Phases of Liberation in Northwestern Cambodia: Conversations with Peang Sophi.* Clayton, Victoria: Monash University Centre of Southeast Asian Studies, 1976.

Chatterjee, Partha. *The Nation and Its Fragments: Colonial and Postcolonial Histories.* Princeton, NJ: Princeton University Press, 1993.

Claeys, Jean Yves. *Angkor.* Paris: Éditions Hoa-Qui, 1948.

Clancy-Smith, Julia, and Frances Gouda, eds. *Domesticating Empire: Race, Gender and Family Life in French and Dutch Colonialism.* Charlottesville: University of Virginia Press, 1998.

Clifford, James T. *Routes: Travel and Translation in the Late Twentieth Century.* Cambridge, MA, and London: Harvard University Press, 1997.

Coedès, George. *Les collections archéologiques du Musée national de Bangkok.* Paris and Brussells: Van Oest, 1928.

Cohn, Bernard. *Colonialism and Its Forms of Knowledge: The British in India.* Princeton, NJ: Princeton University Press, 1996.

Collard, P. *Cambodge et Cambodgiens: Metamorphose du royaume khmer par une methode française de protectorat.* Paris: Société d'éditions géographiques, maritimes et coloniales, 1925.

Coombs, Annie E. *Reinventing Africa: Museums, Material Culture and Popular Imagination in Late Victorian and Edwardian England.* New Haven, CT: Yale University Press, 1994.

Corfield, J. *The Khmers Stand Up.* Clayton, Victoria: Monash Asia Institute, Southeast Asia Working Paper No. 32, 1994.

———. *The Royal Family of Cambodia.* Khmer Language and Cultural Centre. 2nd ed. 1993.

Corporations cambodgiennes. *Les Corporations cambodgiennes.* Phnom Penh: Imprimerie Henry, 1942.

Dagens, Bruno. *Angkor: La forêt de pierre.* Paris: Gallimard, 1989.

Daguerches, Henri. *Le kilomètre 83.* Paris: Calman-Levy, 1913.

Damrong, Prince. *Miscellaneous Articles.* Bangkok: Siam Society, 1962.

Debré, J. *Cambodge: La revolution dans la forêt.* Paris: Flammarion, 1976.

Delaporte, Louis. *Voyage au Cambodge: L'architecture khmer.* Paris: Librairie Ch. Delagrave, 1880.

Democratic Kampuchea. "What Is the Virtue, the Quality, the Reality and the Responsibility of Democratic Kampuchea in the Past, Present and Future?" Unpublished paper. N.d.

Derrida, J., P. de Man, J. Hillis Miller, H. Bloom, and G. Hartman, eds. *Deconstruction and Criticism.* London: Routledge and Kegan Paul, 1979.

Dorsenne, Jean. *Sous le soleil des bonzes.* Paris: Éditions Émile-Paul Frères, 1934.

Doumer, Paul. *L'Indochine française (souvenirs): Nouvelle édition.* Paris: Librairie Vuibert, 1930.

Dreyfus, P. *Le Cambodge économique.* Paris: Giard et Brière, 1910.

Duara, Prasenjit. *Rescuing History from the Nation: Questioning Narratives of Modern China.* Chicago: Chicago University Press, 1995.

Ducoroy, Maurice. *Ma trahison en Indochine.* Paris: Les Éditions internationales, 1949.

Dumarçay, Jacques. *The Palaces of Southeast Asia: Architecture and Customs.* Trans. and ed. Michael Smithies. Singapore: Oxford University Press, 1991.

Dumoulin, H., ed. *Buddhism in the Modern World.* New York: Collier Books, 1976.

Duncan, Carol. *Civilizing Rituals: Inside Public Art Museums.* London: Routledge, 1995.

Duras, Marguerite. *Un barrage contre la Pacifique.* Paris: Éditions Gallimard, 1950.

Duras, Marguerite, and Xavière Gauthier. *Les parleuses.* Paris: Éditions de Minuit, 1974.

Durtain, L. *Dieux blancs, hommes jaunes.* Paris: Ernest Flammarion, 1930.

Ebihara, May. "Interrelations between Buddhism and Social Systems in Cambodian Peasant Culture." In *Anthropological Studies in Theravada Buddhism,* ed. Manning Nash. New Haven, CT: Yale University Southeast Asia Program Studies, 1966.

———. "Social Organization in Sixteenth and Seventeenth Century Cambodia." *Journal of Southeast Asian Studies* 15, no. 2 (September 1984): 280–295.

Edwards, Penny. "Half-Cast: Staging Race in British Burma." *Journal of Postcolonial Studies* 5, Issue 3 (November 2002): 279–293.

———. "Making a Religion of the Nation and Its Language: The French Protectorate and the Dhammakay, 1890–1945." In *History, Buddhism, and New Religious Movements in Cambodia,* ed. J. Marston and E. Guthrie, 63–85. Honolulu: University of Hawai'i Press, 2004.

———. "Mixed Metaphors: Other Mothers, Dangerous Daughters and the Rhetoric of Child Removal in Burma, Australia and Indochina." *Balayi: Culture, Law and Colonialism* 3, no. 6 (July 2004): 41–61.

———. "Propa-Gender: Marianne, Joan of Arc and the Export of French Gender Ideology to Cambodia." In *Promoting the Colonial Idea: Propaganda and Visions of Empire in France,* ed. T. Chafer and A. Sackur, 116–130. London: Macmillan, 2002.

———. "Relocating the Interlocutor: Taw Sein Ko (1864–1930) and the Itinerancy of Knowledge in British Burma." *South East Asia Research* 12, no. 3 (November 2004): 277–335.

———. "Restyling Colonial Cambodia (1860–1945): French Dressing, Indigenous Custom and National Costume." *Fashion Theory: The Journal of Dress, Body and Culture* 5, issue 4 (November 2001): 389–416.

———. "Taj Angkor: Enshrining l'Inde in le Cambodge." In *France, and "Indochina": Cultural Representations,* ed. Kathryn Robson and Jennifer Yee, 13–27. Lanham, MD: Lexington Books, 2005.

———. "Time Travels: Locating *Xinyimin* in Sino-Cambodian Histories." In *Globalizing Chinese Migration: Trends in Europe and Asia,* ed. P. Nyíri and I. Saveliev, 254–290. Burlington, Eng.: Ashgate Press, 2002.

———. "Womanizing Indochina: Fiction, Nation and Cohabitation in Colonial Cambodia, 1890–1930." In *Domesticating the Empire: Race, Gender and Family Life in French and Dutch Colonialism,* ed. J. Clancy-Smith and F. Gouda, 108–130. Charlottesville: University of Virginia Press, 1998.

———. "Cambodge: The Cultivation of a Nation, 1880–1945." PhD diss., Monash University, 1999.

Edwards, Penny, and Chan Sambath. "Ethnic Chinese in Cambodia." In *Interdisciplinary Research on Ethnic Groups in Cambodia: Final Reports,* ed. W. Collins, 109–175. Phnom Penh: Centre for Advanced Studies, 1997.

EFEO, *Chercheurs d'Asie.* Paris: EFEO, 2002.

Eickelmann, Dale F. *Knowledge and Power in Morocco: The Education of a Twentieth-Century Notable.* Princeton, NJ: Princeton University Press, 1985.

Empire colonial de la France: L'Indochine. Paris: Librairie coloniale Augustin Challamel, n.d.

Encyclopédie par l'image: Indochine française. Paris: Librairie Hachette, n.d.

Ennis, T. "The French Administration and Problems in Indochina." PhD diss., University of Minnesota, 1935.

Evans, Grant, and Kelvin Rowley. *Red Brotherhood at War: Vietnam, Cambodia and Laos since 1975.* London: Verso, 1990.

Falasca-Zamponi, Simonetta. *Fascist Spectacle: The Aesthetics of Power in Mussolini's Italy.* Berkeley: University of California Press, 1997.

Faraut, F. G. *Astronomie cambodgienne.* Phnom Penh, 1910.

Far Eastern Association of Tropical Medicine. *L'Indochine française: Receuil de notices rédigées* à l'occasion du Xe Congrès de la Far Eastern Association of Tropical Medicine Hanoi (Tonkin) 24–30 November 1938. Hanoi: Imprimerie G. Taupin and Co., 1938.

Faucheur, P. le. Lettre sur le Cambodge. Paris: Challamel Aîné, 1872.

Fernand, Nathan. L'Indochine. Paris, 1939.

Fillieux, C. Merveilleux Cambodge. Paris: Société continentale d'éditions modernes illustrées, 1962.

Filoz, N. Cambodge et Siam: Voyage et séjour aux ruines des monuments khmers. Paris: Librairie Gedalge, 1896.

Findling, J., and K. Perle, eds. Historical Dictionary of World's Fairs and Expositions 1851–1988. New York: Greenwood Press, 1990.

Florida, Nancy. Writing the Past, Inscribing the Future: History as Prophecy in Colonial Java. Durham, NC: Duke University Press, 1995.

Forest, Alain. Le Cambodge et la colonisation française: Histoire d'une colonisation sans heurts (1897–1920). Paris: l'Harmattan, 1980.

———. Le culte des génies protecteurs au Cambodge: Analyse et traduction d'un corpus des textes sur le Néakta. Paris: l'Harmattan, 1992.

Foucault, Michel. Power/Knowledge: Selected Interviews and Other Writings, 1972–1977. New York: Harvester Press, 1980.

Franck, Harry. East of Siam. New York: Century, 1926.

French, Lindsay. "Hierarchies of Value at Angkor Vat." Paper presented at the 96th Annual Meeting of the American Anthropological Association, Washington, DC, 1997.

Frieson, Kate. "Sentimental Education: Les sages femmes and Colonial Cambodia," 14. Paper presented at an international workshop on Gender and the Transmission of Values and Cultural Heritage(s) in South and Southeast Asia, Belle van Zuylen Institute, Amsterdam University, 23–24 May 2000.

Furnivall, J. Colonial Policy and Practice: A Comparative Study of Burma and Netherlands India. Cambridge: Cambridge University Press, 1948.

Gallocher, Pierre. Marseille: Zigzags dans le passé: IV. Marseille: P. Tacussel, 1995.

Ganguly, Debjani. "Hierarchy and Its Discontents." PhD thesis, Australian National University, Canberra, 2001.

Garnier, Francis. Voyage d'exploration en Indo-Chine. Paris: Librairie Hachette, 1885.

Garnier, Léon. Notice sur Francis Garnier. Paris: Imprimerie Émile Martinet, 1882.

Gas-Faucher, F. En sampan sur les lacs du Cambodge et à Angkor. Marseille: Typographie et Lithographie Barlatier, 1922.

Gastaldy, P. La Cochinchine. Saigon: Société des études indochinoises, 1931.

Geertz, Clifford. Available Light: Anthropological Reflections on Philosophical Topics. Princeton, NJ: Princeton University Press, 2000.

Gellner, Ernest. Encounters with Nationalism. Oxford: Blackwell, 1994.

Gerny-Marchal, Mary. Enthousiasmes recueillements et poèmes khmèrs. Paris, 1945.

Gervais-Courtellemont, Vandelet et al. L'Indochine. Paris: Librairie Firmin-Didot et Cie., n.d. [ca. 1902].

Ghosh, Manomohan. A History of Cambodia from the Earliest Times to the End of the French Protectorate. Calcutta: Oriental Book Agency, 1968.

Girardet, Raol. L'idée coloniale en France. Paris: La table ronde, 1972.

Girbat, P. P., et al. Les colonies françaises au début du XXe siècle: Cinq ans de progrès (1900–1905) Tome III. Marseille: Barlatier, 1906.

Goscha, Chistopher. Vietnam or Indochina? Contesting Concepts of Space in Vietnamese Nation-

alism 1887–1954. Copenhagen: Nordic Institute of Asian Studies, NIAS Report Series, No. 28, 1995.

Gouda, Frances. *Dutch Culture Overseas: Colonial Practice in the Netherlands Indies 1900–1942,* 194–236. Amsterdam: Amsterdam University Press, 1995.

Grauclaude, Henri le. *Le réveil du peuple Khmer: Notes en marge d'un voyage au Cambodge de M. Robin, Gouverneur Général de l'Indochine.* Hanoi: Éditions de la Presse populaire de l'Empire Annam, 1931.

Greenfield, Jeannette. *The Return of Cultural Treasures.* 2nd ed. Cambridge: Cambridge University Press, 1996.

Groslier, George. *Angkor.* Evieux: Imprimerie Ch. Herissey, n.d.

———. *Danseuses cambodgiennes anciennes et modernes.* Paris: Augustin Challamel, 1913.

———. *Eaux et lumières.* Paris: Société d'éditions géographiques, maritimes et coloniales, 1931.

———. *À l'ombre d'Angkor.* Paris: Augustin Challamel, 1916.

———. *Recherches sur les Cambodgiens.* Paris: Augustin Challamel, 1921.

———. *Le retour à l'Argile.* Paris: Éditions Émile-Paul Frères, 1929.

Guesdon, J. *Dictionnaire cambodgien–français, première partie.* Paris: Librairie Plon, 1930.

Hall, W. D. *The Youth of Vichy France.* Oxford: Clarendon Press, 1981.

Hammer, Ellen J. "The Emergence of Vietnam." Unpublished manuscript. New York International Secretariat, Institute of Pacific Relations. June 1947.

Hansen, Anne. "Khmer Identity and Theravada Buddhism." In *Cambodian Religion: New Studies,* ed. John Marston and Elizabeth Guthrie. Honolulu: Hawai'i University Press, 2004.

Hansen, Anne. "Religion and Identity in Turn-of-the-century Cambodia." Paper presented at the Annual Meeting of the Association of Asian Studies, Washington DC, March 1998.

———. "Ways of the World: Moral Discernment and Narrative Ethics in a Cambodian Buddhist Text." PhD diss., Harvard University, 1999. Honolulu: University of Hawai'i Press, forthcoming.

Harris, Ian. "Buddhism in Extremis." Unpublished paper, 12. Lancaster University, 1998; Since published in *Buddhism and Politics in Twentieth Century Asia,* ed. Ian Harris. London: Cassell, 1999.

———. *Cambodian Buddhism: History and Practice.* Honolulu: Hawai'i University Press, 2005.

Harry, Myriam. *L'Indochine.* Vincennes: Les arts graphiques, 1912.

Heder, Steve. "Cambodia's Democratic Transition to Neoauthoritarianism." *Current History,* December 1995, 425–429.

———. "The Khmer Krom Reaction to Its Decline and the Emergence of Son Ngoc Thanh." Unpublished MS, n.d.

Heder, Stephen, and Judy Ledgerwood, eds. *Propaganda, Politics and Violence in Cambodia: Democratic Transition under United Nations Peace-keeping.* New York: M. E. Sharpe, 1996.

Henrique, Louis, ed. *Les colonies françaises: III, colonies et protectorats de l'Indochine.* Paris: Maison Quantin, 1889.

Hervey, H. *Travels in Indochina.* London: Thornton Butterworth Ltd., 1928.

Herzfeld, M. *Cultural Intimacy: Social Poetics in the Nation State.* London: Routledge, 1997.

Hobsbawm, Eric. *Nations and Nationalism since 1780: Programme, Myth, Reality.* Cambridge: Cambridge University Press, 1994.

Hobsbawm, Eric, and Terence Ranger, eds. *The Invention of Tradition.* Cambridge: Cambridge University Press, 1983.

Hoffenberg, Peter. *An Empire on Display: English, Indian, and Australian Exhibitions from the Crystal Palace to the Great War.* Berkeley: University of California Press, 2001.

Hustvedt, Siri. *What I Loved.* London: Hodder and Stoughton, 2003.

Hutchinson, J. *The Dynamics of Cultural Nationalism.* London: Allen and Unwin, 1987.

Igout, Michel. *Phnom Penh: Then and Now.* Bangkok: White Lotus, 1993.

L'Illustration. Special issue. *L'Exposition coloniale internationale de Paris 1931.* Paris: L'Illustration, 1931.

Ishii, Yoneo. *Sangha, State and Society: Thai Buddhism in History.* Honolulu University of Hawai'i Press, 1986.

Iukanthor, Areno. *Destin d'empire.* Paris: Pierre Bossuet, 1935.

————. *Au seuil du narthex khmère: Boniments sur les conflits de deux points cardinaux.* Paris: Éditions d'Asie, 1931.

Jackson, Karl, ed. *Cambodia 1975–1978.* Princeton, NJ: Princeton University Press, 1989.

Jackson, Peter A. *Buddhadāsa: Theravada Buddhism and Modernist Reform in Thailand.* Chiangmai: Silkworm, 2003.

————. *Buddhism, Legitimation and Conflict: The Political Functions of Urban Thai Buddhism.* Singapore: Institute of Southeast Asian Studies, 1989.

Jacobs, Judith. "The Deliberate Use of Foreign Vocabulary by the Khmer: Changing Fashions, Methods and Sources." In *Context, Meaning and Power,* ed. Mark Hobart and Robert Taylor. Ithaca, NY: Cornell University Southeast Asia Program, 1986.

————. *The Traditional Literature of Cambodia.* Oxford: Oxford University Press, 1996.

Jamieson, Neil. *Understanding Vietnam.* Berkeley: University of California Press, 1995.

Jessup, H., and T. Zephir, eds. *Sculpture of Angkor and Ancient Cambodia: Millennium of Glory.* Exh. cat. Washington, DC: National Gallery of Art, 1997.

Johnson, Paul. *Modern Times: The World from the Twenties to the Eighties.* Rev. ed. New York: Harper Collins, 1991.

Kapferer, Bruce. *Legends of People, Myths of State: Violence, Intolerance and Political Culture in Sri Lanka and Australia.* Washington and London: Smithsonian Institution, 1988.

Karpelès, Suzanne. "'Un épisode du Ramayana Siamois': Extrait des Études Asiatiques, publiées a l'occasion du 25e anniversaire de l'EFEO." Hanoi-Haiphong: Imprimerie d' Extrême-Orient, 1926.

Keyes, Charles. "Towards a New Formulation of the Concept of Ethnic Group." *Ethnicity* 3 (1976): 203–213.

Keyes, Charles F., et al., eds. *Asian Visions of Authority: Religion and the Modern States of East and Southeast Asia.* Honolulu: University of Hawai'i Press, 1994.

Khieu, Samphan. *Cambodia's Economy and Industrial Development.* Trans. Laura Summer. Ithaca, NY: Cornell University Southeast Asia Program, Data Paper 111, 1979.

Khing, Hoc Dy. *Écrivains et expressions littéraires du Cambodge au XXème siècle.* Paris: L'Harmattan, 1993.

Kiernan, Ben. *How Pol Pot Came to Power.* London: Verso, 1985.

————. *The Pol Pot Regime: Race, Power and Genocide in Cambodia under the Khmer Rouge, 1975–1979*. New Haven, CT: Yale University Press, 1996.

Kiernan, Ben, and Chanthou Boua, eds. *Peasants and Politics in Kampuchea, 1942–1981*. London: Zed Press, 1982.

King, Anthony. *Urbanism, Colonialism and the World Economy: Cultural and Spatial Foundations of the World Urban System*. London: Routledge, 1989.

Kirsch, A. Thomas. "Modernizing Implications of Nineteenth Century Reforms in the Thai Sangha." In *Religion and Legitimation of Power in Thailand, Laos, and Burma*, ed. Bardwell L. Smith. Chambersburg, PA: ANIMA Books, 1978.

Knight, Stephen. *Robin Hood: A Complete Study of the English Outlaw*. Oxford: Blackwell, 1994.

Kohn, Hans. *The Idea of Nationalism*. New York: Macmillan, 1945.

Lagrillière-Beauclerc, E. *À travers L'Indochine*. Paris: Librairie Ch. Tallander, 1900.

Lajonquière, L. de. *Inventaire descriptif des monuments du Cambodge: Tome III*. Publications EFEO, 1911.

————. "Le voyage de l'envoyé Cambodgien Son Diêp à Paris en 1900." In *Récits de voyages asiatiques: Genres, mentalités, conceptions de l'espace*, ed. Claudine Salmon, 367–383. Paris: EFEO, 1996.

Lamant, Pierre. "La création d'une capitale par le pouvoir colonial: Phnom Penh." In *Péninsule indochinoise études urbains*, ed. P. B. Lafont. Paris: L'Harmattan, 1991.

Langlois, Walter G. *André Malraux: The Indochina Adventure*. New York: Praeger, 1966.

Leclère, Adhémard. *Le bouddhisme au Cambodge*. Paris: Ernest Leroux, 1899.

————. *Livres sacrés*. Paris: E. Leroux, 1906.

Leclère, Thierry, ed. *Les sourires d'Angkor*. Paris: Télérama, 1997.

Ledgerwood, Judy L. "Politics and Gender: Negotiating Conceptions of the Ideal Woman in Present Day Cambodia." *Asia Pacific Viewpoint* 37, no. 2 (August 1996): 139–152.

Lefebvre, Jean. *The Production of Space*. Oxford: Blackwell, 1991.

Lemire, Ch. *L'Indochine: Cochinchine française: Royaume de Cambodge, Royaume d'Annam et Tonkin*. Paris: Challamel Aîné, 1884.

Lester, Robert C. *Theravada Buddhism in Southeast Asia*. Ann Arbor: University of Michigan Press, 1973.

Lévi, Sylvain, ed. *Indochine*. Paris: Sociétés d'éditions géographiques, maritimes et coloniales, 1931.

Lévi-Strauss, Claude. *Structural Anthropology*. New York: Basic Books, 1963.

Lewis, N. *A Dragon Apparent: Travels in Cambodia, Laos and Vietnam*. London: Eland Books, 1982.

Locard, Henri. "The Khmer Rouge Gulag 17 April 1975–7 January 1979." Unpublished MS, 1995.

Lopez, Donald S., Jr. *Curators of the Buddha: The Study of Buddhism under Colonialism*. Chicago: University of Chicago Press, 1995.

Loti, Pierre. *Un pèlerin d'Angkor*. Paris: Calman-Lévy, 1912.

Lowenthal, David. *The Past Is a Foreign Country*. Cambridge: Cambridge University Press, 1985.

Malleret, Louis. *Le cinquantenaire de l'École française d'Extrême-Orient*. Paris: Boccard, 1953.

Malraux, André. *La voie royale*. Paris: Gallimard, 1930. [English ed. *The Royal Way*. New York: Harrison Smith and Robert Haas, 1935.]

Mannika, Eleanor. *Angkor Vat: Time, Space and Kingship*. Sydney: Allen and Unwin, 1997.

Marchal, Henri. *Le décor et la sculpture khmers*. Paris: Vanoest, 1951.

Marchal, S. *Costumes et parures khmèrs*. Paris and Brussells: Librairie Nationale d'art et d'histoire, 1927.

Marquet, J. *La France mondiale au XXe siècle, Indochine*. Paris: Delalain, 1931.

Marr, David. *Vietnamese Tradition on Trial, 1920–1945*. Berkeley: University of California Press, 1981.

———. *Vietnam 1945: The Quest for Power*. Berkeley: University of California Press, 1995.

Marston, John. "Cambodia 1991–94: Hierarchy, Neutrality and Etiquettes of Discourse." PhD diss., University of Washington, 1997.

———. "Khmer Rouge Songs." Unpublished MS, 1990.

Marston, J., and E. Guthrie, eds. *History, Buddhism, and New Religious Movements in Cambodia*. Honolulu: Hawai'i University Press, 2004.

Martin, Marie Alexandrine. *Cambodia: A Shattered Society*. Berkeley: University of California Press, 1994.

Maspéro, Georges, ed. *Un empire colonial français: L'Indochine française—L'Indochine économique, l'Indochine pittoresque*. Vol. 2. Paris: les éditions G. Van Oest, 1930.

———. *L'Empire khmer: Histoire et documents*. Phnom Penh: Imprimerie du Protectorat, 1904.

Mendelson, E. Michael. *Sangha and State in Burma: A Study of Monastic Sectarianism and Leadership*. Ithaca, NY: Cornell University Press, 1975.

Meyer, C. *La vie quotidienne des Français en Indochine* 1860–1910. Paris: Hachette, 1985.

Meyer, Jean, et al. *Histoire de la France coloniale des origines à 1914*. Paris: Armand Colin, 1990.

Meyer, Roland. *Indochine française: Le Laos*. Hanoi: Imprimerie d'Extrême-Orient, 1930.

———. *Komlah: Visions d'Asie*. Paris: Éditions A. Gérard, n.d. Reprint of 1929 original.

———. *Le Propos du Vieux Colonial*. Paris: Éditions A. Gerard, n.d. Reprint of 1929 original.

———. *Saramani: Danseuse cambodgienne*. Paris: Librairie Charpentier et Fasquelle, 1922.

Migot, André. *Les Khmers: Des origines d'Angkor au Cambodge d'aujourd'hui*. Paris: Le livre contemporaine, 1960.

Milner, Anthony C. *The Invention of Politics in Colonial Malaya: Contesting Nationalism and the Expansion of the Public Sphere*. Hong Kong: Cambridge University Press, 1995.

Mommsen, Wolfgang J., and Jürgen Osterhammel, eds. *Imperialism and After: Continuities and Discontinuities*. London: Allen and Unwin, 1986.

Monod, E. *L'exposition universelle de 1889*. Paris: E. Dentu, 1890.

Monod, G. *Le Cambodgien*. Paris: Larousse, 1931.

Morizon, Réné. *Monographie du Cambodge*. Hanoi: Imprimerie d'Extrême-Orient, 1931.

Mosse, George. *The Nationalization of the Masses*. Reprint. Ithaca, NY: Cornell University Press, 1991.

Mouhot, Henri. *Diary: Travels in the Central Parts of Siam, Cambodia, and Laos during the Years 1858–1861*. Ed. Christopher Pym. Kuala Lumpur: Oxford University Press, 1966.

———. *Travels in Siam, Cambodia, and Laos, 1858–1860.* Singapore: Oxford University Press, 1989.

Moura, Jean. *Le royaume du Cambodge.* Vol. 2. Paris: Librairie de la Société asiatique de l'École des langues orientales vivantes, 1883.

Muan, Ingrid. "Citing Angkor: The Cambodian Arts in the Age of Restoration, 1918–2000." PhD diss., Columbia University, 2001.

Muel-Dreyfus, Francine. *Vichy et l'éternel féminine.* Paris: Éditions du Seuil, 1996.

Mul, Bunchan. *Kuk Noyobay* (Political prison). Phnom Penh, 1971.

Muller, Greg. "Visions of Grandeur, Tales of Failure: The Establishment of French Colonial Rule in Cambodia and the Life of Thomas Caraman, 1840–1887." PhD diss., University of Zurich, 2002. *Colonial Cambodia's "Bad Frenchmen": The Rise of French Rule and the Life of Thomas Caraman, 1840–1887.* London: Routledge, forthcoming.

Musée Guimet. *Musée national des arts asiatiques Guimet.* Paris: Beaux Arts, 1993.

Le Myre de Vilers. *Les institutions civiles de la Cochinchine (1879–1881).* Paris: Émile-Paul, 1908.

National Gallery of Australia. *The Age of Angkor: Treasures from the National Museum of Cambodia.* Exh. cat. Canberra: National Gallery of Australia, 1992.

Népote, Jacques. "Liaisons nouvelles sino-khmères." *Péninsule* (1995): 138–151.

Népote, Jacques, and Khing Hoc Dy. "Literature and Society in Modern Cambodia." In *Essays on Literature and Society in Southeast Asia,* ed. Tham Seong Chee. Singapore: Singapore University Press, 1981.

Nicolas, P. *Notices sur l'Indo-chine: Cochinchine, Cambodge, Annam, Tonkin, Laos, Kouang-Tchéou-Ouan publiées à l'occasion de l'Exposition Universelle de 1900.* Paris: Ministère des Colonies, 1900.

Nora, Pierre, ed. *Les lieux de mémoire: Tome II: La Nation (II).* Paris: Gallimard, 1986.

Norindr, Panivong. *Phantasmatic Indochina: French Colonial Ideology in Architecture, Film and Literature.* Durham, NC: Duke University Press, 1996.

Orient des Provencaux: Les expositions coloniales. Marseille: Musée de la Vieille-Charité, 1982.

Osborne, Milton. *The French Presence in Cochinchina and Cambodia.* Ithaca, NY: Cornell University Press, 1969.

———. "History and Kingship in Contemporary Cambodia." *Journal of Southeast Asian History* 7, no. 1 (March 1966): 1–14.

———. "Peasant Politics in Cambodia: The 1916 Affair." *Modern Asian Studies* 12, no. 2 (1978). 217–243.

———. *Sihanouk: Prince of Light, Prince of Darkness.* Sydney: Allen and Unwin, 1994.

Pannetier, A. *Notes cambodgiennes : Au coeur du pays khmer.* Paris: Payot, 1921.

Pavie, Auguste. *Á la conquête des coeurs.* Paris: Presses Universitaires de France, 1947.

———. *Contes populaires du Cambodge, du Laos et du Siam. Collection des contes et chansons populaires.* Paris: Leroux, 1903.

Peleggi, Maurizio. *The Politics of Ruins and the Business of Nostalgia.* Bangkok: White Lotus, 2002.

Petit, M., ed. *Les colonies françaises: Petite encyclopédie coloniale.* Paris: Librairie Larousse, 1903.

Phal, Makhali. *The Young Concubine.* New York: Random House, 1942.

Pieterse, Jan Nederveen, and Bhikhu Parekh, eds. *The Decolonization of Imagination: Culture, Knowledge and Power.* London: Zed Books, 1995.

Pinet, Hélène. *Ornement de la durée.* Paris: Musée Rodin, 1987.

Poirier, R. *Les expositions internationales du XIXe siècle.* Paris: Librairie Plon, 1958.

Ponchaud, François. "Social Change in the Vortex of Revolution." In *Cambodia 1975–1978: Rendezvous with Death,* ed. Karl D. Jackson. Princeton, NJ: Princeton University Press, 1989.

Ponder, H. *Cambodian Glory.* London: Thornton Butterworth, 1936.

Porée, G., and E. Maspéro. *Moeurs et coutumes des Khmèrs.* Paris: Payot, 1938.

Porée-Maspéro, Eveline. "Notes sur les particularités du culte chez les Cambodgiens." *BEFEO* 44 (1947–1950): 619–620.

Poulot, Dominique. *Musée, Nation, Patrimoine, 1789–1815.* Paris: Guillamard, 1997.

Pourtalès, Guy de. *Nous à qui rien n'appartient.* Paris: Flammarion, 1931.

Pouvourville, Albert de. *L'heure silencieuse.* Paris: Éditions du monde nouveau, 1923.

———. *Histoire Populaire des colonies françaises: I: L'Indochine.* Paris: Éditions du Vélin d'Or, n.d.

Recouly. *À travers L'Indochine et les pays voisins: Pistes, fleuves, et jungles.* Paris: Les éditions de France, 1932.

Reddi, V. M. *A History of the Cambodian Independence Movement 1863–1955.* Tiruparti: Sri Venkastesvara University Press, 1973.

Rémusat, Gilberte de Coral. *l'Art khmer: Les grands étapes de son evolution.* Paris, Van Oest, 1951.

Renan, Ernest. *Mélanges d'histoire et des voyages.* Paris: Calmann-Lévy, 1898.

———. *Qu'est-ce qu'une nation?* Paris: Calmann-Lévy, 1882.

Reynolds, Craig. "Buddhist Cosmography in Thai History, with Special Reference to Nineteenth-Century Culture Change." *Journal of Asian Studies* 35, no. 2 (February 1976): 203–220.

———, ed. *National Identity and Its Defenders: Thailand, 1939–1989.* Clayton, Victoria: Monash Asia Institute, 1991.

Reynolds, Frank E. *Civic Religion and National Community in Thailand. Journal of Asian Studies* 36, no. 2 (February 1977): 267–282.

Richer, Denis. *Histoire de la restauration des temples d'Angkor à travers les évenements politiques du Cambodge.* Phnom Penh: Graphicroots, n.d.

Rondet-Saint, Maurice. *Choses de l'Indochine contemporaine.* Paris: Plon-Nourrit, 1916.

Rotalier, Mlle A. de. *Comme les jours passent: Croquis d'Indo-Chine et de Tunisie.* Hanoi: Taupin et cie., 1943.

Royle, Nicholas. *The Uncanny.* Manchester: Manchester University Press, 2003.

Said, Edward. *Culture and Imperialism.* New York: Alfred A. Knopf, 1993.

———. *Orientalism.* New York: Pantheon, 1978.

Salaun, L. *L'Indochine.* Paris: Imprimerie Nationale, 1903.

Sarraut, Albert. *La mise en valeur des colonies françaises.* Paris: Payot, 1923.

Savage, V. *Western Impressions of Nature and Landscape in Southeast Asia.* Singapore: Singapore University Press, 1983.

Schama, Simon. *Landscape and Memory.* London: Harper Collins, 1995.

Schneider, W. *An Empire for the Masses: The French Popular Image of Africa, 1870–1900.* London: Greenwood Press, 1982.

Schwartzberg, Joseph E. "Introduction to Southeast Asian Cartography." In *Cartography in the Traditional East and Southeast Asian Societies, Volume Two, Book Two,* ed. David Woodward, chap. 16. Madison: University of Wisconsin Press, 1994.

Shaffer Yamada, Teri. "The Spirit Cult of Klang Moeung in Long Beach, California." Paper presented at the Annual Meeting of the Association of Asian Studies, Washington, DC, 27–30 March 1998.

Shils, Edward. "The Intellectuals in the Political Development of the New States." *World Politics* 12 (3 April 1960), 329–368.

Sihanouk, Norodom. *La monarchie cambodgienne et la croisade royale pour l'Independence.* Phnom Penh: Ministry of National Education, n.d.

———. *Les paroles de Samdech Preah Norodom Sihanouk.* Phnom Penh Ministry of Information, October–December 1967.

Sinha, Mrinalini. *Colonial Masculinity: The "Manly" Englishman and the "Effeminate Bengali" in the Late Nineteenth Century.* Manchester: Manchester University Press, 1995.

Smail, John. "On the Possibility of an Autonomous History of Modern Southeast Asia." In *Autonomous Histories, Particular Truths: Essays in Honour of John Smail,* ed. Laurie Sears. Madison: University of Wisconsin, Center for Southeast Asian Studies, 1993.

Smith, Anthony D. "Ethnic Election and Cultural Identity." *Ethnic Studies* 10 (1993): 9–25.

———. "Ethnic Sources of Nationalism." *Survival* 35, no. 1 (Spring 1993): 48–62.

Smith, Bardwell L., ed. *Religion and the Legitimation of Power in Thailand, Laos, and Burma.* Chambersburg, PA: ANIMA Books, 1978.

Smith, Donald E. *Religion and Politics in Burma.* Princeton, NJ: Princeton University Press, 1965.

Sreang, Chheat. "The Cambodian Khum from 1897 to 1919 and Its Contemporary Relevance." MA thesis, The Royal University of Phnom Penh, 2004.

Stoler, Ann Laura. *Race and the Education of Desire: Foucault's History of Sexuality and the Colonial Order of Things.* Durham, NC: Duke University Press, 1995.

Suttantaprija In. *Niries Nokorvat* (Journey to Angkor Vat). Phnom Penh: Buddhist Institute, 1969.

Swearer, Donald K. *The Buddhist World of Southeast Asia.* New York: State University of New York Press, 1995.

Tambiah, S. J. *The Buddhist Saints of the Forest and the Cult of Amulets.* Cambridge: Cambridge University Press, 1984.

Tarling, Nicholas. *A Sudden Rampage: The Japanese Occupation of Southeast Asia 1941–1945.* London: Hurst and Company, 2001.

Taylor, J. L. *Forest Monks and the Nation-State: An Anthropological and Historical Study in Northeastern Thailand.* Singapore: ISEAS, 1996.

Teston, E., and M. Percheron. *L'Indochine moderne: Encyclopédie administrative touristique, artistique et économique.* Paris: Librairie de France, 1931.

Tath, Huot. *Kalyanamit roboh knom kii Samdec Sanghariec Chuon Nath* (My soul mate, venerable Samdec Sanghariec Chuon Nath). Phnom Penh: Buddhist Institute, 1993.

Thion, Serge. "Remodelling Broken Images: Manipulation of Identities towards and beyond the Nation: An Asian Perspective." In *Ethnicities and Nations: Processes of In-*

terethnic Relationships in Latin America, Southeast Asia and the Pacific, ed. R. Guidieri, F. Pellizzi, and S. Tambiah. Austin: University of Texas Press, 1988.

Thiounn, Samdach Chaufea. *Danses cambodgiennes.* Phnom Penh: Bibliothèque Royale du Cambodge, 1931.

Thomas, Nicholas. *Colonialism's Culture: Anthropology, Travel and Government.* Melbourne: Melbourne University Press, 1994.

Thompson, Ashley. "Changing Perspectives: Cambodia after Angkor." In *Sculpture of Angkor and Ancient Cambodia: Millennium of Glory,* ed. Helen I. Jessup and Thierry Zephir. Exh. cat. Washington, DC: National Gallery of Art, 1997.

———. "Text and Temple: The Memorialization of Angkor Vat." Paper presented at the annual meeting of the Association of Asian Studies, Boston, 11–14 March 1999.

———. "The Myth of the Saviour, or the Future of Cambodia's Past." Paper presented at the Monash University Conference on Cambodia: Power, Myth and Memory, December 1996.

Thomson, John. *The Straits of Malacca, Siam and Indo-China: Travels of a Nineteenth-century Photographer.* Singapore: Oxford University Press, 1993.

Tissandier, A. *Cambodge et Java: Ruines khmères et javanaises 1893–94.* Paris: G. Masson, 1896.

Todorov, Tzvetan. *On Human Diversity: Nationalism, Racism and Exoticism in French Thought.* Trans. Catherine Porter. Cambridge, MA: Harvard University Press, 1993.

Tricon, A., and Ch. Bellan. *Chansons cambodgiennes.* Saigon: Albert Portail, 1921.

Tully, J. "Cambodia in Sisowath's Reign." PhD thesis, Monash University, Victoria, 1993.

———. *Cambodia under the Tricolour: King Sisowath and the Mission Civilisatrice 1904–1927.* Monash Asia Institute, 1997.

Um, Khatharya. "Brotherhood of the Pure: Cambodian Nationalism." PhD diss., University of California, Berkeley, 1990.

Vercel, Roger. *Le fleuve: Les grandes heures de la vie de Francis Garnier.* Paris: Les éditions de la nouvelle France, 1946.

Vercoutter, Jean. *The Search for Ancient Egypt.* New York: Thames and Hudson, 1992.

Vergo, Peter, ed. *The New Museology.* London: Reaktion Books, 1991.

Vickery, Michael. *Kampuchea: Politics, Economics and Society.* London: Frances Pinter, 1986.

Weber, Eugene. *France: Fin de siècle.* Cambridge, MA: Harvard University Press, 1986.

Weber, Max. *On Charisma and Institution Building: Selected Papers.* Chicago: University of Chicago Press, 1968.

Wheatley, Paul. *Nagara and Commandery: Origins of the Southeast Asian Urban Tradition.* Chicago: University of Chicago Department of Geography Research Paper, 1983.

Wiener, Margaret J. *Invisible Realms: Power, Magic and Colonial Conquest in Bali.* Chicago and London: University of Chicago Press, 1995.

Willmott, W. "The Chinese in Cambodia." *Journal of South East Asian History* 7, no. 1 (March 1966).

Winichakul, Thongchai. *Siam Mapped: A History of the Geobody of a Nation.* Honolulu: University of Hawai'i Press, 1994.

Wright, Gwendolyn. *The Politics of Design in French Colonial Urbanism,* 303. Chicago: University of Chicago Press, 1988.

———. "Tradition in the Service of Modernity: Architecture and Urbanism in French Colonial Policy 1900–1930." *Journal of Modern History,* no. 59 (June 1987): 291–316.

Zeldin, Theodore. *France 1848–1945: Politics and Anger.* Oxford: Oxford University Press, 1978.

———. *A History of French Passions 1848–1945: Volume Two: Intellect, Taste and Anxiety.* Oxford: Clarendon Press, 1993.

Zito, Angela, and Tani E. Barlow, eds. *Body, Subject and Power in China.* Chicago: University of Chicago Press, 1994.

INDEX

ABOUT THE AUTHOR

Penny Edwards is an assistant professor of Southeast Asian studies at the University of California, Berkeley. She has authored numerous articles on culture, colonialism, gender, and national identity in Cambodia and Burma, and is the joint editor of two volumes on Chinese diaspora: *Beyond China: Migrating Identities* and *Lost in the Whitewash: Aboriginal-Asian Encounters in Australia, 1901–2001.* Educated at London, Oxford, Cornell, and Monash universities, she holds degrees in Chinese, international relations, and history.

Production Notes for Edwards | *Cambodge*

Jacket design by Santos Barbasa Jr.

Text based on a series design by Richard Hendel with text in Garamond Three and display in Gill Sans

Composition by BW&A Books, Inc.

Printing and binding by The Maple-Vail Book Manufacturing Group

Printed on 60 lb. Text White Opaque, 426 ppi